# THE
# ENCYCLOPEDIA
## OF
# CANADA

MANITOBA

SASKATCHEWAN

COAT OF ARMS OF THE
PROVINCES OF MANITOBA AND SASKATCHEWAN

# The
# ENCYCLOPEDIA
## *of*
# CANADA

GENERAL EDITOR

W. STEWART WALLACE, M.A. (Oxon.), F.R.S.C.

*Librarian, University of Toronto*

## Volume V
### NEWTS — SIKSIKA

UNIVERSITY ASSOCIATES OF CANADA
Limited
TORONTO

PRINTED IN CANADA BY
MURRAY PRINTING COMPANY, LIMITED, TORONTO
1940

# CONTRIBUTORS OF SPECIAL ARTICLES

## VOLUME V

**North West Company**—W. S. WALLACE, Esq., M.A., editor of *Documents relating to the North West Company.*

**Nova Scotia**—Professor GEORGE E. WILSON, M.A., Ph.D., Professor of History, Dalhousie University.

**Oak**—Professor R. C. HOSIE, B.Sc.F., M.A., Faculty of Forestry, University of Toronto.

**Oblates**—Rev. Father OVILA-A. MEUNIER, O.M.I., D.Ph., L.J.C., Secretaire des "Semaines d'Etudes Missionnaires du Canada", University of Ottawa.

**One Big Union**—W. H. POOLE, Esq., M.A., formerly Lecturer in Political Economy, University of Alberta.

**Ontario**—F. LANDON, Esq., M.A., Librarian of the University of Western Ontario.

**Oriental Immigration**—D. C. MASTERS, Esq., D.Phil., Extension Department, University of Toronto.

**Pacific Salmon**—Professor J. R. DYMOND, M.A., Director of the Royal Ontario Museum of Zoology.

**Paulist Fathers**—Rev. Father FRANCIS BROOME, C.S.P., St. Peter's Church, Toronto.

**Penology**—H. A. AIKEN, Esq., Toronto.

**Periodicals**—W. S. WALLACE, Esq., M.A., Librarian, University of Toronto.

**Pine**—Professor R. C. HOSIE, B.Sc.F., M.A., Faculty of Forestry, University of Toronto.

**Presbyterian Church**—The Rev. W. G. WALLACE, D.D., Toronto.

**Prince Edward Island**—H. A. AIKEN, Esq., Toronto.

**Public Utilities**—Professor A. BRADY, M.A., Ph.D., Department of Political Science, University of Toronto.

**Pulp-and-Paper Industry**—Professor H. A. INNIS, Ph.D., Department of Political Science, University of Toronto.

**Quebec (Province)**—ÆGIDIUS FAUTEUX, Esq., F.R.S.C., Librarian, Civic Library, Montreal.

**Quebec (City)**—Col. G. E. MARQUIS, Librarian, Legislative Library, Quebec.

**Quebec Conference**—Professor W. M. WHITELAW, M.A., Ph.D., formerly Assistant Professor of History, McGill University, and author of *The Maritimes and Canada before Confederation.*

**Queen's University**—E. C. KYTE, Esq., Librarian, Queen's University, Kingston.

**Reciprocity**—D. C. MASTERS, Esq., D.Phil., formerly of the Extension Department, University of Toronto.

**Recollets**—The Rev. Father JUSTIN DE MONTAGNAC, O.M.Cap., of the Société Historique d'Ottawa.

**Redemptorist Fathers**—The Rev. Father L. X. AUBIN, C.S.S.R.

**Roman Catholic Church**—The Rev. Father E. C. LEBEL, M.A., Professor of English, St. Michael's College, Toronto.

**Royal Bank of Canada**—C. P. C. DOWNMAN, Esq., Publicity Department, Royal Bank of Canada.

**Rural Credit**—W. T. EASTERBROOK, M.A., formerly Maurice Cody Fellow, University of Toronto.

**St. Lawrence Waterway Project**—Professor GEORGE W. BROWN, M.A., Ph.D., Department of History, University of Toronto, and editor of the *Canadian Historical Review*.

**Salish**—His Honour Judge F. W. HOWAY, LL.B., F.R.S.C., County Court, New Westminster British Columbia.

**Saskatchewan**—WALTER C. MURRAY, Esq., LL.D., F.R.S.C., President, University of Saskatchewan.

**Sekani**—His Honour Judge F. W. HOWAY, LL.B., F.R.S.C., County Court, New Westminster, British Columbia.

**Separate Schools**—Miss MAY NEWTON, M.A., University of Toronto Library.

# KEY TO ABBREVIATIONS

*Bull. rech. hist.—Bulletin des recherches historiques* (Lévis, P.Q., 1895—).

*Can. hist. rev.—The Canadian historical review* (Toronto, 1920—).

*Can. mag.—The Canadian magazine* (Toronto, 1893—).

*Coll. Nova Scotia Hist. Soc.—Collections of the Nova Scotia Historical Society* (Halifax, 1880—).

*Dict. nat. biog.*—Leslie Stephen and Sidney Lee (eds.), *Dictionary of national biography* (63 vols. and supplements, London, 1885-1912).

*fl.—floruit* (flourished).

n.d.—no date.

n.p.—no place of publication.

*Ont. Hist. Soc. papers and records—Ontario Historical Society papers and records* (Toronto, 1899—).

q.v.—*quod vide* (which see).

*Trans. Roy. Soc. Can.—Transactions of the Royal Society of Canada* (Ottawa, 1883—).

# N

*Continued*

**Newts.** See **Salamanders.**

**New Waterford,** a town in Cape Breton county, Nova Scotia, on the Sydney and Louisburg Railways, 14 miles north-east of Sydney, and 8 miles west of Glace Bay. It derives its name from a nearby lakelet known as lake Waterford. It is chiefly a mining town; but fishing and farming are carried on in the neighbourhood. It has schools, theatres, a general hospital, and a weekly newspaper (*Times*). Pop. (1934), 7,745.

**New Westminster,** a city and port of British Columbia, on the Fraser river, 15 miles from the gulf of Georgia on the Pacific ocean, and served by the Canadian National, Canadian Pacific, and Great Northern Railways. An electric railway connects the city with Vancouver, 12 miles to the north-west. The site of the city was selected in 1859 by Colonel R. C. Moody (q.v.), and was the first capital of the colony of British Columbia until 1868. After the two colonies of British Columbia and Vancouver island were united as British Columbia, the capital was removed to Victoria. The place was first known as Queensborough; but Queen Victoria was asked to name the capital of the new colony, and she suggested New Westminster, in honour of ancient Westminster in England. Thus the popular name, "the Royal City", has been given to it. There was a widely destructive fire here in 1898, and several of the principal streets have been rebuilt. There are Anglican and Roman Catholic cathedrals, Columbia and St. Louis colleges, eight public and high schools, hospitals, and a penitentiary. New Westminster has a good harbour, which was greatly improved by the aid of a $700,000 loan being granted for that purpose by the Dominion government. This is the only fresh-water port in western Canada. The river here is a mile wide. Ocean liners make regular calls. The industries include salmon, fruit, and vegetable canneries, oil refinery, iron foundry, lumber, pulp and paper mills. There is a daily paper (*British Columbian*). Pop. (1931), 17,524. Consult *Manual of provincial information* (Victoria, 1929).

**Niagara,** a district in Upper Canada created by proclamation in 1800, by the division of the Home district into the Newcastle, Home, and Niagara districts. It was abolished, with the other judicial districts in Canada West, in 1849.

**Niagara District Bank,** with head office at St. Catharines, Canada West, took advantage of W. H. Merritt's Free Banking Act of 1850 to come into existence. In 1855, under a new charter, the bank was transferred from the Free Banking Act to all the privileges of an ordinary bank, with an authorized capital of $1,000,000. As the bank found difficulty in raising this capital within the specified period of 5 years, the term was, in 1857, extended to 1861, and, in 1861, to 1866. In 1863 the capital stock requirement was reduced to $400,000. The bank had a fairly successful career until it suffered large losses, through the failure of Jay Cooke and Co., and others, in 1873.

In 1875 it was amalgamated with the Imperial Bank of Canada.

**Niagara falls,** one of the highest cataracts in the world, is on the Niagara river, about 20 miles from lake Erie, and about 14 miles from its mouth in lake Ontario. It has a height of 160 feet. Goat island, half a mile long and a quarter of a mile wide, extends to the brow of the precipice, and divides the falls into two parts, the American falls, and the Canadian or Horseshoe falls. The first description of the falls, from actual observation, is found in Hennepin (q.v.) in 1678; but probably the falls were visited by Europeans before this. Since then the falls have been described by innumerable visitors. They are the result of the Niagara river having eaten its way back from the escarpment at Queenston Heights; and it is estimated that this process has taken 25,000 years. See C. M. Dow, *Anthology and bibliography of Niagara falls* (2 vols., Albany, 1921).

**Niagara Falls,** a city in Welland county, Ontario, on the Niagara river, overlooking the Niagara falls, 24 miles north-west of Buffalo, and 40 miles south-east of Toronto, on the Canadian National, Canadian Pacific, and several railways of the United States. It was originally named Clifton, or Suspension Bridge, after its English prototype at the Severn gorge, near Bristol. The place became important with the building of the bridge over the Niagara river to connect the Canadian railway lines with those of the United States. It soon became an international gateway; and its proximity to the falls as well as the enormous electric power-plants constructed to utilize the water-power, made an important industrial city, the home of Canadian factories for many well-known United States firms. Beautiful Queen Victoria Park, along the gorge, attracts many tourists.

The city contains 7 public schools, a technical school, a business college, a collegiate institute, good hotels, and several churches. Three steel arch bridges span the river. The principal industries are foundries, locomotive shops, cereal mills, canning factories, knitted goods, silverware, office equipment, toilet preparations, and concrete blocks. Niagara Falls was incorporated as a city in 1903. Pop. (1931), 19,046.

**Niagara Historical Society,** a society founded at Niagara-on-the-lake, Ontario, in 1895. Since 1896 it has published 41 numbers of *Transactions*, in addition to its *Annual reports*. The society has an excellent museum at Niagara-on-the-Lake and a comprehensive collection of early Ontario books and newspapers.

**Niagara-on-the-Lake,** a town in Lincoln county, Ontario, situated at the mouth of the Niagara river on lake Ontario, 15 miles west of the Niagara falls, on the Michigan Central Railway. Niagara is the oldest town in the province. It was settled by Loyalists at the close of the American Revolution, and was selected by Simcoe (q.v.) in 1792 as the capital of Upper Canada, and named by him Newark. In 1793, however, he moved the capital to York (now Toronto). Later known as Niagara, the settlement was given its present name to distinguish it from the cities of Niagara Falls. The place was the scene of many stirring events at the beginning of the nineteenth century. In 1813 it was burned by the retreating American army. Niagara, being a point of great historic interest, is a popular summer resort. There are daily steamer connections with Toronto and other ports. The town contains four churches, an historical museum, high and public schools, and a public library. Niagara had the first public library in Upper Canada, and also the first newspaper. To-day there is a weekly newspaper (*Advance*). The manufacturing establishments are two canning factories, a jam factory, three basket factories, and a planing mill. Niagara is in the celebrated fruit-farming region. Pop. (1931),

NIAGARA FALLS

1,228. See William Kirby, *Annals of Niagara* (Lundy's Lane Historical Society, 1896; 2nd ed., Toronto, 1927), and Janet Carnochan, *History of Niagara* (Toronto, 1914).

**Niagara river** flows in a northerly direction from lake Erie into lake Ontario and is part of the boundary between the state of New York and the province of Ontario. The name is derived from an old Indian name, *Onguiaahra*. Of the many meanings given to the word the most suitable is "the thunderer of waters". The river may have been visited by Étienne Brûlé (q.v.), a protégé of Champlain (q.v.), in 1611 or 1612 and is shown on the map published in Champlain's *Travels* in 1632. It was visited by La Salle (q.v.) and Dollier de Casson (q.v.) in 1669. In 1679 there was erected at the mouth of the river a fur-trading post which became one of the line of forts by which it was proposed to restrict the English colonies to the sea. In 1759 the fort was captured by a British expedition under Prideaux (q.v.) and Johnson (q.v.). The Niagara frontier was the principal scene of hostilities during the War of 1812-14 and also in the Fenian raids of 1866.

The river, 34 miles in length and with an average width of 3,500 feet, is the principal drainage outlet of the four upper Great lakes. It is navigable from its source to the upper rapids, a distance of 20 miles, and for 7 miles from Queenston to its mouth. The current is rapid in the upper navigable portion where the average fall is about 0.5 feet per mile; the total fall of the lower 7 miles is 0.5 feet. Navigation between lakes Erie and Ontario is, of course, carried on over the new Welland canal, which can admit vessels with a draught of 30 feet. Three miles below its source the river is divided into two by Grand island, which is 12 miles long and from 2 to 7 miles in width. The intermediate section of the river, 7 miles in length, includes a series of rapids and Niagara falls and has a total fall of 315 feet. The rapids commence about 3 miles below Grand island and, after a course of a little over half a mile, terminate in the falls. Below the falls the river runs with great impetuosity between perpendicular cliffs for 3 or 4 miles in a comparatively narrow channel from which it emerges at Queenston. In this section are two rapids below the first of which is "the Whirlpool", where an angle in the river causes a reflex in the current. Between Queenston and Fort Erie the river is spanned by a number of bridges, including the most recently constructed, the Peace bridge from Fort Erie to Buffalo. See also **Niagara falls.**

**Niccolite,** a mineral consisting of the arsenide of nickel. It usually occurs massive, but occasionally is found in hexagonal crystals. It is brittle, has a hardness of about 5.5, and has a specific gravity of 7.5. It is readily recognized because of its metallic lustre and pale copper-red colour, from which it gets the common name of copper-nickel. It is found most abundantly in veins associated with smaltite and silver. When exposed to a moist atmosphere, it oxidizes very rapidly, and forms the hydrous arsenate of nickel known as annabergite or nickel bloom. It is one of the prominent minerals in the silver deposits of Cobalt, Ontario. Formerly it was used as an ore of nickel.

**Nichikun lake** is at the head of the Eastmain river, in the Ungava area in northern Quebec. The lake is irregular in form, containing a great number of bays of large extent. It is filled with islands, on one of which the Hudson's Bay Company has maintained a trading-post since the beginning of the last century. The frequency of frosts in September and even in the summer in the Nichikun area prevents the growing of grain. The area of the lake is 150 square miles.

**Nichol, Robert** (1774?-1824), soldier and legislator, was born in Dumfriesshire, Scotland, about 1774. He was a relative of the Hon. Robert Hamilton (q.v.), and came to Canada before 1795. He settled in Norfolk county, Upper Canada, and here he became the local agent of Col. Thomas Talbot (q.v.). In 1812 he was appointed by General Brock quartermaster-general of the militia of Upper Canada, and he served in this capacity during the War of 1812-15. In 1812 he was also elected to represent Norfolk in the Legislative Assembly of the province, and he continued to represent this constituency until 1821. He then became judge of the Surrogate Court of the district of Niagara; and on May 3, 1824, he met his death near Queenston, Upper Canada, when driving in a snow storm from Niagara to his home in Stamford township. His horses having missed their way, he was precipitated over the bank of the Niagara gorge, and was "literally dashed to pieces". See E. A. Cruikshank, *A sketch of the public life and services of Robert Nichol* (Ont. Hist. Soc., papers and records, 1922) and *Some letters of Robert Nichol* (Ont. Hist. Soc., papers and records, 1923).

**Nichol, Walter Cameron** (1866-1928), lieutenant-governor of British Columbia (1921-6), was born at Goderich, Ontario, on October 15, 1866, the son of Robert Nichol, barrister, and grandson of Col. Robert Nichol (q.v.). He was educated in Hamilton, Ontario, and in 1881 joined the staff of the Hamilton *Spectator*. From 1888 to 1896 he was editor of the Hamilton *Herald*. In 1897 he went to British Columbia, and became editor of the Victoria *Province*, then a weekly newspaper. In 1898 he removed the *Province* to Vancouver, and made it a daily paper, with great success. From 1921 to 1926 he was lieutenant-governor of British Columbia; and he died at Victoria, British Columbia, on December 19, 1928. In 1897 he married Quita, daughter of Charles Greenwood Moore, M.D., of London, Ontario.

**Nichol,** a township in Wellington county, Ontario, traversed by the Grand river and by the Canadian National and Canadian Pacific Railways. See A. W. Wright (ed.), *Pioneer days in Nichol* (Mount Forest, Ontario, 1924).

**Nicholls, Frederic** (1856-1921), senator of Canada, was born in England on November 23, 1856. He was educated in Germany, and came to Canada in 1874. He was a pioneer in electrical development in Canada, and became president of the Canadian General Electric Company, as well as of many other corporations. In 1917 he was called to the Senate of Canada; and he died at Battle Creek, Michigan, on October 25, 1921. In 1875 he married Florence (d. 1909), daughter of Commander Graburn, R.N.; and by her he had several children.

**Nicholson, Francis** (1660-1728), governor of Nova Scotia (1713-15), was born in 1660, and entered the British army in 1678. He was appointed lieutenant-governor of New York in 1686, and of Virginia in 1696, governor of Maryland in 1694, and of Virginia in 1698. He was an advocate of a vigorous policy against Canada; and in 1710 he was in command of the expedition that captured Port Royal. In 1713 he was made governor of Nova Scotia, but he left the colony in 1715; and in 1719 he was appointed governor of South Carolina. He held this nominal post until his death in London on March 5, 1728. The *Dictionary of national biography* states that he was knighted in 1720; but no confirmation of this statement has been found. He was the author of the *Journal of an expedition for the reduction of Port Royal* (London, 1711; reprinted by the Nova Scotia Historical Society, 1879) and *An apology or vindication of Francis Nicholson, governor of South Carolina* (London, 1724).

**Nickel,** a silver-white metal with a brilliant lustre which does not tarnish on exposure to air, and is ductile, hard, and tenacious. The specific gravity varies between 8.27 and 8.93. Its malleability is diminished by adding an admixture of carbon or manganese. It is attracted by the magnet, and may be rendered magnetic by the same means as iron. It is used largely in coinage, and in the making of alloys, particularly nickel steel, monel metal, nickel silver, nickel bronze, and nickel molybdenum iron, in addition to others. It is used in certain types of storage batteries, as a catalyser for the production of edible oils and of soaps, and for a great variety of apparatus used in many industries. Its most common use is for plating other metals to protect them from oxidation.

The chief source of nickel is in the Sudbury basin of northern Ontario, where the ore consists chiefly of nickeliferous pyrrhotite, associated to a greater or less extent with chalcopyrite. The pyrrhotite itself is not a nickel mineral. It is a sulphide of iron which can be scratched by the knife, and has a specific gravity of about 4.6. It has a metallic lustre and a bronze-yellow to copper-red colour, which is readily tarnished to a reddish-bronze. It has a black streak, and is magnetic. Disseminated through the pyrrhotite are minute specks of pentlandite (q.v.) and polydymite (q.v.), the chief nickel sulphides. In addition to these, the mineral niccolite (q.v.) has also at times been an important source of nickel, and a brass-yellow sulphide called millerite was important at the Lancaster Gap mine in Pennsylvania.

*Nickel Industry.* Canada supplies approximately 90 per cent. of the world's nickel from the Sudbury deposits of this metal's ore. The industry so developed has been largely responsible for stimulating the steadily mounting consumption of nickel by engineering and manufacturing activities all over the world. The span of this Canadian industry stretches over only half a century, but the history of nickel goes back to ancient times when primitive metal workers forged from nickel-iron meteorites implements superior to their best production from native ores. Although occurrence of nickel ore in Canada was reported as early as 1848 and an authentic discovery in the Sudbury district was recorded in 1856, it was not until the uncovering in 1883 of an important outcropping of supposedly copper ore, in a cut being made for the Canadian Pacific Railway, that the foundation for Canada's nickel industry was laid. Even so its potentialities were not recognized, first because of the extreme difficulty in separating the nickel, and secondly, because world consumption of the metal made any increase in production a drug on the market. In the final decade of the nineteenth century, both these difficulties were overcome. Development of the Orford process in the United States and of the Mond (or Carbonyl) process in England provided efficient bases for mass production. With certain refinements, they both are still in use, the Orford process now being the established method in Canada. During the same period, demonstrations abroad of nickel's important contribution to industry as an alloying element with steel opened a new and almost limitless market for the metal. As a result, Canada forged steadily ahead as a producer, passing New Caledonia soon after the turn of the century. At present, Canada's output is more than ten times that of its nearest competitor.

The value of nickel as an alloying element with steel stimulated its production during the World War, but it has been in the post-war period that the metal has won an even larger market. The chief factor in inaugurating this significant change was the rapid growth of the automotive industry, which consumed tremendous tonnages of steels containing from ½ to 5 per cent. of nickel. At the same time, research and development, undertaken by the Canadian producers, and stimulated among other industries, have established nickel and alloys of nickel in a steadily expanding variety of industrial applications. Notable among these are railways, airplanes, Diesel engines, radio, heavy chemicals, textiles, food processing, and machine tools. Its use in the manufacture of stainless steels and of nickel cast-irons has contributed materially to the spread of this metal throughout the industrial world. In recent years, monel metal, the nickel-copper alloy made directly from the selected ores, has added to its industrial and engineering applications such uses in the household field as provision of the material for sinks, table-tops, hot-water storage-tanks, washing machines, kitchen tools, and the trim on ranges and refrigerators. The result is that nickel of Canadian origin is in the water gates at Boulder Dam, the galleys and engine-rooms of ocean liners, the exterior trim of the Empire State Building, the traffic markers of London streets, the filter screens of Cuban sugar-mills, and countless other applications, wherever industry and transportation have progressed beyond the primitive stage. More than 1,000 alloys containing nickel are now trade-marked by their manufacturers.

Because the nickel-bearing ores of the Sudbury district also contain copper in large quantities and gold, silver, selenium, tellurium, and the platinum metals in commercial quantities, the mining and treating of these ores has become one of the great Canadian industries, expending millions of dollars annually, not only for payrolls, but also for fuel and power, supplies, freight, and taxes.

The two companies now actively mining are Falconbridge Mines, which operates one mine and a smelter in the Sudbury district, and ships its matte to Norway for refining there, and the International Nickel Company of Canada (q.v.), which alone provides the world with the bulk of its nickel supply, which ranks fifth among the copper-producing companies of the world, and which now leads Russia in production of the platinum metals. It is, as well, the sole producer of monel metal. Included in the organization are the Frood Mine, a mill, smelter, and electrolytic copper-refinery at Coppercliff, an electrolytic nickel refinery at Port Colborne, Ontario, a carbonyl-process refinery at Clydach, Wales, a precious-metals refinery at Acton, London, and rolling mills at Birmingham, England, and Huntington, West Virginia. A world-wide selling organization is supplemented by bureaus of information in London, Paris, Frankfurt, Milan, New York, and Tokyo.

See A. P. Coleman, *The nickel industry, with special reference to the Sudbury region, Ontario* (Ottawa, Mines Branch, 1913) and the *Report of the Royal Ontario Nickel Commission* (Toronto, 1917).

**Nickinson, John** (1808-1864), actor-manager, was born in London, England, in 1808. In early youth he enlisted in the 28th Regiment; but he obtained his discharge in 1835, with the rank of colour-sergeant, and emigrated to the United States. Here he became an actor; and from 1848 to 1852 he played at the Olympic Theatre, New York. In 1852 he came to Toronto, Canada, and from 1853 to 1858 he was manager of the Royal Lyceum Theatre in Toronto. He was a pioneer in theatrical management in Canada; and his daughter Charlotte (Mrs. Daniel Morrison) became a distinguished actress. He died at Cincinnati, Ohio, in 1864.

**Nicola river,** a tributary of the Thompson river, in the Kamloops district of British Columbia, rises in Nicola lake, and is 97 miles long.

**Nicolet, Jean** (1598?-1642), explorer, was born at Cherbourg, France, about 1598, the son of Thomas Nicolet and Marguerite Delamer. He came to Canada in 1618 in the service of the fur-trading company, and immediately on his arrival, was sent to l'Ile des Allumettes to learn the Algonquin language, and here he spent two years. The next eight or nine years were spent among the Nipissings. After the capture of Quebec in 1629, Nicolet remained loyal to the French, and returned to the country of the Nipissings, where he stayed until July, 1633. He was then recalled to Quebec, and became clerk and interpreter of the Company of One Hundred Associates. In 1634, under Champlain's instructions, he explored lake Michigan as far as Green bay, ascended Green bay and Fox river to an Indian village west of lake Winnebago, and made a treaty of peace with the tribes. In October, 1642, he was named *commis général* of the Company of One Hundred Associates during the absence of Le Tardif. A month later, he was drowned while hastening to Three Rivers to prevent the death of a captive, belonging to a tribe in alliance with the Iroquois, whom the Algonquins were torturing. He married on October 7, 1642, Marguerite Couillard, by whom he had one daughter. See A. Gosselin, *Jean Nicolet et le Canada de son temps* (Quebec, 1905); B. Sulte, *Jean Nicolet et la découverte du Wisconsin* (Revue canadienne, 1910); and C. W. Butterfield, *History of the discovery of the North-West by John Nicolet in 1634, with a sketch of his life* (Cincinnati, 1881).

**Nicolet,** a county in Quebec, bounded on the north by the river St. Lawrence, on the east by Lotbinière county, on the south by Arthabaska county, and on the west by Yamaska county. It is named after the Nicolet river, which waters it. The Canadian National Railway crosses it. Chief town, Bécancour. Pop. (1931), 28,673. See Abbé J. E. Bellemare, *Histoire de Nicolet* (Arthabaska, 1924).

**Nicolet,** a town in Nicolet and Yamaska county, Quebec, on the Nicolet river and the Canadian National Railway, 10 miles north of Three Rivers. The river, after which the town is named, was called "Du Pont" by Champlain (q.v.), but was later renamed after Jean Nicolet (q.v.), the explorer. The town is the centre of the Nicolet diocese, and contains a Roman Catholic cathedral. There is a normal school, a seminary, a boarding school, a commercial academy, a court house, and a hospital. The three largest manufacturing concerns in the town are an optical company, a construction company, and a knitting mill. Pop. (1931), 2,868.

**Nigel, peak,** is in Alberta, in the Rocky mountains. It is in lat. 52° 14', long. 117° 10', and has an altitude of 10,535 feet. It was named by J. Norman Collie in 1898, after Nigel Vavasour, a mountain-climbing companion.

**Nightflowering Catchfly.** See **Catchfly.**

**Nighthawk** (*Chordeiles minor*), a bird closely related to the whip-poor-will. It is not, as its name suggests, a hawk, but rather a member of the family *Caprimulgidae*, a group of birds known as the goatsuckers. Nighthawks are largely active at night or in the evening. They nest in bald exposed situations in wild forested areas, or on the flat gravel roofs of large buildings about cities. These birds are common residents of urban centres and their erratic beating flight, their notes, and their aerial dives, accompanied by the "zooming" sound of their wings, are familiar sights and sounds of town and country alike. The species is found throughout Canada north to the limit of trees.

**Nightshade** (*Solanum nigrum* L., *Solanaceae*), a low, much-branched annual, with stem rough on the angles, leaves ovate, wavy-toothed, and flowers white, in small lateral drooping clusters. The calyx is spreading; the corolla wheel-shaped, and 5-lobed; the stamens exerted. The fruit is a globular black berry. It grows in rich open and shaded ground across Canada, blooming from July to September.

**Nile Expedition.** On August 26, 1884, Lord Wolseley telegraphed to the governor-general of Canada suggesting that Lieut.-Colonel F. C. Denison (q.v.), who had been his orderly officer in the Red River expedition of 1869-70, should organize a detachment of Canadian *voyageurs* to aid him in the campaign on the Nile, in Egypt and the Soudan, for the relief of General Gordon at Khartoum. Denison organized a corps of nearly 400 *voyageurs*, skilled in river navigation, and set sail for Egypt on September 15. The Canadian boatmen served with distinction throughout the campaign in the Soudan; and their services were mentioned in despatches, and in the vote of thanks to the troops moved in the House of Commons. This was the first occasion on which a contingent of Canadian troops took part in an imperial war overseas.

**Nine-bark** (*Physocarpus opulifolius* (L.) Maxim., *Rosaceae*), a shrub, from 3 to 7 feet tall, with long branches on which the old bark is loose and separates into numerous thin layers. The leaves are roundish to heart-shaped, somewhat 3-lobed, and smooth. The flowers are white, borne in clusters which terminate the branches. The fruit is very conspicuous, forming loose inflated membranaceous purple pods. It is found along the rocky banks of streams in Quebec and Ontario, and is often cultivated.

**Ninety-Two Resolutions.** These resolutions were passed in the Legislative Assembly of Lower Canada in February, 1834, and constituted a sort of declaration of rights on the part of the *patriote* party. They were drafted by A. N. Morin (q.v.), but were inspired by L. J. Papineau (q.v.). They demanded the application of the elective principle to the political institutions of the province, after the American model; but did not advocate, in any explicit way, the introduction of responsible government. Lord Aylmer (q.v.), the governor-general of Canada at that time, in an analysis of the resolutions, maintained that "eleven of them represented the truth; six contained truth mixed with falsehood; sixteen were wholly false; seventeen were doubtful; twelve were ridiculous; seven repetitions; fourteen consisted of abuse; four were both false and seditious; and the remaining five were indifferent." The text of the resolutions will be found in W. P. M. Kennedy (ed.), *Statutes, treaties, and documents of the Canadian constitution* (Oxford, 1930).

**Nipigon House,** a Hudson's Bay Company post built about 1775 at the north end of lake Nipigon. It was abandoned shortly after the union of the Hudson's Bay and North West Companies in 1821, and a new post, called Wabinosh House, was constructed on Wabinosh bay, in the north-west angle of the lake, near the site of the North West Company's Fort Duncan (q.v.). About 1850 Wabinosh House was removed ten miles to the south, and was re-established as Nipigon House on its present site.

**Nipigon lake** and **river** are in the Thunder Bay district of Ontario. The lake is about midway between the Albany river and Thunder bay, at the head of lake Superior, into which it is drained by the Nipigon river. The name is an Indian word meaning "deep clear-water lake". The known history of this region dates back to 1678 when the French explorer La Tourette, a brother of Duluth, founded a fort at the mouth of lake Nipigon, in the attempt to cut off trade from the Hudson's Bay Company. The lake is elliptical in general outline; its longest diameter, a little west of north, is 70 miles, and its shortest is 50 miles. The depth of water is very great, and, in some parts, a line of 540 feet has failed to touch bottom. Lake Nipigon is thickly studded with islands, of which, it is estimated, there are more than 1,000. The shore on the southern side is deeply indented by large bays, and, on the northern, Ombabika bay is nearly 20 miles long with an entrance only a mile wide. The shores on the south and west are bolder and the water is deeper than on the north and east. The surrounding country and the islands are undulating and hilly, but level tracts of considerable extent occur in some places. The largest tract of good land is in the south-western side of the lake. The climate appears to be as well-suited for agriculture as that in the greater part of the province of Quebec. The timber is principally white spruce, white birch, aspen, poplar, balsam, fir, tamarac and white cedar. The lake has an area of 1,590 square miles. The river abounds in trout and, like the lake, its waters are very clear. It is about 30 miles long.

**Nipisiguit river** is in Northumberland and Gloucester counties, New Brunswick. After flowing east for the greater part of its course, it turns north and discharges into Nipisiguit bay, the southern arm of Chaleur bay. The river is about 100 miles in length. Its name is a Micmac Indian word meaning "the river that dashes roughly along". The river is celebrated for its fine large salmon, and has many rapids and falls. Twenty miles from Bathurst, which is at the mouth of the river, are the Great falls which consist of 4 leaps with a total height of 140 feet. At the foot of each are deep basins and below the falls, for about a mile, a number of pools and rapids. About 7 miles from Bathurst are the Crosberry falls, which consist of a series of small falls. The mountainous scenery of the district is characterized by gloom and grandeur. It is visited each year by a large number of tourists.

During its early history the district was chiefly important as a centre of Recollet and Jesuit activity; in 1620 the Recollets founded a mission, which was followed in 1644 by a Jesuit mission. Soon afterwards, in addition to holders of large grants from the French crown, the district was also occupied by a small number of Acadians, who were much increased after 1750 and still more after the expulsion. See N. E. Dionne, *Miscou* (Canada Français, 1889), and William F. Ganong, *A Monograph of historic sites in the province of New Brunswick* (Transactions of the Royal Society of Canada, ii, 1889).

**Nipissing,** a district in northern Ontario, is bounded on the west by Sudbury and Parry Sound districts, on the south by Haliburton, Hastings, and Renfrew counties, on the east by the Ottawa river and Renfrew county, and the northern tip reaches up to Timiskaming district. Nipissing used to include the present districts of Parry Sound, Sudbury, and part of Timiskaming. It was named after lake Nipissing, and was created a district by the proclamation of April 17, 1858; and in 1877 it was made a "temporary judicial district." Algonquin park, a forest reserve 56 miles long by 48 wide, was set apart in Nipissing district in 1893; and part of the Timagami forest reserve is also within its boundaries. Pop. (1931), 41,207.

**Nipissing House,** a Hudson's Bay Company post at the east end of lake Nipissing, on the historic route of the fur-traders from the Ottawa to lake Superior. The post was moved before 1850 to one of the islands on lake Nipissing; and after the building of the Canadian Pacific Railway it was transferred to North Bay, about five miles to the north.

**Nipissing lake** is in Ontario, northeast of lake Huron and nearly midway between it and the Ottawa river. The name means "little water", compared with the big water of Georgian bay. It was probably discovered by Étienne Brûlé, a protégé of Champlain, in 1610 or 1611, and was visited by Champlain himself in 1615. With the French river, the Mattawa, and the Ottawa, it once formed part of the *voyageur* route from Montreal to the west. The lake is irregular in shape, its shores are bold, and it contains many islands. It discharges into the Georgian bay by the French river; eastward it is separated by only a short portage from Turtle lake and Little river, a tributary of the Ottawa. It is 50 miles in length, 35 miles at its greatest breadth, and has an area of 330 square miles.

**Nisbet, James** (1823-1874), missionary, was born at Hutchisontown, Glasgow, Scotland, on September 8, 1823. He became a minister of the Canada Presbyterian Church, and was its first missionary in the Canadian West. He founded the town of Prince Albert in 1866; and he died at Kildonan, Manitoba, on September 20, 1874. See E. H. Oliver, *The Presbyterian Church in Saskatchewan, 1866-1881* (Trans. Roy. Soc. Can., 1934).

**Nivert, Désiré Amable Chrétien** (1605?-1661), missionary, was born at Calais, France, about 1605. He became a Recollet, and came to Canada, where he took part in the mission to the Hurons. He died in Canada in 1661.

**Niverville, Joseph Claude Boucher de.** See **Boucher de Niverville, Joseph Claude.**

**Nixon,** a village in Norfolk county, Ontario, on the Canadian National Railway, 5 miles from Simcoe. Pop. (1934), 250.

**Nobleton,** a village in York county, Ontario, 27 miles north-west of Toronto, 5 miles from Kleinburg, the nearest railway station. Pop. (1934), 300.

**Noel, Mrs. John Vavasour** (1815-1873), novelist, was born in Ireland on December 22, 1815. She emigrated to America in 1832, and for a number of years conducted a seminary for young ladies in Savannah, Georgia. In 1847 she removed to Canada, and settled in Kingston. There she died on June 21, 1873. She was the author of *The abbey of Rathmore, and other tales* (Kingston, 1859), *The cross of pride* (Canadian Illustrated News, 1863), and *The secret of Stanley Hall* (Saturday Reader, Montreal, 1865).

**Nokomis,** a town in Saskatchewan, is situated at the junction of the main line of the Canadian National Railway and of the Regina-Saskatoon branch of the Canadian Pacific Railway. It is the centre of a fine grain-growing country and has three elevators. It was incorporated as a town in 1908. The name Nokomis is taken from Longfellow's *Hiawatha*. Pop. (1931), 445.

**Nolin, Jean Baptiste** (*fl.* 1777-1819), an Indian trader, who settled at Sault Ste. Marie, and acted there in some capacity for the North West Company for many years. As early as 1777, he was in partnership with Venant St. Germain (q.v.), and purchased from Alexander Henry (q.v.) the fort at Michipicoten, on lake Superior. In his later years he appears to have been a merchant at Sault Ste. Marie; and in 1819 he sold out his interests there to C. O. Ermatinger (q.v.), and went to live at Pembina, on the Red river.

**Nomenclature.** See **Place-Names.**

**Nominingue,** a village in Labelle county, Quebec, on the Canadian Pacific Railway, 23 miles north-west of Labelle, and 104 miles north-west of Montreal. It is named after the neighbouring lake and river, and is an Indian word signifying "red paint", from the iron ochre found in the vicinity, and used by the Indians for painting their faces. Pop. (1931), 493.

**Nootka,** a tribe of Indians on the west coast of Vancouver island and the extreme north-western corner of the state of Washington. It is a branch of the Wakushan linguistic group—the other being the Kwakiutl (q.v.). Nootka is an Indian word, but was not originally used by the Indians as a tribal name; it was applied by Capt. Cook (q.v.) to the sound, and by extension now includes the surrounding country and people. The Spaniards in 1774 were the first Europeans to see these Indians; but it was Capt. Cook who in 1778 uncovered the wealth of furs and brought traders to the Nootka. These Indians lived in shed-like houses formed of posts covered with split cedar. They changed their residence with the seasons, having a summer and a winter village. Shelter and food supply governed their location. The ocean and ocean beach furnished the greater part of their sustenance. They were great whalers. Their canoes, made from the trunk of the cedar, were fine sea-worthy craft, artistically decorated, capable of holding ten or a dozen men. In them they ventured far to sea in fishing and northward and southward on their war expeditions. Gilbert Malcolm Sproat (q.v.), who lived for five years amongst them, had difficulty in ascertaining anything definite regarding their religion. He says they worshipped the sun and moon, and believed vaguely in a superior being, Quawteaht, whose home was in a delightful land, abounding in all that they valued; but they had no priestly class. Though usually peaceful so far as the whites were concerned, these Indians captured the *Boston* in 1803, the *Tonquin* in 1811, and the *Kingfisher* in 1864. As a result of the last outrage, H.M.S. *Sutlej* bombarded and destroyed a number of their villages in Clayoquot sound; but the criminals were not captured, and the villages were rebuilt. The Nootka are slowly and steadily decreasing in number. In 1845 Warre and Vavasour estimated the whole Wakushan family (Nootka and Kwakiutl) at 40,805. This was merely a wild guess. Sproat in 1860 stated that the twenty villages of the Nootka on Vancouver island contained 1,723 adult males. In 1906 their entire population was 2,159, and in 1911, 1,984 persons. See G. M. Sproat, *Scenes and studies of savage life* (London, 1868), and Robert Brown (ed.), *The adventures of John Jewitt* (London, 1896).

**Nootka sound,** an inlet on the west coast of Vancouver island, between lat. 49° and 50°. Juan Perez, a Spanish explorer, visited its mouth in 1774; but it was actually discovered and named by Capt. James Cook (q.v.) in 1774. A British sea-captain, John Meares (q.v.), built a fort here, at Friendly Cove, in 1788; and in 1789 this was seized by the Spaniards, who held the post until 1795. This event led to a controversy, known as the Nootka controversy, between Great Britain and Spain, involving the question of the sovereignty of the north Pacific coast. The controversy nearly led to war, but in 1790 Spain agreed to pay an indemnity for the seizure of buildings and vessels at Nootka, and allowed British subjects equal rights to trade and settlement north of the 38th parallel of latitude, thus withdrawing for the first time from her claim to exclusive sovereignty over the north Pacific coast of America, south of Alaska. The name Nootka was given by Capt. Cook under the impression that it was the Indian name of the locality, but this impression appears to have been erroneous. For various conjectures as to the explanation of the name, see J. T. Walbran, *British Columbia coast names* (Ottawa, 1909).

**Noranda,** a town in Témiscamingue county, Quebec, on the shore of Tremoy lake, and on the Canadian National Railway, one mile north of Rouyn, and 138 miles north of Témiscamingue. It owes its existence to the discovery of the valuable ores hidden in the earth in this region; and it is particularly famous for the immense smelter built here by Noranda Mines (q.v.). Pop. (1931), 2,246.

**Noranda Mines,** a company owning and operating the Horne mine, a copper-gold property, and a customs concentrator and smelter, at Noranda, Quebec. The name is formed by a combination of North and Canada. In February, 1922, a syndicate, of which the moving spirits were S. C. Thompson and H. W. Chadbourne, optioned the claims of two prospectors named E. H. Horne and E. J. Miller on the shores of lake Osisko. In May, 1922, was incorporated Noranda Mines, Ltd., with James Y. Murdoch as president, which took over the Horne claim and a number of other properties acquired by the syndicate. The success of the company's operations really dated from August, 1923, when diamond-drilling followed by underground work revealed great wealth of ore. In addition to the Horne mine, including the smelter and plant, the company owns claims in the Porcupine area and at Red lake, Ontario. The company produces blister copper, containing precious metals, which is refined by the Canadian Copper Refiners, Ltd., at Montreal East, Quebec, into electrolytic copper. While the mine is primarily a copper producer, the value of its gold production can be adjusted owing to the flexibility of its ore bodies. See *History of Noranda Mines, Limited* (Empire Mining and Metallurgical Congress, 1927), *Annual Financial Review, Canadian*, July, 1934; *Canadian Mining Journal*, April, 1934; *Financial Post Survey of Mines, Canada and Newfoundland*, 1933; *Gold*, April, 1934; B. F. Townsley, *Mine-Finders* (Toronto, 1935).

**Nordheimer, Samuel** (1824-1912), capitalist, was born at Memelsdorf, Germany, in 1824, of Jewish parentage. He emigrated to the United States about 1839; and later he founded, with his brother Abraham, the firm of A. and S. Nordheimer, dealers in musical supplies, at Kingston, and then at Toronto, Ontario. He became president of the Federal Bank of Canada, and director of many financial corporations. In 1887 he was appointed German consul for Ontario; and in 1904 he was decorated with the order of the Red Eagle. He died at Toronto on June 29, 1912. In 1871 he married Edith Louise, daughter of James Boulton, of Toronto, and for many years president for Canada of the Imperial Order of the Daughters of the Empire; and by her had one son and seven daughters.

**Norfolk,** a county on the north shore of lake Erie, is bounded on the east by Haldimand county, on the north by Brant county, on the north-west by Oxford county, and on the west by Elgin county. The county was created by John Graves Simcoe (q.v.) in July, 1792, and was called after Norfolk county in England. The first settlers were United Empire Loyalists, and for many years lumbering was the chief industry. Now, however, the county is mainly agricultural. Tobacco-growing is an important industry, and there are extensive apple orchards, and large poultry and livestock farms. There is a government reforestation area of 1,645 acres at St. Williams, and another of 1,800 acres at Turkey Point, and there are many private plantations also. County town, Simcoe. Area, 400,800 acres. Pop. (1931), 31,359. See illustrated pamphlet issued by the Norfolk Chamber of Commerce (Simcoe, 1931); Henry Smith Johnson, *Norfolk place-names* (Norfolk Historical Society, 1934); J. A. Bannister, *Early educational history of Norfolk county* (University of Toronto Press, 1926); E. A. Owen, *Pioneer sketches of Long Point Settlement*, (Toronto, 1898); *Historical atlas of Norfolk county* (Toronto, 1877); and *Oxford and Norfolk gazetteer* (Woodstock, 1867).

**Norfolk Historical Society,** a society which has a museum of historical antiquities in the public library at Simcoe, Ontario. Its documents are deposited in the Norfolk registry office. The Chadwick Academy, an historic

NORANDA MINES, ROUYN, QUEBEC

*Photograph by Canadian Airways Limited*

private school near Vittoria, is owned by the society.

**Normanby, Marquis of.** See **Mulgrave, George Augustus Constantine, Earl of.**

**Normand, Louis Philippe** (1863-1928), president of the Privy Council of Canada (1921), was born at Three Rivers, Quebec, on September 21, 1863. He was educated at Laval University (M.D., 1886), and practised medicine at Three Rivers, of which he was repeatedly mayor. From September to December, 1921, he was president of the Privy Council in the Meighen administration. In 1922 he was elected president of the Medical Council of Canada. He died at Three Rivers on June 27, 1928.

**Normandin,** a village in Lake St. John county, Quebec, on the Canadian National Railway, 70 miles from St. Bruno. It was named after Joseph Laurent Normandin, the surveyor who mapped the Lake St. John district in 1733. It is the centre of an agricultural district, with cheese and butter factories; and it is also a lumbering centre. Pop. (1931), 773.

**Normans.** A large proportion of the first settlers in Canada during the French régime came from Normandy. It has been estimated that the first generation of Normans in Canada numbered 800 families, with over 5,000 children. The result has been seen in the strong Norman influence on the French-Canadian mode of speech and in the influence of Norman domestic architecture on that of New France. See E. Vaillancourt, *La conquête du Canada par les Normands* (Montreal, 1930).

**Norquay, John** (1841-1889), prime minister of Manitoba (1878-86), was born in the Red River Settlement, Assiniboia, on May 8, 1841. He was educated at St. John's Academy, Winnipeg, under the Right Rev. David Anderson (q.v.); and in 1871 he was elected to represent High Bluff in the first Legislative Assembly of Manitoba. He continued a member of the Assembly until his death. He was appointed minister of public works in the first administration of Manitoba in 1871; he became provincial secretary in 1875, and minister of public works again in 1876; and in 1878 he was called upon, with Joseph Royal (q.v.), to form a government. He was prime minister from 1878 to 1887, when he resigned to become a railway commissioner. He died at Winnipeg, on July 5, 1889. In 1862 he married Elizabeth, daughter of George Setter, of Poplar Point, Manitoba.

**Norquay, mount,** is in Alberta, north-west of Banff, in lat 51° 12′, and long. 115° 39′. It is named after the Hon. John Norquay (q.v.), sometime premier of Manitoba, who climbed it in 1887 or 1888. It has a height of 8,275 feet.

**Norris, Tobias Crawford** (1861-1936), prime minister of Manitoba (1915-22), was born in Brampton, Ontario, on September 5, 1861. He went to the North West as a youth, with his parents, and became a farmer. In 1896 he was elected to the Legislative Assembly of Manitoba; in 1909 he became leader of the Liberal opposition; and in 1915 he became prime minister of the province. He was defeated in the general elections of 1922; and in 1927 he resigned the leadership of the Liberal party in Manitoba, to contest a seat in the Canadian House of Commons. In 1929 he was appointed a member of the Board of Railway Commissioners for Canada; and he died in Toronto on October 28, 1936. His term of office as prime minister of Manitoba saw the introduction into the province of female suffrage, minimum wage laws, and "prohibition".

**Norse Voyages.** It is now generally admitted that the Norse settlers in Greenland visited the coast of north-eastern America about 1000 A.D., and perhaps for years afterwards, thus antedating the discovery of America by Columbus by nearly 500 years. The evidence for the Norse voyages to America consists not only in the sagas of Eric the Red, the Flat Island Book, and the Hawk's Book (narratives set down in writing long after the events which they purport to describe), but also in several Icelandic vellums and in a passage in the writings of Adam of Bremen. It is recorded in at least six vellums that in 1121 Eric Gnupsson, who was appointed by Paschal II "bishop of Greenland, and Vinland *in partibus infidelium*", went in search of Vinland, which was the site of the Norse attempts at colonization in North America. Dr. Fridtjof Nansen, the Norwegian explorer, has, in his *In northern mists* (2 vols., London, 1911), sought to show that the mythical element in the sagas is so pronounced that no reliance can be placed in their details; and he admits no more than the bare fact that the Norsemen reached America by way of Greenland, probably in search of timber, which is lacking in Greenland. All attempts to determine the site of Vinland he rejects as based on unreliable evidence. It is true that there are apparently mythical elements in the sagas, and it is also true that great changes must have taken place in the shoreline of North America since 1000 A.D., but most scholars have refused to follow Dr. Nansen in discounting completely the details of the sagas, and numerous attempts, some of them most ingenious, have been made to identify the sites of Helluland, Markland, and Vinland, the various places mentioned in the sagas. Vinland has been placed as far north as Hamilton inlet in Labrador, and as far south as Long Island sound in Connecticut. The latest theory advanced is that it was in the valley of the St. Lawrence.

The literature relating to the Norse voyages has been extensive. The more important discussions of the problem are to be found in A. M. Reeves, *The finding of Wineland the good* (London, 1890); J. E. Olson, *The voyages of the Northerners* (New York, 1906); M. L. Fernald, *Notes on the plants of Wineland the good* (Rhodora, 1910) and *The natural history of ancient Vinland* (Bulletin of the American Geographical Society, 1915); Fridtjof Nansen, *In northern mists* (2 vols., London, 1911); W. H. Babcock, *Early Norse visits to North America* (Washington, 1913); W. A. Munn, *The location of Helluland, Markland, and Wineland from the Icelandic sagas* (St. John's, Newfoundland, 1914); William Hovgaard, *The voyages of the Norsemen to America* (New York, 1914); H. P. Steensby, *The Norsemen's route from Greenland to Wineland* (Copenhagen, 1917); A. Fossum, *The Norse discovery of America* (Minneapolis, 1918); G. M. Gathorne-Hardy, *The Norse discoveries of America* (Oxford, 1921); H. Hermansson, *The Vinland voyages* (Geographical Review, 1927); and W. Bovey, *The Norse voyages to North America* (Trans. Roy. Soc. Can., 1936).

**North Battleford,** a city in Saskatchewan, at the junction of the Saskatchewan and Battle rivers, 90 miles north-west of Saskatoon, on the Canadian National and Canadian Pacific Railways. The city lies upon the bank of the river two miles north of Battleford, which was the capital of the North West Territories from 1877 to 1883, taking its name from its position at the "ford of Battle river", on which in the early days the Indians fought many battles. The growth of North Battleford at the expense of Battleford is because the Canadian Northern Railway line to Edmonton (254 miles distant) was run on the north side of the river. The city has public and separate schools, a collegiate institute, a convent, seven churches, a public library, and an armoury. The industries include a cold-storage plant, creameries, a sash-and-door factory, aërated water works, a brewery, three elevators, and stock-yards. Jack Fish lake, in the district, attracts many summer visitors. Pop. (1931), 5,986.

**North Bay,** a city in Nipissing district, Ontario, is situated on the north shore of lake Nipissing. The first tree was cut on the site about 1880, and the Canadian Pacific Railway reached it in 1882, when the settlement of the place was inaugurated. The city received its name from its location on lake Nipissing. It was incorporated as a town in 1890, and as a city in 1925. It is served by the Canadian Pacific, Canadian National, and Temiskaming and Northern Ontario Railways. On account of its geographical position, the city is known as the "Gateway to the North". It is the distributing centre for northern Ontario, and is the capital and judicial seat of the district of Nipissing. It has a collegiate institute, a normal school, a technical school, an academy, a boy's college, and a tri-weekly newspaper (*Nugget*). Pop. (1931), 15,528.

**North, cape,** the northern extremity of Prince Edward island. It was named by Jacques Cartier (q.v.) in 1534 "Cap des Sauvages", from the fact that an Indian here beckoned to Cartier to land. The present name first appears in Holland's map of 1765.

**North Devon island.** See **Devon island.**

**Northern Alberta Railways,** a merger of railways formed in 1929, when the Edmonton, Dunvegan, and British Columbia Railway, the Central Canada Railway, and the Alberta Great Waterways Railway were purchased jointly by the Canadian Pacific and Canadian National Railways. The Edmonton, Dunvegan, and British Columbia Railway was opened between Edmonton and Spirit river, Alberta, in 1915-16; and the Central Canada Railway, opened between McLennan and Peace river in 1916, and the Alberta and Great Waterways Railway, opened between Carbondale and lac la Biche in 1917, were operated at first as branches of the E. D. and B. C. Railway. In 1920, the Central Canada and the Alberta Great Waterways Railways were taken over by the Canadian Pacific for five years, under an agreement with the Alberta government; from 1925 to 1929 they were operated by the government; and in 1929 they were taken over, with the E. D. and B. C. Railway, by the Canadian Pacific and Canadian National Railways, and came under their joint operation as the Northern Alberta Railways. Several extensions of the system have taken place since that date.

**Northern Bank,** a bank incorporated in 1903, with headquarters in Winnipeg. In 1908 it was amalgamated with the Crown Bank, under the name of the Northern Crown Bank.

**Northern Crown Bank,** a chartered bank formed in 1908 by the merger of the Crown Bank, founded in 1903, with headquarters in Toronto, Ontario, and the Northern Bank, founded in 1903, with headquarters in Winnipeg, Manitoba. This merger of small banks was taken over by the Royal Bank of Canada in 1918.

**Northern Railway of Canada,** a line of railway opened from Toronto to Collingwood, by way of Bradford and Barrie, during the years 1853-55. It was named originally the Ontario, Simcoe, and Huron Railway; but was re-named the Northern Railway of Canada in 1858. Branch lines were built from Collingwood to Meaford (1872) and from Allandale to Gravenhurst (1875); and in 1879 the Hamilton and North Western Railway was absorbed by the Northern Railway, which became the Northern and North Western. The system was taken over by the Grand Trunk Railway in 1888.

**North Hatley,** a village in Stanstead county, Quebec, at the outlet of lake Massawippi, and on the Boston and

Maine Railway, 12 miles south of Sherbrooke. Pop. (1934), 550.

**North Indian lake** is in northern Manitoba, in the valley of the Churchill river, between the 57th and 58th parallels of north latitude. It has an area of 150 square miles.

**North Kootenay pass** is in the Rocky mountains, on the boundary between British Columbia and Alberta, at the head of Pincher creek, a tributary of the Flathead river, in the Kootenay district, and has an elevation of 6,774 feet. This historic pass is an example of a duplex summit, the two passes, north and south, being separated by a local mountain, 600 feet above the passes. The north pass, which contains the trail, is 25 feet higher than the south pass. Blakiston of the Palliser expedition crossed it in 1858, and is said to have been the first white man to do so.

**North river** crosses the counties of Terrebonne, Argenteuil, and Two Mountains, Quebec, and empties into the lake of Two Mountains, an enlargement of the Ottawa at its junction with the St. Lawrence. At its mouth the North is divided into two channels by a small island. Boats and rafts can ascend it in spite of rapids. It is 75 miles long, and drains a basin of 860 square miles.

**North Somerset island.** See **Somerset island.**

**North Stukely,** a village in Shefford county, Quebec, 14 miles from Waterloo, and 8 miles from South Stukely, the nearest railway station. It is named after Stukely, a village in Huntingdonshire, England. Pop. (1934), 1,000.

**North Sydney,** a town in Cape Breton county, Nova Scotia, about three miles from the coal fields at Sydney Mines and the farming sections of Bras d'Or and Boularderie, is situated on the north side of Sydney harbour. It is on the Canadian National Railway and has regular steamboat service with Newfoundland, with St. Pierre and Miquelon, and, in addition, with Neil's harbour, Ingonish, Bay St. Lawrence, and through the Bras d'Or lakes with Baddeck and Whycocomagh. At North Sydney is the coal shipping pier of the Nova Scotia Steel and Coal Company. It is also the winter port of Cape Breton's fishing industry. A feature which has contributed greatly to its prosperity is the cable office of the Western Union Company, which forms a connecting link between Canada and Europe, with an operating staff of about three hundred. It has a hospital, a convent, and a weekly newspaper (*Herald*). It was named, like Sydney (q.v.), after Thomas Townshend, first Viscount Sydney. Pop. (1931), 6,139.

**Northumberland,** a county in New Brunswick, facing the gulf of St. Lawrence, and bounded on the north by Gloucester and Restigouche counties, on the west by Victoria and York counties, and on the south by Sunbury and Kent counties. It was created in 1785, and its name was suggested either by its contiguity to Westmorland county (before Kent county was created), or by its proximity to Northumberland strait. It is drained by the Miramichi river, with its many tributaries; and is one of the most heavily timbered parts of the province. Chief town, Newcastle. Pop. (1931), 34,124.

**Northumberland,** a county on the north shore of lake Ontario, bounded on the west by Durham county (with which it is united for judicial purpose), on the north by Peterborough, and on the east by Hastings. It was one of the nineteen counties set apart by John Graves Simcoe (q.v.) in July, 1792, and was called after the English shire. Settlement was at first mainly Irish. The county town is Cobourg. Area, 494,075 acres. Pop. (1931), 31,452. See E. Edwin Dodds, *Directory of Northumberland and Durham* (Port Hope, 1880), and Sutherland's *Directory of Northumberland and Durham* (Woodstock, 1865).

**Northumberland strait,** the passage between Prince Edward Island and the mainland of Nova Scotia and New Brunswick. It was named by Des Barres (q.v.) after H.M.S. *Northumberland*, the flagship of Admiral Lord Colville of Culross, at whose request Des Barres was seconded in 1764 from the Royal American Regiment to undertake the survey of the Nova Scotian coast under the Admiralty.

**North Vancouver,** a city of British Columbia, in the district of Burrard, on the north shore of Burrard inlet and opposite Vancouver city, with which it is connected by bridge, ferry, and railroad. It was incorporated in 1906. The industries include shipbuilding, engineering works, wood-working factories, and lumber mills. There is a deep-sea water frontage, and a fine boulevard, 150 feet wide. The scenic drives, good fishing, and shooting attract many tourists. In the vicinity are Crown mountain (5,600 feet), the Lions (6,500 feet), and Grouse mountain (4,350 feet). Pop. (1931), 8,510.

**Northwest Angle inlet,** a bay of the lake of the Woods, on the international boundary between Canada and the United States. At the head of the inlet is the point accepted by Great Britain and the United States as "the north-west angle" or north-western-most point of the lake of the Woods. See **Boundaries.**

**North-West Coal and Navigation Company Railway,** a railway line in the North West Territories, between Dunmore and Lethbridge, opened for traffic in 1885. In 1890 it was absorbed by the Alberta Railway and Coal Company; in 1893 it was leased to the Canadian Pacific Railway; and in 1897 it was purchased by it.

**North West Company,** an organization formed in the years following the British conquest of Canada, for the exploitation of the fur-bearing regions of the Canadian North West. It was not, like the Hudson's Bay Company, a chartered company, but was merely a pool or syndicate of fur-trading firms or individuals, formed to abate the evils of competition; and though it came later to be dominated by the Montreal firm of McTavish, Frobisher, and Company (later McTavish, McGillivrays, and Company), it never lost its character as a partnership. To this feature of its constitution it owed, indeed, in large measure both its success and its failure. Its wintering partners, with a personal stake in the fortunes of the company, proved much more aggressive than the poorly-paid employees of the Hudson's Bay Company; and in the race for the furs which opened up the whole of the Canadian North West, from lake Superior to the Pacific ocean and from the sources of the Mississippi to the Arctic sea, the Nor'Westers easily outdistanced the Hudson's Bay men. On the other hand, when the rivalry between the North West Company and the Hudson's Bay Company came to a head over Lord Selkirk's establishment of a colony on the Red river, cutting across the North West Company's line of communications with the interior, the loose organization of the Nor'Westers proved to be a severe handicap, as compared with the unified control of the Hudson's Bay Company.

Just when the North West Company was first formed, is difficult to determine. At an early date signs of concentration among the fur-traders in the far North West were apparent; and in 1775 Alexander Henry (q.v.) describes a pool or merger of interests on the Saskatchewan. There are references to "the North West Company" as early as 1776. But the first union of interests of which we have definite knowledge was the sixteen-share concern formed in 1779. The agreement on which this was based apparently broke down; but it was succeeded by a new agreement in 1783, and this is the date at which

the North West Company has commonly been said to have begun. The 1783
company had to meet the competition
of a rival organization of Montreal
merchants, known as Gregory, McLeod,
and Company, in the service of which
Sir Alexander Mackenzie (q.v.) began
his career; but in 1787 this company
was absorbed by the North West Company, and a new agreement was made,
under which the North West Company
was reorganized on the basis of twenty
shares, instead of sixteen. Opposition
to the North West Company developed
again after 1793, and in 1800 there was
formed a "New North West Company",
to which the name of XY Company
came to be applied. After a severe
contest, the XY Company was in 1804
absorbed in the North West Company,
and was given a quarter interest in the
new concern, which was reorganized on
the basis of one hundred shares. The
agreement of 1804 was the constitution
under which the company operated for
the rest of its life.

The development of the North West
Company's trade during these years
was spectacular. Its operations were
confined at first to the lake Superior
region, the valleys of the Red and
Assiniboine rivers, and the Saskatchewan river. But in 1778 Peter Pond
(q.v.) reached lake Athabaska; in 1789
Alexander Mackenzie (q.v.) followed
the Mackenzie river to its mouth on
the shores of the Arctic ocean, and in
1793 crossed the Rocky mountains,
and reached salt water on the Pacific
coast; and in 1811 David Thompson
(q.v.) explored the Columbia river to
its mouth. The opening up of these
vast new territories, constituting a
veritable "Empire of the North", over
which the company held sway, converted the North West Company into
one of the first examples of "big business"
on the North American continent; and its
wilderness headquarters, situated first
at Grand Portage on lake Superior, and
after 1805 at Fort William, became in
the height of the season a town of
several thousand inhabitants. Fortunes
were made in the fur-trade; but these
fortunes went to the individual partners,
rather than to the North West Company, which consequently built up no
reserve fund, and was indeed in the
position of a creditor of many of its
partners.

When, therefore, the Earl of Selkirk
(q.v.), who had acquired a controlling
interest in the Hudson's Bay Company,
challenged the North West Company
to a life-and-death struggle by establishing on the banks of the Red river in
1812 a colony which cut athwart of the
North West Company's line of communications, the North West Company
found itself ill-equipped to meet the
long struggle that followed. Not only
was it at a disadvantage in meeting the
intensive competition in the fur-trade
(for the costs of shipping furs by Hudson bay were half of what they were
for transporting furs by the long canoe-
route to Montreal), but it had no
reserves to meet the costs of this
ruinous competition or of the expensive
and prolonged law-suits in which the
North West Company became involved.
It is not possible to describe here in
detail the duel which took place between
Lord Selkirk and the Nor'Westers in
the years following 1812—a duel which
first became acute with the massacre
of Seven Oaks (q.v.) in 1815, and
culminated in the capture of Fort
William by Lord Selkirk in 1816 and
the subsequent arrest of Lord Selkirk
in 1817; but the results of the struggle
were painfully apparent. The Hudson's
Bay Company invaded areas, such as
the Athabaska country, which they
had hitherto left to the Nor'Westers;
and the Nor'Westers devoted all their
energies to the prosecution of the
struggle with the Hudson's Bay men,
instead of to the prosecution of the fur-
trade. On the face of things, the North
West Company did not come out of the
contest badly. They won, on the whole,

a victory in the courts; and Lord Selkirk, his health shattered, retired to the south of France, to die an early and untimely death in 1820. But the victory was a Pyrrhic one. By 1820 the financial position of the North West Company had become so acute that no attempt was made to balance its books; and in 1821 it was driven to accept absorption in the Hudson's Bay Company.

It has been usual to say that in 1821 the Hudson's Bay Company and the North West Company were united or amalgamated; and it is true that the wintering partners of the North West Company were given an interest in the Hudson's Bay Company, and the directors of the North West Company were ultimately given shares in the Hudson's Bay Company. But the fact is that the North West Company in 1821 passed out of existence; the fur-trade was diverted from Montreal to Hudson bay; Fort William sank into the category of a third-rate post; and in 1839 Washington Irving was able to write the epitaph of the Nor'Westers in these famous words: "The feudal state of Fort William is at an end; its council chamber is silent and desolate; its banquet hall no longer echoes to the auld-word ditty; the lords of the lakes and the forests are all passed away."

*Bibliography.* For an account of the history of the North West Company, see G. C. Davidson, *The North West Company* (Berkeley, California, 1918); H. A. Innis, *The North West Company* (Can. hist. rev., 1927); and W. S. Wallace (ed.), *Documents relating to the North West Company* (Toronto, The Champlain Society, 1934). Much material relating to the history of the Company will be found in L. R. Masson (ed.), *Les bourgeois de la Compagnie du Nord-Ouest* (2 vols., Quebec, 1889-90); C. M. Gates (ed.), *Five fur-traders of the north-west* (Minneapolis, Minn., 1933), and the journals or narratives of Alexander Henry the elder (q.v.), Alexander Henry the younger (q.v.),

G. Franchère (q.v.), D. W. Harmon (q.v.), Sir Alexander Mackenzie (q.v.), Duncan McGillivray (q.v.), J. B. Perrault (q.v.), Peter Pond (q.v.), David Thompson (q.v.), and Nicholas Garry (q.v.). Reference should be made also to Marion O'Neil, *The maritime activities of the North West Company, 1813 to 1821* (Washington Historical Quarterly, 1930), and to the following papers by R. Harvey Fleming, *McTavish, Frobisher and Company, of Montreal* (Can. hist. rev.), *Phyn, Ellice and Company, of Schenectady* (Contributions to Canadian Economics, 1932), and *The origin of "Sir Alexander and Company"* (Can. hist. rev., 1928).

**North West Mounted Police.** See **Royal Canadian Mounted Police.**

**North West Rebellions.** The introduction of civilization into the Canadian North West brought about two successive rebellions on the part of the Métis or half-breeds who were the children of the early fur-trade—the first in 1869-70, and the second in 1885. Attempts have been made to show that the first of these was not really a rebellion against the British crown, but was merely an assertion of the basic rights of British citizens; and there is much to be said for this point of view. But the term "rebellion" has long been applied to both episodes; and both had much in common. They were led by the same leader, Louis Riel (q.v.); they were brought about by similar causes; and they had equally unfortunate results. To call them both rebellions is not therefore a complete misnomer.

*1. The Rebellion of 1869-70.* Prior to 1869, the North West was under the government of the Hudson's Bay Company; but in that year the Hudson's Bay Company resigned its suzerainty over this territory to the crown, on condition that it retained certain small areas about its forts, a certain proportion of lands to be granted in the future, and the sum of £300,000 from the Canadian government. It is sometimes said that Canada acquired the North West by purchase; but this is hardly an accurate statement of the facts. What actually happened was that the Hudson's Bay Company resigned its control of the North West to the crown, on condition that it received £300,000 as compensation; and that the crown then conveyed these territories to the Canadian government. Before the transfer was completed, Canada sent out a contractor to build a road from Red river to the lake of Woods, and surveyors to lay out the country in townships and sections for settlement. This greatly alarmed the Métis, across whose lands the surveyors ran their lines, and who feared that their lands and homesteads would be taken from them. The Canadian government made the mistake also of making arrangements for the government of the North West without even consulting the inhabitants; and these felt that they were being bought and sold like sheep in the market. When the Canadian government appointed William McDougall (q.v.) lieutenant-governor of Rupertsland and the North West Territories, the Métis decided to oppose his entrance into the new territory; and when he arrived, *viâ* St. Paul, at the border town of Pembina, he found an armed force of Métis behind a barricade blocking his progress. He foolishly published a proclamation announcing his appointment as lieutenant-governor, only to find that the Canadian government had refused to take over the North West until the troubles ceased; and he was then compelled to make an ignominious retreat to Ottawa.

Meanwhile, the Métis had taken matters into their own hands. The governor of the Hudson's Bay Company, William McTavish (q.v.), was ill; and in any case he now lacked the necessary authority to take action. The half-breeds seized Fort Garry, and in November they set up here a provisional government. As president of this provisional government they chose Louis Riel (q.v.), a young French half-breed of good education, but of unstable mind and character. During the winter of 1869-70, and during the spring and summer of 1870, the Riel government remained in control at Fort Garry. A group of English loyalists under Major C. A. Boulton (q.v.) attempted to dislodge the rebels, but were defeated and captured. Donald A. Smith, afterwards Lord Strathcona (q.v.) was sent out by the Canadian governor as a commissioner to treat with the rebels; but, though he conducted himself with great sagacity, and did much to curb the rebels, he was little more than a prisoner. He was not able to prevent the judicial murder by Riel of a loyalist prisoner named Thomas Scott; and the murder of Scott, who was an Orangeman, roused in English-speaking Canada the bitterest feelings. In the spring of 1870 a military expedition was dispatched to the West under the command of Colonel (afterwards Field-Marshal) Wolseley; and after following the old route of the fur-traders, it arrived at Fort Garry on August 24. As it approached, Riel and his associates fled without fighting, and took refuge in the United States.

*2. The Rebellion of 1885.* The second North West Rebellion broke out in the valley of the North Saskatchewan. Here had settled a number of the half-breeds of the fur-trade, on oblong farms abutting on the river. Some of these were half-breeds from the Red river valley, who, after having been granted farms of 240 acres in the Red river district, had sold out, and moved west to the Saskatchewan. To all these native settlers the building of the Canadian Pacific Railway across the prairies brought a serious threat. They had enjoyed a monopoly of the transportation business on the western prairies; and of this the railway threatened to rob them. The buffalo, on which they had relied for a livelihood, had disappeared, and their farms had become their chief source of livelihood. The government surveyors, who had come out with the railway, had proceeded to run their lines with a mathematical precision which ignored the rights of the half-breed owners of oblong farms; and the half-breeds became fearful that they would be again dispossessed. Their cousins, the Indians, had recently been granted reserves on which they could settle; but no provision had been made for them. They saw white settlers coming into the country, and in some cases receiving title to parts of their farms; and they became panic-stricken. Representations were made on their behalf to the Canadian government, but, with an obtuseness which it is difficult to understand, the government ignored these representations.

In 1884 the half-breeds on the Saskatchewan sent a delegation to Louis Riel (q.v.), who was teaching school in Montana, to come up and help them. He accepted their invitation; and for a time devoted himself to attempting to obtain the redress of the half-breeds' grievances by constitutional means. But gradually he became wilder and more extreme; and in the spring he set up a provisional government at Batoche, on the South Saskatchewan. A detachment of North West Mounted Police, sent to nip the rebellion in the bud, were defeated by the half-breeds under Gabriel Dumont (q.v.); and the fat was in the fire. For a time there was danger of an Indian rising; and the Indians under Big Bear (q.v.) actually massacred most of the whites at the Hudson's Bay Company post of Frog Lake. The North West Mounted Police were forced to abandon first Fort Carlton and later Fort Pitt; and the whites in the Saskatchewan valley were forced to take refuge within the stockades at Battleford.

The news of the Duck Lake disaster roused the Canadian government to action. A force of Canadian militia was organized, under General Middleton (q.v.), the general officer commanding the Canadian militia; and between four and five thousand militiamen were rushed to the West by way of the newly-built Canadian Pacific Railway. General Middleton divided his force into three columns. The main force detrained at Qu'Appelle, and pushed north-west toward Batoche. A second column, under Colonel Otter (q.v.), proceeded north from Swift Current to the relief of Battleford; and a third column, under General Strange (q.v.), marched north from Calgary to Edmonton. Otter was the first to reach his objective. After being checked by a band of Crees under Poundmaker (q.v.) at Cutknife creek, he succeeded in relieving Battleford. Middleton was held up by the half-breeds at Fish creek, on the South Saskatchewan, but after a delay he resumed his march, and on May 12 he defeated the main body of Riel's half-breeds at Batoche. Meanwhile, General Strange had reached Edmonton, and was closing in on Big Bear and his Crees. Riel was captured a few days after Batoche, and later in that summer, on July 2, Big Bear surrendered. With his capture, the rebellion was over.

In the autumn of 1885, Riel and some of the other leaders of the rebellion were tried at Regina on charges of high treason, and were found guilty. Riel was hanged in the Police Barracks at Regina in November, 1885, though there were many who believed that he should properly have been confined instead to a lunatic asylum. Eight of the Indian ring-leaders in the rebellion were also hanged; though Poundmaker and Big Bear both escaped with prison sentences. The execution of Riel caused grave repercussions in Canadian politics, for his compatriots in French Canada were almost unanimous in demanding the remission of his sentence. But Sir John Macdonald (q.v.) was determined that he should pay the price for the mad folly of his second armed outbreak.

"He shall die," Macdonald exclaimed, with unwonted fierceness, "though every dog in Quebec bark in his favour."

*Bibliography.* The story of the two rebellions has been told, in the light of the most recent research, in G. F. G. Stanley, *The birth of the western provinces* (London, 1936), and in A. L. Burt, *The romance of the prairie provinces* (Toronto, 1930). Two volumes by eye-witnesses of both rebellions are C. A. Boulton, *Reminiscences of the North West rebellions* (Toronto, 1886), and G. T. Denison, *Soldiering in Canada* (Toronto, 1900).

The traditional English view of the rebellion of 1869-70 is found in R. G. MacBeth, *The making of the Canadian West* (Toronto, 1898), and in the various histories of Manitoba. The point of view of the French-Canadian half-breeds has been set forth in the Rev. A. G. Morice, *A critical history of the Red River insurrection* (Winnipeg, 1935), and in several papers by A. H. de Trémaudan, notably in *Louis Riel's account of the capture of Fort Garry* (Can. hist. rev., 1924), and *The execution of Thomas Scott* (Can. hist. rev., 1925).

An account of the rebellion of 1885 will be found in the blue paper entitled *Report on the suppression of the rebellion in the North West* (Ottawa, 1886), C. P. Mulvany, *The history of the North West rebellion* (Toronto, 1885), N. F. Black, *History of Saskatchewan and the North West Territories* (2 vols., Regina, 1913), W. B. Cameron, *The war trail of Big Bear* (Toronto, 1926), and in the various histories of the Royal North West Mounted Police.

**North West River House,** a Hudson's Bay Company post at the upper end of lake Melville, at the outlet of Grand lake, opposite the mouth of Hamilton river, in Labrador. It was established in 1836, near the site of an old French trading-post, and was first named Fort Smith. The name was changed in 1840 to North West River

House. The post has been in continuous operation to the present.

**North West Territories,** the name originally applied in 1870 to the whole of the Hudson's Bay Company's territories (known as "Rupert's Land and the North West Territory") handed over to Canada in that year. The exact limit of these territories was not defined, but they included, under the royal charter of the Hudson's Bay Company, all those territories watered by the rivers flowing into Hudson bay. The Hudson's Bay Company had had four departments, the Montreal department, the Northern and Southern departments, and the Columbia department. Of these, only the Northern and Southern departments were those in which the Company had, by its charter, suzerain rights; and it was these departments that were later constituted the "North West Territories". Out of them was carved in 1870 the province of Manitoba, and in 1905 the provinces of Saskatchewan and Alberta. Their government was organized by the North West Territories Act passed by the Canadian parliament in 1875, when they were placed under a lieutenant-governor and council. In 1876 the provisional district of Keewatin was created, and was placed under the government of the lieutenant-governor of Manitoba until 1905. In 1882 the districts of Saskatchewan, Assiniboia, Alberta, and Athabaska were created, and in 1888 were given a legislature, with local responsible government; but in 1905 these districts disappeared with the creation of the provinces of Saskatchewan and Alberta. In 1895 the provisional districts of Mackenzie, Ungava, and Franklin were created; but in 1912 Ungava was annexed to the province of Quebec. At the same time, the boundaries of the provinces of Ontario, Manitoba, Saskatchewan, and Alberta were extended north to the 60th parallel of latitude; and this line became the southern boundary of the

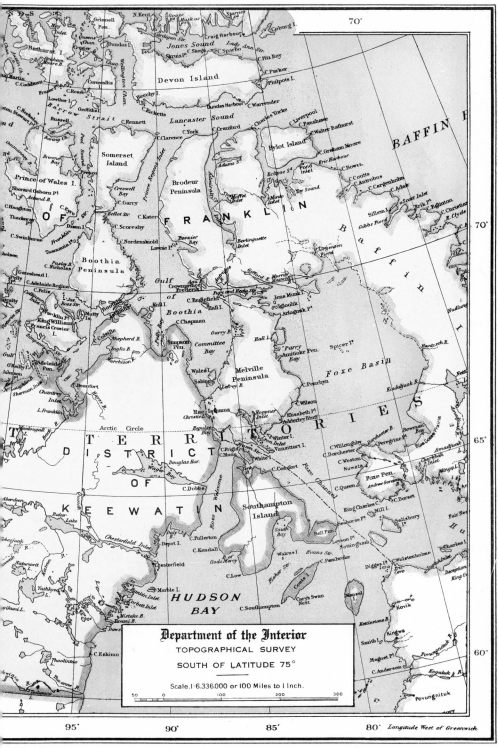

Department of the Interior

TOPOGRAPHICAL SURVEY

SOUTH OF LATITUDE 75°

Scale.1:6.336.000 or 100 Miles to 1 Inch.

districts of Keewatin and Mackenzie. Since 1912 the North West Territories have been confined therefore to the provisional districts of Keewatin, Mackenzie, and Franklin. In 1905 the government of the North West Territories ceased to be vested in a lieutenant-governor and council, and was vested in a commissioner and council appointed by the Dominion government, and under the minister of the Interior. The area of the North West Territories, including the Yukon Territory (which is a separate administrative unit), is no less than 1,516,785 square miles—or nearly half the area of the United States.

**Norway House,** a Hudson's Bay Company fort on the north end of Fort island in Little Playgreen lake, opposite the mouth of the Gunisao river, in Manitoba. The original fort which bore this name was built about 1800 at the entrance to Playgreen lake, near the northern end of lake Winnipeg; and the name is said to have originated from the fact that in 1815 some Norwegians were driven hither from the Selkirk colony. This post was burnt in 1825; and its occupants then moved to a post, about 25 miles distant, at the mouth of the Gunisao or Jack river, which was known as Jack River House. On Fort island, opposite this post, they proceeded to build in 1826-8 the present Norway House, a large post 150 yards square, surrounded by a picket palisade 15 feet high; and until the coming of the railway, Norway House was an important distributing point for the supplies that came from York Factory for the interior. It was there that the governor of the Hudson's Bay Company, Sir George Simpson (q.v.), had for many years his western headquarters; and it was there that the Northern Council of the Hudson's Bay Company met annually. Here, too, the Rev. J. Evans (q.v.) invented the Cree syllabic characters, and did the first printing in the Canadian west, and here the transfer of Rupert's Land to the crown was arranged in 1869. See R. Watson, *The story of Norway House* (Can. Geographical Journal, 1930).

**Norval,** a village in Halton county, Ontario, on the Credit river, and on the Canadian National Railway, 2 miles from Georgetown. Pop. (1934), 400.

**Norwich,** a village in Oxford county, Ontario, is situated on Otter creek, 17 miles south-east of Woodstock (q.v.). It is served by the Canadian National Railways, and has a condensed milk plant, vinegar works, and other factories. The township in which it is situated was surveyed in 1795. It was incorporated as a village in 1876, and takes its name from the city of Norwich, in Norfolk, England. It has a high school, a public library, and a weekly newspaper (*Gazette*). Pop. (1931), 1,158.

**Norwood, Robert Winkworth** (1874-1932), clergyman and poet, was born at New Ross, Lunenburg county, Nova Scotia, on March 27, 1874, the son of the Rev. Joseph W. Norwood and Edith, daughter of Capt. Harding. He was educated at King's College, Windsor, Nova Scotia (B.A., 1897; D.C.L., 1921), and was ordained a priest of the Church of England in 1898. He was rector successively of charges in Bridgewater, Nova Scotia, in London, Ontario, in Philadelphia, Pennsylvania, and in New York. He died at New York on September 28, 1932. He was the author of several volumes of poetry, *His lady of the sonnets* (Boston, 1915), *The witch of Endor* (Toronto, 1916), *The piper and the reed* (Toronto, 1917), *The modernists* (New York, 1918), *The man of Kerioth* (New York, 1918), *Bill Boram* (New York, 1921), and *Mother and son* (New York, 1925), and *Issa* (New York, 1931). He was also the author of four volumes of prose, *The heresy of Antioch* (New York, 1928), *The steep ascent* (New York, 1928), *The man who dared to be God* (New York, 1929), and *His glorious* *body* (New York, 1930). See A. D. Watson, *Robert Norwood* (Toronto, 1924); *Can. Bookman*, June, 1927; and *Can. Bookman*, October, 1932.

**Norwood,** a town in Peterborough county, Ontario, on the river Ouse and on the Canadian Pacific Railway, 18 miles east of Peterborough. The town is the centre of a rich agricultural district. Dairying is carried on extensively. There is a large creamery and a stock food mill. Norwood has four factories which produce wooden ware of various kinds. The public buildings include high and public schools, two armories, a public library, and the town hall. A weekly paper (*Register*) is published. Pop. (1931), 756.

**Notre Dame,** a village in Kent county, New Brunswick, on the Cocague river, and on the Canadian National Railway, 13 miles from Buctouche. Pop. (1934), 400.

**Notre Dame de Portneuf.** See **Portneuf.**

**Notre Dame des Anges,** a village in Portneuf county, Quebec, on the Batiscan river, and on the Canadian National Railway, 27 miles east of St. Tite. Pop. (1931), 543.

**Notre Dame du Portage,** a village in Témiscouata county, Quebec, on the south shore of the St. Lawrence river, 2 miles from Chemin du Lac, a station on the Canadian National Railway. It is so named from the fact that it was the northern end of the old road from Rivière-du-Loup to the Madawaska (called the Portage Road), and that this road followed in part the old portage from Trois Pistoles to the Madawaska. Pop. (1934), 500.

**Notre Dame mountains,** a spur of the Appalachian range of mountains which extends into Canada, and forms the table-land of Gaspé and the Shickshock mountains. They rise to between 3,000 and 4,000 feet. The name was given to them by Champlain (q.v.) in honour of the Virgin Mary.

**Nottawasaga bay,** a large bay on the south shore of the Georgian bay, the entrance to which lies between cape Rich and Christian island. The Nottawasaga river empties into it, 8 miles east of Collingwood. The name is derived from the Algonkian words *Nahdoway* (Iroquois) and *saga* (outlet of river), and has reference to the fact that the river was the route by which the Iroquois came north to attack the Algonkin.

**Nottingham island** is a small island in the Hudson strait in the North West Territories, north-east of Mansel island. It is about 37½ miles long, and 18 miles at extreme width. It was named by Luke Foxe (q.v.) on his voyage of 1631, after the Earl of Nottingham, then lord high admiral.

**Nottaway river** flows from Mattagami lake, into Rupert's bay, at the south-east end of James bay, in the Abitibi territory, Quebec. The name is an Indian word meaning "Iroquois". It has been calculated that the rapids and falls of the river are capable of producing 50,000 horse-power 150 miles from the height of land, 400,000 at a distance of 250 miles, and a total force of about a million horse-power. The river abounds in fish, and is particularly noted for sturgeon. It is 205 miles long, and drains a basin of 2,800 square miles.

**Novar,** a village in the Parry Sound district of Ontario, on the Canadian National Railway, 10 miles north of Huntsville. Pop. (1935), 400.

**Nova Scotia.** Nova Scotia, the most eastern of the Canadian provinces, lies between lat. 43° 25' and 47° and between long. 59° 40' and 66° 25'. With a total area of 21,068 square miles, it is almost equal to the combined area of Holland and Belgium. The length of the province is 381 miles, and its width varies from 50 to 150 miles. The province is made up of the main peninsula, joined to New Brunswick by the narrow isthmus of Chignecto, and the island of Cape

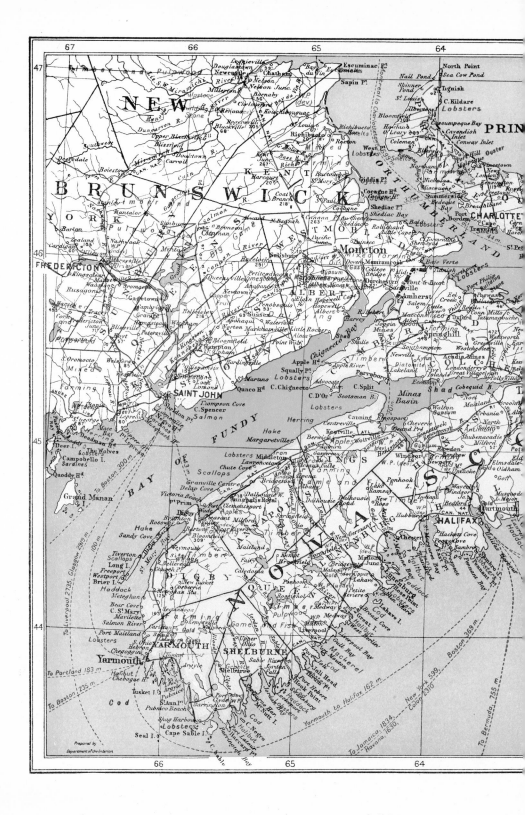

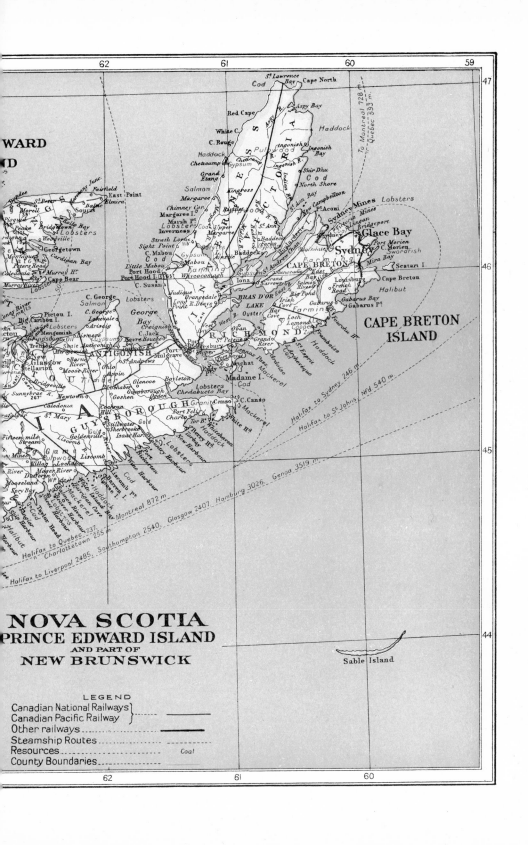

47

St. Lawrence Bay　Cape North
Cod
Red Cape　Aspy Bay

WARD
D

White C.　Haddock
C. Rouge

To Montreal 728 m.
Quebec 595 m.

Haddock　Ingonish
Chetacamp　Ingonish Bay
Pulpwood
Chetacamp R.　Ingonish
Gypsum
Grand　Skir Dhu
Etang　Cod
North Shore

Fairfield　Salmon
East Point　Margaree
Elmira
Souris
Chimney Cor.　Kingross
Margaree I.　New Campbellton
Marsh Pt.　St. Ann　Pt. Aconi　Lobsters
Inverness　Upper　St. Ann's Bay　Sydney Mines
Cow Bay　Margaree　Victoria Mines
Strath Lorne　Baddeck　Bridgeport
Sight Point　Forks　Glace Bay
Baddeck
Cod　Port Morien
C. Mabou　Gypsum　St. Andrews Chan.　C. Morien
Little Mabou　Mabou　Iona　CAPE BRETON　Swordfish
Port Hood　Whycocomagh　Mira Bay
Port Hood I.　Gypsum　Grand　Salmon　Scatari I.
C. Susann　Narrows　River
Irish　Big Pond
Judique　Orangedale　Cove　Louisburg
BRAS D'OR　Farming
C. George　Salmon　Loch R. Denys　LAKE　French
C. George　Lakevale　B. Oyster　Road
Lobsters　Arisaig　Hay　Loch　Gabarus Bay
Pictou I.　George　Cove　Lomond　Gabarus Pt.
Big Caribou I.　Bay　Copper　Halibut
Lobsters　Craignish　B. Oyster　Fourchu Pt.
C. Jack　Loch　CAPE BRETON
Havre Boucher　RICHMOND　Framboise
ANTIGONISH　Port　St. Esprit　ISLAND
Mulgrave　Port Royal　Mackerel
St. Andrews　Petit　L'Ardoise
GUYSBOROUGH　Inhat　Grande
Glencoe　Madame I.　River
Boylston　Cod
Lobsters
Chedabucto Bay
C. Canso
Canso
Granite　Mackerel
Port Felix
Torr B.　Whitehaven
Whitehead
White Hd.

NOVA SCOTIA
PRINCE EDWARD ISLAND
AND PART OF
NEW BRUNSWICK

Halifax to Sydney 246 m.
Halifax to St. John's N'f'd 540 m.

Montreal 872 m.
Halifax to Quebec 737.
Charlottetown 255 m.　Hamburg 3026.　Genoa 3519 m.
Glasgow 2407.
Southampton 2540.
Halifax to Liverpool 2485.

Sable Island

LEGEND
Canadian National Railways
Canadian Pacific Railway
Other railways
Steamship Routes
Resources　　　　Coal
County Boundaries

Breton, which is separated from the rest of the province by the narrow strait of Canso. Cape Breton is substantially 100 miles in length and 87 miles in width, and encloses the salt-water lakes of the Bras d'Or. The backbone of the province is made up of low ranges of hills running roughly east and west. Geologically, the country is the result of two great foldings, the Caledonian, which occurred at the close of the Silurian and the beginning of the Devonian age and accounts for the hills parallel to the Atlantic ocean, and the Hercynian, which occurred after the coal beds of Nova Scotia were laid down and accounts for the ranges of hills in the northern part of the province. The Atlantic coast line is bold and rugged and comparatively barren. It is a drowned coast, and abounds in excellent harbours. Between the hills in the northern part of the province the valleys are fertile, and here is found the agricultural wealth of the province. The chief mineral resource is coal, though there are great deposits of gypsum and widely scattered deposits of gold. The climate is not unlike that of southern Ontario, though somewhat modified by the presence of the ocean. The autumn lasts long, and the spring comes late. The greatest precipitation is in the winter, the average for the year being 35 inches.

*History.* The province first received its present name in the early seventeenth century. In 1621 King James I of England and VI of Scotland "by and with the consent of his Scottish council" granted to Sir William Alexander (afterwards the Earl of Stirling) the territory now forming the three Maritime provinces, the Gaspé peninsula, and the island of Anticosti. Sir William hoped to found a proprietary colony, and to it he gave the name of Nova Scotia. The King could claim the right to dispose of the territory on the basis of prior discovery by the Cabots and its conquest by Argall in 1613.

The new colony was not a success. In 1628 a settlement was begun at Port Royal by Sir William Alexander's son, who brought out some 70 settlers and built a new fort, afterwards known as the Scots' Fort. The following year Lord Ochiltree attempted to found another settlement in Cape Breton. The latter settlement was broken up by Captain Daniel of Dieppe, and the former was abandoned at the command of King Charles I in 1631. The country was to be returned "waist and unpeopled" to the French king, but the efforts of Sir William were not without their results. He had put the name Nova Scotia on the map of America; he had given the present province of Nova Scotia its coat-of-arms and its flag; a few stray Scots remained in the country to be absorbed by the Acadians; and in order to raise money and to get settlers he had founded the order of the baronets of Nova Scotia (q.v.).

The treaty of St. Germain-en-Laye in 1632 restored the country to France. Nova Scotia became Acadia again. In 1654 an English force under Major Robert Sedgwick (q.v.) captured the French posts in Acadia, but in 1667 by the treaty of Breda the land was again restored to France. In 1690 Sir William Phips (q.v.) captured Port Royal, but by the treaty of Ryswick in 1697 French control of Acadia was again recognized. Finally in 1710, Port Royal after a gallant defence by Subercase, was captured by Colonel Francis Nicholson (q.v.). The town was renamed Annapolis Royal, and along with "all Nova Scotia, or Acadia" passed into the possession of Great Britain by the Treaty of Utrecht in 1713.

"All Nova Scotia" did not include Cape Breton or Prince Edward Island (or, as they were known to the French, Ile Royale and Ile St. Jean); and, according to the French, it did not include the country to the north of the isthmus of Chignecto. Much diplomatic chicanery was devoted to the subject. The

French proceeded to build a fortress in Cape Breton at Louisbourg, and, in the years immediately after 1713, tried to induce the Acadians to leave their homes, which were now in British territory, and to settle within the French lines.

An English governor and a small English garrison were stationed at Annapolis Royal. The Acadians were given twelve months within which they were to take an oath of allegiance to the king, but this they steadily refused to do. In spite of various attempts and many threats, little was done, and matters were allowed to drift. The French at Louisbourg also gave up their attempts to move the Acadians, being satisfied to obtain most of their provisions from them.

The Acadians grew and multiplied. The census of 1671 gave their number as 441, but by the time of the English conquest in 1710 the number had increased to over 2,000, and by the time of the expulsion it had reached 12,000.

In 1744 the long peace came to an end. In 1745 the men of Massachusetts, by a fine stroke of audacity, took Louisbourg, but by the treaty of Aix-la-Chapelle in 1748 it was restored to France, which proceeded to add greatly to its strength. It remained a refuge for privateers and a threat to the traders and fishermen of New England.

The British government now decided to take effective possession of Nova Scotia and to establish a settlement that would be a counterpoise to Louisbourg. The chief prompter in the drama was Governor Shirley (q.v.) of Massachusetts. The result was the founding of Halifax on Chebucto harbour. On June 21, 1749, the Hon. Edward Cornwallis (q.v.) arrived with some 2,500 settlers, and began the laying out of the new town. During the next three years some 2,500 "foreign Protestants" arrived, most of them Germans, but including a few French and Swiss. In 1753 the majority of these

were settled in what is now the county of Lunenburg.

The French at Louisbourg were alarmed at the founding of Halifax, and stirred up the Indians to attack the new settlement. They also did their best by threats, compulsion, and persuasion to induce the Acadians to migrate to French territory. In this they were partly successful, and so might be said to have begun the dispersion of the Acadians. On the other hand, the English governor at Halifax gave the Acadians three months in which to take the oath of allegiance. Their claim to be neutral could not be allowed. Stubbornly the Acadians refused. Cornwallis and his successor Hopson (q.v.) temporized, but finally Governor Lawrence (q.v.) in 1755, with the Seven Years' War already a reality in America, took action. Some 6,000 Acadians were transported to the various American colonies. In 1758 there was a second expulsion from Prince Edward Island. Some escaped to the woods, many wandered back from the southern colonies. In 1762 an unsuccessful attempt was made at a further expulsion, and in 1764 some 600 Acadians, of their own free will, sailed for the West Indies.

In 1758 Louisbourg fell; in 1759, Quebec; and in 1763, by the Peace of Paris, all Canada passed into the possession of England. Gradually the Acadians who remained in the province took the oath of allegiance, and were granted new lands. Most of them settled on the shores of St. Mary's bay and around Pubnico, and their descendants now form about one-tenth of the population of the province of Nova Scotia.

Upon the expulsion of the Acadians, Governor Lawrence was anxious to fill their places with settlers from New England. In 1758 and 1759 he issued proclamations promising free lands and setting forth the advantages of Nova Scotia. As a result, between 1760 and 1765, nearly 8,000 New Englanders came to the province. A few who were interested in the fisheries settled on the south-eastern shore of the province, but the majority settled on the abandoned lands of the Acadians. With the coming of the new settlers, Nova Scotia was transformed into a genuine English possession. About the same time, some 200 Ulster Presbyterians came into the province as a result of the efforts of the soldier of fortune and land speculator, Alexander MacNutt (q.v.). The only other considerable immigration before the coming of the Loyalists was some 800 from Yorkshire who settled in what is now Cumberland county, and about 200 from the Highlands of Scotland who settled in what is now Pictou county.

With the founding of Halifax, the government moved there from Annapolis Royal. At first it consisted of a governor and a council, but in 1758, very much against the wishes of Governor Lawrence, but in accordance with the wishes of the New Englanders in Halifax (who were rapidly taking the place of the disbanded soldiers and sailors who had founded the town), and in accordance with instructions received from England, the first popular Assembly was elected.

In 1763 Cape Breton and Prince Edward Island had been annexed to Nova Scotia. In 1769 the latter was separated and has remained separate ever since.

The American Revolutionary War brought distress and hardship to Nova Scotia. Many of the recently arrived settlers from New England could not but sympathize with their fellow-countrymen. A few left the province; four delegates from Cumberland went to the Continental Congress at Philadelphia. Machais in Maine became a centre for attacks on the province, privateers hovered about the coast and made descents on various places, an attempt (originating among a group of Cumberland people) was made to capture Fort Cumberland. Governor Legge (q.v.) was unpopular and suspicious. It is probably a true statement that the majority of the people were passively disloyal.

When the United States was granted its independence, a new era opened in the history of Nova Scotia. Some 35,000 Loyalists came to the colony. One almost immediate result was the setting up of two new colonies in 1784. New Brunswick and Cape Breton were separated from Nova Scotia, the latter, however, to be re-united, much against its will, with Nova Scotia in 1820. In Nova Scotia the population was doubled. Many of the newcomers had been men of wealth and influence in the American colonies, they had given proof of their loyalty, and they now thought that they ought to have a privileged position in their new home. With this opinion the English government concurred, and during the next generation there were many clashes between the pre-Loyalists and the Loyalists.

The Napoleonic wars brought wealth to Nova Scotia. The lumber trade and ship-building developed rapidly. The expenditures of the army and particularly of the navy brought much money into Halifax. Nova Scotia competed with New England in the fisheries and for the West Indian trade. With the passing of the Embargo Act by the American government in 1806 and with the outbreak of the War of 1812, wealth poured into the province. Privateering became a great industry. The anti-war feeling of the Federalists in New England gave Nova Scotia the benefits of war without its hardships.

With peace came depression, made worse by a series of bad harvests. As the country recovered, and particularly with the prosperity that followed the passing of Huskisson's Trade Acts in 1825, Nova Scotia entered on the golden period of her history. There was a confidence and a patriotism that it is hard to exaggerate. There was an imperial feeling that was only partly checked by disappointment that the English government did not see fit to exclude the Americans from the fisheries and the West Indian trade. (That more was not done was not the fault of Nova Scotians: they bitterly resented the concessions granted to American fishermen by the convention of 1818, and the restoration to Americans of their old rights in the West Indian trade in 1830.) Education was supported with enthusiasm, and literature was cultivated as it never was before or has been since. Haliburton (q.v.), McCulloch (q.v.), and Howe (q.v.) won reputations that reached far beyond the bounds of the colony.

During the early years of the nineteenth century the province received its last great wave of immigration. This wave came mainly from northern Scotland, and (to a lesser extent) from southern Ireland. Most of the Scottish settlers went to the northeastern part of the province and to Cape Breton.

In the thirties and forties, the province was convulsed by the struggle for responsible government. Events in the twenties prepared the way. American influence, differences caused by religion, differences between the country and Halifax, all played their part. Opinion was growing against the wealthy pro-Anglican, anti-democratic, office-holding class who controlled, and thought that they ought to control, the government of the colony. The Council of Twelve sitting in secret, combining executive, legislative, and judicial functions, had for years been the real centre of power. Joseph Howe, after his trial for libel in 1835, became the leader of the movement for reform. The struggle went on under two governors, Sir Colin Campbell (q.v.) and Lord Falkland (q.v.). Both were forced to leave the colony, but when in 1848 their successor, Sir John Harvey (q.v.), accepted a popular government led by James B. Uniacke (q.v.), it could be said that the struggle

for responsible government had been won.

Although some six miles of railway began to operate in 1839, it was not until 1854 that real railway-building began. By the time of Confederation 145 miles had been built, and in 1876 railway connection was established with central Canada.

In 1854 the legislature of Nova Scotia ratified the Reciprocity Treaty which had been negotiated with the United States. The essential terms were the reciprocal abolition of duties on nearly all the products of the farm, the forest, the mines, and the fisheries, and the reciprocal opening of the inshore fisheries of both countries. The treaty was brought to an end in 1866 by the United States, but while it lasted it proved a great benefit to Nova Scotia. The outbreak of the American Civil War in 1861 further increased the prosperity of the province.

In 1867 Nova Scotia entered Confederation under circumstances and after a struggle which have left their mark on the province. In September, 1864, delegates of the Maritime provinces met at Charlottetown to discuss Maritime union. There they were joined by delegates from Canada, who proposed that a union of all the British North American provinces be considered instead. The result was the Quebec Conference and the Seventy-two Resolutions. In Nova Scotia bitter opposition developed to the scheme. Local patriotism, distrust of Canadians and their ways, doubts as to the wisdom of the terms of union, fear as to the fiscal policy that the union might bring, were all intensified by the refusal of the provincial prime minister, Charles Tupper (q.v.), to consult the electors on the subject. The opposition found a leader in Joseph Howe, who roused the province against the scheme, but was unable to prevent it going into effect, although he carried his case to London. In the first election for the Dominion

MVNIT·HÆC·ET·ALTERA·VINCIT

Armorial Achievement of Nova Scotia
Granted by King Charles I.
in 1625.

House, Nova Scotia elected eighteen
anti-Confederates to one Confederate.
When Howe in 1869 agreed to drop his
opposition in return for better financial
terms for his province, he lost much of
his popularity, but he established a
precedent. Although only one political
election (1886) was actually conducted
(and won) on a platform of secession,
Nova Scotia has had a sense of grievance
from the day when she became a province in the Dominion of Canada. The
sense of grievance has diminished or
swelled according to the economic conditions of the province, but it has never
vanished. Whether Confederation was
to blame or not, Nova Scotia feels that
her economic progress "has failed to
keep pace with the other provinces of the
Dominion". In 1926 and in 1934 two
royal commissions (the Duncan and
the Jones commissions) investigated,
and reported in favour of "better
terms" for the province. In recent
years the growth of the coöperative
movement and the development of the
tourist traffic have shown much promise.
In 1928 the Legislative Council of Nova
Scotia was abolished.

*Fisheries.* Fish is one of the three
chief exports of the province to markets
outside Canada. In 1928 the catch was
valued at $11,427,491, but in 1933 it
had declined to $6,010,601. The in-
dustry employs from 19,000 to 20,000
people, and brings in from eight to nine
per cent. of the total net production of
the province. Until recent times the
cod was without a rival, but the lobster
has now taken first place. Within the
cod fishery itself, there has been a great
decline in the dried fish industry and a
steady expansion in the market for
fresh fish in central Canada. The
fisheries are under the jurisdiction of
the Dominion government, and a station
for research is maintained at Halifax
by the Biological Board of Canada.

*Agriculture.* The amount of land
available for agriculture is limited.
According to the census of 1931 only
32.41 per cent. of the total land area
of the province is held as farm land, and
only 6.36 per cent. classed as improved, and 5.62 per cent. as "natural
pasture". Generally speaking, agriculture is of the mixed farming type and,
apart from apples, relies on the domestic
market, which it is unable fully to
supply. The Annapolis valley has
specialized in apple-growing, and has
built up an important market in Great
Britain. The development of the industry has been mainly since 1900, and in
spite of depression and competition has
continued to grow. In 1935 the crop
was 1,800,000 bbl., valued at $4,266,000.
The control of agriculture is divided
between the Dominion and the Provincial governments. The former maintains a farm and a station, and the
latter a college of agriculture at Truro.
The gross agricultural revenue of Nova
Scotia for the year 1931 was estimated
at $24,029,000.

*Lumbering.* Fish, apples, and lumber
are the three great natural products
that Nova Scotia ships to markets outside Canada. Nearly three-quarters of
the area of the province can be classed
as forest land. Most of it has passed
into private ownership, but on what the
province still owns the timber is disposed of by means of licences to cut.
The work is largely done by small
portable mills, and in many cases the
industry is carried on in close connection
with farming and fishing. The development of the pulp-and-paper industry
has greatly added to the value of the
forest lands of the province.

*Mining.* Gold is found in widely
scattered but limited amounts. There
are great deposits of gypsum about
Windsor (the chief producing centre),
in Colchester and Antigonish counties,
and in Cape Breton island. There are
important salt deposits at Malagash.
The outstanding mineral resource is
coal. Nova Scotia possesses the only
extensive bituminous deposits of good
quality east of Alberta and the only

deposits on the Atlantic coast of North or South America. The output varies, but approximately 6,000,000 tons are mined annually or considerably more than one-third of the total amount mined in Canada. There are four chief fields, the Joggins-Springhill and New Glasgow fields on the mainland, and the Inverness and Sydney fields in Cape Breton. The latter produces about three-quarters of the total. The greater part of the deposit is submarine. Coal is shipped to Montreal and further west, the distance being determined by the fiscal policy of the Dominion government.

*Manufacturing.* As a manufacturing centre Nova Scotia has the advantage of her coal resources and of cheap water transportation, but she has the disadvantage of being at the extreme east of the protected Canadian market. According to the 1931 census, the total gross value of the products of the manufacturing establishments of the province was $70,679,503 and the number of employees was 16,175. The iron and steel industry was the most important. Other leading industries are fish-curing and packing, pulp-and-paper, central electric stations, railway rolling stock, butter and cheese, biscuits and confectionery, saw-mills, printing and publishing, petroleum products, sugar refining.

*Transportation.* Halifax is one of the chief winter ports of Canada. In summer there are regular sailings to England, to St. John's, Newfoundland, and to Boston, New York, and the West Indies. The Canadian National with its terminals at Halifax is the principal railway. It serves the eastern and south-western part of the province extending to Sydney and Yarmouth. The Canadian Pacific Railway has running rights from St. John (New Brunswick) to Halifax, and controls the Dominion Atlantic Railway running from Windsor Junction and from Truro to Yarmouth and with steamship con-

nection at Digby with St. John. From Yarmouth there is a regular steamship connection with Boston.

The highways of the province have been greatly improved and extended in recent years. Over $7,000,000 was spent on them in 1935, and by the close of that year there were over 8,000 miles of improved roads in the province.

*Education.* Primary education is free and compulsory; secondary education is free, but optional. According to the strict letter of the law, there are no separate schools in Nova Scotia; but a compromise has been arranged in those sections where the Roman Catholic Church is strong. Higher education has suffered because of religious rivalries and jealousies. Dalhousie-Kings at Halifax, Acadia at Wolfville, and St. Francis Xavier at Antigonish are the chief degree-granting institutions. Dalhousie is undenominational, Kings is Anglican, Acadia is Baptist, and St. Francis Xavier is Roman Catholic.

*Population.* At the first census after Confederation, in 1871, the population of Nova Scotia stood at 387,800. By 1921 it had increased to 523,837, but in the next decade the number dropped to 512,846. The increase since 1871 has been mainly in the eastern part of the province, owing to the development of coal-mining and the industries connected with it. While the population of the western part increased only 7.5 per cent., the increase in the eastern part was 46.7 per cent.

The representation in the Dominion House of Commons, which once stood at 21, has now dropped to 12.

*Bibliography.* Books dealing specifically with Nova Scotia are T. C. Haliburton, *An historical and statistical account of Nova Scotia* (2 vols, Halifax, 1829); B. Murdoch, *A history of Nova Scotia* (3 vols., Halifax, 1865-7); D. Campbell, *Nova Scotia* (Montreal, 1873); D. Allison, *History of Nova Scotia* (3 vols., Halifax, 1916); and J. B. Brebner, *New England's outpost* (New

LEGISLATIVE BUILDINGS OF NOVA SCOTIA AT HALIFAX

York, 1927). See also Report of the Royal Commission on Maritime Claims, 1926; Report of the Royal Commission, Provincial Economic Inquiry, 1934; various county histories, and the *Collections* of the Nova Scotia Historical Society.

**Nova Scotia Historical Society,** a society founded at Halifax in 1878. It has published 22 volumes of *Collections*, containing many valuable papers on the history of the Maritime provinces. See Archdeacon F. W. Vroom, *Fifty years of the Nova Scotia Historical Society* (Collections of the Nova Scotia Historical Society, vol. xxii, 1933).

**Nova Scotian Institute of Science,** a society founded in Halifax in 1862 as the Nova Scotian Institute of Natural Science, and incorporated in 1890 under its present name. It published 16 volumes of *Proceedings and transactions* between 1863 and 1926.

**Nova Scotia Railway,** a railway line built from Halifax to Truro, Nova Scotia, between 1855 and 1858, and extended to Pictou Landing in 1867, with the object of giving Halifax access to the gulf of St. Lawrence. In 1858 a branch was opened to Windsor, Nova Scotia. The whole railway was taken over by the Intercolonial, as soon as the latter was in operation. See R. R. Brown, *The Nova Scotia Railway, 1854-1872* (Railway and Locomotive Historical Society, bulletin No. 23).

**Noyelles, Charles Joseph Fleurimont de** (*fl.* 1720-1750), was commandant at Detroit in 1720, in 1728, and again in 1738-41. In 1743 he was charged with continuing La Vérendrye's discoveries in the West, and in 1747 he made a journey to Michillimakinac, but the Indians were so menacing that he turned back. He set out again in June, 1748, and took possession of Fort La Reine, and sent the sons of La Vérendrye (q.v.) to found Fort Bourbon and Fort Paskoyac. He was recalled in 1750. See L. A. Prud'homme,

*Les successeurs de La Vérendrye* (Trans. Roy. Soc. Can., 1906).

**Nueltin lake** lies west of Hudson bay, between the 99th and 100th meridians of west longitude, and on the boundary between Manitoba and the North West Territories. The name is from the Indian word for "island". The lake is drained by the Thlewiaza river, which empties into Hudson bay. Its area is 336 square miles, of which 76 are in Manitoba and 260 in the North West Territories.

**Numismatics** is the science which treats of coins and medals. Though the collections of coins has never attained the popularity of the collection of postage-stamps, it is of earlier origin. As early as 1862 a number of collectors of coins in Montreal formed "the Numismatic Society of Montreal", later known as the Numismatic and Antiquarian Society of Montreal; and this society published, between 1872 and 1916, the *Canadian Antiquarian and Numismatic Journal* (1st series, 1872-86; 2nd series, 1889-94; 3rd series, 1899-1916). Outstanding numismatists in this society were Alfred Sandham (q.v.) and R. W. McLachlan (q.v.). The chief books dealing with numismatics in Canada are Alfred Sandham, *Coins, tokens, and medals of the Dominion of Canada* (Montreal, 1869; 2nd ed., 1872); J. Leroux, *Le medaillier du Canada* (Montreal, 1888), and *Atlas numismatique du Canada* (Montreal, 1883); and P. N. Breton, *Histoire illustrée des monnaies et jetons du Canada* (Montreal, 1894). See also **Currency.**

**Nursey, Walter R.** (1847-1927), author, was born in Crostwick, Norfolk, England, in 1847, the son of the Rev. P. F. Nursey. He emigrated to Canada in 1865, and was successively a farmer, a banker, a civil servant, a fur-trader, and an organizer for the Conservative party. In 1909 he was appointed inspector of public libraries in Ontario; and he died in Toronto on March 14,

1927. He was the author of *The story of Isaac Brock* (Toronto, 1908), and with Alexander Begg (q.v.) joint author of *Ten years in Winnipeg* (Winnipeg, 1879).

**Nursing.** Among the people of New France, and among the Roman Catholic French-speaking people of Canada since the British conquest, nursing has been carried out by the sisters of such religious orders as the Grey Nuns (q.v.). These orders have developed their own training-courses for nurses; and Laval University in Quebec has established a school of nursing (École des Garde-Malades). Among the people of English-speaking Canada, nursing was for many years in a very backward condition. Until near the end of the nineteenth century, most hospital nurses were women without training or education, like Charles Dickens's Sarah Gamp. Their social status was hardly superior to that of the domestic servant; and their moral character was not always above reproach. One of the first hospitals to attempt to raise the standard of nursing was the Montreal General Hospital. In 1875, this hospital, after consultation with the famous Florence Nightingale, imported from the Nightingale School in England a lady superintendent (who was Canadian by birth), a sister, and four trained nurses, to reorganize the nursing service; and it was intended to establish a training school in Canada. But the experiment proved premature. Jealousy and public criticism brought about very soon the return of the Nightingale nurses to England; and the Montreal General Hospital reverted to the system of untrained nurses. The first hospital to establish a training school for nurses was the General and Marine Hospital at St. Catharines, Ontario, in 1874; and the first graduates of this training school received their certificates in 1879. A training school for nurses was opened in connection with the Toronto General Hospital in 1881; and the first gradu-

ates received their certificates in 1883. The early years of this school were, however, full of trouble; and it was not until the appointment of Mary A. Snively as superintendent of nurses in 1884 that the new order of things was firmly established. In the Montreal General Hospital a training school was established in 1890, under Norah Livingston; and it may be said that the early history of nursing in Canada has been largely the history of these two women. Miss Snively was superintendent of nurses at the Toronto General Hospital from 1884 to 1910; and Miss Livingston was superintendent of nurses at the Montreal General Hospital from 1890 to 1919. Other hospitals soon followed the lead of Toronto and Montreal. The Victoria General Hospital in Halifax organized its training school for nurses in 1892; in the Ottawa General Hospital the Grey Nuns established a training school for lay nurses in 1898; the Royal Victoria Hospital training school in Montreal was begun in 1894; the Winnipeg General Hospital has had a training school since 1887; and the Royal Jubilee Hospital in Victoria since 1890. To-day virtually every large hospital in Canada has its school for nurses.

In 1907 there was formed a "Canadian Society of Superintendents of Training Schools for Nurses"; and in 1908 this led to the formation of the Canadian National Association of Trained Nurses, which was re-christened in 1926 the Canadian Nurses Association. This association has done much to raise the standard of the profession of nursing in Canada.

During the Great War many Canadian nurses enlisted for service with the Canadian Army Medical Corps, and all were given commissioned rank—a striking illustration of the status acquired in such a short time by the nursing profession.

An interesting development of the period since the Great War has been the development of training for nurses in the universities of Canada. About 1920 there sprang up a demand for the training of public health nurses; and, generally with the assistance of the Canadian Red Cross, courses in public health nursing were inaugurated at Dalhousie University, McGill University, the University of Toronto, the University of Western Ontario, the University of Alberta, and the University of British Columbia. The course at Dalhousie was later discontinued; but at some of the other universities the courses have developed into full-fledged undergraduate departments, leading, in most cases, to a degree. In the University of Toronto the course in nursing has led to the organization in 1933 of a School of Nursing, subsidized by the Rockefeller Foundation; and in this school both undergraduate and graduate work is carried on, as well as experimental work in the training of public health nurses.

See L. L. Dock (ed.), *A history of nursing*, vol. iv (New York, 1912); *Pioneers of nursing in Canada* (Montreal, Canadian Nurses Association, 1929); *A brief history of the Canadian Nurses Association* (Winnipeg, 1927); Margaret Isabel Lawrence (ed.), *History: The School for Nurses, Toronto General Hospital* (Toronto, 1931); and the calendars of the various universities in which public health nursing is taught.

**Nutarawit lake** lies west of Hudson bay, between the 98th and 99th meridians of west longitude, in the North West Territories. The name is from the Indian for "dead-child". The lake has an area of 350 square miles.

**Nutcracker** (*Nucifraga columbiana*), a bird closely allied to the crows and jays, which inhabits the mountains of British Columbia and a part of Alberta. It is approximately the size of a robin and largely gray in colour. The wings and central tail feathers are dark, and both wings and tail are marked with white. Like the other members of its family, it is not a songster. The species seldom wanders eastward from its normal haunts.

**Nuthatch,** a name used for three species of Canadian birds, smaller than a sparrow and superficially suggestive of the woodpeckers. They obtain their food from crevices in tree bark as they move head foremost down the trunk, with a series of short abrupt progressions. The name nuthatch is derived from "nuthack", the term first applied to an European species because of its habit of breaking nutshells with its bill. The white-breasted nuthatch (*Sitta carolinensis*) occurs in the more southern portion across the whole of Canada. The red-breasted nuthatch (*Sitta canadensis*) occupies the forested north in summer, and is a visitant in southern areas in the autumn and winter. The pygmy nuthatch (*Sitta pygmaea*) occurs in southern British Columbia.

# O

**Oak,** the name of the trees belonging to the genus *Quercus* Linnaeus. Approximately three hundred species have been described, and over fifty of these are found in North America, but many of them are difficult to identify. The number occurring in Canada is not definitely known, but the following are recognized: red oak (*Q. borealis* Michaux), black oak (*Q. velutina* La Marck), pin oak (*Q. palustris* Muenchhausen), bur oak (*Q. macrocarpa* Michaux), white oak (*Q. alba* Linnaeus), swamp white oak (*Q. bicolor* Willdenow), chinquapin or chestnut oak (*Q. muhlenhergii* Engelmann), dwarf chinquapin or dwarf chestnut oak (*Q. prinoides* Willdenow). These all occur in eastern Canada, and are mainly confined to the southwestern peninsula of Ontario. One other tree, Oregon white oak (*Q. garryana* Douglas), is found only in British Columbia.

The oaks are readily separated into two groups. The black or red oaks, including the first three species above, have leaves with pointed and bristle tipped lobes and fruits requiring two seasons to mature; the white oak group includes the remaining six, which have leaves with rounded lobes and fruits maturing in one season.

In general, the leaves are characteristically lobed or toothed and never confused with those of other trees. The flowers are unisexual; the staminate (male), being in long, narrow, pendant catkins, may be seen hanging in bunches as the leaves are unfolding; the pistillate (female) are less conspicuous, occurring singly or in small clusters and close observation is required to see them; both kinds may be seen on the same tree. The fruit is a nut or acorn partly enclosed in a cuplike structure covered with overlapping scales. Leaves and fruits are used in separating the species, which may be found described in Sargent's *Manual of the trees of North America.*

Oak wood is hard, strong, tough, and durable. It presents a decided pattern when sawn, and is universally used for flooring, furniture, interior trim, and many special purposes; but there is comparatively little oak timber produced in Canada.

**Oakes, Forrest** (d. 1783), fur-trader, was an English merchant who came to Canada in the earliest days of British rule. He was a partner in the firm of Mackenzie and Oakes in Quebec in 1761; and he was in Montreal in February, 1762, when he ran foul of the soldiers, during the period of military rule, and was tried by court-martial. He is said to have been a son of Sir Hildebrand Oakes (see *Dict. Nat. Biog.*); but this is impossible, though there was evidently some relationship between them. He engaged in the Indian trade; and in 1779 he became one of the parties to the formation of the original North West Company; but his firm was not included in the agreement of 1783-4, for he died in Montreal in 1783. His will is preserved in the Court House at Montreal; and it reveals the fact that he left property in the parish of Handsworth, Staffordshire, England. He left one son, John Meticamish Oakes, evidently a half-breed, who was a minor, and two sisters, Jemima (d. 1809), the wife of Lawrence Ermatinger (q.v.), and Margaret, who had married in 1767 Edward William Gray, afterwards sheriff of Montreal. Another sister, who would appear to have predeceased him, married in 1770 Edward Chinn, an early Indian trader at Michilimackinac.

**Oak Lake,** a town in Manitoba, on the Assiniboine river, and on the main line of the Canadian Pacific Railway, 32 miles west of Brandon. It was earlier known as Flat Creek. In a grain and stock-farming district, it has a high school and a weekly newspaper (*News*). Pop. (1931), 473.

**Oakland,** a village in Brant county, Ontario, 10 miles south of Brantford, and 2 miles from Scotland, the nearest railway station. Pop. (1934), 250.

**Oak river,** a tributary of the Assiniboine river, which rises in Brandon county, Manitoba, and joins the Assiniboine near the Sioux Indian reservation.

**Oak River,** a village in Marquette county, Manitoba, on the Miniota branch of the Canadian Pacific Railway, 40 miles north-west of Brandon. It has a port on Oak river, and a weekly newspaper (*Post*). Pop. (1935), 240.

**Oakville,** a town of Halton county, Ontario, situated at the mouth of Sixteen Mile creek, on lake Ontario, and on the Canadian National and Canadian Pacific Railways, 22 miles west of Toronto. The town has a good harbour; and boat-building is included in the industries, with planing-mills, the manufacture of aluminium ware, paint, sashes, and doors. There are five churches, public, separate, and high schools, and a public library. Two weekly newspapers (*Record* and *Star*) are published. Pop. (1931), 3,857. There are also small villages named Oakville in Carleton county, New Brunswick, and in Macdonald county, Manitoba.

**Oakwood,** a village in Victoria county, Ontario, 8 miles south-west of Lindsay, on the Canadian National Railway. Pop. (1934), 300.

**Oates, mount,** is in the Rocky mountains, in the Kootenay district of British Columbia, on the Alberta boundary, west of the headwaters of Wood river. It has an altitude of 10,220 feet. It was named in 1914 in honour of Capt. L. E. G. Oates, one of Capt. R. F. Scott's four companions in his last attempt to reach the South Pole in 1912. All of the party perished, but Oates—"a very gallant gentleman"—sacrificed himself in the hope of saving his companions.

**Oblates.** The congregation of the Missionary Oblates of Mary Immaculate was founded in 1816 by Charles Joseph Eugène de Mazenod, who became bishop of Marseilles in 1837. The primary object of this congregation was to repair the havoc caused by the French Revolution in the religious field by replacing religious orders which had all been expelled from France during those tragic years. To-day the Oblates are established in all countries of Europe. They can also be found in South Africa, where they are carrying on missionary work in Natal, Transvaal, Kimberley, Basutoland, Cimbebasia, and Belgian Congo. In Asia, the dioceses of Colombo and Jaffna, in Ceylon, as well as the missions in the Indo-Chinese peninsula, are the achievement of the enterprising zeal of the Oblate Fathers. In Western Australia, South and North America, from the Atlantic to the Pacific, from the gulf of Mexico to the Arctic ocean, flourishing work is carried on under the able direction of these devoted priests and lay-brothers.

The year 1841 saw the first appearance of the Oblates in Canada. Only six were sent from France to lay the foundation of evangelical work, but this is to-day carried on by over 1,500 members, occupying five canonical provinces and five mission districts. Remaining faithful to the chief aim of the Congregation, the Eastern province has particularly excelled in conducting retreats or missions among rural and industrial populations. Travelling from village to village, from town to town, the Oblates have, within the past century, spread the Good Word in practically every parish of Quebec, Ontario, and the Maritime provinces, where the poor were most numerous and spiritual needs the greatest.

Furthermore, fulfilling the wishes expressed by the bishops, the Fathers gladly undertook to visit regularly the numerous camps of the Canadian lumberjacks. Every winter, in the vast forests of the Saguenay, the St. Maurice, the Gatineau, the Ottawa, and other river districts, can be seen scores of missionaries travelling from shanty to shanty on snowshoes. In so doing, the Sons of Mazenod have, for the last seventy-five years, brought to these rugged men of the woods their share of moral and religious care.

Invited by the archbishop of Quebec to preach the Gospel to the nomadic Indian tribes scattered throughout his large diocese, the Oblates, soon after their arrival in Canada, started this great work of Christianization. Moreover, the bishop of Montreal entrusted to their zeal the missions of the Ottawa and Hudson bay districts. In 1845, Bishop Provencher (q.v.) also called upon them to fill the vacancies created in his vicariate by the successive departures of the secular priests under his jurisdiction, who had never numbered more than five at any one time. In 1857, there remained only one secular priest in the diocese of St. Boniface, then covering western Canada. Yearly increasing in number, the Oblates carried on the great cause of Christianity and civilization along the shores of the Saskatchewan, the Fraser, the Mackenzie, and even the Yukon. Throughout these vast, wild regions, they taught the Indian to respect and tolerate, if not to like, the new methods of morality and progress which came to him.

They were apostles of peace during the troubled days of 1885, and while the construction of railways was going on. Moreover, they adorned western cities with cathedrals and churches, schools and colleges, charitable institutions and establishments. Finally, they contributed to the betterment of existing local economic and political conditions; to the development of geographical and idiomatic knowledge; to the writing and publishing of complete dictionaries, and of other works.

In such a brief article, it is impossible to recall all the deeds of the Oblates in Western as well as in Eastern Canada, where they have contributed to the creation of a large number of parishes, particularly in the dioceses of Ottawa, Haileybury, Chicoutimi, and of the gulf of St. Lawrence. In these various centres they also assisted in the organization of religious congregations. To give a more comprehensive view of the educational activities of the Oblate Fathers, mention must be made of the following colleges established or maintained by the order: Victoria, in New Westminster; St. Albert, in Gravelbourg; St. Boniface and St. Paul's, in Winnipeg; St. Patrick's, in Ottawa; the Edmonton, Gravelbourg, and Ottawa Seminaries, and, finally, the University of Ottawa. Special mention should also be made of the religious work initiated among the Germans, Poles, and Ruthenians in western Canada and still carried on, except among the Ruthenians.

Among other social and cultural activities which are also encouraged by the Oblate Fathers, one might mention: "L'Association Canadienne-Française d'Education de l'Ontario", "L'Association d'Education du Manitoba", "L'-Association Canadienne-Française de l'-Alberta", the "Young Catholic Workers" (J.O.C., J.O.C.F.), and the "Young Catholic Students" (J.E.C., J.E.C.F.). Lately, a national association was founded for the purpose of promoting scientific interest in missionary problems. The president and secretary of this new society are both Oblate Fathers.

If reference were to be made to celebrated shrines established in Canada by the Oblate Congregation, it would undoubtedly be proper to mention Cap de la Madeleine, Mont Joli, and Ville Marie, in the province of Quebec; St. Lawrence, in Manitoba; and lake St. Ann, in Alberta.

The congregation comprises within its ranks men of the highest type, such as Brother Moffette, Fathers Lacasse, Lacombe (q.v.), Tabaret, and Morice, Bishops Grouard (q.v.), Grandin (q.v.), Breynat, and Turquetil, Archbishops Taché (q.v.) and Langevin (q.v.), and Cardinal Villeneuve.

*Bibliography.* For the work of the Oblates in Canada, see T. Ortolan, *Cent ans d'apostolat*, vol. vi (Paris, 1932), A. G. Morice, *History of the Catholic church in western Canada* (2 vols., Toronto, 1910), and P. Duchaussois, *Mid ice and snow* (London, 1923).

**O'Brien, Cornelius** (1843-1906), Roman Catholic archbishop of Halifax (1882-1906), was born in Prince Edward Island on May 4, 1843. He was educated at St. Dunstan's College, Charlottetown, and at the College of the Propaganda, Rome, Italy, and in 1871 he was ordained a priest of the Roman Catholic Church. From 1871 to 1873 he was a teacher in St. Dunstan's College; from 1873 to 1874 he was principal priest at the cathedral at Charlottetown; and from 1874 to 1882 he was parish priest at Indian River. In 1882 he succeeded Archbishop Hannan (q.v.) as archbishop of Halifax; and he remained in oversight of the see until his death at Halifax on March 9, 1906. In 1882 he was chosen a charter member of the Royal Society of Canada, and in 1896, he was its president. He was the author of *Philosophy of the Bible vindicated* (Charlottetown, 1876), *Mater admirabilis* (Montreal, 1882), a

novel entitled *After weary years* (Baltimore, 1885), *Saint Agnes, virgin and martyr* (Halifax, 1887), *Aminta, a modern life drama* (New York, 1890), and *Memoirs of the Right Rev. Edmund Burke* (Ottawa, 1894). See Katherine Hughes, *Archbishop O'Brien* (Ottawa, 1906).

**O'Brien, Edward George** (1798-1875), pioneer settler, was born at Woolwich, England, on January 9, 1798. He first served as a midshipman in the British navy, and then as an officer in the army. About 1830 he came to Canada, and settled at Shanty Bay, on lake Simcoe, Upper Canada. He became a justice of the peace and a lieut.-colonel in the militia, and was active in suppressing the rebellion of 1837. He died in the summer of 1875. He married Mary Sophia, daughter of the Rev. Edward Gapper; and by her he had several children.

**O'Brien, Lucius James** (1796-1870), surgeon, was born in Woolwich, England, in 1796, and became a surgeon in the British army. Soon after his brother, Edward George O'Brien (q.v.), he came to Canada in 1832, and settled at Thornhill, Upper Canada. In 1837-8 he was chief military surgeon at Toronto, and from 1845 to 1853 he was professor of medical jurisprudence in King's College (University of Toronto). From 1848 to 1856 he was also editor of the *Patriot* of Toronto. Later, having lost his money, he became secretary to the Hon. William Cayley (q.v.), and obtained an appointment in the office of the receiver-general of Canada. He died in Ottawa on August 14, 1870.

**O'Brien, Lucius Richard** (1832-1899), president of the Royal Canadian Academy of Arts (1880-90), was born at Shanty Bay, Upper Canada, on August 15, 1832, the son of Lt.-Col. E. G. O'Brien (q.v.). He was educated at Upper Canada College, and in 1847 entered an architect's office. He became a civil engineer; and also a painter in water colours. In 1872 he became a member of the Ontario Society of Artists, and from 1873 to 1880 was vice-president of this society. In 1880 he was selected as a charter member of the Royal Canadian Academy of Arts, and he was elected its first president, holding office from 1880 to 1890. Chiefly a landscape artist, he was especially noted for his pictures of scenery in the Rocky mountains. He died in December, 1899. He was twice married, (1) in 1860 to Margaret, eldest daughter of Capt. Andrew St. John, of Orillia, Upper Canada; and (2) in 1888 to Katherine Jane, third daughter of the Ven. Archdeacon Brough, of London, Ontario.

**O'Brien, William Edward** (1831-1914), politician, was born at Thornhill, Upper Canada, on March 10, 1831, the eldest son of Lt.-Col. E. G. O'Brien (q.v.). He was educated at Upper Canada College; and became a farmer. He was called to the bar of Upper Canada in 1874, but never practised law. In 1882 he was elected to represent Muskoka in the Canadian House of Commons as a Conservative, and he retained his seat until 1896. He was a prominent member of the Equal Rights Association, and was one of the "noble thirteen" who voted for the disallowance of the Jesuits' Estates Act in 1888. He opposed also the Manitoba School Bill of the Tupper government in 1896. He died at Shanty Bay, Ontario, on December 22, 1914. In 1864 he married Elizabeth, only daughter of Col. R. R. Loring, London, and widow of J. F. Harris, London, Ontario. In 1882 he became lieut.-colonel commanding the 35th Battalion (Simcoe Foresters) of the Canadian militia; and during the North West rebellion of 1885 he commanded the York and Simcoe regiment.

**Observatory inlet,** an arm of Portland inlet, with a length of 29 miles and an average width of 2½ miles, in the Cassiar district of British Columbia. It was named by Vancouver (q.v.) in 1793, because he set up his observatory here to correct his positions.

**O'Callaghan, Edmund Bailey** (1797-1880), journalist and historian, was born at Mallow, Ireland, on February 27, 1797. He was educated in Paris, France, and came to Canada in 1823. He studied medicine at Quebec, Lower Canada, and was admitted to practice in 1827. From 1834 to 1837 he represented Yamaska in the Legislative Assembly of Lower Canada, and during the same period he was the editor of the Montreal *Vindicator*, the organ of the Society of Friends of Ireland. He was actively implicated in the rebellion of 1837, and escaped to the United States. He there became the historian and archivist of the state of New York. In this capacity, he compiled *The documentary history of the state of New York* (4 vols., Albany, 1850-51), and edited *Documents relating to the colonial history of the state of New York* (11 vols., 1856-61). He published also *The late session of the provincial parliament of Lower Canada* (Montreal, 1836), *Jesuit relations of discoveries and other occurrences* (pamphlet, New York, 1847; French translation, Montreal, 1850); and *The history of the New Netherlands* (New York, 1846; 2nd ed., 2 vols., 1848). He died in New York on May 27, 1880. See F. S. Guy, *Edmund Bailey O'Callaghan* (Washington, D.C., 1934).

**Ocean Falls,** a town and port in Range 3 of the Coast district of British Columbia, at the head of Cousins inlet, off Fisher channel. It is the site of the pulp-and-paper mills of the Pacific Mills, Ltd., which furnish the chief business of the port; and it has a high school, a hospital, and some government offices. Pop. (1934), 1,000.

**Ochotona.** See **Pika.**

**O'Connor, Dennis** (1841-1911), Roman Catholic archbishop of Toronto (1899-1908), was born in the township of Pickering, Upper Canada, on March

28, 1841. He was educated at St. Michael's College, Toronto, and in France; and was ordained a priest of the Roman Catholic Church in 1863. From 1863 to 1870 he was a professor in St. Michael's College, Toronto, and from 1870 to 1890 he was superior of L'Assomption College, Sandwich, Ontario. In 1890 he was consecrated bishop of London, Ontario; and in 1899 he became third archbishop of Toronto. He retired from the archiepiscopate in 1908, and he died at Toronto on June 30, 1911.

**O'Connor, John** (1824-1887), politician and judge, was born in January, 1824, at Boston, Massachusetts. His parents, who had come to the United States in 1823, removed to Canada in 1828, and settled in Essex county, Upper Canada. He was called to the bar of Upper Canada in 1854 (Q.C., 1872). He sat for Essex in the Legislative Assembly of Canada from 1863 to 1864, and in the Canadian House of Commons from 1867 to 1874. In 1878 he was elected to the Commons for Russell, and he represented this constituency until 1884. From 1873 to 1874 he was minister of inland revenue, and then postmaster-general, in the Macdonald government; in 1879 he became president of the Council; in 1880 he was re-appointed postmaster-general; and later in the same year he became secretary of state. In 1884 he was appointed a puisne judge of the Court of Queen's Bench in Ontario; and he sat on the bench until his death at Cobourg, Ontario, on November 3, 1887. In 1849 he married Mary, daughter of Richard Barrett, formerly of Killarney, Ireland; and by her he had nine children. He was the author of *Letters addressed to the governor-general on the subject of Fenianism* (1870). See D. B. Read, *Lives of the judges* (Toronto, 1888).

**Oddfellows, Independent Order of.** The origin of this fraternal and benevolent society is uncertain, as is also that of its peculiar name. It was in 1813 that a number of lodges met and organized the Manchester Unity of Oddfellows, from which the order spread to the United States and Canada. Though lodges seem to have existed in Halifax, Nova Scotia, earlier, it was not until 1843 that the first lodge was formed in the province of Canada. It is said that in that year two Americans, John H. Hardie and George Matthews, established the Prince of Wales Lodge at Montreal. In 1844 the American Grand Lodge constituted the Grand Lodge of Canada, and installed its officers; and in 1845 the first lodge in Upper Canada was formed. In 1847 the Grand Lodge of British North America was constituted; and for a few years the order prospered. Then it fell, about 1851, into a decline; and had it not been for the interest and support of the Grand Lodge of the United States, it might have collapsed in Canada. At present the order has extended into all the Canadian provinces, though it is especially strong in Ontario. The headquarters of the order in North America are at Baltimore, Maryland; but Canadian Oddfellowship has its own organization. It contains four divisions, subordinate lodges, Rebekah lodges, subordinate encampments, and cantons. Women are admitted as members into what is called "the Rebekah branch". The governing body is the Sovereign Grand Lodge. The order holds as cardinal principles the Fatherhood of God and the Brotherhood of Man, and carries on a very large service of relief among its more needy members and their families. It has a number of homes for aged and indigent members and orphan children; and the total of the benefits paid by it is very large. See *History of Odd Fellowship in Canada, 1855-1875* (Brantford, Ontario, 1879), and W. S. Johnston, *Oddfellowship in Ontario* (Toronto, 1923).

**Odell, Jonathan** (1737-1818), clergyman, physician, author, and provincial secretary of New Brunswick (1784-1818), was born in Newark, New Jersey, on September 25, 1737, the son of John Odell and Temperance, daughter of Jonathan Dickinson, president of Princeton College. He was educated at the College of New Jersey, and then at Newark; and after graduating (M.A., 1854) he studied medicine, and became a surgeon in the British army. While in the West Indies, he resigned his commission; and went to England to study for holy orders. He was ordained deacon in 1766 and priest in 1767, and was appointed rector in Burlington, New Jersey. After the American Revolution, in which he served as a captain in a loyal New Jersey regiment, he accompanied Sir Guy Carleton (q.v.) to England; and in 1784 he came out to New Brunswick, where he was appointed provincial secretary, registrar of records, and clerk of the council; and these offices he held continuously until 1812, when his only son William Franklin (q.v.), succeeded him. He died in Fredericton, New Brunswick, on November 25, 1818. He married Anne DeCou on May 6, 1772; and by her he had one son and three daughters. He wrote a number of patriotic verses which were very popular among the Loyalists, and were collected and published by Winthrop Sargent under the title *Loyal verses of Stansbury and Odell* (Albany, 1860).

**Odell, William Franklin** (1774-1844), provincial secretary of New Brunswick (1812-44), was born in Burlington, New Jersey, on October 19, 1774, the only son of the Rev. Jonathan Odell (q.v.) and Anne DeCou. He studied law, and was called to the bar of New Brunswick in 1806. He succeeded his father as provincial secretary of New Brunswick in 1812, and he held this office for thirty-two years until his death. In 1817 he was appointed one of the commissioners to enquire into the boundary between New Brunswick and the United States. He died at

Fredericton, New Brunswick, on December 25, 1844. He married Elizabeth, daughter of the Rev. Elisha Newell, of New Jersey; and by her he had three daughters and one son. See J. W. Lawrence, *Judges of New Brunswick and their times* (St. John, New Brunswick, 1907).

**Odell, William Hunter** (1811-1891), senator of Canada, was born at Fredericton, New Brunswick, on November 26, 1811, the only son of William Franklin Odell (q.v.). He was educated at King's College, Fredericton (B.A., 1832), and in 1838 was called to the bar of New Brunswick. The same year he was appointed deputy provincial secretary, registrar, and clerk of the Executive Council; and in 1847 he was made a judge of the court of common pleas in New Brunswick. From 1850 to 1867 he was a member of the Legislative Council of the province; and in 1865-6 he was postmaster-general in the government formed in opposition to Confederation. In 1867 he was appointed by royal proclamation a senator of the Dominion of Canada; and he sat in the Senate until his death, at Halifax, Nova Scotia, on July 26, 1891. He married the eldest daughter of the Hon. Henry Bliss, of Halifax. See J. W. Lawrence, *The judges of New Brunswick and their times* (St. John, New Brunswick, 1907).

**Odelltown, Battle of.** See **Lacolle, Battle of.**

**Odessa**, a village in Lennox county, Ontario, on the Canadian National Railway, 11 miles east of Napanee. The site was founded under the name of Mill Creek. In 1854 it was named Odessa by the Post Office authorities. The Crimean War had broken out in that year and there was much activity at Odessa, the southern port of Russia, hence the name. The village has a textile mill, and a cheese factory. Pop. (1931), 732.

**O'Donoghue, William B.** (d. 1878), rebel, was an Irishman who was, at the outbreak of the Red River rebellion of 1869-70, a professor in St. Boniface College, Winnipeg. He was "secretary to the treasury" in Riel's provisional government; and on the arrival of the troops he escaped to the United States. He was not included in the amnesty granted to Riel (q.v.) and Lépine (q.v.), on account of his supposed connection with a projected Fenian invasion of Manitoba; but the clemency of the Crown was extended to him in 1877. He died at St. Paul, Minnesota, on March 26, 1878.

**O'Donohue, John** (1824-1902), senator of Canada, was born at Tuam, Galway, Ireland, on April 18, 1824. He emigrated to Canada in 1839, and engaged in mercantile pursuits in Toronto. He studied law, and was called to the bar in Ontario in 1869 (Q.C., 1880). In 1874 he was elected to represent Toronto East in the Canadian House of Commons, but was unseated on petition, and defeated. In 1882 he was called to the Senate of Canada; and he sat in this House until his death on December 7, 1902. In 1848 he married Charlotte Josephine, daughter of Dr. Bradley, of Toronto.

**Ogden, Charles Richard** (1791-1866), attorney-general of Lower Canada (1833-42), was born on February 6, 1791, the son of the Hon. Isaac Ogden (q.v.) and Sarah Hanson. He was educated at Three Rivers and at Montreal, and he was called to the bar of Lower Canada in 1812 (K.C., 1816). From 1814 to 1824, and from 1830 to 1833, he represented Three Rivers in the Legislative Assembly of Lower Canada; in 1823 he was appointed solicitor-general of Lower Canada, and in 1833 attorney-general. As such it was his duty to deal with the rebels of 1837 and 1838; and he incurred, on account of his activ-

ity during this period, the hostility of the French Canadians. In 1840 he was appointed a member of the Special Council of Lower Canada; and in 1841 he countersigned, as attorney-general, the proclamation bringing into effect the union of Upper and Lower Canada. In 1841 he was again elected to represent Three Rivers in the Legislative Assembly; and he entered the first government of the Union as attorney-general for Lower Canada. In 1842, however, while he was on leave of absence, the government resigned; and though he protested that he had been appointed "during good behaviour", and not "during pleasure", he ceased to be attorney-general—the first victim of the new theory of responsible government. In 1844 he went to live in England, and was called to the English bar. He eventually obtained an appointment as attorney-general of the Isle of Man, and later, in 1857, as district registrar at Liverpool. Both these offices he held until his death in February, 1866. He was twice married, (1) to Mary, daughter of General Coffin, and (2) to Susan, daughter of Isaac Winslow Clarke. By his second wife he had four sons and one daughter. See W. Ogden Wheeler, *The Ogden family in America* (Philadelphia, 1907).

**Ogden, Isaac** (1739-1824), judge, was born in New Jersey in 1739, the son of the Hon. David Ogden. During the American Revolution he adhered to the loyalist cause, and the property of his family was confiscated. He went to England, on the evacuation of New York, in 1783; and in 1788 came to Canada. Here he was appointed a judge of the Admiralty Court at Quebec. In 1796 he became a puisne judge of the court of King's Bench at Montreal; and he retained this post until failing health compelled his resignation in 1818. He died in England in 1824. See W. Ogden Wheeler, *The Ogden family in America* (Philadelphia, 1907).

**Ogden, Peter Skene** (1794-1854), fur-trader, was born in Quebec, Lower Canada, in 1794, the son of the Hon. Isaac Ogden (q.v.) and Sarah Hanson. He entered the service of the North West Company as a clerk in 1811; and from 1811 to 1818 he was stationed at Isle à la Crosse. He was transferred to the Columbia department in 1818; and in 1820 he was made a partner of the Company. In 1823, after the union of 1821, he was given the rank as a chief trader in the Hudson's Bay Company, and in 1835 he became a chief factor. He spent most of his life, after 1818, on the Pacific slope; and he died near Oregon city on September 27, 1854. It has been said that he was the anonymous author of *Traits of American Indian life and character* (London, 1853); but this is not certain. For a fuller account of his life, see T. C. Elliott, *Peter Skene Ogden* (Quarterly of the Oregon Historical Society, 1910).

**Ogden, mount,** is in the Kootenay district of British Columbia, between the Yoho river and Sherbrooke creek, in Yoho Park in the Rocky mountains. It is in lat. 51° 28′ and long. 116° 24′, and has an altitude of 8,805 feet. It was named in 1904, after J. G. Ogden, vice-president of the Canadian Pacific Railway.

**Ogden, mount,** is on the boundary line between British Columbia and Alaska in the Cassiar district. It is in lat. 58° 25′, and long. 133° 22′, and has an altitude of 7,441 feet. It was named after Herbert G. Ogden of the United States Coast and Geodetic Survey, who carried on original explorations, and made maps in 1893, on the basis of which the present international boundary hereabouts was determined.

**Ogden, mount,** is in the Cassiar district of British Columbia, south of Ominiceta creek, head of the Omineca river. It is in lat. 55° 55′, and long. 125° 53′, and has an altitude of 6,500 feet.

**Ogema,** a village in Saskatchewan, on the Weyburn-Lethbridge branch of the Canadian Pacific Railway, 75 miles south of Regina. It is in a general farming district, and has a high school, a library, and a weekly newspaper (*South Country Times*). Pop. (1934), 400.

**Ogilvie, Alexander Walker** (1829-1902), senator of Canada, was born at St. Michel, near Montreal, Lower Canada, on May 7, 1829, the son of Alexander Ogilvie. In 1854 he founded the firm of A. W. Ogilvie and Co., millers and grain merchants. From 1867 to 1871, and from 1875 to 1878, he represented Montreal West in the Legislative Assembly of Quebec; and in 1881 he was called to the Senate of Canada. He sat in the Senate until shortly before his death in Montreal, on March 31, 1902. In 1854 he married Sarah, daughter of William Leney, of Longue Pointe; and by her he had several children. See J. A. Gemmill, *The Ogilvies of Montreal* (Montreal, 1904).

**Ogilvie, John** (1722-1774), clergyman, was born in New York in 1722, and was educated at Yale University (B.A., 1748; M.A., 1751). He was ordained a priest of the Church of England, and became a chaplain with the colonial forces in the Seven Years' War. From 1760 to 1764 he was stationed at Montreal, and he was the first Protestant clergyman in Montreal. His register of births, deaths, and marriages in Montreal from 1760 to 1763 is still in existence. He died in New York on November 26, 1774. See A. H. Young, *The Reverend John Ogilvie* (Ont. Hist. Soc., Papers and Records, 1925).

**Ogilvie, William** (1846-1912), commissioner of the Yukon (1898-1901), was born at Ottawa, Upper Canada, on April 7, 1846, the son of James Ogilvie and Margaret Halliday. He was educated in Ottawa, and in 1869 was admitted to practice as a provincial and Dominion land surveyor. Between 1875 and 1898 he carried out many surveys and explorations in the Canadian West, and notably in the Mackenzie river and Yukon districts. He was in the Yukon Territory at the time of the "gold rush" of 1898; and from 1898 to 1901 he was commissioner in the Yukon for the Dominion government. He died in Winnipeg on November 13, 1912. His reminiscences were published posthumously under the title *Early days on the Yukon* (Toronto, 1913).

**Ogilvie, mount,** is on the boundary between British Columbia and Alaska, in the Cassiar district. It is in lat. 58° 51', and long. 134° 15', and has an altitude of 7,700 feet. It is named after William Ogilvie (q.v.), who made field surveys from 1893 to 1895, and aided in making the maps upon the basis of which the present international boundary was determined.

**Ogilvy, John** (1769?-1819), merchant, was born in Scotland about 1769. He came to Canada about 1790, and became a partner in the firm of Parker, Gerrard, and Ogilvy. This was the firm that joined with Forsyth, Richardson, and Co. to form the XY Company; and John Macdonald of Garth (q.v.) says in his autobiography that in 1798 John Ogilvy was "at the head of the XY Co." He signed the agreement of 1804, by which the XY and North West Companies were amalgamated; and thus acquired in the North West Company an indirect interest. In 1817 he was appointed a commissioner, under the Treaty of Ghent, for determining the boundaries of British North America; and he died, while engaged in this capacity, at Sandwich, Upper Canada, on September 28, 1819. A portrait of him is in the McCord National Museum, in Montreal.

**Ogoki river,** a tributary of the Albany river, in the Thunder bay and Cochrane districts of Ontario. The name is an Indian word meaning "swift river". It rises north-west of lake Nipigon, and flows into the Albany just east of the 86th parallel of longitude.

**O'Grady, William John** (d. 1840), priest and journalist, was born in Ireland, and was ordained in the diocese of Cork. He went to Brazil with a party of Irish immigrants; and later he came to Upper Canada in 1828. He was given charge of the mission at York (Toronto), but he came into conflict with the bishops, and he became one of the leaders of the advanced wing of the Reform party. In 1832 he became the editor of the *Canadian Correspondent;* and in 1834 this paper was merged with W. L. Mackenzie's *Colonial Advocate,* under the name of *Correspondent and Advocate.* O'Grady died in Whitby, Upper Canada, in 1840.

**O'Hanly, John Lawrence Power** (1829-1912), civil engineer and author, was born at Waterford, Ireland, on June 24, 1829, the son of Patrick O'Hanly and Bridget Power. He came to Canada as a young man, and became a land surveyor and civil engineer. He was employed on the Intercolonial Railway, the Southern Railway, the Canadian Pacific Railway, the Ottawa and Gatineau Railway, and the Ontario Pacific Railway; and on the Ontario and Quebec boundary survey, and on surveys in Manitoba and the North-West. He died at Ottawa on March 22, 1912. He was the author of *The Intercolonial Railway* (Ottawa, 1868), and *The political standing of Irish Catholics in Canada* (Ottawa, 1872).

**O'Higgins, Harvey** (1876-1929), author, was born at London, Ontario, on November 14, 1876. He was educated at the University of Toronto, but did not graduate. He was at first a journalist in Toronto; but he soon obtained an *entrée* into the best American periodicals, and he then removed to the United States. He died at Martinstown, New Jersey, on February 28, 1929. His chief publications were *The smoke-eaters* (New York, 1905), *Don-o'-dreams*

(New York, 1906), *A grand army man* (New York, 1908), *Old clinkers* (Boston, 1909), *The adventures of detective Barney* (New York, 1915), *The secret springs* (New York, 1920), *Some distinguished Americans* (New York, 1922), *Julie Crane* (New York, 1924), and *Clara Barron* (New York, 1926). He collaborated also in a number of works—with Judge B. Lindsey in *The beast* (New York, 1910), with F. J. Cannon in *Under the prophet in Utah* (New York, 1911), with Judge Lindsey in *The doughboy's religion* (New York, 1920), with E. H. Reade in *The American mind in action* (New York, 1924), and with Harriet Ford in the following plays: *On the hiring line* (New York, 1909), *The Argyle case* (1912), *The dummy* (1913), *Polygamy* (1914), and *Main street* (1921).

**Oil City,** a village in Lambton county, Ontario, on the Michigan Central Railway, 18 miles south-east of Sarnia. Pop. (1934), 300.

**Oil Industry.** See **Petroleum Industry.**

**Oil Shale,** a dark shale impregnated with petroleum, which probably has originated from disintegration of organic material in the original mud from which the shale was formed. Important deposits of oil shale in Canada are found in New Brunswick, Nova Scotia, and the northern parts of Ontario, Manitoba, and Saskatchewan.

**Oil Springs,** a village in Lambton county, Ontario, on the Michigan Central Railway, 21 miles south-east of Sarnia. It has oil wells. Pop. (1934), 800.

**Ojibwa.** See **Chippewa.**

**Ojibway lake,** the name applied to a glacial lake which once existed to the north of the height of land in eastern Canada, as the ice-sheet receded toward Hudson bay. The so-called clay belt of northern Quebec and Ontario represents the deposits in this lake. Its outlet is not certainly known. As the ice reached Hudson bay, the lake was drained off, leaving as its successors the Abitibi lakes and other smaller bodies of water. See A. P. Coleman, *Glacial and post-glacial lakes in Ontario* (Toronto, 1922).

**Oka,** a village in the county of Two Mountains, Quebec, situated on the north bank of the lake of Two Mountains, opposite Vaudreuil. The name is an Algonkian word signifying "doré", and has reference to the number of these fish formerly found in the lake of Two Mountains. For many years the village was the headquarters of the Indian agent who looked after the Iroquois and Algonkin concentrated here; but it is now chiefly notable for the Trappist monastery and farm established nearby in 1881. Connected with the monastery is a school of agriculture. See Ubald Paquin, *La Trappe d'Oka* (Montreal, 1934).

**Okak,** a mission station for the Eskimo, founded by the Moravian brethren on the east coast of Labrador in 1778. It is 120 miles north-west of Nain.

**Okanagan lake** is in the Osoyoos district of British Columbia, between the 49th and 51st parallels of latitude, and at the head of the Okanagan river. The Okanagan valley is a famous fruit-farming district. The lake is 69 miles long from north to south, varies in width from ¾ to 2½ miles, and has an area of 127.2 square miles.

**Okanagan Landing,** a village in the Osoyoos district of British Columbia, on the east side of Okanagan lake, 5 miles south-west of Vernon, and the terminus of the Sicamous branch of the Canadian Pacific Railway. Pop. (1930), 150.

**Okanagan Mission,** a settlement in the Similkameen district of British Columbia, on the east side of Okanagan lake, 5 miles from Kelowna, the nearest railway station. Pop. (1931), 300.

**Okanagan river,** a stream which flows from the southern end of Okanagan lake in a southerly direction across the

KELOWNA, OKANAGAN VALLEY, BRITISH COLUMBIA

international boundary, and falls into the Columbia river about 70 miles south of the boundary. Its length in Canada is about 43 miles.

**Okotoks,** a town in Alberta, on the Sheep river, and on the Macleod-Calgary branch of the Canadian Pacific Railway, 27 miles south of Calgary, and 80 miles north of Macleod. The name is a Blackfoot word meaning "lots of stones", in reference to the ford of Sheep river on the Calgary-Macleod trail. It is in a mixed farming and horse-breeding district; and it is the shipping point for the Turner valley oil fields. It has a weekly newspaper (*Review*). Pop. (1931), 760.

**Olds,** a town in Alberta, on the Calgary-Edmonton branch of the Canadian Pacific Railway, 57 miles north of Calgary, and 137 miles south of Edmonton. It was named, when the railway was built, after George Olds, sometime traffic manager of the Canadian Pacific Railway. Situated in the heart of a rich grain-growing and stock-raising district, it has eleven grain elevators, and is the site of the provincial school of agriculture. It has a high school and a weekly newspaper (*Gazette*). Pop. (1931), 1,056.

**Old-squaw** (*Clangula hyemalis*), a common Arctic nesting duck, characterized by the long pointed central tail feathers. The male is conspicuously patterned with dark brown and white. Females are more dully coloured. Old-squaws are common winter visitors along both sea coasts in winter and on the Great lakes. The species is also known as the "long-tailed duck" and the "coween."

**Olga lake,** in the basin of the Nottaway river, and south-east of Mattagami lake, in Abitibi territory, Quebec, is 16 miles in length, and has an area of 50 square miles.

**Olier de Verneuil, Jean Jacques** (1608-1657), priest, was born in Paris, France, on September 20, 1608. He

was for many years *curé* of the parish of St. Sulpice in Paris; and in 1640 he took a leading part in forming the company which established the Sulpician settlement at Montreal. He continued to be interested in the missions of Canada until his death, which took place in Paris on April 2, 1857; and his letters, which contain a narrative of the Sulpician missions in Canada, were published posthumously under the title, *Lettres et correspondance du Père Olier de Verneuil sur les établissements de la foi dans la Nouvelle France* (Paris, 1674). See Abbé Faillon, *La vie et les œuvres de Jean Jacques Olier de Verneuil* (Paris, 1855).

**Oliver, Edmund Henry** (1882-1935), educationist and historian, was born at Eberts, Kent county, Ontario, on February 8, 1882, and was educated at the University of Toronto (B.A., 1902; M.A., 1903) and at Columbia University (Ph.D., 1905). From 1905 to 1909 he was lecturer in history in McMaster University, Toronto; from 1909 to 1914 he was professor of history and economics in the University of Saskatchewan; and from 1914 to his death he was principal of St. Andrew's College, Saskatoon. In 1930 he was elected moderator of the United Church of Canada. He died at Round Lake, Saskatchewan, on July 11, 1935. He was a doctor of divinity of Emmanuel College, Toronto, of Queen's University, Kingston, and of the Union College of British Columbia. In 1921 he was elected a fellow of the Royal Society of Canada, and in 1934 president of Section Two. He was the author of *Roman economic conditions* (Toronto, 1907), *The Canadian North West, its early development and legislative records* (2 vols., Ottawa, 1914), *The winning of the frontier* (Toronto, 1930), and a series of papers on the history of Saskatchewan in the *Transactions* of the Royal Society of Canada. See C. Mackinnon, *Life of Principal Oliver* (Toronto, 1936).

**Oliver, Frank** (1853-1933), minister of the interior for Canada (1905-11), was born in Peel county, Ontario, in 1853, the son of Allan Bowsfield. As a young man, he adopted his mother's maiden name, and went west in 1873 to Winnipeg, and in 1876 to Edmonton, where he founded the *Edmonton Bulletin* in 1880. Of this journal he remained the proprietor until 1923. He was elected to the North West Council in 1883 and to the Legislative Assembly of the North West Territories; and he represented first Alberta, and then Edmonton, in the Canadian House of Commons from 1896 to 1917. From 1905 to 1911 he was minister of the interior in the Laurier administration. From 1923 to 1928 he was a member of the Board of Railway Commissioners for Canada. He died at Ottawa on March 31, 1933. In 1881 he married Harriet, daughter of Thomas Dunlop, of Prairie Grove, Manitoba; and by her he had one son and four daughters. In 1930 he was made an LL.D. of the University of Alberta.

**Oliver, John** (1856-1927), prime minister of British Columbia (1918-27), was born at Hartington, Derbyshire, England, on July 31, 1856, the son of Robert Oliver and Emma Lomas. He came to Canada with his parents in 1870; and in 1877 he went to British Columbia, where he became a rancher. He was elected to represent Delta in the Legislative Assembly of British Columbia in 1900, and was chosen leader of the Liberal opposition in 1905. He was defeated in 1909, and did not return to the legislature until 1916, when he became minister of railways and agriculture in the Brewster cabinet. On the death of Brewster (q.v.) in 1918, he succeeded to the prime ministry; and he retained power until his death at Victoria, British Columbia, on August 17, 1927. In 1886 he married Elizabeth Woodward, of Mud Bay, British Columbia, and by her he had five sons and three daughters. See James Morton, *Honest John Oliver* (London, 1933).

**Oliver,** a town in the Similkameen district of British Columbia, on the Okanagan river, and on the Penticton branch of the Canadian Pacific Railway, 25 miles south of Penticton. It is the centre of the southern Okanagan irrigation project of the British Columbia government. Pop. (1934), 300.

**Olivier, Louis Auguste** (1816-1881), judge and author, was born at Berthier-en-haut, Lower Canada, in 1816. He was called to the bar of Lower Canada in 1839 (Q.C., 1864). From 1863 to 1867 he represented the Lanaudière division in the Legislative Council of Canada; and in 1867 he was called to the Senate of Canada. In 1873 he was appointed a judge of the Superior Court of Quebec for the district of Joliette; and he sat in this court until his death, at Joliette, Quebec, on September 18, 1881. He contributed to *Le répertoire national* (Montreal, 1848-50) an *Essai sur la littérature du Canada* and some poetry. See P. E. Roy, *L. A. Olivier* (Lévis, 1891).

**Olivine,** a rock-forming mineral consisting of silicate of magnesia and ferrous iron. It crystallizes in the orthorhombic system, but is most commonly found in granular masses or as disseminated grains in rock. It has a hardness of 6.5 to 7, and a specific gravity of about 3.25. The lustre is vitreous, and commonly it is coloured olive-green. Transparent material free from flaws, it is highly prized as a gem stone, sold under the names of olivine, peridot, and chrysolite. The mineral is readily altered, possibly by the direct action of steam, to form serpentine. It is particularly abundant in basic igneous rocks, including olivine basalts, olivine gabbros, and the different varieties of peridotites.

**Ombabika bay,** the mouth of the Ombabika river in lake Nipigon, in the Thunder Bay district of Ontario. The name is an Indian word meaning "a gap between two promontories."

**O'Meara, Frederick Augustus** (1814-1888), clergyman and translator, was born in Wexford, Ireland, in 1814, and educated at Trinity College, Dublin (B.A., 1837). He took holy orders in the Church of Ireland, and in 1838 was sent as a missionary to Canada. For twenty years he was a missionary among the Ojibwa Indians on Manitoulin island; and in his later years he was rector of Port Hope, Ontario. He died at Port Hope, suddenly, on December 17, 1888. He translated into Ojibwa the *Book of Common Prayer* (Toronto, 1853), the *New Testament* (Toronto, 1854), and (with the Rev. Peter Jacobs) the *Pentateuch* (Toronto, n.d.). With Peter Jacobs, he also compiled a *Hymn book for the use of Ojibway Indian congregations* (Toronto, n.d.).

**O'Meara, Thomas Robert** (1864-1930), principal of Wycliffe College, Toronto, was born in Georgetown, Ontario, on October 16, 1864, the son of the Rev. F. A. O'Meara (q.v.). He was educated at the University of Toronto and at Wycliffe College, Toronto; and was ordained a priest of the Church of England in 1888. From 1887 to 1906 he was engaged in parochial work in Toronto; and in 1906 he was appointed second principal of Wycliffe College. He died at Toronto on January 10, 1930. See *The jubilee volume of Wycliffe College* (Toronto, 1927).

**Omemee,** a village in Victoria county, Ontario, on the Pigeon river, and on the Canadian National Railway, 10 miles south-east of Lindsay. Known first as Williamstown, and then as Metcalfe, it was re-named Omemee about 1857, after the Omemee or "Pigeon" sub-tribe of the Mississaga Indians; and it was incorporated as a village in 1874. It has a high school. Pop. (1934), 500. See W. Kirkconnell, *Victoria county centennial history* (Lindsay, Ontario, 1921).

**Omineca river,** a tributary of the Finlay river, in the Cassiar district of British Columbia. It flows around the Cariboo mountain range on the north, and is 140 miles long.

**One Big Union.** The One Big Union, generally referred to as the O.B.U., came into existence at Calgary, Alberta, in March, 1919. The organization was largely an outcome of the World War, with its resulting dislocations in industry, and political and social unrest. It might also be said that it was a tangible expression of disapproval of the existing forms of labour organization in Canada at that time. In 1918 the Trades and Labour Congress of Canada had held its annual convention in the city of Quebec, which was attended by a number of delegates from the four western provinces. At this meeting eight resolutions were introduced by certain of these representatives. The substance of these resolutions was practically the same, and called upon the Trades and Labour Congress to re-organize the Canadian labour movement into a "modern and scientific organization by Industry instead of by Craft". These resolutions all met with defeat, and, as a result, it was decided to hold a delegate conference previous to the next meeting of the Trades and Labour Congress for the purpose of giving the western membership of the Congress an opportunity of formulating a policy which they might consider would be progressive, and one which it was believed would receive the support of the eastern delegates. This proposal for the western conference was later taken in hand by the British Columbia Federation of Labour, a body which was then under charter from the Trades and Labour Congress of Canada, but which has since lapsed.

The conference, which met at Calgary in March, 1919, was attended by 237 delegates from western labour bodies and two from Ontario. Although it had been previously stated that the meeting was not intended as a secessionist movement, the second resolution adopted favoured the immediate reorganization of the workers "along industrial lines, so that by virtue of their industrial strength, the workers may be better prepared to enforce any demand they consider essential to their maintenance and well-being". It was further resolved that the conference recommend that the existing branches of international organizations should sever their connections with such bodies and coöperate in the formation of an industrial organization of all workers. It was also decided that a referendum on the question be submitted to the entire Canadian trade union membership, and also that a proposed plan of the new organization, which on the report of the policy committee became known as the One Big Union, be presented at the same time.

A second meeting of the advocates of the One Big Union was held in Calgary on June 11, 1919, when the constitution tentatively agreed to in March, with certain amendments, was ratified. The following quotation from the preamble to this constitution shows clearly the aims and purposes of the One Big Union: "The One Big Union seeks to organize the wage earners according to class and class needs and calls upon all workers to organize irrespective of nationality, sex, or craft into a workers' organization so that they may be enabled to more successfully carry on the every-day fight over wages, hours of work, etc., and prepare ourselves for the day when production for profit shall be replaced by production for use."

Directly after the formation of the One Big Union, the organization added considerably to its membership. Many members of certain craft unions, principally those connected with railway shop work, identified themselves with the new industrial union. At the close of the year 1919 the reported membership was 41,150, comprised in 101 local units. The Trades and Labour Congress of Canada opposed the One Big Union, as did also the various international craft bodies, whose long established form of organization along craft lines was being challenged.

The name of the One Big Union has been associated consistently with the Winnipeg strike of 1919; although the advocates of the One Big Union have disclaimed repeatedly any connection between the strike and their propaganda. The Winnipeg strike, however, resulted in a rather severe denunciation of the principle of paralysing industry through use of the general strike, and the One Big Union, dedicated to this line of advance, has declined in numerical strength since that time. In 1933 the general secretary reported 46 local units in Canada with a membership of 23,300.

An account of the organization, strength, and activities of the One Big Union can be found in the *Annual reports on labour organization in Canada* published by the Department of Labour, Ottawa, Canada. The reports of 1919 and 1920 are particularly useful for the early history of the organization. An excellent analysis of the underlying philosophy of the One Big Union and its general relation to the labour movement in Canada is contained in H. A. Logan, *Trade union organization in Canada* (Chicago, 1928).

**Oneida.** See **Iroquois.**

**O'Neill, John** (1834-1878), Fenian leader, was born at Drumgallon, county Monaghan, Ireland, on March 8, 1834. He emigrated to the United States in 1848; and after a varied career served as a cavalry officer in the American Civil War. He joined the Fenian brotherhood, and in May, 1866, he was the leader of the Fenian force which crossed the Niagara river, captured Fort Erie, and fought at Ridgeway. He was later appointed "inspector-general" of the Fenian forces; and in

May, 1870, he again attempted an invasion of Canada, but was turned back at Eccles Hill near the Vermont border. Finally, in October, 1871, he invaded Canadian territory a third time, but without the support of the Fenian council, when he seized Pembina on the Red river. He was, however, arrested by United States troops, and the invasion came to nought. In his later years, he was the agent for a firm of land speculators in Nebraska; and he died at Omaha on January 7, 1878. He was the author of an *Address . . to the officers and members of the Fenian brotherhood* (1868), and an *Official report . . . on the attempt to invade Canada* (1870).

**Onion lake** is in Saskatchewan, near the Alberta boundary, and between the 53rd and 54th parallels of latitude. According to an old Indian legend, the beautiful daughter of a Cree chief drowned herself in the lake because her lover, who had been bewitched, cursed her for eating onions. The lover followed his adored one to a watery grave. See J. H. McCormick, *Lloydminster* (London, 1924).

**Onion, Wild** (*Allium cernuum* Roth., *Liliaceae*), a strong-scented, pungent herb. The leaves are linear, flattened and strongly keeled, and rise from a coated bulb. The flower stalk is naked, angular, and nodding at the apex, and bears a loose or drooping cluster of rose-coloured flowers. The perianth segments are all alike, dry, and more or less persistent. It is found in the prairie provinces and Ontario.

**Onondaga.** See **Iroquois.**

**Ontario** is the second largest in area and the largest in population of the provinces of Canada. Situated between Quebec on the east and Manitoba on the west, it has an area of 407,262 square miles. Its population, as shown by the census of 1931, was 3,431,683. It is the leading province of the Dominion both industrially and in agri-

culture; it stands first in mineral productions; and it is second only to Quebec in lumbering and in developed water-power. Of its area, 41,382 square miles are water. The lakes and rivers within its bounds or forming a part of its boundaries are of the utmost consequence, not only in their influence upon climate and fertility, but also as outlets for trade and as sources of power.

No other province exhibits such variety of agriculture as may be found within Ontario. The western peninsula, inclosed by lakes and connecting rivers, is the most temperate region of Canada, while all portions of the table-land region are modified in climate to some degree by surrounding waters. In the Niagara district and along the shores of lake Erie, peaches, grapes, and other small fruits are produced in abundance and with little danger from frost. Forage crops and coarse grains are grown everywhere, while tobacco, beans, and sugar beets form important crops in the south-western counties. Dairy farming extends from the Ottawa and St. Lawrence river districts into the counties of western Ontario. In northern Ontario, where pioneer conditions still prevail, the process of clearing the land is itself made remunerative by the sale of the pulp-wood.

The industrial development of the province has been particularly marked since 1900. Cheap hydro-electric power, ample transportation facilities, abundant raw materials, and a developing home market have given stimulus to a varied manufacturing. Many American industries have established Canadian branches in Ontario in order to share in Canadian trade or to secure the advantages of imperial trade agreements.

The boundaries of the province consist for the most part of lakes and rivers. On the east the division between Ontario and Quebec is marked by a line drawn due south along the meridian of 79° 30′ from James bay to lake

Timiskaming, thence by the Ottawa river flowing south-eastward, but near the mouth of that stream deflected southwardly to the St. Lawrence river. On the south and west the St. Lawrence and its chain of lakes and rivers constitute the boundary as far as Pigeon river. Thence it follows small rivers and lakes (including Rainy lake and Rainy river) to the lake of the Woods, which forms the corner boundary between Ontario, Manitoba, and the state of Minnesota. Here an artificial line begins, being the eastern boundary of Manitoba, continuing northward to about the 53rd degree, and thence north-easterly to Hudson bay. The boundary then follows the shores of Hudson bay and James bay to the point due north of lake Timiskaming, already mentioned. The province is nearly a thousand miles in breadth, and is the same distance from its most southerly to its most northerly boundary.

The early explorations of the present province of Ontario were related to the fur-trade, to religion, and to the search for a western sea. Champlain (q.v.) in 1615 ascended the Ottawa river to the Mattawa and by lake Nipissing and French river entered the Georgian bay. Later he accompanied a Huron war-party southward by the Trent system. Jean Nicolet (q.v.), sent by Champlain to extend trade relations with Indians in the region of lake Michigan, was the first white man to reach the rapids of the St. Mary's river. Pierre Esprit Radisson (q.v.) and Médard Chouart, Sieur de Groseilliers (q.v.), relatives by marriage, went westward beyond Sault Ste. Marie, probably in 1658, and returned by the north shore of lake Superior. In 1661 they pushed northward from lake Superior towards Hudson bay, their exploration being a factor in the establishment of the Hudson's Bay Company. Prior to 1669 all westward exploration had been carried on by the Ottawa river route, but in that year Louis Jolliet (q.v.), who had been sent to report upon stories of copper deposits near lake Superior, returned by way of lake Huron and lake Erie. Near the present city of Hamilton he met a party under La Salle (q.v.), which had come from Montreal. La Salle's main party crossed lake Erie, and moved inland toward the Ohio river; but two Sulpician priests, Galinée (q.v.) and Dollier de Casson (q.v.), determined to follow the north shore of lake Erie. Bad weather prevented them from going far during the autumn of 1669, and they spent the winter near the present site of Port Dover, continuing their journey in the spring of 1670 on to the upper lakes. In 1731-2 La Vérendrye and his sons reached the lake of the Woods. Many others contributed to the store of geographical knowledge of the area now embraced in the province of Ontario, but then a part of New France.

When France ceded her North American possessions to Great Britain in 1763, there were few settlers in the area bounded by the Great lakes, and these were chiefly in the vicinity of the Detroit river. The region, however, was far from unknown, for it had been traversed by explorers and missionaries, fur-traders and hunters for more than a century. It was a great virgin area awaiting the coming of settlers, and the first of these arrived within a quarter century after the conquest. They were the refugee Loyalists of the American Revolution, and by the circumstances under which they came and by their character they profoundly influenced the future of the province. Loyalty to the British cause cost them homes and wealth and drove them into exile, but it made them founders of a new British colony. Within a year after the peace there were about ten thousand of them in the region west of the Ottawa river. For the British authorities in Canada their arrival created problems of an unprecedented character. Many had lost all their possessions, and there were few who were not in need. The British government came to their aid with rations, clothing, seed, implements, and livestock, built mills for their use, and pushed surveys with vigour, so that they might be securely established. Yet, despite all that was done for them, their privations were many. Though most of them had been farmers before coming to Canada, the primitive conditions of Canadian pioneer life brought trials and disappointments that sorely tested their resolution and patience.

The Loyalist settlements were along the St. Lawrence river west of Longueil, on the bay of Quinte, and in the vicinity of the Niagara and Detroit rivers. In the settlements on the St. Lawrence and the bay of Quinte an effort was made to keep together as far as possible men who had served in the same regiment. Loyalists from western Pennsylvania and southern New York came chiefly to the Niagara district, where the men of Butler's Rangers were also placed. The loyal Six Nations Indians were given lands along the Grand river emptying into lake Erie.

In addition to the administrative problems arising out of this large accession of population, the British authorities in Canada soon found themselves facing a constitutional problem. The Loyalists were of English tradition and accustomed to a large measure of self-government. They now found themselves under an instrument of government, the Quebec Act, which made no provision for self-government. The Quebec Act may or may not have been a wise measure in 1774, but the policy which it expressed had been nullified by the events which followed, and it was soon evident that a new policy for Canada would have to be devised. This new policy was expressed in the Constitutional Act of 1791, by which provision was made for the division of Quebec into two provinces, Upper and Lower Canada, the first of which would include the area in which the Loyalists had been settled. The new province was to have a lieutenant-governor and a council of not less than seven members, appointed by the Crown, together with an elected Legislative Assembly of not less than sixteen members. The Act further made provision for the creation of a colonial aristocracy and for the setting up of what was plainly intended to be an established church to be supported out of public funds.

This new system of government was set in operation by Colonel John Graves Simcoe (q.v.), who met his first Assembly at Newark (Niagara) in September, 1792. Simcoe was a man of marked ability and many virtues. He promoted the building of roads and the opening up of the country for settlement. He gave encouragement to immigration from the United States, and in large measure sought the welfare of the people under his charge. Though he regarded the Loyalist as the best possible settler, he offered land also to non-Loyalist elements from the republic, about 30,000 of whom came in his time. These newcomers were scrutinized with care, and were placed in townships well away from the border to avoid the contamination of republican ideas. Simcoe's successors in office continued his immigration policy, though with less care in selection, so that by 1812, when the province had a population of about 77,000, fully three-fifths of this number were non-Loyalist, land-hungry Americans, most of them preferring the republican form of government to the pseudo-aristocracy of Upper Canadian rule, and voicing their discontent through the members whom they succeeded in electing to the Assembly.

The Upper Canada Assembly in its early sessions enacted legislation of a basic character. English civil law, trial by jury, and courts were provided while local government of a simple character was also established. Serious mistakes were, however, also made at this time. Simcoe's ardent admiration for the British constitution and the support which he gave to the aristocratic provisions of the Constitutional Act started a train of evils which troubled the province for almost half a century. At a very early date the chief offices tended to be concentrated in the hands of a small group of people, chiefly Loyalists, who used their place and influence to acquire large areas of the public lands which they held tax-free for speculative purposes. As early as 1806 discontent was widespread in the province and found its leadership in men of Irish birth like William Weekes (q.v.) and Robert Thorpe (q.v.). Little headway, however, was made against the well-entrenched governing group in the period before the War of 1812.

Upper Canada as a province was but twenty years old when hostilities arose between Great Britain and the United States. The conflict was a phase of the great European struggle with Napoleon, but had its peculiarly North American background as well. Desire on the part of American frontiersmen to possess the rich lands of Upper Canada had much to do with the fervour for war which was voiced in Congress by the western members. The popular American opinion, in the West at least, that the conquest of Canada would offer no difficulties, was probably encouraged by the knowledge that a majority of Upper Canada's people were of recent American origin and would probably welcome republican rule.

The declaration of war, on June 19, 1812, was followed by an invasion of the province on the Detroit river border. The problem of Canadian defence was difficult, since there were but 4,450 British regulars in the province, and not more than 4,000 each of Canadian regulars and Canadian militia. Upper Canada, which alone among the provinces was seriously invaded, had not more than 100,000 population, as opposed to the 6,000,000 white people in the United States, though it must be admitted that certain sections of the republic were apathetic, if not actually opposed to the war. Upper Canada was fortunate, however, in the leadership of Sir Isaac Brock (q.v.). With energy and great skill, he at once took the offensive, forced Hull to surrender at Detroit in August without the firing of a shot, and then in October defeated an invading force at Queenston Heights on the Niagara frontier. Here he fell leading his men in the attack. The end of the year saw not a foot of Canadian territory in American hands.

The year 1813 was less auspicious for British arms. The Americans secured possession of the lower lakes, captured York, the provincial capital, in April, and in the following September, after a naval victory on lake Erie, forced Procter (q.v.) to withdraw from his position on the Detroit river. Following closely on his retreating army, the American forces completely defeated him on October 5, at Moraviantown on the Thames river. The enemy were unsuccessful, however, in operations of this year against Kingston and Montreal.

The year 1814 saw another invasion on the Niagara frontier. The opposing forces met on July 25 at Lundy's Lane, and there fought what proved to be the bloodiest battle of the war. The Canadians held the superior enemy force in a stubborn contest and on the following day the American troops withdrew across the river. By this time, with Napoleon sent into exile, Britain was at last able to provide military aid for her colonies, and 16,000 of Wellington's troops were sent out to America. At sea the British navy also began to exert a pressure that was more effectual than that of the troops which were sent out. The New England states had been opposed to the war from the beginning, and by 1814 even the western "War Hawks" were tiring

THE LEGISLATIVE BUILDINGS OF ONTARIO AT TORONTO

of their efforts to capture Upper Canada. Peace negotiations were under way by the middle of the year 1814, and were consummated in the Treaty of Ghent, which was signed on December 24, 1814. As far as Canada was concerned, the war had been purely defensive, and in the final outcome not a foot of territory was lost.

The years of war had important effects upon Upper Canada. American aggression ended the possibility that the province might fall peacefully into the hands of the United States. British connection was henceforth assured. A new national pride and loyalty was born out of the sacrifices and endurance of the war. But there were other effects, less happy in their character. The Loyalists, regarding themselves as having saved the province for Great Britain, were more than ever convinced of their right to dictate its affairs. For the next two decades this assumption contributed to the political strife. The war also brought its usual accompaniments of extravagance, increased drinking, and generally lowered moral standards.

Some interesting economic changes may also be set down to the influence of the war. Money having been plentiful between 1812 and 1814, the former long credits ceased and the people became accustomed to paper money. The way was paved for banks, the first of which received its charter less than three years after the war. The prosperity of the war years was followed by the inevitable depression, and with depression came a revival of discontent. The exclusion of American immigration reduced land sales and slowed up development. Promises of land to those who had served as volunteers were slow in being fulfilled, though friends of the government seemed to experience no difficulty in securing for themselves large areas of wild lands, which, like the clergy reserves, remained unoccupied, unimproved, and free from taxation. In a province where the majority of the people were not members of the Church of England, the special privileges enjoyed by that body stirred envy and resentment. The influential group, the so-called Family Compact, seemed more firmly entrenched than in the past, controlling both the Executive and Legislative Councils and invariably having the ear also of the lieutenant-governor. There was little hope of political reform being achieved under such conditions.

Despite the turmoil in Upper Canada in the period from 1815 to 1840, the province experienced considerable growth and advancement. Within a decade after the war, the population had reached 150,000; by 1830 it was above 200,000; and in the next decade it increased to 430,000. In 1831-2 more than 100,000 people came to the British provinces, most of them to Upper Canada. The industrial revolution and the close of the Napoleonic wars were factors in producing one of the great migrations of the nineteenth century.

Movements for reform in Upper Canada coincided in point of time with reform movements in England and with the era of "Jacksonian democracy" in the United States. The Upper Canadian Reformers, strongest in numbers in the country districts, were often vague in their proposals for change, but in general they aimed to secure an elective Legislative Council and some kind of responsibility on the part of the Executive back to the Assembly. Once these gains were secured, they believed they would be able to control legislation. In general their resources were small, and during most of the period of agitation they lacked experienced leadership. Since the fight had to be waged in the Assembly, they set out to elect a majority of their own number to that body and succeeded both in 1824 and in 1828. In the latter election William Lyon Mackenzie (q.v.) entered the Assembly, and was soon the acknowledged leader of the reform group. On the part of the governing group, there was an apparent determination to surrender nothing. In the session of the Assembly during 1829-30 no less than 58 bills passed by the Assembly were thrown out by the Legislative Council, many of the measures being of importance to the welfare of the province.

The elections of 1830, brought on by the death of King George IV, resulted in the defeat of the Reformers and the new Assembly, controlled by the Family Compact, stupidly proceeded to a persecution of Mackenzie by repeatedly expelling him, after each of which expulsions he was promptly re-elected by his constituents. The British government showed some alarm at these proceedings, which made Mackenzie a popular hero, and contributed to his election as the first mayor of the city of Toronto in 1834.

In January, 1836, Sir John Colborne (q.v.), who had been lieutenant-governor since 1829, was succeeded in office by Sir Francis Bond Head (q.v.), who soon found himself in conflict both with his advisers and with the Assembly, and finally dissolved the Assembly in 1836. The election of a majority favourable to the governor, in a contest marked by considerable violence, seemed to turn Bond Head into a veritable despot, and convinced the more violent Reformers that attainment of their ends by constitutional methods was not possible. The uprising at York which was the sequel of these developments was quickly quelled, but throughout the province a seething unrest continued during 1838. The British government, shocked by the Upper Canada troubles and by an even more sanguinary uprising in Lower Canada, immediately despatched Lord Durham (q.v.) to Canada to make an investigation. His stay in the country was brief, and his observations were in some respects incomplete, but his report was of the utmost importance, and his recommendations of far-reaching character. He proposed a union of Upper and Lower Canada (and an even wider union of British provinces in America) under one legislature in which the English population were to be assured of control. Furthermore, he advocated the principle of responsible government, "entrusting the management of public affairs to persons who have the confidence of the representative body".

Upper Canada as a political entity theoretically ceased to exist on February 10, 1841, when the Union Act came into force. For the next quarter century it was geographically known as Canada West. The government of the now united Canada consisted of a governor, an appointed Legislative Council of not less than twenty members, and an Assembly in which each of the uniting provinces had an equal representation of forty-two members (after 1853 sixty-five each). The Family Compact in Upper Canada, foreseeing a loss of privilege and control, resisted for a time, but in the end gave assent to the new plan. The next decade was almost wholly occupied in the working out of the experiment of responsible government, the process being terminated when in 1849 Lord Elgin (q.v.) gave his assent to the highly contentious Rebellion Losses Bill by which the principle was definitely acknowledged that in matters of domestic concern the governor must act on the advice of his Canadian advisers.

In the period between the Act of Union and Confederation Upper Canada made a steady growth, though somewhat slower than in the earlier period. Immigration lessened in volume as compared with the 'thirties, and there was a falling off in quality as well. The arrival of shiploads of poor Irish during the 'forties created problems of health and relief that taxed both provincial and municipal effort. The population increased from 430,000 in 1840 to more than a million and a half in 1867, at which time three-fifths were of Canadian origin. The majority continued to be engaged in agriculture. The Crimean War and the American Civil War stimulated farm production, while the Reciprocity Treaty with the United States, in force between 1854 and 1866, widened the Canadian producer's market. Machinery came into much wider use on the farms, and there was considerable improvement in live-stock and in the quality of seed grain. Coöperative cheese-making, introduced from New York state about 1863, started the dairying industry on its long and prosperous history. Agricultural societies, farm journals, and agricultural exhibitions all contributed to the knowledge of a more scientific type of farming. Land under cultivation in Upper Canada increased four-fold between 1840 and 1867. Wheat, which was the chief staple, increased in production from three million bushels to nearly twenty-five million bushels between 1840 and 1860; but after the Civil War period there was a tendency toward a more diversified farming than hitherto.

The decade of the 'fifties was an era of railway-building. The Grand Trunk Railway, upon which work began in 1853, had at one time as many as 14,000 men employed in construction; and by 1856 Montreal and Toronto were joined. Two years later the road had been extended to London, and by 1859 it was at Sarnia. In the same period the Great Western Railway was built to connect Toronto with Windsor, while the Northern Railway linked Toronto with Collingwood on the Georgian bay. One immediate effect of the railway building was to reduce to insignificance many of the smaller lake ports which had hitherto been outlets for provincial trade. On the other hand, the railways stimulated many industries, particularly wood-working and iron-working industries, by opening up wider markets.

Political changes in the period covered by the Act of Union were less spectacular than in the preceding period. Responsible government involved the creation of political parties and new men began to come to the front. In Upper Canada the two more conspicuous figures were John A. Macdonald (q.v.) and George Brown (q.v.). Macdonald showed his political skill in 1854 when out of a congeries of factions he formed the new Liberal-Conservative party, becoming its real head within the next two years. Brown became leader of the Clear Grits, an ultra reform group in Upper Canada, and through his newspaper, the *Globe*, wielded enormous influence over the political opinions of the rural population. Between Macdonald and Brown there was an intense rivalry and at times considerable ill-feeling. The political situation was complicated by the prevailing view that the administration must have the backing of a majority from each of the two united provinces. Between 1854 and 1862 there were no less than ten different ministries; and by 1864 the rival forces were so evenly matched that government was becoming impossible, and the union appeared ready to fall apart.

It was in this critical period that Brown "by an act of self-abnegation unparalleled in Canadian politics" agreed to enter a coalition with Macdonald in order to explore the possibilities of a confederation of all the British provinces in North America. Already in the Maritime provinces, consideration was being given to the idea of a federation, though in a more local way, and a conference of delegates from the eastern provinces had been called to meet at Charlottetown in September, 1864. The Canadian government asked permission to send delegates to Charlottetown, and received a favourable reply. At Charlottetown it was decided to hold another and more general conference at Quebec in October. At the Quebec conference, lasting sixteen days and attended by representatives of all the provinces, including Newfoundland, agreement was reached upon a plan for a federal union which would have a parliament of two houses, the upper house appointed and the lower house elected upon a basis of representation by population. Each province was to retain its legislature to deal with matters of purely provincial concern, these being distinctly enumerated in the Act passed in London. The question of the larger union was not submitted to popular vote. The new Dominion of Canada, brought into being by the British North America Act, was composed of Nova Scotia, New Brunswick, and the united province of Canada, which now, however, was divided into the two provinces of Ontario and Quebec. On July 1, 1867, the Dominion officially came into existence.

Union of the provinces involved the subordination of each to the central authority in certain fields where hitherto they had been autonomous. Such matters, for example, as defence, post-office, customs, and excise came under federal control. It was soon observed that the larger political arena tended to attract the more outstanding political figures and that the provincial legislatures took second place in public interest.

It was necessary for the federal government to set up new provincial administrations in both Ontario and Quebec. For the leader of the first government in Ontario Sir John Macdonald (q.v.) chose John Sandfield Macdonald (q.v.), a Scottish Catholic Reformer who had been critical of Confederation, but was prepared to accept the new order of things. Macdonald's régime in Ontario was of brief duration, for under the skilful leadership of Edward Blake (q.v.) the Liberal opposition jockeyed the administration into a position where it was forced to resign. In 1871 there began a period of Liberal rule that lasted for thirty-three years, during

twenty-four years of which Oliver Mowat (q.v.) was prime minister. In spirited controversies with the federal government over questions of provincial rights, Mowat was almost uniformly victorious. Agriculture and education were both advanced in Mowat's time, while effort was also made to secure more effective control of the liquor traffic. When Mowat retired in 1896 to join the new Laurier cabinet at Ottawa he was succeeded by A. S. Hardy (q.v.), and when the latter retired in 1899 George W. Ross (q.v.) took office.

The Conservatives, led by James P. Whitney (q.v.), came into office in 1905. Development of northern Ontario, extension of the provincial boundaries, hydro-electric power development, and enlargement of educational facilities were prominent in their achievements. At the death of Sir James Whitney in 1914, he was succeeded by Sir William Hearst, whose tenure of office coincided with the Great War, during which the history of Ontario became merged to a greater degree than usual in the history of the Dominion. Apart from the war effort, temperance legislation stood out among matters of more domestic concern.

Post-war unsettlement joined with other causes to defeat the Hearst administration in the elections of 1919, and there was brought into power a combination of the United Farmers of Ontario and the Labour party under the leadership of E. C. Drury. Drury's government lacked experience and cohesion, and went down to defeat in 1923 after but one term of office. The new Conservative administration was headed by G. Howard Ferguson. On the retirement of Ferguson in 1930 to become Canadian high commissioner at London, he was succeeded by George S. Henry. Henry's government was badly defeated in 1934, when the Liberals under Mitchell F. Hepburn scored one of the most decisive victories in the history of the province.

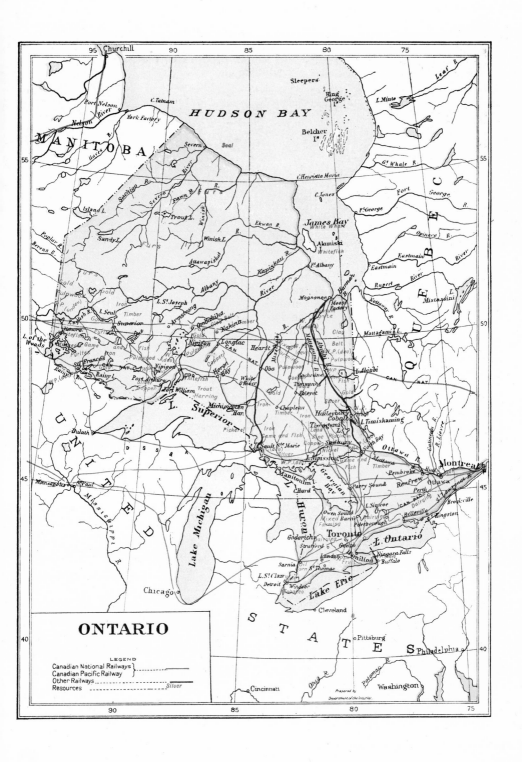

## ONTARIO

LEGEND
Canadian National Railways
Canadian Pacific Railway
Other Railways
Resources

*Prepared by Department of the Interior.*

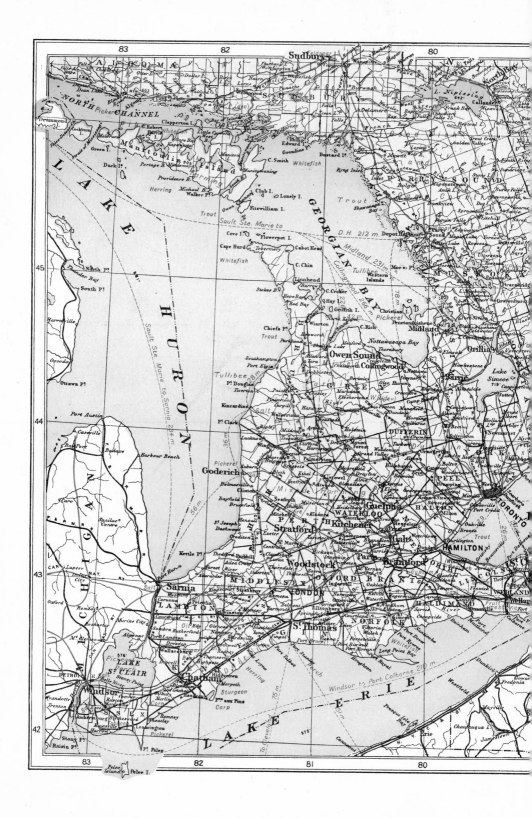

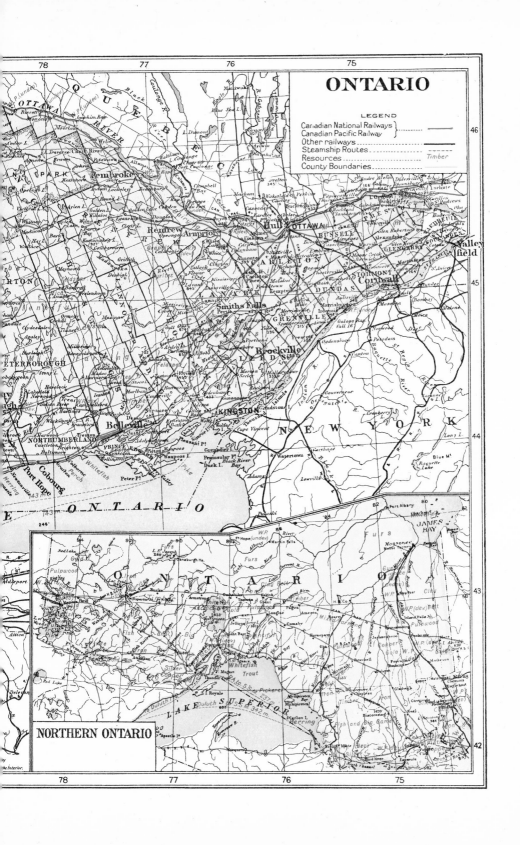

# ONTARIO

LEGEND

Canadian National Railways
Canadian Pacific Railway
Other railways
Steamship Routes
Resources ........................... Timber
County Boundaries

# NORTHERN ONTARIO

High expectations had been raised at the time of Confederation as to the economic benefits which would come to Ontario from the union with the other provinces. Actually there was a slowing up of development as compared with the growth in earlier decades. British immigration lessened in volume at the very time the lure of the United States was most powerful with the youth of Ontario. The fall in prices after the American Civil War bore particularly hard upon the farmers, who also found their nearest large market closed by hostile American tariffs. Even the development of the Canadian North West had an initial adverse effect upon Ontario by drawing away many of its younger men, though at a later date the western provinces became important markets for Ontario manufactured products.

The high American tariff was met after 1878 by a higher Canadian tariff, thereby giving the Canadian manufacturer an advantage in the home market. The development of the West further widened industrial opportunity, and by 1900 the factory disputed the supremacy of the farm in Ontario. The census of 1881 had shown nearly twice as many people on the farms as in the towns and cities of the province, but twenty years later the numbers had become almost equal, while a decade later less than half the population was rural.

While western development gave Ontario industry its first great impetus, two other factors also operated to promote industrial growth, namely, the development of hydro-electric power under government auspices and with municipal coöperation, and the spectacular rise of the mining industry in the northern part of the province.

As early as 1883, during the construction of the Canadian Pacific Railway, deposits of nickel had been discovered near Sudbury which eventually turned out to be the most valuable deposits known anywhere in the world. In 1903, during the construction of the Temiskaming and Northern Ontario Railway, discoveries of silver made the Cobalt region immediately world-famous. Discoveries of gold were subsequently made at Porcupine (1909) and at Kirkland Lake (1912) which attracted similar widespread attention. Enormous capital investments were made in these and in other mining fields of lesser importance. Ontario, as a result of these discoveries, soon led the Canadian provinces in mining production, and ranked as one of the world's greatest mineral fields. In 1932, of Canada's mineral production valued at $79,509,-239, Ontario produced 43.5 per cent. Accompanying the mining development in the northern areas there was also a large agricultural development in the clay belt, where thousands of new settlers, many of them French Canadians, staked out farms.

By the parliamentary legislation of 1912 the northern area of Ontario was increased in extent by 146,400 square miles. Much of this area has been only roughly explored, and its resources and possibilities are as yet but little known.

*Bibliography.* The chief authorities are W. Canniff, *History of the settlement of Upper Canada* (Toronto, 1869), A. Fraser, *A history of Ontario, its resources and development* (2 vols., Toronto, 1907), A. Shortt and A. G. Doughty (eds.), *Canada and its provinces*, vols. xvii and xviii (Toronto, 1914), W. L. Smith, *Pioneers of old Ontario* (Toronto, 1923), W. A. Langton (ed.), *Early days in Upper Canada* (Toronto, 1926), J. E. Middleton and F. Landon, *The province of Ontario* (4 vols., Toronto, 1927), and E. C. Guillet, *Early life in Upper Canada* (Toronto, 1933).

**Ontario,** a county on the north shore of lake Ontario, is bounded on the east by the counties of Durham and Victoria, on the west by York county, lake Simcoe, and Simcoe county, and the narrow northern boundary touches

Muskoka county. The name was first given by Simcoe (q.v.) to a group of islands, including Wolfe, Howe, and Amherst islands; but by an Act passed in 1851, which became effective in 1854, the present county was formed of part of York county, and called after lake Ontario. The early immigration was Irish and "Pennsylvania Dutch". The county is 66 miles long, and its width is 18 miles at the south end and about 8 to 5 at the north. The county town is Whitby. Pop. (1931), 59,667. See Emily P. Weaver, *The counties of Ontario* (Toronto, 1913); W. H. Higgins, *Life and times of Joseph Gould* (Toronto, 1887); and *Ontario county gazetteer* (Toronto, 1885).

**Ontario Agricultural College.** In 1873 the Ontario government purchased a farm on the outskirts of Guelph, Ontario, and in 1874 it opened here the Ontario School of Agriculture. In 1880 the name of this school was changed to "the Ontario Agricultural College and Experimental Farm"; and in 1887 the course at the college, which had hitherto been for two years, was extended for three years. At the same time the college was affiliated with the University of Toronto, and the degree of B.S.A. (bachelor of scientific agriculture) was instituted. In 1903 the Macdonald Institute for domestic science was established in connection with the college; and in 1908 a summer school for teachers was inaugurated. In addition to the work of instruction, which has resulted in the training of nearly 40,000 graduates of the college, a great deal of valuable research work has been done; and the *Bulletins* issued by the college have exercised a most salutary and beneficial effect on agriculture in Ontario and elsewhere. The presidents of the college have been William Johnston (1875-9), James Mills (1880-1904), G. C. Creelman (1904-20), J. B. Reynolds (1920-8), and G. I. Christie (1928—).

**Ontario Bank,** a bank founded in 1857 by a group which included the Hon. John Simpson (q.v.), who subsequently became the president. In its origin and for years afterwards, it was an eminently sound institution. Its failure in 1906 threatened extensively to increase the criticisms, already widespread, of the banking system of Canada. Many newspapers at this time demanded some system of external bank inspection. The unfortunate effects of this failure would have been greater had not the larger banks come to the partial rescue of the institution, and allayed the fears of its creditors. At the time of its failure, the Ontario Bank had a paid-up capital of $1,500,000, and total assets of over $17,000,000.

**Ontario Educational Association,** an organization founded in 1861 as the Teachers' Association of Canada West. Shortly afterwards the name was changed to the Ontario Teachers' Association, and in 1892 it became the Ontario Educational Association. It publishes the *Proceedings* of its annual meetings.

**Ontario Historical Society,** a society originally established at Toronto, on September 4, 1888, under the name of the Pioneer Association of Ontario, which was changed in 1891 to the Pioneer and Historical Association of the Province of Ontario. At the 11th annual meeting in 1898, it was reorganized as the Ontario Historical Society. It has issued *Annual reports* since 1889 (since 1922 entitled *Annual reports and proceedings*), 30 volumes of *Papers and records* since 1899, the *Correspondence of Lieutenant-Governor John Graves Simcoe*, collected and edited by Brig.-General E. A. Cruikshank (Toronto, vols. i-v, 1923-31), and the *Correspondence of Hon. Peter Russell*, collected and edited by Brig.-General E. A. Cruikshank and A. F. Hunter (Toronto, vols. i-iii, 1932-6).

**Ontario, lake,** the smallest and most easterly of the 5 Great lakes. The name, which probably refers to the Niagara escarpment, means "rocks standing high or near the water." The lake was discovered in 1615 by Étienne Brûlé (q.v.), who was closely followed by Champlain (q.v.) and the Huron expedition on their way to fight the Iroquois. By 1668 the north shore of the lake had been fully explored by the French, and mission stations extended beyond the present site of Burlington. The lake area was the scene of hostilities during the Seven Years' War, when Montcalm's capture of Oswego in 1756 was followed by the surrender to the British of Fort Frontenac in 1758 and Niagara in 1759. During the War of 1812, it was again the scene of hostilities, including the capture and destruction of York (Toronto) in 1813.

The lake is situated between 43° 10' and 44° 10' n. lat. and between 74° and 78° w. long., and is bounded on the north by the province of Ontario and on the south by the state of New York. It is roughly elliptical; its major axis, 180 miles long, lies nearly east and west, and its greatest breadth is 53 miles. Its area is 7,540 square miles; its greatest depth is 738 feet, and its average depth much in excess of that of lake Erie. Lake Ontario receives its chief supply from the Great lakes through the Niagara river. Its other principal tributaries are the Trent from the north and the Genesee, Oswego, and Black from the south. The east end of the lake, where it is 30 miles wide, is crossed by a chain of 5 islands. The lake has its outlet near Kingston, where it discharges into the St. Lawrence river between a group of islands. Elsewhere it is practically free from islands. It never freezes over except near land, but the harbours are closed from mid-December to mid-April. On the north side, in Ontario, the shore rises gradually and spreads into broad plains which are a thickly settled agricultural country. Both in the Niagara peninsula of Ontario and in New York a ridge extends along the south shore at a distance of 3 to 8 miles from the lake. The low ground between this ridge and the shore is a celebrated fruit-growing district, which has earned for the Niagara peninsula the name of the "garden of Ontario". It abounds in vineyards and in peach, apple, and pear orchards.

The completion of the new Welland canal has made possible the passage from lake Ontario to the upper lakes of vessels with a draught of 20 feet. The commerce on the lake consists chiefly in grain and other products shipped from upper lake ports, through the Welland canal, to the St. Lawrence river; coal shipped from American ports on the south shore to Canadian ports on the lake, to Canadian and American ports on the St. Lawrence, and to upper lake ports; lumber from Canadian ports; and pleasure traffic. On the north side, the Murray canal, 11 feet deep below the lowest lake level, extends from Presqu'isle bay to the head of the bay of Quinte. The Trent canal, a series of lakes and rivers connected by short canals, will, when completed, provide 6-foot navigation from lake Ontario to Georgian bay. It is now navigable for 224 miles from the lake to the Severn river. The Rideau canal, with locks of a minimum depth of 5 feet, extends from the St. Lawrence at Kingston to Ottawa. The Oswego canal, which will accommodate boats drawing 10½ feet, provides an outlet to the Hudson river and New York city.

**Ontario Library Association,** an association founded in Toronto in 1900 to promote the welfare of libraries and to extend their sphere of usefulness to the schools and the public in general. It publishes the *Proceedings* of its annual meetings.

**Ontario Research Foundation,** a research institute founded in Toronto in 1928 by the Ontario government and private donors, for the purpose of aiding the industries of Ontario by research into their scientific problems. The Foundation has built elaborately equipped laboratories in Queen's Park, Toronto, and has conducted investigations into a wide variety of scientific and industrial problems. The chairman of the Foundation is Sir Joseph Flavelle, Bart., and the director is Dr. H. B. Speakman. It has issued an *Annual report* since 1928. See H. B. Speakman, *The Ontario Research Foundation and its work* (Proceedings of the Engineering Society, Queen's University, September, 1931).

**Ontario, Simcoe, and Huron Railway.** See **Northern Railway of Canada.**

**Ontario Society of Artists,** an organization formed in 1872, with headquarters in Toronto, with the object of encouraging and fostering original art, the promotion of the interests of professional artists, the holding of annual exhibitions of art, and the establishment of a National Gallery and a School of Art. The society was incorporated in 1877, and re-incorporated in 1898. Its members have played a part in the formation of the Royal Academy of Art, the founding of the National Art Gallery, and the opening of the Toronto College of Art. It has held annual exhibitions of the work of its members, and has published catalogues of these exhibitions. See R. F. Gagen, "History of art societies in Ontario" in J. Castell Hopkins (ed.), *Canada, an encyclopædia*, vol. v (Toronto, 1898).

**Oolakan.** See **Oolichan.**

**Oolichan,** or Candle-fish (*Thaleichthys pacificus*), a small smelt-like fish of British Columbia, which in the spring runs from the sea into the rivers in immense numbers. It is characterized by the excessive fatness of its flesh, which contains so much oil that it is said, when it is dried and a wick is drawn through the body, it may be used as a candle. The Indians catch this fish in large numbers for the purpose of making a nutritious oil; and this oil was formerly an important article of trade among the Indians of northern British Columbia. It was transported from the Nass river outward to the Queen Charlotte islands, and inland by what is still known as the Grease trail to the upper Skeena river.

**Oomiak.** See **Umiak.**

**Opazatika river,** a tributary of the Moose river, in northern Ontario, which takes its rise in Opazatika lake, a few miles east of Brunswick lake. It is about 180 miles long.

**Opossum.** The Virginia opossum (*Didelphis virginiana*) is a member of the order *Marsupialia*, animals having a pouch or "marsupium" in which the young are kept, during part of their development. The opossum is an animal about the size of a large house cat, with long rather coarse grayish fur, a scaly prehensile tail, and a pointed face. This animal is a rare wanderer in southwestern Ontario from its normal range, which is farther south.

**Ops,** a township in Victoria county, Ontario, created in 1821. Its name is a Latin word meaning "riches" or "abundance".

**Oquassa Trout,** a char (q.v.), one of the derivatives or relatives of the Arctic char. Specimens identified as this form have been taken in the gulf of St. Lawrence and along the Labrador coast.

**Orange Association of British North America.** The Orange Society, as it exists to-day, was founded in Ireland in 1795; though the first Orange societies or clubs existed in Great Britain as early as 1686, and had as their object the selection of William of Orange as king of Great Britain and Ireland—whence the name. Orangeism appears to have been introduced into Canada about 1820; but it was not until 1830 that a Grand Lodge for British North America was formed at Brockville, Upper Canada, under the presidency of Ogle Robert Gowan (q.v.), who was in 1832 appointed "deputy grand master of all the provinces of British North America."

The Orange Association is technically a secret society; but its only secrets are its annual passwords and the signs by which members recognize one another. Its constitution and objects are public property. In its constitution, it is declared to have been formed "by persons desirous of supporting, to the utmost of their power, the principles and practices of the Christian religion, to maintain the laws and constitution of the country, afford assistance to distressed members of the Association, and otherwise promote such laudable and benevolent purposes as may tend to the due ordering of religion and Christian charity, and the supremacy of law, order, and constitutional freedom." In the words of a former grand master, the Association "lays no claim to exclusive loyalty, or exclusive Protestantism; but it admits no man within its pale whose principles are not loyal, and whose creed is not Protestant."

Since the Association was founded in Canada, it has spread to all the provinces of the Dominion of Canada; and there are now Provincial Grand Lodges in every province, with primary, district, and county lodges under them, as well as kindred or subsidiary orders, such as the Orange Young Britons, Loyal True Blues, and the Ladies' Orange Benevolent Association.

One of the rules of the Association has always been that on July 12, the members shall meet and parade to celebrate the victory won at Boyne by William, Prince of Orange, over the forces of James II. These demonstrations have on various occasions been accompanied by disorder; but recently they have been more peaceful, as the objects of the Association have been better understood. In Canada, the Association has been frequently accused of being subservient to the Conservative party; but on occasion they have proved their independence of that party, as, for instance, in the controversy over the Manitoba school question in 1896. On the other hand, when the Association sought incorporation by Act of the Dominion parliament, the incorporation bill was opposed by the Liberals in parliament, and was defeated.

Among the grand masters of the Association have been some of the outstanding men in Canadian public life— such as the Hon. John Hillyard Cameron (q.v.), Sir Mackenzie Bowell (q.v.), the Hon. N. Clarke Wallace (q.v.), the Hon. T. S. Sproule (q.v.), and the Hon. J. W. Edwards (q.v.).

See O. R. Gowan, *Orangeism, its origin and history* (3 vols., Toronto, 1859), and N. Clarke Wallace, "Sketch of the Orange order in Canada", in J. Castell Hopkins, *Canada: An encyclopædia of the country*, vol. vi (Toronto, 1900).

**Orange Lily.** See **Lily.**

**Orange Root.** See **Golden Seal.**

**Orangeville,** the shire-town of Dufferin county, Ontario, situated on the Credit river and on the Canadian Pacific Railway, 45 miles north-west of Toronto. In 1832 the site of the town was known as Mills, because of a flour-mill and a saw-mill. In 1844 Orange Lawrence bought both mills, and the place was named Orangeville in honour of its chief industrialist; and to-day mills are used for the principal manufactures, flour, lumber, and knitting. The town has several churches, public and high schools, a hospital, a court house, and a public library. A newspaper (*Banner*) is published weekly. Pop. (1931), 2,614.

**Orchid.** See **Lady's Slipper.**

**Orchis, Showy** (*Orchis spectabilis* L., *Orchidaceae*), one of the most beautiful orchids, and the first to bloom in the spring. It is a fleshy perennial, bearing 2 basal, oblong, shining leaves between which the 4-angled flower stalk rises. The flowers are borne in a loose spike, and each is subtended by a leaf-like, lanceolate bract. The arching upper lip of the flower is purple-pink, the lower lip is white and wavy in outline. It grows in rich moist woods from New Brunswick to Ontario.

**Oregon,** the name formerly applied to the valley of the Columbia and the adjacent territories on the Pacific slope, but now confined to the state of Oregon. Over the origin of the name a controversy has raged; but it is probable that it is a version of the name applied by the Indians to the Columbia river about the middle of the eighteenth century. It first appears in print in its present form in the *Travels* of Jonathan Carver (q.v.) in 1778; but it is found as early as 1765 in the form of "Owragan" or "Ourigan" in a report on western exploration submitted to the Privy Council by Major Robert Rogers (q.v.), and clearly has reference to the Columbia river. It was first explored by David Thompson (q.v.), and was exploited by the North West Company, and later by the Hudson's Bay Company. A brief foothold obtained by the Americans at Fort Astoria near the mouth of the Columbia in 1811 came to an end with the surrender of Astoria in 1813; but after 1830 large numbers of American settlers found their way into the Oregon country over the Oregon trail. Between 1818 and 1846 there was a protracted dispute between Great Britain and the United States over the international boundary in the Oregon country; but this was at last, in 1846, fixed at the 49th parallel of latitude. See **Boundaries.**

The literature of Oregon is voluminous. See C. W. Smith, *Pacific Northwest Americana: A checklist* (New York, 1921). Special reference, however, may be made to J. Dunn, *History of the Oregon territory* (London, 1846); C. G. Nicolay, *The Oregon territory* (London, 1860); H. G. Lyman, *History of Oregon* (4 vols., New York, 1903); J. Schafer, *A history of the Pacific north-west* (New York, 1905); W. I. Marshall, *The acquisition of Oregon* (2 vols., Seattle, 1911), and C. H. Carey, *History of*

*Oregon* (Chicago, 1922), and *A general history of Oregon prior to 1861* (Portland, 1935).

**Orford lake,** a small body of water in Brome county, Quebec, lying south of mount Orford. It is nearly 1,000 feet above sea level.

**Oriental immigration.** Since 1885 Canada, and particularly British Columbia, has been faced with the problem of Oriental immigration—especially Chinese, Japanese, and East Indian. The objection to Orientals is not so much racial, social, or religious, as chiefly economic; accustomed as they are to long hours, low wages, and a low standard of living, the Asiatics are able to underbid the white man in selling his labour. Doubtless the other three above-mentioned factors contribute to the problem, but they would lose much force if the economic difference could be eliminated. The Orientals cannot be assimilated without very great difficulty. Moreover, governments, churches, and social organizations have made little effort to Canadianize them. The fact that comparatively few are naturalized, shows that there is no great drive to change their allegiance. The Orientals stand well in industry, as is shown by the intensive agriculture which is carried on by the Chinese and Japanese. These Asiatics vary from the intelligent, successful, loyal, and philanthropic citizen down to the debased habitués of the opium-joint. Many display great indifference to sanitation, to the fundamentals of hygiene, and to what the intelligent Canadian regards as the common decencies of life. The Orientals are chiefly in British Columbia, which, in 1931, had 58 per cent. of the Chinese and over 94 per cent. of the Japanese in Canada.

Chinese immigration to America appears to have commenced in 1849, and the first immigrants had reached British Columbia before 1870. Their early occupations were as laundrymen and domestic servants, although, in 1872, they were already employed in the coal mines of the province. In 1885 Chinese immigrants, upon entering Canada, were required to pay a poll tax of $50; this was increased to $100 in 1901, and to $500 in 1904. Extensive Chinese immigration continued, however, until it practically ceased after passage of the Chinese Immigration Act of 1923. In 1931 there were 46,519 Chinese in Canada. For the most part they are transients who plan to return eventually to China, and who are therefore content to live in dilapidated areas in the hearts of cities. A few only have brought with them wives and children. In the eastern provinces, the Chinese are chiefly engaged in the laundry business. In British Columbia they are engaged in every kind of work, particularly in the lumbering and fishing industries. Large numbers are employed on fruit and vegetable farms. They are very successful truck farmers, although the Chinese, who are transients, lease, while the Japanese buy their farms and equipment.

Japanese immigration commenced about 1896; and, by the year 1900, 12,000 had entered Canada. Japanese immigration was particularly active between 1906 and 1908, in which period over 11,000 entered the country. In 1908 Canada negotiated an agreement with the Japanese government, by which the number of Japanese immigrants entering Canada were limited to about 400 per annum. After that year Japanese immigration experienced a marked decrease. In 1931 there were 23,342 Japanese in Canada. The Japanese are more ambitious than the Chinese, and crowd into all lines of industry, in competition with the white man. Like the Chinese, they are engaged in the lumber camps and the pulp mills. In addition to their success as truck farmers, the Japanese have the advantage of the Chinese in the production of fruit, and they excel in the fishing industry.

East Indian immigration was negligible until 1907, when 2,124 East Indians arrived in Canada. As a result of certain restrictive measures by the Canadian government, including a regulation under section 38 of the Immigration Act of 1910, East Indian immigration has, since 1908, been comparatively small. Although East Indians already domiciled in Canada were, after 1919, allowed to bring in their wives and minor children, there were only 418 entries between 1921 and 1930. In 1931 there were 5,795 East Indians domiciled in Canada. Most of them are Sikhs from the Punjab. They have been employed only in the lowest kinds of manual labour. They are very slow and seem incapable of hard, continuous exertion. Their diet is light, and they are not adapted to the rigorous climate of Canada. See W. G. Smith, *A study in Canadian immigration* (Toronto, 1920); James S. Woodsworth, *Strangers within our gates* (Toronto, 1909); and Tein-Fang Cheng, *Oriental immigration in Canada* (Shanghai, 1931).

**Oriental Languages.** The fact that the Oriental languages are written in unfamiliar scripts has made the study difficult for the ordinary man, and the vocabularies present even a greater difficulty. The Royal Asiatic Society of England, and, later, the American Oriental Society, have done much during the past century to stimulate intelligent interest in this study; and archæological research in Egypt, Palestine, Syria, and Mesopotamia has been rewarded by rich discoveries, which throw much light on Eastern customs and manners of life. The clearer light upon the Old Testament and on the background of the New Testament is an invaluable result.

Into Canada articles and objects of many kinds have been brought, to find a place in museums and libraries. In the Royal Ontario Museum, Toronto, is housed a very fine collection covering the history, literature and customs of the East. But it is in the colleges that the study of Oriental languages is systematically prosecuted. King's College, Windsor, Nova Scotia—which in 1923 moved to Halifax and became federated with Dalhousie University—was teaching Hebrew in 1814. A few years later (1829) Hebrew was on the curriculum of the University of New Brunswick. In 1852 the Arts course in McGill University, Montreal, embraced the study of Oriental languages. In 1845 J. M. Hirschfelder was teaching Hebrew in King's College, Toronto (the University of Toronto), and in 1889 there was appointed to the chair of Oriental Languages Professor J. F. McCurdy (q.v.), who initiated in this University the honour and post-graduate courses in Semitics, which have helped students in the application of historical criticism in the interpretation of the Bible. The study of Hebrew is now universal in Canadian universities or colleges, both in the older and in the newer provinces. The study of Arabic and Syriac has not been so fully developed.

**Orillia,** a town in Simcoe county, Ontario, 84 miles north of Toronto, is situated on lake Couchiching, at the northern extremity of lake Simcoe. There has been much speculation as to the origin of the name. It is probably derived from a Spanish word meaning "border, bank, shore", and may have been bestowed on the place by Sir Peregrine Maitland, the lieutenant-governor of Upper Canada (1818-28), who had fought under Wellington in Spain in the Peninsular War. Some students claim that it is from the Indian word *orelia*, which the red men applied to a berry growing in the neighbouring bush. The site of the town was surveyed in 1822. It is on the Canadian Pacific Railway and is at the junction of the Midland and Northern divisions of the Canadian National Railway. It is the centre of a fine mixed farming and fruit-growing country and has numerous industries, such as factories

for making agricultural implements, stoves, and mining and lumbering machinery, as well as flour mills and planing mills and a well-equipped sea-going motor cruiser plant. In Orillia is the Ontario Hospital for the Feeble-minded, one of the best equipped institutions in Canada. An object of great interest is the magnificent monument to Champlain, which was designed by the late Vernon March, a brilliant young English sculptor. There is a collegiate institute, a public library, a memorial hospital, and two weekly newspapers (*News-Letter* and *Packet and Times*). Pop., about 8,000; and there is a tributary population of over 20,000.

**Oriole,** a name used in North America, with prefixes, for certain birds which are members of the blackbird family, *Icteridae.* The Baltimore oriole (*Icterus galbula*) is an orange and black species which inhabits the southern settled portions of Canada from the Rocky mountains to the Atlantic. Its nest is a remarkable example of bird architecture; it is felted and woven with plant fibre into a hanging pocket, usually at the extremity of some wind-tossed branch. Bullock's oriole (*Icterus bullocki*) occurs in the southern part of British Columbia and Alberta, and the orchard oriole (*Icterus spurius*) is found in southern Manitoba and southern Ontario. The latter species weaves a nest from green grass.

**Orleans, island of,** is in the St. Lawrence river, close to the city of Quebec. It is 20 miles long, and 5 miles wide, and has a road girdling it of 42 miles in length. It is the home of some of the earliest settlers in America, who settled here soon after 1651. The original settlers came mostly from northern and central France, and its population remains really French to this day. The island, known to the Indians as "Minigo", was called "Island of Bacchus" by Jacques Cartier (q.v.), the name being changed later in honour of the Duke of Orleans, son of the French king. Ste. Famille, on the north-eastern side, the most attractive parish, commands a splendid view, and has one of the oldest and finest churches on the St. Lawrence. The people are self-supporting, farming, spinning and weaving, building their houses, canoes and sailing sloops. Fine wood-carving is extensive, and the houses are veritable museums. See Abbé L. E. Bois, *L'Ile Orléans* (Quebec, 1896), and Marius Barbeau, *The island of Orleans* (Canadian Geographical Journal, 1932.).

**Ormstown,** a village in Châteauguay county, Quebec, on the Canadian National Railway, 50 miles from Montreal. It is named after Orms Ellice, one of the sons of Alexander Ellice (q.v.), who purchased the seigniory of Beauharnois (in which the village is situated) in 1763. The chief industry is dairying. Pop. (1931), 842.

**Ornithology,** the branch of the science of zoology dealing with birds. The beginnings of the science in Canada dates from the days of the early explorers. It is to Champlain (q.v.), for example, that we owe the first list of birds in Acadia. Later, some of the officers of the Hudson's Bay Company made valuable contributions to the science, notably Thomas Hutchins (d. 1790), governor of Fort Albany from 1774 to 1782, and Samuel Hearne (q.v.), whose *Journey* contained 50 pages devoted to the birds of northern Canada. To American ornithologists, and especially to the famous Audubon, the study of birds in southern Canada owed its first impulse; but it is worthy of note that by 1820 Charles Fothergill (q.v.) had begun in Upper Canada the scientific study of birds, though the results of his investigations have not yet been published. For many years ornithology in Canada continued to be almost wholly the object of study by amateurs. Dr. A. M. Ross (q.v.), whose *Birds of Canada* was published in 1871, and Thomas McIllwraith (q.v.), whose *Birds*

*of Ontario* was first published in 1887, were both private students of ornithology. With the introduction of natural history as a subject of instruction in Canadian universities after 1850, some attention was devoted to ornithology in academic institutions; and small museum collections of birds were gradually developed in these institutions. But it was not until the founding of such great museums as the Victoria Memorial Museum in Ottawa and the Royal Ontario Museum in Toronto that the study of ornithology in Canada acquired a truly modern scientific basis. It is to the Museum in Ottawa that we owe the most recent and authoritative treatise on Canadian ornithology, P. A. Taverner's *The birds of Canada* (Ottawa, 1934). See also **Birds.**

**Oro,** a township and village in Simcoe county, Ontario. The township was created in 1820. The village is ten miles south of Orillia, on the Canadian National Railway, with a port on lake Simcoe, and has a population of 100. The name is the Spanish word for "gold", and was probably chosen by Sir Peregrine Maitland (q.v.), who had served in Spain during the Peninsular War.

**Oromocto river** rises in York, Charlotte, and Sunbury counties, New Brunswick, and flows north into the St. John river, which it enters 11 miles below Fredericton. The name is a Malecite Indian word meaning "good river", in the sense of being easy for canoe navigation. An Indian burial ground was located at the mouth of the river. The river is an excellent mill-stream, and is navigable for vessels drawing 8 feet of water for 20 miles above its outlet. Some of its branches abound in salmon and trout.

**Oronhyatekha** (1841-1907), supreme chief ranger of the Independent Order of Foresters, was born on the Six Nations Indian reservation, near Brantford, Upper Canada, on August 10,

1841. He was educated at the Industrial School on the reservation, at the Wesleyan Academy, Wilbraham, Massachusetts, at Kenyon College, Ohio, and at the University of Toronto. The Prince of Wales, on his visit to Canada in 1860, was so interested in him that he was invited to continue his studies at Oxford University; and here he qualified himself as a physician. On his return to Canada he practised, first at Frankford, Ontario, and then at London, Ontario. He was here initiated into the Order of Foresters, and in this order he rapidly rose to the position of chief executive. In 1881 he was elected supreme chief ranger of the order, and this position he continued to occupy until his death. In 1889 the head office of the order was moved to Toronto, and here Oronhyatekha lived during his later years. He died at Savannah, Georgia, on March 3, 1907. In 1863 he married Ellen Hill, a great-granddaughter of Joseph Brant (q.v.). He was the author of a *History of the Independent Order of Foresters* (Toronto, 1894).

**Orono,** a village in Durham county, Ontario, on the Orono creek, 5 miles north of Newcastle, on the Canadian National Railway, and 9 miles south of Pontypool, on the Canadian Pacific Railway. It is in an apple-growing district, and has an evaporator and canning factory, as well as a flour mill, a creamery, and a foundry. It has a high school and a weekly newspaper (*News*). Pop. (1934), 900.

**Orr, Rowland Beatty** (1852-1933), physician and archæologist, was born at Kleinburg, Ontario, on March 16, 1852, of Irish parentage. He was educated at the University of Toronto (M.B., 1877), and studied medicine in London and Edinburgh. He practised medicine in Toronto; and was prominent in local politics. In 1911 he was appointed curator of the Provincial Museum in Toronto; and from 1911 to 1924 he edited the *Annual Archæological Report*, printed as an appendix to the report of the minister of education in Ontario. He died in Toronto on May 28, 1933.

**Orthoclase.** See **Feldspar.**

**Osage,** a village in Saskatchewan, on the Arcola branch of the Canadian Pacific Railway, 56 miles from Regina. Pop. (1934), 250.

**Osborne, Mrs. Marion,** *née* **Francis** (1871-1931), poet and dramatist, was born at Montreal, Quebec, on May 14, 1871, the daughter of George Grant Francis. In 1892 she married Charles Lambert Bath (d. 1897), and in 1902 Colonel Henry Campbell Osborne. For many years she lived in Toronto; but from 1920 to her death she lived in Ottawa. There she died on September 5, 1931. She was the author of *Poems* (London, Chiswick Press, 1914), *The song of Israfel and other poems* (Toronto and London, 1923), *Flight Commander Stork* (Toronto, 1925), a lyrical drama entitled *Sappho and Phaon* (Toronto, 1926), and a prose comedy, *The point of view*, included in V. Massey (ed.), *Canadian plays from Hart House Theatre*, vol. i (Toronto, 1926).

**Osgoode, William** (1754-1824), judge, was born in England in March, 1754. He was educated at Christ Church, Oxford (M.A., 1777), and was called to the bar from the Inner Temple. In 1792 he was appointed first chief justice of Upper Canada, was commissioned a member of the Legislative Council, and appointed speaker of the Council. In 1794 he became chief justice of Lower Canada. In 1801 he retired from the bench on a pension, and returned to England; and he died in London on January 17, 1824. He was the author of a pamphlet on *The laws of descent* (London, 1779). See W. R. Riddell, *William Osgoode* (Can. Law Times, 1921).

**Osgoode Hall,** the home of the Law Society of Upper Canada, the body which controls legal education in Ontario. It contains also the judges' chambers and law courts of Ontario. Built in 1832, it was first named Lawyers' Hall, and was later re-named after the Hon. William Osgoode (q.v.), the first chief justice of Upper Canada. Additions were made to it in 1833, in 1845, and in 1860. See the Hon. W. R. Riddell, *The legal profession in Upper Canada* (Toronto, 1915), and *Osgoode Hall* (Can. Hist. Ass. Report, 1922).

**Oshawa,** a city in Ontario county, Ontario, situated on lake Ontario and on the Canadian National and Canadian Pacific Railways, 32 miles east of Toronto. Its history dates from 1795 when Lieut.-Governor Simcoe (q.v.) built a military road, known as the Kingston road between the site of the city and Kingston, 160 miles distant. In 1835 the hamlet was known as Shea's Corners. When a post-office was established in 1842, the name was changed to Oshawa, an Indian term meaning "crossing a stream". It was incorporated as a town in 1879, and as a city in 1924. Oshawa is a modern city, with good public buildings, schools, four parks, a Carnegie library, fifteen churches, a hospital, and a golf course. Industries employ a third of the population; there are large automobile works, woollen and textile mills, foundries, steel spring and sheet metal works, plate glass and pottery works, leather goods and radio factories. The local electric railway connects all industrial plants with the transcontinental railways. A newspaper (*Times*) is published four times a week. Pop. (1931), 23,439. Consult T. E. Kaiser, *Historic sketches of Oshawa* (Oshawa, 1921).

**Osler, Britton Bath** (1839-1901), lawyer, was born in the township of Tecumseth, Simcoe county, Upper Canada, on June 19, 1839, the second son of the Rev. Featherston Lake Osler and Ellen Free Pickton. He was educated at the Barrie Grammar School, and in 1862 obtained the degree of LL.B. at the University of Toronto. He was called to the bar of Upper

Canada in 1862 (Q.C., 1876), and practised law, first in Dundas, then in Hamilton, and lastly in Toronto. From 1874 to 1880 he was crown attorney for the county of Wentworth; and after moving to Toronto in 1882 he rapidly acquired a reputation as the foremost criminal lawyer in Canada. He was prosecuting counsel in the trials at Regina arising out of the Riel rebellion in 1885, and in the trials of McGreevy (q.v.) and Connolly in 1891. He died at Atlantic City, New Jersey, on February 5, 1901. He was twice married, (1) in 1863 to Caroline (d. 1895), daughter of Capt. Henry Smith, H.E.I.C.S., and (2) in 1897 Elizabeth Mary, eldest daughter of A. G. Ramsay, of Hamilton.

**Osler, Sir Edmund Boyd** (1845-1924), financier, was born in the township of Tecumseth, Simcoe county, Upper Canada, on November 20, 1845, the son of the Rev. Featherston Lake Osler and Ellen Free Pickton. He was educated at the Dundas Grammar School, and began his career as a clerk in the Bank of Upper Canada. When that bank failed in 1866, he became a stockbroker; and he was a member of the Toronto Stock Exchange until 1903. In 1901 he was elected president of the Dominion Bank; and he was a director of the Canadian Pacific Railway. From 1896 to 1917 he represented West Toronto as a Conservative in the Canadian House of Commons. He died at Toronto on August 5, 1924. In 1872 he married Annie Farquharson (d. 1910), daughter of James L. Cochran, of Aberdeen, Scotland; and by her he had several children. He was created a knight bachelor in 1912.

**Osler, Featherston** (1838-1924), judge, was born at Newmarket, Upper Canada, in 1838, the eldest son of the Rev. Featherston Lake Osler and Ellen Free Pickton. He was educated at the Barrie and Bond Head Grammar Schools, and was called to the bar of Upper Canada in 1860 (Q.C., 1879). He practised law in Toronto, and in

1879 he was appointed a puisne judge of the Court of Common Pleas in Ontario. In 1883 he became a judge of the Court of Appeal in Ontario; and this post he retained until his retirement from the bench in 1910. From 1910 to his death he was president of the Toronto General Trusts Corporation. He died at Toronto on January 16, 1924. In 1861 he married Henrietta (d. 1902), daughter of Captain Henry Smith, H.E.I.C.S.

**Osler, Sir William, Bart.** (1849-1919), physician and author, was born at Bond Head, Upper Canada, on July 12, 1849, the youngest son of the Rev. Featherston Lake Osler and Ellen Free Pickton. He was educated at Trinity College School, Port Hope, at Trinity University, Toronto, at McGill University (M.D., 1872); and he studied in London, Berlin, and Vienna. From 1874 to 1884 he was on the staff of the medical school at McGill University; from 1884 to 1889 he was professor of clinical medicine at the University of Philadelphia; from 1889 to 1905 he was professor of medicine at Johns Hopkins University, Baltimore; and from 1905 to his death he was regius professor of medicine in the University of Oxford. He died at Oxford on December 29, 1919. In 1892 he married Grace Lindsee Revere, widow of Dr. S. W. Gross, of Philadelphia. He was an LL.D. of McGill University (1895), of Aberdeen University (1898), of Edinburgh University (1898), of the University of Toronto (1899), of Yale University (1901), of Harvard University (1904), of Johns Hopkins University (1905); a D.C.L. of Trinity University (1902); and a D.Sc. of Oxford University (1904) and Leeds University (1910). In 1898 he was elected a fellow of the Royal Society, and in 1911 he was created a baronet of the United Kingdom.

He published numerous monographs and papers on medical subjects, including a work on *The principles and practice of medicine* (New York, 1892), which went into many editions; and he edited a medical encyclopedia entitled *The system of medicine* (7 vols., London, 1907-10). But his reputation rests chiefly on his addresses and less technical publications: *Science and immortality* (London, 1904), *Æquanimitas, and other addresses* (London, 1904), *Counsels and ideals* (Oxford, 1905), *Thomas Linacre* (Oxford, 1908), *An Alabama student, and other essays* (Oxford, 1908), and *A way of life* (Oxford, 1914).

See H. Cushing, *The life of Sir William Osler* (2 vols., Oxford, 1925); E. G. Reid, *The great physician* (Oxford, 1931); and *Contributions to medical and biological research, dedicated to Sir William Osler . . . by his pupils and co-workers* (2 vols., New York, 1919).

**Osnabruck Centre,** a village in Osnabruck township, Stormont county, Ontario, 5 miles from Wales, the nearest railway station, and 15 miles west of Cornwall. The township was named in honour of one of the sons of George III, who was hereditary lord of Osnabruck in Hanover, Germany. Pop. (1934), 200.

**Osnaburgh House,** a Hudson's Bay Company post at the east end of lake St. Joseph, in northern Ontario. It was built in 1786 to checkmate the inroads of the North West Company, was rebuilt in 1794, was closed from 1810 to 1815, and has been in operation from 1815 to the present. It was sometimes called Albany House.

**Osoyoos lake,** an expansion of the Okanagan river, at the international boundary between British Columbia and the United States. It is 7 miles long.

**Osprey** (*Pandion haliaetus*), a fish-eating hawk distributed sparingly over the whole of Canada, except the more southerly portions. Although the osprey is a large long-winged species, it does not approximate an eagle in size. One of the most remarkable adaptations for special food habits is possessed by this bird; the soles of the feet are equipped with small, sharp, horny spikes which assist in holding their slippery prey. The osprey hunts over shallow bays and rivers, and upon sighting a fish near the surface dives from the air into the water, striking feet first.

**O'Sullivan, Michael** (1784-1839), judge, was born at Cahir, Lismore, Ireland, on May 4, 1784, the son of John O'Sullivan and Eleanor O'Donell. He came to Canada at an early age, and was educated at the College of Montreal. He studied law under Denis Benjamin Viger (q.v.), and was called to the bar of Lower Canada in 1811 (K.C., 1831). He served in the militia during the War of 1812-4, and distinguished himself at the battle of Châteauguay. He was one of the first editors of *Le Canadien;* and from 1814 to 1824 he represented Huntingdon in the Legislative Assembly of Lower Canada. In 1833 he was appointed solicitor-general of Lower Canada; and in 1838 he became chief justice of the court of King's Bench at Montreal. He died at Montreal on March 7, 1839. In 1809 he married Cécile, daughter of Pierre Berthelet. See F. J. Audet, *Michael O'Sullivan* (Les Annales, 1924).

**Oswego Tea** (*Monarda didyma* L., *Labiatae*), an odorous, aromatic, perennial herb, with erect, hairy, acutely 4-angled stems, and ovate to lanceolate, acutely-toothed leaves. The flowers are very showy, borne in bright red, close clusters or heads, surrounded by floral bracts which are tinged with red. The calyx is 5-toothed and reddish; the corolla, tubular, elongated, 2-lipped with slightly expanded throat; stamens and style exerted beyond the corollatube. It blooms in moist damp woods and along streams in midsummer in western Quebec and Ontario.

**Otonobee river** rises in Peterborough county, Ontario, in a chain of lakes and flows into Rice lake. The name is an Indian word meaning "mouthwater", so called from the place where the river empties into Rice lake through a delta.

It was discovered in 1615 by Champlain (q.v.), when on his way, in company with the Huron Indians, to attack the Iroquois.

**Ottawa.** See **Chippewa.**

**Ottawa,** a district in Upper Canada, created in 1816 by the separation from the Eastern district (q.v.) of the counties of Prescott and Russell. It was abolished, with the other districts in Canada West, in 1849.

**Ottawa,** a former county of Quebec, lying north of the Ottawa river, with Hull as its county town. It comprised what is now Hull county and parts of the adjacent counties.

**Ottawa,** a city in Carleton county, Ontario, is the capital of the Dominion of Canada. It is situated at the junction of the Ottawa and Rideau rivers. On June 4, 1613, Samuel Champlain (q.v.) in charge of a party of explorers, reached the mouth of the Gatineau river, opposite the eastern part of the present city of Ottawa, on his voyage in search of a north-west passage to China. He was attracted by the region, but over two centuries were to pass before any real attempt was made at settlement, and the site of Ottawa remained a forest-clad wilderness. The actual founding of the city was not until 1826, when Colonel John By (q.v.) of the Royal Engineers, who built the Rideau canal at an outlay of £1,000,000, constructed rude frame barracks for his men where the parliament buildings now stand, as well as a residence for himself in what is now Major's Hill Park. In the same year, the first church, now St. Andrew's, was built. In 1832 the Rideau canal was completed, thus providing a waterway for trade between Upper and Lower Canada. In 1847 the village of Bytown was incorporated as a town, and on December 18, 1854, the town was incorporated as the city of Ottawa. In 1857, Queen Victoria selected Ottawa as the capital of Canada, and this choice was ratified by the Canadian parliament in 1859. On July 1, 1860, King Edward VII, then Prince of Wales, laid the corner stone of the original parliament building. The first session of parliament was opened on June 8, 1866. During this session Confederation became an actuality, and on July 1, 1867, the birthday of the new Dominion was duly celebrated.

Ottawa has an area of 5,295¼ acres; owns its water-works and electric light system; has over fifty elementary schools; two collegiate institutes; two normal schools; one technical school; one high school of commerce; one university; fifteen colleges; a public library; and three daily newspapers, two in English (*Journal* and *Citizen*) and one in French (*Le Droit*). It has over fifty government buildings, including the Parliament Buildings, the Victoria Memorial Museum, the Dominion Observatory, the Royal Mint, and the Public Archives; twenty-two parks and squares, over eighty miles of paved streets including the Federal District driveways, and almost sixty miles of electric street railways. The city is served by the Canadian National, Canadian Pacific, and Ottawa and New York (New York Central) Railways. It is the centre of a great power and lumbering region and has about 460 industries —wood products, paper mills, watch factories, etc. The Central Canada Exhibition is held in Ottawa annually. The grounds and buildings are owned by the city, and are leased to the Exhibition Association.

The city is governed by a board of control, composed of the mayor and four controllers, and a council of eighteen aldermen, elected annually. The mayor and controllers are elected by general vote, the aldermen by wards, two for each ward. The mayor, by virtue of his office, is chairman of the board of control, is one of the police commissioners, and represents the city council on all committees and commissions appointed by council.

The name Ottawa was first applied to the river, and was later bestowed on the city. Various explanations are given for its origin. According to some authorities it is from an Indian word *atawa*, or *otawah*, meaning to extinguish, referring to the mist rising from Chaudière falls in the vicinity of the city. But it is more probably from the term *adawe* (to trade), the Indians of the northern stretches of the river being noted traders in furs in the days of the French régime. In the Jesuit *Relations* these Indians are referred to as *Outaouak*, and later missionaries and explorers called them *Outaowa*. After 1700 they were called the *Outaouais*, but finally the form became fixed as Ottawa, and was used to designate the "Grand River of the Algonquins". There are in all some thirty spellings of the word. Population, about 130,000, and if the suburbs are included, over 160,000.

See A. Wilson, *A history of old Bytown and vicinity* (Ottawa, 1876); Sir J. D. Edgar, *Canada and its capital* (Toronto, 1898); A. H. D. Ross, *Ottawa past and present* (Toronto, 1927); Blodwen Davies, *The charm of Ottawa* (Toronto, 1932); and T. M. Longstreth, *Quebec, Montreal, and Ottawa* (New York, 1933).

**Ottawa and New York Railway,** a line opened in 1898 between Ottawa and Cornwall, Ontario, and leased to the New York Central Railway in 1916.

**Ottawa and Prescott Railway,** a line opened in 1854 between Ottawa and Prescott, Ontario, chiefly for the transportation of lumber. It was purchased by the Canadian Pacific Railway in 1884.

**Ottawa, Arnprior, and Parry Sound Railway,** a line opened between Ottawa and Parry Sound, Ontario, in 1896, and consolidated with the Canada Atlantic Railway in 1899.

**Ottawa Canals.** See **Canals.**

**Ottawa Literary and Scientific Society,** incorporated by Act of the Legislature on December 24, 1869, at

OTTAWA FROM THE AIR

*Photograph by Royal Canadian Air Force*

Ottawa, to further the cultivation of literature and science. It was an amalgamation of two societies: the Bytown Mechanics Institute and Athenæum, founded first in 1847, and reorganized in 1853, and the Natural History Society of Ottawa, organized in 1863. The society published its *Transactions* for the years from 1898 to 1907 (Nos. 1-4).

**Ottawa river,** the largest tributary of the St. Lawrence. It rises in the Laurentian plateau in Quebec, between the 47th and 48th parallels of latitude, flows westward to lake Timiskaming, then follows a south-easterly course and discharges into the St. Lawrence above Montreal island. It was named after a tribe of Indians living on Manitoulin island and the shores of Georgian bay. It was first visited in 1610 by Étienne Brûlé (q.v.), a protégé of Champlain (q.v.). Champlain himself explored the Ottawa to Allumette island in 1613, and in 1615 he followed it to the Mattawa before turning off toward Georgian bay. By 1625 a regular intercourse had been established between the Hurons of Georgian bay and the French on the St. Lawrence; until the beginning of the nineteenth century, it was the great highway to the west over which the fur-trade was carried on. During the seventeenth century the trade of the Ottawa was menaced by Iroquois attacks, and in 1660 Dollard (q.v.) and his sixteen companions made their heroic stand at the Long Sault rapids, mid-way between Montreal and the site of Ottawa. After the conquest the North West Company at first kept the Ottawa valley fairly free of settlers. At the beginning of the nineteenth century came the settlement of the valley and with it the commencement of the lumbering industry, the construction of canals, and the employment of steam, at first on the river and later on its banks.

The Ottawa is 696 miles long and drains an area of more than 56,000 square miles. It is composed largely of deep and wide basins or lakes connected by falls and heavy rapids, including the Johnston rapids, above the Mattawa river, the Chats rapids, which are 3 miles in length and end in the Chats falls, below which are the Deschênes rapids, and, above the city of Ottawa, the Chaudière falls, which, with the rapids for 6 miles above, represent a drop of 60 feet. Between the Chaudière and the mouth of the river are the Long Sault and the Carillon rapids. The principal lakes in the course of the river are Grand Victoria, Expanse, des Quinze, Timiskaming, Seven League, Upper Allumette, Coulonge, Deschênes, and Two Mountains. The Ottawa is broken by a number of islands, including 3 at its mouth, Jésus, Montreal, and Perrot; between Ottawa and Pembroke are Allumette and Calumet islands. Its chief tributaries on the left bank are the Rouge, North Nation, Lièvre, Gatineau, Coulonge, and Dumoine; and on the right bank are the South Nation, Mississippi, Madawaska, Petawawa, and Rideau. The banks of the river are wooded with pine, hemlock, spruce, balsam, fir, cedar, oak, maple, and birch; and these made the Ottawa for one hundred years the centre of the lumbering industry in Canada. The Ottawa has great potentialities as a source of power, and has been estimated as capable of producing 2 million horse power. The construction of the St. Anne, Carillon, and Grenville canals has made possible the passage from Montreal to Ottawa of vessels drawing 9 feet. See George Shortt, *The Ottawa river* (Canadian Geographical Journal, February, 1931), and J. L. Gourlay, *History of the Ottawa valley* (Ottawa, 1896).

**Ottawa, University of.** See **University of Ottawa.**

**Otter, Sir William Dillon** (1843-1929), soldier, was born near Clinton, Ontario, on December 3, 1843, the son of Alfred William Otter and Anna de la Hooke. He was educated at the Toronto Model School and Upper Canada College; and entered the volunteer militia in 1861. He was adjutant of the Queen's Own Rifles during the Fenian raid of 1866, and became lieut.-colonel commanding the regiment in 1874. He entered the permanent militia in 1883; and during the North West Rebellion of 1885 he commanded the column which marched on Battleford. Later he captured the Indian chief Poundmaker (q.v.). He commanded the first contingent of troops sent to the South African War in 1899, and was wounded in action in 1900. From 1908 to 1910 he was chief of the general staff at Ottawa, with the rank of brigadier-general; from 1910 to 1912 he was inspector-general, with the rank of major-general; and during the Great War he was director of internment operations. He died at Toronto on May 6, 1929. Created a C.B. in 1900 and a C.V.O. in 1908, he was made a K.C.B. in 1913; and he was made an LL.D. of the University of Toronto in 1922. He was the author of *The guide* (Toronto, 1880), a military manual which went into many editions.

**Otter** (*Lutra canadensis*). This member of the weasel family (*Mustelidae*) is highly specialized for aquatic life. The long slim body, rounded head, and tapering tail allow it to slip through the water with minimum resistance. Short legs with webbed toes drive it at a speed that enables it to capture the swiftest fish, and the dense coat of sleek brown fur is almost impervious to penetration by water. Essentially an aquatic animal, it is never found far from watercourses, though at times it will travel some distance overland from one body of water to another. Its food is principally fish and crayfish, but muskrats, beaver, ducks, and even frogs are eaten when encountered. Its den is usually located in the bank of a lake or stream or in a hollow log, and here the single litter of from one to four young is born in the spring. Both parents participate in the care and training of the young until they are able to look after themselves. Otters are nowhere common, but may be found throughout Canada as far north as the Arctic circle. Throughout all this vast range, the otters are remarkably uniform both in coloration and size. The fur has long been renowned as both beautiful and durable; consequently, it is much sought after by trappers, and is an important item in the Canadian fur-trade.

**Otterville,** a village in Oxford county, Ontario, on Otter creek, and on the Canadian National Railway, 16 miles west of Woodstock. It has grist and saw mills and some small factories. Pop. (1934), 700.

**Ouananiche,** a form of the Atlantic salmon which does not go to sea, but spends its whole life in freshwater lakes. The best known ones are those of lake St. John in the province of Quebec, but similar "land-locked" varieties are said to occur in other lakes of Quebec. They are very highly regarded as game fish. Similar freshwater forms of the Atlantic salmon are found in some lakes in New Brunswick and Maine, and in lake Wenern in Sweden. See E. T. D. Chambers, *The ouananiche and its Canadian environment* (New York, 1896).

**Ouimet, Gédéon** (1823-1905), prime minister of Quebec (1873-4), was born at Ste. Rose, Lower Canada, on June 3, 1823, the son of Jean Ouimet and Marie Boutron *dit* Major. He was educated at the colleges of St. Hyacinthe and Montreal, and was called to the bar of Lower Canada in 1844 (Q.C., 1867). From 1857 to 1861 he was Conservative member for Beauharnois in the Legislative Assembly of Canada; and from 1867 to 1875 he sat for Two Mountains in the Legislative Assembly of Quebec. He was attorney-general in the Chauveau administration in Quebec from 1867 to 1873; and from 1873 to 1874 he was prime minister of Quebec, with the portfolios of minister of public instruction and provincial secretary. In 1876 he was appointed superintendent of education for Quebec; and this post he held for twenty years, after which he retired on a pension. He was appointed also in 1895 to the Legislative Council of Quebec. He died at Quebec on April 23, 1905. In 1850 he married Jane, daughter of Alexis Pellant, of Montreal; and by her he had six children. He was a D.C.L. of Bishop's College, Lennoxville, and an LL.D. of Laval University.

**Ouimet, Joseph Alderic** (1848-1916), politician and judge, was born at Ste. Rose, Lower Canada, on May 20, 1848, the son of Michel Ouimet, J.P., and Elizabeth Filiatrault St. Louis. He was educated at the College of Ste. Thérèse and at Victoria University, Cobourg, Ontario (LL.B., 1869), and was called to the Quebec bar in 1870 (Q.C., 1880). He became head of the law firm of Ouimet, Emard, and Maurault, of Montreal. From 1873 to 1896 he represented Laval as a Liberal-Conservative in the Canadian House of Commons; and from 1887 to 1891 he was the speaker of the House. He was sworn of the King's Privy Council for Canada in 1891, and from 1892 to 1896 he was minister of public works in the successive Abbott, Thompson, and Bowell cabinets. In 1896 he was appointed a puisne judge of the Court of King's Bench of Quebec; and he retired from the bench in 1906. He died at Montreal on May 12, 1916. In 1874 he married Marie Thérèse, daughter of Alfred Chartier La Rocque, of Montreal; and by her he had several children. From 1879 to 1889 he was lieut.-colonel commanding the 65th Mount Royal Rifles. He saw service in the Fenian raids of 1870 and in the North West rebellion of 1885; and in 1888 he was president of the Dominion Rifle Association.

**Ouimet, Joseph Alphonse** (1845-1900), judge, was born at St. Eustache, Lower Canada, on November 17, 1845, the son of Louis Ouimet and Marguerite Goulet. He was educated at St. Mary's Jesuit College and at the College of

Montreal, and was called to the bar of Lower Canada in 1868. For a number of years he practised law in Montreal in partnership with his cousin, Joseph Alderic Ouimet (q.v.); and he became professor of administrative law in Laval University, Montreal. In 1885 he was appointed a special commissioner to report on the causes of the North West rebellion; and in 1886 he was chairman of the royal commission to examine into claims for compensation arising out of the rebellion. The same year he was appointed a puisne judge of the Superior Court of Quebec; and in 1894 he was made a judge of the Court of Queen's Bench in Quebec. He died on December 19, 1900. He married, in 1868, Elmina, daughter of F. Poirier, Montreal. In 1878 he was made an LL.D. of Laval University, Montreal.

**Outardes river,** in Saguenay county, Quebec, falls into the St. Lawrence river 12 miles east of the Bersimis river. It is so named from the large number of wild geese (*outardes*) which frequent the river in the spring and autumn. It has a length of about 300 miles, and is interrupted by many falls and rapids which are capable of developing considerable water-power.

**Outlook,** a town in Saskatchewan, on the Canadian Pacific Railway, 75 miles south-west of Saskatoon. It is in a farming and stock-raising district, and has a weekly newspaper (*Outlook*). It is the site of Outlook College, which is maintained by the Norwegian Lutheran Church of Canada. Pop. (1931), 712.

**Outram, Joseph** (1803-1885), author, was born on the Clyde, near Glasgow, Scotland, in 1803, settled in Nova Scotia in 1861, and died at Halifax in 1885. He was the author of *Nova Scotia, its condition and resources* (Edinburgh, 1850) and *A handbook of informtaion for emigrants to Nova Scotia* (Halifax, 1864).

**Outram, mount,** is in Alberta, in the Rocky mountains. It is in lat. 51° 53′ and long. 116° 52′, and is named after

Sir James Outram, Bart. (1864-1925), noted mountain-climber and author of *In the heart of the Canadian Rockies* (New York, 1923).

**Outremont,** a city in Jacques Cartier county, Quebec, 5 miles north-east of Montreal, on the Canadian Pacific and Canadian National Railways. Outremont dates from 1875, when it replaced the name Côte-Ste. Catherine, a settlement founded in the early years of the nineteenth century by the Sulpician Fathers, or Christian Brothers. The name of the city was suggested by that of the home of the Le Bouthillier family, the principal residence in the village. The house was probably so called because it was "on the other side of Mount Royal". The city has few industries, being principally a residential suburb of its great metropolitan neighbour. Strict building regulations and other ordinances have eliminated undesirable features of city life. It became a town in 1895, and was incorporated a city in 1915. Pop. (1931), 28,641.

**Ouzel.** See **Dipper.**

**Oven-bird** (*Seiurus aurocapillus*), a small bird which belongs to the North American wood-warbler family, *Compsothlypidae*, and occurs throughout wooded parts of Canada east of the Rocky mountains. It is olive-green above, with an orange-brown crown, and white below with dark streaks. Its name is derived from the shape of the nest it constructs, the materials being arched over in the form of a roof, which suggests a "Dutch oven". The oven-bird is somewhat peculiar for its gait, since it does not hop, but rather walks. Dense woods are its favourite haunt.

**Owen Sound,** a city in Grey county, Ontario, situated on the Georgian bay at the mouth of the Sydenham river. It is served by the Canadian National and Canadian Pacific Railways, and has steamboat connection with Fort William as well as weekly steamboat service with Manitoulin island, Sault Ste. Marie, and Mackinac island. It is an agricultural centre, and has numerous industries—furniture, agricultural implements, etc.—and a grain elevator of 4,000,000 bushels capacity. Cheap power is obtained from Eugenia falls. The townsite was surveyed by Capt. William Fitzwilliam Owen in 1812. The village was incorporated as a town in 1857, and was then named after the original surveyor. Its incorporation as a city took place in 1920. It has a collegiate institute, a technical school, a business college, a public library, and a daily evening newspaper (*Sun-Times*). Pop. (1931), 12,839. See J. M. Kilbourn, *Reminiscences of the first settlers of Owen Sound* (Ont. Hist. Soc., Papers and Records, 1920).

**Owikeno lake** lies 4 miles east of the head of Rivers inlet, at the head of the Wannock river, in the Coast district of British Columbia. It has an area of 62,720 acres.

**Owl,** the English name for the nocturnal birds of prey. These birds have certain affinities to the goatsuckers, a group to which the whip-poor-will belongs, and also to the parrots. Their body feathers are fluffy, and the wing feathers are soft-edged, which makes possible noiseless flight. They are further characterized by a rounded or heart-shaped disc of feathers forming a "face", and by their large eyes, which are directed forward. Some species possess pairs of feather tufts on the head, termed "ears" or "horns". The horned owl (*Bubo virginianus*) is the largest Canadian species; it is nearly two feet in length. The smallest species, the pygmy owl, which is found in Canada only in British Columbia, is little more than half a foot in length. For an account of the owls in Ontario, see Royal Ontario Museum of Zoology, *Handbook No. 2*, Toronto.

**Oxbow,** a town in Assiniboia district, Saskatchewan, on the Souris branch of the Canadian Pacific Railway, 257 miles west of Winnipeg, and 41 miles north-east of Estevan. It is in a fertile farming and stock-raising district, and has three grain elevators. It has also a high school and a weekly newspaper (*Herald*). Pop. (1931), 585.

**Oxenden, Ashton** (1808-1892), Anglican bishop of Montreal, and metropolitan of Canada (1869-78), was born at Broome Park, Canterbury, England, on September 20, 1808, the fifth son of Sir Henry Oxenden, Bart. He was educated at Harrow and at University College, Oxford (B.A., 1831; M.A., 1859; D.D., 1869), and was ordained a priest of the Church of England in 1833. For twenty years he was vicar of Pluckley in Kent; and in 1869 he was elected bishop of Montreal and metropolitan of Canada. Ill-health compelled his retirement from this bishopric in 1878; and he died at Biarritz, France, on February 22, 1892. He was the author of numerous theological and devotional works; but the only books by him which have special reference to his life in Canada are *My first year in Canada* (London, 1871) and *The history of my life: An autobiography* (London, 1891). After his death there was published his *Plain sermons, with a memoir of the author* (London, 1893).

**Ox-eye Daisy.** See **Daisy.**

**Oxford,** a county in Ontario, is bounded on the south by Elgin and Norfolk counties, on the east by Norfolk, Brant, and Waterloo counties, on the north by Waterloo and Perth counties, and on the west by Middlesex and Elgin counties. It was erected in 1798 from municipalities formerly belonging to Norfolk and York counties, and named after Oxfordshire in England. The townships of Zorra and Nissouri were added in 1821. A large colony of Highlanders settled in Zorra about 1830; and by 1852 the population was 32,000, nearly one-third of which had been born in the British Isles, mainly in Scotland. County town, Woodstock. Pop. (1931),

47,825. See G. R. Pattullo, *Leaves from an early note-book* (Ont. Hist. Soc., Papers and Records, 1919); W. A. MacKay, *Pioneer life in Zorra* (Toronto, 1899); *Oxford and Norfolk gazetteer* (Woodstock, 1867); and Emily P. Weaver, *The counties of Ontario* (Toronto, 1913).

**Oxford,** a town in Cumberland county, Nova Scotia, is situated on the river Philip at the head of the tide, and on the Canadian National Railway, between Oxford Junction and Pictou. It has a number of industries, and produces engines and milling machinery, furniture, etc. The Oxford tweeds and blankets, manufactured in the town, have won a high reputation. There are three rivers running through Oxford, and before bridges were erected, and when oxen were used in transportation, the rivers were forded by the oxen, hence the name Ox-ford. Pop., about 1,500.

**Oxford Historical Society** of Woodstock, Ontario, was reorganized in 1930. Some of the papers read at the society's meetings have appeared in the local press.

**Oxford House,** a Hudson's Bay Company post at the north-east end of Oxford lake on the Hayes river route from York Factory to lake Winnipeg. The original post was built in 1798, but was succeeded by a second in 1816, which has been in regular operation to the present date. It was an important post when York Factory was the chief shipping port of the Hudson's Bay Company, and the furs were brought down thither in York boats. See S. J. C. Cumming, *Oxford House* (Beaver, 1929).

**Oxford lake** lies north-east of lake Winnipeg, in Manitoba, about the 96th meridian of west longitude. It has an area of 155 square miles.

**Oxford Mills,** a village in Grenville county, Ontario, 4 miles west of Kemptville, the nearest railway station. Pop (1924), 400.

**Oxley, James Macdonald** (1855-1907), writer of books for boys, was born at Halifax, Nova Scotia, on October 22, 1855, the son of James Black Oxley, a merchant, and Ellen Macdonald. He was educated at the Halifax Grammar School, at Dalhousie University (B.A., 1874), and at Harvard University. He was called to the bar of Nova Scotia in 1878, and for five years he practised law in Halifax. From 1883 to 1891 he was legal adviser to the department of marine and fisheries at Ottawa; and he then entered the service of the Sun Life Assurance Company at Montreal. During his last years he lived in Toronto; and he died here on September 9, 1907. In 1887 he published *Bert Lloyd's boyhood* (Philadelphia), the first of a long series of stories for boys which were widely popular. Perhaps his best known book was *Archie of Athabasca* (Boston, 1893), published also as *Archie McKenzie, the young Nor' Wester* (London, 1894).

**Oyama,** a village in the Osoyoos district of British Columbia, on the Canadian National Railway (Kamloops-Vernon-Kelowna branch), and on the west side of Long lake, 12 miles south of Vernon. It has a high school. Pop. (1930), 400.

**Oyen,** a village in Alberta, on the Canadian National Railway, 192 miles west of Saskatoon. It has six grain elevators, a school, and a weekly newspaper (*News*). Pop. (1934), 401.

**Oyster Industry.** Oysters are bivalve molluscs which inhabit shallow ocean beds with muddy bottoms. For many years Prince Edward Island was the home of the oyster industry of Canada; and Malpeque oysters were famous all over North America. Early in the twentieth century, however, the Prince Edward Island oyster fishery began to decline, through over-exploitation; and the oyster fisheries of New Brunswick rose in importance. These, in turn, have declined. But the Canadian government has, within recent years undertaken the restoration of the industry through the development of oyster farming. Favourable areas in Prince Edward Island have been seeded; and investigations and experiments in the culture of the oyster have been carried on at Malpeque bay, Prince Edward Island, and in Shediac bay, New Brunswick, by the Canadian department of fisheries. The Commission of Conservation (q.v.) devoted some attention to the oyster industry (see J. Stafford, *The Canadian oyster*, Ottawa, 1913); and more recently the Biological Board of Canada, at some of its stations on the Atlantic, has devoted much research into the culture of the oyster, especially at Ellerslie, Prince Edward Island. The Atlantic oyster has been introduced into Pacific coast waters, but without much success. There is a native species on the Pacific coast of good flavour, but rather small in size, which has become increasingly important commercially in recent years. A large Japanese species has also been introduced on the west coast.

# P

**Paardeberg, Battle of,** an engagement in the South African War in which the Canadians were employed, and which resulted in the capture of General Cronje's force. It began on February 18, 1900, when Lord Roberts's force, which had relieved Kimberley, surrounded Cronje's army of 6,000 men, north of Paardeberg Drift on the Modder river. An attack on this day, in which the Canadians distinguished themselves, proved abortive; and for eight days the British beleaguered the Boer laager. Then, on the night of February 26, the order was given to attack again. The Canadians led the assault, but were held up 50 yards from the Boer trenches by a devastating rifle fire which forced them to retire, with severe casualties. The next morning, however, the Boers hoisted the white flag; and General Cronje and his force surrendered.

**Pabos,** a settlement in Gaspé county, Quebec, on Pabos bay, between the Grand and Petit Pabos rivers, and on the Atlantic, Quebec, and Western Railway, 65 miles from Gaspé. The name is of uncertain origin, and has been attributed to both Micmac and Basque sources. The chief industries are fishing and lumbering; but general farming has of recent years developed rapidly. The parish is officially known as Ste. Adelaide de Pabos. Pop. (1930), 2,652.

**Pacific Cable.** See **Cables.**

**Pacific Fur Company,** the company formed by John Jacob Astor (q.v.) in 1810, for the purpose of engaging in the fur-trade on the Pacific coast of North America. The servants of this company founded Fort Astoria at the mouth of the Columbia river in 1811.

**Pacific ocean,** the largest of all bodies of water on the globe, washes the west coast of America, and extends from America to the east coast of Asia, and from the Arctic to the Antarctic oceans. It has an area estimated at 70,000,000 square miles; and at the equator it is 10,000 miles wide. The North Pacific narrows as it approaches the Arctic circle, until it reaches Bering strait, by which it communicates with the Arctic ocean. The first European to lay eyes upon it was Balboa, the Spanish governor of Darien, who crossed the isthmus of Panama in 1513, and named it "the South Sea". The name "Pacific" was given to it by Magellan, the Portuguese navigator who crossed it in 1521. The west coast of North America was explored by the Spaniards, by the Russian sailor Bering (q.v.), by Cook (q.v.), Vancouver (q.v.), and others; and it was first reached overland from Canada by Sir Alexander Mackenzie (q.v.) in 1793. The Pacific, though not so important as the Atlantic as an avenue for trade, gives Canada access to Japan, China, Australia, New Zealand, and India. The North Pacific has long been famous for its seal-fisheries, now almost extinct. See G. H. Scholefield, *The Pacific, its past and future* (London, 1919).

**Pacific Salmon.** The salmon of the Pacific belong to five species, of which the following are the scientific and common names: (1) *Oncorhynchus nerka*, sockeye, blue back, or redfish, (2) *Oncorhynchus kisutch*, coho or silver salmon, (3) *Oncorhynchus tschawytscha*, spring, king, tyee, or chinook salmon, (4) *Oncorhynchus gorbuscha*, humpback or pink salmon, and (5) *Oncorhynchus keta*, dog or chum salmon. Pacific salmons extend from California to Alaska on the American side and from Siberia to Japan on the Asiatic side of the Pacific. They constitute the most valuable commercial fisheries of Canada, the annual production of salmon in normal times being valued at fifteen million dollars. They are marketed principally in the canned condition, although some, principally springs and cohos, are sold fresh or frozen. The sockeye was the first species to be exploited commercially because of its superior quality, but as the supply of this species declined and the demand increased, the less valuable species, including the pink and chum salmons, were utilized. The life history of the Pacific species is similar to that of the Atlantic salmon in that spawning occurs in fresh water and the young pass the early portion of their lives there. The time spent in fresh water varies from species to species and in the same species from place to place. In the sockeye the young usually spend one year in a lake before going to sea, but some go to sea during their first summer, while a few spend two winters in the lake In the pink and chum the fry go to sea during their first summer. Most sockeye mature in their fourth year; pinks and chums, in their second year; some springs live as much as six or seven years. After spawning, all species of Pacific salmon die. In this they differ from Atlantic salmon, which return to the sea after spawning and make two or more migrations to fresh water for spawning during their lives. The salmon runs to some of the rivers of British Columbia have been greatly reduced through overfishing and otherwise. This is particularly true in the case of sockeye salmon in the Fraser. Since the salmon returning to this river to spawn are taken both in United States and Canadian waters, satisfactory measures for the improvement of these fisheries are impossible until an international agreement for the control of the taking of fish bound for this river has been arrived at.

**Pacific Scandal,** the name applied to the episode which resulted in 1873 in the resignation of the first government of the Dominion of Canada. In the general elections of 1872, Sir John Macdonald (q.v.) was so indiscreet as to seek contributions to the funds of the Liberal-Conservative party from Sir Hugh Allan (q.v.), who headed the syndicate to which had been granted the charter for building the Canadian Pacific Railway. The Liberal opposition obtained evidence of this fact, and charged that Macdonald had sold the charter for building the railway in return for large contributions to his party's campaign funds. This led to the resignation of the Macdonald government in 1873, owing to the defection of some of its supporters, who were not prepared to defend at the polls the government's action. In the general elections that followed, the Liberal-Conservative party was overwhelmingly defeated; but in five years' time the Canadian people either forgot the episode or changed their opinion about it, and Macdonald was returned to power by a majority as great as that by which he had been defeated in 1873. Sir Charles Tupper (q.v.) always maintained that the "Pacific Scandal" should have been known as the "Pacific Slander"; and it is possible that Macdonald's acceptance of campaign funds from Sir Hugh Allan was merely a grave indiscretion, rather than a serious moral offence. See also **History, Political.**

**Page, Rhoda Ann** (1826-1863), poet, was born in Hackney, England, in 1826, and came to Canada in 1832. In 1856 she married a Mr. Faulkner, and went to live near Rice lake, Ontario, where she died in 1863. She was the author of a volume of verse entitled *Wild notes from the backwoods* (Cobourg, Ontario, 1850).

**Painchaud, Charles François** (1782-1838), priest and educationist, was born at the Ile aux Grues, Quebec, on September 9, 1782, the son of François Painchaud and of Marie-Angélique Drouin. He was educated at Quebec, and was ordained a priest in 1805. From 1806 to 1814 he was a parish priest on the shores of the bay of Chaleurs; and in 1814 he went to Ste. Anne de la Pocatière. Here he founded, in 1829, the classical college of Ste. Anne de la Pocatière; and he had a profound influence on education in French Canada. He died at Ste. Anne de la Pocatière on February 8, 1838. See N. E. Dionne, *Vie de C. F. Painchaud* (Quebec, 1894); C. Bacon, *Éloge de messire C. F. Painchaud* (Ste. Anne de la Pocatière, 1864); and H. Têtu, *Souvenirs inédits sur l'abbé Painchaud* (Quebec, 1893).

**Painted Cup** (*Castilleja coccinea* (L.) Spreng., *Scrophulariaceae*), a hairy perennial or biennial herb with simple, seldom-branched stem, 6 inches to 1 foot high. The root leaves are clustered, oblong and mostly entire, the stem leaves are cut, those nearest the flowers being 3-cleft, the lobes toothed and brilliant scarlet towards the tip. The calyx is 2-cleft, and yellowish in colour, about the length of the pale yellow corolla; the upper lip of the corolla is keeled and flattened laterally; stamens are 4 in number, 2 long and 2 short; and the fruit is a many-seeded capsule. It grows in low sandy ground from the Atlantic coast to Manitoba. There are several species, which are very similar, common to the prairie provinces.

**Painting.** See **Art.**

**Paisley,** a village in Bruce county, Ontario, at the confluence of the Teeswater and Saugeen rivers, and on the Canadian National Railway, 86 miles north-west of Guelph. It is named after Paisley in Scotland. It has flour and alfalfa mills, a fruit-box factory, and a creamery, as well as a public library and a weekly newspaper (*Advocate*). Pop. (1934), 724.

**Pakenham,** a village in Lanark county, Ontario, on the Mississippi river, and on the Canadian Pacific Railway, 10 miles north of Almonte. It was named after General Sir Edward Michael Pakenham (1778-1815), who was killed while in command of the British forces at the battle of New Orleans. It is in a farming and lumbering district. Pop. (1934), 700.

**Palermo,** a village in Halton county, Ontario, 7 miles north-west of Oakville. Pop. (1934), 200.

**Palladium,** a silver-white to steel-gray metal of the platinum group. It is nearly as hard as platinum, but is less ductile, and has a specific gravity of about 11.5. It is used in jewellery to replace white gold, and in the electrical trades and for electro-plating table utensils. In the chemical industry, palladium is useful in the reduction and hydrogenation of organic compounds. Practically all the Canadian production is from the Sudbury nickel-copper ores.

**Palliser, John** (1807-1887), explorer, was born on January 29, 1807, the eldest son of Wray Palliser, of county Waterford, Ireland. In 1847 he set out on a hunting expedition in north-western America; and he later described his experiences in *Solitary rambles and adventures of a hunter in the prairies* (London, 1853). In 1857 he was appointed to command an expedition sent out by the British government to explore British North America between the parallels of 49° and 50° north latitude and 100° and 115° west longitude. He spent the years 1857-1861 in discharging this commission; and his report was issued in the British parliamentary papers for 1863. He died unmarried at Comragh, county Waterford, Ireland, on August 18, 1887. In 1877 he was created a C.M.G.

**Palliser pass,** in the Rocky mountains, lies at the head of Palliser river, in the Kootenay district of British Columbia, and has an altitude of 6,836 feet. It is named after Captain John Palliser (q.v.).

**Palliser range,** a chain of mountains in Alberta, named after Captain John Palliser (q.v.). Palliser's range is on the Palliser exploration map, 1859.

**Palmer, Edward** (1809-1889), politician and judge, was born at Charlottetown, Prince Edward Island, on September 1, 1809, the son of James B. Palmer, a barrister, and Millicent, daughter of Benjamin Jones, of London, England. He was educated at Charlottetown, studied law under his father, and was called to the bar in 1831 (Q.C., 1857). From 1835 to 1860 he was a member of the Legislative Assembly of Prince Edward Island for Charlottetown and Royalty; and from 1860 to 1873 he was a member of the Legislative Council. He repeatedly held office in the Island administration. From 1848 to 1851 he was solicitor-general; for some months in 1854 he was attorney-general; in 1859 he became president of the council; and he was again attorney-general from 1863 to 1869, and from 1872 to 1873. He was a delegate to the Charlottetown conference on the union of the Maritime provinces in 1864, and to the Quebec conference later in the same year. He opposed Confederation on the basis of the Quebec Resolutions; but in 1873 threw his influence in favour of union. In 1873 he was appointed a judge of the Queen's county court, Prince Edward Island; and in 1874 he was appointed chief justice of the Supreme Court of the Island. This office he held until his death on November 3, 1889. He married Isabella, daughter of Benjamin Tremain, of Quebec; and by her he had nine children.

**Palmer, mount,** is in the Kootenay district of British Columbia, at the eastern termination of Sir Sandford range, in the Selkirk mountains, north of Gold river. It is in lat. 51° 40' and long. 117° 47'; and is named after Howard Palmer, who explored the locality in 1908-12. There is also a Palmer mount in the Coast district of British Columbia, north of Puntzi lake, in Range 3. It is in lat. 52° 15' and long. 124° 03', and has an altitude of 4,346 feet.

**Palmerston,** a town in Wellington county, Ontario, on the Canadian National Railway, 42 miles north-west of Guelph. In 1822 the place was named to commemorate Lord Palmerston (1784-1865), prime minister of England. The town contains five churches, a Carnegie library, and a hospital. The chief industries are railway shops, a butter factory, a cheese factory, and a grist mill. A newspaper (*Observer*) is published weekly. Pop. (1931), 1,543.

**Pambrun, Pierre Chrysologue** (1792-1841), fur-trader, was born at L'Islet, below Quebec, Lower Canada, on December 17, 1792, the son of André Dominique Pambrun. He served in the Canadian *Voltigeurs* under Salaberry in the War of 1812, and took part in the battle of Châteauguay. After the war, in 1815, he entered the service of the Hudson's Bay Company; and in 1816 he was taken prisoner by the *bois-brulés* of the North West Company on the Qu'Appelle river. In 1821 he was stationed at Cumberland House; and in 1824 he was transferred to the Pacific slope. Here he spent the remainder of his life. He died at Fort Walla Walla, in the Oregon country, in 1841, as the result of injuries received when breaking in a wild horse. Just before his death, in 1840, he had been promoted to the rank of chief trader. About 1821, at Cumberland House, he married the half-breed daughter of Edward Umfreville (q.v.); and she was still living, in the state of Washington, in 1878. One of his sons, Pierre Chrysologue, entered the service of the Hudson's Bay Company, and was met by Lord Milton and Dr. Cheadle in the foothills of the Rocky mountains in 1868. An account of the life of the elder Pierre Chrysologue Pambrun will be found in J. Tassé, *Les*

*Canadiens de l'Ouest* (2 vols., Montreal, 1878).

**Panet, Bernard Claude** (1753-1833), Roman Catholic bishop of Quebec (1825-33), was born in Quebec on January 9, 1753, the second son of Jean Claude Panet (q.v.). He was educated at the Quebec Seminary, and in 1778 was ordained a priest of the Roman Catholic Church. In 1781 he became *curé* of the parish of Rivière-Ouelle; and served in this parish for nearly forty-five years. In 1806 he was appointed co-adjutor to Bishop Plessis (q.v.) with the title of bishop of Saldes *in partibus;* and in 1825 he became bishop of Quebec. He died at Quebec on February 14, 1833. See P. G. Roy, *La famille Panet* (Lévis, 1906).

**Panet, Charles Eugène** (1829-1898), deputy minister of militia and defence (1875-98), was born at Quebec on November 27, 1829, the son of the Hon. Philippe Panet (q.v.). He was educated at the Quebec Seminary and at the Jesuit College, Georgetown; and in 1854 he was called to the bar of Lower Canada. In 1874 he was called to the Senate of Canada; but in 1875 he resigned his seat in the Senate to accept the position of deputy minister of militia and defence, and he retained this position until shortly before his death at Ottawa on November 22, 1898. He was thrice married; and he had sixteen children. In 1886 he was gazetted a colonel in the Canadian militia. See P. G. Roy, *La famille Panet* (Lévis, 1906).

**Panet, Jean Antoine** (1751-1815), speaker of the Legislative Assembly of Lower Canada (1792-1814), was born at Quebec on June 8, 1751, the eldest son of Jean Claude Panet (q.v.). In 1772 he was admitted to practice as a notary public, and in 1773 as a barrister. In 1792 he was elected to represent the upper town of Quebec in the Legislative Assembly of Lower Canada; and he was a member of the Assembly continuously until 1814, for the upper town of Quebec until 1808, for Huntingdon until 1814, and again for the upper town of Quebec in 1814. During the whole of this period, except for about two years between 1794 and 1797 when he was a judge of the court of common pleas, he was speaker of the Assembly, being elected in all seven times. At the beginning of 1815 he was appointed a member of the Legislative Council; but he survived his appointment only a few months, dying at Quebec on May 17, 1815. In 1779 he married Louise Philippe, daughter of surgeon-major Philippe Louis François Badelard; and by her he had fifteen children. See P. G. Roy, *La famille Panet* (Lévis, 1906).

**Panet, Jean Claude** (1720-1778), judge, was born in Paris, France, in 1720, the son of Jean Nicolas Panet and Marie Madeleine Françoise Foucher. He emigrated to Canada as a soldier in the troops of the Marine, and in 1741 was admitted to practice as an attorney. In 1744 he was appointed royal notary in Quebec, and in 1751 an assessor of the Sovereign Council. He was present at Quebec during the siege of 1759, and remained in the city after its capture. In 1760 he was appointed by General Murray (q.v.) chief clerk of the superior court of Quebec, and in 1765 clerk of the court of common pleas in Quebec. In 1766 he resigned this post, and the next year he was admitted to practise as a barrister. In 1775 he was named a justice of the peace for Quebec, and in 1776 a judge of the court of common pleas for Quebec. He was thus the first French-Canadian judge under British rule. He died at Quebec on February 28, 1778. In 1747 he married Marie-Louise, daughter of Claude Barolet; and by her he had fourteen children. He was the author of a *Journal du siège de Québec*, published by the Literary and Historical Society of Quebec in its *Manuscripts*, fourth series (Quebec, 1875). See P. G Roy, *La famille Panet* (Lévis, 1906).

**Panet, Louis** (1794-1884), senator of Canada, was born at Quebec on March

19, 1794, the third son of the Hon. Jean Antoine Panet (q.v.). He was admitted to practice as a notary public in Lower Canada in 1819. In 1852 he was appointed a member of the Legislative Council of Canada, in 1867 of the Legislative Council of Quebec, and in 1871 of the Senate of Canada. He resigned from the Senate, on account of ill health, in 1874; and he died at Quebec on May 15, 1884. In 1820 he married Marie Louise, daughter of Dr. Frederic W. Oliva; and by her he had five children. See P. G. Roy, *La famille Panet* (Lévis, 1906).

**Panet, Philippe** (1791-1855), judge, was born at Quebec on February 28, 1791, the second son of the Hon. Jean Antoine Panet (q.v.). He served in the Canadian *Voltigeurs* during the War of 1812, and was present at the battle of Châteauguay. In 1817 he was called to the bar of Lower Canada; and from 1816 to 1824 and from 1830 to 1832 he represented Northumberland in the Legislative Assembly of the province. In 1831 he was appointed by Lord Aylmer (q.v.) a member of the executive council of Lower Canada; and in 1832 he was gazetted a judge of the court of King's Bench for the district of Quebec. In 1838 he was suspended from the bench by Sir John Colborne (q.v.); but he resumed his seat in 1840, and continued to occupy a seat on the bench until his death at Quebec on January 15, 1855. In 1819 he married Marie Luce, daughter of Pierre Casgrain; and by her he had twelve children. See P. G. Roy, *La famille Panet* (Lévis, 1906).

**Panet, Pierre Louis** (1761-1812), judge, was born in Montreal on August 2, 1761, the eldest son of the Hon. Pierre Méru Panet (q.v.). In 1780 he was admitted to practice as a notary public and barrister in Montreal; and in 1783 he was appointed clerk of the court of common pleas in Quebec. In 1792 he was elected to represent Cornwallis in the Legislative Assembly of Lower Canada, and he opposed the election of his cousin, Jean Antoine

Panet (q.v.), as speaker of the House. In 1795 he was appointed a judge of the court of King's Bench at Montreal, in succession to his cousin, Jean Antoine Panet, and he sat on the bench in this court until his death. In 1800 he was elected to represent Montreal East in the Legislative Assembly; but in 1801 he was appointed a member of the executive council. He died at Montreal on December 2, 1812. In 1781 he married Marie Anne Cerré; and by her he had twelve children. See P. G. Roy, *Le famille Panet* (Lévis, 1906).

**Panet, Pierre Méru** (1731-1804), executive councillor of Lower Canada, was born in Paris, France, in 1731, the fourth child of Jean Nicolas Panet and Marie Françoise Foucher, and brother of Jean Claude Panet (q.v.). He joined his brother in Quebec in 1746, and in 1754 he was appointed royal notary for Montreal. In 1761 he was named clerk of the court of captains of militia in Montreal, during the period of military rule; and in 1768 he became a notary public and barrister in Montreal. In 1778 he succeeded his brother as a judge of the court of common pleas for Quebec, and he sat on the bench until his retirement in 1784. In 1791 he was appointed a member of the executive council of Lower Canada; and he died at Montreal on June 15, 1804. In 1754 he married Marie Anne Trefflé Rottot, and by her he had seventeen children. See P. G. Roy, *La famille Panet* (Lévis, 1906).

**Panet,** a village in Montmagny county, Quebec, 9 miles from Daaquam Station on the Canadian National Railway. It was named after the Hon. Pierre Louis Panet (q.v.). Pop. (1934), 300.

**Pangman, John** (1808-1867), legislative councillor of Lower Canada, was the son of Peter Pangman (q.v.) and was born on November 13, 1808. He inherited his father's estate at Mascouche, Lower Canada, and was the seignior of Lachenaie. In 1837-8 he was a member of the Legislative Council of

Lower Canada. He died on January 5, 1867. He was twice married, (1) in 1835 to Marie Henriette, daughter of the Hon. Janvier Lacroix, by whom he had three sons and two daughters, and (2) in 1857 to Georgiana, daughter of Dr. Robertson, of Montreal, by whom he had one son.

**Pangman, Peter** (1744?-1819), fur-trader, was born in New England, of German descent, about 1744. He engaged in the fur-trade; and in 1767 his name appears in the Michilimackinac licences as trading to the Mississippi. In 1774 he transferred his energies to the Saskatchewan; and he was engaged in the fur-trade on the Saskatchewan almost continuously until 1790. In 1783 he joined Gregory, McLeod, and Co.; and in 1787, when this firm was absorbed by the North West Company, he became a partner in the North West Company. He retired from the fur-trade about 1794; and in that year he purchased the seigniory of Lachenaie, in Lower Canada; and here he died on August 28, 1819. He had a half-breed son, commonly known after him as "Bastonnais Pangman", who was prominent in the Seven Oaks affair on the Red river in 1816; and in 1796 he married Grace MacTier, by whom he had one son (q.v.) and one daughter.

**Pangman, mount,** is on the boundary between British Columbia and Alberta, at the head of the Valenciennes river, in the Rocky mountains, in the Kootenay district. It is in lat. 51° 46', and long. 116° 58', and has an altitude of 10,420 feet. It is named after Peter Pangman, fur-trader (q.v.).

**Pangnirtung,** a mission station and a post of the Canadian Mounted Police, on Baffin island, at the head of Cumberland sound. The name is Eskimo for "the place of the caribou stag". The village, which is the centre for about 400 Eskimo, has a Church of England hospital.

**Papaw,** a tree belonging to the genus *Asimina* Adanson. Six species are known, one only (*A. triloba* Duval) occurring in Canada, where it is confined to southern Ontario. It is readily recognized by its leaves, which are without teeth, 8 inches to a foot in length, with a long tapered base, and broadest above the middle. The fruit, which is edible, is very variable in shape, usually three or more inches long, and contains a few large flat seeds. The wood is of no importance commercially.

**Paper-Making.** See **Pulp and Paper Industry.**

**Papin, Joseph** (1825-1862), lawyer and politician, was born at L'Assomption, Lower Canada, on December 14, 1825, was educated at L'Assomption College, and studied law in Montreal. He was one of the early members of the Institut Canadien of Montreal, of which he was president in 1847, and he was described as the "Danton" of the *Parti rouge*. From 1854 to 1857 he represented L'Assomption in the Legislative Assembly of Canada. He was then appointed counsel to the corporation of Montreal; and he died at L'Assomption on February 23, 1862.

**Papinachois river** is a tributary of the St. Lawrence river, flowing into it below the Bersimis river, on the north shore in Saguenay county. It has a length of 35 miles.

**Papineau, Denis Benjamin** (1789-1854), commissioner of crown lands for Canada (1844-7), was born in Montreal on November 13, 1789, the son of Joseph Papineau (q.v.) and Marie-Rosalie Cherrier, and the younger brother of Louis Joseph Papineau (q.v.). He did not share his brother's political views, and he took no part in the rebellions of 1837-8. In 1842 he was elected to represent Ottawa county in the Legislative Assembly of Canada; and in 1844, at the invitation of Sir Charles Metcalfe (q.v.), he entered the executive council as commissioner of crown lands. It was he who introduced the bill authorizing the official use of the French language in the Assembly; though the bill did not become law until 1848, under the Baldwin-Lafontaine administration. He failed, however, to win over the support of any considerable number of French Canadians, and his partial deafness hindered his effectiveness both in the assembly and in the cabinet. In 1847, therefore, he was persuaded to retire from office; and later in the same year he withdrew from the Assembly. Until his brother, Louis Joseph, returned from exile in 1846, he devoted his energies to the development of his father's seigniory of La Petite-Nation, to which he had gone as a settler in 1809, and he was its directing spirit. In 1853 he founded Papineauville. He died at Plaisance, Canada East, on January 20, 1854. In 1813 he married Louise Angélique, daughter of Michel Cornud, a merchant of Quebec; and he had by her five sons and four daughters. The best-known of his sons were Denis Emery Papineau (1819-1898), a notary public who represented Ottawa county in the Legislative Assembly of Canada from 1858 to 1861, and the Hon. Augustin Cyrille Papineau (1829-1913), who was a judge of the superior court for the district of Montreal.

**Papineau, Joseph** (1752-1841), notary public and politician, was born at Montreal, on October 16, 1752, the son of Joseph Papineau and Marie-Josèphe Beaudry. He was educated at the Montreal and Quebec Seminaries, and was commissioned a surveyor in 1773 and a notary public in 1780. In 1776 he was one of two volunteers who carried dispatches from Montreal to Sir Guy Carleton (q.v.) at Quebec, through the American lines. He sat in the Legislative Assembly of Lower Canada from 1792 to 1804, and from 1809 to 1814, for Montreal county or Montreal East. In 1801 he bought the seigniory of La Petite Nation, on the Ottawa river;

and here he lived until 1818, when he sold the seigniory to his son Louis Joseph (q.v.), and went to live in Montreal. Here he died on July 8, 1841. In 1779 he married Marie-Rosalie Cherrier; and by her he had seven sons and three daughters. See L. O. David, *Les deux Papineau* (Montreal, 1896) and *Biographies et portraits* (Montreal, 1876).

**Papineau, Louis Joseph** (1786-1871), rebel, was born in Montreal on October 7, 1786, the son of Joseph Papineau (q.v.) and Rosalie Cherrier. He was educated at the Quebec Seminary, and was called to the bar of Lower Canada in 1811. He served as an officer in the Canadian militia during the War of 1812, and was present at the capture of Detroit. In 1814 he was elected to represent Montreal West in the Legislative Assembly of Lower Canada; in 1815 he was chosen speaker of the Assembly; and he sat for Montreal West continuously, and he occupied the speaker's chair almost continuously, until the rebellion of 1837-8. During this period he came to be regarded as the leader of the French-Canadian reformers or *patriotes*, and their chief spokesman. In 1820 Lord Dalhousie (q.v.) induced him to accept a seat in the executive council; but he found his advice disregarded, and soon resigned from the council. In 1822 he took a leading part in opposing the abortive union bill of that year, and went to London with John Neilson (q.v.) to protest against it. After this he became bitterly hostile to the British government in Canada; and not even Lord Gosford (q.v.) was able to conciliate him. His policy resulted in the rebellion of 1837, though he himself took no active part in the rebellion, and fled to the United States soon after the outbreak of hostilities. He remained in the United States until 1839, vainly endeavouring to bring about American intervention in the Canadian struggle; and then he went to France. He lived in Paris until, in 1844, the Canadian government granted an amnesty to the rebels of 1837; and under the amnesty he returned to Canada. Here he re-entered politics; and from 1848 to 1851 he represented Saint Maurice, and from 1852 to 1854 Deux-Montagnes, in the Legislative Assembly of Canada. But he did not regain his former command-ing position in the House; and in 1854 he retired to private life, on his seigniory of La Petite Nation, on the Ottawa river. Here he died, at his manor-house of Montebello, on September 23, 1871. In 1818 he married Julie Bruneau; and by her he had several children. One of his daughters was the mother of Henri Bourassa, noted politician and publicist, and former director of *Le Devoir*.

Papineau's place in Canadian history is difficult to define. Though he was re-garded as the leader of the *patriotes* for so many years before 1837, he was, as the historian Christie has pointed out, a man who followed, rather than led, public opinion. Nor were his political views enlightened. He was not an advocate of responsible government; but his solution of the difficulties of Lower Canada lay in an elective upper house. His apparent vacillation and pusillanimity at the time of the rebellion of 1837 brought much discredit on him; and in his later days he lost almost entirely his hold on his compatriots. He lent his support to the Institut Canadien, and he may be regarded as having been a sort of godfather to the *Parti rouge*. Herein lies, perhaps, his chief importance in Canadian history.

See A. D. DeCelles, *Papineau* (Mont-real, 1905), and *Papineau, Cartier* (To-ronto, 1904); E. Circé-Côté, *Papineau, son influence* (Montreal, 1924); L. O. David, *Les deux Papineau* (Montreal, 1896); N. Story, *Papineau in exile* (Can. hist. rev., 1929), and R. Rumilly, *Papineau* (Paris, 1934).

**Papineau, Samuel** (1670-1737), pioneer, was born in Montigny, Poitou, near Bordeaux, France, in 1670. He was a soldier, and came to Canada in 1695. In 1699 he obtained a grant of land from the Sulpicians in the seigniory of Ville Marie (Montreal), at Côte St. Michel; and he died at Sault-au-Recollet, Montreal, in 1737. In 1704 he married Catherine Quevillon, of Rivière des Prairies; and he became the founder of the Papineau family in Canada. His descendants are to be found, not only in the different provinces of Canada, but also in the United States and in England. He was surnamed Montigny, after his place of origin, to distinguish him from others who had taken the name of Papineau, like the Papineau surnamed Deslauriers and the Papineau surnamed Fortville. These had taken the name Papineau, as some of their people had married into the Papineau family. Even to-day some of the Papi-neaus are known by the name of Mon-tigny.

**Papineau, Talbot Mercer** (1883-1917), lawyer and soldier, was born at the manor-house of Montebello on March 25, 1883, the son of Louis Joseph Papineau and Caroline Rogers, of Philadelphia, and the great-grandson of the Hon. Louis Joseph Papineau (q.v.). He was educated at Oxford University (B.A., 1908), and on his return to Canada was called to the Quebec bar. In August, 1914, he joined the Princess Patricia's Canadian Light Infantry; he won the Military Cross in France, and rose to the rank of major. He was killed at Paschendaele on October 30, 1917. He was the author of "An open letter to Mr. Henri Bourassa" in *Canadian nationalism and the war* (Montreal, 1916). With his death, a career of great promise was cut short.

**Papineauville,** a village in Papineau county, Quebec, on the Ottawa river, and on the Canadian Pacific Railway, 85 miles west of Montreal. Founded in 1853, it was incorporated in 1896, and was named in honour of Louis Joseph Papineau (q.v.), whose family owned the seigniory of La Petite Nation, in which the village is situated. The principal industries are farming, lumbering, and dairying; and the village contains a juniorate and novitiate of the Marists and two convents. Pop. (1931), 954.

**Parent, Amand** (1818-1907), clergyman, was born at Quebec, Lower Canada, in 1818, the son of French-Canadian Roman Catholic parents. In 1840 he was converted to Protestantism, and in 1856 he became a missionary of the Methodist Church, the first French-Canadian to be ordained in this denomination. He died at Waterloo, Quebec, on February 18, 1907. He wrote an autobiography, entitled *The life of the Rev. Amand Parent* (Toronto, 1887), describing "fifty-seven years' experience in the evangelical work in Canada, thirty-one years in connection with the [Methodist] Conference, and eight years among the Oka Indians."

**Parent, Étienne** (1801-1874), journalist, was born at Beauport, near Quebec, Lower Canada, on May 2, 1801, and was educated at the College of Nicolet and the Quebec Seminary. From 1822 to 1825 he was editor of *Le Canadien* in Quebec; and in 1831, after several years devoted to the study of law, he revived this journal, and again became its editor. In this position he achieved an unrivalled place in French-Canadian journalism. He supported L. J. Papineau (q.v.) up to the outbreak of the rebellion of 1837; and, though he did not take part in the rebellion, he was arrested in 1837 and imprisoned. In 1841 he was elected for the county of Saguenay to the first Legislative Assembly of united Canada; but in 1842 a serious deafness, contracted in prison, compelled him to resign his seat. In the same year he gave up the editorship of *Le Canadien*, and accepted the post of clerk of the executive council. In 1847 he was appointed under-secretary for Lower Canada; in 1867 he became under-secretary of state for the Dominion; and he retired from office in 1873. He died at Ottawa on December

22, 1874. After his entrance into the civil service, he exerted an influence through public lectures which he delivered before the Institut Canadien and elsewhere; and these were collected and published after his death under the title *Discours* (Quebec, 1878). See B. Sulte, *Mélanges historiques* (Montreal, 1928).

**Parent, Simon Napoléon** (1855-1920), prime minister of Quebec (1900-05), was born at Beauport, near Quebec, Lower Canada, on September 12, 1855, the son of Simon Polycarpe Parent and Lucie Bélanger. He was educated at Laval University (LL.L., 1881; LL.D., 1902), and was called to the bar of Quebec in 1881 (Q.C., 1899). From 1890 to 1905 he represented St. Sauveur as a Liberal in the Legislative Assembly of Quebec; from 1894 to 1905 he was mayor of Quebec; from 1897 to 1900 he was commissioner of lands, mines, and forests in the Marchand administration; and from 1900 to 1905 he was prime minister of Quebec. In 1905 he was appointed chairman of the National Transcontinental Railway Commission, and this position he retained until the defeat of the Laurier government in 1911. He was then appointed chairman of the Quebec Streams Commission; and he died at Montreal on September 7, 1920. In 1877 he married Clara, daughter of Ambroise Gendron; and by her he had a family of four sons and four daughters. In 1902 he was made an LL.D. of Bishop's College, Lennoxville, Quebec.

**Paris,** a town in Brant county, Ontario, situated at the confluence of the Nith and Grand rivers, on the Canadian National and Canadian Pacific Railways, 60 miles south-west of Toronto. An electric railway runs to Brantford (7 miles) and to Galt (14 miles). The place was known as "The Forks of the Grand River" until 1836, when the name was changed to Paris, both for convenience and because of the crude plaster of Paris found in the

PARIS 87 PARKER

locality. The industries include alabastine works, the manufacture of knitted goods, needle works, screendoor and refrigerator factories. Paris is the centre of a rich farming and dairy district. Gypsum deposits are found in the vicinity. The town contains several churches, a splendid community building, a public library, and high, public and separate schools. There is a weekly newspaper (*Paris Star*). Pop. (1931), 4,137.

**Paris, Treaty of (1763)**. This was the treaty of peace, signed on February 10, 1763, which brought to a close the Seven Years' War between Great Britain and France, and by which France ceded Canada to Great Britain. "Canada, with all its dependencies, as well as the island of Cape Breton, and all the other islands and coasts in the gulph and river of St. Lawrence," was handed over to Great Britain; and, in return, the King of Great Britain granted "the liberty of the Catholick religion to the inhabitants of Canada", agreed that the French inhabitants of Canada might withdraw from Canada without hindrance, and gave to French fishermen "the liberty of fishing in the gulph of St. Lawrence" and "the liberty of fishing and drying on a part of the coasts of the island of Newfoundland", as well as the ownership of the islands of St. Pierre and Miquelon, "to serve as a shelter to the French fishermen." Louisiana remained a French possession; but the French posts on the upper Mississippi were ceded to Great Britain, with all the territories occupied by the French fur-traders in the Old North West. For the text of the treaty, see W. Houston, *Documents illustrative of the Canadian constitution* (Toronto, 1891).

**Paris, Treaty of (1783)**. This was the treaty of peace, signed on September 3, 1783, between Great Britain and the United States of America, which brought to an end the American Revolutionary War. By it, Great Britain acknowledged

"the said United States . . . to be free, sovereign, and independent states"; and defined the boundaries between them and what remained of British North America. It granted also to American citizens fishing rights on the banks of Newfoundland and in the gulf of St. Lawrence. An attempt was made to protect the interests of the American loyalists by an agreement that creditors should "meet with no lawful impediment" to the recovery of their debts, and that the American Congress should "earnestly recommend it to the legislatures of the respective states, to provide for the restitution of all estates, rights, and properties which have been confiscated, belonging to real British subjects"; but these clauses remained almost wholly a dead letter. For the full text of the treaty, see W. P. M. Kennedy (ed.), *Documents of the Canadian constitution, 1759-1915* (Toronto, 1918).

**Parke, Thomas** (d. 1864), surveyorgeneral of Canada (1841-5), was a native of Wicklow county, Ireland, who came to Canada in 1820, and became a builder and architect. From 1834 to 1840 he represented Middlesex in the Legislative Assembly of Upper Canada; and from 1841 to 1844 in the Assembly of united Canada. From 1841 to 1845 he was surveyor-general of Canada, but without a seat in the executive council. He died at St. Catharines, Canada West, on January 29, 1864.

**Parker, Daniel McNeill** (1822-1907), physician and politician, was born at Windsor, Nova Scotia, on April 28, 1822, the son of Francis Parker. He was educated at Windsor and at Horton Academy and he studied medicine at Edinburgh University. He practised medicine and surgery for many years in Halifax; and his name became a household word in Nova Scotia. In 1867 he was called to the Legislative Council of Nova Scotia; and he sat in the Council until 1898. He died at Halifax, Nova Scotia, on November 4,

1907. See W. F. Parker, *Daniel McNeill Parker, M.D.: His ancestry and a memoir of his life* (Toronto, 1910).

**Parker, Sir Horatio Gilbert, Bart.** (1862-1932), author, was born at Camden East, Ontario, on November 23, 1862, the eldest son of Joseph Parker. He was educated at the Ottawa Normal School and at Trinity University, Toronto; and was ordained in 1882 a deacon of the Church of England, but did not take orders. In 1885 he went to Australia, and there engaged in journalism. In 1889 he went to England, and turned to the writing of fiction. He achieved a great success as an historical novelist, and entered politics in England. From 1900 to 1918 he represented Gravesend in the British House of Commons, and he became a leading figure in the Unionist party. He was created a knight bachelor in 1902, a baronet in 1915, and a privy councillor in 1916. He died in London, England, on September 6, 1932. In 1895 he married Amy (d. 1925), daughter of Ashley Van Fine, New York. He was the author of the following novels or collections of short stories: *Pierre and his people* (London, 1892), *The chief factor* (New York, 1893), *The trespasser* (London, 1893), *Mrs. Falchion* (London, 1893), *The translation of a savage* (London, 1894), *The trail of the sword* (London, 1895), *When Valmond came to Pontiac* (London, 1895), *An adventurer of the north* (London, 1895), *A Romany of the snows* (New York, 1896), *The pomp of the Lavilettes* (Boston 1896), *The seats of the mighty* (London, 1896), *The battle of the strong* (London, 1898), *The liar* (Boston, 1899), *The hill of pains* (Boston, 1899), *The lane that had no turning* (London, 1900), *The right of way* (London, 1901), *A pardonable liar* (Boston, 1902), *Donovan Pasha* (London, 1902), *A ladder of swords* (London, 1904), *The march of the white guard* (New York, 1906), *The weavers* (London, 1907), *Northern lights* (London, 1909), *Cumner's son* (London, 1910), *The going*

*of the white swan* (New York, 1912), *The judgment house* (London, 1913), *The money master* (London, 1915), *You never know your luck* (London, 1915), *The world for sale* (London, 1916), *Wild youth and another* (London, 1919), *No defence* (London, 1920), *Carnac's folly* (London, 1922), *The power and the glory* (London, 1925), *Tarboe* (London, 1927), and *The promised land* (London, 1928). He was also the author of two books of verse, *A lover's diary* (Chicago, 1894; new ed., London, 1901) and *Embers* (London, privately printed, 1908), a book of travel, *Round the compass in Australia* (London, 1892), and a book on the Great War, *The world in the crucible* (London, 1915). With Claude G. Bryan, he wrote *Old Quebec* (London, 1903), and with Richard Dawson, *The land, the people, and the state* (London, 1910). In 1913 a collected edition of his works was published in New York.

**Parker, William** (1760?-1831), merchant, was born about 1760 in Kilmarnock, Scotland, and came to Canada before 1787. He became the senior partner of Parker, Gerrard, Ogilvy, and Co., which was one of the supply firms of the XY Company. He returned to Great Britain at an early date; and died in London, England, at his house in John Street, America Square, on June 18, 1831, aged 71 years. In his obituary notice he is described as "one of the oldest Canada merchants in London".

**Parkhill,** a town in Middlesex county, Ontario, on the Canadian National Railway, lying midway between Stratford and Sarnia, 40 miles east and west respectively. The town contains five churches, high, public, and separate schools, and a public library. Parkhill is in a farming district; cattle and hogs are shipped in considerable quantities. The industries include saw-mills, brick and tile making, and egg crate factories. A newspaper (*Gazette*) is published. Pop. (1931), 1,030.

**Parkin, Sir George Robert** (1846-1922), educationist and author, was born at Salisbury, New Brunswick, on February 8, 1846, the son of John Parkin. He was educated at the University of New Brunswick (B.A., 1868; M.A., 1873; LL.D., 1894), and at Oxford University. From 1868 to 1872 he was headmaster of the Bathurst Grammar School; from 1874 to 1889 of the Collegiate School, Fredericton; and from 1895 to 1902 of Upper Canada College, Toronto. In 1889 he made a lecture tour of the Empire, at the request of the Imperial Federation League; and in 1902 he was appointed organizing representative of the Rhodes Scholarship Trust. This position he held until his death at London, England, on June 25, 1922. In 1878 he married Annie Connell, daughter of William Fisher, of Fredericton, New Brunswick; and by her he had one son and four daughters. In 1898 he was created a C.M.G., and in 1920 a K.C.M.G. He was a D.C.L. of Trinity University, Toronto (1898), and an LL.D. of McGill University (1903). His chief publications were *Reorganization of the British Empire* (London, 1882), *Round the Empire* (London, 1892), *Imperial federation* (London, 1892), *The great Dominion* (London, 1895), *Edward Thring, headmaster of Uppingham school* (London, 1898), *Sir John Macdonald* (Toronto, Makers of Canada, 1908), and *The Rhodes scholarships* (Toronto, 1912). See Sir J. Willison, *Sir George Parkin* (London, 1929).

**Parkin, John Buckworth** (1816-1875), criminal lawyer, was born at Dewsbury, Yorkshire, England, in 1816, the son of the Rev. Edward Parkin. He came to Canada in 1818, with his father, who was appointed rector of the Church of England at Chambly, Lower Canada; and he was called to the bar of Lower Canada in 1837. He became perhaps the most famous criminal lawyer of his day in Canada; and he died at Quebec in December, 1875. See C.

Langelier, *J. B. Parkin* (Bull. rech. hist., 1897).

**Parks, William Arthur** (1868-1936), palæontologist, was born at Hamilton, Ontario, on December 11, 1868. He was educated at the University of Toronto (B.A., 1892; Ph.D., 1900; LL.D., 1936); and he became a fellow in geology at this university in 1893. He became head of the department of geology, and director of the Royal Ontario Museum of Palæontology; and he retained these positions until shortly before his death at Toronto on October 3, 1936. He was a fellow of the Royal Society of London and of the Royal Society of Canada, and was elected president of the latter in 1926. In 1925 he was elected president of the geological section of the British Association for the Advancement of Science, and in 1927 president of the Palæontological Society of America. He was the author of *Building and ornamental stones of Canada* (2 vols., Ottawa, 1912-14), and co-author with A. P. Coleman of *Elementary geology, with special reference to Canada* (London, 1922); and he was especially noted for the work he did on the dinosaurs of Alberta, with regard to which he published several studies.

**Parksville,** a village on the east coast of Vancouver island, in British Columbia, on the Canadian Pacific Railway, 22 miles north-west of Nanaimo. Pop. (1930), 300.

**Parr, John** (1725-1791), governor of Nova Scotia (1782-91), was born in Dublin, Ireland, on December 20, 1725, the son of John Parr, of Belturbet, county Cavan. He was educated at Trinity High School, and entered the British army as an ensign in 1744. In 1771 he reached the rank of lieutenant-colonel; and in 1782 he was appointed governor of Nova Scotia. It was during his period of office that the Loyalist migration to Nova Scotia took place, and that New Brunswick was made a separate province; and Saint John, New

7

Brunswick, was first named Parrtown in his honour. His commission was changed in 1786 to that of lieutenant-governor of Nova Scotia, instead of governor; and he was thus the last to hold the post of governor and commander-in-chief of Nova Scotia. He died at Halifax on November 25, 1791. In 1761 he married Sara, daughter of Richard Walmesley, of Lancashire; and by her he had three sons and two daughters. See J. S. Macdonald, *Memoir of Governor John Parr* (Coll. Nova Scotia Hist. Soc., 1910), with portrait.

**Parrsboro,** a town in Cumberland county, Nova Scotia, on the north shore of the basin of Minas, and on the Cumberland Railway and Coal Company's line which connects at Springhill with the Canadian National Railway. The name was given in honour of John Parr (q.v.), governor of Nova Scotia from 1782 to 1791. The town has a harbour; and from it are shipped coal and lumber. There is a weekly newspaper (*Record*). Pop. (1931), 1,919.

**Parr-Town.** See **Saint John.**

**Parry, Sir William Edward** (1790-1855), sailor and explorer, was born at Bath, England, on December 19, 1790. He entered the British navy as a midshipman in 1803, and served throughout the Napoleonic wars. In 1818 he accompanied Capt. (afterwards Sir John) Ross (q.v.) on his expedition to the Arctic; in 1819-20 he commanded another expedition, which penetrated to Melville island; in 1821-3 he was in command of an expedition which reached the western end of Fury and Hecla strait; and in 1824-5 he commanded a fourth expedition, but had the misfortune to lose one of his ships in Prince Regent inlet. From 1825 to 1829 he was hydrographer to the admiralty; and in his later years he held a variety of positions. He died at Ems, Germany, whither he had gone for medical treatment, on July 8, 1855. He was knighted in 1829, and was promoted to the rank

of rear-admiral in 1852. He was the author of a *Journal of a voyage for the discovery of a north-west passage from the Atlantic to the Pacific, performed in the years 1819-20* (London, 1821), *Journal of a second voyage for the discovery of a north-west passage, performed in the years 1821-3* (London, 1824), *Journal of a third voyage for the discovery of a north-west passage, performed in the years 1824-5* (London, 1826), and *A narrative of an attempt to reach the North Pole in boats fitted for that purpose, and attached to H. M. ship Hecla, in the year 1827* (London, 1828). An abridgement of the three volumes relating to the north-west passage was published in 5 vols. (London, 1828). See E. Parry, *Memoirs of Rear-Admiral Sir W. Edward Parry, Kt.* (London, 1857).

**Parry, cape,** a promontory on the Arctic coast of the Mackenzie district, at the eastern end of Franklin bay. It was named by Richardson (q.v.) in 1826 after Captain William Edward Parry (q.v.).

**Parry Sound,** a district in northern Ontario, is bounded on the north by the French river and lake Nipissing, on the west by the Georgian bay, on the south by the Muskoka district, and on the east by the Nipissing district. It was called after the town of Parry Sound, which got its name from Sir William Edward Parry (q.v.), the Arctic explorer. It was formed of part of Nipissing district, and made a territorial district in 1870, but was not made a judicial district until 1914. Its boundaries include hundreds of lakes, and the fishing and game is very good. It is about 60 miles square. Pop. (1931), 25,900.

**Parry Sound,** the shire-town of the Parry Sound district of Ontario, situated on the small arm of Georgian bay from which it took its name in 1870, at the mouth of the Seguin river, 150 miles north of Toronto, on the Canadian

National and Canadian Pacific Railways. There is steamship connection with Chicago, Sault Ste. Marie, and other ports. The Seguin river, flowing into the sound at this point, is not navigable, but that adds to the rugged charm of the locality. Parry Sound is known as the gateway to the highlands, and is a popular summer resort, with numerous islands in a good harbour. The town has five churches, two public schools, a high school, and a business college. The chief industries are railway repair shops, machine shops, a saw-mill, and planing mills. There are two weekly newspapers (*Parry Sound Canadian* and *North Star*). Pop. (1931), 3,512.

**Parsnip.** See **Cow Parsnip,** and **Water Parsnip.**

**Parsnip river** rises in the Cariboo district of British Columbia, at 54° 123°, and flows north-west to its junction with the Peace river near the 56th parallel of north latitude. It was discovered by Sir Alexander Mackenzie (q.v.), on his journey to the Pacific in 1793, and, with the Peace, became an important avenue for the fur-trade and further exploration. In 1805 Simon Fraser (q.v.) built a trading-post upon its upper waters. The river is 160 miles in length.

**Parties, Political.** See **History, Political.**

**Parti Rouge,** the name of the Liberal or radical party which sprang up in Lower Canada after the dawn of responsible government in 1849. It owed its inspiration chiefly to Louis Joseph Papineau (q.v.), who returned to Canada in 1844 after having imbibed in the United States and France advanced liberal or republican ideas; but other leaders of the party were A. A. Dorion (q.v.), Joseph Doutre (q.v.), Louis Michel Viger (q.v.), and L. A. Dessaulles (q.v.). Sir Wilfrid Laurier (q.v.) began his political career in the ranks of this party. The platform of the party included universal suffrage, the abolition of property qualifications for members of the legislature, the abolition of tithes and seigniorial tenure, and the wide application of the principle of election to public office. It also opposed the interference of the church in politics; and some of its members were distinctly anti-clerical. The Institut Canadien (q.v.) owed its foundation to members of this group; and the history of the party was closely linked with that of the Institut Canadien. As time went on, the ideas of most of the members of the party moderated; and by Confederation it had merged with the Liberal party in the province of Quebec. See J. S. Willison, *Sir Wilfrid Laurier and the Liberal party* (2 vols., Toronto, 1903).

**Partridge,** a name with a rather confused application, but applying to upland game birds. Strictly, from the ornithologists' viewpoint, it should designate the small species of game birds, such as the "bob-white" (*Colinus virginianus*) and the "mountain quail" (*Oreortyx picta*). The word, however, is rather generally used in Canada for the ruffed grouse (*Bonasa umbellus*). An upland bird, properly known as the European partridge (*Perdix perdix*), has been introduced in various parts of the more southern and settled sections of Canada. It is larger than the bob-white, but smaller than the ruffed grouse, and inhabits open country. Its introduction for purposes of sport has been successful, but the wisdom of such practices in relation to the welfare of native game birds is questionable.

**Partridge Berry** (*Mitchella repens* L., *Rubiaceae*), a small evergreen herb, with smooth trailing stems, and opposite round-ovate shining leaves, which are sometimes variegated with fine white lines. The flowers are very fragrant, and are borne in pairs united by their ovaries. The corolla is white or pinkish, funnel-form, and bearded on the inside. The fruit is a scarlet berry which persists and may be found on the vines along with the present year's flowers. It is common in dry woods, creeping over the roots of trees, especially conifers, across the continent.

**Pas, The.** See **The Pas** and **Fort Pasquia.**

**Paspebiac,** a village in Bonaventure county, Quebec, on the north shore of Chaleur bay, and on the Atlantic, Quebec, and Western Railway, 110 miles west of Gaspé. The name is derived from the Micmac *pipsequiac*, meaning "cloven shoal", and is descriptive of the conformation of the natural basin forming the harbour. The chief industries are lumbering and fishing; and the place is also a summer resort. Pop. (1934), 1,800.

**Passamaquoddy bay,** an inlet of the bay of Fundy, between Maine and New Brunswick. It extends inland for about 15 miles, including the estuary of the St. Croix river, which empties into it; and it has an average breadth of about 10 miles. It contains many islands, and has an irregular shore-line, with many harbours. There are three entrances to the bay, known as the East, Middle, and West Passages, which are guarded by lighthouses. The name is an Indian (Passamaquoddy) word meaning "where the pollock are."

**Passenger Pigeon.** See **Pigeon.**

**Paterson, Charles** (d. 1788), fur-trader, was a trader from Montreal whose name first appears in the fur-trade licences in 1770. He appears on the Saskatchewan in 1774, and in the winter of 1775-6 he made, with Alexander Henry (q.v.) and William Holmes (q.v.), an overland journey to the Assiniboine. He formed a partnership with John McGill (q.v.), and the firm of McGill and Paterson held two shares in the sixteen-share North West Company formed in 1779. About 1783, however, he withdrew from the North West trade, for his name is not found among the partners of the North West Company of that year; and shortly

afterward he became the director for the trade of the Michilimackinac Company in lake Michigan. He was drowned in lake Michigan, off a point still known as Paterson's point, on September 10, 1788; and a vivid account of his death has been left us by J. B. Perrault (q.v.), who was an eyewitness. He had a brother, Allan, who was in partnership with him after 1780, but who retired from the fur-trade after his death, and who married in 1784 Cornelia, the daughter of Capt. John Munro, of Matilda.

**Paterson, Thomas William** (1852-1921), lieutenant-governor of British Columbia (1909-14), was born at Darvel, Ayrshire, Scotland, on December 6, 1852, the son of William Paterson and Margaret Pearson. He came to Canada with his parents in 1855, and was educated in Oxford county, Ontario. He became a railway contractor, built a section of the Canadian Pacific Railway north of lake Superior, and later built a number of railways in British Columbia. From 1902 to 1903 he represented North Victoria in the Legislative Assembly of British Columbia, and from 1903 to 1907 he represented the Islands. In 1909 he was appointed lieutenant-governor of British Columbia; and his term of office expired in 1914. He died at Victoria, British Columbia, on August 29, 1921. In 1886 he married Emma, daughter of the Hon. George Riley, a senator of Canada.

**Paterson, William** (1839-1914), minister of customs for Canada (1897-1911), was born in Hamilton, Upper Canada, on September 19, 1839, the son of James and Martha Paterson, of Aberdeen, Scotland. His parents died from cholera in 1849, and he was adopted by the Rev. Dr. Ferrier, a Presbyterian minister. He was educated at Hamilton and at Caledonia, Haldimand county, Upper Canada, and he went into business in Brantford, Upper Canada. Here he established himself in 1863 as a manufacturer of biscuits and confectionery, and built up a successful business. From 1872 to 1896 he represented South Brant in the Canadian House of Commons; and during the latter part of this period he became one of the leaders of the Liberal party in the House. In 1896 he was defeated for South Brant, but was returned for North Grey, and was appointed controller of customs, and in 1897 minister of customs, in the Laurier administration. This department he administered continuously until the defeat of the Laurier government in 1911, sitting successively for North Grey (1896-1900), for North Wentworth (1900-4), and for Brant (1904-11). In 1902 he was a delegate to the Imperial Conference; and in 1911 he was one of the ministers who negotiated the abortive reciprocity agreement at Washington. He died at Picton, Ontario, on March 18, 1914. In 1863 he married Lucy Olive, daughter of T. C. Davies, of Brantford.

**Paterson-Smyth, John.** See Smyth, John Paterson.

**Patricia,** a district in the extreme north-west of Ontario, is bounded on the north by Hudson bay, on the east by James bay, on the west by the province of Manitoba, and on the south by Kenora, Thunder Bay, and Cochrane districts, or the Albany river. After being part of the "disputed territory" between Manitoba and Ontario, this huge district was added to the province of Ontario in 1912 by the Ontario Boundaries Extension Act of the Dominion government. It was called after Princess Patricia, then in Canada with her father, the Duke of Connaught, who was governor-general of Canada. The district was annexed for judicial purposes to the judicial district of Kenora in 1927, and was called "the Patricia portion" of Kenora. Pop. (1931), 3,973.

**Patrick, Alfred** (1811-1892), civil servant and author, was born in Kingston, Upper Canada, in 1811, and was educated at York, (Toronto) under the Rev. John Strachan (q.v.). He entered the civil service in 1827, and in 1873 was appointed clerk of the House of Commons. He retired on pension in 1880; and he died at Niagara-on-the-Lake on July 18, 1892. He was the author of a *Digest of "Precedents or decisions" by the select committees appointed to try the merits of Upper Canada contested elections, from 1824 to 1849* (Montreal, 1849).

**Patriotes,** the name applied by themselves to the French-Canadian rebels of 1837-8. See A. D. DeCelles, *The "patriotes" of '37* (Toronto, 1916).

**Patrons of Industry.** See **Farmers' Movements.**

**Patterson, Andrew Dickson** (1854-1930), portrait painter, was born at Picton, Ontario, on June 30, 1854, the son of the Hon. Christopher Salmon Patterson (q.v.). He was educated at Upper Canada College, Toronto, and he studied painting in England. He became a portrait-painter in much demand for the painting of Canadian public men; and his work was exhibited at the Chicago and St. Louis World's Fairs and at the Pan-American Exhibition at Buffalo in 1901. In 1886 he was elected a fellow of the Royal Canadian Academy. He died at Montreal, Quebec, on July 31, 1930.

**Patterson, Christopher Salmon** (1823-1893), judge, was born in London, England, in 1823, of Irish parentage, and was educated at the Royal Academical Institution, Belfast, Ireland. He came to Canada in 1845, and in 1851 was called to the bar of Upper Canada (Q.C., 1872). In 1874 he was appointed a judge of the court of Appeal in Ontario; and in 1888 a judge of the Supreme Court of Canada. He died on July 24, 1893. In 1853 he married the daughter of Andrew Dickson, of Glenconway, Antrim, Ireland.

**Patterson, Edward Lloyd Stewart** (d. 1932), banker and author, was born in Strathroy, Ontario, the son of the Rev. Robert Stewart Patterson. He was educated at Gibraltar and in England; but in 1888 returned to Canada, and entered the service of the Eastern Townships Bank at Sherbrooke. In this bank, which was absorbed by the Canadian Bank of Commerce in 1912, he rose to the rank of assistant general manager; and in the Canadian Bank of Commerce he became super-intendent of the Eastern Townships branches. He retired on pension in 1930; and he died at Toronto, Ontario, on September 4, 1932. He was the author of *Banking principles and practice* (New York, 1917), *Domestic and foreign exchange* (New York, 1918), and *Canadian banking* (Toronto, 1932), and, with M. B. Foster, he was co-author of a volume on *Banking* (New York, 1931).

**Patterson, George** (1824-1897), clergyman and historian, was born at Pictou, Nova Scotia, on April 30, 1824, the son of Abraham Patterson and Christiana, daughter of the Rev. James MacGregor (q.v.). He was educated at Pictou Academy and at Dalhousie University (LL.D., 1896); and he was ordained a minister of the Presbyterian Church in 1849. For twenty-seven years he was minister of Green Hill, Pictou; and then he became minister at New Glasgow, Nova Scotia. He died at New Glasgow, Nova Scotia, on October 26, 1897. In 1851 he married Margaret, daughter of Hugh McDonald (q.v.), of Antigonish, Nova Scotia. In addition to a number of historical contributions to the Transactions of the Royal Society of Canada, of which he was elected a member in 1889, he was the author of a *History of the county of Pictou* (Montreal, 1877), and of the following biographies, *Memoir of the Rev. James MacGregor* (Halifax, 1859), *Memoirs of the Revds. S. F. Johnston and J. W. Matheson and Mrs. Mary J. Matheson* (Pictou, 1864), *Missionary life among the cannibals, being the life of the Rev. John Geddie* (Toronto, 1882), and *Sketch*

*of the life and labours of the Rev. John Campbell* (New Glasgow, 1889).

**Patterson, James Colebrooke** (1839-1929), lieutenant-governor of Manitoba (1895-1900), was born in Armagh, Ireland, in 1839, the son of the Rev. James Patterson. He was educated in Dublin, and came to Canada in 1857. After teaching school for a number of years, he was called to the bar of Ontario in 1876, and practised law in Windsor, Ontario. From 1874 to 1878 he represented North Essex in the Legislative Assembly of Ontario; and from 1878 to 1895 he represented successively the constituencies of Essex, North Essex, and West Huron in the Canadian House of Commons. From 1891 to 1895 he was a member of the Abbott, Thompson, and Bowell administrations, holding in turn the portfolios of secretary of state and minister of militia and defence. From 1895 to 1900 he was lieutenant-governor of Manitoba. He then retired to private life, and he died at Ottawa on February 17, 1929.

**Patterson, Walter** (d. 1798), governor-in-chief of the island of St. John (1769-84) and then lieutenant-governor (1784-7), was born in Ireland, the son of William Patterson, of Foxhall, county Donegal. He entered the British army, and saw service in America with the 8th Regiment. In 1769 he was appointed governor-in-chief and captain-general of the island of St. John (Prince Edward Island); and, except for the years 1775-80, which he spent on leave in England, he administered the affairs of the island until 1787. In 1784, however, his commission as governor was withdrawn, and he was appointed lieutenant-governor, and in 1787 he was recalled to answer "serious and secret charges" against him. He was succeeded in the government by Edmund Fanning (q.v.), but did not return to England until 1789. He died in London, England, on September 6, 1798, in great poverty. In 1770 he married in England Hester

Warren; and by her he had "at least four children". By Margaret Hyde, who was ostensibly his wife in Charlottetown, he had two daughters.

**Patterson, William John** (1815-1886), author, was born in Glasgow, Scotland, in 1815, and after some time spent in journalism in the United States, he settled in Montreal. In 1863 he was appointed joint secretary of the Board of Trade and Corn Exchange Association in Montreal, and he held this post until his death in Montreal on June 12, 1886. He was the author of a large number of pamphlets and trade reports, notably *Commercial relations of the British North American provinces* (Montreal, 1866), *Some plain statements about immigration, and its results* (Ottawa, 1872), *Descriptive statement of the great water highways of the Dominion of Canada* (Montreal, 1874), *Brief notes relating to the resources, industries, commerce, and prospects of Newfoundland* (Montreal, 1876), *Two trade letters* (Montreal, 1876), *Another trade letter* (Montreal, 1876), *Trade letter No. IV* (Montreal, 1880), and *The Dominion of Canada* (Montreal, 1883). He published also *Annual reports on the commerce of Montreal* from 1863 to 1882; and also a series of *Statements relating to the home and foreign trade of Canada*.

**Patteson, Thomas Charles** (1836-1907), journalist and civil servant, was born at Patney, Wiltshire, England, on October 5, 1836, the son of the Rev. Thomas Patteson. He was educated at Eton and at Merton College, Oxford (B.A., 1858). He then came to Canada, and in 1863 he was called to the bar of Upper Canada, and entered into partnership with the Hon. John Ross (q.v.). In 1872, when the Toronto *Mail* was established as the organ of the Conservative party, he was appointed its managing editor; and he conducted the *Mail* until 1879. He was then appointed postmaster of Toronto; and this post he held until his death at Toronto on September 21, 1907. In 1867 he married Marie Louise, daughter of Ralph Jones, of Port Hope, Ontario. He was the founder of the Ontario Jockey Club, and was the author of a number of pamphlets, notably *Sporting intelligence* (Toronto, 1866), and *Observations on riding* (Toronto, 1901).

**Patton, James** (1824-1888), solicitor-general for Upper Canada (1862), was born at Prescott, Upper Canada, on June 10, 1824, the son of Major Andrew Patton, a native of St. Andrew's, Fifeshire, Scotland. He was educated at Upper Canada College and King's College, Toronto (LL.D., 1858). He was called to the bar of Upper Canada in 1845 (Q.C., 1862), and he began the practice of law at Barrie, Upper Canada. In 1860 he opened an office in Toronto, and he later became head of the firm of Patton, Osler, and Moss. In 1856 he was elected a member of the Legislative Council of Canada for an eight-year term; but on seeking re-election in 1862, after being appointed solicitor-general for Upper Canada in the Cartier-Macdonald government, he was defeated, resigned his portfolio, and retired from political life. In 1878 he ceased to practise law, and from 1881 to his death he was collector of customs at Toronto. He died at Toronto on October 12, 1888. In 1853 he married Martha Marietta, daughter of Alfred Hooker, of Prescott. From 1860 to 1864 he was vice-chancellor of the University of Toronto; and he was the author of the *Canadian constable's assistant* (Toronto, 1852).

**Paulist Fathers.** The Paulist Fathers, known officially as the Missionary Society of St. Paul the Apostle (C.S.P.), were founded in 1858 at New York. The five co-founders were all converts to the Roman Catholic Church, among whom the leader was Father Isaac T. Hecker. The primary external object of the community was to work among the non-Catholics of the American continent. This object is still their principal aim, although they engage in parish work, conduct Catholic missions, novenas, and retreats, and minister to the needs of Catholic students in Newman clubs. The apostolate to non-Catholics is evidenced in missions to non-Catholics, in the publication by the Paulist Press of many doctrinal pamphlets and books, and in the inauguration of a radio station (WLWL) at New York. The Paulist Fathers have charge of the following churches in the United States and Canada: St. Paul's and Good Shepherd in New York City; St. Mary's, Chicago, Illinois; St. Lawrence's, Minneapolis, Minnesota; St. Mary's, San Francisco, California, to which is attached the Catholic Chinese Social Centre; St. Francis de Sales, Winchester, Tennesee; St. Austin's, Austin, Texas; St. Paul's, Los Angeles, California; St. Peter's, Toronto, Canada. They have also Santa Susanna's, Rome, Italy, placed in charge of the Paulists by Pope Benedict XV for the benefit of English-speaking visitors. In addition, the Paulist Fathers have charge of Newman clubs at the University of California, the University of Texas, the University of Toronto, and the University of California at Los Angeles. See *Paulists and their work* (New York, 1933).

**Payne lake** is in northern Quebec, west of Ungava bay, into which it is drained by the Payne river. It is named after F. F. Payne of the Meteorological Service, Toronto. It has an area of 300 square miles.

**Peace river,** the principal tributary of the Mackenzie, rises in British Columbia, in 56° 120° S.E., flows east and breaks through the Rocky mountains into Alberta, after which it follows a north-easterly course until its junction with the Slave river. The name is derived from Peace point on the river, where the Cree and Beaver Indians settled a dispute about adjacent lands. The river may have been reached by the explorer Peter Pond (q.v.) between 1779 and 1781. Mackenzie (q.v.)

dated the first arrival of white traders on the river as in 1786. Mackenzie himself explored the upper waters of the Peace on his journey to the Pacific in 1792-3. The river soon became a main artery of the fur-trade and an avenue for further exploration. The settlement of its valley as an agricultural area did not commence until early in the twentieth century.

To the headwaters of its tributary, the Finlay, the Peace is 1,054 miles in length. The Peace itself pours turbulent waters for 100 miles through majestic mountain passes, then emerges at Hudson's Hope, British Columbia, and winds its way for another 700 miles through a rich agricultural plateau, the famous Peace valley. The soil and climatic conditions of this area are excellently suitable for agriculture, particularly the growing of wheat, oats, and peas. The area of agricultural country in the Peace valley is estimated at 47,000,000 acres. Since the first trek to this district, settlement has been rapid, and the agricultural production of the Peace valley in 1931 exceeded that of Alberta 25 years before. The islands and banks of the river are extensively wooded, chiefly by poplar. Valuable mineral deposits exist in the Peace valley, including coal, gypsum and salt. The two main water powers of the Peace country proper are the rapids of Rocky Mountain canyon and Vermilion falls and rapids, the former of which has an estimated capacity of 94,000 horse-power. Close enough to the Peace to be a factor in economic development are the Alexandra falls on Hay river and the rapids on Slave river between Forts Fitzgerald and Smith. See John M. Imrie, *The valley of the Peace* (Canadian Geographical Journal, June, 1931); H. M. Leppard, *The settlement of the Peace river country* (Geographic Review, January, 1935), and O. A. Dawson and R. W. Murchie, *The settlement of the Peace river country* (Toronto, 1934).

**Peace River,** a town in northern Alberta, on the Peace river, and on the Northern Alberta Railways, 320 miles north-west of Edmonton. It has long been a centre of the fur-trade; is in a growing agricultural district; and it has saw-mills, a creamery, brick and lime works, a hospital, and two weekly newspapers (*Northern Gazette* and *Record*). Pop. (1934), 864. See O. A. Dawson and R. W. Murchie, *The settlement of the Peace river country* (Toronto, 1934), and Mary P. Jackson, *On the last frontier* (London, 1935).

**Peace River pass,** the gorge through the Rocky mountains cut by the Peace river. This was the route through the mountains taken by Sir Alexander Mackenzie (q.v.) on his epoch-making journey to the Pacific in 1793. He passed through the northerly part of the mountains by the Peace river, turned south up the Parsnip river, and crossed the continental divide at a place about 70 miles west of the present boundary between Alberta and British Columbia. Simon Fraser (q.v.) also followed this route when he explored the Fraser in 1805, and established the first trading post on the western side of the mountains; but in later years the route fell into comparative disuse.

**Peach.** See **Cherry.**

**Peachland,** a village in the Osoyoos district of British Columbia, on the west side of Okanagan lake, 20 miles north of Penticton. It has a high school, and is noted for its orchards. The nearest railway is at Vernon, at the head of Okanagan lake. Pop. (1930), 500.

**Peck, Edmund James** (1850-1924), missionary and grammarian, was born at Rusholme, near Manchester, England, on April 15, 1850. He spent over ten years in the British navy; but in 1875 he entered the training institute of the Church Missionary Society, and in 1876 was sent as a missionary to the Eskimo in Hudson bay. Here he re-mained for the greater part of his life. He died in Toronto, Ontario, on September 10, 1924. His *Eskimo grammar* was published by the Geographic Board of Canada (Ottawa, 1919; new ed., 1931). See A. Lewis, *The life and work of E. J. Peck among the Eskimos* (London, 1904).

**Pedagogy,** or the science of education, has been taught in normal schools in most of the provinces of Canada for the greater part of a century. See **Education, Primary,** under the sub-heading of "Teacher-Training". It has been only, however, since the dawn of the twentieth century that the subject has found a formal place in the curricula of colleges and universities. One of the first, if not the first, university to establish a course in pedagogy was Acadia, which offered it as an elective course in 1901. A faculty of education (now the Ontario College of Education) was created at the University of Toronto in 1907, and a chair in education was founded at McGill University in 1908. Queen's University organized a school of education in 1912, but this was discontinued in 1920. Pedagogy is now taught, and teachers are trained, in the following colleges and universities: Prince of Wales College, Charlottetown, Prince Edward Island; Acadia, Dalhousie, and St. Francis Xavier Universities, Nova Scotia; Mount Allison University and the University of New Brunswick, New Brunswick; Laval University, McGill University, the Institute of Pedagogy (Montreal), and Bishop's University, Quebec; the University of Toronto, Ontario; the University of Manitoba; the University of Saskatchewan; the University of Alberta; and the University of British Columbia.

**Pedley, James William** (1856-1933), clergyman and author, was born at Chester-le-Street, Durham, England, in 1856. He was educated at McGill University (B.A., 1884), and became a Congregationalist minister. He was the pastor of churches in Georgetown,

Ontario, in Vancouver, British Columbia, and in London and Toronto, Ontario. He died in Toronto on May 24, 1933. He was the author of a *Biography of Lord Strathcona and Mount Royal* (Toronto, 1915).

**Peel, Paul** (1859-1892), painter, was born in London, Ontario, in 1859, the son of John Peel. He studied art at the Pennsylvania Academy of Fine Arts in Philadelphia; and in 1880 he went to London, England, and entered the Royal Academy. In 1887 he went to Paris, where he studied under Gérôme, Boulanger, and Constant; and here he worked for the rest of his short life. In 1889 his picture, "Life is bitter," was awarded honourable mention at the Salon; and in 1890 his famous "After the bath," representing the slender nude figures of children before a fire, was awarded a gold medal. In 1890 he came to Canada, and held a sale of his pictures in Toronto; but he returned to France, and he died at Paris on October 25, 1892. In 1890 he was elected a fellow of the Royal Canadian Academy of Arts.

**Peel,** a county in Ontario, is bounded on the east by York county, on the west by Halton and Wellington counties, and on the north by Dufferin and Simcoe counties. In 1788 it was part of the "Nassau District", later called the "Home District". For many years it was part of York county, but in 1865 it was made a separate county. Settlement began about 1807, but received a check during the War of 1812-5, and there was very little settlement until 1819. Peel is called after Sir Robert Peel (1788-1850). The county town is Brampton. Pop. (1931), 28,156. The Perkins Bull Historical Foundation is publishing a series of histories of the county of Peel, amongst which have appeared the following: *From medicine-man to medical man* (Toronto, 1934); *From rattlesnake hunt to hockey* (Toronto, 1934); *From Brock to Currie* (Toronto, 1935); and *From the Boyne to Brampton* (Toronto,

1936). See also *Illustrated atlas of Peel county* (Toronto, 1877); Peel County Municipal Council, *Description of roads* (Brampton, 1880); and Emily P. Weaver, *The counties of Ontario* (Toronto, 1913).

**Peel sound,** the passage between Somerset island and Prince of Wales island, in the Franklin district of the North West Territories, between the 95th and 97th parallels of longitude. It was named after Sir Robert Peel (1788-1850).

**Peerless lake** is in northern Alberta, between the 56th and 57th parallels of latitude and between the 114th and 115th meridians of west longitude. It is so called from the "peerless" beauty of its blue water. It has an area of 75 square miles.

**Pefferlaw,** a village in York county, Ontario, on the Black river, and on the Canadian Northern Ontario Railway, 60 miles north-east of Toronto. Pop. (1934), 200.

**Pegmatite,** a very coarse-grained rock which occurs in veins or dikes. Commonly pegmatite has much the composition of granite, and consists of quartz microcline and either muscovite or biotite. These dikes are the home of many rare minerals, and it is common to find intimate intergrowth of quartz and feldspar called graphic granite, because in cross section the quartz crystals resemble certain ancient types of writing. These dikes are the chief source of the commercial feldspar, microcline, which is employed in the manufacture of pottery.

**Pekan.** See **Fisher.**

**Pelee island** is the southernmost portion of Canada (except for Middle island, which is negligible in size), in lake Erie, just north of the lake Erie shore of the state of Ohio. It lies in lat. 41° 36′, and according to the Salter survey of 1834, it comprised 11,549 acres, of which 5,413 acres were marsh. The name is derived from the

French *pelée*, meaning "bare" or "bald". In 1823, William McCormick purchased Pelee island for $500, but it already had a history, having been leased by Thomas McKee from the Indians in 1788. In 1834, William McCormick moved to the island to found an ancestral estate for his family alone, but already other names are found amongst the inhabitants. Later descendants sold parts of the island, which became one of great opportunities for grape-growing and wine-making, and, after Dr. John F. Scudder started the dredging of the marshes in 1885, of vegetable and tobacco raising. Tobacco is the main product of the island taken as a whole. The climate is healthful, but as visitors who come to live there generally stay, the island is mainly possessed by all-year round residents. See Raymond Knister, *Pelee Island* (Canadian Geographical Journal, 1933), and J. J. Bell, *Pelee Island, a misnomer* (Can. mag., 1909).

**Pelican,** a name applied with specific prefixes to the large fish-eating waterfowl, remarkable for the enormous pouch formed by the extensible skin between their long lower jaws. One species, the white pelican (*Pelecanus erythrorhynchos*), is locally common in the western provinces. It nests on low islands in the prairie lakes. During migration an occasional straggler is observed east of the Ontario-Manitoba boundary. Two races of the brown pelican (*Pelecanus occidentalis*), both of which are of more southern distribution, are occasionally recorded at southern points in Canada along the sea coasts.

**Pelican lake** lies west of lake Winnipegosis, Manitoba, and between the 52nd and 53rd parallels of north latitude. It has an area of 80 square miles.

**Pelletier, Sir Charles Alphonse Pantaléon** (1837-1911), lieutenant-governor of Quebec (1908-11), was born at Rivière Ouelle, Lower Canada, on Janu-ary 22, 1837, the youngest son of J. M. Pelletier and Julie Painchaud. He was educated at the College of Ste. Anne de la Pocatière and at Laval University (B.L., 1858), and was called to the bar of Lower Canada in 1860 (Q.C., 1879). From 1869 to 1877 he sat for Kamouraska as a Liberal in the Canadian House of Commons; and he represented Quebec East in the Legislative Assembly of Quebec from 1873 to the abolition of dual representation in 1874. In 1872 he was one of the founders of the *parti national*. In 1877 he was called to the Senate of Canada, and from 1877 to 1878 he was minister of agriculture in the Mackenzie administration. From 1896 to 1901 he was speaker of the Senate; but in 1904 he resigned from the Senate, and was appointed a judge of the Superior Court of Quebec. This position, in turn, he resigned in 1908, to accept appointment as lieutenant-governor of Quebec. He died in office, at Quebec, on April 29, 1911. He was twice married, (1) in 1862 to Suzanne, daughter of the Hon. C. E. Casgrain, and (2) in 1866 to Virginie, daughter of the Hon. M. P. de Sales La Terrière; and he had one son. In 1878 he was created a C.M.G.; and in 1898 a K.C.M.G.

**Pelletier, Louis Philippe** (1857-1921), postmaster-general of Canada (1911-14), was born at Trois Pistoles, Quebec, on February 2, 1857, the son of Thomas Philippe Pelletier and Caroline, sister of Sir Louis Napoléon Casault (q.v.). He was educated at the College of Ste. Anne de la Pocatière and at Laval University, Quebec, and was called to the bar in 1880. He was a member of the Quebec legislature from 1888 to 1904; and he was provincial secretary in the Boucherville and Taillon governments from 1891 to 1896, and attorney-general in the Flynn government from 1896 to 1897. In 1911 he was elected to represent Quebec county in the Canadian House of Commons; and from 1911 to 1914 he was postmaster-general in the Borden government. He retired from office, because of ill-health, in 1914, and was appointed a judge of Supreme Court of the province of Quebec. He died at Quebec on February 8, 1921.

**Pelly, Sir John Henry, Bart.** (1777-1852), governor of the Hudson's Bay Company, was born on March 31, 1777, the eldest son of Henry Hinde Pelly, of Upton House, Essex, England. He became a director of the Hudson's Bay Company in 1806, deputy-governor in 1812, and governor in 1822. He died at Upton House on August 13, 1852. In 1840 he was created a baronet of the United Kingdom. In 1807 he married Emma, daughter of Henry Boulton, of Thorncroft, Surrey; and by her he had a large family. Several places in the Hudson's Bay Territories were named after him. See D. R. Pelly, *The Pelly family in England*, printed for private circulation (1912).

**Pelly, Robert Parker** (*fl.* 1790-1825), governor of Assiniboia (1823-5), was born in England on January 10, 1790, and was a cousin of Sir John Henry Pelly, Bart. He was a captain in the East India Company's service; but from 1823 to 1825 he was governor of Assiniboia in the Hudson's Bay Company's territories. The date of his death does not appear to be known. See D. R. Pelly, *The Pelly family in England*, printed for private circulation (1912).

**Pelly lake** is in the North West territories, about the 66th parallel of north latitude, in the basin of Backs river. It was discovered in 1834 by Sir George Back (q.v.), a famous Arctic explorer, and named after Sir John Henry Pelly (q.v.), governor of the Hudson's Bay Company (1822-51). It has an area of 331 square miles.

**Pelly river** rises in the Yukon territory near its eastern boundary and between the 62nd and 63rd parallels of north latitude, and flows in a north-westerly direction until its junction with the Yukon river. It was discovered in 1840 by Robert Campbell (q.v.) of the Hudson's Bay Company, who had ascended the Liard and the Frances rivers in his search for a great river flowing toward the west or north-west. Campbell named his discovery after Sir John Henry Pelly (q.v.), governor of the Hudson's Bay Company (1822-51). The river is 330 miles in length.

**Pemaquid,** a post on the coast of what is now the state of Maine, between the mouths of the Penobscot and Kennebec rivers. It was established by the English in 1677, captured by the Abnaki in 1689, rebuilt by the English in 1692, and captured by the French under Iberville (q.v.) in 1697. See J. H. Cartland, *Ten years at Pemaquid* (Pemaquid Beach, 1899) and V. H. Paltsits, *Depredations at Pemaquid* (Portland, Maine, 1905).

**Pembina.** See **Fort Pembina.**

**Pembina river,** in southern Manitoba, rises near the American border, in Morton county, and flows eastward; it crosses the boundary line into the United States between the 99th and 98th meridians of west longitude and joins the Red river at St. Vincent just before it enters Canada. The name is an Indian word meaning "summer-berry". It is possible that La Vérendrye (q.v.) and his sons may have ascended the Red river to the entrance of the Pembina before 1737. It is a rapid, turbid stream, abounding in pike and other fish, and occasionally widening into beautiful lakes.

**Pembroke,** a town in Renfrew county, Ontario, situated on the Indian Muskrat and Ottawa rivers, and on the Canadian Pacific and Canadian National Railways, 96 miles north-west of Ottawa. A settlement was formed here in 1843, and it was named in honour of the Hon. Sidney Herbert, son of the Earl of Pembroke, who was prominent in the British navy at that time. The town possesses several churches and public schools, a collegiate institute, a convent, and two hospitals. The industries include lumber mills, machine shops, foundries, a steel furniture factory, and two creameries. Good hunting and trout fishing are to be had in Algonquin national park, about 10 miles west of Pembroke. In the season there is a ferry running hourly to Allumette island. Pembroke has a weekly newspaper (*Standard-Observer*). Pop. (1931), 9,368.

**Pemmican,** a form of concentrated food derived by the western fur-traders from the Indians of the Plains. It was composed of buffalo meat, dried in the sun and pounded fine, and mixed with melted fat; and would keep for many months in a temperate climate. One pound of pemmican had a food value equivalent to six pounds of fresh meat. It was therefore a food easily transported; and it seems certain that the discovery of pemmican played its part in enabling the early fur-traders from Montreal to reach and exploit the Athabaska country. The name is derived from a Cree word signifying "a mixture", or "something mixed with fat". See B. Cameron, *The romance of pemmican* (Can. mag., 1902).

**Penetangore river,** in Bruce county, Ontario, consists of two principal branches which flow westward and unite at the town of Kincardine before entering lake Huron on its eastern shore. The name is the corruption of an Indian name, *No-benem-tow-gaugh*, meaning "the river with the sand on one side". The river is exceedingly serpentine, and runs through a broad valley composed of rich flats, which lie at a depth of 50 or 60 feet below the natural surface of the adjoining table land. During dry weather, the water in both streams becomes very low. See Norman Robertson, *The history of the county of Bruce* (Toronto, 1906).

**Penetanguishene,** a town in Simcoe county, Ontario, is situated on an inlet of the Georgian bay, 100 miles north of

Toronto. It is on the Canadian National Railway, and has steamboat connection with all Great lakes ports. The oldest historical spot in Canada, west of the city of Quebec, it was visited by Father Le Caron (q.v.) in 1615, and a little later in the same year by Champlain (q.v.). Here too rested Brébeuf (q.v.) and Lalemant (q.v.) and other devoted missionaries to Huronia. In 1793 John Graves Simcoe (q.v.), after whom the county is named, visited the harbour with a view to establishing there a military and naval station. This was done in 1813. A blockhouse was built, a magazine for ammunition established on Magazine island, officers' quarters erected and vessels outfitted. In 1825 Sir John Franklin (q.v.) landed here on his way to the Arctic regions. In 1830 the government of Upper Canada opened a post office and in 1878 the first train arrived. The town has a number of prosperous industries, and is a popular summer resort. It has a weekly newspaper (*Herald*). The name is of Indian origin, and means "the place of the white rolling sands". Pop. (1931), 4,035. See A. C. Osborne, *Old Penetanguishene*, in *Pioneer papers*, published by the Simcoe County Pioneer and Historical Society (Barrie, 1917).

**Penitentiaries.** See **Penology.**

**Penny, Edward Goff** (1820-1881), journalist, was born in Hornsey, London, England, on May 15, 1820, and came to Canada in 1842. He joined the staff of the Montreal *Herald*, and eventually became its editor and one of its proprietors. He was an opponent of Confederation, and published a pamphlet entitled *The proposed British North American confederation: Why it should not be imposed upon the colonies* (Montreal, 1867). In 1874 he was called to the Senate of Canada; and he died at Montreal on October 11, 1881. In 1857 he married Eleanor (d. 1881), daughter of Oliver Smith, of Montreal. See A. G. Penny (ed.), *The annexation movement* (Can. hist. rev., 1924).

**Pennyroyal** (*Hedeoma pulegioides* (L.) Pers., *Labiatae*), a strong-scented little plant found throughout the greater part of the country and flowering in mid-summer. It is low, erect, branched, with the stem 4-angled, and the leaves oblong to ovate. The flowers are in loose axillary whorled clusters; the corolla is purplish blue, small, 2-lipped, and hairy. It grows in dry sandy soil in open woods and fields from Nova Scotia westward.

**Penology.** In 1867 the Dominion government, when it came into being, took over the penal institutions that had been, up to that time, under provincial control. In 1854 a prison containing 80 cells was erected at Halifax, but when it was inspected in 1867 it was found to be dirty and utterly lacking in discipline. New Brunswick at the time of Confederation had a prison near Saint John, with machinery sufficient to keep 80 inmates busy in the manufacture of tubs, brooms, and clothespins. It had neither school nor library. The Dominion government in 1867 took over from Ontario an institution located at Kingston which had been first occupied in 1835, and was considered a very superior institution. In 1911 the new penitentiary building at Prince Albert, Saskatchewan, was projected. This building is regarded as the finest in the penitentiary service, and was the first of a series of notable prison buildings that have since the year 1911 been erected in Canada.

To-day, as Canada is controlled politically by a Dominion government, by provincial legislatures, and by county and city councils, so Canadian penal institutions are controlled by these same units of government. The Dominion government has full charge of penitentiaries and has as its wards in these institutions all persons sentenced by a court for a period of two or more years in a penal institution. The provincial legislatures in a number of cases have provincial institutions that are directly and immediately under their control

through a departmental officer. Ontario has four such institutions; New Brunswick and Nova Scotia have county and city gaols partly under the control of the provincial legislature and partly under the control of a city or of a county council; the county jails of Prince Edward Island are directly under the control of the provincial legislature. Ontario has county and city gaols in addition to its provincial institutions. The department of Justice is charged with the administration of the various penitentiaries of Canada. Seven institutions are included in the system, the two largest of which are at Portsmouth, Ontario, and St. Vincent de Paul, Quebec, while the other five are at Dorchester, New Brunswick; Prince Albert, Saskatchewan; Stony Mountain, Manitoba; New Westminster, British Columbia; and Collins Bay, Ontario. In the fiscal year 1933-4 the average daily population of these institutions was 4,358, but a decline was shown for the fiscal year ending March 31, 1935, the penitentiary population averaging 3,895.

Kingston penitentiary at Portsmouth, Ontario, is a standard Dominion penitentiary. It is a massive, walled, limestone structure with a very superior library and hospital, varied workshops, a large farm, an effective school plant, and two chapels. Inmates are housed in small, clean, well-furnished, well-equipped cells that rise four tiers high, back to back, in enormous well-lighted stone buildings that spread out like the points of a star from a vast central dome. The inmates are forced to keep themselves clean and tidy; are fed, in their cells, large quantities of rough, wholesome food; are given all the work that can possibly be found or created for them; are sometimes confined to their cells on bread and water, or otherwise strictly disciplined; are granted tobacco; are given shortened sentences for good behaviour within the institution; are granted a hearing on each complaint against them, but no control in the government of the penitentiary; are supplied with good books and magazines and encouraged to read them; are taught to read and write and to pass high school and college entrance examinations if capable; are taught any one of fifteen different trades; have a small daily wage put to their credit; are seldom entertained either by moving pictures or concerts, and are never allowed to play games or to take part in any athletic activities. An inmate who shows himself worthy may be released on parole, but there is no system of classification within the penitentiary itself. Contrary to a common belief in the United States, the lash is not used in Canadian penitentiaries for the purpose of discipline. Inmates are lashed under but two conditions, namely, when the court so orders in the sentence, and when the minister of justice grants permission at the request of a warden through the superintendent, in a very extreme case of insubordination. Penitentiary chaplains had their salaries practically doubled a few years ago, which is some indication of the increased respect with which these officers are coming to be regarded in the service. Their work is to hold religious services with the inmates each Sunday, and to arrange conferences with them on spiritual matters during the week. In the past the prevailing idea has been that penitentiaries were a place of punishment only; that it was of small moment whether men were kept in idleness, made to break stones, or given clean, interesting, useful work to do, so long as society was protected from them. Penitentiaries are now fast being regarded as industries—factories to manufacture government material and to remake men. From depraved, neglected, diseased, and crooked material received, their object is to turn out, as their product, good citizens, reformed, and fully qualified to take their places in the world of work.

Nine institutions in various parts of Canada may be classified as industrial farms. These institutions have in common excellent farms and adequate housing accommodation. Meals are not as palatable as in the penitentiaries, but are better than those served in the old-style jails. Each institution has workshops, and a number of the farms pay a small wage to inmates. The old-style jails located west of lake Superior are, four in Manitoba, one in Alberta, and one in British Columbia. Ontario has 46 gaols; Quebec has 25; Nova Scotia has 22; New Brunswick 15; and Prince Edward Island three, making a total for Canada of 111 institutions that may properly be called old-style jails. They are clean, and few inmates escape from them. They have neither schools nor chaplains; neither full-time medical officers nor libraries. It is here that the hardened offender initiates impressionable youths into the ways and means of becoming professional criminals.

A complete survey of Canadian juvenile institutions reveals a total of 24 industrial schools, detention homes, training schools, etc., which are of uneven quality as to equipment, staff, and management. Some of these institutions are organized as a group of families. The boys eat as family groups, sleep and dwell as family groups, and are controlled in family groups. They are trained by a group of experts, including a psychologist. The boys are selected on the basis of age, intelligence, and misdemeanour committed; and are trained in self-government, religion, and the use of money. Juveniles under the age of 16 years to the number of 7,453 were found guilty of various offences in a recent year. Of this total, 5,144 were convicted of "major" offences and 2,309 of "minor" offences, terms which correspond very nearly to "indictable" and "non-indictable" offences, as applied to adults.

Consult M. H. Smith, *Prisons and a changing civilization* (London, 1934); J. E. Jones, *Pioneer crimes and punish-*

*ments* (Toronto, 1924); L. W. Fox, *The modern prison* (London, 1934); F. W. Harland-Edgecumbe, *Prison life in England and North America* (London, 1934), and S. H. Blake, *Our faulty gaol systems* (Toronto, 1896).

**Pense,** a village in Saskatchewan, on the main line of the Canadian Pacific Railway, 17 miles west of Regina. It is in a farming district, and has a weekly newspaper (*Herald*). Pop. (1935), 300.

**Pentagoët.** See **Castine.**

**Pentecost River,** a village in Saguenay county, Quebec, on the north shore of the St. Lawrence, 55 miles below Seven Islands, at the mouth of the Pentecost river. It is a lumbering village. Pop. (1934), 450.

**Penticton,** a city in the Yale district, British Columbia, is situated at the southern extremity of Okanagan lake. It is a divisional point of the Kettle Valley Railway, and a steamboat service connects it with the Canadian Pacific Railway at Okanagan Landing. The name is of Indian origin, and means "the meeting of the ways". Penticton, because of the irrigation system owned and controlled by the municipality, has become famous as a fruit-growing centre, producing apples, apricots, peaches, and other soft fruits of an exceptionally high quality. The city has a high school, a municipal hall, a tourist hotel, and a weekly newspaper (*Herald*). Pop. (1931), 4,640.

**Pentlandite,** a mineral consisting of sulphide of nickel and iron. It is usually massive and disseminated in pyrrhotite. It may be distinguished from pyrrhotite by the presence of a good cleavage, which is octahedral, showing that the mineral is cubic in crystallization. In lustre it is metallic, and it has a light bronze-yellow colour. Occasionally masses 2 in. to 3 in. in diameter are found, but usually it requires microscopic examination to recognize the mineral in the ore. It is probably the chief source of the nickel extracted from the nickeliferous pyrrhotite in the Sudbury district, Ontario.

**Pepperell, Sir William, Bart.** (1696-1759), soldier, was born at Kittery Point, Maine, on June 27, 1696. For many years he was a member of the Council of Massachusetts; and in 1744 he was appointed to command the expedition sent by the English colonies to reduce Louisbourg. In fitting out this expedition, he engaged his whole fortune. He succeeded, with the aid of the British fleet, in capturing Louisbourg in 1745; and in 1746 he was created a baronet. He died on July 6, 1759. See Usher Parsons, *The life of Sir William Pepperell, Bart.* (Boston, 1855).

**Pepperidge.** See **Black Gum.**

**Pepper-root.** See **Toothwort.**

**Percé,** a village in Gaspé county, Quebec, on the gulf of St. Lawrence, 36 miles south of Gaspé basin, and on the Gaspé branch of the Canadian National Railway. It is named after the famous Percé Rock (or Pierced Rock), an island 1,500 feet long and 288 feet high, pierced by a central arch 50 feet in height, which faces it, and has long been a picturesque sea-mark. The village, which is the county town of Gaspé county, is an important fishing centre. Pop. (1931), including the whole municipality, 1,520. See John M. Clarke, *L'Ile Percée, the finial of the St. Lawrence, or Gaspé Flaneries* (New Haven, Conn., 1923), and Alice Wetherell, *The pageantry of Percé* (Canadian Geographical Journal, 1931).

**Perch,** a common spiny-finned freshwater fish (*Perca flavescens*) of eastern North America, closely related to a very similar fish found in northern Europe and Asia, it is marked with a series of black vertical bars. It does not reach a large size, ten inches being about the maximum size normally attained. It is taken to some extent as a commercial fish, especially in lake Erie. It is prized also by rod and line fishermen, especially by boys, since it usually bites readily and is generally distributed. It is a fine pan fish, its flesh being sweet and firm. Spawning occurs in the spring. Off the Pacific coast of America occurs a family of marine fish, members of which are often known as perch, *e.g.*, viviparous perch, white perch, etc. A more suitable name for them is surf-fish (q.v.). The cunner (q.v.) of the Atlantic coast is sometimes called blue perch.

**Perdue,** a village in Saskatchewan, on the Canadian Pacific Railway, 44 miles south-west of Saskatoon. It is in a farming district, and has a weekly newspaper (*Record*). Pop. (1934), 300.

**Peridotite,** a series of plutonic rocks consisting essentially of olivine and one or more dark minerals. Feldspar is completely lacking. Many varieties have been made depending upon the dark mineral that is associated with the olivine. By alteration the rock is converted into serpentine. These rocks are important sources of platinum, chromite, asbestos, and the diamond.

**Péribonka,** a parish in the Lake St. John county, Quebec, on the east side of lake St. John, near the mouth of the Great Péribonka river. It was here that the French novelist Louis Hémon laid the scene of his celebrated novel *Maria Chapdelaine*. The parish is an agricultural and lumbering district. Its name is an Indian word meaning "river cutting through the sand" or "place where the sand is displaced". Pop. (1931), 672.

**Péribonka river** flows between Chicoutimi and Lake St. John counties, Quebec, and empties into lake St. John, of which it is the largest tributary. The river is navigable for small steamboats for a distance of 9 or 10 miles. About 20 miles above lake St. John is a series of 7 falls, covering a distance of 5 or 6 miles, and capable of producing 300,000 horse-power. The river passes through magnificent country which is well-wooded, particularly with spruce. It is 300 miles long, at several points a mile in width, and drains a basin of 12,000 square miles.

**Periodicals.** The periodical literature of Canada covers a vast field. It ranges from daily to annual publications, and it embraces newspapers, almanacs, literary magazines, learned and scientific journals, and trade journals—classes of periodicals which often shade into one another. Of these, almanacs and newspapers are dealt with separately. See **Almanacs** and **Journalism**.

Literary periodicals in Canada have been generally short-lived; but there are a few that deserve especial mention. The first literary periodical to be published in any of the provinces of Canada was the monthly *Nova Scotia Magazine* (Halifax, 1789-93). Almost contemporary with it was the *Quebec Magazine* (Quebec, 1792-4). The first literary periodical to enjoy any length of life, however, was the *Literary Garland* (Montreal, 1838-51). This was followed by the *Canadian Monthly* (Toronto, 1872-8), continued as *Rose-Belford's Canadian Monthly* (Toronto, 1878-82), by the *Week* (Toronto, 1883-96), and by the *Canadian Magazine* (Toronto, 1893—). This last, it should be explained, was the fifth periodical of this title to be launched. The first was the *Canadian Magazine and Literary Repository* (Montreal, 1823-5); then followed the *Canadian Magazine*, edited by W. Sibbald, and the *Canadian Literary Magazine*, edited by John Kent (q.v.), both published in York (Toronto) for a few months in 1833; and lastly, there was the *Canadian Magazine*, edited by R. Ridgeway in Toronto in 1871-2. Mention should be made also of the *Canadian Review and Magazine* (Montreal, 1824-6).

In the twentieth century some of the outstanding literary periodicals in English have been, besides the *Canadian Magazine*, the following: The *Westminster* (1896-1916), the *New Brunswick Magazine* (1898-1904), *Acadiensis* (1901-8), *Maclean's Magazine* (1896—), *Satur-*

8

*day Night* (1887—), the *University Magazine* (1902-20), *Queen's Quarterly* (1893—), the *Canadian Forum* (1920—), the *Dalhousie Review* (1921—), and the *University of Toronto Quarterly* (1931—).

Among French-Canadian literary periodicals the most noteworthy have been the *Bibliothèque Canadienne* (1825-30), the *Revue Canadienne* (1864-1922), *Les Soirées Canadiennes* (1861-5), followed by *Les Nouvelles Soirées Canadiennes* (1882-8), *La Nouvelle-France* (1902-18), the *Canada Français* (1918—), and the *Revue Trimestrielle Canadienne* (1915—).

In the field of learned and scientific journals, reference should be made to the *Canadian Journal* (1852-78), continued as the *Proceedings of the Royal Canadian Institute* (1878—), the *Canadian Entomologist* (1868—), the *Canadian Field Naturalist* (1887—), the *Canadian Journal of Medicine and Surgery* (1897—), the *Review of Historical Publications relating to Canada* (1897-1918), continued as the *Canadian Historical Review* (1920—), the *Canadian Alpine Journal* (1907—), the *Canadian Defence Journal* (1923—), the *Canadian Bar Review* (1923—), the *Canadian Journal of Religious Thought* (1924—), the *Canadian Journal of Research* (1929—), the *Canadian Geographical Journal* (1930—), the *Canadian Journal of Economics and Political Science* (1935—), and the *Canadian Law Journal* (1935—).

Canadian trade journals are numerous, and many of them are of long standing, such as the *Bookseller and Stationer*, which began publication in Toronto in 1884, and the *Canadian Textile Journal*, which began publication in Montreal in 1883. There have been also a great number of religious periodicals, and many of these have had a long history.

Of annual publications, apart from the *Reports* and *Proceedings* of various historical, literary, and scientific societies and associations, special mention should be made of the *Canada Year Book* (1867—), and the *Canadian Annual Review* (1902—).

For an account of Canadian literary periodicals, see Dorothea D. Tod and Audrey Cordingley, *A bibliography of Canadian literary periodicals, 1789-1900* (Trans. Roy. Soc. Can., 1932). For information regarding the duration of individual periodicals and the libraries in which they may be found, see W. Gregory (ed.), *The union list of serials* (New York, 1928), and G. H. Locke and W. S. Wallace (eds.), *A joint catalogue of the periodicals and serials in the libraries of the city of Toronto* (4th ed., Toronto, 1934).

**Periwinkle** or Myrtle (*Vinca minor* L., *Apocynaceae*), a smooth trailing hardy plant with creeping stems, glossy evergreen leaves, ovate-oblong in shape, and pale blue flowers borne on slender stalks in the axils of the leaves. The corolla is funnel-form with spreading lobes. It is found along roadsides, escaped from cultivation, everywhere, blooming from April to June.

**Perley, Sir George Halsey** (1857-1938), acting prime minister of Canada on several occasions, was born at Lebanon, New Hampshire, on September 12, 1857, the son of William G. Perley and Mabel Ticknor Stevens. He was educated at the Grammar School in Ottawa, where his father had engaged in the lumber trade, and at Harvard University (B.A., 1878). He carried on the lumber business founded by his father in the Ottawa valley; and in 1904 he was elected to represent Argenteuil in the Canadian House of Commons. He continued to represent this constituency in the Commons from that date up to his death January 4th, 1938, with the exception of the years from 1917 to 1925, during most of which he was in England. In 1911 he was appointed a minister without portfolio in the Borden government; from 1914 to 1922 he was high commissioner of Canada in London; and in 1916-7 he was minister of the overseas military forces of Canada. He was secretary of state in the short-lived Meighen administration of 1926; and he was a minister without portfolio in the Bennett administration formed in 1930. As senior privy councillor, he was repeatedly during the years 1930-5 acting prime minister. In 1884 he married Annie Hespeler (d. 1910), daughter of Ward H. Bowlby, K.C., Berlin (Kitchener), Ontario, by whom he had one daughter; and in 1913 he married, secondly, Emily Colby, daughter of the Hon. Thomas White (q.v.) He was created a K.C.M.G. in 1915, and a G.C.M.G. in 1933; and in 1932 he was appointed an imperial privy councillor. He died at Ottawa, January 4, 1938.

**Perley, Moses Henry** (1804-1862), writer on the natural history of the Maritime provinces, was born at Maugerville, New Brunswick, on December 31, 1804, the son of Moses Perley and Mary Perley. He was educated at Saint John, New Brunswick, and in 1830 was called to the bar, but practised law only for a short time. He had a varied career. For several years he was engaged in the lumbering business; in 1841 he was appointed special commissioner for Indian affairs in New Brunswick; in 1847 he was sent to England to secure aid in railway-building; he was then employed in investigating the fishery grounds of New Brunswick; from 1851 to 1853 he was engaged in the compilation of trade statistics in connection with the Reciprocity Treaty of 1854; in 1854 he was a commissioner for carrying out the terms of this treaty; and in 1861 he became the editor of the *Colonial Empire* of Saint John, New Brunswick. He died on board H.M.S. *Desperate* off Forteau, Labrador, on August 17, 1862. In 1829 he married Jane, daughter of Isaac Ketchum; and by her he had eight children. He founded the Natural History Society of New Brunswick; and, besides many articles in periodicals, he published the following: *Report on the*

*condition . . . of the Indian tribes of New Brunswick* (Fredericton, n.d.); *Report on the forest trees of New Brunswick* (Fredericton, 1847); *Report on the fisheries of the gulf of St. Lawrence* (Fredericton, 1849); *Report on the fisheries of the bay of Fundy* (Fredericton, 1851); *Catalogue of fishes of New Brunswick and Nova Scotia* (Fredericton, 1851); *Report on the sea and river fisheries of New Brunswick* (Fredericton, 1852); and *Handbook of information for emigrants to New Brunswick* (Saint John, 1854). A lecture *On the early history of New Brunswick*, delivered by him at Saint John in 1841, was edited with notes by W. F. Ganong (Saint John, 1891).

**Perrault, Jean Baptiste** (1761-1844), fur-trader, was born at Three Rivers, Canada, in 1761, the son of Jean Baptiste Perrault and Marie LeMaitre. He was educated at Quebec, and entered the fur-trade about 1783. For ten years he was a trader in the Illinois country; but in 1793 he entered the service of the North West Company as a clerk. He was stationed in the Fond du Lac department until 1799; and from 1799 to 1805 he was in charge at the Pic, on lake Superior. From 1805 to 1806 he was on the St. Maurice and Ottawa rivers; and in 1806 he left the employ of the North West Company. He was subsequently employed by the Pacific Fur Company, by an independent trader, and by the Hudson's Bay Company; but he retired from the service of the Hudson's Bay Company in 1821, and settled at Sault Ste. Marie. Here he died in 1844. He married an Indian woman; and by her he had at least nine children. His *Narrative*, a translation of which has been published in the *Michigan Pioneer and Historical Collections*, vol. 37, 1909-10, is one of the most interesting and valuable documents relating to the history of the fur-trade.

**Perrault, Jean Baptiste Olivier** (1773-1827), executive and legislative councillor of Lower Canada, was born at Quebec on July 22, 1773. He was called to the bar of Lower Canada in 1799, and in 1808 was appointed advocate-general of the province. In 1812 he was appointed a judge of the court of King's Bench for the district of Quebec, and the same year he was sworn of the Executive Council of Lower Canada. In 1818 he became also a member of the Legislative Council. He died at Quebec on March 19, 1827. See P.G.R., *L'Hon. Jean-Baptiste-Olivier Perrault* (Bull. rech. hist., 1902).

**Perrault, Joseph François** (1753-1844), author and educationist, was born in Quebec on June 2, 1753, the son of a fur-trader. He was educated at the Quebec Seminary; and he was engaged in the western fur-trade until 1781. He then began business by himself in Montreal, but he did not prosper, and he turned instead to the study of law. He was called to the bar in 1790; in 1795 he was appointed clerk of the peace at Quebec; and in 1802 he became prothonotary at Quebec. This position he held for the rest of his life. Though largely self-educated, he took a great interest in education and scientific agriculture, and he established at his own expense model schools and experimental farms. He published a large number of books and pamphlets, mainly of a legal or educational character; among them, however, were an *Abrégé de l'histoire du Canada* (5 vols., Quebec, 1832-6) and an autobiography, entitled *Biographie de Joseph-François Perrault . . . écrite par lui-même, à l'âge de quatre-vingt ans, sans lunettes, à la suggestion de Lord Aylmer* (Quebec, 1834). He died at Quebec on April 4, 1844. In 1783 he married Ursule, daughter of Major Richard McCarthy; and by her he had two sons and three daughters. See P. B. Casgrain, *La vie de Joseph François Perrault* (Quebec, 1898).

**Perrault, Joseph Xavier** (1838-1905), agriculturist, was born in Quebec, Lower Canada, on May 28, 1838, the son of Lieut.-Col. Joseph Xavier Perrault, and the grandson of Joseph

François Perrault (q.v.). He was educated at the Quebec Seminary; and he studied agriculture at the University of Durham and at the Royal College at Cirencester, England, and at the National School of Agriculture, Grignon, France. He returned to Canada, and in 1857 he was appointed secretary of the Board of Agriculture. In 1863 he was returned to the Legislative Assembly of Canada for Richelieu; but he opposed Confederation, and was defeated in 1867. In 1887 he founded the Chamber of Commerce at Montreal; and he was the first farmer in Quebec to import Ayrshire cattle and Percheron stallions. He occupied various temporary official positions; and in 1903 he was appointed a secretary of the Royal Transportation Commission. He died on April 9, 1905. In 1866 he married C. F. Couillard, of Montreal. He was an officer of the Legion of Honour of France; and he was the author of a number of books and pamphlets on agricultural and political subjects, notably of a *Traité d'agriculture pratique* (Montreal, 1865).

**Perré, Henri** (1828-1890), painter, was born at Strasbourg, Alsace, in 1828. He took part in the insurrection of 1849 in Saxony, and afterwards fled to the United States. His later years were spent in Canada, and he was for a time on the staff of the Ontario School of Art, the first art school in Toronto. In 1880 he became a charter member of the Royal Canadian Academy; and he died in Toronto in 1890. He painted in a conventional manner, but he did some important work as a landscape-painter.

**Perrot, François Marie** (*fl.* 1669-1691), governor of Montreal (1670-84), was captain of a regiment of Auvergne. In 1669 he was named governor of Montreal by the Sulpicians, and came to Canada with Talon (q.v.) in 1670, arriving at Quebec on August 18. In 1672 he obtained the concession of île Perrot above Montreal, where he established a trading-post, and carried on an illegal traffic with the Indians, exchanging brandy for furs. He encouraged and protected the lawless bands of *coureurs de bois*, and his conduct became so tyrannical that Frontenac (q.v.) had him arrested, imprisoned, and tried before the Superior Council at Quebec in 1674. He was then sent to France and kept for three months in the Bastille; but on his release the governorship of Montreal was restored to him. In 1684, he was appointed governor of Acadia. His malpractices continued here, and, in 1687, he was succeeded by Menneval (q.v.). He remained at Port Royal as a trader; in 1690 he was taken prisoner by Phips (q.v.); and he lost his life at Martinique in 1691. He married, in 1669, Madeleine Laguide Meynier, the niece of Jean Talon (q.v.); and he had by her six children. See P. G. Roy, *François Marie Perrot* (Bull. rech. hist., vol. ii).

**Perrot, Nicolas** (1644?-1717), voyageur, was born in France in 1644. He came to Canada as a child, and was employed by the Jesuits from 1660 to 1665, and, a year later, by the Sulpicians. For the next ten years he was engaged in the fur-trade, and often acted as interpreter for the Algonkin. He became one of the best-known figures of the Upper Lake region. In 1684 he induced a number of the western tribes to join La Barre (q.v.) in his campaign against the Iroquois; and his influence was later of great service to Denonville (q.v.) and Vaudreuil (q.v.). About 1693 he discovered the lead mines of the Mississippi. Because of the decree which abolished all trading privileges, the last ten years of his life were spent in poverty. During this period he composed his memoirs, which were published in 1864 under the title of *Mémoire sur les mœurs, coustumes et religion des sauvages de l'Amérique septentrionale*, with notes by the Jesuit Tailhan; and the book affords an interesting picture of the life of the tribes in the North West. Perrot died on August 13, 1717. He married, sometime after 1665, Madeleine Raclot, by whom he had nine children.

**Perrot island,** or île Perrot, lies at the junction of the Ottawa and St. Lawrence rivers, and is crossed by the Montreal-Toronto highway. It was named after François Marie Perrot (q.v.), governor of Montreal in 1670, to whom the island was granted in 1672. For many years it was a centre for the illicit trade with the Indians during the French period. It is now largely agricultural. Pop. (1930), 1,300.

**Perry, Peter** (1793-1851), politician, was born at Ernestown, near Kingston, Upper Canada, in 1793, the son of Robert Perry, a United Empire Loyalist. He had little education, but by force of character early became an outstanding member of the Reform party in Upper Canada. In 1824 he was elected, with M. S. Bidwell (q.v.), to represent Lennox and Addington in the Legislative Assembly, and he continued to represent this constituency until his defeat in the elections of 1836, partly as the result of the dissemination of a pamphlet by Egerton Ryerson (q.v.) entitled *Peter Perry picked to pieces*. He then left the bay of Quinte region, and opened a general store at a place henceforth known as "Perry's Corners" (now Whitby, Ontario). He did not re-enter public life until 1849, when he became one of the founders of the "Clear Grit" party, and was elected to the Legislative Assembly of united Canada for the east riding of York. He died, not long afterwards, at Saratoga Springs, New York, on August 24, 1851. See G. M. Jones, *The Peter Perry election and the rise of the Clear Grit party* (Ont. Hist. Soc., papers and records, 1914).

**Perth,** a county in the western part of the province of Ontario, is bounded on the west by Huron county, on the north by Wellington county, on the east by Waterloo county, and on the south by Middlesex and Oxford counties. It was originally part of the "Huron

Tract" sold to the Canada Company (q.v.) in 1828. From 1841 to 1850 the county was united with the counties of Huron and Bruce, but withdrew under the Municipal Act of 1850, made effective in 1853. Perth was named after Perthshire in Scotland, from which a large number of early settlers came. The county town is Stratford. Pop. (1931), 51,392. See William Johnston, *History of Perth county, 1825-1902* (Stratford, 1903), and *Illustrated historical atlas of Perth county* (Toronto, 1879).

**Perth,** the county town of Lanark county, Ontario, is situated on the Tay canal and on the Canadian Pacific Railway, 57 miles south-west of Ottawa. In 1847 a settlement was founded here, and named after Perth, Scotland. The canal connects Perth with Ottawa, Kingston, and ports of the Great lakes. The town is in a fine farming district, surrounded by numerous beautiful lakes. It has four churches, public and separate schools, a collegiate institute, and a public library. The manufacturing establishments prepare toilet goods, chemicals, soap, shoes, woollens, felt, iron sleighs, knitted goods, aërated waters, sashes and doors. Two weekly papers are published (*Courier* and *Expositor*). Pop. (1931), 4,099. See A. Hayden, *Pioneer sketches in the district of Bathurst* (Toronto, 1925).

**Perth,** a village in Victoria county, New Brunswick, on the St. John river, and on the Canadian Pacific Railway, 50 miles north of Woodstock. It has a saw-mill, wood-working and canoe factories, and wholesale businesses in drugs and groceries. It has also a weekly newspaper (*Victoria County News*). Pop. (1934), 1,854.

**Petawawa,** a village in Renfrew county, Ontario, situated on the Ottawa river, opposite Allumette island, and on the Canadian Pacific Railway, 10 miles north-west of Pembroke. A settlement was established here in 1857. The name

is a corruption of the Algonkian word *pitwewe*, meaning "when one hears a noise like this", that is, the voice of the waters, according to the Indian fancy. A pulp-and-paper mill in the village takes advantage of the good water-power in the vicinity. Pop. (1934), about 350.

**Peterborough,** a county in the centre of the province of Ontario, is bounded on the north by Haliburton county, on the east by Hastings county, on the west by Victoria and Durham counties, and on the south by Northumberland county, of which it was once "the north riding". It was not until 1863 that the county of Peterborough was separated from the county of Victoria. In 1818 a small colony of settlers came out from the north of England, and settled in Smith township; and in 1825 about 2,000 settlers were brought out by the Hon. Peter Robinson (q.v.) from Ireland. The lift locks on the Trent Valley canal in Peterborough county are among the largest in the world. The county is called after the Hon. Peter Robinson (q.v.). Its area is about 35 to 40 miles. Pop. (1931), 43,958. See *History of the county of Peterborough* (Toronto, 1884); T. W. Poole, *Sketch of the early settlement and subsequent progress of the town and county of Peterborough* (Peterborough, 1867); Frances Stewart, *Our forest home* (Montreal, 1902); W. A. Langton, *Early days in Upper Canada* (Toronto, 1926); and *Illustrated history of the county of Peterborough* (Toronto, 1879).

**Peterborough,** a city in Ontario, the county town of Peterborough county, situated on both banks of the Otonabee river, on the Canadian National and Canadian Pacific Railways, 72 miles north-east of Toronto. The name commemorates the Hon. Peter Robinson (q.v.), who in 1825 founded the town. It was previously known as Indian Plain or Scott's Landing. It was incorporated as a city in 1905. The Otonabee river at this point falls 50 feet in several miles, and provides abundant power for the industries, which include farm-implement mills, hydraulic machinery works, clock-making, textile factories, paper mills, cereal food factories, tent and awning manufacturing mills, and the building of the celebrated motor-boats. Many products are exported *via* the railways, the Trent canal system, and lake Ontario. The countryside is picturesque, and the city is well-planned. There are several parks, a Roman Catholic cathedral, a conservatory of music, seventeen churches, eleven schools, a normal training-school for teachers, a collegiate institute, a technical school, and a business college. The Kawartha lakes, the Otonabee river, and Rice lake attract summer tourists to the district. A daily newspaper (*Examiner*) is published. Pop. (1931), 22,327. See T. W. Poole, *Sketch of the early settlement and subsequent progress of the town and county of Peterborough* (Peterborough, 1867).

**Peter Pond lake** lies at the headwaters of the Churchill river in northern Saskatchewan near the Alberta boundary. It is named after Peter Pond (q.v.) the first white man to visit and map it; he wintered on the Athabaska river in 1778. It has an area of 302 square miles.

**Peters, Frederick** (1852-1919), prime minister of Prince Edward Island (1891-7), was born in Charlottetown, Prince Edward Island, on April 8, 1852, the son of the Hon. James Horsfield Peters and Mary, daughter of Sir Samuel Cunard, Bart. (q.v.). He was educated at King's College, Windsor, Nova Scotia (B.A., 1871), and was called to the bar at the Inner Temple, London, in 1876, and to the bar of Prince Edward Island and of Nova Scotia the same year (Q.C., 1894). He was elected to represent Charlottetown as a Liberal in the Island Assembly in 1890; and from 1891 to 1897 he was prime minister and attorney-general. In the latter year he resigned, and removed to British Columbia. Here he practised law until his death at Prince Rupert, British Columbia, on

July 29, 1919. In 1888 he married the youngest daughter of the Hon. J. H. Gray (q.v.), of Charlottetown.

**Peterson, Sir William** (1856-1921), principal of McGill University (1895-1919), was born at Edinburgh, Scotland, on May 29, 1856, the fifth son of John Peterson and Grace Anderson. He was educated at Edinburgh University (B.A., 1875), at the University of Göttingen, and at Corpus Christi College, Oxford (M.A., 1883); and in 1879 he was appointed assistant professor of humanity in Edinburgh University. From 1882 to 1895 he was principal of University College, Dundee; and in 1895 he was appointed principal of McGill University, Montreal, Canada. This post he occupied until his retirement in 1919, and he died in London, England, on January 4, 1921. In 1885 he married Lisa, daughter of William Ross, of Glenearn, Perthshire, Scotland. In 1901 he was created a C.M.G., and in 1915 a K.C.M.G. He was an LL.D. of St. Andrew's University (1885), of Princeton University (1896), of New Brunswick University (1900), of Yale University (1901), of Johns Hopkins University (1902), of Queen's University, Kingston (1903), of Aberdeen University (1906), of the University of Toronto (1907), and of Harvard University (1909). He was the author of *Canadian essays and addresses* (London, 1915), and the editor of a number of Latin texts. See C. Macmillan, *McGill and its story* (Toronto, 1921).

**Petitclair, Pierre** (1813-1860), poet and dramatist, was born at Quebec in 1813. His later years were spent on the Labrador coast. He was the author of three comedies, *Griphon ou la vengeance d'un valet* (Quebec, 1837), *La donation* (Répertoire nationale, 1848), and *Une partie de campagne* (Quebec, 1865). Some of his verses are printed in J. Huston (ed.), *Le répertoire national* (Montreal, 1848-50). He died at Pointe-au-Pot, Labrador, on August 15, 1860.

See L. M. Darveau, *Nos hommes de lettres* (Montreal, 1873).

**Petitcodiac river,** in Albert and Westmorland counties, New Brunswick, empties into Shepody bay, off Chignecto bay, the north-east arm of the bay of Fundy. The name is a Micmac Indian word meaning "the river bends round in a bow". The river was a favourite Indian route between the Cumberland or Beauséjour region and Quebec. Large Acadian settlements, originally established at the head of the bay of Fundy, spread in part after 1676 to adjacent districts, including the Petitcodiac. Some Acadians, after the expulsion, were permitted by the Nova Scotian government in 1767 to return and found a small settlement at Fox Creek on the Petitcodiac. Subsequently a few loyalists came to the district. The river, which is 100 miles long, is navigable for large vessels up to a distance of 25 miles, for vessels of 60 or 80 tons for 12 miles farther to the head of tide, and for boats and canoes for 50 miles. It is fed by a number of rivers and creeks, of which the principal are Weldon and Strong creeks and the Coverdale and Pollett rivers. The river is an important fertilizer of rich and extensive marshes on its banks, which produce abundant hay. The celebrated "Albert coal" is shipped from Hillsborough, and above it are extensive wharves, from which plaster of Paris is also shipped. The famous tidal bore, which flows up the river past Moncton at a height of from 3 to 5 feet, is a great attraction for tourists. This curiosity results from the fact that the tide is forced through a comparatively narrow channel with steep banks on either side.

**Petite Nation river,** in Quebec, near the 75th meridian of west longitude, flows into the Ottawa river, on its left bank, between the Lièvre and Rouge rivers. The river crossed the hunting grounds of a division of the Algonkin, called by the French, the "Petite Nation" to distinguish them from an-other division called "the Nation". It is 55 miles in length and drains a basin of 110 square miles.

**Petitot, Emile Fortuné Stanislas Joseph** (1838-1917), missionary and geographer, was born at Grancey-le-Château, near Marseilles, France, in 1838. He became a priest in the Oblate order; and in 1862 he was sent to the Canadian North West as a missionary. He served as a missionary in various parts of what are now the provinces of Alberta and Saskatchewan until 1882. He then returned to France, and in 1886 he became the parish priest of Mareuil-les-Meaux. Here he died on May 29, 1917. He published a number of valuable works dealing with the geography, anthropology, and linguistics of the Canadian North West: *Dictionnaire de la langue Dènè-Dindjié* (Paris, 1876), *Vocabulaire français-esquimau* (Paris, 1876), *Monographie des Esquimaux Tchiglit du Mackenzie et de l' Anderson* (Paris, 1876), *Monographie des Dènè-Dindjié* (Paris, 1876), *Traditions indiennes du Canada Nord-ouest* (Paris, 1886), *Les Grands Esquimaux* (Paris, 1887), *En route pour la mer glaciale* (Paris, 1888), *Quinze ans sous le cercle polaire* (Paris, 1889), *Origine Asiatique des Esquimaux* (Rouen, 1890), *Autour du grand lac des Esclaves* (Paris, 1891), and *Exploration de la région du grand lac des Ours* (Paris, 1893). See A. G. Morice, *L'abbé Émile Petitot et les découvertes géographiques au Canada* (Le Canada Français, 1921).

**Petitot river** rises in the North West territories, between the 116th and 117th meridians of west longitude, crosses the north-west corner of Alberta and the north-east corner of British Columbia, and enters the Liard at Fort Liard. It was named after Father Émile Petitot (q.v.), a missionary in the Mackenzie district from 1862 to 1878. It is 260 miles long.

**Petroleum Industry.** Petroleum is a mixture of hydrocarbons, the com-

THE TURNER VALLEY OIL FIELDS, ALBERTA

position and properties of which vary in different regions. Its products include crude oil, gasoline, kerosene, gas and fuel oil, lubricating oil, grease, paraffin wax, and asphalt. The development of the motor-car has brought about a great growth in the consumption of most of these products in recent years; and the petroleum industry now ranks eighth in importance among all industries in Canada.

Canada possesses in the Turner valley in Alberta an oil-field of distinct importance; but the crude oil produced in Canada is less than 10 per cent. of the total consumption. The refining of petroleum products is carried on by about thirty different companies; but by far the most important of these are the Imperial Oil Company, the British American Oil Company, the McColl-Frontenac Oil Company, and the Shell Oil Company. Of these the Imperial Oil has the lion's share of the business. These companies largely control the distribution of petroleum products in Canada. They have either established their own service stations, or they rent their service stations to independent operators on well-understood conditions. There are, however, a large number of service stations owned by private operators, who buy from the oil companies. These independent service stations are perhaps on the increase, for the oil companies have found it difficult to ensure economical and satisfactory administration of their own service stations, or even of those leased to others. There have been complaints of an attempt to create a monopoly of the petroleum business in Canada on the part of the large oil companies; and many efforts have been made, by cutting prices, to force out of business independent distributors. But, on the whole, the independent distributor has held his own. Certainly, competition has not been eliminated in the distribution of petroleum products in Canada; and it does not seem likely that it will be.

The independent operator in Canada, able to buy in the cheapest market, and with a personal stake in the business, will often be able to compete on even terms with the employee or agent of a vast corporation.

Canadian exports of petroleum products are relatively unimportant. Apart from border movements into the United States, most of the Canadian exports go to such nearby customers as Newfoundland, St. Pierre and Miquelon, Bermuda, and Alaska, the total consumption of which is small. See F. J. McCarthy, *The petroleum trade of Canada* (United States Commerce Reports, October 12, 1931) and L. Dubé, *La production et la distribution de l'essence au Canada* (École des Hautes Études Commerciales de Montréal, vol. iv, 1934).

**Petrolia,** a town in Lambton county, Ontario, situated on the Sydenham river, and on the Canadian National and the Michigan Central Railways, 16 miles south-east of Sarnia. The place was named in 1867 by the first postmaster, Patrick Barclay. The origin of the name is derived from petroleum, the production of which is the staple industry of the locality. The town was incorporated in 1874. It is the centre of a huge oil district; and contains two refineries, and has ample facilities for the storage of oil and for the manufacture of oil-well supplies. Petrolia is also in a good farming, fruit-growing, and dairying area. A suitable clay for the manufacture of bricks and tiles is another economically important resource. A weekly newspaper (*Advertiser-Topic*) is published. Pop. (1931), 2,596.

**Petuns.** See **Tobacco Nation.**

**Pewee.** See **Flycatcher.**

**Phalarope,** a name applied in a general way to any member of one of the shore-bird families, *Phalaropodidae*. In general appearance, they closely resemble their allies the sandpipers, but the peculiar lobed flaps of skin bordering the toes, which form a special adaptation for swimming, are not to be found in any of the other shore-birds. Three species occur in Canada, the red phalarope (*Phalaropus fulicarius*), the northern phalarope (*Lobipes lobatus*) and Wilson's phalarope (*Steganopus tricolor*). The first two mentioned are Arctic nesting species, and the latter inhabits the southern portion of the western provinces.

**Pharmacy.** Prior to Confederation there appears to have been little or no restriction on the sale of drugs in Canada. Apothecaries, druggists, and chemists were free from governmental regulation; and the sale of drugs was frequently combined with that of books and other articles. In 1849 an Act of the legislature of the old province of Canada prohibited the use of strychnine for certain purposes; and in 1859 an Act of the same legislature regulated the sale of strychnine and other poisons. But it was not until 1871 that the legislature of Ontario, for example, passed a Pharmacy Act restricting the sale of drugs to the members of a College of Pharmacy, created by the same Act. Since then all the other provinces of Canada have followed the lead of Ontario. In 1882 the Ontario College of Pharmacy created a school or college for the training of pharmacists, and in 1891 this college was affiliated with the University of Toronto, so that graduates of the college could proceed to the degree of Phm.B. (bachelor of pharmacy). A similar school has been established by Laval University at Quebec.

**Pheasant,** a name restricted in Canada to an introduced, semi-wild, fowl-like bird, characterized by the resplendent colour of the male and the long pointed tail of both sexes. The ancestry of this bird was never exactly recorded; it has been cultivated in Europe for several centuries. The general appearance of the pheasant makes it appear certain that it represents, largely, the form *Phasianus colchicus*, but hy-

bridization with other forms has repeatedly taken place. The name "ring-necked pheasant" is perhaps the most nearly accurate and applicable of any. Pheasants are well established in the southern parts of British Columbia and Ontario. The fostering of this rather artificial type of game is done at the neglect of native game birds.

**Philately,** the hobby or business of collecting postage-stamps, had its first beginnings in Canada about the time of Confederation. The first postage-stamps were issued in the United States in 1847; and by 1859 American collectors of postage-stamps were already busily at work. The first postage-stamps were not issued in the provinces of British North America until 1851; and it is probable that philatelists sprang up in Canada somewhat later than in the United States. The hobby has spread until it has become with many collectors a business; and it is estimated that there are in Canada to-day over 30,000 collectors of postage-stamps. Of the early stamps of the British North American provinces, such as the province of United Canada, Nova Scotia, New Brunswick, Prince Edward Island, British Columbia, and Vancouver Island, many issues now bring large sums of money. The black twelve-penny postage-stamp issued by the old province of Canada has a catalogue price of $1,750, if unused, and $1,200, if used. A pair of these stamps are reputed to be worth $5,000. Even the commoner three-penny beaver stamp of old Canada has a catalogue price of between $25 and $75, according to the issue. Some of the early postage-stamps of Nova Scotia, New Brunswick, and Prince Edward Island command prices ranging upwards of $100. Even the earlier issues of the Dominion of Canada are at a high premium. These prices are dictated solely by scarcity, and by the desire of wealthy collectors to complete their collections; and because of the many trifling peculiarities of different issues even of the same postage-stamp, the quest of completeness is a veritable will-o'-the-wisp. There is no substantive value behind these rare postage-stamps; but because of the widespread competition among philatelists, the prices of postage-stamps have held up even when the prices of sound commercial stocks have gone down. For an account of Canadian philately, see F. Jarrett, *B. N. A. Book: Stamps of British North America* (Toronto, 1929).

**Philipsburg,** a village in Missisquoi county, Quebec, on the east shore of Missisquoi bay, two miles north of the international boundary. It was named after Philip Ruiter, agent for Thomas Dunn (q.v.), who owned land in this region; and it was created a village in 1846. It has a marble quarry; and a Canadian customs office is located here. Pop. (1931), 638.

**Phillipps, Richard** (1661?-1750), governor of Nova Scotia (1719-49), was born about 1661, the second son of Richard Phillipps and Frances Noel. At the Revolution of 1688 he entered the service of William of Orange, and was present at the battle of the Boyne in 1690. In 1712 he became colonel of the 12th Regiment of Foot, and in 1717 of the 40th Regiment. In 1719 he was appointed governor of Placentia and captain-general of Nova Scotia. From 1720 to 1722 he administered in person the affairs of Nova Scotia; but he then returned to England, and, with the exception of the years 1729-31, his duties were performed by deputies. He ceased to draw his salary as governor in 1749, and he died on October 15, 1750.

**Phillipps-Wolley, Sir Clive Oldnall Long** (1854-1918), author, was born at Wimborne, Dorsetshire, England, on April 3, 1854, the son of R. A. L. Phillipps, F.R.G.S. He was educated at Rossall School, England; and, after serving for some years as British consul at Kertch, Russia, he studied law, and was called to the bar from the Middle Temple in 1884. In 1876 he inherited the Wolley estate at Woodhall, Hamwood, Shropshire, and assumed the Wolley arms and name. In 1896 he removed to British Columbia; and he lived in Victoria, Vancouver Island, for the rest of his life. He died at Somenos, British Columbia, on July 8, 1918. He was created a knight bachelor in 1915; and in 1913 he was elected a fellow of the Royal Society of Canada. Among other books, he published *Sport in the Crimea and Caucasus* (London, 1881), *Savage Svânetia* (London, 1883), *The trottings of a tenderfoot* (London, 1884), *A sportsman's Eden* (London, 1888), *Snap* (London, 1890), *Gold, gold in Cariboo* (London, 1893), *Big game shooting* (London, 1894), *The Queensberry cup* (London, 1895), *One of the broken brigade* (London, 1897), *The Chicamon stone* (London, 1900), *Songs of an English Esau* (London, 1902), and *Songs from a young man's land* (London, 1920).

**Phillips, John Arthur** (1842-1907), journalist and author, was born in Liverpool, England, on February 25, 1842, the son of Arthur Phillips, of Barbados, West Indies, and Mary Ann Griffith. He was educated in Barbados; but became a journalist in New York in 1865, and in Canada in 1870. He lived first in Montreal, and after 1878 in Ottawa. Here he died on January 8, 1907. In 1875 he married Ivy Sarah Parsons. He was the author of *Thompson's turkey, and other Christmas tales* (Montreal, 1873), *From bad to worse* (Montreal, 1877), *The ghost of a dog* (Ottawa, 1885), and *Out of the snow, and other stories* (Ottawa, 1886); and he collaborated with C. R. Tuttle in his *Illustrated history of the Dominion* (Boston, 1878).

**Phipps, George Augustus Constantine, Earl of Mulgrave.** See **Mulgrave, George Augustus Constantine, Earl of.**

**Phips, Sir William** (1651-1695), governor of Massachusetts, was born in Maine on February 2, 1651, of humble parents. He became a ship's carpenter in Boston, married a wealthy widow, became a ship-owner, and in 1687 he succeeded in raising a Spanish treasure-ship off Haiti, an exploit for which he was knighted. In 1690 he was given command of a New England expedition against Port Royal in Acadia. He captured Port Royal; and later in the year he proceeded against Quebec. He made his way up the St. Lawrence to the basin of Quebec; but he was not able to capture the citadel. In 1692 he was appointed first royal governor of Massachusetts; but he was recalled in 1694 to London to meet charges of maladministration, and he died in London, on February 18, 1695, during the hearing of these charges. See Carl Von Doren (ed.), *The life of Sir William Phips* (New York, 1929); H. O. Thayer, *Sir William Phips* (New York, 1927); and E. Myrand, *Sir William Phips devant Québec: Histoire d'un siège* (Quebec, 1893).

**Phlogopite.** See **Mica.**

**Phlox** (*Phlox divaricata* L., *Polemoniaceae*), a perennial herb with spreading or ascending stems, which are clammy to the touch, and oblong-ovate or lance-ovate opposite leaves. The lilac or bluish-coloured flowers are borne in spreading, loosely flowered terminal clusters. The calyx has 5 slender, awl-shaped teeth; the corolla is salver-shaped, 5-lobed, with the lobes wedge-shaped and notched at the apex, and has a long tube. It is found blooming in May and June in damp woods from western Quebec to Manitoba.

**Phoebe.** See **Flycatcher.**

**Phoenix,** a former mining town in the Similkameen district of British Columbia, on the Canadian Pacific and Great Northern Railways, 4 miles east of Greenwood and 25 miles from Grand Forks.

**Phosphate Rock,** a sedimentary rock which consists of the accumulation of bones of prehistoric vertebrate animals to some extent, and the excreta of flesh-eating and fish-eating animals and birds. This rock is used in the manufacture of fertilizers in the same way as apatite. Extensive but thin deposits are found in Alberta, Saskatchewan, and British Columbia.

**Phyn, James** (1742-1821), merchant, was born on March 12, 1742, a son of George Phyn, of the Corse of Monelly, in Scotland, and his wife Janet Simpson. He was thus an uncle of the Hon. John Forsyth (q.v.) and his brothers, and of the Hon. John Richardson (q.v.). He came to America before 1763, for in that year he became a partner of John Duncan, an Indian trader of Schenectady, in a firm which came to be known in 1767 as Phyn, Ellice, and Co. In 1774 he left for England, to found in London the firm of Phyn, Ellice, and Co., which was destined to play for many years an important rôle in the history of the Canadian fur-trade. It was a party to the formation of the XY Company in 1798; and on the union of the XY and North West Companies in 1804, it became one of the regular supply houses of the North West Company. Phyn retired from the Company about 1805, and he died near Schenectady, New York, on November 2, 1821. About 1768 he married in Schenectady the daughter of Dr. John Constable, a friend of Sir William Johnson; and by her he had at least two sons. Some account of his life in America will be found in R. H. Fleming, *Phyn, Ellice and Company of Schenectady* (Contributions to Canadian Economics, IV, 1932).

**Physics.** Since James Loudon (q.v.) established in 1878 in the University of Toronto the first physics laboratory in Canada, much important work in physics has been carried out in Canadian laboratories. Special reference should be made to the researches of Professor H. L. Callendar and Professor (now Lord) Rutherford at McGill University and those of Sir J. C. McLennan (q.v.)

at the University of Toronto; but many other Canadian physicists have made notable contributions in many phases of physics. See A. N. Shaw, "The progress of physics in Canada," in *The Royal Society: Fifty years' retrospect* (Toronto, 1932).

**Piapot,** a village in the Maple Creek district of Saskatchewan, on the Canadian Pacific Railway. It is named after Piapot, a Cree chief. Pop. (1931), 300.

**Pic.** See **Fort Pic.**

**Pichon, Thomas** (1700-1783), traitor and author, was born at Vire, Calvados, France, on September 20, 1700. He became a lawyer, and then entered the service of the French king. In 1751 he came to Cape Breton as secretary to the governor; and in 1755 his treason in providing the English with military information resulted in the capture by the English of Fort Beauséjour. He went in 1756 to live in England; and there he died in 1783. He was the anonymous author of *Lettres et mémoires pour servir à l'histoire naturelle, civile, et politique du Cap Breton* (The Hague, 1760), translated into English under the the title, *Genuine letters and memoirs relating to the natural, civil, and commercial history of the islands of Cape Breton and Saint John* (London, 1760). See G. Lanctot, *Le traitre Pichon* (Bull. rech. hist., 1930).

**Pickerel.** In Canada this name is commonly applied to the pike-perch (*Stizostedion vitreum*). In the United States, the same name is used for small and medium-sized specimens of the pike (*Esox lucius*), and for a series of the smaller relatives of the pike. The word properly means a small pike (pike-rel), and the use of the name pickerel for the pike-perch without the descriptive adjective "yellow" should be discouraged. Similarly, the use in the United States of the name pike for the pike-perch, without the descriptive adjective "wall-eye", is equally objectionable. The so-called blue pickerel

is merely a colour phase of the yellow species.

**Pickerel Weed** (*Pontederia Cordata* L., *Pontederiaceae*), a stout, perennial, aquatic herb developed from a thick horizontal rootstock. The stem or scape bears a single, large, arrow- or heart-shaped leaf, and a dense spike of blue flowers, which is subtended by a spathe-like bract. Each flower is tubular and 2-lipped, the upper lip of 3 ovate lobes, with the middle the longest, and the lower lip of 3 linear spreading lobes. There are 6 stamens, 3 long and protruding, and 3 very short. It grows along the borders of ponds and streams, and margins of shallow lakes, from Nova Scotia to Manitoba, and blooms from June to September.

**Pickering,** a village in Ontario county, Ontario, on Duffin's creek, and on the Canadian National Railway, 22 miles east of Toronto, and about 3 miles from Pickering harbour on lake Ontario. It is named after the township in which it is situated, which was organized in 1792 as Edinburgh township, but the name of which was later changed to Pickering, after the town of Pickering in Yorkshire. It is in a farming district, and has an excelsior factory, a continuation school, and a weekly newspaper (*News*). Pop. (1934), 606. See William R. Wood, *Past years in Pickering* (Toronto, 1911).

**Pickering College,** near Newmarket, Ontario, is a residential school for boys founded in 1842 at Picton, Ontario, by the Society of Friends. About 1872 it was removed to Pickering, Ontario, from which it derives its present name, and it continued here until the main building was burnt to the ground in 1906. The school was then removed to Newmarket, Ontario. It was closed from 1917 to 1927; but since it has re-opened it has obtained a deservedly high reputation. Special emphasis is laid in the school on vocational training. The headmaster, since 1927, has been Joseph McCulley, B.A. (Oxon.).

**Pickthall, Marjorie Lowry Christie** (1883-1922), author, was born at Gunnersbury, near Cheswick, London, England, on September 14, 1883, the daughter of Arthur C. Pickthall and Helen Mallard. She came to Canada with her parents in 1889, settled in Toronto, and was educated at Bishop Strachan School. From an early age she contributed poems and stories to the magazines and newspapers; and before her first book appeared, her genius was recognized. In 1912 she went to England, and she remained there until 1919. Then she went to live in British Columbia, first in Victoria, and then in Vancouver. Here she died suddenly on April 19, 1922. Her first book was a little volume of poetry, entitled *Drift of pinions* (Montreal, 1912); and this was followed by *The lamp of poor souls, and other poems* (Toronto, 1917), *The wood carver's wife, and later poems* (Toronto, 1922), *Little songs* (Toronto, 1925), and *Complete poems* (Toronto, 1936). In addition to some juvenile stories, she published two novels, *Little hearts* (London, 1915) and *The bridge* (London and New York, 1922), and a collection of her short stories was published posthumously under the title *Angels' shoes and other stories* (London, 1923). See L. Pierce, *Marjorie Pickthall, a book of remembrance* (Toronto, 1925), with portrait and bibliography; and J. D. Logan, *Marjorie Pickthall* (Halifax, 1922).

**Picquet, François** (1708-1781), missionary, was born in Bourg-en-Bresse, France, on December 6, 1708, the son of humble parents. He joined the congregation of St. Sulpice in 1729, was ordained a priest, and in 1735 was sent to Canada as a missionary. He obtained a great influence with the Algonkin and Nipissing Indians; and in 1749 he built a fort at La Présentation (now Kingston, Ontario). He fought at the head of his Indians during the Seven Years' War, and was wounded at the siege of Quebec in 1759. A price having been placed on his head by the English, he escaped in Indian dress after the battle of the Plains of Abraham, and made his way overland to New Orleans. In 1762 he returned to France, and he died in poverty at the home of his sister, a peasant woman of the village of Verjon, on July 15, 1781. See A. Chagny, *Un défenseur de la Nouvelle-France: François Picquet, "le Canadien"* (Montreal, 1913).

**Picton,** a town in Hallowell township, Prince Edward county, Ontario, on the bay of Quinte, and on the Canadian National Railway, 18 miles south-east of Belleville. That part of the town on the west side of the creek flowing through it was originally known as Hallowell, after Benjamin Hallowell, a United Empire Loyalist who was a brother of Chief Justice Elmsley (q.v.); but shortly after 1815 the group of houses on the east side of the creek were named Picton, after Sir Thomas Picton, a British general who fell at the battle of Waterloo. The name Hallowell or Hallowell Bridge persisted as late as 1837; but when the town was incorporated in 1845, the name Picton was adopted. It is the centre of a rich mixed-farming country, and has several industries allied to agriculture. The chief products manufactured in Picton are cream, butter, and cheese, mitts and gloves, canned vegetables, and evaporated fruits. The town has seven churches, a collegiate institute, a public library, and two weekly newspapers (*Gazette* and *Times*). The Picton *Gazette* is one of the oldest newspapers in Ontario, and celebrated its centenary in 1930. Pop. (1931), 3,580.

**Pictou,** a county in Nova Scotia, on the southern shore of Northumberland strait. It has a shoreline about 50 miles long, and it extends into the interior more than 20 miles. On the south it is bounded by Guysborough county, on the east by Antigonish county, and on the west by Colchester county. The first settlers came from Philadelphia on the *Hope* in 1767; and they were followed in 1773 by Scottish Highlanders on the *Hector* in 1773. The county was created by Act of the legislature in 1836. Though hilly, it is fertile; and it contains rich mines of coal and iron ore. County town, Pictou. Pop. (1931), 39,018. See Rev. G. Patterson, *A history of the county of Pictou, Nova Scotia* (Montreal, 1877; new ed., Pictou, 1916) and Rev. J. P. MacPhie, *Pictonians at home and abroad* (Boston, Mass., 1914).

**Pictou,** the county town of Pictou county, Nova Scotia, is situated on Pictou harbour, an arm of the strait of Northumberland. It is on the Canadian National Railway, and is Nova Scotia's most northern port for outlet to the gulf of St. Lawrence, having steamboat connection with Halifax, Prince Edward Island, and the Magdalen islands. Originally a Micmac village stood on its site. In 1762 a grant of 200,000 acres in the vicinity was made to a group of Philadelphians, among whom was Benjamin Franklin. But no real progress in settlement was made until 1773 when 200 Highlanders from Scotland arrived on the ship *Hector*. Many of the present inhabitants of Pictou trace their ancestry back to these early Highland settlers. Various explanations are given for the origin of the name, but the one generally accepted locally is that it was derived from the Indian word *Piktook*, meaning "bubbling water". Its main industries are coal-mining, lumbering, and deep sea fishing. It has a central public school, an academy (the famous Pictou Academy), a convent, and a weekly newspaper (*Advocate*). Pop. (1931), 3,152.

**Piegan.** See **Siksika.**

**Pierreville,** a village in Yamaska county, Quebec, on the river St. Francis, near its entrance into the St. Lawrence, 28 miles north-east of Sorel, on the Canadian National Railway. The place, at one time known as St. Thomas, received its present name to commemorate Pierre, son of Laurent Philippe, grantee of the seigniory. The chief industries are ship-building and saw-mills. Pop. (1931), 1,352.

**Pigeon,** the term used by ornithologists in a rather general way for members of the bird family *Columbidae*. There is, however, a tendency to regard the smaller members of this family as doves, though there is actually no sharp distinction between a pigeon and a dove. The term "pigeon", with a prefix, has been given specific application in the case of the band-tailed pigeon (*Columba fasciata*), an inhabitant of south-western British Columbia, and also the passenger pigeon (*Ectopistes migratorius*), which is now extinct. This bird at one time occurred in vast numbers over the central and southern parts of Canada east of the Rocky mountains. Although all the factors contributing to its extinction are probably not known, there is no doubt that man was the principal agency of its destruction. The species reached its low ebb at the close of the nineteenth century, and the last known individual died in captivity in 1914. For an account of this species, see W. R. Mershon, *The passenger pigeon* (New York, 1907) and Margaret H. Mitchell, *The passenger pigeon in Ontario* (Toronto, 1935).

**Pigeon river** flows into Pigeon bay on the north-west side of lake Superior, near the 48th parallel of north latitude, and forms part of the international boundary between Thunder Bay district, Ontario, and the state of Minnesota. The river was first mentioned, as the best means of penetrating to the west, in 1722 in the report of a French officer named Pachot, and was for many years part of the canoe route from Grand Portage.

**Pigweed.** See **Amaranth** and **Lamb's Quarters.**

**Pika** (Genus *Ochotona*). The pika looks like a small tailless rabbit with short legs and gray-buff fur. The Canadian distribution of this animal includes the Rocky mountains, the southern mountain ranges of British Columbia, and the interior of the Yukon. The pika makes its home among the tumbled masses of rock slides. The squeaking bleat with which it greets an intruder resembles the call of no other animal, but this penetrating call has a ventriloquistic quality and is difficult to locate. Another characteristic of the pika is its habit of gathering piles of hay, and stacking them about the rock heap in which it lives. Pikas are active during the day, and so are often seen sunning themselves or pattering about on the rocks. The young number three or four to a litter, and are born in late spring or summer.

**Pike** (*Esox lucius*), one of the best known of freshwater fishes, generally distributed throughout Canada and the northern United States, as well as through northern Asia and Europe. In western Canada, it is found only northward. Because of its wide distribution, it is one of the most widely known of fishes. Although lacking many of the qualities of a first-class game fish, it is widely popular, largely perhaps on account of the size to which it grows and the readiness with which it takes many types of lures. In southern Canada, where the waters have been longer fished, the average weight of the pike taken by fishermen is about five pounds. As one goes north the average weight increases until in the virgin waters of the more remote areas thirty-pounders are sometimes reported. The pike is a voracious feeder, preying on many kinds of smaller fish.

**Pike-perch**, a freshwater fish closely related to the perch. Two species occur in northern North America: *Stizostedion vitreum*, commonly called yellow pickerel, or just pickerel (q.v.); also known as wall-eyed pike (abbreviated to pike), and doré. The other species, *Stizostedion canadense*, is known as the sauger or sand pickerel. The yellow pickerel is

the commoner and more widely distributed, occurring in rivers and lakes from New Brunswick to Great Slave lake. In the larger lakes, it is a commercial species of some importance; it also provides considerable sport to rod-and-line fishermen. It is excellent as a food fish. It is said sometimes to reach a weight of 20 pounds, but fish over 10 pounds in weight are ordinarily not taken now. The sauger is a much smaller species, with more restricted distribution. It is found sparingly from the St. Lawrence through the Great lakes and southward.

**Pilchard,** a marine fish belonging to the herring family, also known as sardine (q.v.).

**Pilot Mound,** a village in Manitoba, on the Pembina branch of the Canadian Pacific Railway, 125 miles south-west of Winnipeg. It was originally on a high landmark of the early settlers, but was moved to its present site, 2 miles distant, when the railway was built in 1884. It is in a general farming district, and has a weekly newspaper (*Sentinel*). Pop. (1934), 500.

**Pimpernel** (*Anagalis arvensis* L., *Primulaceae*), a low, spreading or procumbent herb, mostly annual, with opposite, ovate, sessile leaves, shorter than the flower stalks, which are solitary in their axils. The flowers are scarlet or white, the corolla being wheel-shaped with 5 broad divisions. They close quickly at the approach of rain, and because of this feature are often called "poor-man's weather vane". The plant grows in waste sandy fields everywhere, blooming from June to August.

**Pincher Creek,** a town in the Macleod district of Alberta, on Pincher creek, a tributary of the Oldman river, and on the Crowsnest branch of the Canadian Pacific Railway. The name appears in surveyors' reports as early as 1880, and is said to have originated in the fact that a pair of horseshoe pincers or pinchers found in an Indian camp near the creek was identified as belonging to a party of prospectors from Montana killed by Indians in 1864. The chief industries of the neighbourhood are coal-mining, lumbering, cattle-ranching, and farming; and the town has a high school and a weekly newspaper (*Echo*). Pop. (1931), 1,024.

**Pine,** the name of the trees belonging to the genus *Pinus* Duhamel of the family *Pinaceae*. Eighty species are known, nine of which occur in Canada, forming two well-established groups, the soft and the hard pines. The former, with leaves in bundles of five, and with fruits thin scaled and mostly pendulous, include northern white pine (*Pinus strobus* Linnaeus), western white pine (*P. monticola* D. Don), limber pine (*P. flexilis* James), and whitebark pine (*P. albicaulis* Engelmann). The hard pines with their leaves in bundles of two or three, and with cone scales quite thick and woody, and frequently bearing a prickle or spine, include red or Norway pine (*P. resinosa* Solander), western yellow pine (*P. ponderosa* Lawson), pitch pine (*P. rigida* Miller), jack pine (*P. banksiana* Lambert), and lodgepole pine (*P. contorta* Loudon).

All pines are evergreens, with needle-like leaves which are clustered in bundles of from two to five (one species, not native, has solitary leaves). The leaves vary in length from one to fifteen inches, and afford ready identification for the majority of the species. The flowers are unisexual, with both staminate (male) and pistillate (female) on the one tree. They are minute, borne in pairs on a small scale, the scales arranged in a spiral manner on a central woody axis, forming little cone-like structures which may be seen on the trees in early summer, the male at the base of the shoots, the female mostly terminal. After fertilization takes place, the pistillate flowers develop slowly, taking at least two growing seasons to mature into the fruit, which is also cone-like in appearance, but has become hard and woody;

usually only the central scales bear seeds, two per scale, each provided with a wing which aids in the distribution of them and offers a further means of identification.

In the recognition of the species, few difficulties arise. Northern white pine resembles western white pine in foliage, these two having fine leaves about four inches long, but the cones of the latter are almost twice as large, being from six to eighteen inches. Similarly, limber pine resembles whitebark pine, both having stout rigid foliage less than three inches long, but the cone of the former is four to ten inches in length, and splits open at maturity to release the seeds, whereas whitebark pine has a short globose cone rarely over three inches long, which does not split open at maturity, but remains closed and retains the seed for some years. Red, jack, and lodgepole pines have practically all of their leaves in bundles of two, while yellow and pitch pines have their leaves in bundles of three. The red pine has leaves four to six inches long; jack pine has very short leaves rarely two inches; and lodgepole pine leaves are somewhat longer up to three inches. The latter two may be separated readily by the fruit, the cones of lodgepole pine being prickled and opening to release the seeds, while those of jack pine are smooth-scaled and remain closed for many years: they are also the most persistent, and remain on the branches often throughout the life of the tree. The leaves of pitch pine are about half the length of those of yellow pine, being usually around four inches long, and the cones seldom reach three inches, whereas yellow pine cones are usually four or five inches in length.

Pines are widely distributed throughout the northern hemisphere. Northern white and red pine range from Newfoundland to Manitoba, and rarely extend north of the height of land dividing the waters of the St. Lawrence and the Great lakes from those of Hudson

9

bay. These two reach their best development in the Great lakes region and the valley of the Ottawa river, where they are frequently found in pure stands on sandy soils. Jack pine is found right across Canada from Nova Scotia to Alberta and the valley of the Mackenzie, but it is more northerly in habit than any of the other pines, and seldom occurs south of Muskoka in Ontario. Pitch pine has a very limited range in Canada, extending from the northeastern states barely across the international boundary into New Brunswick, Quebec, and Ontario, entering Ontario at the Thousand islands in the St. Lawrence. Western white pine, limber pine, whitebark pine, yellow pine, and lodgepole pine are western species. The former ranges throughout southern British Columbia at altitudes below 3,500 feet. Limber pine and whitebark pine are small, mostly limby and crooked, rarely forty feet high, found in the Rocky mountain region at altitudes of 3,000 to 7,000 feet, and are of no commercial importance. Yellow pine is confined to the drier portions of the southern interior of British Columbia, extending as far north as Vavenby on the north Thompson river. Lodgepole pine has a wide range, covering most of British Columbia, into the Yukon on the north and Alberta on the east; because of its varied habitats, it is extremely variable in its characteristics, and for a considerable time was known as two distinct species, *Pinus contorta* Douglas, the coast form, and *P. murrayana* Balfour, the inland or Rocky mountain form; in fact, some authorities still maintain this distinction.

In the lumber industry of Canada, the pines have always held an important position. For many years northern white pine alone produced approximately one-quarter of the present total cut, and still furnishes the best known lumber on the North American continent. The wood is light and soft and easily carved; it shrinks little on drying,

is easily seasoned, holds its shape and takes nails without splitting, and thus is much prized for pattern-making and as a general utility wood. The wood of western white pine is very similar in its properties, and these two species form the white pine lumber of commerce, known commonly as Weymouth pine in Europe. The other soft pines are of no commercial importance. The hard pines have mostly a harder and more resinous wood and some of them are valuable for structural timbers, notably red pine. Much of the hard pine lumber is, however, used as white pine, and is frequently sold as such. Jack and lodgepole pines are much favoured for railway ties.

**Pine river,** in Manitoba, lies between the 51st and 52nd parallels of north latitude, and flows north-east into lake Winnipegosis. The Pine River Indian reserve is situated near the river.

**Pine river,** in the Peace river district of British Columbia, is a tributary from the south of the Peace river, which it enters below Fort St. John. It is 130 miles in length.

**Pinhey, John Charles** (1860-1912), artist, was born at Ottawa, Canada, on August 24, 1860, the son of John Hamnet Pinhey and Constance Pinhey. He studied art at the Central School of Art, Toronto, and later at the Académie Julien and the École des Beaux-Arts in Paris. On his return to Canada, he had his studio for many years at Hudson Heights, Quebec, on the lower Ottawa river; and he achieved a considerable reputation as a painter of figure studies. In 1897 he was elected a member of the Royal Canadian Academy of Arts; and he died at Montreal on September 7, 1912.

**Pinkham, William Cyprian** (1844-1928), Anglican bishop of Calgary (1888-1928), was born at St. John's, Newfoundland, on November 11, 1844, the son of William Pinkham. He was educated at the Church of England

Academy, St. John's, Newfoundland, and at St. Augustine's College, Canterbury, England; and was ordained a priest of the Church of England in 1869. In 1887 he was elected bishop of Saskatchewan, and in 1888 bishop of Calgary. This latter position he held for forty years. He died at Calgary, Alberta, on July 18, 1844. In 1887 he was made a D.C.L. of Trinity University, Toronto, and a D.D. of St. John's College, Winnipeg.

**Pinnacle mountain** is in Alberta, south-west of mount Temple. It is in latitude 51° 21', longitude 116° 13', and has an altitude of 10,062 feet.

**Pintail** (*Dafila acuta*), a pond or river duck which nests largely in western Canada, but also occurs eastward in summer in the more northerly part of its range. The male has a seal-brown head; the upper parts are finely marked in grays, and below and on the breast it is white. The central tail feathers are narrow, elongated, and pointed. The female is, in general effect, grayish brown, resembling a female mallard. On migration this species appears in the east, where it frequents marshes and smaller bodies of water.

**Pipefish,** long slender little fishes of wide distribution in the sea. Only a single species is common on each of the Atlantic and Pacific coasts of Canada. They are of no commercial importance.

**Pipes, William Thomas** (1850-1909), prime minister of Nova Scotia (1882-4), was born at Amherst, Nova Scotia, on April 15, 1850, the son of Jonathan Pipes of Amherst Point. He was educated at Amherst, and at Acadia College, and became headmaster of the Sydney academy. He was called to the bar in 1875 (Q.C., 1890), and was elected to the Legislative Assembly of Nova Scotia in the Liberal interest for Cumberland in 1882. He became the leader of the government without office and without salary, on August 3, 1882,

and resigned on July 15, 1884. In 1887 he was made judge of probates for Cumberland. In 1898, he was appointed to the Legislative Council, and entered the Murray administration without portfolio. He became commissioner of public works and mines for Nova Scotia in 1905, and attorney-general in 1907. In 1906 he retired from the Legislative Council, and was elected to the Legislative Assembly for Cumberland. He died in Boston on October 7, 1909. He married Ruth Eliza (d. 1894), daughter of David McElmon, on November 23, 1876.

**Pipestone,** a village in Manitoba, on the Arcola branch of the Canadian Pacific Railway. Pop. (1934), 300.

**Pipit,** a designation for two species of Canadian birds belonging to the family *Motacillidae*, a group of birds largely found in the Old World. They are somewhat smaller than the common sparrow, obscurely coloured, and possessing rather sharp, warbler-like bills and elongated nails on the hind toes. The American pipit (*Anthus spinoletta*) nests in the Arctic, but occurs southward in flocks in the winter. Sprague's pipit (*Anthus spraguei*) is a common inhabitant of the southern parts of the prairie provinces, where it nests.

**Pipmakan lake** is in Chicoutimi county, Quebec. The name is the Montagnais for "spear", and the lake is said to be named in remembrance of the last fight between the Montagnais and Iroquois, which took place on the mountain overlooking the lake. It has an area of 90 square miles.

**Pipsissewa,** or Prince's Pine (*Chimaphila umbellata* (L.) Nutt., *Ericaceae*), a little evergreen herb with shining foliage and clusters of very fragrant pinkish or white flowers. The stem is leafy; the leaves are whorled, lance-shaped, and sharply toothed. The flowers are in loose terminal clusters; the corolla is of 5 rounded, widely-spreading petals; the stamens are 10, with violet-coloured anthers; the pistil with a disk-like stigma. This plant is a delightful surprise in dry woods in mid-summer from Nova Scotia to the Pacific.

**Pitcher Plant,** or Side-Saddle Flower (*Sarracenia purpurea* L., *Sarraceniaceae*), a bog plant which develops a tuft of pitcher-shaped hollow leaves. These have a broad lateral wing and an erect open hood, and are purple-veined and smooth on the outside and clothed with stiff reflexed hairs on the inside. They persist over the winter. The flowers are solitary, nodding, on the end of naked flower stalks about 1 to 2 feet tall. The blossom is round, with 5 green sepals, 5 incurved, side-saddle-shaped, deep purple-red petals, and a 5-angled, umbrella-shaped style. The pitcher plant is commonly found in peat bogs and wet sphagnum places from Labrador to the Rockies, flowering in May. The pitcher-shaped leaves are generally half full of water, in which insects are trapped.

**Pitt island** is in the Pacific ocean, and is the largest of the Pitt archipelago group. It is situated off the coast of British Columbia, in the Coast district, between Banks island and the mainland, and is 57 miles long, and 6 to 13 miles wide. Pitt island was named by Vancouver (q.v.), in 1793, after the prime minister of England, William Pitt, second son of the Earl of Chatham. Several other islands in the Pacific bear this name.

**Pitt Meadows,** a village in the New Westminster district of British Columbia, on the main line of the Canadian Pacific Railway, 22 miles east of Vancouver. Pop. (1930), 500.

**Pitt river,** a tributary of the Fraser river, in British Columbia, which has its mouth about 5 miles east of New Westminster. It has a length of 52 miles.

**Piuze, Liveright** (1754-1813), physician, was born in Warsaw, Poland, on February 2, 1754, and emigrated to America in his youth. He became a medical officer in the American army during the war of the Revolution, was afterwards kidnapped by Indians, was handed over to the English at Niagara, and ultimately settled as a licensed surgeon and apothecary at Rivière-Ouelle, on the south shore of the St. Lawrence. There he died on April 22, 1813. His autobiography was translated into French by J. R. Piuze, and was published, under the title *Récit des aventures de Liveright Piuze*, in the *Bulletin des recherches historiques*, 1919.

**Place-names.** Until the end of the nineteenth century, the greatest confusion prevailed both in regard to geographical names in Canada and in regard to their spelling. The post-office and the railway did much to fix Canadian place-names; but even these were frequently at variance. It was not until the establishment of the Geographic Board of Canada in 1897 that order began to be brought out of chaos. This body has been active since that time, and is still active, in making decisions with regard to Canadian place-names, their orthography, and their origin. These decisions have been embodied in a series of reports and miscellaneous publications. See **Geographic Board of Canada.** The province of Quebec has also created a Geographic Board, or Commission de Géographie under the department of Lands and Forests; and this board has issued a *Dictionnaire des rivières et lacs de la province de Québec* (Quebec, 1925). The geographic division of the department of lands in British Columbia has published a *Geographical gazetteer of British Columbia* (Victoria, 1930). In addition a number of studies of place-nomenclature in Canada have been published by individuals. Notable among these are Thomas J. Brown, *Nova Scotia place-names* (North Sydney, 1922), W. F. Ganong, *A monograph of the place nomenclature of the province of New Brunswick* (Trans. Roy. Soc. Can. 1896), James White, *Place-names in*

*Quebec* (Geographic Board of Canada, 9th Report, 1910), W. F. Moore, *Indian place-names in Ontario* (Toronto, 1930), and G. H. Armstrong, *The origin and meaning of place-names in Canada* (Toronto, 1930).

**Plagioclase.** See **Feldspar.**

**Plaice,** an important food fish (*Pleuronectes platessa*) of England and north Europe. This species is not found in Canadian waters, and the name is sometimes in Canada applied to other species of flatfishes (q.v.).

**Plaisance,** a village in Papineau county, Quebec, on the north shore of the Ottawa river, at the mouth of the North Nation river, and on the Canadian Pacific Railway, 5 miles north of Papineauville. Pop. (1934), 700.

**Plamondon, Antoine** (1804-1895), painter, was born at Lorette, near Quebec, Lower Canada, on February 28, 1804. He went to Paris to study painting in 1826, and became a pupil of Guérin. On his return to Quebec, he painted many portraits and numerous pictures for churches. He became a member of the Royal Canadian Academy of Arts in 1880; and he died at Pointe-aux-Trembles, Quebec, on September 4, 1895. See G. Bellerive, *Artistes-peintres canadiens-français* (Quebec, 1925).

**Plamondon, Marc Aurèle** (1823-1900), journalist, politician, and judge was born in Quebec, Lower Canada, the son of Pierre Plamondon and Aimée Mondion, on October 16, 1823. He was educated at the Quebec seminary, and was called to the bar in 1846. In 1848 he was one of the founders of the Institut Canadien of Quebec, and its first president; and in 1855 he was one of the founders and the editor of *Le National*, the organ of the Reform party in Lower Canada. In 1874 he was made a puisne judge of the Supreme Court of Quebec; and he retired on pension in 1897. He died on August 4, 1900. In 1859 he married Mathilde L'Ecuyer, of Quebec.

**Plane-Tree.** See **Sycamore.**

**Plantagenet,** a village in Prescott county, Ontario, on the Nation river, one mile from Plantagenet Springs, on the Canadian Pacific Railway, and 41 miles from Ottawa. It is named after the township in which it is situated. Pop. (1934), 500.

**Plantain** (*Plantago major* L., *Plantaginaceae*), a common rough weed with thick, leathery, ovate leaves, 5-7 ribbed, forming a rosette pressed flat to the ground. The leaf stems are channeled. The flowers are small and inconspicuous, and are produced in long slender spikes. Flowers part in 4's, and the stamens are characteristically purple. It is a persistent, succulent weed, abundant in fields and gardens and low rich soil throughout the Dominion. See also **Water Plantain.**

**Planté, Joseph Bernard** (1768-1826), politician, was born at Pointe-aux-Trembles, near Quebec, on December 19, 1768. He was educated at the Quebec Seminary, and became a notary public. He represented Hampshire in the Legislative Assembly of Lower Canada from 1796 to 1808; and he was one of the founders of *Le Canadien*. From 1809 to 1826 he represented Kent in the Legislative Assembly of the province. He died at Quebec on February 13, 1826. See F. J. Audet, *Joseph-Bernard Planté* (Trans. Roy. Soc. Can., 1933).

**Plaster Rock,** a village in Victoria county, New Brunswick, on the Canadian Pacific and Canadian National Railways. Pop. (1934), 400.

**Platinum,** a silver-white metal which has a specific gravity of about 21.5. It is much harder than silver and gold, and on that account is highly prized for use in jewellery. It is also extensively used in the electrical trades, for thermocouples, electroplating, and as a catalyst in the manufacture of sulphuric acid. It is insoluble in all acids except aquaregia, and for this reason finds extensive use in chemical laboratories. The two principal sources of platinum are native platinum, which occurs principally in placer deposits; but the original source is principally in peridotite and serpentine rocks. This type of material is recovered in small quantities near Tulameen in British Columbia. The other source is the mineral sperrylite, which is an arsenide of platinum occurring with the nickel-copper ores in the Sudbury district, Ontario. This mineral is tin-white to silver-white in colour, has a specific gravity of 10.6, and crystallizes in cubes with pyritohedral faces. It is the chief source of the platinum production in Canada.

**Plattsburg, Battle of,** an engagement in the War of 1812 which took place near Plattsburg, New York, on the western shore of lake Champlain, 25 miles south of the international boundary, on September 11, 1814. Sir George Prevost (q.v.), the governor-general of Canada, having been reinforced by over 10,000 of the Duke of Wellington's veterans, had been ordered to take the offensive against the Americans, and on September 1, 1814, invaded the United States by way of lake Champlain, with a force of over 7,000 picked soldiers. He was held up by a numerically inferior American force near Plattsburg, at the mouth of the Saranac river; and, being obsessed with the idea that naval control of lake Champlain was essential to him, he waited for ten days until the British flotilla on lake Champlain, under Captain Downie, was able to go into action. On September 11, Downie engaged the American flotilla in the Plattsburg bay; but he himself was killed in the engagement, and the British flotilla suffered a decisive defeat. Meanwhile, Prevost had ordered an advance on the American land defences; but when the British flotilla was defeated, he promptly withdrew his troops, and made a precipitate retreat into Canada. For his defeat at Plattsburg he was recalled as governor-general of Canada, and was ordered to face a court-martial. He died in 1815, before the court-martial took place; and no one can tell what the result of the court-martial would have been. There is no doubt that Prevost, whatever his merits as a civil governor, was unduly cautious as a military commander; and it is certain that a more aggressive general, like Brock (q.v.), would have swept all opposition before him. But, on the other hand, it is difficult to see what substantial advantages would have accrued to the British from success at Plattsburg; and success might easily have led Prevost into the position in which Burgoyne (q.v.) had found himself a generation earlier. It is probable that Prevost was never whole-heartedly in favour of the strategy imposed on him, and welcomed the opportunity to withdraw from a campaign for which he had no liking. Over his defeat and withdrawal, a vehement controversy broke out; and in many quarters his conduct of the campaign was condemned as supine and pusillanimous. But it is worthy of note that the Duke of Wellington was "inclined to think he was right". After all, the defence of Canada and the safety of his army was his chief consideration; and there are times when discretion is the better part of valour. See Sir C. P. Lucas, *The Canadian War of 1812* (Oxford, 1906). For some account of the controversy over the battle, see *The letters of Veritas* (Montreal, 1815), and *Some account of the public life of the late Lieutenant-General Sir George Prevost, Bart.* (London, 1823).

**Plattsville,** a village in Oxford county, Ontario, on the Nith river, and 4 miles from Bright, on the Canadian National Railway. Pop. (1934), 800.

**Playgreen lake,** in Manitoba, lies north of lake Winnipeg, of which it is, properly speaking, an arm. Out of Playgreen lake flows the Nelson river. The lake is so called from the accumulation of a brightly green water-weed on certain of its parts, particularly at its entrance. Cree names for the lake are "treeless island lake" and "egg-gathering lake". It is full of bare rocky islets, on which are found large quantities of gulls' eggs. The fishing in the lake forms one of the principal sources of food for Norway House, a Hudson's Bay Company trading post, which is situated at its head. Sturgeon of good quality are taken throughout the summer. The area of the lake is 257 square miles. The route between Norway House, on Playgreen lake, and York Factory, at the mouth of the Nelson, was the trunk line of the Hudson's Bay Company's fur-trade; during the middle period of the nineteenth century, it declined in importance with the improvement in transportation between Red river and the United States.

**Playter, George Frederick** (1811?-1866), clergyman and author, was born about 1811, and became a minister of the Wesleyan Methodist Church in Upper Canada in 1833. From 1844 to 1846 he was editor of the *Christian Guardian*, Toronto, and from 1847 to 1849 he edited the *Prince Edward Gazette*, Picton. He died at Frankford, Canada West, on October 24, 1866. He was the author of *The history of Methodism in Canada* (Toronto, 1862), of which only Vol. I was published.

**Plebiscite.** See **Referendum.**

**Plessis, Joseph Octave** (1763-1825), Roman Catholic bishop of Quebec (1806-25), was born near Montreal, Quebec, on March 3, 1763, the son of humble parents. He was educated in the College of Montreal and the Seminary of Quebec. He became secretary to Bishop Briand (q.v.), and in 1786 he was ordained a priest. In 1788 he became secretary to Bishop Hubert; in 1792 he was appointed curé of Quebec; and in 1801 he was consecrated a bishop and made coadjutor to Bishop Denault. In 1806 he succeeded the latter as bishop of Quebec; and he opposed vigorously the policy adopted by Sir James Craig

(q.v.), in regard to the French Canadians. He came to an agreement, however, with Sir George Prevost (q.v.), and during the War of 1812 he played an important part in ensuring the loyalty of the French Canadians. In 1818 he was nominated archbishop of Quebec, but he did not assume the title. In the same year he was appointed a member of the Legislative Council of Lower Canada; and in 1822 he opposed the projected union of Upper and Lower Canada. He interested himself in education; and the colleges of Nicolet and St. Hyacinthe were founded under his régime. He died at Quebec on December 4, 1825. A sermon which he preached on the occasion of the naval victory of the British in the Mediterranean in 1798 was printed during his lifetime (Quebec, 1799); and his *Journal de deux voyages apostoliques dans le Golfe Saint-Laurent et les provinces d'en bas, en 1811 et 1812* was published in the *Foyer canadien*, 1865. See Rev. J. B. A. Ferland, *Notice biographique sur Mgr. J. O. Plessis* (Foyer Canadien, 1863), tr. by T. B. French (Quebec, 1864; 2nd ed. 1878).

**Plessisville,** a village in Megantic county, Quebec, on the Canadian National Railway, 35 miles south-west of Quebec. The settlement was named to commemorate the Rt. Rev. Joseph Octave Plessis (q.v.), who became bishop of Quebec in 1801. The village was incorporated in 1855. The industries include machine shops and foundries, butter and cheese factories, saw-mills and planing mills, and a large shoe-factory. Hunting and fishing (the Blanche river is about a mile from the village) enjoy great popularity in the surrounding district. Pop. (1931), 2,540.

**Pletipi lake,** in Saguenay county, Quebec, lies at the source of the Outardes river. It is very irregular in shape, and forms 5 great bays which themselves form a great number of smaller bays. It has many tributary rivers, of which the most considerable is the source of the Outardes river. The lake is very deep and abounds in fish. It contains a great number of islands, which are, for the most part, wooded. Its shores are wooded by white spruce, cypress, tamarac, wild cherry, fir, etc. The soil, which is covered with thick moss, is sandy and rocky. The adjacent country to the west and south is a great marshy plain. The area of the lake is 138 square miles.

**Plover,** a group name for members of one of the shore-bird families, *Charadriidae.* Certain members of this group are moderately large, approaching the size of a pigeon, and their heavy muscular bodies have made them particularly attractive to sportsmen. The black-bellied plover (*Squatarola squatarola*) and the golden plover (*Pluvialis dominica*) are the most favoured. Both species nest in the far north, and migrate to southern South America in the autumn. The golden plover is now becoming scarce.

**Plum.** See **Cherry.**

**Plumas,** a village in Manitoba, on the Canadian National Railway, 50 miles north-west of Portage la Prairie. It has a weekly newspaper (*Standard and Glinella Gazette*). Pop. (1934), 350.

**Plumb, Josiah Burr** (1816-1888), speaker of the Senate of Canada (1887-8), was born at East Haven, Connecticut, in 1816, the son of the Rev. Elijah Griswold Plumb and Grace Hubbard Burr. He was for many years manager of the State Bank at Albany, New York. At the end of the American Civil War he settled in Canada; and in 1874 he was elected to represent Niagara in the Canadian House of Commons, as a Conservative. He became a friend and confidant of Sir John Macdonald (q.v.); and when defeated for North Wellington in 1882, he was appointed a member of the Senate of Canada. In 1887 he was made speaker of the Senate, and he presided over the Senate until his death at Niagara, Ontario, on March 12, 1888. In 1849 he married the youngest daughter of the Hon. Samuel Street, of Niagara Falls, Upper Canada; and by her he had three sons and three daughters.

**Plum Coulée,** a village in Manitoba, on the Pembina branch of the Canadian Pacific Railway, 63 miles from Winnipeg. It is named after Plum creek, which flows through it. Pop. (1931), 456.

**Plymouth Brethren.** With the beginning of Brethrenism certain names are connected, but usually John Nelson Darby, of Irish descent, though born in London (1800), is claimed as the founder. Trinity College, Dublin, was its academic birthplace; his followers were called "Darbyites" in Ireland. The term "Plymouth" soon came to be the designation for the new sect in England, for in that city was the first meeting of Brethren; before long it had a membership of over one thousand. It is a religious society formed on the platform of evangelical Calvinism; it rejects belief in an official ministry, claiming all male members to be on an equal footing and to have an equal right to exhort in its meetings. The sect has never made much progress in Canada; the census of 1931 reports only 6,983 belonging to it—mostly in Ontario and British Columbia. Consult William Blair Neatby, *History of Plymouth Brethren* (London, 1901).

**Point au Baril,** a summer resort in the Parry Sound district of Ontario, on the east side of the Georgian bay, 30 miles north of Parry Sound. The Canadian National Railway station is at the bottom of a deep, island-studded bay, 6 miles from the point from which it takes its name. The origin of the name is uncertain; but it is probably derived from the fact that in the days of the fur-trade the point was marked by a barrel as a buoy.

**Pointe au Père.** See **Father Point.**

**Pointe-aux-Trembles,** a town in Hochelaga county, Quebec, on the Canadian National Railway, 10 miles from Montreal. The place was named by the early settlers, in 1674, because of the aspen trees with quivering leaves found growing there. There are three churches, two public schools, and a college for boys. Pop. (1931), 2,970.

**Pointe-aux-Trembles.** See **Neuville.**

**Pointe Claire St. Joachim,** a town in Jacques Cartier county in the province of Quebec, on lake St. Louis, and on the Canadian National and Canadian Pacific Railways, 14 miles west of Montreal. The village is on a small point of land from which a clear view may be had of the bays on each side of the lake; hence the origin of the name. The settlement was founded in 1713; and the town was incorporated in 1911. It contains an important brick-manufacturing plant. Pop. (1931), 2,935.

**Pointe du Lac,** a village in St. Maurice county, Quebec, on the north shore of lake St. Peter, 8 miles west of Three Rivers. Pop. (1934), 600. See A. Dugré, *La Pointe-du-Lac* (Three Rivers, 1934).

**Point Edward,** a village in Lambton county, Ontario, on the Canadian National Railway, 2 miles north of Sarnia. Its docks are part of the Sarnia harbour. Pop. (1934), 900.

**Pointe Gatineau,** a village in Hull county, Quebec, situated at the junction of the Ottawa and Gatineau rivers, on the Canadian Pacific Railway, 6 miles from Ottawa. The town takes its name from the Gatineau river, and was established in 1876. Pop. (1931), 1,926.

**Pointe Lévy.** See **Lauzon.**

**Point Fortune,** a village in Vaudreuil county, Quebec, on the Ottawa river, and on the Montreal-Ottawa line of the Canadian Pacific Railway, 55 miles north-west of Montreal, and opposite the village of Carillon, just south of the boundary between Ontario and Quebec. It is named after either William Fortune, who settled here about the close of the nineteenth century, or

Joseph Fortune, an early surveyor. It was formerly an important point in the navigation of the Ottawa river; but it is now merely the centre of an agricultural district. Pop. (1931), 305.

**Point Levy.** See **Lauzon.**

**Poirier, Pascal** (1852-1933), senator and author, was born at Shediac, New Brunswick, on February 15, 1852, of French-Acadian descent. He was educated at St. Joseph's College, Memramcook (B.A., 1872), and was called to the bar of Quebec in 1877, and that of New Brunswick in 1887. From 1872 to 1885 he was postmaster of the House of Commons, Ottawa; and in 1885 he was called to the Senate of Canada. He remained a member of the Senate until his death at Shediac on September 25, 1933. In 1879 he married Anna, sister of Alphonse Lusignan (q.v.). In 1899 he was elected a member of the Royal Society of Canada; and he was the author of *L'origine des Acadiens* (Montreal, 1874), *Le Père Lefebvre et l'Acadie* (Montreal, 1898), *Le parler Franco-Acadien et ses origines* (Quebec, 1928), and a number of historical papers contributed to the Transactions of the Royal Society of Canada.

**Poison Hemlock.** See **Hemlock, Poison.**

**Poison Ivy,** or Poison Oak (*Rhus Toxicodendron* L., *Anacardiaceae*), a low shrub, scrambling over stumps and trees by means of aerial rootlets. The long-stalked leaves are divided into 3, ovate, pointed leaflets, bright green and shining above and pale and slightly hairy beneath. In the autumn the leaves take on rich autumnal colours. The flowers are seldom noticed, being small, greenish or whitish, in loose clusters in the axils of the leaves. The fruit cluster is more often noticed, consisting of a small compact cluster of dun-coloured, round, smooth berries with ridges at intervals. It grows commonly in thickets and dry woods from Nova Scotia to British Columbia. It is the worst vegetable poison in America, causing severe skin irritations.

**Poison Oak.** See **Poison Ivy.**

**Poison Sumach,** or Swamp Sumach (*Rhus Vernix* L., *Anacardiaceae*), a shrub or small tree with long compound leaves bearing 7-13 leaflets. These are lanceolate, entire, green on both sides with reddish stalks. The flowers are small, green, borne in long loose open clusters, appearing in June. The fruit is round, smooth, and dun-coloured; by this it is very easy to distinguish it from the harmless sumachs, which have red fruits. Like the other members of this genus, this form takes on brilliant autumn coloration. It is found growing in low wet ground and swamps in Ontario.

**Poisson, Adolphe** (1849-1922), poet, was born at Gentilly, Lower Canada, on March 14, 1849. He was educated at the Quebec Seminary and at the College of Nicolet; and in 1874 he was called to the bar of Quebec, and was appointed registrar of the county of Arthabaska. He published four volumes of poetry: *Chants canadiens* (Quebec, 1880), *Heures perdues* (Quebec, 1894), *Sous les pins* (Montreal, 1902) and *Chants de soir* (Arthabaska, 1917). He died at Arthabaska, Quebec, on April 22, 1922. In 1882 he married Amélie, daughter of A. Coté, Quebec.

**Pokeweed** (*Phytolacca decandra* L., *Phytolaccaceae*), a tall, stout, smooth-stemmed perennial 6-10 feet high, with an unpleasant odour and large poisonous root. The stems are purple-pink or bright red; the leaves are large, alternate and veiny; the flowers white or pinkish, growing in slender clusters opposite each leaf, having a calyx of 5 petal-like sepals, no corolla, and 10 stamens; the fruit is a dark purplish berry, ripe in the autumn. It may be found growing in low rich ground from New Brunswick to Ontario.

**Police.** The development of a paid and uniformed civil police, for the enforcement of law and order, has been a development of the last century, in Canada as in most other countries. In New France, the intendant was charged with the oversight of "justice, police, and finance"; but he had no police force to assist him. He seems to have relied mainly on the captains of militia in the parishes for what assistance he had. After the British conquest, the military appear for many years to have performed what police duties were required in emergencies; though with the organization of townships under the Quebec Act both in Upper and in Lower Canada, the English custom of appointing unpaid constables for the term of a year began. These constables were ordinary citizens, like the watchmen who guarded the gates of English towns in the Middle Ages, and they served without pay. It was not until after Sir Robert Peel introduced into the streets of London in 1829 a force of paid and uniformed policemen, known after him as "Bobbies" and "Peelers", that modern police appeared in Canada. One of the first, if not the first, city to employ a police force in Canada was Toronto, which engaged in 1835 the services of a chief constable and five policemen—though it was not until several years later that these policemen obtained uniforms. Montreal was still without modern police protection when, in 1849, the Parliament Buildings were burned down by a mob of rioters.

During the past century, however, the idea of a paid and uniformed police has undergone a remarkable development. Not only have the numbers of policemen vastly increased, so that cities like Montreal and Toronto have now police forces numbering over 1,000 men, and even small towns have police forces; but the work of the police has become more specialized. Not only have municipalities their police forces, but since Confederation both the Dominion and the provinces have established police forces. The Dominion created in

1873 the North West Mounted Police, which became in 1920 the Royal Canadian Mounted Police (q.v.); and this magnificent force now, in addition to patrolling what remains of the North West Territories, devotes itself mainly to enforcing the laws passed by the Dominion parliament, such as those pertaining to immigration, customs, etc. Practically all the provinces have formed police forces also, whose chief duty is to patrol the provincial highways, and to look after the enforcement of laws passed by the provincial legislatures. Even among the municipal police, there has been specialization. In the larger cities, the police are now usually divided into special squads or departments. There may be a detective department, composed of plain-clothes policemen; a morality department, which concerns itself with offences against morality; a motor-cycle squad, which deals primarily with breaches of the traffic regulations and other similar matters. Special kinds of police have been created, to deal with special kinds of crime.

Finally, there has been an extension of the sphere of a policeman's duties. A hundred years ago, a policeman's chief duty was the arrest of criminals; and this is still perhaps his chief duty. But he is now expected not only to arrest trouble-makers, but to prevent trouble. He regulates traffic; he makes the round of houses when their occupants are absent; he takes charge of lost children and lost articles; he stops runaway horses, and shoots mad dogs; he even escorts old people and little children across busy intersections; and he sometimes acts as the friend of dumb animals. He plays a part in modern life which was not contemplated one hundred years ago.

There has been no study published of the development of police work in Canada, though it is a subject of profound importance in the social history of the country.

**Polish immigration** into Canada has been chiefly into Manitoba and Saskatchewan. In 1931 there were 145,000 Poles in Canada. They have settled chiefly in the cities, and every little town in western Canada has its Polish colony. In Saskatchewan are several agricultural communities where the Poles are making excellent progress and, in some places, becoming comparatively well-to-do. Most of the Poles who reach Canada are country peasants or workingmen from cities and towns; they are poor, illiterate, and with a code of morals of their own. Without money and education, they can only join with the Ruthenians in the rough work of development in western Canada. Yet many of the sons and daughters of the earliest arrivals are fast coming to the front in various lines of Canadian public life. The Poles are very enthusiastic about education, and social conditions among them are rapidly improving: modern homes are being built to replace the old-fashioned, mud-plastered, and thatched huts. Practically all of the Poles are Roman Catholic; but, since their arrival, they have organized the Polish Independent Church, which retains most of the ritual and services of the Roman Catholic Church, but which repudiates the authority of the Pope. The Poles are intensely patriotic and cherish the love of Poland; national societies, such as the Polish Alliance, foster the traditions and keep alive the memory of the homeland. See J. T. M. Anderson, *The education of the New-Canadian* (New York, 1918), and James S. Woodsworth, *Strangers within our gates* (Toronto, 1909).

**Political History.** See **History, Political.**

**Political Science.** See **Social Science.**

**Pollack,** a marine fish belonging to the same family as the cod-fish and, like it, found on both sides of the Atlantic. It is a food fish of considerable value, especially excellent when fresh

**Pollard, Richard** (1752-1824), missionary, was born in 1752. He came to Canada in 1775, and in 1787 he settled on the Detroit river. He became the sheriff of the Western district of Upper Canada; but in 1802, owing to the scarcity of clergymen coming from the Mother Country, he took holy orders in the Church of England; and he was missionary at Sandwich, Upper Canada, from 1802 to his death on November 6, 1824. See A. H. Young, *The Revd. Richard Pollard* (Ont. Hist. Soc., Papers and Records, 1929).

**Polydymite,** a mineral consisting of sulphide of iron and nickel. Occasionally it is found in octahedral crystals, but more frequently it is massive. It has a metallic lustre and a light gray to steel-gray colour. Its hardness is about 4.5 and specific gravity 4.75. In a moist atmosphere it oxidizes rapidly, forming a crumbly mass with some sulphates of iron and nickel. It is an important constituent of the nickel ores of Sudbury, Ontario.

**Pond, Peter** (1740-1807?), fur-trader and explorer, was born in Milford, Connecticut, on January 18, 1740. After serving as a soldier in the French and Indian wars, he became a fur-trader at Detroit, and was for ten years or more engaged in the fur-trade on the upper Mississippi. In 1775 he made his first expedition to the Canadian North West; and in the development of the fur-trade here he played an important part. In 1778 he established the first post in the Athabaska country; and he appears to have reached later Great Slave lake. In 1783 he became one of the partners in the North West Company; but the murder of John Ross (q.v.) by some of his men in 1787, being the second murder with which he had been connected in the West, brought about his retirement from the fur-trade, and in 1790 he sold his share in the company to William McGillivray (q.v.). He returned to the United States, and became for a time a special agent of the American government in its dealings with the Indians. In his later years, he returned to New England, and he died about 1807 a poverty-stricken and forgotten old man. The maps which he drew of his explorations in the North West were among the first which exercised an influence over future events. A full account of his life and work is to be found in H. A. Innis, *Peter Pond, fur-trader and adventurer* (Toronto, 1930). The most recent edition of the fragment of his *Narrative* which has come down to us is in C. M. Gates (ed.), *Five fur-traders of the North West* (Minneapolis, 1933).

**Pond Lily, Yellow** (*Nymphaea advena* Ait., *Nymphaeaceae*), an aquatic herb developed from a thick horizontal rootstock. There are 2 types of leaves formed, the floating, which are large, round to heart-shaped with a deep sinus, and the submerged, which are small, thin membraneous, and nearly round. The flowers are showy, yellow tinged with purple on the inside, somewhat globular in shape. The calyx is of 6 petal-like sepals; the corolla of numerous small thick fleshy petals, which resemble the numerous stamens; the pistil single, with a disk-like, many-rayed stigma. It grows along the borders of ponds and slow moving streams from Labrador and Nova Scotia to the Rockies, and blooms from April to September.

**Ponds Inlet,** a post of the Canadian Mounted Police and of the Hudson's Bay Company, at the northern end of Baffin island. It was named by John Ross (q.v.) in 1818 after John Ponds (1767-1836), astronomer-royal. See Douglas S. Robertson, *To the Arctic with the Mounties* (Toronto, 1934).

**Pondweed** (*Potamogeton natans* L., *Najadaceae*), an aquatic herb with simple or sparingly-branched, jointed stem, and 2 kinds of leaves. The floating ones are elliptical, with a much elongated petiole, and are heart-shaped at the base, while the submerged ones are grass-like. The flowers are pale, small, and inconspicuous, united to form cylindrical spikes, which are developed above the water surface. The flower parts are in fours. This weed is common in ponds and quiet streams, and blooms from July till September.

**Ponoka,** a town in Alberta, on the west bank of the Battle river, and on the Calgary and Edmonton branch of the Canadian Pacific Railway, 62 miles south of Edmonton. The name is a Blackfoot word signifying "a red deer", and pronounced Pŏn-ō-kaw' by the Indians. Nearby is Look Out hill, from which the Indians in time of war scanned the surrounding prairies. The town is the centre of a lumbering, ranching, and mixed farming district. It is the site of a provincial hospital for the insane; and it has a weekly newspaper (*Herald*). Pop. (1931), 836.

**Pont-à-Buot,** a village in Westmorland county, New Brunswick, on the Missaquash river, 5 miles from Sackville. The English equivalent of the name is "Buot's Bridge". The name "Pointe-de-Bute", by which it is commonly known, is a corruption. Pop. (1934), 300.

**Pontbriand, Henri Marie Dubreuil de** (1708-1760), Roman Catholic bishop of Quebec (1741-60), was born in Vannes, France, in January, 1708. He was ordained a priest of the Roman Catholic church, about 1732, and in 1741 he was consecrated in Paris bishop of Quebec. He came out to Canada the same year, and he administered the affairs of the diocese of Quebec until the capture of Quebec in 1759. He then retired to Montreal; and here he died on June 8, 1760. See A. Gosselin, *L'église du Canada depuis Mgr de Laval jusqu'à la conquête, 3e partie* (Quebec, 1914).

**Pont-Gravé, François Gravé, Sieur de** (*fl.* 1554-1629), sailor and trader, was born at St. Malo, France, in 1554. He became interested in the Canadian fur-trade, and was connected with almost all the early attempts at colonization in Canada. He was an associate of Chauvin in 1599, of Monts (q.v.) in 1604-7, of Champlain (q.v.) in 1608-23. He was in Quebec in 1629, but thereafter he disappears from view. See H. P. Biggar, *The early trading companies of New France* (Toronto, 1900).

**Pontiac** (d. 1769), chief of the Ottawa, is said to have been born on the Maumee river in 1720, but may have been born earlier than this, since he was said in 1763 to be "about fifty years of age". He has been described as the organizer and guiding spirit of the widespread uprising of the Indian tribes in the "Old North West" in 1763-4, and this uprising has been long known as "Pontiac's Conspiracy". It is probable, however, that this conception of him is a mistake. His authority seems to have been confined to the Indians who were actually with him when, in May, 1763, he laid siege to Detroit. The garrison of Detroit, under Major Henry Gladwyn (q.v.), was able to withstand the attempts of the Indians to capture the fort; and in November, 1763, Pontiac withdrew to his winter quarters on the Maumee river. He continued on the warpath during 1764; but in 1765 he made peace with the English, and he observed this peace during the remainder of his life. It is probable that his attack on Detroit, like the Indian disturbances elsewhere, was mainly due to the instigation of some of the French inhabitants of the western country. He was murdered in the Illinois country in the early part of 1769, according to some accounts by an Indian bribed by an English trader, and according to another account during a drunken brawl. Even before his death, the mythopœic imagination was busy with his reputation; for in 1766 Major Robert Rogers (q.v.) published a tragedy with the title *Ponteach* (reprinted, with notes and introduction, by Allan Nevins, 1914), in which he plays the part of the hero. The book, however, that definitely established Pontiac in the popular imagination was Francis Parkman, *The conspiracy of Pontiac* (Boston, 1851). See also T. G. Marquis, *The war chief of the Ottawas* (Toronto, 1915), E. O. Randall, *Pontiac's conspiracy* (Ohio Archaeological and Historical Quarterly, 1903), F. B. Hough (ed.), *Diary of the siege of Detroit* (Albany, 1860), and M. A. Burton (ed.), *Journal of Pontiac's conspiracy* (Detroit, 1912).

**Pontiex,** a village in the Maple Creek district of Saskatchewan, on the Moose Jaw-Shaunavon branch of the Canadian Pacific Railway. Pop. (1934), 500.

**Pont Rouge,** a village in Portneuf county, in the province of Quebec, on the Canadian Pacific Railway, 25 miles north of Quebec city. The name of the place commemorates a red bridge erected by the early settlers about 1769. Pop. (1931), 1,353.

**Pontypool,** a village in Durham county, Ontario, on the Canadian Pacific Railway, 10 miles north of Millbrook. Pop. (1934), 300.

**Poor Clares.** The Order of the Poor Clares, founded in Umbria, Italy, in 1212, by Saints Francis and Clare of Assisi, is entirely contemplative, with Papal enclosure and solemn vows, and was instituted to afford spiritual assistance to the Catholic church in all her needs, and particularly to the First Franciscan Order, by the daily and midnight recital of the Divine Office, mental prayer, silence, work, austere penance, and the practice of the most strict evangelical poverty. The monastery of the Poor Clare-Colettines of Valleyfield, Quebec, was founded in 1902 by Bishop J. M. Emard, first bishop of Valleyfield, and five nuns from the monastery of Lourdes, two of whom were French and three Canadians. By the mother-houses of Lourdes and Lyons, the monastery of Valleyfield descends directly from the Poor Clare-Colettine community of Bourg-en-Bresses, the associates of St. Coletta, who, during the fifteenth century, restored the order to its primitive fervour.

The monastery of Poor Clare-Colettines of the Rivière-du-Loup was founded by Cardinal R. M. Rouleau, archbishop of Quebec, on April 29, 1932, with six nuns and two extern sisters from the monastery of Valleyfield.

There is also a community of English-speaking Poor Clares in Victoria, British Columbia, founded by the monastery of New Orleans.

**Pope, James Colledge** (1826-1885), prime minister of Prince Edward Island (1865-7 and 1870-2) and minister of marine and fisheries for Canada (1878-82), was born at Bedeque, Prince Edward Island, on June 11, 1826, the second son of the Hon. Joseph Pope, of Charlottetown, and Lucy, daughter of Captain Colledge. He was educated in England; and in 1849 he went to California during the "gold rush". He returned to Prince Edward Island, however, and there engaged in shipbuilding and other mercantile enterprises. He was a member of the Legislative Assembly of Prince Edward Island, for Prince county from 1857 to 1867, and for Charlottetown from 1872 to 1873; he became a minister without portfolio in the Palmer administration in 1859, colonial secretary in the Gray administration from 1863 to 1865, prime minister of Prince Edward Island from 1865 to 1867, from 1870 to 1872, and again for a few months in 1873. He opposed the entrance of the Island into Confederation, both on the basis of the Quebec Resolutions of 1864 and on the terms secured by the Haythorne government in 1873; but in 1873 he succeeded in bringing about federation on more favourable terms, and was elected a member of the Canadian House of Commons for Prince county. He was defeated in 1874, and from 1875 to 1876 he again represented Prince county in the provincial Assembly; but in 1876 he was re-elected to the House of Commons, this time for Queen's county, and he continued to represent this constituency until 1882. From 1878 to 1882 he was minister of marine and fisheries in the Macdonald government; but owing to ill-health he ceased to administer his department in 1881. He died at Summerside, Prince Edward Island, on May 18, 1885. In 1852 he married Eliza, daughter of Thomas Pethick, of Charlottetown; and by her he had eight children.

**Pope, John Henry** (1824-1889), minister of agriculture for Canada (1871-3 and 1878-85) and minister of railways and canals (1885-9), was born in the Eastern Townships, Lower Canada, in 1824, the son of John Pope and Sophia Lahern. He was educated at the Compton High School, in the Eastern Townships, and first devoted himself to agriculture. In 1857 he was elected to represent Compton as a Liberal-Conservative in the Legislative Assembly of Canada, and this constituency he represented continuously, first in the Assembly, and then in the House of Commons, until his death thirty-two years later. In 1864 he was one of those who conducted the *pourparlers* which brought about the great coalition; and in 1871 he was sworn of the privy council and became minister of agriculture in the Macdonald government. He resigned with his colleagues at the time of the "Pacific Scandal" in 1873; but he was one of the chief lieutenants of Sir John Macdonald (q.v.) in opposition, and in 1878, when Macdonald came back to power, he resumed his old portfolio. In 1885 he exchanged it for that of minister of railways and canals, and this portfolio he held until his death at Ottawa on April 1, 1889. In 1880 he went to England with Macdonald and Tupper in connection with the contract for the building of the Canadian Pacific Railway; and it was partly through his influence on Macdonald that the government saw the contractors through the financial difficulties which several times

threatened to overwhelm them. Though not an orator, he was an exceedingly shrewd practical politician.

**Pope, Sir Joseph** (1854-1926), under-secretary of state for Canada (1896-1909) and under-secretary of state for External Affairs (1909-1926), was born at Charlottetown, Prince Edward Island, on August 16, 1854, the son of the Hon. William Henry Pope (q.v.), one of the Fathers of Confederation. He was educated at Charlottetown, but removed to Ottawa in 1878. From 1882 to 1891 he was private secretary to Sir John Macdonald (q.v.), and he was appointed Macdonald's literary executor. In 1896 he was appointed under-secretary of state for Canada, and for thirty years he was a distinguished figure in the public life of Canada. In 1903 he was associate secretary to the Alaska Boundary Tribunal, and in 1906 he was British plenipotentiary at the Pelagic Sealing Conference in Washington. He was made a C.M.G. in 1901, a C.V.O. in 1908, and a K.C.M.G. in 1912. He died at Ottawa on December 2, 1896. In 1884 he married Henriette, daughter of Sir Henri Taschereau (q.v.); and by her he had five sons and one daughter. He was the author of *Jacques Cartier, his life and voyages* (Ottawa, 1890), *Memoirs of the Right Hon. Sir John Alexander Macdonald* (2 vols., Ottawa, 1894; new ed., Toronto, 1930), *The royal tour of 1901* (Ottawa, 1903), and *The day of Sir John Macdonald* (Toronto, 1915); and he edited *Confederation documents* (Toronto, 1895) and *The correspondence of Sir John Macdonald* (Toronto, 1921). He left an autobiography in manuscript, but this has not yet been published.

**Pope, William Henry** (1825-1879), politician and judge, was born at Bedeque, Prince Edward Island, on May 29, 1825, the eldest son of the Hon. Joseph Pope, of Charlottetown, and Lucy, daughter of Captain Colledge. He was educated in England, studied law under Edward Palmer (q.v.) in Charlottetown, and was called to the bar of Prince

Edward Island in 1847. In 1859 he was appointed colonial secretary of the Island, though without a seat in the executive council; and from 1863 to 1873 he represented Belfast in the Legislative Assembly of the Island. He was an advocate of Confederation, and was in 1864 a delegate to both the Charlottetown and Quebec Conferences. In 1873 he was appointed judge of the county court of Prince county, Prince Edward Island; and this office he held until his death at Summerside, Prince Edward Island, on October 7, 1879. In 1851 he married Helen, daughter of Thomas Desbrisay, of Charlottetown; and by her he had eight children, of whom Sir Joseph Pope, the biographer and literary executor of Sir John Macdonald (q.v.), was the eldest. He was the author of *The confederation question considered from the P.E.I. point of view* (Charlottetown, 1866).

**Poplar,** the name of the trees belonging to the genus *Populus* Linnaeus. Poplars are also frequently called aspens and cottonwoods. Some thirty species are known, eight of which are native to Canada. Many exotic species, amongst them silver poplar (*P. alba* Linnaeus), recognized by the dense, silvery-white down on the under surface of the leaf, and the tall, erect lombardy poplar (*P. nigra italica* Du Roi) have been introduced and are growing naturally all through the older portion of eastern Canada. The native species are the aspen (*P. tremuloides* Michaux), found all across Canada; the balsam poplar (*P. balsamifera* Linnaeus), also occurring throughout Canada; the largetooth aspen (*P. grandidentata* Michaux) from Ontario eastward south of the height of land dividing the watersheds of the Great lakes and Hudson bay; the eastern cottonwood (*P. deltoides* Marshall), a scattered tree throughout the river valleys in the southern prairie provinces and in the southern part of eastern Canada; the lanceleaf cottonwood (*P. acuminata* Rydberg), confined

to the banks of streams in southern Alberta, and of no commercial importance; the black cottonwood (*P. trichocarpa* Hooker), the western counterpart of balsam poplar, occurring from Alaska southward through coastal British Columbia, and one of the largest and most rapid-growing broad-leaved trees in Canada; and the narrowleaf cottonwood (*P. angustifolia* James), confined to the banks of streams in southern Alberta and Saskatchewan, and unimportant.

The trees flower before the leaves appear. The flowers are of two kinds, staminate (male) and pistillate (female), these being arranged in drooping catkins, and only one kind on a tree. Thus all poplar trees, like willows, do not bear fruit. The fruit is mature by the time the leaves are fully grown, and consists of a slender stalk bearing little pods, which on splitting open release innumerable minute, downy seeds. The leaves are, in general, broad for their length, singly placed, deciduous, and provided with long, mostly flattened stalks. They offer a ready means of separating the species. The leaf of the aspen is the smallest, and is nearly orbicular, about one and one-half inches long, and very long-stalked. Balsam poplar and western cottonwood leaves are practically indistinguishable, ovate in shape and three to four inches long; these two are separated through their fruits, the latter having a fruit pod which splits into three parts, rather than into the two or four parts characteristic of all other poplars. Largetooth aspen has an oval to orbicular leaf provided with very few, large, irregular teeth on the margin; and eastern cottonwood, frequently called deltoid poplar, gets its name from the fact that its leaves are equilateral triangular in shape. The two prairie species are readily separated. The narrowleaf cottonwood has a willow-like leaf, two to three inches long, and one-half to one inch broad, whereas lanceleaf cottonwood leaves are much broader and taper at both ends.

As a group the poplars are fast-growing, short-lived trees and cover vast areas of forest land following fires. They are as yet of slight importance in the lumber industry, but frequently form a useful nurse crop to the more important evergreens, and therefore have an economic importance frequently overlooked.

**Population.** See **Census.**

**Porcher island** lies off the mouth of the Skeena river, in Range 5 of the Coast district of British Columbia. It is 20 miles long and 20 miles wide.

**Porcupine.** The porcupine (*Erethizon dorsatum*) occurs throughout the forested regions of Canada, abundant in some areas, rare in others. This large, slow-moving rodent with its defensive armour of sharp quills is well known to most people. When the animal is alarmed the quills, which normally lie hidden in the long coarse hair, are erected into a bristling protection. The tail is filled with loosely set quills, and on being touched the porcupine strikes with it at the attacker. It is from this habit of the animal that the myth of the porcupine throwing its quills has arisen. The quills are barbed, and on entering the victim can be removed only with difficulty. If not removed or broken off, the quills work deeper and deeper, often resulting in grave injury or death. This is the common fate of animals attempting to prey upon the porcupine. Essentially a tree-dwelling animal, feeding on twigs and the succulent inner bark of trees, the porcupine is sometimes accused of destroying timber, especially young growth, but in most cases the injuries caused by the animal are of slight importance. The porcupine has a fondness for salt, and will often gnaw tool handles for the salty taste left by the perspiration from the hands of the user. The porcupine does not hibernate, but is active throughout the winter, and the one or two young are born in the spring.

**Porcupine,** a mining town in the Cochrane district of Ontario, on a spur of the Temiskaming and Northern Ontario Railway, 40 miles south of Cochrane. It began as a mining camp after the discovery of gold in the neighbourhood in 1909; and the name spread to the whole area, in which were developed such mines as Hollinger and Dome. Pop. (1934), 200.

**Porcupine river** rises in the north-west part of the Yukon territory, within 30 miles of the Yukon river, in approximately latitude 65° 30′, describes a great semi-circular curve to the north-east, enters Alaska, and joins the Yukon near the 145th meridian of west longitude. It was discovered in 1842 by John Bell (q.v.), a chief trader of the Hudson's Bay Company, who explored it to a point near the international boundary in that year and, two years later, to its junction with the Yukon. The river, which is approximately 150 miles in length, flows through a valley generally wide and shallow. Near the international boundary occurs a stretch of swift water, known as the Ramparts, where the river narrows to 75 yards and rushes through a walled valley or canyon. In its upper parts the river banks rise steeply from the water's edge to a height of 300 or 500 feet. The adjoining country is wooded by spruce and poplar.

**Porlier, Jacques** (1765-1839), fur-trader, was born in Montreal in 1765, and was educated there. He went to Green bay, on lake Michigan, and engaged in the fur-trade about 1791. He was elected a member of the Beaver Club of Montreal in 1801; and he became a partner of the South West Company. He died at Green bay on July 12, 1839. Further details about him will be found in J. Tassé, *Les Canadiens de l'Ouest*, vol. i (Montreal, 1878).

**Portage,** a carrying-place between two bodies of navigable water, from the French *porter* (to carry).

**Portage du Fort,** a village in Pontiac county, Quebec, on the Ottawa river, near Shawville, on the Canadian Pacific Railway, 50 miles north-west of Hull. It takes its name from the fact that there once stood on the Ottawa river, near the site of the village, a fort in which were stored provisions for the lumber camps of the district, and which was reached by means of a portage. Pop. (1931), 297.

**Portage La Loche.** See **Methye Portage.**

**Portage la Prairie,** a city in Manitoba, on the Assiniboine river, and on the Canadian National and Canadian Pacific Railways, 56 miles west of Winnipeg. The name is French for "prairie portage". It was here that the fur-traders crossed from the river to lake Manitoba, about 15 miles to the north. The locality was known as far back as 1739 as a carrying-place from the river to the lake used by the Assiniboin Indians on their trading expeditions to the English posts on Hudson bay. The city stands on the site where La Vérendrye (q.v.) built Fort La Reine in 1738. In 1832 a post was established by the Hudson's Bay Company about two miles from the centre of the present city. The post was moved nearer the city in 1866, and moved again in 1870. It was destroyed by fire in 1913, and has not been rebuilt. Portage la Prairie was incorporated as a city in 1907. The chief industries are flour mills, oatmeal mills, foundries, machine works, brick works, and an aërated water works. It is in an excellent district for farming and stock-raising. The city owns extensive park lands which, with lake Manitoba, make it a popular summer resort. There are nine churches, kindergarten and public schools, a collegiate institute, an industrial school for boys, and an Indian school. A daily newspaper (*Graphic*) is published. Pop. (1931), 6,597.

**Port Alberni.** See **Alberni.**

**Port Alfred,** a town in Chicoutimi county, Quebec, on the Saguenay river, 60 miles from its mouth, and 4 miles from Bagotville, which is on the Canadian National Railway. The place was named in honour of Alfred Dubuc, who had large holdings of pulpwood in the parish, which is known as St. Edouard de Port Alfred. The district is a great source of attraction to tourists during the summer months. Pop. (1931), 2,342.

**Port Arthur,** a city located at the north-western end of lake Superior on Thunder bay, Ontario. It occupies a series of terraces rising 400 feet from the shores of the bay. It is served by the Canadian Pacific, Canadian National and Port Arthur-Duluth Railways, and is 570 miles north-west of Toronto, about half-way between the Atlantic and Pacific oceans. Originally known as Dawson's, it became Prince Arthur's Landing, in honour of Prince Arthur, afterwards Duke of Connaught, whose regiment, commanded by Colonel (afterwards Viscount) Wolseley, landed here in 1870, the year of the Riel rebellion. As the place became settled, the name was changed, and Port Arthur was founded in 1883, and was incorporated as a city in 1907. The city is substantially built, and owns its own public utilities. There are churches of practically all denominations, public schools, a collegiate institute, a technical school and government offices. Port Arthur is the judicial centre of Thunder Bay district. The terminals for handling grain have been the admiration of the country. There are 16 elevators with a total capacity of 49,000,000 bushels; one of the largest shipbuilding plants in Canada, with a drydock 720 feet in length; several lumber mills; woodworking plants; foundries; machinery works; and pulp-and-paper mills. The district is a health resort and a tourist

GRAIN ELEVATORS, PORT ARTHUR, ONTARIO

centre for fishing and hunting. A fine scenic motor highway connects Port Arthur with Duluth, Minnesota, 179 miles to the south-west, and an electric railway with Fort William, 3 miles away. The neighbourhood is rich in minerals. There is a daily newspaper (*News-Chronicle*). Pop. (1931), 19,818. See T. L. Tanton, *Fort William and Port Arthur* (Ottawa, 1931).

**Port Borden,** a village and artificial harbour on the south coast of Prince Edward Island, opposite cape Tormentine on the mainland of New Brunswick. It is the terminus of the Canadian National Railways car-ferry crossing Northumberland strait. Pop. (1934), 300.

**Port Burwell,** a village and harbour in Elgin county, Ontario, on the north shore of lake Erie, 40 miles west of Long point, and a terminus of a branch line of the Canadian Pacific Railway, which connects here with a car-ferry for Ashtabula, Ohio. The village was founded in 1817 by Mahlon Burwell (q.v.), after whom it was named, and it was incorporated as a police village in 1900. It is a port of entry, and large quantities of coal are imported. Fishing is also a local industry. Pop. (1934), 700.

**Port Burwell,** a post of the Canadian Mounted Police, at the northern extremity of Labrador, and at the entrance to Hudson strait. It is named after H. M. Burwell, C.E., who was stationed here as an observer in 1885-6.

**Port Carling,** a village and summer resort in the Muskoka district, Ontario, on the Indian river, which connects lake Muskoka with lake Rosseau. It was first settled in 1865, and was named after the Hon. John Carling (q.v.). In summer it is connected by steamboat with Gravenhurst. Pop. (1934), 400.

**Port Churchill. See Churchill.**

**Port Colborne,** a town in Welland county, Ontario, situated on the northeast shore of lake Erie, at the entrance of the Welland ship canal, and on the

Canadian National Railway, 25 miles south of St. Catharines. The town was named in memory of Sir John Colborne (q.v.). The harbour, which can accommodate the largest vessels on the Great lakes, is on both sides of the canal entrance, and is protected by extensive breakwaters. All municipal facilities are available in the town. Several industries are established: a large nickel-refining plant, cement works, a modern elevator, and an iron-ore smelter. The port is a trans-shipping point from the West to Montreal. The educational institutions are a high school, three public schools, and a public library. Pop. (1931), 6,503.

**Port Coquitlam,** a city in British Columbia, situated at the junction of Pitt and Fraser rivers, 17 miles east of Vancouver, on the Canadian Pacific Railway. The name Coquitlam is that of a Salish tribe in the locality speaking the Cowichan dialect. Fruit-farming is successfully carried on in the neighbourhood. Fishing and hunting and splendid scenery attract many tourists. Pop. (1931), 1,312.

**Port Credit,** a town in Peel county, Ontario, situated at the mouth of the Credit river on lake Ontario, on the Canadian National Railway, 12 miles west of Toronto. The town takes its name from the Credit river (q.v.). The port was formerly of some importance in shipping, but the harbour works have been allowed to decay. The channel into the river is used by fishing craft only, as the depth of water is not more than $4\frac{1}{2}$ to 5 feet. The fishing industry is becoming important. The other industries are a starch factory, a brick works, fruit-growing, and farming. A weekly newspaper (*News*) is published. Pop. (1931), 1,635.

**Port Dalhousie,** a village in Lincoln county, Ontario, is situated on the south side of lake Ontario at the entrance to the old Welland canal. It owes its origin to the building of the first Welland canal, completed in 1829. At the time of the building of the second Welland canal, the settlement had only fourteen houses; but its growth was steady, and in 1862 it was incorporated as a village and was named after Lord Dalhousie (q.v.), governor of Canada (1920-8). Pop. (1931) about 1,700; but in summer this is increased to about 3,000.

**Port Daniel,** a village and harbour in Bonaventure county, Quebec, on the north shore of Chaleur bay, and on the Gaspé-Matapedia branch of the Canadian National Railways, 45 miles southwest of Percé. Exports are chiefly lumber and fish. On Port Daniel bay there are three villages, Port Daniel Centre and Port Daniel East and West, with a combined population of about 2,000.

**Port Dover,** a village in Norfolk county, Ontario, situated on the north shore of lake Erie, on the Canadian National and Lake Erie Northern Railways, 40 miles south-west of Hamilton. The place was named after Dover, England. The harbour is located at the mouth of the Lynn river. A commercial fishing fleet operates from the port. The other industries are farming, lumbering, canning, ship-building, cereal food manufacturing, and the making of greenhouses in the largest plant in Canada. Natural gas and hydro-electric power are to be had in abundance. Port Dover is a popular summer resort. It has a weekly newspaper (*Maple Leaf*). Pop. (1931), 1,707.

**Port Dover and Lake Huron Railway,** a railway line opened in 1875 between Port Dover and Stratford, Ontario. In 1880 it took over the Stratford and Huron Railway; and it became part of the Georgian Bay and Lake Erie Railway. Later, it was absorbed by the Grand Trunk Railway.

**Port Dufferin,** a village in Halifax county, Nova Scotia, on the Salmon river, 80 miles east of Dartmouth, the nearest railway station. It is a fishing village; and there are gold mines in the neighbourhood. Pop. (1934), 650.

**Port Elgin,** a village in Bruce county, Ontario, situated on the eastern shore of lake Huron, and on the Canadian National Railway, 28 miles north-west of Walkerton. The place was named in 1851 in honour of the Earl of Elgin (q.v.), governor-general of British North America. The port's chief industries are commercial fishing, a brush and broom factory, a planing mill, and a machine shop. The village has several churches, public and high schools, and a public library. A sandy beach and a golf course attract summer tourists. A weekly newspaper (*Times*) is published. Pop. (1931), 1,305. There is also a village named Port Elgin in Westmorland county, New Brunswick, on the Canadian National Railway, 20 miles from Sackville. Pop. (1931), 600.

**Port Essington,** a settlement in Range 5 of the Coast district of British Columbia, on the Skeena river, 12 miles from its mouth. It is a port of call for coastwise steamships. Pop. (1934), 400.

**Port Greville,** a village in Cumberland county, Nova Scotia, on the north shore of Greville bay, on Minas channel. It is a port of entry, but the nearest railway is at Parrsboro. The harbour is dry at low tide.

**Port Hammond.** See **Hammond.**

**Port Haney,** a village and steamer landing in the New Westminster district of British Columbia, on the north side of the Fraser river, and on the main line of the Canadian Pacific Railway, 26 miles east of Vancouver, and 2 miles east of Port Hammond. It has three churches and a school, and is a port of call for steamers. Pop. (1930), 1,000.

**Port Hardy,** a village on Hardy bay, on the north-east coast of Vancouver island. It has a government wharf, and ships call weekly or bi-weekly.

**Port Hastings,** a village and harbour in Inverness county, Nova Scotia, on the east shore of the strait of Canso, 4 miles north of Port Hawkesbury. It is a coal-shipping port for the Inverness

Mines on the Canadian National Railway. Pop. (1934), 600.

**Port Hawkesbury,** a town in Inverness county, Nova Scotia, on the east shore of the strait of Canso, and on the Canadian National, Inverness, and Cape Breton Railways. It is adjacent to Point Tupper, the docking terminal of the car-ferry over the strait of Canso; and it is connected with Halifax through a weekly steamship service. It exports fish, and imports general merchandise. It has two large cold-storage plants for fish, a large and modern creamery, and a weekly newspaper (*Victoria-Inverness Bulletin*). Pop. (1934), 1,000.

**Port Hood,** a village and harbour on the west coast of Cape Breton island, Nova Scotia, and on the Canadian National Railway, 23 miles from Inverness. It was formerly a coal-shipping port of the Inverness Coal Company. Pop. (1934), 800. See D. S. McIntosh, *Port Hood harbour* (Trans. Nova Scotia Institute of Science, vol. xv).

**Port Hope,** a town in Durham county, Ontario, is situated on lake Ontario, 63 miles east of Toronto. It is served by the Canadian National and the Canadian Pacific Railways, has an excellent harbour, and is an industrial centre, producing tiles, enamel ware, and preserved and canned goods, etc. There was a trading post on its site, at the Mississaga village of Cochingomink, as early as 1778. A trader name Peter Smith built the first log cabin on its site, and the settlement came to be known as Smith's Creek. For a time it was called Toronto. United Empire Loyalists began to settle there about 1792, and in that year Mydert Harris, an arrival from Annapolis Royal, Nova Scotia, became the first permanent settler. In 1817, the village was given the name Port Hope, probably in honour of Colonel Henry Hope (q.v.), who had been a friend of the Loyalist settlers. The name was confirmed by the legislature of Upper Canada on

March 6, 1834. Port Hope is the home of Trinity College School for boys, and has a high school, a public library, a hospital, and a daily newspaper (*Guide*), with a weekly edition established in 1831. Pop. (1931), 4,723. See W. A. Craick, *Port Hope historical sketches* (Port Hope, 1901).

**Portland,** a village in Leeds county, Ontario, on Rideau lake, and on the Canadian National Railway. Pop. (1934), 300.

**Portland canal.** See **Portland inlet.**

**Portland inlet,** a body of water extending for 25 miles in a north-easterly direction from the northern end of Chatham sound, in the Cassiar district of British Columbia. Its northern continuation, with a length of 70 miles, is known as Portland canal, and was declared by the Alaska boundary commission of 1903 to be the boundary between British and American territory. The name Portland was given to both inlet and canal by Vancouver (q.v.) in 1793, in honour of the ducal house of Portland.

**Portland point,** a small promontory at the mouth of the St. John river, in New Brunswick. It was the site of the first English settlement in this locality. See W. O. Raymond, *At Portland point* (New Brunswick Magazine, 1898).

**Port Latour,** a village in Shelburne county, Nova Scotia, on a harbour of the Atlantic coast, 10 miles from Barrington, and 21 miles from Shelburne. It derives its name from the fact that Claude de La Tour (q.v.) built a fort here in the early part of the seventeenth century. Pop. (1934), 750.

**Portlock, Nathaniel** (1748?-1817), mariner, was born in England about 1748, and became a master mariner. He was in command of a fur-trading expedition which visited the coast of British Columbia in 1787; and he was the author of *A voyage round the world* (London, 1789). He died at Greenwich hospital, in England, on September 12, 1817.

**Port McNicholl,** a village in Simcoe county, Ontario, situated on an artificial harbour, 5 miles east of Midland at the foot of Sturgeon bay, the south-eastern part of Georgian bay, and on the Canadian Pacific Railway. The place was founded in 1909 by the Canadian Pacific Railway Company, and named in honour of an executive of the company, David McNicoll, or McNicholl (1852-1916). The port is a grain and transfer point and terminal of the Canadian Pacific Railway's upper lake steamship service. An elevator with a capacity for 7,000,000 bushels is used for grain, flour, and general freight. Pop. (1931), 1,074.

**Port Maitland,** a village and harbour in Haldimand county, Ontario, near the mouth of the Grand river, on lake Erie, and on the Toronto, Hamilton, and Buffalo Railway. Car ferries run between this harbour and Ashtabula, Ohio. The chief local industry is fishing. There is also a fishing village named Port Maitland in Yarmouth county, Nova Scotia, 10 miles north of Yarmouth, at the entrance to the bay of Fundy.

**Port Mann,** a village and steamer landing in the New Westminster district of British Columbia, on the south side of the Fraser river, and on the Canadian National Railway, 4 miles east of New Westminster. Pop. (1934), 300.

**Port Medway,** a village and harbour in Queen's county, Nova Scotia, at the mouth of the Medway river, and 3 miles from Medway station on the Canadian National Railway. By highway it is 12 miles from Liverpool and 20 miles from Bridgewater. The chief exports are pulpwood and fish. Pop. (1934), 670.

**Port Menier,** a village on Ellis bay, at the west end of Anticosti island, in the gulf of St. Lawrence. It was founded in 1895 by Henri Menier, a wealthy French chocolate-manufacturer, who purchased the island of Anticosti; but is now owned by the Consolidated Paper Corporation, which have a pulpwood plant here, but have in recent years been compelled to suspend operations. Pop. (1935), 300. See also **Anticosti island.**

**Port Moody,** a city in British Columbia, situated at the head of Burrard inlet, on the main line of the Canadian Pacific Railway, 12 miles east of Vancouver. The city was incorporated in 1913; but the place received its name in 1860, bestowed on it by Captain Richards, H.M. surveying vessel *Plumper*, in honour of Colonel (afterwards Major-General) Richard Clement Moody (q.v.), who commanded the sappers and miners who opened up most of the roads in the early days of British Columbia. Lumbering is the main industry; but there are also two oil refineries, one of them on the opposite side of the inlet. It has a high school. Pop. (1931), 1,260.

**Port Morien,** a fishing town and harbour in Cape Breton county, Nova Scotia, on the east coast of Cape Breton island, and on the Sydney and Louisburg Railway, 6 miles from Glace Bay. It exports fish, and imports general merchandise. Pop. (1934), 1,000.

**Port Mouton,** a village and seaport in Queen's county, Nova Scotia, on an inlet of the Atlantic, and on the Canadian National Railway, 10 miles from Liverpool. It was named "Port du Mouton" by Monts (q.v.) in 1604, from the fact that here a sheep (*mouton*) jumped overboard and was nearly drowned. Pop. (1934), 800.

**Port Mulgrave,** a village and harbour in Guysborough county, Nova Scotia, on the west side of the strait of Canso, and on the Canadian National Railway. It is the western terminus of the car-ferry over the strait of Canso, connecting with Port Hawkesbury. Fish, lumber, and pulpwood are exported. Pop. (1934), 400.

**Portneuf,** a county in Quebec, bounded on the south by the river St. Lawrence, on the west and north by Champlain county, and on the east by Quebec county. It is named after the Portneuf river flowing through it; and this river was probably so named because of the "new port" (*port neuf*) at its mouth. It is traversed by the Canadian Pacific and Canadian National Railways. Chief town, Cap Santé. Pop. (1931), 35,890.

**Portneuf,** a village in Portneuf county, Quebec, at the mouth of the Portneuf river, and on the Canadian Pacific and Canadian National Railways, 37 miles west of Quebec. It is the most important industrial centre on the north shore of the St. Lawrence between Quebec and Three Rivers, and has paper mills, saw-mills, a foundry, a steel construction plant, a tannery, butter factories, and a cheese factory. Pop. (1934), 2,000.

**Port Perry,** a village in Ontario county, Ontario, situated on lake Scugog, and on the Canadian National Railway, 48 miles north-east of Toronto. A settlement was established here in 1873, and named in honour of George Perry, M.P.P. The village has four churches, high and public schools, and a public library. The chief industries are flour- and saw-mills, and harness making. Farms, orchards, and rose and dahlia gardens are in the neighbourhood. Fishing and duck-shooting attract tourists. A weekly newspaper (*Star*) is published. Pop. (1931), 1,163.

**Port Razoir.** See **Shelburne.**

**Port Robinson,** a village in Welland county, Ontario, on the Welland branch of the Canadian National Railways, and on the Welland canal, 4 miles north of Welland. It was the southern terminus of the original Welland canal, which here joined the Welland river. Pop. (1934), 400.

**Port Roseway.** See **Shelburne.**

**Port Rowan,** a village in Norfolk county, Ontario, on Long Point bay, and the terminus of the South Norfolk branch of the Canadian National Railways, 15 miles south-west of Simcoe. It was founded in 1825, and was later named in honour of Sir William Rowan (q.v.). It has grist, saw, and planing mills, a high school, and a weekly newspaper (*News*). Pop. (1934), 672.

**Port Royal.** See **Annapolis Royal.**

**Port Ryerse,** a village in Norfolk county, Ontario, on lake Erie, 10 miles south of Simcoe, the nearest railway station. In the early days of the province it was a place of some importance; but its importance long ago declined. Pop. (1934), 100. See George J. Ryerse, *Port Ryerse, its harbour and former trade* (Ont. Hist. Soc., Papers and Records, 1923).

**Port Sandfield,** a summer resort in the Muskoka district, Ontario, between lakes Joseph and Rosseau. It was named after the Hon. John Sandfield Macdonald (q.v.).

**Port Simpson,** a village and seaport in Range 5 of the Coast district of British Columbia, on the Pacific coast, opposite Dixon entrance, 550 miles north of Vancouver, and 30 miles north of Prince Rupert. It was named after Capt. Æmilius Simpson (d. 1831), an officer of the Hudson's Bay Company who founded Fort Simpson at the mouth of the Nass river, a port transferred in 1834 to the present site of Port Simpson. The village has a school and a hospital. Pop. (1934), 750.

**Portsmouth,** an incorporated village in Frontenac county, Ontario, on lake Ontario, 2 miles west of Kingston, with which it is connected by electric railway. It is the site of the Portsmouth Penitentiary and of a lunatic asylum. Pop. (1934), 2,500.

**Port Stanley,** a village and harbour in Elgin county, Ontario, on the north shore of lake Erie, at the mouth of Kettle creek, 60 miles west of Long point. It is the southern terminus of the London and Port Stanley Electric Railway, and is a summer resort. It is also a centre of the fishing industry. Pop. (1934), 900.

**Port Stanley,** a village and summer resort in the Muskoka district, Ontario, on Mary lake and on the north branch of the Muskoka river, 12 miles from Huntsville. Pop. (1934), 200.

**Port Sydney,** a village and summer resort in the Muskoka district, Ontario, on Mary lake and on the north branch of the Muskoka river, 12 miles from Huntsville. Pop. (1934), 200.

**Port Wade,** a small village in Annapolis county, Nova Scotia, on the north-west shore of Annapolis basin, opposite Digby. It has a government wharf which was built for the shipping of iron ore, but is now used only for shipments of lumber.

**Port Weller,** a harbour on the south shore of lake Ontario, 3 miles east of Port Dalhousie, at the entrance to the new Welland ship canal. It was named after George H. Weller, sometime superintendent engineer of the old Welland canal, with whom the idea of building the new canal originated.

**Port Williams,** a village and harbour in King's county, Nova Scotia, on the south bank of the Cornwallis river, 6 miles from its mouth on Minas basin, and on the Dominion Atlantic Railway, 5 miles from Kentville. It is a rich apple-growing district, and large shipments of apples are made from this port. Pop. (1934), 950.

**Postage Stamps.** See **Philately.**

**Post Office.** During the French régime there was no postal service in Canada, except a system of official couriers, established in 1721, between Quebec and Montreal, whose chief duty was to carry government dispatches, but who carried also private letters. With the British conquest, however, Canada came under the British post-office, which had been established as

early as the end of the seventeenth century, and which early extended its operations to the British colonies in North America. A post-office was established in Halifax in 1755, and postal communication was opened with both Boston and London; and in 1763 post-offices were opened in Quebec, Three Rivers, and Montreal, with communication by means of courier between Montreal and New York. Later, when the thirteen colonies to the south had declared their independence, a deputy postmaster-general was appointed for the remaining British North American colonies, with headquarters in Quebec; and the postal arrangements in British North America continued to be under his control, as a subordinate of the post-master-general in Great Britain, until the middle of the nineteenth century.

This state of affairs gave rise to grave complaints. It meant that the people of British North America had no voice in the control of their own postal service. The deputy postmaster-general at Quebec was independent even of the governor-general of Canada; and could alone decide where post offices were to be established. The years between 1783 and 1850 saw, it is true, a remarkable development of the post office in British North America. In 1788 communication was opened overland by courier between Quebec and Halifax. In 1792 a postal convention was concluded with the United States, whereby the United States post-office engaged to act as the intermediary for the conveyance of mails between Canada and Great Britain. York (Toronto) had a post-office as early as 1800; and between 1816 and 1827 the number of post-offices in Upper and Lower Canada increased from 19 to 114. These were mainly on a trunk line of communication between Halifax, Quebec, Montreal, York, and Amherstburgh, with routes branching off to such places as Sherbrooke, St. John's, Hull, Hawkesbury, Perth, and Richmond—over which couriers travelled at varying intervals. But many pioneer communities remained without a postal service. As late as 1835, for example, the settlers at Barrie, on lake Simcoe, had to travel forty miles to the nearest post-office, at Newmarket. The postal rates were, moreover, exorbitantly high. One hundred years ago it cost ninepence to send a letter consisting of a single folded sheet of paper from Montreal to York (Toronto), and over four shillings from York to England, by way of Halifax. If there were more than one sheet of paper, the charge was four times as great. The charge on newspapers was four shillings a copy per annum; and it was one of the anomalies of those times that the revenue from newspapers went into the pocket of the deputy postmaster-general as a perquisite of his office.

Despite the discontent, however, it was not until the advent of responsible government that the control of the post-office in British North America was handed over to the governments of the British North American provinces in 1847-51. The result was a vindication of those who had advocated this reform. The number of post-offices underwent a rapid increase, so rapid that in Canada proper it was doubled in five years, trebled in ten, and quadrupled in fifteen; and at the same time the postal rates were reduced to one-third of what they had been, with the result that within ten years the revenue from this source was double what it had been in 1851. A feature of the lower rates was the introduction of the postage stamp. Hitherto letters had been paid for usually on delivery, with the result that letters carried long distances were sometimes refused. The postage stamp compelled people to pre-pay their letters, and thus proved more economical and business-like.

In 1867 the post-offices of the various provinces were taken over by the new Dominion government, and were placed under the charge of the postmaster-general of Canada, who was made a member of the Canadian government. Since then great advances have been made. The number of post-offices in Canada has grown to such an extent that there is now hardly a community of any size in Canada outside the Arctic circle that has not a post-office. The delivery of mail has been accelerated, first by the railway, secondly by the motor-car, and thirdly by the aeroplane. At the same time, the cost of postage has been reduced to a minimum. In 1878 Canada became a member of the Universal Postal Union, the object of which is to promote intercharge of correspondence among the nations of the world. In 1897 imperial penny postage (2 cents per half-ounce) was introduced; and while it has not been possible to maintain this rate, it has not since that time been greatly exceeded. About 1875 the post-card was introduced; and later a parcel post was inaugurated, so that Christmas presents, for example, could be sent by post instead of by express. Special rates have been established for books; and newspapers are now delivered by post at a fraction of their cost of delivery, since they are deemed to have an educational influence. Lastly, in 1908, a system of rural mail delivery was inaugurated. This has been developed until there are to-day about 250,000 rural mail boxes served by the post-office, and has proved a great boon to the Canadian farmer.

Since Confederation, the Canadian post-office has established a number of auxiliary services, such as the issuance of money orders and postal notes and the establishment of post-office savings banks; and these also have undergone a spectacular development.

While the post-office in Canada has never been a profit-producing department, it has, unlike many other public services, nearly always paid its way, and has remained an outstanding example of the success of public ownership of public utilities.

For the history of the post-office in British North America, see W. Smith, *The history of the post office in British North America, 1639-1870* (Toronto and Cambridge, 1920). For current statistics in regard to the post-office, see the *Canada Year Book*.

**Pothier, Jean Baptiste Toussaint** (1771-1845), legislative and executive councillor of Lower Canada, was born at Montreal on May 16, 1771, the son of Louis Toussaint Pothier, a fur-trader, and Louise Courault. In 1812 he organized and commanded a corps of voyageurs for the defence of the lakes. From 1824 to 1838 he was a member of the Legislative Council of Lower Canada; from 1838 to 1839 of the Executive Council; and from 1838 to 1841 of the Special Council. He died at Montreal on October 22, 1845. In 1820 he married Anne Françoise, daughter of Lieut.-Col. Ralph Henry Bruyères, R.E. See E. Z. Massicotte, *L'honorable Toussaint Pothier* (Bull. rech. hist., 1920).

**Potlatch,** the word used to denote the great winter ceremonials held among the Indian tribes of the north Pacific coast from Oregon to Alaska. The word has passed into popular speech from the Chinook jargon (q.v.), into which it was adopted from the Nootka word for "giving" or "a gift". Although they varied in different localities, potlatches were mainly marked by the giving away of quantities of goods, frequently blankets. The giver sometimes went so far as to strip himself of nearly everything but his house; but he obtained his reward in the esteem of his fellows, and when others "potlatched", he received something back from them. The idea underlying the potlatch is that "it is more blessed to give than to receive". The potlatch was formerly accompanied by dancing, singing, and feasting, as well as by secret rites such as the raising of carved poles, the slitting of ears, noses, and lips for ornaments, and the tattooing of children. See W. M. Halliday, *Potlatch and totem* (London, 1935).

**Potts, John** (1838-1907), general secretary of education for the Methodist Church (1886-1907), was born at Maguire's Bridge, county Fermanagh, Ireland, in 1838. He came to Canada in 1855, and was educated at Victoria University, Cobourg. In 1861 he was ordained a minister of the Methodist Church, and he held successive charges in many parts of Ontario. In 1886 he was appointed general educational secretary of the Methodist Church, and he held this position until his death at Toronto on October 16, 1907. Early in life he married Margaret, daughter of John Breden, of Kingston. He was a D.D. of the Wesleyan University of Ohio (1878) and of Victoria University (1894).

**Poundmaker** (1826-1886), Indian chief, was born near Battleford, North West Territories, in 1826. In 1881, as a chief of the Cree nation, he acted as guide of the Marquis of Lorne (q.v.) and his party from Battleford to Calgary, during the vice-regal tour of the North-West; and in 1885 he was persuaded by Louis Riel (q.v.) to take part in the second North-West Rebellion. He commanded the Indians at the skirmish of Cut Knife Creek and at Batoche. After the capture of Riel, he surrendered himself to General Middleton (q.v.), was tried at Regina, and was sentenced to three years' imprisonment. He was released after a year's confinement; but he died shortly afterward, on July 4, 1886, while on a visit to Crowfoot, chief of the Blackfoot Indians, at Gleichen, near Calgary.

**Poutré, Félix** (1816?-1885), patriot or spy, was born in Lower Canada about 1816, and is reputed to have taken some part in the patriot rebellion of 1837-8. He was imprisoned at Montreal, probably as a government agent employed to spy upon his fellow-prisoners, and he is said to have escaped punishment by feigning madness. He later published a pamphlet giving an account of his experiences, under the title *Échappé de la* *potence* (Montreal, 1862; 2nd ed., Montreal, 1884), and this was translated into English under the title *Escaped from the gallows* (Montreal, 1862). He became a popular hero; and Louis Fréchette (q.v.) embodied his story in an historical drama entitled *Félix Poutré*. His claims to fame as a patriot have, however, been seriously questioned; and it is probable that he was an *agent provocateur*. See L. A. Lapointe, *Documents inédit sur Félix Poutré* (Bull. rech. hist., 1927), and G. Lanctot, *La fin d'une légende* (Revue Franco-Americaine, 1913).

**Poutrincourt, Jean de Biencourt de.** See **Biencourt de Poutrincourt, Jean de.**

**Powassan,** a village in Parry Sound district, Ontario, on the South river, near lake Nipissing, and on the Canadian National Railway, 20 miles south of North Bay. The chief industries are lumbering, fishing, farming, and brick-making. The town has a continuation school and a weekly newspaper (*News*). Pop. (1934), 650.

**Powell, Grant** (1819-1904), under-secretary of state for Canada, was born in York (Toronto), Upper Canada, on September 2, 1819, the third son of Grant Powell, M.D., and Elizabeth Bleeker, and grandson of the Hon. William Dummer Powell (q.v.). He was educated at Upper Canada College; and in 1839 he entered the office of the civil secretary of Upper Canada. In 1883 he was appointed under-secretary of state for Canada; and he retired on pension in 1896. He died at Ottawa on January 28, 1904.

**Powell, Henry Watson** (1733-1814), soldier, was born in England in 1733, and entered the British army. He came to Canada in 1776 in command of the 53rd Foot, became a brigadier-general, and was successively in command at Ticonderoga, Montreal, Niagara, and Quebec. He returned to England at the close of the American Revolutionary War, and in 1801 became a general. He died at Lyme, England, on July 14, 1814.

**Powell, Walker** (1828-1915), soldier, was born at Waterford, Upper Canada, on May 20, 1828, the son of Israel Wood Powell and Melinda Boss. He was educated at Victoria University, Cobourg. From 1857 to 1861 he represented Norfolk in the Legislative Assembly of Canada; and in 1862 he became deputy adjutant-general of Upper Canada. In 1868 he was appointed deputy adjutant-general of Canada, and in 1875 adjutant-general, with the rank of colonel in the militia. He held this office until his retirement on pension in 1896; and he had much to do with the organization of the militia system of the Dominion. He died at Ottawa on May 6, 1915. He married (1) in 1853 Catherine Emma Culver (d. 1855), and (2) in 1857 Mary Ursula Bowlby; and he had six children. In 1885 he was created a C.M.G.

**Powell, William Dummer** (1755-1834), chief justice of Upper Canada, was born in Boston, Massachusetts, in 1755, the son of John Powell and Jane Grant. He was educated in England and in Holland, and in 1779 he was called to the English bar from the Middle Temple. The same year he came to Canada, and was admitted to practise as an attorney in the province of Quebec. He practised law in Montreal, and in 1783 was one of the delegates sent to England to petition for the repeal of the Quebec Act. In 1789 he was appointed the first judge of the court of Common Pleas in the district of Hesse. In 1794 he was appointed a judge of the court of King's Bench in Upper Canada; and in 1816 he became chief justice of this court. At the same time he was appointed speaker of the Legislative Council of the province. He retired from the bench in 1825; and he died at Toronto on September 6, 1834. In 1773 he married Anne, daughter of Dr. J. Murray, of Norwich, England; and by her he had five sons and three daughters. See W. R. Riddell, *The life of William*

*Dummer Powell* (Lansing, Mich., 1924); and C. C. James, *William Dummer Powell, a critical incident* (Trans. Roy. Soc. Can., 1912).

**Powell River,** a town in the Comox district, British Columbia, is situated on a fine harbour 78 miles north-west of Vancouver. It derives its name from a short river, the Powell, which formerly drained the waters of Powell lake and Goat lake. This river is now dammed for the production of hydraulic electric power. The main industry is the manufacture of newsprint paper. An excellent boat service is provided between Powell River and Vancouver by the Canadian National Railway, the Canadian Pacific Railway, and the Union Steamship Company; and there is a daily airplane service. Pop. (1931) about 2,200; but with the surrounding villages it is over 4,000.

**Power, Lawrence Geoffrey** (1841-1921), speaker of the Senate of Canada (1901-5), was born at Halifax, Nova Scotia, on August 9, 1841, the son of Patrick Power (q.v.) and Ellen Gaul. He was educated at St. Mary's College, Halifax (B.A., 1858) and at Harvard University (LL.B., 1866); and was called to the bar of Nova Scotia in 1866 (K.C., 1905). From 1867 to 1877 he was clerk of the House of Assembly of Nova Scotia; and in 1877 he was called to the Senate of Canada. From 1901 to 1905 he was speaker of the Senate; and in 1905 he was sworn of the Imperial privy council. He died at Halifax on September 12, 1921. In 1880 he married Susan O'Leary, of West Quoddy, Nova Scotia. He received the honorary degree of LL.D. from Ottawa University in 1901.

**Power, Michael** (1804-1847), Roman Catholic bishop of Toronto (1842-7), was born in Halifax, Nova Scotia, on October 17, 1804. He became a priest of the Roman Catholic Church, and was curé of La Prairie, Lower Canada, until 1841. In that year he was nominated bishop of the western part of the diocese of Kingston; and in 1842 he was consecrated first bishop of Toronto. He espoused the cause of the Jesuits in Upper Canada; and for a time he was chairman of the council of public instruction in Upper Canada. He died in Toronto on October 1, 1847.

**Power, Patrick** (1815-1881), politician, was born in the county of Waterford, Ireland, on March 17, 1815, the son of Lawrence Power. He emigrated to Nova Scotia with his father in 1823, and was educated in Halifax. He went into business in Halifax, and became a supporter of Joseph Howe (q.v.). In 1867 he was elected as an anti-confederation candidate in Halifax county in the Canadian House of Commons; and he sat in the House of Commons from 1867 to 1872, and from 1874 to 1878. He died at Halifax, on February 23, 1881.

**Prairie Chicken.** See **Grouse.**

**Prairie du Chien,** a settlement founded by French fur-traders on the Upper Mississippi, four miles above the mouth of the Wisconsin river. It was named after a Fox chief named Le Chien. During the War of 1812 it was captured by a combined force of British and Indians under Lieut.-Col. William McKay (q.v.).

**Precambrian Shield.** See **Canadian Shield.**

**Preeceville,** a village in Saskatchewan, on the Assiniboia river, and on the Canadian National Railway, 30 miles from Canora. It has a high school and a weekly newspaper (*Progress*). Pop. (1934), 250.

**Preference, Imperial.** See **Imperial Preference** and **Tariffs.**

**Préfontaine, Joseph Raymond Fournier** (1850-1905), minister of marine and fisheries for Canada (1902-5), was born at Longueuil, Lower Canada, on September 16, 1850, and was educated at St. Mary's College, Montreal, and at McGill University (B.C.L.,

1873). He was called to the bar of Quebec in 1873 (Q.C., 1893), and practised law for many years in Montreal. He represented Chambly in the Legislative Assembly of Quebec from 1875 to 1881, and in the Canadian House of Commons from 1886 to 1896. In 1896 he was returned to the Commons for Maisonneuve; in 1898 he was elected mayor of Montreal; and in 1902 he was appointed minister of marine and fisheries in the Laurier government. He died at Paris, France, on December 26, 1905. In 1876 he married Hermantine, daughter of the Hon. J. B. Rolland, a senator of Canada.

**Prehistory.** When human history in Canada began, is a matter of conjecture. There are those who have attempted to prove that man in America antedated the Ice Ages. There is no doubt that American mastodons of pre-glacial times must have migrated to America from Asia by way of the land bridge that once existed between Siberia and Alaska; and if mastodons found their way over this land bridge, why not man? On the other hand, no sure proof of the existence of man in America before the Ice Age has been found; and if there were men in Canada before the Ice Age, it is certain that they could not have survived the Ice Age, in Canada at least. Until proof of the contrary is forthcoming, therefore, it must be assumed that the history of man in Canada does not begin until post-glacial times.

The inhabitants of Canada, before the coming of the Europeans, were what we know now as Indians—a name bestowed on them as a result of the mistaken belief of the early explorers that the West Indies were the East Indies. For a time, it was thought that the Indians were not the original inhabitants of America, but were preceded by a race known as "the Mound Builders"—so called from the burial mounds found in many parts of the United States. It is now believed, however, that these mounds were built by the Indians themselves, and not by any prior race. It is thus probable that the Indians were the first human inhabitants of America; and the theory has been advanced that they were indigenous to America. Certainly, the similarity between the languages of the American Indian and those spoken in other parts of the world is slight. But the evidence of anthropology seems to suggest that the Indian migrated originally from Asia. His racial characteristics are Mongoloid; and many of his cultural characteristics are Mongoloid also. Even the linguistic evidence suggests an Asiatic origin; for it has recently been demonstrated that there are similarities between some of the Indian languages and primitive Chinese, not in words, but in the system whereby the same words in different "tones" have widely different meanings. There are also suggestive similarities between Indian music and primitive Chinese music.

If, as seems certain, the Indians of Canada came originally from Asia, it is probable that they came by way of the land bridge that formerly existed between Siberia and Alaska; though it is by no means impossible that they may have come after the land connection was broken, for even to-day the passage across Bering strait by way of the Aleutian islands is not impossible for primitive craft, and there are well-authenticated cases of Chinese and Japanese junks having been blown ashore on the coast of north-western America. It is, indeed, possible that the Indians of South America may have come originally from Polynesia by way of the South Sea islands, or by way of a land connection which may have once existed between Polynesia and South America. But, however they may have come, there is now little doubt that the American Indians came originally from Asia.

The Eskimo, who inhabit the northern fringe of the North American continent, used to be thought a different race from the Indians. But recent investigation has shown that they too are of Mongoloid origin, and probably entered America by way of Bering strait. Their language has affinities with Turkish, Hungarian, and Finnish, rather than with the languages of other American tribes—a fact which suggests that they may have been a later migration. But they are in origin not essentially different from the other inhabitants of Canada in prehistoric times.

The aborigines of Canada never developed, except in a most primitive and rudimentary way, the art of writing. Consequently, our knowledge of them, during the many thousands of years which elapsed before the coming of the Europeans and the dawn of written history, is slight. It is mainly derived from the researches of archæologists. These have made it clear that in some parts of the Americas the Indians developed a considerable civilization. The Indians of South and Central America constructed magnificent stone buildings, the ruins of many of which are still standing; they understood the working of the softer metals; they made elaborate and artistic pottery; and they seem to have known something of surgery and of astronomy. The Indians of Canada, however, remained much more primitive. Their clothing was the skin of animals; and they lived on the fruits of the chase. Few of them cultivated the soil; and these grew only Indian corn or maize, planted in the natural clearings of the forest. They were still, at the coming of the white man, in the nomadic stage of society, one tribe warring with another for its hunting-grounds; and we can only guess at the widespread movements of population that must have taken place in Canada in prehistoric times. Even after the coming of the first European explorers, there were profound changes of habitat among the Indians with regard to which our information is negligible. The history

of the Indian inhabitants of Canada before the coming of the white man is, and will probably always remain, an almost impenetrable mystery. See S. Leacock, *The dawn of Canadian history* (Toronto, 1914). See also **Indians.**

**Premier.** See **Prime Minister.**

**Premonstratensian Fathers** (O. Proem.). The Premonstratensian Canons were founded in 1120 by St. Norbert at Prémontré, near Laon, France. To-day the order is widely spread in most European countries, and is also represented in the United States and Canada. In Canada the Fathers are engaged in colonization and parish works in the dioceses of Edmonton and Vancouver.

**Presbyterian Church.** Among the earliest settlers in Canada were to be found Presbyterians—Huguenots from France, and "Reformed" people from Holland and Germany. United Empire Loyalists from the United States also provided their quota. But the predominant elements in Canadian Presbyterianism came from Scotland and the north of Ireland. In the half-century prior to 1867, there was a large immigration from the British Isles. Wherever the Scottish or the Scots-Irish elements abounded, Presbyterianism became firmly rooted; a notable example of this was the Pictou district in Nova Scotia. The divisions in the Presbyterianism of Scotland found their way overseas, and by 1860 there were at least eight distinct and self-governing Presbyterian bodies —three in the Canadas and five in the Maritime provinces. In order of formation, these were as follows: the synod of the Presbyterian Church of Nova Scotia (1817); the synod of the Presbyterian Church of Canada, in connection with the Church of Scotland (1831); the synod of New Brunswick, in connection with the Church of Scotland (1833); the synod of the United Presbyterian Church of Canada, in connection with the United Presbyterian Church of Scotland (1834); the synod of the (Free)

Presbyterian Church of Canada (1844); the synod of the Free Church of Nova Scotia (1844); the synod of the (Free) Presbyterian Church of New Brunswick (1845); and the synod of the Church of Scotland in Nova Scotia and Prince Edward Island (1854). In 1860 the number was reduced to seven by the union of two synods in Nova Scotia; in 1861 the union of two synods of the Canadas resulted in the formation of the "Canada Presbyterian Church"; and in 1866 two New Brunswick synods became one. So that when, in 1867, the Dominion of Canada came into being, the number of separated Presbyterian bodies had been reduced from eight to five. The number was still further reduced the next year by the union of the synod of New Brunswick and the synod of the Church of Scotland in Nova Scotia and Prince Edward Island, neither of which, however, had been a synod of the Scottish national church, but entirely self-governing.

*1867-1875.* In 1868, within the newly-formed Dominion, there were four Presbyterian bodies—the synod of the Presbyterian Church of Canada in connection with the Church of Scotland and the synod of the Maritime provinces in connection with the Church of Scotland, both of which had only a nominal relationship with the parent Scottish Church, and the general assembly of the Canada Presbyterian Church and the synod of the Presbyterian Church of the lower provinces, neither of which was even nominally connected with the Church of Scotland.

The political confederation of 1867 turned the dream of a dominion-wide Presbyterian Church into a firm resolve and definite purpose in many minds. Committees of the various bodies were appointed to explore the possibility of union, and in 1870 a joint committee was formed to consider and to make recommendations to the several synods. This committee, finding itself in substantial agreement, drafted a basis of union, in which the Scriptures of the Old and New Testaments were declared to be the supreme standard of faith, the Westminster Confession to be the subordinate standard, and in which fraternal relations with other Presbyterian Churches were warmly urged. The Basis of Union was earnestly debated throughout the various synods. The first and second clauses were slightly amended, and the third was dropped. In addition, Christ was definitely declared to be the "Head of the Church and Head over all things to the Church", and the form of Presbyterian Church government, and the directory of public worship, of the Westminster Assembly, were made general guides to worship and polity. Among the clauses attached to the Basis, the Church professed "Christian affection toward the whole Church of God", and made needful provision for congregational procedure, for the support of ministers' widows and orphans, for the disposal of property, for theological education, and for the prosecution of missionary work at home and abroad. Required legislation was obtained in the various provinces; the union of the four churches was formally consummated in a memorable gathering in Victoria Hall, Montreal, on June 15, 1875; and "The Presbyterian Church in Canada" was launched upon its way. Some twenty-five congregations refused from a variety of reasons to concur in the union, but in the later years they passed, one by one, into the union.

*1875-1925.* Presbyterianism has always stood for an educated ministry, and therefore in this new, far-reaching land the Presbyterian Church established its training schools at several centres. The Pictou Academy, in which theological classes had been held since 1820, finally united with the Free Church College in Halifax, which dates from 1848, to form the Presbyterian College, Halifax—the oldest college of the Canadian Church. The charter of Queen's University, Kingston, Ontario, dates from 1841, and its first session from 1842; the University ceased in 1912 to be strictly denominational, and, in place of the faculty of theology, a separately organized theological college was established. Knox College, Toronto, came into being in 1844 as a result of the disruption in the Church of Scotland; it was not incorporated, however, until 1858. Morrin College was established in 1861 in the city of Quebec, but gradually declined, and finally ceased its operations, as the Presbyterian College, Montreal, grew in importance and influence. This latter secured its charter in 1865, and began its work of instruction in 1867, a unique feature being the training of French Protestant students for the ministry. As western Canada opened up, colleges were established in the various provinces—Manitoba College, Winnipeg (1871); Westminster Hall, Vancouver (1907); Robertson College, Edmonton (1911); and St. Andrew's College, Saskatoon (1914).

In the missionary field at home and abroad, the Presbyterian Church in Canada has ever been in the forefront. The eastern section of the Church has the honour of having done pioneer work among non-Christian peoples, for its work in the New Hebrides was begun in 1848, and that in Trinidad in 1868. The whole Church caught the inspiration, and missions were established in Formosa (1871), Central India (1877), North China (1888), British Guiana (1884), Korea (1895), and South China (1901). Evangelism, education, and medicine indicate the three special departments of missionary service. It was, however, in the newer and more needy districts of this vast dominion that the Church expended most freely its labour and sacrifice. Not alone in the Maritimes and in Quebec, but especially in northern Ontario and in the sparse settlements of the Canadian west. Following the building of the Canadian Pacific Railway, people of the eastern provinces and also from other lands, of many races and languages, responded to the urge of the mine, the forest, and the soil. For the scattered communities the Church recognized its share of responsibility, and daringly undertook the task, with other branches of the Christian church, of providing them with ordinances of religion. The story is full of heroic endeavour and of signal achievement, in which on every page is written the record of the noble ministry of the Women's Missionary Society, especially through its hospitals and school homes, even as in the lands beyond the sea the same society rendered honourable service among women and children.

The Westminster Confession remained the standard of faith and order, subordinate only to the Scriptures, but gradually the critical method of interpreting the Scriptures was being generally followed. Whilst the Church continued to place high emphasis on the spirituality of worship, congregations were given a large measure of liberty in regard to its order and conduct. Parental duty in the training of children was everywhere stressed, but as a help Sabbath schools and young people's societies were established within the Church. The creation of a Board of Social Service and Evangelism evidenced the Church's interest along important lines. All through these years, moreover, concern was given to the well-being of ministers, in active service and retired, and to that of ministers' widows and orphans, and valuable assistance was rendered to needy congregations in the erection of their churches and manses. In all these regards was to be seen the unfolding life of a great church.

From 1875 onwards the numerical growth of the Church was large and steady. The number of synods had by 1925 increased from 5 to 8, of presbyteries from 33 to 79, of ministers from 579 to 1,685, of elders from 3,412 to 12,754, and of annual contributions to the missionary, educational, and benevolent schemes of the Church from $93,610 to $1,187,824.

So also had there been a very decided growth in union sentiment. Within five years after Confederation, the Dominion of Canada had become continent-wide; with scattered forces its religious needs could not be met. Hence the union of the Presbyterian Churches in 1875, of the Methodist Church in 1887 and in 1883-4, and the formation of the Congregational Union in 1906. But the colossal task, especially in the growing West, needed something more. Plans were evolved with a view to prevent overlapping and to bring about co-operation; but even this was not enough. Independent unions began to emerge. In 1912 the General Assembly adopted a resolution, postponing the larger union with the Methodist and Congregational bodies, with a view to securing greater unanimity. This action only stimulated the formation of additional independent unions. The parent churches saw the peril of further delay, and soon committed themselves to the principles of organic union. There were other considerations, but many contend that the frontier forced the issue.

The vote in the General Assembly of 1916 was 406 to 90 in favour of the proposed union, but, because of the Great War then in progress, the matter was held up meantime. At the Winnipeg Assembly of 1922, legal counsel were instructed to prepare "such draft bills, as would be necessary to the consummation of this Union, and further to prepare such legislation, as would conserve the rights and interests of all parties involved". At Port Arthur, in 1923, the General Assembly, by a vote of 427 to 129, "determined to proceed forthwith to the consummation of Union with the Methodist Church and the Congregational Churches of Canada upon the terms of the draft bills presented". The enabling Act of Parliament was enacted in 1924, and on June 10. 1925, the Presbyterian Church in Can-

ada passed "without loss of its identity" into the United Church of Canada. See **Church Union.** Unionists claim that presbytery, synod, and general assembly are preserved in the United Church, though under slightly different names, that the permanent pastorate is the ideal and the right of a congregation to call its minister is preserved, and that there is nothing in the Basis of Union that is alien to Presbyterian belief.

There were a very large number of Presbyterians who refused to concur in this union. The Presbyterian Church Association was called into being, and was very vigorous in its opposition to the policy of the Church, even as the Unionist leaders with great earnestness supported the policy. Feeling ran very high, and opposition was crystallized. When the Assembly of 1925, meeting in College Street Presbyterian Church, Toronto, was adjourning to meet with the sister churches in the inaugural meeting of the United Church, seventy-nine of the commissioners protested that "the resolutions adopted by the General Assembly of 1916, approving of the said 'Basis of Union', together with all things since done to implement the said resolutions, were beyond the power of that or any other General Assembly", and claimed that it was "lawful for them, together with such other Commissioners as might adhere to them, to continue in session, and to adopt such measures as might be competent for the continuance of the Presbyterian Church in Canada". In accordance with this protest and claim, these commissioners adjourned to meet again in Knox Church, Toronto, and there reaffirmed the claim of right to be the fifty-first General Assembly of the Presbyterian Church in Canada. Since that date, the continuing Presbyterian Church has applied itself with energy and enthusiasm to perfect its organization and to carry forward its various departments of service. The increases from 1925 to 1932 are as follows:

11

ministers, from 558 to 711; elders, from 4,879 to 6,191; communicants, from 154,243 to 180,956; contributions to budget fund, from $302,150 to $450,813.

Pursuant to the United Church of Canada Act, by which incorporation was granted to the United Church, a commission was appointed to determine the equities of the non-concurring congregations; this commission had as its chairman the Right Hon. Mr. Justice (later Sir) Lyman Duff, and numbered nine persons in all. It dealt with the division of home mission and foreign mission properties of the Church, and of the institutions and loans of the various boards, between the United Church and the non-concurring congregations. Provincial Acts followed; that of the legislature of Ontario determined that "the estate, right, title and interest of the corporation of Knox College, Toronto, be vested in trustees for the Church of the non-concurring congregations of the Presbyterian Church in Canada"—with some special provision for contents, library, and principal's residence. In Quebec somewhat similar action was taken in regard to the Presbyterian College, Montreal. Instead of the bitterness of strife, the horizon seems to promise friendly rivalry between the two churches in their endeavour to further the interests of Christianity at home and abroad.

*Bibliography.* The chief authorities are Rev. William Gregg, *History of the Presbyterian Church in Canada* (Toronto, 1885), J. T. McNeill, *The Presbyterian Church in Canada (1875-1925)* (Toronto, 1925), and the Rev R. G. MacBeth, *The burning bush and Canada* (Toronto, 1926). Mention should also be made of W. Stanford Reid, *The Church of Scotland in Lower Canada* (Toronto, 1936), and John M. MacLeod, *History of Presbyterianism on Prince Edward Island* (Chicago, 1904).

**Prescott, Robert** (1725-1816), governor-in-chief of Canada (1797-1807), was born in 1725 in Lancashire, England.

He entered the British army, and in 1757 served in the expedition against Rochefort, as a captain in the 15th Foot. In 1758 took part in the expedition against Louisbourg; and in 1759 he was aide-de-camp to General Amherst (q.v.). He served in America during the War of the American Revolution, and was present at the battle of the Brandywine. He then served in the West Indies, and in 1794 he was appointed governor of Martinique; but his health failed, and he returned to England in 1795. In 1796 he was sent to Canada as lieutenant-governor of Lower Canada, and administrator of the government of Canada; and in 1797 he was appointed governor-in-chief, in succession to Lord Dorchester (q.v.), and in 1798 he was promoted to be full general. He returned to England in 1799; but he retained his appointment as governor until 1807, and his duties were performed by deputies. He settled at Rosegreen, near Battle, Sussex, England; and here he died on December 21, 1816.

**Prescott,** a county in the extreme eastern tip of the province of Ontario, is bounded on the east by the county of Vaudreuil in the province of Quebec, on the north by the Ottawa river, on the west by Russell county (with which it is united for judicial purposes), and on the south by Glengarry and part of Stormont counties. It was set apart in 1798 and named after Major-General Robert Prescott (q.v.), who was governor-general of Canada (1797-1807). The county town is L'Orignal. Area, about 20 by 30 miles. Pop. (1931), 24,576. See C. Thomas, *History of Argenteuil and Prescott* (Montreal, 1896).

**Prescott,** a town in Grenville county, Ontario, is situated on the St. Lawrence river opposite the city of Ogdensburg, New York state, at the head of the rapids in the river, and at the lowest point to which the largest lake boats can be brought with safety. It is served by the Canadian Pacific and Canadian National Railways; and there is a ferry service to Ogdensburg. It was founded by Colonel Edward Jessup (q.v.) and was laid out in town lots in 1810. It was incorporated as a town in 1834. During the War of 1812, in the first house erected by Colonel Jessup, the plans were laid for the capture of Ogdensburg. To the east of the town is the old windmill, now used as a light-house, where the battle of Windmill Point (q.v.) was fought. Within the town itself is Fort Wellington, which played a prominent part in the War of 1812. It is now under the Dominion Parks Branch of the Dominion government, and is used as a museum to perpetuate the early history of the country. Just west of Prescott is the little Blue Church and cemetery in which is erected a beautiful monument to the memory of Barbara Heck (q.v.), the founder of Methodism in Upper Canada. Prescott was named after Major-General Robert Prescott (q.v.), governor-in-chief of British North America. It is the centre of a good agricultural district; and it has a terminal grain elevator, several factories, lumber mills, a distillery, and a silk mill, as well as a high school, a public library, a radio broadcasting station, and a weekly newspaper (*Journal*). Pop. (1931), 2,984.

**Presentation Brothers.** The Institute of the Presentation Brothers was founded in the year 1802 by Edmund Rice, in the city of Waterford, Ireland. It continued a diocesan congregation until 1889, when the government of the Institute was placed in the hands of a superior general and council. Pope Leo XIII, by a brief dated 1889, formally approved of the new constitution; and in 1899 the order was finally confirmed by the same pontiff. The Christian education of youth constitutes the chief end of the Institute, after the sanctification of its own members. The mother house is in Cork, Ireland. The first Presentation Brothers came to Canada in 1910, with the approbation of Archbishop Bruchési of Montreal, and at the

invitation of the Very Rev. Canon O'Meara, pastor of St. Gabriel's, Montreal. The provincial house and novitiate are in Longueuil, Quebec, in the diocese of St. John's. Other houses are located in the archdioceses of Montreal, and in the dioceses of Sherbrooke, Quebec, and Alexandria, Ontario.

**President range,** a range of mountains in the Kootenay district of British Columbia, north-west of Emerald lake, Yoho Park, in the Rocky mountains. It is in latitude 51° 30′, longitude 116° 34′, and was named in 1904 after the president of the Canadian Pacific Railway.

**Press.** See **Journalism.**

**Preston,** a town in Waterloo county, Ontario, situated at the confluence of the Speed and Grand rivers, 8 miles south of Kitchener, on the Canadian National and Canadian Pacific Railways. The place received its name about the year 1830 from Squire Scollick, an early settler, and a native of Preston, in Lancashire, England. Sulphur springs were discovered in 1838; and now the town is an excellent health resort, the medicinal springs and sulphur baths attracting many to the hotels and sanitarium. There are three large parks, six churches, and a public library. Electric railway lines run to Kitchener, Waterloo, Hespeler, Paris, Brantford, and Port Dover. The industries include wood-working machinery works; flour mills; woollen factories; office, school, and household furniture works. A weekly newspaper (*Prestonian*) is published. Pop. (1931), 6,280. For fuller particulars see Otto Klotz, *Sketch of the history of Preston* (Waterloo Hist. Soc., Kitchener, Ont., 1917).

**Prevost, Sir George, Bart.** (1767-1816), governor-in-chief of Canada (1811-5), was born on May 19, 1767, the eldest son of Major-General Augustine Prevost. He entered the British army, was gazetted a captain in the 25th Foot in 1784, and became a major in the Royal Americans in 1790. In 1794-6 he

PREVOST

saw active service in St. Vincent, West
Indies; and in 1798 he was appointed
military governor of St. Lucia, with the
rank of brigadier-general. He was so
successful in conciliating the good will
of the French population of the island
that, in 1801, he was appointed civil
governor. In 1802 he became governor
of Dominica, and in 1805 he drove the
French from this island. In 1808 he was
appointed lieutenant-governor of Nova
Scotia, with the rank of lieutenant-
general; and he administered the affairs
of this province with general approval
until, in 1811, he was transferred to
Quebec as administrator of the government of Lower Canada. Later in the
same year he became governor-in-chief
of the Canadas; and he was commander-
in-chief of the British forces in Canada
during the War of 1812. As governor,
he performed a signal service in conciliating the good will of the French Canadians, who had been roused to hostility
by the conduct of Sir James Craig (q.v.);
but as commander-in-chief he was
personally responsible for two of the
most humiliating episodes of the War
of 1812, the withdrawal after the successful attack on Sackett's Harbour in
1813, and the defeat at Plattsburg in
1814. In 1815 he was recalled to face
court-martial in connection with the
Plattsburg episode; but he died at
London, England, on January 5, 1816, a
week before the court-martial was due
to be held. In 1789 he married Catherine
Anne, daughter of Major-General John
Phipps, R.E.; and by her he had one
son and two daughters. In 1805 he was
created, for his services in the West
Indies, a baronet of the United Kingdom. See R. Christie, *Memoirs of the
administration of the colonial government
of Lower Canada by Sir J. Craig and Sir
G. Prevost* (Quebec, 1818); *The letters of
Veritas* (Montreal, 1815); *The Canadian
inspector* (Montreal, 1815); and E. B.
Brenton, *Some account of the public life
of the late Lieut.-Gen. Sir G. Prevost,
Bart.* (London, 1823).

**Price, David Edward** (1826-1883),
senator of Canada, was born in Quebec
in 1826, the eldest son of William Price,
the founder of Chicoutimi. He became
the senior partner of the firm of Price
Brothers and Co. From 1855 to 1864 he
represented Chicoutimi and Saguenay
in the Legislative Assembly of Canada;
in 1864 he was elected to the Legislative
Council; and in 1867 he was called to
the Senate. He died at Quebec on
August 22, 1883.

**Price, James Hervey** (1797-1882),
commissioner of crown lands for Canada
(1848-51), was born in Cumberland,
England, in 1797. He came to Canada
in 1828, and was called to the bar of
Upper Canada in 1833. He allied himself with the advanced Reformers, but
held aloof from the Rebellion of 1837.
From 1841 to 1851 he represented the
first riding of York in the Legislative
Assembly of Canada, and from 1848 to
1851 he was commissioner of crown
lands in the second Baldwin-Lafontaine
administration. In 1851 he was defeated
in South York; and shortly afterward
he returned to England, where he spent
the remainder of his days. He died at
Shirley, near Southampton, England,
on July 13, 1882.

**Price, Sir William** (1867-1924),
manufacturer and politician, was born
at Talca, Chili, on August 30, 1867,
the son of Henry Ferrier Price and
Florence Rogerson. He was educated
at Bishop's College School, Lennoxville,
Quebec, and at St. Mark's School,
Windsor, England; and in 1886 he
entered the firm of Price Brothers and
Co., lumber and paper manufacturers,
Quebec. In 1889 he became president,
managing director, and sole partner of
this company; and he conducted the
business until his death. From 1908 to
1911 he represented Quebec West in the
Canadian House of Commons; and in
1912 he was appointed chairman of the
Quebec Harbour Commission. He was
accidently killed on October 2, 1924,
while inspecting his timber-limits at

Kenogami, Quebec. In 1894 he married Æmilia Blanche, daughter of R. Herbert Smith; and by her he had six children.

**Priceville,** a village in Matane county, Quebec, on the Metis river, 3 miles south of Grand Metis. It is the site of a lumber-mill of Price Brothers, after whom the village is named. Pop. (1931), 2,310.

**Priceville,** a village in Grey county, Ontario, on the Saugeen river, 35 miles south of Owen Sound. Pop. (1934), 400.

**Prickly Lettuce.** See **Lettuce.**

**Prideaux** (Prĭd'-ō), **John** (1718-1759), soldier, was born in Devonshire, England, in 1718, the son of Sir John Prideaux, Bart. He entered the British army, and rose to the rank of brigadier-general. He commanded the expedition sent in 1759 to capture Fort Niagara from the French; and he was killed during the siege of the fort, on July 19, 1759, a few days before the fort surrendered. He was buried in the chapel of the fort on July 28.

**Priests of St. Mary of Tinchebray** (S.M.T.), a religious congregation founded at Tinchebray, France, in 1851 for the renovation of Christian morals in Catholic countries and for the propagation of Christian civilization among the pagan nations. In 1904 this congregation was introduced in Canada by Archbishop Legal, O.M.I., and undertook the colonization of fifteen parishes in Alberta. The congregation is represented to-day in the dioceses of Edmonton, Prince Albert, and Montreal.

**Priests of the Blessed Sacrament** (S.S.S.), a religious congregation founded in Paris in 1856 by the Blessed Peter-Julian Eymard, and approved by the Holy See in 1863. Its aim is the perpetual adoration of the Blessed Eucharist, solemnly exposed in its sanctuaries. Several associations have been grafted upon this religious society to allow all those who so desire to affiliate with the congregation. In Canada, over 2,500 priests led by Cardinal Villeneuve are enrolled in the "Priests' Eucharistic League". The Aggregation of the Most Blessed Sacrament, another organization, comprises the majority of Catholic parishes. In connection with these societies, publications are issued dealing with the Blessed Sacrament. The congregation undertakes the preaching of forty-hour devotions, eucharistic tridiums, and retreats in parishes and colleges. It is also particularly interested in the preparation of children for their first holy communion.

**Priests of the Sacred Heart of Jesus** (S.C.J.), a religious society founded in 1877 at St. Quentin, diocese of Soissons, France, by the Very Rev. Canon Léon Dehon. This society was first approved by the Pope in 1888, and finally approved in 1906. At the end of the year 1934, it numbered five bishops, two prefects apostolic, 1,500 professed members, and 1,400 student candidates. The special object of the society is to offer to the Sacred Heart of Jesus a worship of love and atonement by lives of zeal and piety. From the beginning, the society has devoted itself to various works of zeal, among which are to be mentioned, principally, both home and foreign missions. The society founded several parishes in Alberta, in 1910. They are now founding establishments in Quebec and Ontario, for the purpose of recruiting missionaries.

**Prime Ministers.** The term "prime minister" was not, of course, introduced into the terminology of Canadian government until the advent of responsible or parliamentary government, of which the office of prime minister is one of the conventions. Until comparatively recent times, the office of prime minister, even in Great Britain, had no legislative basis, but was merely the result of the fact that the person so designated had been entrusted with the task of forming a government. Originally the prime minister always held some portfolio, such as the presidency of the council or the headship of some department of government; only in recent years has the office been sometimes regarded as a portfolio in itself, and been given a legislative basis.

Actually, however, the term "prime minister" did not come into common usage in Canada until Confederation. Between 1849, when full responsible government dawned in Canada, and 1867, when Confederation became an accomplished fact, the term was inapplicable because of the quasi-federal character of the government of "united Canada" and the existence of twin heads of the government. It is true that Robert Baldwin (q.v.) always insisted that Louis Lafontaine (q.v.) was prime minister of the "Great Ministry" that brought responsible government into effect; but in actual practice, the government was regarded as having two heads, one from Upper Canada and the other from Lower Canada. In the MacNab-Morin government of 1854, for instance, A. N. Morin (q.v.) was frequently referred to as "the French-Canadian prime minister"; though it was Sir Allan MacNab (q.v.) to whom the governor had applied to form a government. Even in the Maritime provinces the term "prime minister" does not seem to have obtained any vogue until after 1867.

When, however, Lord Monck (q.v.) invited Sir John Macdonald (q.v.) to form the first government of the Dominion in 1867, he was most explicit as to the position he should occupy. "In authorizing you to undertake the duty of forming an administration for the Dominion of Canada," he wrote, "I desire to express my strong opinion that, in the future, it shall be distinctly understood that the position of First Minister shall be held by *one* person, who shall be responsible to the governor-general for the appointment of the other ministers, and that the system of dual First Ministers, which has hitherto prevailed, shall be put an end to." Since that time, the office of prime minister has been a recognized feature of the government both of the Dominion of Canada and of the Canadian provinces.

The prime ministers of the Dominion have been as follows:

Right Hon. Sir John A. Macdonald (1867-73).
Hon. Alexander Mackenzie (1873-8).
Right Hon. Sir John A. Macdonald (1878-91).
Hon. Sir John J. C. Abbott (1891-2).
Right Hon. Sir John Thompson (1892-4).
Hon. Sir Mackenzie Bowell (1894-6).
Hon. Sir Charles Tupper (1896).
Right Hon. Sir Wilfrid Laurier (1896-1911).
Right Hon. Sir Robert Borden (1911-20).
Right Hon. Arthur Meighen (1920-1).
Right Hon. W. L. Mackenzie King (1921-6).
Right Hon. Arthur Meighen (1926).
Right Hon. W. L. Mackenzie King (1926-30).
Right Hon. R. B. Bennett (1930-5).
Right Hon. W. L. Mackenzie King (1935—).

The prime ministers of the provinces have been as follows:

### PRINCE EDWARD ISLAND

Hon. L. C. Owen (1873-6).
Hon. L. H. Davis (1876-9).
Hon. W. W. Sullivan (1879-89).
Hon. N. McLeod (1889-91).
Hon. F. Peters (1891-7).
Hon. A. B. Warburton (1897-8).
Hon. D. Farquharson (1898-1901).
Hon. A. Peters (1901-8).
Hon. F. L. Haszard (1908-11).
Hon. J. A. Mathieson (1911-7).
Hon. A. E. Arsenault (1917-9).
Hon. J. H. Bell (1919-23).
Hon. J. D. Stewart (1923-7).
Hon. A. C. Saunders (1927-30).
Hon. W. M. Lea (1930-1).
Hon. J. D. Stewart (1931-3).
Hon. W. J. P. MacMillan (1933-5).
Hon. W. M. Lea (1935-6).
Hon. Thane A. Campbell (1936—).

### NOVA SCOTIA

Hon. H. Blanchard (1867).
Hon. W. Annand (1867-75).
Hon. P. C. Hill (1875-8).
Hon. S. H. Holmes (1878-82).
Hon. John S. D. Thompson (1882).
Hon. W. T. Pipes (1882-4).

Hon. W. S. Fielding (1884-96).
Hon. G. H. Murray (1896-1923).
Hon. E. H. Armstrong (1923-5).
Hon. E. N. Rhodes (1925-30).
Hon. G. S. Harrington (1930-3).
Hon. Angus L. Macdonald (1933—).

### NEW BRUNSWICK

Hon. A. R. Wetmore (1867-72).
Hon. G. E. King (1872-8).
Hon. J. J. Fraser (1878-82).
Hon. D. L. Hanington (1882-3).
Hon. A. G. Blair (1883-96).
Hon. James Mitchell (1896-7).
Hon. H. R. Emmerson (1897-1900).
Hon. L. J. Tweedie (1900-7).
Hon. William Pugsley (1907).
Hon. C. W. Robinson (1907-8).
Hon. J. D. Hazen (1908-11).
Hon. J. K. Flemming (1911-4).
Hon. G. J. Clarke (1914-7).
Hon. J. A. Murray (1917).
Hon. W. E. Foster (1917-23).
Hon. P. J. Veniot (1923-5).
Hon. J. B. M. Baxter (1925-31).
Hon. C. D. Richards (1931-3).
Hon. L. P. D. Tilley (1933-5).
Hon. A. A. Dysart (1935—).

### QUEBEC

Hon. P. J. Chauveau (1867-73).
Hon. G. Ouimet (1873-4).
Hon. C. E. B. de Boucherville (1874-6).
Hon. H. G. Joly (1876-9).
Hon. J. A. Chapleau (1879-82).
Hon. J. A. Mousseau (1882-4).
Hon. J. J. Ross (1884-7).
Hon. L. O. Taillon (1887).
Hon. H. Mercier (1887-91).
Hon. C. E. B. de Boucherville (1891-2).
Hon. L. O. Taillon (1892-6).
Hon. E. J. Flynn (1896-7).
Hon. F. G. Marchand (1897-1900).
Hon. S. N. Parent (1900-5).
Hon. Sir L. Gouin (1905-20).
Hon. L. A. Taschereau (1920-36).
Hon. M. Duplessis (1936-39).
Hon. J. A. Godbout (1939—).

### ONTARIO

Hon. J. Sandfield Macdonald (1867-71).
Hon. Edward Blake (1871-2).
Hon. Sir Oliver Mowat (1872-96).

Hon. A. S. Hardy (1896-9).
Hon. Sir George W. Ross (1899-1905).
Hon. Sir J. P. Whitney (1905-14).
Hon. Sir W. H. Hearst (1914-9).
Hon. E. C. Drury (1919-23).
Hon. G. Howard Ferguson (1923-30).
Hon. George S. Henry (1930-34).
Hon. Mitchell F. Hepburn (1934—).

### MANITOBA

Hon. A. Boyd (1870-1).
Hon. N. A. Girard (1871-2).
Hon. H. J. H. Clarke (1872-4).
Hon. N. A. Girard (1874).
Hon. R. A. Davis (1874-8).
Hon. John Norquay (1878-87).
Hon. D. H. Harrison (1887-8).
Hon. T. Greenway (1888-1900).
Hon. H. J. Macdonald (1900).
Hon. Sir R. P. Roblin (1900-15).
Hon. T. C. Norris (1915-22).
Hon. John Bracken (1922—).

### SASKATCHEWAN

Hon. Walter Scott (1905-16).
Hon. W. M. Martin (1916-22).
Hon. C. A. Dunning (1922-6).
Hon. J. G. Gardiner (1926-9).
Hon. J. T. M. Anderson (1929-34).
Hon. J. G. Gardiner (1934-5).
Hon. W. J. Patterson (1935—).

### ALBERTA

Hon. A. Rutherford (1905-10).
Hon. A. L. Sifton (1910-7).
Hon. Charles Stewart (1917-21).
Hon. H. Greenfield (1921-5).
Hon. J. E. Brownlee (1925-34).
Hon. R. G. Reid (1934-5).
Hon. William Aberhart (1935—).

### BRITISH COLUMBIA

Hon. J. F. McCreight (1871-2).
Hon. A. De Cosmos (1872-4).
Hon. G. A. Walkem (1874-6).
Hon. A. C. Elliott (1876-8).
Hon. J. Walkem (1878-82).
Hon. R. Beaven (1882-3).
Hon. W. Smythe (1883-7).
Hon. A. E. B. Davie (1887-9).
Hon. J. Robson (1889-92).
Hon. T. Davie (1892-5).
Hon. J. H. Turner (1895-8).

Hon. C. A. Semlin (1898-1900).
Hon. Joseph Martin (1900).
Hon. J. Dunsmuir (1900-2).
Hon. E. G. Prior (1902-3).
Hon. R. McBride (1903-15).
Hon. W. J. Bowser (1915-6).
Hon. H. C. Brewster (1916-8).
Hon. John Oliver (1918-27).
Hon. J. D. McLean (1927-8).
Hon. S. F. Tolmie (1928-33).
Hon. T. D. Pattullo (1933—).

**Primrose.** See **Evening Primrose.**

**Primrose lake** is on the boundary between Alberta and Saskatchewan, about the 55th parallel of north latitude. Its name is derived from the fact that it was surveyed on Primrose day, April 19, 1909. It has an area of 181 square miles, of which 173 are in Saskatchewan and 8 in Alberta.

**Prince, John** (1796-1870), soldier and politician, was born in England in March, 1796. He was educated at Hereford, and in 1813 obtained a commission as a subaltern in the 1st Regiment of Herefordshire militia. In 1815 he began the study of law and in 1821 he was called to the English bar. He emigrated to Canada in 1833, and settled at Sandwich, Upper Canada. During the disturbances on the Canadian border following the rebellion of 1837, he was active in repelling American filibusters; and on December 4, 1838, he commanded the force of Canadian militia which repelled a body of invaders which crossed from Detroit to Windsor. Five prisoners taken by him were shot as outlaws. In 1836 he was elected to represent Essex in the Legislative Assembly of Upper Canada; and after 1841 he represented this constituency in the Legislative Assembly of united Canada until 1854, and the Western division in the Legislative Council from 1856 to 1860. Never a party man, his political course was erratic; and in his later days he was an advocate of Canadian independence. In 1860 he was appointed judge of the district of Algoma; and he

died at Sault Ste. Marie, Ontario, on November 30, 1870.

**Prince,** a county in Prince Edward Island, comprising the north-west part of the island. It is traversed by the Canadian National Railway. Chief town, Summerside. Pop. (1931), 31,500.

**Prince Albert,** a city in Saskatchewan, situated on the North Saskatchewan river and on the Canadian Pacific and Canadian National Railways, 80 miles north of Saskatoon. In 1866 the site of the city was named after the Prince Consort by the Rev. James Nisbet (q.v.), who established a Presbyterian mission station in the locality in that year. Previously there were about half-a-dozen settlers in the district, which went by the general term of Saskatchewan River Settlement. The city contains an Anglican and a Roman Catholic cathedral, seven churches, seven public schools, two separate schools, a collegiate institute, two business colleges, and an armory. The industries include creameries, breweries, a brick yard, a flour-mill, a cold-storage plant, saddlery works, an iron foundry, sheet metal works and marble and granite works. Here is the gateway to Prince Albert National Park. There is an all-weather highway from the United States border, 350 miles south, to the park. In a recent season 30,000 visitors registered at the park. Prince Albert is a picturesque city, with facilities for boating, bathing, fishing, shooting, etc. There is a large sanitarium situated in a pine forest near the river. About 2,000 square miles of forest land extend northwards from the city. Prince Albert was incorporated as a city in 1904. A daily paper (*Herald*) is published. Pop. (1931), 9,905. See the *Publications* of the North-West Historical Society.

**Prince Albert National Park,** a reservation in Saskatchewan, comprising a beautiful woodland country specially noted for its maze of connected waterways. From its headquarters at Was-

LEGISLATIVE BUILDINGS OF PRINCE EDWARD ISLAND AT CHARLOTTETOWN

kesiu Beach, a canoe may reach either Hudson bay or the mouth of the Mackenzie river in the Arctic ocean. See M. B. Williams, *Prince Albert National Park* (Ottawa, Dept. of the Interior, 1928).

**Prince Albert sound,** a deep and wide inlet on the western side of Victoria island, in the Franklin district of the North West Territories. It was named in 1852 by Sir R. Collinson (1811-1883), Arctic explorer, after Prince Albert, the consort of Queen Victoria.

**Prince Edward,** a county in the province of Ontario, has been made an island in lake Ontario by the cutting of the Murray canal, 5 miles long, which now divides it from Northumberland county, and its northern coast is separated from Hastings county by the bay of Quinte. It was called by the French "Presqu'Isle de Quinte", but was renamed in honour of the Duke of Kent, after his visit there. Prince Edward became a separate county in 1831. Its county seat is Picton. Area, 241,500 acres. Pop. (1931), 16,693. See *Illustrated atlas of the counties of Hastings and Prince Edward* (Toronto, 1878); and M. B. Williams, *Ontario's island county* (Can. Geog. Journal, 1934).

**Prince Edward Island,** a province of Canada, is an island lying in the south of the gulf of St. Lawrence, and separated from New Brunswick on the east and Nova Scotia on the south by Northumberland strait. It is the smallest province in the Dominion, being 120 miles in length, and, with an average width of 20 miles, covers an area of 2,184 square miles. The island is almost trisected by the deep indentations of Malpeque bay and by the mouth of the Hillsborough river. The lowland surface is relieved by a low range of hills; the coast is low; and the rivers short. All parts of the island are close to the sea. The climate is milder than that of the mainland, and is not subject to extremes. The mean annual temperature at Char-

lottetown is 41 degrees. Precipitation averages 40 inches. Fogs are rare. Prince Edward Island is divided into three counties—King's county, Queen's county, and Prince county. King's county is situated at the eastern end of the province; the shire town is Georgetown. Queen's county occupies the middle part of the island, and contains Charlottetown, the capital of the province. Prince county is at the west end of the island; Summerside is its shire town.

The island was known as St. John's island till 1799. As early as 1780 confusion caused by the resemblance of the name to St. John's, Newfoundland, and St. John, New Brunswick, had led Governor Patterson (q.v.) to propose that it be changed to New Ireland, and an Act was passed for the purpose in 1780, but was disallowed because the name of New Ireland was already appropriated. In 1799 the name was changed to Prince Edward, in compliment to the Duke of Kent, then commanding the British troops in North America, who later became the father of Queen Victoria. The Micmac Indian name of the island is *Abagweit*, meaning "Home on the wave".

The earliest discovery of the island is not satisfactorily known. The tradition that John Cabot (q.v.) sighted the island in 1497 is not sufficiently authenticated to be accepted as history. In 1534 Jacques Cartier (q.v.) visited the island, which he thought a part of the mainland. He named it the Isle of St. John, having arrived on St. John's day. In 1603, Champlain (q.v.) took possession of it on behalf of the king of France; and in 1663 it was granted to Captain Doublet, but he, failing to establish the stipulated settlements, forfeited his interest in it. In subsequent years several attempts were made to settle the island. In 1719 the Comte de St. Pierre unsuccessfully tried to establish fisheries and a trading company. The island was captured by the British in 1745, but was restored to France three years later. In 1758, after

Louisbourg fell, the British again took possession, without much resistance, and since that time the island has continued to form a part of the British Empire. In 1763, when Prince Edward Island was annexed to Nova Scotia, the British government surveyed the place, and township lots of some 20,000 acres each were laid out. These lands were granted extensively to favourites at court, who agreed to settle them within ten years in the proportion of one person to each 200 acres, the settlers to be European Protestants or persons who had lived at least two years in British North America. In this manner the whole of the island had been disposed of by 1767. Much of the land fell into the hands of non-residents, and there arose a system of absentee landlordism which proved detrimental to the colony's welfare. In 1860 a system of compulsory purchase was advocated to remedy the evil, and it was ultimately adopted. The constitution of the colony was definitely settled, and in 1773 the first House of Assembly met. The conference which paved the way for federation was held at Charlottetown in 1864, but the colony did not join the Dominion until 1873, although the question was debated annually. The Dominion government paid $800,000 to the provincial government to buy out the landlords. Of the 843,981 acres thus acquired, practically all has been sold as freehold.

Agriculture is the chief industry of the island. Its rich red soil, with a climate tempered by the surrounding waters of the gulf, and yet free from the rigours of Atlantic storms, offers great inducements to the pursuit of agriculture. About 85 per cent. of the entire area is cultivable. Oats and potatoes form the chief crops, supported by turnips, wheat, barley, hay, and clover. Sheep-raising is increasing in importance; swine and poultry are raised for the Montreal market; beef cattle and horses are numerous. The dairying industry is of comparatively recent growth, but many factories are making cheese and butter. Prince Edward Island potatoes enjoy a very high reputation; seed potatoes are sent to the markets of the southern United States. There is a Dominion experimental station of 173 acres at Charlottetown. Thick beds of mussel mud, or oyster mud, are found in all bays and river mouths. The deposit, often many feet thick, consists of organic remains of oysters, mussels, clams, etc. The supply appears almost inexhaustible. It affords a fertilizer of great value, and is applicable to any kind of crop grown in the province.

The fox-farming industry was founded in Prince Edward Island. The first experiments in breeding of foxes dates back to early in the nineteenth century, and since that time fox farms have been established in every province of Canada, in many of the northern states of the United States, and in a few countries in Europe. There are approximately 750 ranches on the island, ranging from two pairs up to several hundred pairs of breeding foxes. Foxes for breeding purposes are exported to all northern countries. A Dominion experimental fox-ranch was established at Summerside in 1925. The fisheries provide employment to both sexes. Lobsters are the principal catch. Cod, mackerel, herring, smelts, oysters, and scallops are caught in great quantities. Almost all of the canned lobster products are exported to France, Great Britain, and the United States.

The trade and commerce of the province is mostly connected with the farming and fishing occupations. The leading industries are butter and cheese; fish-curing and packing; flour and grist-mill products; printing and publishing; castings and forgings; central electric stations; tobacco factories; saw-mills; bread and other baking products; harness and saddlery. The province contains no minerals of economic importance.

The Prince Edward Island Railway is a branch of the Canadian National

Railway, and extends from one end of the island to the other, with several branch spurs serving important centres. The railway is connected with the main system by a railway car ferry operating from Port Borden to cape Tormentine, New Brunswick, a distance of nine miles. The ferry service operates throughout the year. A boat service is provided daily between Pictou, Nova Scotia, and Charlottetown. A regular service is also maintained between Montreal, Prince Edward Island, and Newfoundland. With the exception of the railway car ferry, which is an ice-breaker, all other steamer traffic is in operation only for seven or eight months of the year. Charlottetown is the chief port.

The province is rich in recreational activities. Trout abound in the streams, tidal rivers, and inlets. Sea-bathing in shallow warm water may be enjoyed almost everywhere. There is no large game on the island, as most of the province is settled. Flocks of wild geese, ducks, plover, and snipe are found in the late summer and autumn. There are about 3,700 miles of uncongested roadways, of excellent construction. The principal trees found in the forest land are birch, beech, pine, maple, cedar, and spruce.

There is a free school system of education. All the schools are non-sectarian, and dogmatic religious teaching is prohibited. In a recent year there were 479 schools in operation, with an enrolment of 18,247 pupils. Advanced education is provided at the Prince of Wales College and the Provincial Normal School at Charlottetown: this is the training centre for public school teachers. The course is three years long, and graduates of the college are admitted to the second year (in some cases the third year) at several Canadian universities. St. Dunstan's University, also at Charlottetown, provides instruction for about 200 Roman Catholic students.

Prince Edward Island is more thickly populated than any of the other provinces. Over 97 per cent. of the population are Canadian-born, and practically all are descended from the original settlers. The racial origins are as follows: Scottish, 37.7 per cent.; English, 26.3 per cent.; Irish, 21.1 per cent.; and French, 13.5 per cent. Many Acadian French settled on the island after being deported from Nova Scotia in 1755. Two or three hundred Indians of the Algonkian race are located on two reserves at Lennox island and Morell. There is very little unemployment in the province; and no crime problem, as it is known nowadays. Of 2,485 penitentiary sentences throughout the Dominion in a recent year, there were 16 in Prince Edward Island. Pop. (1931), 88,038.

For fuller details see B. Bremner, *An island scrap book* (Charlottetown, 1932), D. C. Harvey, *The French régime in Prince Edward Island* (New Haven, 1926), A. B. Warburton, *A history of Prince Edward Island* (St. John, N.B., 1923), *British America*, vol. iii, British Empire series (London, 1900), and J. A. Maxwell, *Prince Edward Island and Confederation* (Dalhousie Review, vol. xiii).

**Prince Edward Island Railway,** a railway line connecting the chief centres of population in Prince Edward Island, and opened for traffic in 1874. On the inclusion of Prince Edward Island in the Canadian confederation, it was taken over, in December, 1874, by the Dominion government, and is now part of the Canadian National Railway system.

**Prince George,** a city in the Cariboo district, British Columbia, is situated at the junction of the Nechako and Fraser rivers, 526 miles north of Vancouver and 470 miles east of Prince Rupert. In 1807 Simon Fraser (q.v.) established a North West Company post (Fort George) at or near the site of the present city, and from this point set out to explore the Fraser river. On the amalgamation of the North West and Hudson's Bay Companies, it was taken over by the latter. It was a mere fur-trading post until 1908 or 1909, when the Grand Trunk Pacific Railway, now the Canadian National, was surveyed through to Prince Rupert. Settlement began as construction progressed, and in March, 1915, the municipality was incorporated as the city of Fort George; later in the year the name was changed to Prince George. It is a divisional point on the Canadian National Railway, and is the distributing centre for a region whose main industry is lumbering. Other industries are mining, agriculture, and fur-trading. The place was no doubt named after King George III, the reigning sovereign of England when the original fort was established. It has schools, theatres, hotels, and a weekly newspaper (*Citizen*). Pop. (1931), 2,500, with 500 more in the extra-municipal areas known as South Fort George and Central Fort George.

**Prince of Wales College,** in Charlottetown, Prince Edward Island, was founded in 1860, and was amalgamated with the provincial normal school in 1879. It is not a degree-granting institution, but awards certificates both for its regular courses and for its teacher-training courses. The college offers also a two-year commercial course. It has twenty-five officers of instruction; and it has an enrolment of over 400 students.

**Prince of Wales strait,** the passage between Victoria island and Banks island, in the Franklin district of the North West Territories. It was named after Albert Edward, Prince of Wales (1841-1910), afterwards King Edward VII.

**Prince Patrick island** is in the Arctic archipelago, north-west of Melville island in the Franklin district of the North West Territories. It is about 162 miles long, has an area of 7,100 square miles, and lies between latitude 76° and 77° in longitude 120°. It was discovered by McClintock (q.v.) in 1853, and was named after the Duke of Connaught, one of whose names was Patrick.

**Prince Regent inlet,** the strait between Brodeur peninsula and Somerset island, in the Franklin district of the North West Territories, leading from Lancaster sound to the gulf of Boothia. It was named by Parry (q.v.) in 1819 in honour of the Prince Regent, George Augustus Frederick (1762-1830), afterwards King George IV.

**Prince Rupert,** a city in the Skeena district, British Columbia, is situated on Kaien island, a short distance north of the mouth of the Skeena river. It was named after Prince Rupert, the first governor of the Hudson's Bay Company. It has a spacious, sheltered harbour, well equipped with docks and shipping facilities, shipbuilding and repair yards, and a great floating dry-dock able to accommodate the largest ship afloat. It is 480 miles north-west of Vancouver, in the same latitude as London, England, and about 500 miles nearer the Orient than any other railway terminus on the Pacific. In 1908 the site was a wilderness; in 1909, a tent town; in 1910, the town was incorporated as a city, and in 1914, when it was linked up with the Grand Trunk Pacific (now the Canadian National) Railway, it became its western terminus and a divisional point. Among its industries are shipbuilding, lumbering, and extensive halibut and salmon fisheries that have caused it to be called the Grimsby of the Pacific. It has a regular steamboat service—Canadian National, Canadian Pacific, and Union Steamship Company lines—with Victoria, Vancouver, and Skagway, Alaska; and is the principal grain-port in northern British Columbia. It has eight churches, good public schools, a public library, and two evening newspapers (*Empire* and *News*). Pop. (1931), 6,350.

**Prince's Pine.** See **Pipsissewa.**

**Princess Royal island** is a large elongated island, in the Skeena district

PRINCE GEORGE, BRITISH COLUMBIA

From the East

*Photograph by Royal Canadian Air Force*

# THE

# TRIAL

O F

## DANIEL DISNEY, Esq;

Captain of a Company in His Majesty's 44th Regiment of Foot, and Town-Major of the Garrison of *Montreal*, at the Session of the Supreme-Court of Judicature, holden at *Montreal*, on *Saturday* the 28th Day of *February*, and thence continued by Adjournments to *Wednesday* the 11th Day of *March*, 1767, before the Honourable WILLIAM HEY, Esq; Chief-Justice of the Province of *Quebec*, upon an Indictment containing two Charges, the one for a Burglary and Felony, in breaking and entering Mr. *Thomas Walker*'s House, at *Montreal*, on the Night of the 6th Day of *December*, in the Year 1764, with an Intention to murder the said *Thomas Walker*, the other for feloniously and of Malice aforethought cutting off the Right Ear of the said *Thomas Walker*, with Intention thereby to disfigure him, against the Form of the Statute of 22 and 23 *Car*. II. Cap. i. in that Case made and provided.

---

## QUEBEC:

Printed by BROWN & GILMORE.

M,DCC.LXVII.

THE TITLE-PAGE OF ONE OF THE FIRST BOOKS PRINTED IN CANADA

of British Columbia, in the Caamãno sound, on the east side of Hecate strait, south-east of Pitt island. It is 52 miles long and 27 miles wide. It was named by Captain Charles Duncan, in 1788, after his sloop *Princess Royal*, which was seized by the Spaniards at Nootka in 1789, and used by Quimper in his exploration of the strait of Juan de Fuca in 1790.

**Princeton,** a town in Yale district, British Columbia, is situated at the confluence of the Similkameen and Tulameen rivers, and is on the Canadian Pacific Railway (Kettle Valley branch), 150 miles east of Vancouver. It was named by Sir James Douglas (q.v.) in honour of the visit of Edward, Prince of Wales (later King Edward VII) to Canada. It is essentially a mining town, the district about it producing both coal and copper. Lumbering and mixed farming add to its prosperity. It has a weekly newspaper (*Star*). Pop. (1931), 1,000.

**Princeton,** a village in Oxford county, Ontario, on the Canadian National Railway, 12 miles east of Woodstock. Pop. (1934), 400.

**Princeville,** a village in Stanfold township, Arthabaska county, Quebec, on the Canadian National Railway, 10 miles north-east of Victoriaville. The parish is known as St. Eustèbe de Stanfold, and the village is sometimes known also as Stanfold. It was, however, created a municipality under the name Princeville, after one of the first settlers, Pierre Prince. Pop. (1931), 980.

**Pringle, Jacob Farrand** (1816-1901), judge and historian, was born in Valenciennes, France, on June 27, 1816, the son of Lieut. James Pringle of the 81st Foot and his wife, Ann Margaret Anderson, who later settled in Cornwall, Upper Canada. He was educated at the Cornwall grammar school; and was called to the bar of Upper Canada in 1838. From 1866 to within a short time before his death was county judge of

Stormont, Dundas, and Glengarry. He died at Cornwall on February 1, 1901. In 1844 he married Isabella, daughter of Colonel the Hon. Alexander Fraser, of Fraserfield; and by her he had five sons and five daughters. He was the author of a valuable local history, *Lunenburgh, or the old Eastern District* (Cornwall, Ont., 1890).

**Pringle, John** (1852-1935), missionary, was born in Prince Edward Island in 1852, and was educated at Queen's University, Kingston (B.A., 1875; D.D., 1904). He was ordained a minister of the Presbyterian Church, and he became famous as a missionary in the Yukon at the time of the Klondike "gold-rush" in 1897-8, and afterwards. In 1908 he accepted a charge at Sydney, Cape Breton; and he was a chaplain with the Canadian Expeditionary Force overseas during the Great War. He died at Lowell, Massachusetts, on April 20, 1935.

**Printing.** So far as can be ascertained, there was no printing-press in Canada during the French régime. "Il n'y a d'imprimerie au Canada," wrote the botanist Kalm (q.v.) in 1749. He added the qualification, "quoiqu'il y en ait eu autrefois" (although there was one formerly); but no evidence in support of this last statement has yet been found. It has been maintained that ten years later, in 1759, Mgr. de Pontbriand (q.v.), the bishop of Quebec, printed two of his *mandements* on a small private press in Quebec; but even this contention is difficult of proof, and indeed the probabilities are strongly against it.

The first printing-press to be imported into what is now the Dominion of Canada would appear to have been a press brought to Halifax, Nova Scotia, in 1751, by Bartholomew Green, Jr., the scion of a famous family of Boston printers. Green died, however, only a few weeks after his arrival in Halifax; and the honour of turning out the first product of a printing-press in what is now Canada fell to one of his old associates in Boston, John Bushell. In January, 1752, Bushell printed in Halifax the first number of the *Halifax Gazette*—the first in point of time, of all Canadian periodicals. It is an interesting fact that not only in Halifax, but nearly everywhere else, the beginnings of printing in Canada have been also the beginnings of journalism. The first printing-presses were primarily newspaper presses; and at first any books or pamphlets published were merely by-products. Printing began in New Brunswick with the publication by John Ryan of the *Royal St. John's Gazette* in Parr-Town (Saint John) in 1783. In Quebec, printing began apparently with the appearance of the first number of the famous *Quebec Gazette* (1764-1874), printed by William Brown and Thomas Gilmore, and in Montreal with the appearance of a few books and pamphlets printed by Fleury Mesplet (q.v.), followed by his *Gazette* (now the *Montreal Gazette*) in 1778. In Upper Canada (Ontario) the first printed publications were probably two eight-page pamphlets issued by Louis Roy at Newark (Niagara) in the beginning of 1793, one containing the speeches of Lieutenant-governor Simcoe (q.v.) at the opening and closing of the first session of the legislature of Upper Canada, and the other the laws passed at the first session of the legislature; but these were followed almost immediately by the first number of the *Upper Canada Gazette*, on April 13, 1793. In the Canadian West, printing began with the production by the Rev. James Evans (q.v.) of his Cree spelling-book at Norway House in 1841, on a home-made press, with types manufactured from a few bullets and the lead lining of tea-chests; but the first commercial printing in the West followed the establishment of the *Victoria Gazette*, on June 25, 1858, the *Vancouver Island's Gazette*, in July, 1858, the *British Colonist* in Victoria, in December, 1858, and the *Nor'Wester*, at Winnipeg, on December 29, 1859.

Since the first wooden hand-presses laboriously turned out the early Canadian newspapers and pamphlets, the machine age has revolutionized printing. First, iron presses were introduced, about 1832; then steam-power was applied to printing, between 1840 and 1850; and finally, the invention of the Hoe cylinder press and of the type-setting machines, in the last quarter of the nineteenth century, together with other technical improvements, has completely altered the processes of printing. To-day printing involves a capital outlay in machinery which would have left our grandfathers aghast. But in this development Canada has had small part. It has merely adopted the mechanical advances made in Great Britain and the United States; and it has even lagged behind in some of the refinements of printing. Printing in Canada is still largely of the commercial type; and comparatively few efforts have been made to establish standards of fine printing. There have been established few private presses, with artistic standards; and most commercial printing-houses in Canada have their eyes on dividends rather than on good typography, not realizing that good typography often yields good dividends.

There is no history of the printing art in Canada; but an admirable account of the beginnings of printing in Canada is to be found in Ægidius Fauteux, *The introduction of printing into Canada* (Montreal, 1929).

**Prior, Edward Gawler** (1853-1920), prime minister of British Columbia (1902-3), was born on May 21, 1853, at Dallaghgill, near Ripon, Yorkshire, England, the son of the Rev. Henry Prior and of Hannah Mouncey Kendell. He studied mining engineering at Wakefield, England; and in 1873 he came to Vancouver island as mining engineer for the Vancouver Coal Mining and Land Co. From 1878 to 1880 he was provincial inspector of mines; and he then established himself as a hardware merchant at Victoria. He represented Victoria as a Conservative in the Legislative Assembly of British Columbia from 1886 to 1888, and in the Canadian House of Commons from 1888 to 1902. From December 17, 1895, to July 8, 1896, he was controller of inland revenue in the Dominion government; and in 1902 he became minister of mines in the Dunsmuir ministry of British Columbia. He was again elected to represent Victoria in the provincial Assembly; and on November 21, 1902, he succeeded Dunsmuir (q.v.) as prime minister of British Columbia. On June 1, 1903, however, he was dismissed from office, following the break-up of his cabinet and personal charges levelled against himself; and he thereupon retired to private life. In 1919 he was appointed lieutenant-governor of British Columbia; and he died in office at Victoria, British Columbia, on December 12, 1920. He was twice married, (1) in 1878 to Suzette, daughter of the Hon. John Work (q.v.), by whom he had one son and three daughters, and (2) in 1899 to Genevieve, daughter of Capt. Thomas Wright of San Francisco. For many years he was lieutenant-colonel commanding the 5th Regiment of Garrison Artillery; and he was twice president of the Dominion Artillery Association.

**Prisons.** See **Penology.**

**Pritchard, John** (1777-1856), furtrader, was born in Shropshire, England, in 1777. He came to Canada about 1800, and became a clerk in the XY Company. In 1804 he was stationed at lake Nipigon. He became a clerk in the North West Company in 1805, and from 1808 to 1814 he was in charge of the Souris River post. In 1815 he took service with Lord Selkirk (q.v.), and was appointed a councillor of Assiniboia. He was present at the affair of Seven Oaks in 1816, and was made a prisoner by the half-breeds. Taken to Montreal, he gave evidence in the Selkirk trials. Afterwards he settled on the Red river, and in 1822 he organized the Buffalo

Wool Company. He died at the Red River Settlement in 1856. His narrative of the struggle between Selkirk and the North West Company was published in J. Halkett (ed.), *Narratives of John Pritchard, Pierre Chrysologue Pambrun, and Frederick Damien Heurter* (London, 1819); and some of his letters, written between the years 1805 and 1836 were published by George Bryce (q.v.), under the title *Glimpses of the past* (Middle Church, Manitoba, 1892).

**Privy Councillors.** All members of the Canadian cabinet are *ipso facto* members of the King's Privy Council for Canada, and are entitled to be termed "Honourable" for life. A few others, such as Lord Strathcona (q.v.) and the Hon. G. Howard Ferguson, have been sworn of the Privy Council for Canada, though not Dominion cabinet ministers. A limited number of Canadian cabinet ministers, including most of the Canadian prime ministers, have also been sworn of the Imperial Privy Council, and are entitled to be termed "Right Honourable" for life, and to bear after their names the letters "P.C.".

**Proclamation of 1763.** See **Royal Proclamation of 1763.**

**Procter, Henry Adolphus** (1787-1859), soldier, was born in Wales in 1787, and entered the British army. He came to Canada before the outbreak of the War of 1812 as officer commanding the 41st Regiment. In the campaigns of 1812 and in 1813 he was in command in the Amherstburg sector, and he inflicted some reverses on the Americans. In the autumn of 1813, however, he was compelled to retreat, and at the battle of Moraviantown, on October 5, he was defeated by General Harrison. He was court-martialled for his behaviour on this occasion, and was suspended for six months from rank and pay; but he later resumed service in the army, was made a C.B., and rose to the rank of lieutenant-general. He died at his place in Montgomeryshire,

12

Wales, on May 13, 1859. See E. A. Cruikshank, *Harrison and Procter* (Trans. Roy. Soc. Can., 1911).

**Proctor, John James** (1838-1909), journalist and author, was born in Liverpool, England, in 1838, and was educated at Sedburgh in Yorkshire. He came to Canada in 1856, and for several years taught on the staff of Bishop's College, Lennoxville. He then became a journalist, and at the time of his death on December 17, 1909, he was editor of the Quebec *Morning Chronicle*. He was the author of a volume of verse, *Voices of the night and other poems* (Montreal, 1861), and a novel entitled *The philosopher in the clearing* (Quebec, 1897).

**Progressive Party,** a political party formed at a conference called by the Canadian Council of Agriculture at Winnipeg in January, 1920. The party arose out of the success of the United Farmers of Ontario in the Ontario elections of 1919, and was an attempt to enlist in the support of the political ideals of the farmers the other "progressive" elements in the country. The Hon. T. D. Crerar, and later the Hon. Robert Forke (q.v.), led the party in the Dominion; and E. C. Drury, prime minister of Ontario from 1919 to 1923, was an exponent of the ideas of the party in Ontario. With the defeat of the Drury government in Ontario in 1923, the party suffered an eclipse; and ultimately many of the members of the party coalesced with the Liberal party. In 1932 the residue of the party was reorganized as the Co-operative Commonwealth Federation (q.v.). The programme of the party will be found in the *Canadian Annual Review*, 1919. See also **History, Political.**

**Prohibition.** The first Canadian prohibition of the sale of intoxicating liquors took place during the War of 1812, when an Act was passed, as a temporary war measure, to prohibit the exportation of grain and to restrain the distillation of spirituous liquors from grain. A local-option measure known as the Canada Temperance Act was passed in 1878, prohibiting the sale of intoxicating liquors in places that should adopt it. In subsequent years a number of counties and municipalities throughout Canada put the law into force, but the greatest advance in prohibition was made after the outbreak of the World War. In 1915 Saskatchewan closed every bar in the province and greatly reduced the number of dispensaries. A referendum of the people was taken at the latter end of 1916, and as a result the remaining liquor dispensaries were voted out of existence by a majority of seven to one. On June 1, 1916, prohibition became effective in Manitoba; and in July of the same year Alberta voted for prohibition. In September a referendum was taken in British Columbia and prohibition won; in 1920 the question was recommitted to the people, and defeated. After this, liquor was sold under government supervision, in sealed packages. A legislative enactment declared for prohibition in Ontario in the year 1916. Thus by 1921 every province except Quebec and British Columbia had declared for prohibition. Later, all except Prince Edward Island returned to government control. Under Parts I and II of the Canada Temperance Act, provision is made for the prohibition of the sale of intoxicating liquors in counties and cities. A vote taken under these parts in the county of Compton, Quebec, in 1930, in response to a petition for the repeal of the Act in that county, resulted in favour of the repeal, which immediately became effective. Part III of the Act relates to penalties and persecutions, Part IV to the prohibition of the importation and exportation of intoxicating liquors into and from the provinces, while Part V enacts provisions in aid of provincial legislation for the control of the liquor traffic. It is frequently known as the "Scott Act", from the fact that it was sponsored by Sir Richard Scott (q.v.).

Consult W. R. Riddell, *The first Canadian war-time prohibition measure* (Can. hist. rev., 1920), and R. E. Spence, *Prohibition in Canada* (Toronto, 1919). See also **Liquor Control.**

**Protection.** See **Tariffs.**

**Proton,** a village in Proton township, Grey county, Ontario, on the Canadian Pacific Railway, 5 miles from Dundalk. Pop. (1934), 300.

**Proudfoot, William** (1788?-1851), clergyman, was born in Scotland about 1788, and was educated at Edinburgh University. He was ordained a minister of the United Presbyterian Church; and in 1813 was ordained to the charge of Pitrodie, in Perthshire. In 1832 he came to Canada as a missionary, and settled at London, Upper Canada. Here he died on February 10, 1851. On his arrival in Canada, he kept a diary; and his diary and letters are one of the most valuable sources for the social history of Upper Canada at this period. Portions of these have been published in the *Transactions* of the London and Middlesex Historical Society for 1915, 1917, and 1922, and in the *Papers and records* of the Ontario Historical Society for 1931.

**Proudfoot, William** (1823-1903), judge, was born near Errol, Perthshire, Scotland, on November 9, 1823, the son of the Rev. William Proudfoot. He came to Canada with his parents in 1832, and was educated by his father at London, Upper Canada. In 1849 he was called to the bar of Upper Canada, and he became an outstanding equity lawyer. In 1874 he was appointed a vice-chancellor of the Court of Chancery of Ontario; and he held this position until his retirement from the bench in 1890. In 1884 he was appointed professor of Roman law, jurisprudence, and the history of English law in the University of Toronto. He died on August 4, 1903. In 1853 he married the daughter of John Thomson, Toronto; and on her

death in 1871 Emily, daughter of Adam Cook, Hamilton, Ontario.

**Proudfoot, William** (1859-1922), senator of Canada, was born in Colborne township, Huron county, Canada West, on February 21, 1859, the son of Robert Proudfoot and Margaret Darlington, and a nephew of the Hon. William Proudfoot (q.v.). He was educated at Goderich, Ontario, and at Osgoode Hall, Toronto; and was called to the Ontario bar in 1881 (K.C., 1902). From 1908 to 1919 he represented Huron Centre in the Legislative Assembly of Ontario; and from 1917 to 1919 he was leader of the Liberal opposition in the Assembly. Defeated in the elections of 1919, he was called to the Senate of Canada; and he sat in the Senate until his death at Toronto on December 3, 1922. In 1886 he married Marion F. Dickson; and by her he had one son and one daughter.

**Proulx dit Clément, Jean Baptiste** (1846-1904), priest and author, was born at Ste. Anne, Lower Canada, on January 7, 1846, the son of J. B. Proulx dit Clément and Adeline Lauzon. He was educated at the College of Ste. Thérèse de Blainville, and was ordained a priest of the Roman Catholic Church in 1869. From 1870 to 1874 he was a missionary in Manitoba. In 1889 he was appointed vice-rector of Laval University, Montreal; and he died at Ottawa on March 1, 1904. He published several dramatic works and a large number of books and pamphlets dealing with controversial questions in the Roman Catholic Church in Canada. His best known work was *L'enfant perdu et retrouvé, ou Pierre Cholet* (Mile-End, 1887; 2nd ed., Montreal, 1892).

**Provancher, Léon** (1820-1892), priest and naturalist, was born at the village of Courtnoyer, Lower Canada, the son of Joseph-Étienne Provancher and Geneviève Hébert. He was educated at the College of Nicolet, and was ordained a priest of the Roman Catholic Church in 1844 In 1868 he founded *Le Natura-*

*liste Canadienne*, which he edited until
his death, and in 1888 he founded also
*La Semaine Religieuse de Québec*. In 1879
the French government made him an
officer of the French Academy; in 1880
Laval University conferred on him the
degree of D.Sc.; and in 1887 he was
elected a member of the Royal Society
of Canada. He died at Cap Rouge, near
Quebec, on March 23, 1892. He was
the author of an *Essai sur les insectes
et les maladies qui affectent le blé* (Montreal, 1857), a *Traité élémentaire de
botanique* (Quebec, 1858), *La flore canadienne* (2 vols., Quebec, 1862), *Le verger
canadien* (Quebec, 1862), *Les oiseaux du
Canada* (Quebec, 1874), *L'echo du Cal-
vaire* (Quebec, 1883), *Histoire du Canada*
(Quebec, 1884), and *De Québec à Jerusa-
lem* (Quebec, 1884). See V. A. Huard,
*La vie et l'œuvre de l'Abbé Provancher*
(Paris, 1926).

**Provencher, Joseph Alfred Norbert**
(1843-1887), journalist and Indian
agent, was born at La Baie du Febvre,
Lower Canada, on January 6, 1843. He
was educated at the Nicolet seminary,
and was called to the bar of Lower Canada in 1864. In 1866 he became editor
of *La Minerve*, the chief Conservative
journal in Montreal. In 1869 he was
appointed a member of the provincial
council of the North West Territories;
and he was an intermediary between the
Métis and the Canadian authorities
during the first Riel rebellion. From
1870 to 1876 he was an Indian commissioner in the North West Territories.
He returned to Montreal in 1881, and
in 1884-5 was editor-in-chief of *La
Presse*. He died in Montreal on October
28, 1887. He was one of the founders of
the *Revue Canadienne*; and in the early
volumes of this periodical appeared a
number of essays by him.

**Provencher, Joseph Norbert** (1787-
1853), Roman Catholic bishop of St.
Boniface (1847-53), was born at Nicolet,
province of Quebec, on February 12,
1787. He was educated at the Nicolet
Seminary, and in 1811 was ordained a
priest of the Roman Catholic Church.
In 1818 he was sent as a missionary to
the North West; and in 1820 he was
appointed bishop of Judiopolis *in partibus*, and apostolic vicar of the North
West. In 1847 he was designated bishop
of St. Boniface; and he died near Winnipeg on June 7, 1853. In 1818 he founded
the College of St. Boniface. His letters
have been published in the *Bulletin de
la Société de St. Boniface*, vol. iii (St.
Boniface, Manitoba, 1913). See D.
Frémont, *Mgr. Provencher et son temps*
(Winnipeg, 1935).

**Provincial Bank of Canada,** or
Banque Provinciale du Canada, was
established in 1900, with head office in
Montreal. It began with a paid-up
capital of less than $1,000,000; but this
has now increased to $4,000,000, and
the bank has a reserve fund of $1,000,-
000. Its branches, which number over
300, are chiefly in the province of Quebec; but it has a number of branches also
in Prince Edward Island, in New Brunswick, and in the French-speaking districts of Ontario adjacent to Ottawa
and Windsor.

**Provost,** a village in Alberta, on the
Canadian Pacific Railway, 150 miles
south-east of Edmonton. It has a high
school and a weekly newspaper (*News*).
Pop. (1934), 500.

**Pruden, John Peter** (1778?-1870?),
fur-trader, was born at Edmonton,
Middlesex, England, about 1778. He
entered the service of the Hudson's
Bay Company in 1791, as an apprentice,
and later as a writer, at York Factory.
From 1798 to 1808 he was on the
Saskatchewan; and from 1809 to 1824
he was in charge of Carlton House. In
1821 he was made a chief trader. He
was in charge of Norway House in
1825-6, but later returned to command
at Carlton House. He was promoted to
the rank of chief factor in 1836; and he
retired from the Company's service in
1837. After his retirement, he lived at
the Red River; and here he died about

1870. His daughter married Chief Trader John McLeod (q.v.).

**Psilomelane.** See **Manganese.**

**Ptarmigan.** See **Grouse.**

**Ptolemy, mount,** is on the boundary of British Columbia and Alberta, north of Corbin in the Kootenay district of British Columbia. It is in lat. 49° 33′, long. 114° 38′, and has a altitude of 9,234 feet. The mountain resembles the head and shoulders of a man lying down and gazing skywards; originally called "Mummy", it was changed to Ptolemy, an Egyptian.

**Public Archives of Canada.** See **Archives.**

**Public Debt.** See **Debt, Public.**

**Public Finance.** See **Finance, Public.**

**Public Health.** Even in a new country like Canada, it became necessary for government to concern itself with public health at an early date. In the centres of population, police regulations with regard to the disposal of garbage and sewage became necessary; and a supply of pure water became one of the earliest concerns of municipal governments. In the cholera epidemics which ravaged Canada during the first half of the nineteenth century, the government was forced to take what measures it could to control the epidemics, though the ignorance of medical science at that time as to the cause of the epidemics rendered them largely helpless. They were able, however, to establish quarantine stations where diseased immigrants were held; and the quarantine station at Grosse Isle below Quebec was established before 1850. It has been only in the twentieth century, however, that the public health activities of the governments of the Dominion and its provinces, and of the larger cities, have reached their present very considerable proportions.

Under the British North America Act, 1867, the oversight of public health in Canada was assigned, in the main, to the provinces; but the Dominion government has in some respects taken the lead in matters of public health, and a Dominion department of health was created in 1919. This department exercises oversight over such matters as quarantine and medical inspection of immigrants, the provision of lazarettos for lepers and hospitals for sick and injured mariners, the control of patent medicines and narcotic drugs, the inspection of food, and the supervision of men employed on public works; and it co-operates with the provinces in the control of venereal disease and in child welfare.

All the provinces of Canada have now departments or bureaux of public health; but most of these have been created since the Dominion department of health was established in 1919. A bureau of public health was created in Saskatchewan in 1909, though it did not become a department of government until 1923; and the department of public health in Alberta dates from 1918. The department of health in Manitoba was organized only in 1928; and those in Prince Edward Island and Nova Scotia date only from 1931. The first school of hygiene or public health in Canada was organized in connection with the University of Toronto in 1927.

Most of the largest centres of population in Canada have now medical health officers; and these exercise a general supervision over the health of the communities of which they have charge, providing sometimes nurses for poorer or destitute families. In outlying communities, the Canadian Red Cross has done a valuable service in providing district nurses.

Socialized medicine has not yet arrived in Canada; but the public health activities of the Dominion, provincial, and municipal governments have gone a long way in this direction. Preventive medicine has since the beginning of the Great War cut the deaths from tuberculosis almost in half, and the deaths from typhoid fever almost to one-tenth of what they were in 1913. Great advances have been made in controlling such scourges as infantile paralysis, and even in reducing the ravages of such ailments as influenza and the common cold.

The ramifications of the public health movement are too numerous to enumerate; but full information regarding them may be had from the *Canadian Public Health Journal* (Toronto, 1910—) and the *Canadian Annual Review*.

**Public Ownership.** See **Public Utilities.**

**Public Utilities.** The term public utility has broadly the same connotation in Canada as in Great Britain and the United States: it is applied to an industry which provides the public in a given area with what are considered necessary services, and has, either through a relatively large initial investment or other conditions, the traits of a natural monopoly — traits which from early times in Great Britain and the United States inevitably tended to bring it within some special form of public control, judicial or administrative. The actual agencies of such control in Canada have been patterned upon those in the older states of the English-speaking world, of which the most important are the specific terms of a franchise, the supervision of rates and service by a public utility commission, and public ownership and operation. Significantly, public ownership and operation as instruments of control are more widely developed in Canada than in the neighbouring United States.

The public utilities of Canada can best be classified and described according as they come under federal, provincial, or municipal jurisdiction. Important utilities within the ambit of federal regulation are the great transcontinental railways and such lines as are declared by Act of parliament to be in "the general interests of Canada", the telegraph companies, two of which are subsidiaries of the railways, radio broadcasting, telephones operating in more than one province, postal service, and those canals that are considered part of the national waterways. Some of these utilities are not merely regulated by, but are under the ownership and operation of, the government. Such are the canals, the Canadian National Railway, operated by a board of directors responsible to the government, and the Canadian National Telegraphs, operated with the Canadian National Railway. In radio broadcasting the federal government owns only a limited number of stations, but the Canadian Broadcasting Corporation, established in 1936 in partial imitation of the British Broadcasting Corporation, is empowered to provide programmes for all the populated areas of Canada, to regulate the programmes and advertising on the air, to prohibit the establishment of privately owned stations, and to pursue the policy of extending the number of public stations. The logical objective of the Broadcasting Act of 1936 is a publicly owned monopoly in radio broadcasting. The postal service, following British and American example, is administered as a department of government.

The outstanding institution designed to regulate federal utilities is the Board of Railway Commissioners, which bears a name that inadequately illustrates its varied and extensive functions. It was established first in 1903 to exercise a control over the rates and service on national railways, it being discovered at the time that non-competitive rates were exorbitant as compared with competitive rates and that the railways had freely exercised their privilege to change rates without notice, to the inconvenience and distress of shippers. The Board of Railway Commissioners was devised as a permanent means of hearing and investigating grievances as to rates. The Board originally consisted of three members appointed for ten years by the governor-general-in-council. In 1908 the number was increased to six. Judicial decisions and amendments to the original Act have greatly enlarged the powers of the commission, and its functions are now partly executive and partly judicial. It may issue mandatory and restraining orders; and in its investigations it can, like a superior court, insist upon the production of necessary documents and the attendance of witnesses. Only standard or maximum rates require the approval of the Board before they are applied. Changes in competitive rates may be applied by the railways without approval provided that they have been advertised, but in case of special grievances all changes in rates can be brought before the Board. Its sanction must also be obtained to the location and construction of new lines, or branch lines, and to all regulations concerning safety and convenience in operation. Unlike, however, its American counterpart, the Interstate Commerce Commission, it has no control over railway financing and the issue of railway securities. Doubtless the crucial dependence of Canada upon foreign capital restrained the federal government from providing the Board with this power. Appeals may be taken from the Board to the governor-general-in-council, or in questions of law and jurisdiction to the Supreme Court of Canada, but appeals allowed by these authorities are few. The regulative powers of the Board have been extended beyond railway rates to those of telephone, telegraph, and express companies which conduct an interprovincial business; for example, the Bell Telephone Company of Ontario and Quebec comes under its regulation. It has also jurisdiction over the price paid for water power, leased from the crown for the development of electrical energy.

Public ownership over federal utilities is more widely developed in Canada than in the United States, a fact which is due less to the wider prevalence of a socialist ideology than to peculiar exigencies in the development of the state and the economy. The essential task in the building of a federation in 1867 and the succeeding years was the more thorough consolidation of the separated portions of British North America through effective means of transport. Hence federal governments constructed such railways as the Intercolonial, and through land grants and bond guarantees assisted private companies in extending their lines to the West. The policy once begun was difficult to discontinue at the point where it became extravagant, mainly because of the political pressure of outlying regions solicitous for railway service and the scarcely less influential, although more secret, pressure of railway contractors. As a result the federal government by 1914 was heavily committed in support of the major lines, except the Canadian Pacific, and, when these lines felt the financial strain in the war and post-war period, the government had little alternative but to assume ownership and operation. Similarly public construction of canals was due to the fact that private corporations could not attempt to improve the vast and valuable waterway of the St. Lawrence which made possible the opening and exploitation of the West. Federal enterprise in such utilities was, therefore, in its origin a basic condition for the expansion of population and social life throughout the Dominion.

The principal utilities under provincial jurisdiction are hydro and other electric power, telephone systems within the province, provincial railways, steam or electric, and the new and important forms of motorized transport. Of these hydro-electric power, owing to its decisive influence in Canadian industry, is undoubtedly the most important, and the consistent trend within the twentieth century has been to subject it more directly to public control, resulting in extensive public ownership and operation. In this development Ontario has taken the lead. At the beginning of the twentieth century the government of this province was content to grant franchises to private companies for the development of power from the Niagara and other rivers. But partly under the influence of British immigrants indoctrinated with the ideas of municipal socialism then current in Great Britain, an opinion favourable to public ownership quickly developed, especially in Toronto and the urban areas of western Ontario. As early as February, 1903, the civic council of Toronto recorded that "the time is certainly here, if it has not been here long ago, when public utilities of this nature should be owned and operated by the government of the province, or by the municipalities". The Ontario Hydro-Electric System had its birth in 1906 as a result of the vigorous drive of these urban municipalities for the public transmission of power. The Commission established in 1906 was engaged merely in transmitting power at cost to such municipalities as desired it, but, under the persistent pressure of the munitions industry for more and cheaper power in the period of the Great War, it began to generate as well as to transmit, and definitely set out to achieve a monopoly of the hydro-electric industry in southern Ontario. Such a development was inevitable, not simply because of natural ambition in the commissioners, but because in this industry genuine economies were to be effected in the linking together of all productive units in a highly co-ordinated system. Over this integrated system some control is exercised by the municipalities, which have commissions to administer the local distributive plants, although there is an effective supervision of the financing, rate-making, and management of these local bodies by the auditors employed by the provincial commission. The provincial government has an ultimately vital direction over the entire hydro-electric system in that it

guarantees the loans for works of expansion and is represented on the commission of three by at least one, and sometimes two members of the cabinet. Thus the Ontario Hydro-Electric System is not as free from actual and potential political interference as the statutory corporations in Australia, or such organizations in Great Britain as the Port of London authority and the Central Electricity Board.

Under the impressive influence of the Ontario Hydro-Electric System, commissions have been established in other provinces, with varying powers of regulation over the private companies and usually with the authority to transmit power, or to generate it for transmission to municipalities. Quebec was tardy in exercising control of the hydro-electric utility, but in 1935 it established a commission of three members with jurisdiction over the production, transmission, and distribution of electricity with the purpose of extending the use of electrical energy to the greatest possible number of citizens. The commission has the important task of co-ordinating the power industry throughout the province. In Nova Scotia there is not merely a public power commission engaged in generation and distribution, but also a board of public utility commissioners authorized to supervise electrical and other utilities, excepting the enterprises under the power commission, and to restrict profit to no more than eight per cent. upon real investment. Such specific limitation of profit is not the practice elsewhere in Canada, but in all the provinces there are utility commissions which attempt to control rates with obviously indirect effects on profit.

Apart from electric power, the telephone as a significant utility is regulated in all the provinces, and in Manitoba, Saskatchewan, and Alberta is mainly owned and operated by the provincial governments. Companies whose activity extends beyond the boundary of a given province, like the Bell Telephone, which serves the major part of Ontario and Quebec, are regulated in service and rates by the Board of Railway Commissioners in Ottawa. Private provincial companies, such as those in the Maritimes, are similarly controlled by the public utility commissions of these provinces. On the prairie are publicly owned and operated telephones, where the crucial problem is that of insuring the efficiency of management and not merely the protection of consumers from the exploitation of a monopolist. Public ownership of telephones was established in this region because the private companies were accused of being slow in satisfying the demand of the farmers for rural service, and it has suffered at times from the popular pressure for extravagant extension of lines, notably during the period of the Roblin government in Manitoba and the Stewart government in Alberta. Moreover, at the outset, the methods of accounting were not above reproach, and administration was bedevilled by the more indefensible forms of political pressure. But the three western provinces have learned from experience. Of late years the administration of the telephones has improved, and their financial record has become respectable.

Municipal utilities are subject to diverse forms of control, which are influenced by both British and American example. In the major urban utilities, such as water, gas, electric light, power, and street railway service, public ownership and operation have been steadily on the increase since the beginning of the twentieth century. Water-works especially are now generally under public management. In the urban areas of Ontario and the western provinces street railway service also tends to be publicly managed. Where public ownership exists, the organs of management are varied, and the following are common types: (1) a small commission appointed or elected to manage the specific utility in question, such as the Toronto Transportation Commission, which operates the street railway and public buses of Toronto; (2) a general utility commission which operates all the utilities within the municipality, and is held responsible for its management to the municipal government; (3) a committee of aldermen which manages the utilities directly. Where the utilities are privately owned and operated, public control is exercised through the terms of a franchise and the regulative powers of provincial utility commissions. The controversy continues as to the respective merits of private and public ownership, and Canadian experience can render no decisive conclusion because the quality of management in both public and private enterprises varies greatly. In the case of the publicly owned and operated municipal utilities, it has commonly been difficult to judge the efficiency of administration, owing partly to the fact that in contrast to the private companies the enterprises are exempt from certain forms of taxation. The lack of tradition in the maintenance of an expert civil service has clearly injured public ownership and operation in Canada, because too often it has resulted in the appointment of "ward-heelers" to positions which should be occupied only by thoroughly-trained men. But whatever the defects in public ownership and operation, the trend of development has been inexorably towards this type of management, and consistent improvement has been noticeable in the quality of the services.

**Pubnico Head,** a village in Yarmouth county, Nova Scotia, on the Pubnico river, and on the Canadian National Railway. It is at the head of Pubnico harbour, and is a fishing village. The name is a corruption of the Indian *Pogomkook*, meaning "land from which the trees have been removed to fit it for cultivation". Pop. (1934), 600.

**Puccoon** (*Lithospermum canescens* (Michx.) Lehm., *Boraginaceae*), a softly-hairy perennial herb with long, deep, red roots. The leaves are linear-oblong, downy beneath and rough with appressed hairs above. The flowers are yellow, sessile, on leafy-bracted spikes; the corolla is salver-form, naked within and twice as long as the calyx. It grows in open woods and plains in sandy soil, from Ontario westward, and blooms in April and May.

**Puffin,** a group name for certain sea birds, somewhat smaller than a crow, with an extraordinary visage due to the variously and highly coloured bill, which is greatly deepened and very much narrowed laterally. The puffins belong to the family of marine birds grouped under the designation *Alcidae*, to which also belong the auks, murres, and guillemots. Of the three species indigenous to Canadian shores, one is found on the Atlantic coast and two on the Pacific.

**Pugsley, William** (1850-1925), minister of public works for Canada (1907-11), was born at Sussex, New Brunswick, the son of William Pugsley. He was educated at the University of New Brunswick (B.A., 1868; B.C.L., 1879; D.C.L., 1884), and was called to the bar in 1872 (Q.C., 1891). For ten years he was reporter to the Supreme Court of Nova Scotia. He represented King's county in the Legislative Assembly of New Brunswick from 1885 to 1892 and from 1899 to 1907; and was solicitor-general of New Brunswick from 1889 to 1892, and attorney-general from 1900 to 1907. In 1907 he became prime minister of New Brunswick, but after a few months of office resigned, and became minister of public works in the Laurier government at Ottawa. He represented Saint John city and county in the Canadian House of Commons from 1907 to 1911, and Saint John city from 1911 to 1918. In 1918 he was appointed lieutenant-governor of New Brunswick; he retired from office in 1923, and was then appointed chairman of the Reparations Commission. He died in Toronto on March 3, 1925. He was twice married, (1) in 1876 to Fannie (d. 1914), daughter of Thomas Parks, Saint John, New Brunswick, and (2) in 1915 to Miss Macdonald, Saint John, New Brunswick.

**Pugwash,** a village in Cumberland county, Nova Scotia, on an inlet of Northumberland strait, and on a branch line of the Canadian National Railway, 30 miles east of Amherst. The name is derived from the Indian *Pagweak*, meaning "shallow water". It is a fishing village, but has also a number of industrial establishments. Pop. (1934), 900.

**Puisaye, Joseph Geneviève, Comte de** (1755-1827), French royalist, was born at Mortagne-en-Perche, France, in 1755, the son of André Louis Charles de Puisaye, marquis de Puisaye. Though, at the outbreak of the French Revolution in 1789, he was numbered among the Reform noblesse, he later became one of the chief royalist leaders. He took refuge in England, and commanded the ill-fated Quiberon expedition in 1795. In 1798 he obtained from the British government a concession of land in the townships of Markham and Vaughan, Upper Canada; and in 1799 he came out with a number of other royalists to found a settlement. The settlement proved a failure, however, and in 1802 Puisaye returned to England. He died at Hammersmith, near London, England, on October 13, 1827. On his return to England he published his *Mémoires* (6 vols., London, 1803-8). See Lucy E. Textor, *A colony of émigrés in Canada* (Toronto, 1904); Janet Carnochan, *The Count de Puisaye* (Niagara Historical Society, No. 15, 1907); Abbé A. P. Gaulier, *Joseph-Geneviève de Puisaye* (Bull. rech. hist., 1913).

**Pulp-and-Paper Industry.** This article is concerned primarily with the use of wood in the manufacture of pulp and paper. The writing of government reports and documents in the French régime and the printing industry after the British conquest were dependent on imports of paper. The paper machine was invented by Louis Robert at the Essone paper mills in France in 1798, and was introduced into England by Henry Fourdrinier in 1803. The first paper mill was begun by Americans at St. Andrew's in Lower Canada in 1804. A second mill was started in the county of Portneuf in 1810. In Nova Scotia, a paper mill was started at Nine Mile river in 1819 by the owner of the *Acadian Recorder*, and in Upper Canada mills were started at Crooks Hollow and in the Don valley in 1825. Two additional mills were started in the Don valley in 1840, of which that owned by the Taylor family became the basis of the Don Valley mill. James Barber received his training in paper-making at Crooks Hollow, and started a plant at Georgetown in 1853. In 1851 Upper and Lower Canada had five mills each, and in 1861 Lower Canada had six. In the next census, Canada had 21 mills, employing 760 hands, and using material valued at $522,573, and selling at $1,071,651 (Ontario 12, Quebec 7, New Brunswick 1, Nova Scotia 1). These mills were concerned with the manufacture of paper from rags.

Paper was made from groundwood by C. Fenerty in Nova Scotia in 1839, but it was not until 1859 that John Thomson began to experiment in the manufacture of paper from wood with the firm of Angus Logan and Co. (formed 1859). He achieved success with the manufacture of soda pulp at Sherbrooke in 1864. New mills were built at Windsor, and production began in 1869, the firm being organized as the Canada Paper Company in 1883. Valleyfield mills began the use of pulp in 1866. Apparently the first groundwood from hydraulic drive was produced successfully at Portneuf in 1880. The sulphate process was introduced by J. R. Barber and C. Riordon at Merrit-

ton in 1885. These interests formed the Toronto Paper Company (Cornwall) in 1880. The first sulphate was made by Bromptons at East Angus in 1907. The Rolland Paper Company began the production of fine papers at St. Jérôme in 1882. These early mills, which shifted gradually from dependence on rags to dependence on wood, were located in the industrial area, and became the basis of the expansion of fine paper production in the next century.

The number of pulp mills increased from 5 in 1881 to 24 in 1891 (Quebec 17, Ontario 3). Exports of woodpulp totalled $168,180 in 1890. In the nineties the demands of Great Britain, of the United States, and of the domestic market supported a marked increase in production of pulp and of paper. Expansion in production of newsprint which followed the use of wood was accompanied by a marked decline in price. In the United States prices declined from 9 cents per lb. in 1870 to 4 cents in 1880 and to 2 cents by the turn of the century. Pulpwood was exported in increasing quantities to the mills of the United States (20,200 cords in 1890 and 62,000 cords in 1900). Increase in the production and export of pulpwood was followed by the production and export of raw materials in the more advanced stage as groundwood pulp. The process involved grinding of the wood by pressure against a rapidly revolving circular stone, and required an abundance of power, obtained chiefly by direct hydraulic drive. The groundwood industry was consequently limited to sites in which water-power was easily available, and quantities of spruce could be obtained at low costs. The Laurentide Pulp Company, with the support of Sir William Van Horne (q.v.), began operations at Grand'Mère on the St. Maurice river in the early nineties. In 1898 it added the production of sulphite, which involved cutting the wood into small chips and cooking it in sulphite liquor as a means of extracting the cellulose fibre. A proportion of about 25 per cent. sulphite pulp, added to 75 per cent. of groundwood, produced newsprint. Laurentide consequently began the production of newsprint and of cardboard paper on a small scale.

A decision of the Privy Council of May 26, 1898, which placed ownership of water-powers definitely under the control of the provinces was followed by a period of relatively rapid development in Ontario and Quebec. The Ontario government continued a policy of embargo on the export of logs cut from crown lands initiated in 1898 by extending it to pulpwood in 1900. It granted concessions to companies on condition that mills were built of specified size as a means of encouraging pulp and paper production in the province. In 1899, as a result of a concession sold to Edward Lloyd, Ltd., publishers of the *Daily Chronicle*, a groundwood pulp mill was built at Sturgeon Falls. Sulphite pulp was purchased on the open market until a sulphite plant was built in 1905, and a forty-ton newsprint plant began production in 1903. The company went into receivership in 1906, and continued in financial difficulties. The Sault Ste. Marie Pulp and Paper Company began operations with a hundred-ton groundwood mill in 1899. A sulphite plant was added, but the company went into receivership in 1903. With government support it eventually became an important producer of groundwood pulp.

Lumber companies which had built up operations around important power-sites and ample supplies of raw material began to turn to the production of pulp and newsprint. In 1903 J. R. Booth installed 15 grinders and produced from 75 to 80 tons of groundwood daily. A paper mill was added in 1905, and sulphite production began in 1908. Difficulties of low water and high freight charges offset the importance of cheap raw material and placed the industry under serious handicaps. On the Quebec

side of the river, the E. B. Eddy Company started the production of sulphite pulp in 1888, and after destruction of their mills in 1900 became concerned in the production of a wide variety of products. As in the case of the Booth mills, operations were handicapped by an uncertain supply of water, but its market for various products was more certain.

In the province of Quebec an order-in-council was passed on June 1, 1901, imposing 65 cents per cord stumpage on all pulpwood cut on crown lands, with a rebate of 25 cents per cord if the pulpwood was manufactured into pulp in Canada. The rebate was offset by a provision under the United States Tariff Act of 1897 imposing a duty of 25 cents per cord on pulp exported to the United States from wood cut on Quebec crown lands. Increasing quantities of pulpwood were exported to the United States from Quebec, and American companies began to acquire limits on a large scale as a means of guaranteeing a continued supply. The embargo in Ontario encouraged Quebec to assist colonization by permitting exports of pulpwood to the United States. Groundwood pulp production developed in relation to the British market in the more easterly parts of the province—at Chicoutimi, Péribonka, Jonquière, Metabetchouan, Quiatchouan, and Clarke City. Similarly in the Maritimes, especially in Nova Scotia, groundwood was exported to both Great Britain and the United States. The industry was handicapped by unevenness of water flow, by high costs of transportation, by inadequate methods of extracting water from the pulp, and by lack of uniformity. The sulphite industry expanded in New Brunswick and in Ontario and Quebec. The Riordon at Hawkesbury and Merritton, and the Bromptons at East Angus were among the chief producers. The competition of skilled manufacturers in Scandinavian countries handicapped production.

Difficulties in the production and export of groundwood in Quebec hastened the construction of newsprint mills. Price Brothers in 1904 assumed control of small pulp and lumber companies with a view to developing the newsprint industry. The Belgo-Canadian Company installed a newsprint machine in 1907. Bromptons purchased the Royal mills (formerly Wm. Angus Co.) in the same year. The specialty mills responded to the increasing demands of the domestic market after 1900, shown in the expansion of Canada Paper Company and the Rolland Paper Company. Reduction of the American tariff on newsprint from $6.00 to $3.75 per ton and free entry of groundwood, from provinces without prohibition regulations, in 1909 (increased to $6.10 on Quebec newsprint and to $8.00 on the Ontario product), the severe drought of the 1908-9 season, increase in stumpage duties, and an embargo on exports of pulpwood from Quebec in 1910 (New Brunswick, 1911), and free entry of newsprint to the United States under the Reciprocity Treaty of 1911 and the tariff of 1913 hastened the migration of the newsprint industry to Canada in the second decade of the century.

Construction of newsprint plants was dependent on the development of hydro-electric power and its transmission from the power-site to the mills. The handicap of fluctuating supplies of water-power was overcome by construction of dams for regulating supply, and the difficulties of sites in which groundwood was made at the point with most effective use of hydraulic drive were removed with the possibility of transmitting power to sites at which the raw material and the finished product could be efficiently handled. Nearly 85 per cent. of the power required for the production of newsprint was used in the manufacture of groundwood. The first transmission line was used at the Barber mill at Georgetown in 1888. In 1909 a transmission line was built by the Canada Paper Company from Shawinigan to Windsor Mills. Power was transmitted by alternating current over increasing distances from the power-site to the mill. Linking up of the groundwood plant to the newsprint mill not only facilitated more efficient use of water-power, but it also eliminated the necessity of drying the groundwood and later reducing it again to slush form.

Expansion after 1911 and during the war period was evident in the establishment of new plants and the addition of new machines to old plants. The Ontario Paper Company at Thorold (controlled by the Chicago *Tribune*) began production in 1912. In the same year Kenogami (Price Brothers) became a producer, and the Lake Superior Paper Company extended its plant. Donnacona (owned by St. Regis and Gould paper interests) came into production in 1913, and in the same year Spanish River (owned by the Mead interests), already in possession of Sturgeon Falls (1911), amalgamated with Lake Superior and began the plant at Espanola. Howard Smith (book and writing) began operations in 1912 and later amalgamated with Crabtrees. The Fort Frances mill (Backus interests) was started in 1914. During the war the Abitibi plant (Ogilvie interests) at Iroquois Falls was built (1916), and the St. Maurice (Union Bag and Paper) at Cap de la Madeleine was completed in 1917. Total daily capacity of newsprint production in Canada reached 2,775 tons in 1919. The war checked exports of sulphite to North America from Scandinavian countries, with the result that rising prices brought rapid expansion. Mattagami, at Smooth Rock Falls, began the production of bleached sulphite in 1916. Riordon interests built the plant at Kippawa and extended the plants at Merritton and Hawkesbury. Provincial began a sulphite plant at Port Arthur and Frasers at Edmundston. The total daily sulphite production capacity in Canada increased 300 tons in 1918. Sulphate pulp (Kraft) expanded with sulphite and newsprint. The Brown Corporation at La Tuque began operations in 1910, Wayagamack at Three Rivers in 1912, Drydens in 1913. Increased production of papers of various grades supported extension of the St. Lawrence mills which absorbed the Montrose in 1912, and later was merged with the Georgetown mills to form the Provincial Paper Company. Interlake Tissue began operations in 1913. Bathurst installed a board mill in 1914. Hinde and Dauch began the production of paper boxes in 1913.

Increased prices (with newsprint at $40.00 per ton in 1914, $60.00 in 1916, $62.00 in 1917, and $69.00 in 1918) and increase in costs of production led to attempts to fix prices by government control in the United States and Canada. R. A. Pringle was placed in control of prices in Canada. He reduced the price of paper to Canadian consumers by exacting a quota from exporters, but difficulties of administration and the appeal of Price Brothers against the constitutionality of the Board of Commerce Act put an end to regulation in 1920. In spite of these attempts to lower the price of newsprint, large numbers of newspapers in Canada disappeared during the war and the post-war period. As a means of meeting problems of marketing during the war, paper companies formed the Export Paper Company in 1916 (Canada Paper Export Company — Price, Laurentide, Belgo-Canadian, Brompton, St. Maurice, 1918).

Following abolition of price control in 1920, prices increased to $130.00, partly as a result of the investment of surplus from war profits in advertising in the United States and favourable exchange rates, only to decline to $80.00 in 1921 and $75.00 in 1922. Sulphite producers suffered from renewed competition from Scandinavian countries with the end of the war and

the release of shipping. The Mattagami Company went into receivership, and the Riordon Company was in difficulties. Toronto Paper was sold to Howard Smith in 1919. Additional newsprint machines were installed in 1920, and in 1921 Laurentide established a record on a new 166″ machine of 1,031 feet per minute. In 1922 International started four machines at Three Rivers, and Abitibi completed installation of seven machines. The Spruce Falls sulphite mill was started at Kapuskasing in the same year. St. Lawrence (Timmins interests) at Three Rivers started two machines, the Fort William Paper Company (Spanish River) two, and older organizations started additional machines in 1923. The pulp concerns dominated by English interests (Becker and Co.) in the Gulf and Maritime regions went into liquidation, and the Ha-Ha Bay Sulphite Company was acquired by Sweezey-Gundy interests and organized as the Port Alfred Pulp and Paper Company. In 1925 International acquired the Riordon properties, and began the development of hydro-electric power on an extended scale on the Gatineau river. Thirteen new machines (with 1,215 tons daily capacity) came into production in 1926. In the same year the St. Maurice Valley Corporation absorbed Belgo-Canadian, St. Maurice Valley, and Canada Paper, and Abitibi acquired Mattagami. Seventeen mills (with 1,900 tons daily capacity) were added in 1927, including four 270″ machines of International on the Gatineau, the Pine falls mill (Spanish River) in Manitoba and the Lake St. John mill at Dolbeau. Canadian production had definitely passed United States production, but increased output and marketing problems led to the formation of the Canadian Newsprint Company. Spanish River and Abitibi were merged, bringing control of Fort William, Manitoba, Ste. Anne, and Murray Bay companies under single direction. In 1928 prices dropped three dollars, and mergers developed on a large scale. The St. Maurice Valley Corporation was joined with Laurentide to form the Canada Power and Paper Corporation. Price Brothers acquired Donnacona, and International secured control of Bathurst and of Cornerbrook in Newfoundland. Abitibi and Canada Power bought the Thunder Bay mill at Port Arthur. In the fine paper industry Alliance Paper Mills amalgamated Lincoln Pulp and Paper, Ritchie and Ramsay, and Georgetown Coated Paper; and Howard Smith purchased Canada Paper from the Canada Power and Paper Company. In the following year (1929) Canada Power and Paper acquired Wayagamack and Port Alfred. In spite of these mergers, the Mersey Paper Company (Killam interests), International (Dalhousie), and Great Lakes (Backus) started new machines, the latter with the world's largest width 304″. Further machines came into production in spite of the depression and a price of $55.20 in 1930—McLaren's, Dalhousie, and Mersey. Anglo-Canadian (Rothermere) joined Canada Power and Paper; Brompton, Lake St. John, and St. Lawrence united to form the St. Lawrence Corporation, and Abitibi secured control of Provincial. Canada Power and Paper entered into an arrangement with the Hearst interests as a protective measure, and Col. J. H. Price resigned in protest from the presidency of the Newsprint Institute. Prices declined to $53.00 in 1931, and necessitated the reorganization under the direction of the Hon. Charles Dunning of Canada Power and Paper as the Consolidated Paper Corporation, in which Anglo-Canadian returned to its independent status. In 1932 Abitibi went into liquidation, Price Brothers defaulted, and the price of newsprint dropped to $46.00.

The development of the pulp-and-paper industry in British Columbia, in spite of the availability of supplies of western hemlock, accessibility to tide water, and ample water-power, began at a later date than in eastern Canada. A paper mill supported by imports of rags from Great Britain was operated near Alberni from 1894 to 1896, but it was not until 1909 that pulp was first manufactured from wood. Legislation was enacted in 1901 to encourage the pulp-and-paper industry by reserved stands granted on 21-year leases. The legislation was repealed in 1903, but four companies secured leases, the Oriental Power and Pulp Company (84,180 acres), the Quatsino Power and Pulp Company (55,669 acres), the Canadian Industrial Company (134,551 acres), and the Bella Coola Development Company (79,999 acres). The Canadian Pacific Sulphite Company (later the Swanson Bay Forests Wood Pulp and Lumber Company) began the production of sulphite in 1909 at Swanson Bay, but difficulties compelled it to suspend operations until it was sold to the Whalen interests in 1916. The British Columbia Sulphite Fibre Company began the production of sulphite pulp in 1912 at Mill creek, and in 1917 also came under the control of the Whalen group, as did the Quatsino Power and Pulp Company, which began to produce pulp in 1918. The Whalen pulp-and-paper mills went into receivership in 1923, and were sold to the British Columbia Pulp and Paper Company in 1925. Plants under the control of this company have been engaged chiefly in the production of sulphite for export largely to Japan and for the domestic market. The Rainy River Pulp and Paper Company began production in 1909, but was forced to close down, and eventually came under the control of the Vancouver Kraft mills, a subsidiary of the Columbia River Paper Mills, Portland, which is planning (1936) to re-open the plant. The Reciprocity Treaty and an embargo on pulpwood cut on crown lands in 1913, stimulated expansion of newsprint production in British Columbia, as it did in eastern Canada. The Powell River Company took over the leases of the Canadian Industrial Company, and began operations in 1912 with two machines of 150″ and 156″. It added two more machines in 1914, two 234″ machines in 1926, and one 226″ 1,400-feet-per-minute machine in 1930. Power was developed at Powell lake (50,000 h.p.) and at Lois river (44,000 h.p.), and an additional machine will increase production to 1,000 tons per day. The Ocean Falls Company took over the leases of the Bella Coola Development Company, and began operations in 1912 with production of groundwood pulp, and after a receivership in 1913 came under the control of the Crown Willamette Paper Company. Newsprint and kraft paper were produced in 1916, paper towels and similar products in 1927 (a large conversion plant was started at Vancouver in 1930), and fibre board containers in 1933. Newsprint was sold to the domestic market, to countries in the Pacific basin, and with opening of the Panama canal to Gulf state ports. The New Westminster Paper Company began the manufacture of tissue paper in 1922, and after loss by fire in 1929 rebuilt its plant. The Sidney Roofing and Paper Company started production of roofing paper and building material at Victoria in 1918, and added a groundwood plant in 1927. The Beaver Cove Lumber and Pulp Company was started in 1919, and taken over by Canadian Forest Products, a subsidiary of International Harvester Company, in 1926.

The increased efficiency of new machines achieved through the introduction of suction couch and press rolls in the post-war period was evident in increasing speed and increasing width. Hydro-electric power facilitated extension of control devices and more effective adaptation of cost accounting systems. Synchronous motors facilitated the use of electric drives in paper mills. Ventilation was improved with larger ma-chines. Increasing efficiency of machines was accompanied by extension of facilities for handling raw materials and finished products. Railways were extended, and chutes and tractors and specially built ships were introduced to lower the costs of pulpwood and meet the larger demands of the mills. Pulpwood storage became increasingly important. Barking drums increased in size, artificial stones were introduced, and magazine grinders were used on a large scale. Economy of power was achieved by grinding at periods of low power consumption, and the introduction of electric steam boilers. Canadian plants such as Dominion Engineering and Port Arthur Shipbuilding became more efficient in the construction of paper mills and pulp-and-paper equipment. The increasing importance of machinery has involved steady decline in the use of labour. The number of men per ton of paper has declined from 6 in 1903 to 1 in 1933. Mergers were arranged to lower costs of pulpwood and reduce the costs of cross freights. Conservation became more urgent along the lines of reducing fire losses, rotation of cutting, planting of trees as in the case of Laurentide, and more efficient government regulation. Ninety-one mills were installed in Canada from 1919 to 1930, and daily capacity increased by 8,360 tons. Capacity doubled from 1926 to 1930. Increased efficiency of more recently constructed mills, decline in prices in spite of favourable exchange rates, and the depression, were followed by receiverships of large groups such as Abitibi, Price Brothers, and Ontario and Minnesota (Backus).

Difficulties of the paper industry concerned with products other than newsprint were a result of a variety of factors. Paperboard mills flourished with the building industry, but suffered severely with the depression. The Canadian Paperboard Company went into bankruptcy in 1930. The Gair Company (New York) has acquired control of

PAPER MACHINES, POWELL RIVER, BRITISH COLUMBIA

PULP AND PAPER MILLS AT RIVER BEND, QUEBEC

numerous box companies in Canada. Paperbox mills and catalogue mills (Madawaska) responded to the demands of hand-to-mouth buying, the development of chain and department stores, and extensive advertising through containers. The Kraft industry (Dryden, Wayagamack, Brown Corporation, Bathurst, and others) has increased with the demands for paper-bags and improved methods of production. Finished papers were handicapped by small mills with lack of diversified production and limited demand, but were protected by substantial tariffs which compelled American publications to be printed in Canada. An artificial silk plant was built by Courtaulds at Cornwall in 1924. Canadian Celanese established a branch at Drummondville in 1926, and Canadian Industries, a celanese plant at Shawinigan Falls in the early thirties. High grade sulphite for rayon became increasingly the object of attention on the part of mills at Kippawa, Athol, New Brunswick (Restigouche Pulp), and St. John's (Royal Pulp formerly, Nashwaak, a subsidiary of the Oxford Paper Company).

The newsprint industry has steadily migrated to Canada as a result of governmental activity and encouragement by the provinces, transportation differentials which favoured the movement of newsprint rather than pulpwood, lower labour costs, cheap water transportation, abundance of raw material, and hydro-electric power. A hundred ton mill requires annually 50,000 cords of pulpwood. Since four tons of raw material (pulpwood, coal or fuel oil, sulphur, limestone, etc.) are necessary to produce a ton of newsprint, accessibility to cheap water transportation has been an important factor. The spruce forests of the lower St. Lawrence and its tributaries, of the Maritimes, and of northern Ontario, have been the chief source of raw material, with the result that lumber mills developed in relation to pine (Booth,

Eddy's) have been less conspicuous in the newsprint industry. Construction of mills on lake Superior, the Ottawa, the St. Maurice, the Saguenay, the St. Lawrence, the gulf of St. Lawrence, and the Atlantic has been a result. Mills dependent on rail transportation, such as at Iroquois Falls, Kapuskasing, Fort Frances, Kenora (1924), and Pine Falls, have been less favourably situated. The improvement of transmission of hydro-electric power has weakened the significance of power-sites, as in the case of mills along the St. Lawrence, such as Anglo-Canadian and Dalhousie; but the enormous demands for power have placed the industry under heavy obligations. A ton of newspaper requires the use of roughly 100 horsepower. Large-scale power development has contributed to the problems of the newsprint industry. International followed a policy of closing American newsprint mills, disposing of the power for other uses, and building Canadian mills in relation both to established and new power-sites. The Gatineau mills used a proportion of power developed in that region for sale to the Ontario Hydro-Electric, as did also the McLaren mills at Buckingham. Delivery of power by International on a contract basis was actually accompanied by the installation of coal-burners. Similarly Grand Falls on the St. John, developed largely by International (1928), supplied power to Dalhousie, and also to Fraser's at Edmundston and Madawaska). The Duke-Pine interests developed the Isle Maligne plant to supply power to newsprint mills at Kenogami and Riverbend and the aluminum industry at Arvida. Abitibi purchased the Island Falls plant from Hollinger, and built the Abitibi Canyon plant. In the latter case, the task was undertaken at too late a date, and the Ontario government assumed the responsibility. The strength of power interests on the St. Maurice, *i.e.* Shawinigan, contributed to the difficulties of Canada Power and Paper.

Mills dependent on direct purchases of power, such as the Ontario Paper Company, Interlake, and Provincial in the Niagara peninsula, have shifted from coal to electric power for steam purposes with low prices during the depression, and back to coal in 1936. The Ontario Paper Company, with its direct purchase of power, and Spruce Falls (Kimberley and *New York Times*) at Kapuskasing, with its power development at Smoky Falls, are illustrations of mills controlled by American publishers. The St. Lawrence Corporation (Timmins) has been conspicuous in its success, partly through dependence on the flexibility of purchased power.

The difficulties of the newsprint industry have been partly a result of expansion to parallel the development of large power-sites and partly a result of the position of organizations producing newsprint as a by-product of power development. Heavy initial investment involved in the development of power-sites and of the construction of paper plants ($50,000 per ton capacity, plus say $50,000 for timber limits) and reliance on rigid instruments of finance such as bonds have made costs unresponsive to changes in price. Highly efficient mills with the advantages of government support and most advanced technique, such as the Mersey and McLarens, continued to come on the market after the beginning of the depression. Capital reorganizations have been an inevitable result, and large units of control have shown signs of weakening. Gefaell interests purchased Great Lakes Paper (1936) and International relinquished control of Bathurst. The newsprint export manufacturers association (Nemac) co-operated with the code authorities under National Recovery Act to stabilize prices at $40.00. Prices increased slightly in 1936 and in 1937. The Murray Bay mill (International) has come into production and Ontario Paper Company is constructing a two-machine mill at

Comeau Bay to come into production in 1938.

The demand for newsprint has been closely dependent on advertising activity and on the efficiency of publishing houses in securing increased circulation. Wars have been important in increasing the consumption of newsprint and in increasing the efficiency of the printing press in securing increased speed. The radio tends to be complementary and competitive, and demands for economy have led to the narrowing of the margin of newspapers, to standardization of size to 20'' (8 columns of 12 ems), and to the emergence of smaller-size papers such as the tabloid. Expansion of press services and of advertising agencies has accompanied the marked improvements in communication and in the distribution of newspapers. The metropolitan press has steadily encroached on the newspapers of smaller centres, forcing amalgamation or abandonment. Compulsory education and the decline of illiteracy have been basic factors in the development of the industry. The power of the press, increased by effective organization and expansion of large units (Hearst and Howard Scripps in the United States; Southam and Sifton in Canada), and difficulties of organization based on the regional character of the production of newsprint in Canada have placed the newsprint industry in a weak position. Newspapers have been slow to secure control of newsprint mills, Riordon and Killam in the Toronto *Mail and Empire* and Lord Atholstan in the News Pulp and Paper Company (St. Raymond, 1910) being the exceptions.

*Bibliography.* Consult N. Reich, *The pulp and paper industry in Canada* (1926); E. A. Forsey, *The pulp and paper industry* (Canadian Journal of Economics and Political Science, 1935); *The Canadian economy and its problems* (Toronto, 1934); A. R. M. Lower, *Settlement and the first frontier* (Toronto, 1936); C. Southworth, *The American-*

*Canadian newsprint paper industry and the tariff* (Journal of Political Economy, 1922); W. L. Crum, *Advertising fluctuations* (Chicago, 1927); R. S. Kellogg, *Pulpwood and wood pulp in North America* (New York, 1923); *The manufacture of pulp and paper* (5 vols., New York, 1927-9); H. Marshall and others, *Canadian-American industry* (New Haven, 1936); *Report of the Royal Commission on pulpwood* (Ottawa, 1924); *Pulp and Paper Magazine* (1903—); and the annual report of the Dominion Bureau of Statistics.

**Punk island** is in lake Winnipeg in Manitoba, 3 miles south-east of Grindstone point.

**Punnichy,** a village in Saskatchewan, on the main line of the Canadian National Railway, 156 miles south-east of Saskatoon. It has a weekly newspaper (*Touchwood Times*). Pop. (1934), 230.

**Punshon, William Morley** (1824-1881), Methodist minister, was born at Doncaster, England, in 1824. He became a minister of the Wesleyan Methodist Church; and in 1868 he came to Canada. As pastor of the Metropolitan Church in Toronto, he assumed an outstanding position as a pulpit orator; and he played an important part in bringing about the union of the Methodist Churches in Canada. In 1873 he returned to England, and he died at Brixton, London, England, on April 14, 1881. See F. W. Macdonald, *Life of W. M. Punshon* (London, 1887).

**Purple-flowering Raspberry.** See **Raspberry.**

**Purple Gerardia.** See **Gerardia.**

**Purslane** (*Portulaca oleracea* L., *Portulacaceae*), a fleshy, prostrate, freely branching herb which grows very rapidly, forming mat-like clusters. The alternate leaves are wedge-shaped and rounded at the apex. The flowers are numerous, pale yellow, and sessile in the axils of the leaves, opening only on sunny mornings. The fruit is a many-seeded capsule. It is very common in gardens, dooryards, and cultivated rich sandy soil in eastern Canada especially, though found to some extent everywhere.

**Puslinch,** a village in Wellington county, Ontario, on the Canadian Pacific Railway, 12 miles south-east of Guelph. The township of Puslinch in which it is situated, was created in 1835, and was named after the birthplace in Devonshire, England, of Lady Colborne, the wife of Sir John Colborne (q.v.). Pop. (1934), 150.

**Pussy Toes.** See **Everlasting.**

**Pyrite,** a mineral consisting of sulphide of iron. It crystallizes in the cubic system, commonly showing cubes upon the faces of which are striations, the striae on adjoining faces being perpendicular to each other. It also crystallizes in pentagonal dodecahedra, or pyritohedra. It is brittle, has a hardness of 6 to 6.5 and a specific gravity of 5. The lustre is metallic, and it is characterized by a pale brass-yellow colour, so that it is frequently mistaken for gold. It is one of the most common of metallic minerals, being found in practically every kind of rock, but more particularly in igneous rocks and also as an important vein mineral occurring in masses of great extent. The bright crystals are sometimes cut for ring stones and sold under the name of marcasite. The chief use, however, of pyrite is as the source of sulphur for the manufacture of sulphuric acid and for the artificial preparation of elemental sulphur. Pyrite frequently contains sufficient gold to be used as an ore of that metal. The chief producing regions in Canada for pyrite have been North Pines, Goudreau, and Queensboro, in Ontario, and the Aldermac mines in Quebec. See A. W. G. Wilson, *Pyrites in Canada: its occurrence, exploitation, dressing, and uses* (Mines Branch, Ottawa, 1913).

**Pyrola.** See **Shin-leaf.**

**Pyroxene,** a group of rock-forming minerals which are characterized by an imperfect prismatic cleavage making angles of about 87° between the cleavage faces. The important orthorhombic pyroxenes are enstatite and hypersthene, which are silicates of magnesia and ferrous iron and are characteristically found in basic igneous rocks. Monoclinic pyroxene includes diopside and augite, in addition to other less common varieties. Diopside is a silicate of calcium and magnesium. It is usually light-coloured, though sometimes dark green, and ranges from transparent to opaque. It is one of the characteristic minerals found with crystalline limestone, and results largely from the contact metamorphism of limestones. Augite, the other important monoclinic pyroxene, is a dark silicate of magnesia and iron with alumina. It is characteristically found in basic igneous rocks, particularly gabbro, anorthosite, and diabase.

**Pyroxenite,** in general a plutonic rock consisting essentially of pyroxene without feldspar and without olivine. The name has also been applied to certain rocks resulting from contact metamorphism of limestone.

**Pyrrhotite.** See **Nickel** and **Iron.**

**Pyrolusite.** See **Manganese.**

# Q

**Quaco.** See **St. Martins.**

**Quadra island** is in the Coast district of British Columbia, between Vancouver island and the mainland, separated from Vancouver island by Discovery passage in a north approach to Georgia strait. It is the southern portion of what was formerly Valdes island. It is 22 miles long and from 1 to 9½ miles wide. It was named after Juan Francisco de la Bodega y Quadra, a Spanish naval officer who explored the coast of British Columbia and Alaska in 1775 and 1779, and who died in 1794.

**Quadra mountain** is on the boundary line between British Columbia and Alberta, north-west of the headwaters of the Vermilion river, in the Rocky mountains. It is in lat. 51° 17′ and long. 116° 09′, and has an altitude of 10,410 feet.

**Quail,** a name in rather general use for the small upland game bird known as the bob-white (*Colinus virginianus*), and also used, with a prefix, as a designation for two related forms, the mountain quail (*Oreortyx picta*) and the California quail (*Lophortyx californica*). The bob-white occurs in Canada only in southern Ontario. It was almost extirpated from this area at the end of the nineteenth century. Protection and the introduction of stock from southern areas have resulted in a rather feeble expansion of its population. The mountain quail and the California quail are not native to Canada, but were introduced from more southern sections of the mountainous West to Vancouver island. See also **Partridge.**

**Quakers.** See **Friends, Society of.**

**Qualicum Beach,** a village on the east coast of Vancouver island, British Columbia, 6 miles north-west of Parksville. It has elementary and high schools. Pop. (1930), 300.

**Qu'Appelle.** See **Fort Qu'Appelle.**

**Qu'Appelle river,** rises in southern Saskatchewan, near the Elbow of the South Saskatchewan river, and flows in an easterly direction through the southern belt until its junction with the Assiniboine, in western Manitoba, between the 50th and 51st parallels of north latitude. The name is derived from a bend in the river which produces a very strong echo. The Qu'Appelle runs through a delightful valley and expands into 8 lakes, where the best of whitefish abound. It is 270 miles in length.

**Quartz,** one of the most common minerals. It crystallizes in the hexagonal system, and is sometimes transparent and colourless, when it is known as rock crystal. Sometimes it is purple, and is then called amethyst. Smoky and brown colours go under the names of smoky quartz and cairngorm stone. Pink varieties are called rose quartz, while good yellow is known as citrine. All these varieties have a glassy lustre. Quartz seldom exhibits cleavage, but is recognized by the fact that it has a shell-like or conchoidal fracture. It has a specific gravity of 2.66, and is harder than a knife, being number 7 in Moh's scale of hardness.

In addition to the crystallized quartz, there are certain varieties which to the naked eye show no trace of crystallization, but when examined under the microscope are found to have certain evidences of crystalline structure. These varieties, because the crystallization is concealed, are said to be crypto-crystalline. The common varieties of crypto-crystalline quartz are chalcedony, agate, jasper, and flint. Quartz is particularly important as a rock-forming mineral, being one of the essential minerals in granite and almost the sole constituent of many sandstones. It is probably better known in the crystallized form in veins and is one of the common vein minerals. It is particularly well known in the gold quartz veins. In addition to its use as a semi-precious stone, large quantities of quartz are used in the manufacture of glass, in steel foundries, in sand-blasting, and in filtration plants. It is used extensively in the manufacture of sand-paper and along with anthracite coal in the manufacture of the artificial abrasive carborundum. It is employed as a flux in certain metallurgical operations, and is used in the manufacture of ferro-silican. See L. Heber Cole, *Silica in Canada*, Parts I and II (Ottawa, Mines Branch, 1923-8).

**Quartzite,** a metamorphosed sandstone in which the bonding material is quartz.

**Quartz Porphyry,** an igneous rock with a porphyritic texture, having as its chief phenocrysts quartz and orthoclase. The ground mass is usually felsitic or microcrystalline. The quartz porphyries are more frequently dike rocks, in contrast to the rhyolites, which are characteristic surface flows.

**Quatsino,** a village in Vancouver island, British Columbia, on the north side of Quatsino sound, west of the entrance to Hecate cove. It has a school and government offices. Pop. (1930), 500.

**Quatsino sound,** the north-westernmost of the deep inlets on the west coast of Vancouver island. It is about 25 miles long. The name is an adaptation of that of the Koskimo Indians, a now almost extinct tribe which formerly inhabited this locality. See D. Jenness, *Fading scenes on Quatsino inlet* (Canadian Geographical Journal, 1934).

**Quebec,** the most easterly of the provinces of Canada, is bounded on the north by Ungava bay and Hudson straits, on the west by Hudson bay, James bay, the Ottawa river, and the province of Ontario, on the south by the states of New York, Vermont, New Hampshire, and Maine, and on the east by the Labrador coast and the gulf of St. Lawrence.

In 1912 the area of Quebec was exactly doubled, and extended to 703,653 square miles through the annexation of the territory of Ungava; but fifteen years later, in 1927, a decision of the Privy Council gave back to the colony of Newfoundland 102,000 of the 351,780 square miles thus added, leaving an actual present area of 594,534 square miles, which leaves Quebec still the largest of the Canadian provinces. The combined area of France, Germany, and Spain exceeds only by 2,600 square miles that of Quebec.

*History.* The history of Quebec dates as far back as the discovery of Canada itself. It was indeed on her soil that Jacques Cartier (q.v.), the envoy of the king of France, landed for the first time in 1534. She did not, however, really begin to exist until 1608, when Samuel de Champlain (q.v.), who had already established a first settlement in Acadia, planted the *fleur-de-lis* on the rock of Stadacona, and definitely chose Quebec as the seat of what was to be New France for more than a century and a half.

The new colony, which ultimately grew into the present Canada, had very humble beginnings, and for a long time its existence was extremely precarious. Twenty years after its foundation, in 1629, when it was captured by the English under Sir David Kirke (q.v.), but two families were yet permanently settled, with a shifting population of

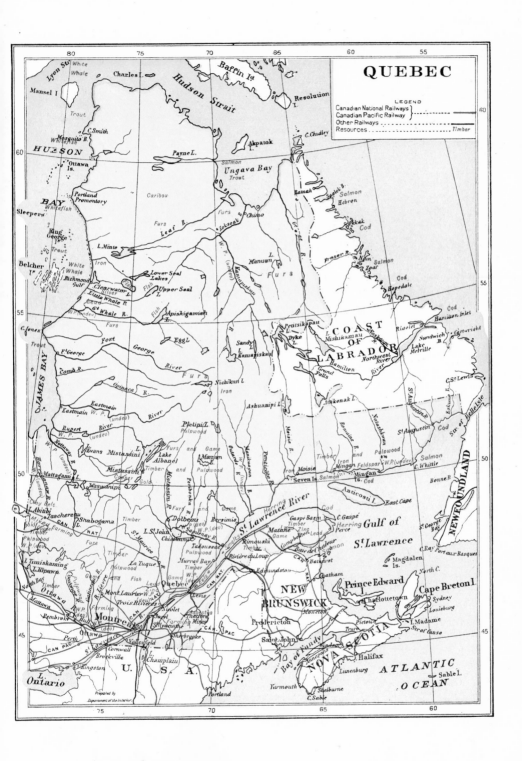

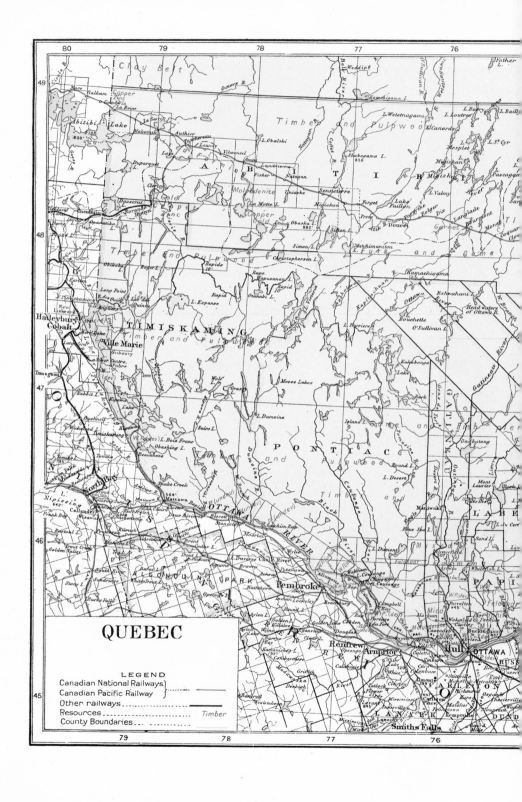

QUEBEC

LEGEND
Canadian National Railways
Canadian Pacific Railway
Other railways
Resources
County Boundaries

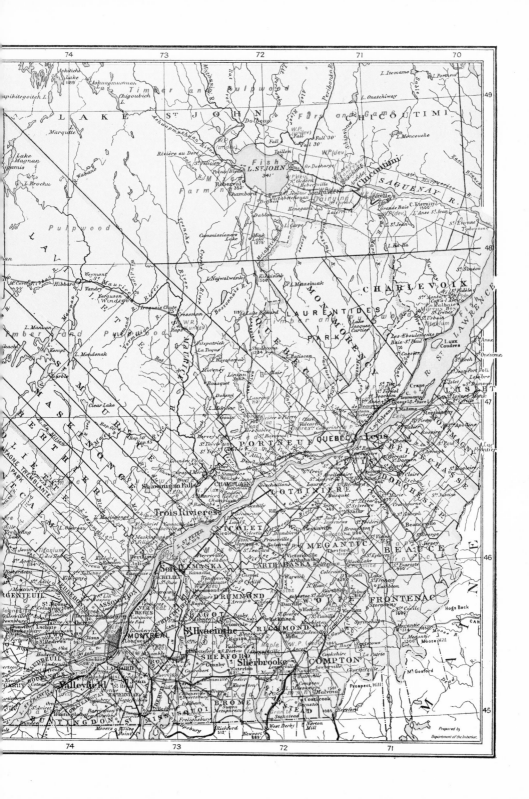

monks, officials, and fur-traders. Restored to the French in 1632 by the Treaty of St. Germain, New France resumed courageously its career. Further penetration of the country was instantly begun, and in the course of a few years Three Rivers and Montreal were successively established. So heavy, however, was the toll of lives levied at that time by continuous incursions of the barbarous Indians that more than once the fate of the colony appeared to be sealed. Relief came at last in 1665 with the timely arrival of the regiment of Carignan. The Indians were kept at bay at least temporarily, and the colonists were for the first time allowed to breathe. A period followed of the most fruitful activity. Under the inspiration of Colbert, then minister of Louis XIV, France had at last decided to inaugurate a real policy of colonization, and the economic direction of the country had been fortunately entrusted to Jean Talon (q.v.), a man of superior ability known in Canadian history as "the Great Intendant". Settlers began to pour in in greater numbers, marriageable girls were sent to insure the creation of families, commerce was regulated, thought was even given to manufacturing industry, but perhaps the most important move of the new intendant was the distribution of the territory into vast seigniories which were destined to expand colonization, and on which a good proportion of the Carignan soldiers effectively settled. Thanks to the powerful impetus thus given, the population increased more than five times in the twenty years which followed. In the meantime, it is true, too many of the young men, attracted by the advantages of fur-trading, or simply by the lure of the wild, deserted the fields and chose to roam through the forest with the Indians, but the evils of that plague were largely redeemed by services of another kind. The great feats of discovery which so early opened the continent of North America would have never been accomplished without the help of the sturdy *coureurs-des-bois* who accompanied Joliet (q.v.), La Salle (q.v.), and Iberville (q.v.) in their search of the Mississippi, and later La Vérendrye (q.v.) in his quest of the Western Sea.

Towards the end of the seventeenth century, New France was at last internally at peace, the Indians having been sufficiently overpowered or having become friendly as a whole, and the colony could have grown much more rapidly had the home government shown the same interest in its welfare as at the time of Colbert. Progress was considerably hampered by continuous petty quarrels between governors and intendants, whose powers were not well defined; and, as a result of a narrow policy, only a slight encouragement was given to local industry. Besides, the influx of settlers had practically ceased, and the population was left to its natural increase, which was, it is true, wonderfully rapid.

Meanwhile the British settlements were thriving in New England and Virginia, and, as was inevitable, there was soon created between them and New France a certain rivalry which periodically broke out into warring conflicts. In retaliation for the numerous and bloody incursions made with the help of Indians on New England towns, the English twice planned to subdue New France, but without success, firstly in 1690, when Sir William Phips (q.v.) was repulsed by Frontenac (q.v.), and secondly in 1711, when Quebec was saved by the wreck of Sir Hovenden Walker's fleet.

As time went on, however, what were only at the beginning frictions occasioned by rivalry in trade gradually developed into a graver conflict, an open contest for territorial supremacy. While English possessions were still confined to the Atlantic seaboard, France, by a continuous advance, had taken hold of the whole centre of the continent from the regions adjoining Hudson bay to the gulf of Mexico, and New France herself had extended her domain proper to the very heart of what are now the United States. Time had come to decide which of the two rivals would become the ultimate master of a country the immense possibilities of which were more than ever apparent. The tension finally came to a break in 1755, and a war was waged which lasted five long years. After various successes which at first elated their hopes, the French gradually lost ground until at the end of 1759 they were cornered in the St. Lawrence valley. Insufficiently aided by the mother country and disheartened by the brazen thefts of Bigot (q.v.) and company, which brought upon the people untold miseries, their courage had to yield finally before the proverbial British tenacity. The real turning-point of the contest, however, was the battle of the Plains, in which, on September 13, 1759, Wolfe (q.v.), the victor, and Montcalm (q.v.), the vanquished, fell clothed in the same shroud of glory. A French victory soon followed, that of Ste. Foy, but it was only a last glowing spark, and could not change the course of events, the colony being already doomed by the capture of Quebec. The capitulation of Montreal in September, 1760, put an end to the contest, but it was only three years later, by the Treaty of Paris in 1763, that New France ceased to exist as such, and was officially transferred, under the name of Canada, from the French to the British crown.

The transition of a population of 60,000 to a new allegiance was naturally fraught with difficulties. On the one hand, the French, or "new subjects" (as they were called), complained, though not too highly at the beginning, that their ancient laws and religious privileges had been done away with; and, on the other hand, the English merchants or "old subjects", though still few in number, claimed more and more of the upper hand and insisted noisily on their growing demands. After years of wrangle, the British House of Commons, moved by a spirit of conciliation, but perhaps stimulated at the end by the troubles which were then bubbling in the American colonies, voted a new constitution called the Quebec Act of 1774, which, among other provisions, restored the ancient civil laws of the majority and conceded a greater liberty for the exercise of their religion. The invasion of the country in the following year by the American rebels put to a victorious test the fidelity of the French Canadians. Resisting a tendency quite natural and all kinds of other inducements, they followed the guidance of their clergy and remained loyal to the Crown, with the exception of small dissenting groups.

After the repelling of the invader, political dissensions were not long in flaming anew between the two rival sections of the community, and in 1791 it was found necessary to frame a second constitution, which like the former one was diversely appreciated. By the new Act the colony was divided into two distinct provinces, namely Lower Canada (or otherwise Quebec), and Upper Canada (later called Ontario). Each of the two provinces was at the same time endowed with a legislature consisting of two branches, a Legislative Council and a Legislative Assembly. In Lower Canada particularly, the legislature provided a new field in which were emphasized the differences already existing. The elected representatives of the majority could not go hand in hand with the appointed Council, and each in turn took up the cudgels. There were also innumerable occasions of quarrel between the governors and the representatives of the people. When the Assembly, after having uselessly claimed during many sessions the absolute control of public expenditure, finally refused in 1826 and later to vote the subsidies required by the administration, the situation became acute. After the adoption of the Ninety-Two Resolutions, especially, in 1834, feelings rose still higher. Papineau (q.v.) and the other reformist leaders went on the stump and aired the grievances of the people throughout the province. This agitation finally culminated in the two rebellions of 1837 and 1838, which were, however, rapidly quashed, like the two coincident ones in Upper Canada.

One of the first steps of the imperial parliament, after the rebellion, was to sanction the legislative union of Upper and Lower Canada, as advised by Lord Durham (q.v.) in his famous *Report*. The new measure conceded an equal representation to two provinces of unequal population and burdened one province with a large part of the other's debts, but it had at least one good point, that of establishing at last the long-expected responsible government. In the end, indeed, Lower Canada did not fare too badly under the new régime, and even managed to prosper. With the exception of a few flurries like the burning of Parliament House in Montreal in 1849, there was no longer any sign of internal trouble.

Lower Canada was one of the first five provinces to enter the pact of Confederation in 1867. It became thereby autonomous once more as to its essential rights, and regained at the same time the ancient official title of "province of Quebec".

*Description*. Fourteen-fifteenths of the province form part of the vast Precambrian or Canadian Shield, which is considered the most ancient geological formation in the universe. The mountains may be classified in three groups, the Laurentians which skirt the St. Lawrence from Labrador to a point not far from the city of Quebec and then recede, leaving a widening lowland between them and the river as far as the Ottawa river; the Appalachians,

a continuation of the chain of the same name in the United States, which run in Canada from the frontier in the neighbourhood of lake Champlain to the city of Quebec, and thence to the gulf, down the St. Lawrence valley and through the Gaspé peninsula; and lastly the Monteregians, situated in the western portion of the St. Lawrence lowlands. In the Laurentians, along the gulf and the river St. Lawrence, the elevations vary from less than 1,000 to over 3,000 feet. Some peaks of the Appalachians rise to 3,000 feet in the Eastern townships, and even to 4,000 in the Gaspé peninsula. The Monteregians are considerably lower, their highest elevation slightly exceeding 1,700 feet.

The province is abundantly watered. Its liquid area, not including tidal waters, comprises 71,000 square miles, compared with 49,300 in Ontario, the nearest rival. The main artery is the river St. Lawrence, which brings transatlantic vessels to the harbour of Montreal, nearly 1,000 miles from the ocean, during seven and a half months of the year. Among the most important tributaries of the St. Lawrence must be mentioned the Ottawa, the St. Maurice, the Richelieu, and the Saguenay. With the exception of the Richelieu, the importance of which is only local, these rivers are navigable only in part, but they have been long used for the floating of timber. There are besides in the province of Quebec numerous lakes of all dimensions, the largest being Mistassini lake, with an area of 840 square miles.

The province extends from the 45th parallel of latitude to 62° 40′ north, and its temperature is therefore of necessity varied. In the upper regions, winters are very long and extremely severe, but in the settled part the seasons do not offer very striking contrasts. While the winters are still cold, the summers are warm and sunny. In general, the climate is considered healthy and favourable to most kinds of culture.

*Population.* The province of Quebec holds the second rank in the Confederation as to population. According to the latest official census, the total number of its inhabitants was 2,874,255 in 1931, compared to 3,431,683 in Ontario, but a recent estimate of the Bureau of Statistics advances the figures for Quebec to 3,062,000 in June, 1935.

An immense majority are of French origin, though Canadian-born, the total being 2,270,059 against 604,000 of all other origins, British or foreign. And all of these, while speaking the two official languages of the country, English and French, with the exception of a negligible minority, claim French as their mother tongue. In many of the rural districts, the population might nearly be said exclusively French-Canadian. The *habitant* is constantly gaining ground even in the Eastern Townships, which were expressly set apart for the settlement of the United Empire Loyalists more than a hundred years ago. There remains in that region only one riding in which the two elements are about equally balanced. In all the others, which were overwhelmingly English-speaking not many years ago, the French have attained to-day a supremacy of number which is unquestionable.

Though it has shown a certain tendency to decrease in the last decade, the birth-rate of Quebec is still the highest in the Confederation, 25.3 per 1,000 inhabitants.

Another noticeable fact in the province of Quebec is the great numerical strength of Roman Catholics, who number 2,463,160 against 411,095 of all other denominations combined.

*Cities and Towns.* Montreal, the largest city of the province, is also the largest of Canada. According to the latest available official census, it was supposed to have six years ago, in 1931, a population of 818,577, but these figures were for the city proper, and did not include Verdun, Outremont, and Westmount, three important cities immediately contiguous but municipally distinct. Montreal claims to-day a population of over a million, exclusive of the aforesaid adjoining towns. Though coming far behind the metropolis, Quebec, the capital of the province, is still in numerical importance the sixth city of Canada, with its population of over 130,000. Leaving aside Verdun, whose 60,000 inhabitants virtually form part of Montreal, the next city in importance is Trois Rivières (Three Rivers), a centre of the pulp industry, whose population exceeds 35,000. Other cities worthy of mention are Hull (29,433), Sherbrooke (28,933), Lachine (18,630), Shawinigan (15,345), St. Hyacinthe (13,448), Chicoutimi (11,877), and Valleyfield (11,411).

*Agriculture.* It is estimated that out of the 335,057,760 acres of land which cover the province of Quebec only 43,745,000, not even an eighth, are suited for agricultural purposes. The reason is that the major part of the land, about 62 per cent., is in too high latitudes to permit the economic production of cereals. However, with approximately 6,000,000 acres under actual cultivation at the present time, the province still retains the third rank in Canadian farm production. In 1934, at a time when low prices were still prevailing, the total value of its field crops was placed at $98,309,000. The principal crops are oats, which yielded in 1934 48,000,000 bushels, valued at $10,757,000, and hay and clover, which yielded in the same year 4,848,000 tons. valued at $57,433,000. Farmers sow very little wheat, not because the soil itself is not as well suited for it as any other, but because it is less profitable owing to other conditions.

The dairying industry is well established in all the settled parts of the province, nearly every parish having its cheese factory and creamery. Quebec produced in 1935 over 30 per cent. of all the creamery butter and about 20 per cent. of all the factory cheese produced in Canada, 72,999,000 pounds of the first, and 20,357,000 of the second.

The making of maple sugar is also an industry of considerable size. In 1935 Quebec produced 5,747,000 pounds of maple sugar and 1,581,000 gallons of maple syrup, respectively 90 per cent. and 70 per cent. of the total production of Canada, which is by itself half the world's supply. The central area of the sugar industry in Quebec is in the Eastern Townships. Other items of importance are honey production, market-gardening, and tobacco-growing. Primitive methods of farming have been rapidly disappearing, especially in late years, thanks to the policy of the government. The placing in every county of farm demonstrators trained in agricultural colleges has been especially helpful in that respect. In 1934 the total value of the agricultural wealth in the province of Quebec was estimated at $965,583,000.

*Fisheries and Game.* Quebec in 1934 ranked fourth among the provinces of Canada in value of fish caught. The value of production of its commercial fisheries, which was exceeded only by British Columbia and two of the Maritime provinces, amounted in that year to $2,303,517. Sea fisheries, which were formerly controlled by the Dominion government, reverted to the province in 1922. They are by far the most important part of the industry. Cod, herring, mackerel, lobster, salmon, and smelts are the principal kinds caught in the salt water of the gulf and of Chaleur bay. The total market value of cod alone exceeded $900,000 in 1934.

Game fish is found in abundance in the numerous streams and lakes of the province. The Gaspé peninsula offers to the angler some of the finest salmon rivers in Canada, and lake St. John is renowned as the home of the best ouananiche.

Quebec is also one of the best big game territories on the continent. Moose, cariboo, deer, and bear are still plentiful in its immense forested lands. The northern regions particularly possess an abundance of fur-bearing animals, whose marketable pelts were valued in 1934 to $1,479,811.

Fish and game in the province of Quebec have not only a commercial importance; they are also an indirect source of revenue in attracting from the outside hosts of tourists and sportsmen, who spend lavishly and add to the local wealth. So far, Quebec is the only province in the Dominion which leases exclusive fishing and hunting rights over large tracts of forest, lake, or river territory.

*Forest Industry.* The forest domain of the province of Quebec, New Quebec not included, is approximately estimated at 165,000,000 acres. It is divided into private forests, which are located principally in the central St. Lawrence valley, and consist of farms sold to settlers by the government, or of old seigniories alienated under the French régime, or of lands conceded to railways, into lots under ticket of lease which become private property after issue of letters patent, and finally into crown lands.

The territory of the Crown itself is divided into forests leased to different parties for a fixed period (about 49,000,-000 acres); into township reserves destined to supply the adjoining villages (787,000 acres); into domanial forests reserved for future requirements of the industry (1,882,000 acres); and lastly into unleased timber limits (about 98,000,000 acres). The unleased forests are in absolute possession of the government, and free from all encumbrance. Chiefly situated in the northern part of the province, in the basins of the St. Lawrence and of Hudson bay, they are known to be rich in merchantable timber, but they have not yet been worked. An inventory is being made of these forests, so that they may be utilized as needs require.

The forests of Quebec are estimated to be worth more than $1,000,000,000. According to recent figures prepared by the Dominion Bureau of Statistics, they contain 61,461,875 cubic feet of softwoods and hardwoods.

In 1934 there were 296,220,000 feet board measure of lumber cut in the province, and the total value of the products of the saw mills was placed at $7,143,396, nearly two-thirds less than in 1926, before the depression.

But the largest by far among the Canadian industries which draw from the forest their raw material is the pulp-and-paper industry; and in this particular domain Quebec holds unquestionably the first rank. In 1934, 2,382,437 cords of wood, mostly spruce (68.1 per cent.) were utilized in the manufactures of pulp in Quebec, and the total production, valued at $36,837,402, was 1,813,096 tons against 1,823,239 in all the other provinces. High as they are, these figures show a considerable decrease when compared with those of 1929, the banner year of the pulp industries. In that year out of 114 pulp-and-paper mills in Canada, 50 were operated in Quebec, and the capital invested in them amounted to $295,505,-402, over 50 per cent. of that in the whole Dominion. As to the total production, it reached 2,174,805 tons, and was valued at $69,295,498.

Quebec stands first not only in pulpwood manufactured, but also in pulpwood consumed. In 1934 it produced 51 per cent. of the total paper production in Canada, namely 1,569,538 tons, valued at $61,837,248. A strong factor in the development of the industry has been the legislative enactment of the Quebec government in 1910 under which all pulpwood cut on crown lands must be manufactured within the Canadian boundary.

On account of its enormous supply of pulpwood still available, of its practically inexhaustible water-power resources, and of its geographical position, unequalled in Canada for trade with Europe and the United States, Quebec bids fair to continue to lead in the production of pulp-and-paper.

Abundant measures are taken by the administration to protect the forests by an extensive system of fire prevention, to prevent the depletion by the establishment of forest reserves in large areas and of nurseries which provide material for distribution or the reclaiming of waste lands by tree planting, and finally by the establishment of various schools of forest researches, of forest rangers, and even of paper-making.

*Mines.* From the fifth rank which she held in the Canadian mineral industry in 1927, the province of Quebec has passed to the third in 1935, the total output of her mines and quarries for that year being valued at $38,897,-127. Until recently the great bulk of minerals produced in the province was of the non-metallic order, such as asbestos, mica, magnesite, and practically all the building materials, granite, lime-stone, marble, etc. To-day more than half of the production is from metals, principally gold and copper. The value of gold production in Quebec has jumped from $172,214 in 1927 to $7,914,556 in 1935, and to $10,950,540 if we include the exchange equalization. During the same period, the value of copper produced has increased from $407,146 to $5,214,177. This phenomenal increase is due to the discovery of important gold quartz veins of considerable extent and of vast deposits of solid sulphides carrying gold and copper in the Timiskaming and Abitibi districts which are the continuation of the highly mineralized rocks of eastern Ontario.

We have yet a very incomplete idea of the mineral potentialities of the province of Quebec, less than 40,000 of her 600,000 square miles having been prospected so far, but geologists are more and more of the opinion that Quebec's mineral resources will before

THE LEGISLATIVE BUILDINGS OF QUEBEC AT QUEBEC CITY

long exceed its agricultural resources. The immense region which lies in the north, in the Ungava district, is reputed totally Precambrian, and, when exploited, it should yield an immense quantity of minerals of all kinds.

Among minerals of the non-metallic class, asbestos holds the first place in Quebec. The important asbestos deposits situated in what is known as the "Serpentine Belt" produced in 1934, 155,980 tons valued at $4,936,826, which is about 80 per cent. of the total consumption of the world. It is so far the principal mineral wealth of the Appalachian region, but it is firmly believed by many that the Eastern Townships themselves have not yet told all their story in respect of mining.

*Manufactures.* The manufacturing industry in Quebec has marked a considerable progress in the present century. Measures taken by the government for the manufacturing of a considerable part of the raw material within the territory of the province, the abundance of water-power and also the general conditions of labour, which are favourable, have induced each year the investment of a larger amount of capital, mostly from the neighbouring United States. This capital, which amounted to $142,403,407 in 1901, had increased to $1,648,872,387 in 1933. As to the total value of manufactured products it increased from $158,287,994 in 1901 to $1,155,201,014 in 1929 at the peak of prosperity. In 1933 that value still amounted to $653,066,534.

Pulp-and-paper making is the principal manufacturing industry of the province, the gross value of its products having amounted in 1933 to $56,474,428. Next in importance are the power plants, the textiles, the smelters, the tobacco factories, the clothing mills, the petroleum refineries, and the leather factories.

Montreal, or more correctly Greater Montreal, remains the largest manufacturing centre, sharing 3,000 of the 8,070 industrial establishments of the province, and a similar proportion of the total capital invested, but the move towards decentralization is yearly increasing. Outside of Montreal, the city of Quebec still has the lead as to value of output, but it is closely followed by Three Rivers, the principal seat of the pulp-and-paper industry. The most important of the other manufacturing towns are Drummondville with its celanese factory; Valleyfield and Magog, with their cotton mills, Shawinigan Falls, Grand'Mère, La Tuque, and East Angus with their pulp mills, Hull, Sherbrooke, St. Hyacinthe, and St. Johns with their varied industries, and finally Arvida with its huge aluminium plant.

*Water-Power.* Of all the Canadian provinces Quebec is the richest in water-power, both potential and developed. To the north of the St. Lawrence, practically the whole territory, including that draining towards Hudson bay and the North Atlantic, is part of the great Laurentian plateau, whose extensive lake and stream system are favourable to the widespread location of water-power sites both great and small. To the south, the topography is somewhat different, but there are still rivers like the Richelieu, the St. François, and the Chaudière with considerable water-power resources.

As far as they are known, the total available power resources of the province of Quebec aggregate 13,064,000 horse-power at ordinary six months' flow, and 8,459,000 at ordinary minimum flow, that is to say continuously available 24 hours per day throughout the year. Of this total 3,700,320 horse-power was already utilized in 1930; and this represents about 50 per cent. of the turbine installation in the whole of Canada.

The outstanding power rivers of the province are the St. Lawrence, which has between two and two-and-a-half million horse-power available between the Ontario boundary and Montreal, the Ottawa river and its Quebec tributaries with from 1,000,000 to 1,600,000 horse-power, the St. Maurice river and its tributaries with upwards of 1,000,000 horse-power, and the Saguenay and its tributaries with from 1,260,000 to 1,530,-000 horse-power. Of these, the St. Maurice river is at present the largest source of power, 602,500 horse-power being already installed on different sites.

To ensure an equal flow of water in the principal rivers serving power stations and manufactures, the government has built four large storage dams, the principal of which is the Gouin dam, with a capacity of 160,000 million cubic feet, in the headwaters of the river St. Maurice.

There were in 1933 in the province of Quebec 96 central electric stations, which, with a capital investment of $606,904,478, supplied power to innumerable industries and generated not less than 9,611,084,000 kilowatt hours of electricity. The production of power through the harnessing of falls and rivers is unquestionably the chief factor in the industrial development of the province of Quebec; it has given impetus to manufactures in many small centres and spread the general use of electricity for commercial, municipal, and domestic purposes.

*Education.* The education system of the province of Quebec is dual, Catholic and Protestant. There is no minister of education, but the department of education is represented in the legislature by the provincial secretary. The non-political head of the department is the superintendent, who is assisted by a French and by an English secretary, the latter of whom is also styled director of Protestant education. All matters concerning taxation, erection of municipalities, election of commissioners and trustees, and civil management of school affairs generally are regulated by the legislature through the Education Act, but the real power in matters of education is vested in a Superior Council of

Public Instruction, of which the superintendent is president *ex-officio*. The Superior Council is made of two committees, one Catholic and one Protestant, which sit separately. The Catholic committee is composed of all the archbishops and bishops of the province and of as many laymen appointed by the government, while the Protestant committee, equal to the former in number, is wholly appointed. Each committee manages independently the educational affairs of the section of the population belonging to its religious denomination. They make all regulations concerning the organization of schools under their control, the government of normal schools, the approval of textbooks, etc., and these regulations have force of law when approved by order-in-council.

The province itself is divided into school municipalities, the limits of which generally coincide with those of the parish, and which are administered by five commissioners elected every three years by the tax-payers. In most of the rural districts, the majority is French and Catholic, but any minority, Protestant or Catholic, has the right of dissenting and of establishing a commission of its own, three in number, governing its own schools. The direct administration of the schools, the appointment of teachers and the levying of taxes according to legislative regulations are under the control of the school commissioners. In important cities or towns, there may be special laws governing the school boards, but in every case Protestants and Catholics attend independently to the education of their own.

There are three grades of schools in the province: schools for primary education, for secondary education, and for superior education. Since 1929 the Catholic primary schools have been divided into five categories: infant, primary, elementary, primary complementary, primary superior, and domestic sciences schools. The Protestant retain the division into elementary, intermediate, and high schools.

While the Protestant committee controls primary education and to some extent secondary education, through the high schools, the Catholic committee controls only the five categories of primary schools and the normal schools intended for the training of primary teachers.

Secondary education is dispensed to the Catholic young men through 21 classical colleges affiliated to one or the other university of the same denomination and to the Catholic young girls through superior teaching convents sometimes also affiliated. These institutions are independent of the control of the Council of Education, but may receive grants from the government on certain conditions.

Of the four universities existing in the province, McGill University in Montreal is non-sectarian, Laval University of Quebec and the University of Montreal are Catholic, and Bishop's College of Lennoxville is Anglican.

There is no compulsory education in the province of Quebec, but school attendance favourably compares with that found elsewhere. During the last quarter of a century the school population has steadily grown out of proportion to the growth of the general population. Another indication of progress is that while the total cost of education was $9,225,771 in 1912, it had amounted in 1933 to $34,591,963.

*Government.* The government consists of a lieutenant-governor appointed by the Dominion government, a Legislative Council appointed for life by the provincial government, and a Legislative Assembly elected for five years. Quebec is the only province in the Dominion which has retained a Legislative Council. While the membership of the Legislative Council is fixed at 24, that of the Legislative Assembly may vary according to circumstances; it is at present 90. The Executive Council is composed as follows: the premier, who may or may not administer a special department, a provincial treasurer, an attorney-general, a provincial secretary, a minister of lands and forests, a minister of colonization, a minister of fisheries, a minister of agriculture, a minister of public works, a minister of roads, a minister of labour, and lastly a minister of municipal affairs and commerce. A certain number of other ministers may also have a seat in the provincial cabinet, but without a portfolio.

In the Dominion parliament, Quebec is represented by 65 members elected to the House of Commons and 24 members appointed for life to the Senate. By virtue of the Canadian constitution itself, Quebec is the pivotal province in the matter of representation. Its quota of 65 members in the House of Commons is unchangeable, while to each of the other provinces is assigned a number of representatives bearing the same proportion to the number of its population ascertained by the preceding census as the number 65 bears to the number of the population of Quebec.

The total ordinary revenues of the province which were of $4,563,432 in 1901 had increased to $31,018,344 in 1934. The net bonded debt for the same year was $97,988,338.

*Arms.* The arms of the province of Quebec are as follows: Or, on a fesse gules, a lion passant guardant or; in chief two fleurs de lis azure and in base three maple leaves slipped vert. To these arms, conceded by royal mandate in 1868, was added in 1883 the oft-quoted motto: *Je me souviens.* See the frontispiece to vol. iii of this *Encyclopedia.*

*Bibliography.* Among the numerous books which may be consulted on the province of Quebec and her people, the following may be mentioned: I. Lebrun, *Tableau statistique et politique des deux Canadas* (Paris, 1832); Robert Christie, *A history of the late province of Lower*

*Canada* (6 vols., Montreal, 1848-55);
S. Drapeau, *Études sur les developpements de la colonisation du Bas-Canada* (Québec, 1863); E. de Nevers, *L'avenir du peuple canadien-français* (Paris, 1896); A. Siegfried, *Le Canada, les deux races* (Paris, 1906); E. Salone, *La colonisation de la Nouvelle France* (Paris, 1906); L. Arnould, *Nos amis les canadiens* (Paris, 1912); J. C. Hopkins, *French Canada* (Philadelphia, 1913); A. Shortt and A. G. Doughty (eds.), *Canada and its provinces* (Toronto, 1914, vols. xv-xvi); F. X. Garneau, *Histoire du Canada* (6th edition, 2 vols., Paris, 1913-30); L. Hémon, *Maria Chapdelaine* (Montreal, 1916); Sir Thos. Chapais, *Cours d'histoire du Canada* (8 vols., Quebec, 1919-34); L. Groulx, *La naissance d'une race* (Montreal, 1919); L. Groulx, *Lendemains de conquête* (Montreal, 1920); I. Caron, *La colonisation de la province de Québec: Débuts du régime anglais (1760-1791)* (Québec, 1923); A. Rivard, *Chez nous* (Quebec, 1924), translated by W. H. Blake (New York, 1924); J. C. Bracq, *Evolution of French Canada* (New York, 1924); F. O. Call, *The spell of the province of Quebec* (New York, 1926); I. Caron, *La colonisation de la province de Québec: Les Cantons de l'Est (1791-1815);* (Quebec, 1927); G. Bouchard, *Other days, other ways* (Montreal, 1928); G. Vattier, *Esquisse historique de la colonisation de la province de Québec (1608-1925)* (Paris, 1928); G. Vattier, *Essai sur la mentalité canadienne-française* (Paris, 1928); W. Wood (ed.), *Storied province of Quebec* (4 vols., Toronto, 1931); J. C. Sutherland, *The province of Quebec* (Toronto, 1931); B. Davies, *Romantic Quebec* (New York, 1932); W. Bovey, *Canadien, a study of the French Canadians* (London, 1933); G. Langlois, *Histoire de la population canadienne-française* (Montreal, 1932); A. L. Burt, *The old province of Quebec* (Toronto, 1935); Raoul Blanchard, *L'est du Canada français* (2 vols., Montreal, 1935); Raoul Blanchard, *La région du fleuve St-Laurent entre Québec et Montreal* (Grenoble, 1936); and C. N. Boissonnault, *Histoire politique de la province de Québec* (Quebec, 1936).

**Quebec,** a county in the province of Quebec, bounded on the south by the river St. Lawrence, on the west by Portneuf and Champlain counties, on the north by the Lake St. John district, and on the east by Montmorency county. It is watered by the Jacques Cartier, St. Charles, and Montmorency rivers; and it is traversed by the Canadian Pacific and Canadian National Railways. Chief town, Indian Lorette. Pop. (1931), 170,915.

**Quebec,** the capital city of the province of Quebec, and one of the chief ports in Canada, is situated on a lofty rock named by Jacques Cartier (q.v.) in 1535 cape Diamond, at the confluence of the St. Lawrence and St. Charles rivers, 180 miles north-east of Montreal, and 800 miles south-west of the gulf of St. Lawrence. It is served by the Canadian Pacific, Canadian National, and Quebec Central Railways; and it has ferry connection with Lévis, opposite to it on the south shore of the St. Lawrence, which has here a width of nearly a mile. The origin of the name Quebec is open to doubt. It is generally believed to be derived from an Indian word meaning "The river narrows here"; but the theory has recently been advanced that it comes from an Algonkian word meaning "Place where you go back", and is in origin identical with the name of the village of Cobokonk in Ontario. It is the oldest city in Canada. It was the site of the Indian village of Stadacona, which Jacques Cartier visited in 1535, and near which he spent the following winter. It was founded by Samuel de Champlain (q.v.) in 1608, who built a fort (*L'abitation de Québec*) on the site of what is now the lower town, but who erected also in 1620 a fort on top of the rock, in which he built a wooden house, replaced in the time of Montmagny (q.v.) by the first stone Château St. Louis.

THE CITY OF QUEBEC

Viewed from the Tower of the Parliament Buildings

During the French régime, Quebec was the centre of all movements, the headquarters of missionaries, fur-traders, explorers, and military forces in New France. During the wars between France and England, it was the scene of memorable conflicts. It was taken by the English, when still a tiny settlement, in 1629, was held by them until 1632, and was then returned to France. An unsuccessful attempt to capture it was made by Phips (q.v.) in 1690; and another attempt against it was made by the abortive expedition of Sir Hovenden Walker in 1711. In 1759, however, the British under Wolfe (q.v.) captured it after the battle of the Plains of Abraham; and, after the cession of Canada to the British in 1763, it became the capital of the new British colony of Quebec. It was unsuccessfully besieged by the Americans in 1775-6.

On the creation of the province of Lower Canada in 1791, it became the capital of the province, and the seat of the governor-general. After the union of Upper and Lower Canada in 1841, it was for two short periods the capital of the united province. It was incorporated as a city in 1832, and it obtained its present charter in 1840.

Quebec is topographically divided into two sections, the upper and the lower. The lower town, old Quebec, with its narrow, crooked streets, suggests an ancient city of Europe. The upper town is a modern city, with wide streets and handsome public, mercantile, and residential buildings. It is reached by roads cut in the rock, by flights of steps, and by a lift or elevator. The highest point in the upper town, the crest of cape Diamond, is 333 feet above the river, and is crowned by the citadel, a strong, natural fortress with a walled area of 40 acres. From an early date there were fortifications on cape Diamond; but the present defences were built between 1823 and 1832, at a cost of thirty million dollars. Quebec is now the only fortified town in North America.

The harbour at Quebec is extensive, and can afford shelter to a large fleet. Its many wharves can accommodate 30 large steamships at a time; and its grain elevators can hold four million bushels. It is the terminal port of the *Empresses* of the Canadian Pacific steamships. River navigation lasts for about seven months in the year; from December to April ice prevents it, and the buoys are removed. There are two graving-docks capable of doing all necessary repair work. About three miles from Quebec is an airport, which now forms part of the Canadian airports system.

The Quebec bridge, which spans the St. Lawrence seven miles above the city, is a remarkable engineering feat. It is of the cantilever type, and has a span of 1,800 feet, with a central span of 640 feet, the longest of all metallic cantilever bridges in the world. It carries a double-track railway, accommodation for foot traffic, and also a highway. In 1907, when it was being built, it collapsed, with the loss of the lives of 75 workmen; but the Canadian government took over the enterprise, and the bridge was completed in 1917, at a cost of nearly $23,000,000. Another bridge, near Montmorency falls, connects Quebec with the island of Orleans.

Quebec has many industries. Chief among these are newsprint plants, tobacco warehouses, brickworks, foundries, tanneries, boot-and-shoe factories, clothing and corset factories, fur-trading establishments, and breweries. It is the seat of a Roman Catholic archbishop and a Church of England bishop. It has a university (Laval), a Grand Seminary for ecclesiastical students, a Jesuits' College, a famous High School, and a Junior Seminary for boys. Besides several hospitals, it has sanatoria for consumptives, asylums, and refuges. It supports three evening newspapers (*Chronicle-Telegraph*, *Le Soleil* and *L'Action Catholique*) and two morning papers (*L'Evènement* and *Le Journal*).

14

Quebec has become a Mecca of the tourist. Perched on its rock like an eagle's nest—with its quaint houses, some of them nearly three centuries old its narrow, tortuous streets, its cafés, shops, and hotels with French signboards; its steep hills leading from the Lower to the Upper Town; the Plains of Abraham, now the National Battlefields Park, where the fate of New France was sealed; its historic monuments rising everywhere; churches, chapels, monastries, convents proclaiming the faith of its inhabitants; Dufferin Terrace, its unique board-walk, commanding the river; the gorgeous panorama; the proximity of the famous shrine of Ste. Anne de Beaupré and of the Montmorency falls—it draws hundreds of thousands of visitors every year. It is estimated that in 1936 the tourist industry brought into Quebec over $6,000,000. There are many hotels; and the Château Frontenac, owned by the Canadian Pacific Railway, is one of the best appointed hotels in the British Empire. Its site—where the Château St. Louis formerly stood—is unique.

The population of Quebec is about 150,000, of whom nine-tenths are French-speaking.

See Sir J. M. Lemoine, *Picturesque Quebec* (Quebec, 1882), *Maple leaves* (Quebec, 1872), *L'Album du Tourisme* et *Monographies et esquisses* (Quebec, 1885); G. Mercer Adams, *Illustrated Quebec* (Montreal, 1891), *The King's book of Quebec* (Ottawa, 1911); Blodwen Davies, *The storied streets of Quebec* (Montreal, 1929); P. G. Roy, *La ville de Québec sous le régime français* (2 vols., Quebec, 1930), *Le vieux Québec* (Lévis, 1923-1931, 2 vols.), *Les rues de Québec*, (Lévis, 1932), *Les fils de Québec* (Lévis, 1933); William Wood and others, *The storied province of Quebec* (4 vols., Toronto, 1931); A. G. Doughty and N. E. Dionne, *Quebec under two flags* (Quebec, 1905); A. G. Doughty, *The fortress of Quebec* (Quebec, 1904), *The cradle of New France* (Montreal, 1908), *Quebec of*

*yester-year* (Toronto, 1932); A. Basile Routhier, *Québec et Lévis à l'aurore du XXe siècle* (Montreal, 1900); G. M. Fairchild, Jr., *My Quebec scrap-book* (Quebec, 1907); Geo. Gale, *Historic tales of old Quebec* (Quebec, 1923); Ernest Myrand, *Une fête de noël sous Jacques Cartier* (Quebec, 1890), *Les noëls anciens de la Nouvelle-France* (Quebec, 1899); E. Hawkins, *Pictures of Quebec* (Quebec, 1834).

**Quebec Act,** the Act passed by the British parliament in 1774 "for making more effectual provision for the government of the province of Quebec in North America". It superseded the Royal Proclamation of 1763 as the constitution of the colony, and introduced far-reaching changes. It extended the boundaries of the province of Quebec (or Canada) to include the whole of what is known as the Old North West, which comprised the territories bounded by the Ohio river, the Mississippi river, and the southern boundary of the territories granted in 1670 to the Hudson's Bay Company; it substituted the French civil code for the English civil law; and it not only gave freedom of worship to the Roman Catholic Church in Canada, but it virtually endowed it, by ordaining that the Roman Catholic clergy should continue to receive "their accustomed dues and rights". It declared that it was "at present inexpedient to call an Assembly"; and it continued in Canada government by governor and council. The motives actuating the British government in putting this legislation on the statute books have been the subject of prolonged debate, some writers maintaining that the objects of the Act were purely military, and others that the Act was inspired by the same generous policies that have underlain the development of the British Commonwealth of Nations. See V. Coffin, *The province of Quebec and the early American Revolution* (Madison, Wisconsin, 1896), with the review of this book by Adam

Short in *Review of Historical Publications relating to Canada*, vol. i (Toronto, 1897); R. Coupland, *The Quebec Act: A study in statesmanship* (Oxford, 1925); and Charles H. Metzger, *The Quebec Act: A primary cause of the American Revolution* (New York, 1936).

**Quebec Bank,** a bank founded in 1818 by a number of merchants and residents of the city of Quebec who did not consider the newly-organized Bank of Montreal sufficient for the needs of the province. The bank had an initial capital of £52,000. Its first president was J. W. Woolsey, and its first cashier, Noah Freer. The bank was incorporated in 1822 under a very lax charter and, at first, experienced quiet progress, but suffered severely in the great revulsion of 1826-7. The paid-up capital of the bank was a million dollars in 1860 and $2,500,000 in 1890. Until a few years before 1916, its operations were confined to the provinces of Ontario and Quebec, principally to Quebec. In 1916 the Quebec Bank was absorbed by the Royal Bank of Canada, which had formerly possessed few branches in the province of Quebec. The 15 branches of the Quebec Bank closed by the Royal were chiefly in western Canada.

**Quebec Central Railway,** a railway line opened in 1884 between Sherbrooke and St. Francis, Quebec, and later extended to Harlaka Junction. It included also the Lévis and Kennebec Railway, which had been purchased in 1881. In 1912 it was leased to the Canadian Pacific Railway.

**Quebec Conference,** a constitutional convention called on the initiative of the Canadian government to meet at Quebec city on October 10, 1864, to discuss a plan for a federal union of the British North American provinces. It was attended by thirty-three delegates, later known as the "Fathers of Confederation," representing Canada, the three Maritime provinces of Nova Scotia, New Brunswick, and Prince Edward Island, and the colony of Newfoundland. Although each delegation consisted of both Conservatives and Reformers, the complexion of the whole was decidedly Conservative. Canada was represented by its entire coalition cabinet. Each of the Maritime provinces sent a majority of government supporters, including their prime ministers, and a minority from the opposition. Political exigencies made it impossible for Newfoundland to send any member of its executive council.

The negotiations culminating in this conference had two sources. In the Maritime provinces a desire to improve local economic conditions by the elimination of separate provincial governments had resulted in the convocation at Charlottetown in September, 1864, of a Maritime union conference. In Canada, on the other hand, the necessity of loosening the ties between Upper and Lower Canada resulted in June of that year in the formation of a coalition government whose avowed objective was constitutional reform. The proposed Maritime union conference provided the Canadian government with its cue. At Charlottetown a Canadian deputation so persuasively presented a plan for a general federal union that all three Maritime delegations agreed to postpone any further consideration of their local union until an attempt should be made to concert a plan for the larger union. Every delegate who attended the conference at Charlottetown in September also attended the Quebec Conference in October. The preliminary provisional understandings reached at the former materially facilitated the work of the latter.

The conference at Quebec was notable for its brevity. On the eighteenth and final day, in an adjourned session at Montreal, seventy-two resolutions, commonly referred to as the Quebec Resolutions, were adopted, and later became the substantial basis for the British North America Act (q.v.). Several things helped to expedite the work of the "Fathers" at Quebec. The peculiar difficulties inherent in French-Canadian particularism could be resolved in the secret preliminary meetings of the Canadian cabinet. This was the easier because in constitutional and judicial matters Canada had already taken on many of the features of a federation, and Maritime delegates could feel that within the Canadian cabinet stout supporters of provincial rights were guarding their interests. It was understood also that the resolutions would subsequently be subjected to the scrutiny of both provincial legislatures and the British parliament. There were in fact only two subjects on which the conference encountered difficulties. It might perhaps have been better had it encountered more.

After the formal presentation of credentials, Sir E. P. Taché (q.v.), nominal head of the Canadian government, was selected chairman, and Major Hewitt Bernard was appointed executive secretary. After Edward Palmer (q.v.) of Prince Edward Island had made an unsuccessful attempt to submerge Canadian influence at the conference by providing that each province should have but one vote, the real work of the conference began with a discussion of representation in the proposed federal upper house. Although it was known that the Canadians would later insist on representation by population in the federal lower house, no attempt appears to have been made to have upper house representation based on provincial equality. As finally constituted, both houses gave to Canada a decided predominance over all the other provinces together. Prince Edward Island, on the other hand, was to have such an inconsequential representation in both that the Island delegation could only be induced to sign the Quebec Resolutions as authenticating them.

The second critical discussion was on the subject of federal subsidies to prov-

inces. Here too the Maritime provinces were acutely concerned, for they had hitherto relied almost wholly on indirect taxation, which now, it was agreed, must be given to the federal government. On the basis of a computation by Tupper (q.v.) of Nova Scotia, it was decided that the federal government should give to each of the provinces annually a sum equal to eighty cents per head of the population. Even in the conference, however, New Brunswick was successful in securing "better terms", and attempted raids on the federal treasury were to be a feature of subsequent Dominion history.

Little difficulty was encountered in dividing the powers of federal and provincial governments, or in erecting a federal judicial system. Provincial constitutions were conveniently left for each province to arrange for itself. It was unanimously agreed that the new Dominion should build an intercolonial railway; but it was only with difficulty that, in the closing hours of the conference, the Maritime delegates agreed to a resolution looking to the eventual construction of communications from the Great lakes westward. Also reluctantly did they agree to the new Dominion assuming all costs of Canadian defence construction incurred prior to the union. It was an indication of the feeling of urgency in matters of defence, as the American Civil War was drawing to a close.

The Quebec Resolutions received the immediate and energetic support of the Colonial Office. The Canadian legislature passed them by a large majority, Lower Canadian Reformers, who had not been brought into the coalition, being the only opposing group. In Nova Scotia and New Brunswick considerable persistent pressure was needed to secure legislative approval. The legislatures of the two island colonies voted against the confederation scheme. Prince Edward Island did not join the new Dominion until

1873. Newfoundland continued to stand aloof.

See Sir J. Pope (ed.), *Confederation: Being a series of hitherto unpublished documents bearing on the British North America Act* (Toronto, 1895); A. G. Doughty (ed.), *Notes on the Quebec Conference, 1864* (Can. hist. rev., 1920); *Parliamentary debates on the subject of the Confederation* (Quebec, 1865); E. Whelan (ed.), *The union of the British provinces* (Charlottetown, 1865; new ed. by D. C. Harvey, Gardenvale, 1927); J. H. Gray, *Confederation* (Toronto, 1872); R. G. Trotter, *Canadian federation* (Toronto, 1924); and W. M. Whitelaw, *The Maritimes and Canada before Confederation* (Toronto, 1934).

**Quebec Literary and Historical Society.** See **Literary and Historical Society of Quebec.**

**Quebec Resolutions.** See **Quebec Conference.**

**Queen Anne's Lace.** See **Carrot.**

**Queen Anne's War,** the name applied to the North American phase of the War of the Spanish Succession. It began after the accession of Queen Anne to the throne of England in 1702, and was concluded by the treaty of Utrecht in 1713.

**Queen Charlotte,** a village in the Queen Charlotte Island district of British Columbia, on the north shore of Skidegate inlet, 3 miles west of Skidegate, on Graham island. It has a school and an hospital. Formerly it was known as Queen Charlotte City. Pop. (1930), 200.

**Queen Charlotte islands,** a group of islands in the north Pacific ocean, off the coast of British Columbia. It consists of three principal islands, named Graham, Moresby, and Kunghit, which are separated from the mainland by Hecate strait on the east, and Dixon entrance on the north. The two largest islands, Graham and Moresby, measure with two smaller ones, North and Prevost, 180 miles in length, and 60 miles at greatest width, and lie in lat. 52° to 54°, long. 132° to 134°. They were discovered by Captain Cook (q.v.) in 1778. Captain George Dixon examined them in 1787, and named them after his ship, the *Queen Charlotte.* In 1789 Gray named them Washington, and thus they appear on Ingraham's chart of 1791-2, but the earlier name has survived. In 1774, they had been visited by Juan Perez, who named the north point Cabo de Santa Margarita. The islanders are known as Haida, and they number about 5,000. The agricultural capacities are good, especially for potatoes, and the fish and game supply is excellent. Another group of islands called Queen Charlotte lies in the South Pacific ocean, and was discovered in 1767 by Captain Carteret. See F. Poole, *Queen Charlotte islands* (London, 1872).

**Queen Charlotte sound,** the body of water between the northern end of Vancouver island and the mainland of British Columbia, between Aristazabal island on the north and cape Caution, on the mainland, on the south. It was named in 1786 after Queen Charlotte, wife of King George III, by the commander of the *Experiment.*

**Queen Charlotte strait,** the restricted body of water between Vancouver island and the mainland of British Columbia from cape Caution on the north to the several narrow channels north and east of Malcolm island. It is a continuation of Queen Charlotte sound.

**Queen Mary, mount,** is in the Kootenay district of British Columbia. It is one of the Royal Group, and is west of the Palliser river in the Rocky mountains. It is in lat. 50° 39', long. 115° 27', and has an altitude of 10,600 feet. It is named after Her Majesty Queen Mary.

**Queen's,** a county at the south-west angle of Nova Scotia, bordering on the Atlantic, and bounded by Lunenburg county on the east, Annapolis county on the north, and Shelburne county on the west. Settlement began in 1759, and the county was created in 1761. The name "Queen's" was chosen as an expression of loyalty to the monarchy. The shore line is deeply indented, and contains a number of excellent harbours. Among the chief occupations of the inhabitants have been fishing and ship-building. The county town is Liverpool. Pop. (1931), 10,612. See James F. More, *The history of Queen's county, N.S.* (Halifax, 1873).

**Queen's,** a county occupying the central part of Prince Edward Island, between Prince county and King county. Chief town, Charlottetown. Pop. (1931), 37,591.

**Queensport,** a village and harbour in Guysborough county, Nova Scotia, 50 miles from Port Mulgrave, the nearest railway station. It was originally named Crow Harbour, but was re-named in 1897, in honour of Queen Victoria. Pop. (1934), 400.

**Queen's Rangers.** There have been three military units bearing this name in Canadian history. The first was a loyalist light corps raised in 1776, during the American Revolutionary War, and reorganized by Lieut.-Col. John Graves Simcoe (q.v.) in 1777. It continued in active service until 1783, and was then disbanded in New Brunswick. The second was the unit, named after the first Queen's Rangers, and raised in England in December, 1791, for service in Upper Canada. It did garrison duty at Newark (Niagara), York (Toronto), and other places; and it was disbanded in 1802. The third unit was a militia regiment raised in Toronto during the Rebellion of 1837, under the command of Lieut.-Col. Samuel Peters Jarvis (q.v.). It was disbanded shortly after-wards. See G. H. Locke and Margaret Ray, *The Queen's Rangers* (pamphlet, Toronto, 1923).

**Queenston,** a village in Lincoln county, Ontario, on the west bank of the Niagara river, and on the Michigan Central Railway, 6 miles west of Niagara Falls. In 1792 Simcoe (q.v.) had his regiment, the Queen's Rangers, en-camped at the Niagara landing, now Queenston, and it is thought that the name of the village originated from the regiment being stationed there at that time. The village is associated in history with the defence made by the British on Queenston heights in the War of 1812. A monument to General Brock (q.v.) stands on the heights, and is an attractive object of interest. Many people visit Queenston by steamboat during the season of navigation. The population is about 300.

**Queenston Heights, Battle of,** an important engagement on the Niagara frontier in the War of 1812. In the early morning of October 13, 1812, the Ameri-can forces at Lewiston, numbering over 5,000 men, under General Stephen Van Rensselaer, attempted a landing in force at the village of Queenston, opposite Lewiston. They were held in check by the small British force at Queenston; but a party of Americans under Captain Wool succeeded in scaling the cliff of the gorge south of Queenston, and in capturing a battery of one gun on Queenston heights, overlooking the village. General Brock (q.v.), who had galloped up from Fort George, his head-quarters at the mouth of the Niagara river, immediately led an attack on the Americans on the heights, but fell, mortally wounded. A second attack was led by his aide-de-camp, Lieut.-Col. John Macdonell (q.v.), resulted in Macdonell also falling, mortally wound-ed. The Americans were thus able to consolidate their position on the heights. In the meantime, however, Brock's second-in-command, Major-General Sheaffe was bringing up all available re-serves from Fort George; and in the afternoon of October 13 he launched an attack on the American position from the west. The attack was completely successful, and the Americans were either driven over the cliff into the river, or were forced to surrender. Nearly 1,000 Americans were taken prisoners. The British victory was in some measure due to the refusal of the New York militia to cross the river. "The name of Indian, or the sight of the wounded, or the devil, or something else," wrote an eyewitness, "petrified them; not a regiment, not a company, scarcely a man, would go." The death of Brock was a serious loss to the British; but the result of the battle was greatly to encourage the defenders of Canada, and in corresponding measure to depress the morale of the Americans. See Sir C. P. Lucas, *The Canadian War of 1812* (Oxford, 1906), W. Wood (ed.), *Select British documents of the Canadian War of 1812* (4 vols., Toronto, 1920-8), and E. Cruikshank (ed.), *The documentary history of the campaign on the Niagara frontier* (9 vols., Welland, Lundy's Lane Historical Society, 1896-1908).

**Queen's University,** in Kingston, Ontario, owes its origin to the desire of the Synod of the Presbyterian Church in Canada for a ministry trained within the country. As early as 1832 the government of Upper Canada had been petitioned "to endow without delay an institution, or professorships, for the education and training of young men for the ministry in connection with the Synod". This and other representations failing of their object, steps were taken by the Synod to found a college at Kingston on the lines of the Scottish national universities. On October 16, 1841, a royal charter was issued for the establishment of Queen's College, Kingston; and the first classes were opened in March, 1842, with the Rev. Dr. Thomas Liddell (q.v.) as principal. Funds were provided in part by grants from the Presbyterian Church in Scotland and from the Canadian government, and in part by liberal subscriptions from the friends of the young and growing university. In 1867-8, however, the withdrawal of the pro-

vincial grant, and the failure of the Commercial Bank, almost brought financial disaster. But the crisis was met by the determination of Principal Snodgrass (q.v.) and of other self-denying workers, chief among whom was Professor Mackerras (q.v.). The country was canvassed for subscriptions, and as a result $113,000 was added to the endowment.

In 1877 Principal Snodgrass was succeeded by the Rev. G. M. Grant (q.v.), who for a quarter of a century built with brilliant success upon the foundation laid by his predecessors. Under him the university gained rapidly in size and prestige. By 1881 Queen's had new buildings, an enlarged staff, and a great increase of students. In 1887, as the result of an effort in commemoration of the Queen's Jubilee, $250,000 was raised, resulting in further extension, and in the establishment of new professorships.

In 1893 the School of Mining was founded under an Ontario charter, and its rapid growth occasioned the provision in 1900 of two large buildings, Ontario Hall for the departments of physics, geology, and mineralogy, and Fleming Hall for the departments of civil, mechanical, and electrical engineering. Gordon Hall was erected in 1911, and Nicol Hall in 1912. The one was used for the teaching of chemistry, and the other for mining and metallurgy. In 1916 the School of Mining gave up its separate board, and was constituted as a faculty of applied science. In this faculty four-year courses are given in all the divisions of practical science, except architecture. They lead to the degree of B.Sc., and post-graduate work can also be taken towards the M.Sc. degree. The engineering departments have adequate and modern laboratory equipment, and the training in mining and metallurgy is second to none in Canada. It was the School of Mining that was initially responsible for the development of the famous silver deposits of Cobalt; and many of the men responsible to-day for the mining development of northern Ontario are graduates of Queen's.

Since the end of the war, the principal additions to the university buildings have been the Douglas Library, named in memory of Dr. James Douglas (q.v.), a former chancellor of the university, who contributed $150,000 to its cost; Ban Righ Hall, the residence for women; Miller Hall, for the teaching of geology and mineralogy; and the new gymnasium opened in 1931. The buildings have a certain harmony of construction and appearance, being all of the local limestone.

Queen's led the way in co-education. As early as 1870 special classes in English and other subjects were formed for women, and courses leading to a degree were thrown open to them in 1878-1879. In 1880 co-education was extended to the medical course, and in 1883 a separate Women's Medical College was opened and affiliated with Queen's. This College was closed in 1894. The medical faculty of Queen's dates from 1854.

*Library and Museums.* The Library at Queen's is contemporary with the university. Its beginnings, indeed, are even earlier, for in 1839 advocates of the founding of a college were receiving gifts of books from friends in Scotland toward the establishment of a library. After the first few years it grew but slowly, and in 1860 contained about 3,120 volumes. When the university removed from its earlier home to what is now the principal's residence, the library occupied the room at present used as a dining room. From there it went to the old Arts Building (now the Theological Building), where its growth was restricted by limited space. In 1914 Chancellor Douglas offered the money for the erection of a new building; but owing to the outbreak of war its construction was postponed, and not until 1924 was it opened to students. It now contains about 120,000 volumes, as well as many original manuscripts and prints. The departmental libraries for physics, chemistry, mining and metallurgy, geology and mineralogy, biology, medicine, and civil, mechanical, and electrical engineering, are housed in various Halls. The Miller Memorial Museum contains among other things an excellent collection of economic minerals used in industrial processes. The Biological Museum has a large botanical and an excellent zoological collection, and there is also an ethnological collection.

*Medicine.* The work of the medical faculty at present is carried on in three large buildings, which in arrangement and equipment are thoroughly modern. Excellent clinical facilities are available at two local general hospitals and one mental hospital. Both the medical school and the Kingston hospital are rated Grade "A" by the American Medical Association. There are now fifty-six officers of instruction, many of them full time; the length of the course is six years; and the present student registration is 293. Degrees conferred are M.D. and C.M. on completion of the regular course, and, following postgraduate study, D.P.H. and D.Sc.

*Theological College.* The charter of Queen's in 1841 nominated the College to be "for the educating of youth in the principles of Christian religion". At the same time, it stipulated that "no religious test or qualifications shall be required or appointed for any persons admitted or matriculated as scholars within the said college". Though the faculty of theology was under the wing of the Presbyterian Church, classes in Arts were open to all without any reliance upon religious denomination, and Queen's has so remained for nearly a century, truly catholic in its aims and national in its scope. Until some years after the death of Principal Grant, the greatest contribution that the university made to Canadian life and culture was probably in theology and education. From coast to coast gradu-

VIEWS OF QUEEN'S UNIVERSITY AT KINGSTON, ONTARIO

ates of this seat of learning ministered from pulpits and taught in schools. Particularly valuable was this service in the Canadian West, which was at that time practically without university education. The last vestige of denominational connection at Queen's disappeared in 1912, when the Theological College became entirely independent of the Presbyterian Church. Legally, the College is an affiliated institution, but it has always been closely associated with the University and has the same representation upon the University Senate as any of the faculties. Theological degrees are conferred by the University and not by the College.

*Education.* In eastern Canada, the continuous and close association of Queen's with education has been most marked. In Ontario about seventy per cent. of the school inspectors, fifty per cent. of the high school principals, and thirty-five per cent. of the high school teachers are Queen's graduates. No fewer than sixteen graduates or members of staff of the university have served as president of the Ontario Educational Association. In 1907 a faculty of education was established at Queen's by the Ontario government for the purpose of providing professional training for teachers in the secondary schools of the province. In 1920, however, the decision of the government to create in Toronto the Ontario College of Education led to the discontinuance of that work. In extra-mural courses and in the work of summar school, Queen's has led the way, and the value of this work in this field cannot be too highly estimated. In 1919 a new development of the Arts courses produced a department of commerce and business administration; this department, some years later, established a banking and accountancy section, through which, by correspondence, many officers of the chartered banks of Canada and large numbers of accountants have been able to study the advanced principles of their professions. These courses lead to the degrees of B.Com. and M.Com. The extension work of the university, indeed the whole of the extra-mural work, is under the faculty of Arts.

*Sports.* Smaller by far than its nearest university rivals, McGill, in Montreal, and the University of Toronto, Queen's yet can hold its own with either of them in the domain of sport. In rugby football, the senior team at Queen's has won the Gray Cup, emblematic of the intercollegiate championship, nine times in the last fifteen years. In hockey, basketball, and indoor athletics, such as boxing and wrestling, the university teams have also won frequent championships.

*Government.* The financial and administrative management of Queen's is vested in the Board of Trustees, which comprises 37 members. The University Council consists of the Trustees, the Senate, and an equal number of elected graduates. It controls various university elections, and acts in an advisory capacity to the Board of Trustees. The Senate comprises the principal, the vice-principal, the principal of Queen's Theological College, the deans of the three other faculties, and eleven elected professors. It determines all matters of purely academic character which concern the University as a whole, and is the medium of communication between the student organizations and the governing bodies. The faculty boards are composed of the members of the teaching staffs of the respective faculties, and have to do with the administration of the affairs of their particular divisions.

Queen's was the first university in Canada to introduce student self-government, and its administration rests with the Alma Mater Society and the subsidiary faculty organizations.

The University has three regular publications: the *Queen's Quarterly*, a literary magazine of high merit brought out by the University itself; the *Queen's*

*Review*, the monthly periodical of the General Alumni Association; and the *Queen's Journal*, published bi-weekly by the Alma Mater Society during the college session.

The income of the University is derived from three sources: students' fees, revenue from endowment, and assistance from the provincial government.

Queen's University has never been in any sense a local institution, but in service and in influence may be accounted national. Its students are drawn from every province in the Dominion, and only a relatively small number reside in Kingston.

*Principals*. In her history of nearly one hundred years, Queen's has had twelve principals: Rev. Thomas Liddell (1842-6); Rev. John Machar, D.D. (1846-52); Rev. James George, D.D. (1852-7); Rev. John Cook, D.D., LL.D. (1857-60); Rev. William Leitch, D.D. (1860-64); Rev. William Snodgrass, D.D. (1864-77); Rev. George Monro Grant, D.D., LL.D., C.M.G. (1877-1902); Very Rev. D. M. Gordon, D.D. (1902-16); Rev. R. Bruce Taylor (1917-30); W. H. Fyfe, M.A., LL.D., F.R.S.C. (1930-36); and Dr. R. C. Wallace, D.Sc., Ph.D., LL.D., F.R.S.C. (1936—).

See Adam Shortt, *Random recollections of Queen's* (Queen's Quarterly, 1920).

**Quesnel, Frédéric Auguste** (1785-1866), politician, was born at Montreal in 1785, the eldest son of Joseph Quesnel (q.v.). He was called to the bar of Lower Canada, and from 1826 to 1834 he was a member of the Legislative Assembly of Lower Canada. A supporter of Papineau during his earlier career, he broke with his leader over the Ninety-Two Resolutions, and in 1835 failed of re-election to the Assembly. In 1837 he was appointed a member of the Executive Council of the province; and he served as an executive councillor until the Union of 1841. From 1841 to 1844 he sat as the representative of Mont-

morency in the Legislative Assembly of united Canada. He died on July 28, 1866. In 1813 he married Marguerite Denaut (d. 1820); and by her he had two sons and three daughters, all of whom predeceased him. He acquired a fortune in the fur-trade and by speculation, and the bulk of this fortune he left to his nephew, the Hon. Charles Joseph Coursol (q.v.). See E. Z. Massicote, *La famille du poète Quesnel* (Bull. rech. hist., 1917), C. S. Cherrier, *L'honorable F. A. Quesnel* (pamphlet, Montreal, 1878), and F. J. Audet, *L'hon. Frédéric-Auguste Quesnel* (Bull. rech. hist., 1927).

**Quesnel, Joseph** (1749-1809), poet and dramatist, was born at Saint-Malo, France, on November 15, 1749, the son of Isaac Quesnel de la Rivaudais and Pélagie-Jeanne-Marguerite Duguen. He came to Canada in 1779, and took out letters of naturalization a few years later. He was a merchant, but in his leisure moments he wrote poems, epistles, hymns, epigrams, songs, and comedies. His chief compositions were a dialogue in verse, entitled *Le rimeur dépité*, and the following comedies: *Colas et Colinette, Les républicains français*, and *L'Anglomanie*. Of these none was published in his lifetime, except *Les républicains français*, which Bibaud says was printed in Paris; but many of his writings were printed posthumously in the *Bibliothèque canadienne* (9 vols., Montreal, 1825-30) and in the *Répertoire national* (4 vols., Montreal, 1848-50). He died at Montreal in July, 1809. In 1770 he married Marie-Josephte Deslandes; and by her he had thirteen children. See E. Z. Massicotte, *La famille du poète Quesnel* (Bull. rech. hist., 1917).

**Quesnel, Jules Maurice** (1786-1842), fur-trader, was born in Montreal in 1786, the second son of Joseph Quesnel (q.v.). He entered the service of the North West Company, and in 1804 was stationed at Edmonton. In 1808 he accompanied Simon Fraser (q.v.) in his exploration of the Fraser river. He left the service of the North West Company in 1811, and returned to Canada. In 1838 he was appointed a member of the Special Council of Lower Canada; and in 1841 a member of the Legislative Council under the union. He died at Montreal on May 20, 1842. In 1816 he married Marie Josephte Cotté, the daughter of a fur-trader of the North West. See E. Z. Massicotte, *La famille du poète Quesnel* (Bull. rech. hist., 1917).

**Quesnel,** a town in the Cariboo district of British Columbia, at the confluence of the Fraser and Quesnel rivers, and on the Pacific Great Eastern Railway, 220 miles north of Ashcroft. It is named after Jules Maurice Quesnel (q.v.). Besides government offices, it has a school and an hospital. Pop. (1930), 500.

**Quesnel lake** and **river** are in the Cariboo district of British Columbia. The lake, at 52° 121° north-west, is drained by the river into the Fraser river at Quesnel. The river was discovered and named by Simon Fraser (q.v.) after Jules Maurice Quesnel (q.v.), a clerk in the North West Company, who accompanied him when he descended the Fraser in 1808. The lake is 57 miles long, ⅓ to 2 miles wide, and has an area of 104 square miles. The river is 64 miles in length.

**Quevillon, Louis Amable** (1749-1823), wood-carver and architect, was born in 1749 at St. Vincent de Paul, Canada. He was a self-taught artist; but he gathered about him a number of apprentices, and their work is an illustration of one of the first native impulses in Canadian art. He died at St. Vincent de Paul on March 9, 1823. See E. Vaillancourt, *Une maîtrise d'art en Canada* (Montreal, 1920).

**Queylus, Gabriel de Thubière de Lévy de** (1612-1677), superior of the Sulpician missions in Canada (1657-61 and 1668-71), was born in the diocese of Rodez in France in 1612. He entered the Sulpician order, and was ordained a priest in 1645, and in 1657 he came to Canada as first superior of the Sulpician missions in Canada. He returned to France in 1661, and he remained there until 1668; but in 1668 he became for a second time superior of the Sulpicians in Canada. Though he had quarreled with Bishop Laval (q.v.) during his earlier stay in Canada, he now became grand vicar to Laval. He returned to France finally in 1671; and he died at Paris on March 20, 1677.

**Quiblier, Joseph Vincent** (1796-1852), priest and educationist, was born at St. Julien, in the diocese of Lyon, France, on May 24, 1796, and was ordained a priest of the Roman Catholic Church in 1819. He entered the Sulpician order in 1825, and was sent to Canada. From 1831 to 1846 he was superior of the Seminary at Montreal; and he is generally regarded as the organizer of primary education among the French Roman Catholics in Montreal. In 1846 he left Canada, to assume the charge of a parish in London, England; and he died at Issy, France, on September 17, 1852.

**Quill lakes** are in southern Saskatchewan, south-east of Saskatoon and on the 52nd parallel of north latitude. The name is derived from the number of wild fowl which moult at the lakes. Formerly they were called Big Quill and Little Quill. They have an area of 236 square miles.

**Quinan,** a village in Yarmouth county, Nova Scotia, on the Tusket river, 7 miles from Belleville, the nearest railway station. It is in a prosperous agricultural and horticultural district. Until 1885 it was known as Tusket Forks; but in that year it was re-named Quinan, in memory of a deceased pastor of that name. Pop. (1934), 1,000.

**Quinte, bay of,** a long and irregularly shaped inlet of lake Ontario, between the peninsula of Prince Edward county and the mainland of Ontario, west of Kingston harbour. It has a length of about 50 miles, and a width of from 6 to 12 miles. At its western extremity an isthmus of about a mile, which separates it from lake Ontario, is cut by the Murray canal. Its shores were first settled by the United Empire Loyalists of 1784. The name is derived from the Indian village of Kenté (q.v.), where the Sulpicians established a mission station in the seventeenth century. The historical pronunciation of the name is Kăn'tay; but the Geographic Board of Canada has ruled that the word Quinte is to be spelled without an acute accent on the final letter, and this would seem to lend authority to the popular pronunciation of Kwĭn'tee.

**Quintuplets.** See **Dionne Quintuplets.**

**Quinze, lac des,** is an expansion of the upper Ottawa river, in Témiscamingue county, Quebec. The name is derived from that section of the river below the lake, which is named Quinze because of its fifteen rapids in a short stretch of river. The lake has an area of 55 square miles.

**Quinze river,** a stream emptying into the head of lake Temiskaming, in Témiscamingue county, Quebec. It flows from the Quinze lake (or lac des Quinze), and is 15 miles long. It has 15 rapids, which are capable of developing over 32,000 horse-power, and from which it takes its name.

**Quitch Grass.** See **Couch Grass.**

**Quoddy,** an abbreviation in common use for Passamaquoddy (q.v.).

**Quoddy river.** See **Musquodoboit river.**

**Quyon,** a village in Pontiac county, Quebec, on the Canadian Pacific Railway, 32 miles north-west of Hull. It was founded in 1848 and incorporated in 1875. The origin of the name is doubtful. It has been explained as an English variant of the French word *couillon* (projection); but it is more probably of Indian origin. The chief industries are farming and lumbering. Pop. (1931), 793.

# R

**Raby, Augustin** (1702-1782), pilot, was born at Quebec in 1702, and became a pilot and navigator. It was he who piloted the British fleet up the St. Lawrence to Quebec in June, 1759. He died at Quebec on December 19, 1782.

**Rabbit.** See **Hare.**

**Raccoon.** The raccoon (*Procyon lotor*) is a medium-sized animal of rather heavy build, readily identified by the gray-black coat, ringed tail, and the black mask across its face. It is found in British Columbia, Ontario, Quebec, and the Maritimes, but does not penetrate far into the north. The raccoon is nocturnal in its habits, and is seldom seen during the day. An excellent climber, it prefers to make a hollow tree the site for its den, but when trees are not available, it will use crevices among rocks or a burrow. The 'coon (as it is popularly known) will eat nearly anything, berries, nuts, corn, frogs, fish, birds, mammals, or reptiles. It is a good swimmer, and much of its food is found by wading and paddling along streams, marshes, and lake shores. A peculiar habit to which it owes its name "lotor" (meaning "washer") is that of dabbling its food in the water before eating it. The raccoon hibernates in the autumn, and does not appear till warm weather in early spring. The young, two to six in number, are born in late spring, and both male and female parents take part in caring for the family. The ability of this animal to maintain itself in settled districts where scattered wood lots are still available has rendered it a steady source of income to the rural trapper. The fur of the raccoon, being in demand for fur coats, is an important item in the fur-trade.

**Racine, Dominique** (1828-1888), first Roman Catholic bishop of Chicoutimi, was born at Jeune Lorette, near Quebec, on January 24, 1828. He was educated at Quebec, and was ordained a priest of the Roman Catholic Church in 1853. In 1862 he went to Chicoutimi as parish priest, and in 1878 he was elected first bishop of Chicoutimi. He died at Chicoutimi on January 28, 1888. See Abbé V. A. Huard, *L'apôtre du Saguenay* (Quebec, 1895).

**Radcliffe, Thomas** (1794-1841), legislative councillor of Upper Canada, was born in Castle Coote, Roscommon county, Ireland, on April 17, 1794, the eldest son of the Rev. Thomas Radcliffe, of Dublin, Ireland. He entered the British army in 1811, and served as a subaltern in the Peninsular War and in the War of 1812 in Canada. In 1816 he was placed on half-pay, and in 1836 he came to Upper Canada and settled in Adelaide, near London. He commanded a body of militia during the rebellion of 1837; and in 1839 he was appointed a member of the Legislative Council of Upper Canada. He died on Amherst island, Upper Canada, on June 6, 1841.

**Radio.** The administration of radio within Canada is vested in the department of Marine, under the Act of 1927. Dominion jurisdiction was questioned by some of the provinces from time to time, but in 1932 the Judicial Committee of the Imperial Privy Council ruled that the control and regulation of radio communication is within the jurisdiction of the Dominion parliament. The entire art of long-distance radio communication dates from December 12, 1901, when Guglielmo Marconi in Nova Scotia received the first trans-oceanic radio message from his station in England. This class of service includes radiotelegraphy as well as radio-telephony. The present coast station system of 69 stations in Canada con-sists of three chains—one extending from Vancouver to Prince Rupert on the Pacific, another from Port Arthur to the Atlantic ocean in the east, and the third from Port Churchill to Reso-lution island at the entrance to Hudson strait. The Great lakes coast stations connect with those of the east coast, which, in turn, connect with the Hudson bay route chain. There is no direct radio connection between the Great lakes and the Pacific coast chain. Twice daily a number of these stations broad-cast messages to shipping, reporting dangers to navigation, etc. There are 13 direction-finding stations fitted with special apparatus which enables the direction of the incoming radio signal transmitted by a ship to be accurately determined. To assist the direction-finding instrument on board ship, the department of Marine has established radio beacon transmitters at a number of lighthouses and lightships. To insure safety of life at sea, all passenger steamers and freighters plying to and from Canadian ports must carry radio equipment. A radiotelephone service between Canada and Great Britain was first made available to the Canadian public, through the medium of the Bell Telephone Company viâ the American Telegraph and Telephone Company from New York, in March, 1928. In 1932 a direct circuit with Great Britain was opened through the medium of the beam station of the Canadian Marconi Company at Drummondville, Quebec.

Broadcasting of the human voice by radio first commenced in Canada with test programmes carried out by the Canadian Marconi Company in Mont-real in the winter of 1919. Regular organized programmes were commenced in December, 1920, by the same com-pany, on a wave-length of 1,200 metres. In April, 1922, the establishment of broadcasting stations on a general scale commenced, 52 private, commercial, and amateur broadcasting licences having been granted during the fiscal year 1922-23. In 1934, 74 stations were in operation in the Dominion, and the number of licensed receiving sets was 707,625. The licence fee for a broad-casting station is $25 for a period of 6 months, and for a receiving set $2 per annum. Approximately $250,000 is ex-pended annually by the department of Marine for the suppression of inductive interference in the interests of broad-cast listeners.

The Canadian Radio Broadcasting Act, passed in 1932, provided for the establishment of a commission of three to undertake the business of radio-broadcasting in Canada as a national public service and to regulate and control radio broadcasting by other agencies in Canada. This Act was, how-ever, repealed by an Act in 1936 which provided for the constitution of a corporation to be known as the Cana-dian Broadcasting Corporation, and substituted for the commission of three a board of nine governors, under the chairmanship of Leonard W. Brocking-ton, K.C., of Winnipeg. Since broad-casting has been nationalized, six radio stations have been acquired and arrange-ments have been made for broadcasting time on stations from coast to coast, transmission line facilities have been leased to form a coast-to-coast network, and a regular schedule of national, regional, and local programmes has been inaugurated. The system is being developed and extended gradually. The national broadcasting service follows usual broadcasting practices with re-spect to types and variety of entertain-ment provided. The daily broadcasting contains no advertising, direct or indirect, and all Canadian cities are represented in the broadcasting. In the corporation's own studios light operas are produced by its own groups of artists. Leading Canadian orchestras, bands, and choral groups are heard frequently in the national service. During the autumn and winter season the corporation maintains a weekly service by short wave to the outposts in the far north. One of the strongest reasons for establishing government control in Canada was too much advertising on the air. Despite its small budget, the Canadian Radio Corporation has succeeded in bringing radio programmes to vast areas of the Dominion which were previously without any broadcasting service whatever. This valuable public service would not have been attempted by private ownership without a government subsidy, or some kind of assistance. The experiment of government control, however, remains an experiment; and the legislation creating that control is not necessarily permanent.

See M. Denison, *Radio in Canada* (The Annals of the American Academy of Political and Social Science, Philadelphia, January, 1935); *Report of the royal commission on radio broadcasting* (Ottawa, 1929); and A. R. Nilson, *Radio operating questions and answers* (New York and London, 1932).

**Radish, Wild** (*Raphanus Raphanistrum* L., *Cruciferae*), an introduced annual or biennial weed with sparingly-branched stem and rough lyre-shaped leaves, a pale yellowish-green in colour, and bearing a few stiff bristles. The flowers are fewer and larger than in the wild mustard, and a paler yellow, the petals conspicuously veined. The constricted seed pods are the most outstanding feature, and make it very easy to distinguish the two plants. The pod is in 2 distinct sections, the lower small and seedless, the upper cylindrical and constricted between each of the 2-8

seeds. It is a troublesome weed in fields from Newfoundland to Ontario.

**Radisson, Pierre Esprit** (1636?-1710?), explorer and fur-trader, was born in Paris, France, about 1636. He came to Canada in 1651, and settled at Three Rivers. In 1652 he was captured by the Iroquois, but he escaped from them in 1653 and returned to Canada by way of New York, Holland, and France. Between 1654 and 1660 (or, less probably, between 1658 and 1663) he made, with his brother-in-law Chouart des Groseilliers (q.v.), two voyages to the country west of the Great lakes. His own account of these voyages, which was first discovered and printed in 1885, seems to indicate that he reached the Mississippi on one journey and Hudson bay on the other; but grave doubt has been cast on these rather extravagant claims. It is probable, however, that Radisson was the first white man to penetrate to the old North-West.

In 1665 Radisson, as the result of a disagreement with the French authorities, went to England, and offered to lead a trading expedition to Hudson bay. The outcome of this was the foundation in 1670 of the Hudson's Bay Company. In the service of this company Radisson remained until 1676; then he reverted to his French allegiance, returned to Canada, and in 1682 led an expedition against the English on Hudson bay. In 1684, however, he once more entered the service of the Hudson's Bay Company; and for the rest of his life he was either a servant or pensioner of the company. His death seems to have taken place in England about 1710. His account of his journeys has been published by the Prince Society under the title *Voyages of Pierre Esprit Radisson* (Boston, 1885) and in the Canadian Archives Report for 1895 under the title *Relation du voiage du Sieur Pierre Esprit Radisson*.

See N. E. Dionne, *Chouart and Radisson* (Quebec, 1910); W. Upham, *Groseilliers and Radisson* (Minnesota Historical

Collections, 1905); B. Sulte, *Radisson in the north-west* (Trans. Roy. Soc. Can., 1904); G. Bryce, *The remarkable history of the Hudson's Bay Company* (Toronto, 1900) and *Further history of Pierre Esprit Radisson* (Trans. Roy. Soc. Can., 1898); A. T. Adams, *A new interpretation of the voyages of Radisson* (Minnesota History, 1925); D. Frémont, *Pierre Radisson* (Montreal, 1933); and A. T. Adams, *The Radisson problems* (Minnesota History, 1934).

**Radisson,** a village in Saskatchewan, on the main line of the Canadian National Railway from Winnipeg to Edmonton, 520 miles west of Winnipeg, and 300 miles east of Edmonton. It is in a rich grain-growing country, and has five grain elevators, a high school, and a weekly newspaper (*Comet*). Pop. (1934), 362.

**Radium.** See **Uranium.**

**Radium Hot Springs,** a settlement in the Kootenay district of British Columbia, on the Banff-Windermere highway, and on the Canadian Pacific Railway, 9 miles north of lake Windermere.

**Radville,** a town in the Weyburn district of Saskatchewan, on the Souris river, and on the Canadian National Railway, 70 miles south of Regina. It is a railway divisional point, and has four grain elevators, public and separate schools, a convent, and a weekly newspaper (*South Saskatchewan Star*). Pop. (1934), 1,000.

**Rae, John** (1813-1893), explorer, was born near Strowness in the Orkney islands, on September 30, 1813. He studied medicine at Edinburgh University; and in 1833 he was appointed surgeon to the Hudson's Bay Company's ship which visited annually Moose Factory. From 1835 to 1845 he was resident surgeon at Moose Factory; and in 1846 he was sent on his first journey of exploration, which resulted in the survey of the shores of Committee bay. In 1847 he joined the first land expedition in search of Sir John Franklin

(q.v.), under Sir John Richardson (q.v.); and in 1851 he undertook another search for Franklin, in the course of which he covered 5,380 miles, 700 of which were newly discovered coast line. On his return to England, he proposed yet another expedition in search of Franklin; and this expedition, which set out in 1853, resulted in the discovery of Franklin's fate. In his later years Rae lived in London, England; and in 1880 he was elected a fellow of the Royal Society. He died in London on July 22, 1893. In 1860 he married Catharine Jane Alicia, daughter of Major George Ash Thompson, of Ardkill, Londonderry, Ireland; but he left no children. He was the author of *A narrative of an expedition to the shores of the Arctic sea in 1846 and 1847* (London, 1850); and his *Report . . . of the proceedings of the Arctic searching expedition* was printed by order of the House of Commons (London, 1852).

**Rae.** See **Fort Rae.**

**Rae strait,** the body of water to the east of King William island, separating it from the mainland, in the Franklin district of the North West Territories. It was named after Dr. John Rae (q.v.), Arctic explorer.

**Raffeix, Pierre** (1633-1724), priest and cartographer, was born in Auvergne, France, in 1633, and entered the Jesuit novitiate in 1653. He was sent to Canada in 1663, and became a missionary to the Iroquois. He died at Quebec on August 29, 1724. He was the maker of three early maps of Canada: one, dated 1676, describing "the westernmost parts of Canada"; another, dated 1688, describing lake Ontario and the territories of the Five Nations; and a third covering the whole of New France to lake Erie on the west and New England on the south. See Rev. T. J. Campbell, *Pioneer priests of North America*, vol. i (New York, 1908).

**Ragueneau, Paul** (1608-1680), missionary, was born in Paris, France, on March 18, 1608. He joined the Society of Jesus, and was sent to Canada as a missionary in 1636. He joined the Jesuit mission among the Hurons, and he was superior of the mission when it was attacked by the Iroquois in 1649. He brought the remnant of the Huron tribe to Quebec, and he laboured among them until 1662. He then returned to France, and for the rest of his life he acted as agent for the Jesuit missions in Canada. He died at Paris on September 3, 1680. He was the author of *Vie de la Mère St. Augustine, religieuse hospitalière de Québec, en la Nouvelle France,* (Paris, 1672), *Relation de ce qui s'est passé de plus remarquable ès missions des pères de la Compagnie en la Nouvelle France* (7 vols., Paris, 1647-57), and *Mémoires touchant les vertus des Pères de Noue, Jogues, Daniel, Brébeuf, Lallement, Garnier et Chabanel* (Paris, n.d.).

**Ragweed** (*Ambrosia artemisiifolia* L., *Compositae*), a coarse, homely, very common weed; the branching stem is 1-3 feet high, erect and hairy; the leaves are thin, 2-pinnate, the lobes linear, smooth above and pale and hoary beneath. The flowers are unisexual, greenish, and inconspicuous; the staminate heads are borne in long slender branched spikes, each head containing 5-20 staminate flowers; the pistillate heads are sessile at the base of the staminate spike. It is found growing along the roadsides and in waste places everywhere, and is one of the most troublesome plants to hay-fever sufferers.

**Rail,** a name used for the medium or smaller members of the bird family *Rallidae,* to which belong the coot and gallinules. The true rails are characterized by their thin, laterally compressed bodies and their long toes. The Canadian species are entirely marsh-dwelling birds, and are seldom seen, but more often heard. Their cackling, "laughing", and frog-like notes are characteristic sounds of a cat-tail marsh. In colour the rails are all similar; they are cinnamon-brown, greenish-brown, and buff,

patterned with darker markings. The sora (*Porzana carolina*) is the most widely distributed of the rails in Canada. It is a short-billed type.

**Railways.** See **Transportation,** and the names of individual railways.

**Rainbow trout,** a general name applied to several species of trout which develop a red band along the side at spawning time. They are native of western North America, and are found from Alaska to California. All are close relatives or derivatives of the steelhead (q.v.). Spawning occurs in the spring. Several varieties of rainbow trout have been introduced into eastern America and to other parts of the world.

**Raine, Walter** (1861-1934), naturalist, was born in Leeds, England, in 1861. He came to Canada in youth, settled in Toronto, and became an authority on Canadian birds. He was the author of *Bird-nesting in north-west Canada* (Toronto, 1892), and he presented his collection of birds' eggs to the Royal Ontario Museum. He died in Toronto on July 29, 1934.

**Rainy lake** and **river,** in Rainy River district, west of lake Superior and on the boundary between Ontario and Minnesota. The lake, 220 miles west of lake Superior, discharges into the lake of the Woods by the Rainy river which is 100 miles in length. The lake contains over 500 islands, and its banks are covered with small timber. It is 50 miles long, 38½ wide, and has an area of 366 square miles. The name is derived from the Indian name which meant "it is raining all the time"; and it seems to have had reference to the fact that the waterfall connecting the lake and the river gave rise to a sort of mist that looked like rain. The French name was "La Pline". Both the lake and river were discovered by Jacques de Noyon, a French explorer, in 1688.

**Rainy River,** a district which forms a rough triangle in the extreme west of Ontario, bounded on the north by

15

Kenora district and the lake of the Woods, on the east by Thunder Bay district, and on the south by the state of Minnesota. This district was part of the "disputed territory" between Manitoba and Ontario, and it was made part of Ontario by the Privy Council in 1884. It was joined to Thunder Bay district for judicial purposes until 1914, when it became a provisional judicial district. Pop. (1931), 17,359.

**Rainy River,** a town in the Rainy River district of Ontario, at the foot of the lake of the Woods, on the Rainy river, and on the Canadian National Railway, 150 miles east of Winnipeg. It is near the international boundary, and is a divisional point on the railway. It has good steamboat service with Kenora, Fort Frances, and Beaudette, Minnesota. The industries include lumbering, boat-building and repairing, box and barrel factories, dairying, farming, and fishing. Rainy River has several churches, public and separate schools, and a weekly newspaper (*Record*). Pop. (1931), 1,444.

**Râle, Sébastien.** See **Rasles, Sébastien.**

**Rama,** an Indian village in Ontario county, Ontario, on lake Couchiching, and on the Canadian National Railway, 7 miles north-west of Orillia. It is named after Rama township, in which it is situated. The name, which is Spanish for "the branch of a tree", was probably given by Sir Peregrine Maitland (q.v.), who saw service in the Peninsular War.

**Rameau de Saint-Père, François Edme** (1820-1899), historian, was born at Adon, France, in 1820. He became a journalist and man of letters in Paris; and he was the author of two works on the history of Acadia, *La France aux colonies: Acadiens et Canadiens* (Paris, 1859), and *Une colonie féodale* (2 vols., Paris, 1877-89). In 1884 he was elected a corresponding member of the Royal Society of Canada; and in 1889 he was made an LL.D. of Laval University.

He died, suddenly, at Adon on December 15, 1899.

**Ramezay, Claude de** (1657-1724), governor of Montreal (1704-24), was born at Lagesse, France, in 1657, the son of Timothée de Ramezay, a descendant of the Scotch family of Ramsay, and Catherine Tribouillard. He came to Canada in 1685 as a lieutenant in the *troupes de la Marine*, took part in 1686 in Denonville's expedition against the Iroquois, and in 1690 was present at the siege of Quebec. On July 1, 1690, he was appointed governor of Three Rivers; and on May 28, 1699, he was named commander of the royal troops in the colony. In June, 1703, he was made a chevalier of St. Louis, and on May 15, 1704, was appointed governor of Montreal. From 1714 to 1716 he was administrator of New France. He died at Montreal on August 1, 1724. He married, on November 8, 1690, Marie Charlotte Denys, and by her he had sixteen children. See *La famille de Ramezay* (Bull. rech. hist., vols. xvi and xvii), and R. Roy, *De Ramesay* (Bull. rech. hist., vol. v).

**Ramezay, Jean Baptiste Nicolas Roch de** (1708-1771?), commandant of Quebec (1758-9), was born in Montreal on September 4, 1708, the son of Claude de Ramezay (q.v.) and Marie Charlotte Denys. In 1720 he became an ensign, in 1726 a lieutenant, and in 1734 a captain. In 1742 he was given the command of Fort Nipigon on Hudson bay, and in 1746 he was sent to Acadia. On his return to Quebec in 1748, he was made a chevalier of St. Louis; and in the following year was named town major of Quebec. In 1758 he was promoted to the post of King's lieutenant. In 1759, after the flight of Vaudreuil (q.v.), following Montcalm's defeat, he made every effort to save Quebec from the English, but was obliged to capitulate on September 18. He returned to France soon afterward, and lived in Paris. He died about 1771. He married, on December 6, 1728, Louise Godefroy de Tonnancour, and by her he had six children. See *La famille de Ramezay* (Bull. rech. hist., vols. xvi and xvii).

**Ramsay, George, ninth Earl of Dalhousie.** See **Dalhousie, George Ramsay, ninth Earl of.**

**Ramsay, Thomas Kennedy** (1826-1886), judge, was born in Ayr, Scotland, on September 2, 1826. He came to Canada, was called to the bar, and was appointed an assistant judge of the Superior Court of Quebec in 1870, and a puisne judge of the Court of Queen's Bench in 1873. He died at St. Hugues, Quebec, on December 22, 1886. In 1857 he founded the *Lower Canada Jurist;* and he was the author of *Notes sur la coutûme de Paris* (Montreal, 1863; 2nd ed., 1864), *Government commissions of inquiry* (Montreal, 1863), and a *Digested index to the reported cases in Lower Canada* (Quebec, 1865).

**Ramsheg river,** in Cumberland county, Nova Scotia, flows into Wallace bay, and has a length of 25 miles.

**Rand, Silas Tertius** (1810-1889), clergyman and philologist, was born in Cornwallis, Nova Scotia, on May 17, 1810. He was ordained to the Baptist ministry in 1834, and in 1846 he became a missionary among the Micmac Indians of New Brunswick and Nova Scotia. He became an authority on the linguistics and folk-lore of the Micmac, and actually rescued their language from oblivion. Besides translating into Micmac a good part of the Old and New Testaments, he compiled a Micmac grammar (Halifax, 1875) and a Micmac dictionary (Halifax, 1888). He wrote also *A short statement of facts relating to the history, manners, customs, language, and literature of the Micmac tribe of Indians* (Halifax, 1850) and *Legends of the Micmacs* (New York and London, 1894). He died at Hantsport, Nova Scotia, on October 4, 1889. He was a D.D. of Acadia University, and an LL.D. of Queen's University, Kingston.

See J. S. Clark, *Rand and the Micmacs* (Charlottetown, 1899).

**Rand, Theodore Harding** (1835-1900), chancellor of McMaster University (1891-5), was born in Cornwallis, Nova Scotia, in 1835. He was the son of a cousin of Silas Tertius Rand (q.v.). He was educated at Acadia College (B.A., 1860; M.A., 1863; hon. LL.D., 1874), and from 1860 to 1864 he taught in the provincial normal school at Truro, Nova Scotia. From 1864 to 1870 he was superintendent of education for Nova Scotia, and from 1871 to 1883 superintendent of education for New Brunswick. From 1883 to 1885 he was on the staff of Acadia University; and in 1885 he was appointed to the staff of the Baptist College (later McMaster University), Toronto. In 1891 he became the chancellor of this institution; but ill-health compelled his withdrawal from administrative work in 1895; and he died at Fredericton, New Brunswick, on May 29, 1900. He was the author of *At Minas basin, and other poems* (Toronto, 1897), and *Song waves, and other poems* (Toronto, 1900); and he was the editor of an excellent *Treasury of Canadian verse* (Toronto, 1900).

**Randal, Stephen** (1804-1841), journalist, was born in the Eastern townships, Lower Canada, on January 1, 1804. He came to Upper Canada when a young man, as a protégé of the bishop of Quebec. In 1828 he was teaching school in Hamilton, Upper Canada; and about 1832 he became editor of the *Hamilton Free Press*. In 1832-3 he edited also in Hamilton a semi-monthly library journal, named the *Voyager*. About 1836 he went to Hallowell (Picton), and he published there a short-lived periodical named *Randal's Magazine*. He died at Stanstead, Lower Canada on April 27, 1841.

**Randall, Robert** (1766-1834), pioneer, was born in Maryland in 1766. He came to Upper Canada in 1798, and settled at Niagara Falls. Here he built a saw and flour mill, in which was ground the first flour sent from Upper Canada to the British market, and a foundry for the manufacture of the first bar and cast iron made in Upper Canada. He established also a mercantile business at Cornwall. In various parts of the province he acquired valuable lands, including the site of what is now a large part of the city of Ottawa. In 1809, owing to the failure of his British agents, he was arrested and imprisoned for debt; and he lost his various properties. There were irregularities in the disposal of these properties; and for many years he strove, though in vain, to obtain justice from the courts of the province. In 1820 he was elected to the Legislative Assembly of Upper Canada for Niagara; and in 1825 he was elected for Lincoln. During this period he gained the friendship of William Lyon Mackenzie (q.v.), and the latter made Randall's treatment a political issue against the "Family Compact". Randall died near Niagara Falls, Upper Canada, on May 1, 1834; and in his will Mackenzie was named his executor. He was buried at Lundy's Lane.

See H. P. Hill, *Robert Randall and the Le Breton Flats* (pamphlet, Ottawa, 1919).

**Ranken, George** (1828-1856), soldier and author, was born in London, England, on January 4, 1828. He was educated at the Royal Military Academy, Woolwich; and in 1847 he was commissioned a second lieutenant in the Royal Engineers. From 1850 to 1854 he was stationed in Canada; in 1855 he was sent to the Crimea; and on February 28, 1856, he was killed by the explosion of a mine at Sebastopol. He was the author of *The experiment: A farce, in one act* (Quebec, 1854); and his journal and correspondence were later published by his brother under the title *Canada and the Crimea, or Sketches of a soldier's life* (London, 1862).

**Raphael, William** (1833-1914), painter, was born in West Prussia in 1833. He graduated from the Royal School of Art in Berlin, and in 1860 he emigrated to Canada. At Montreal, where he lived for the rest of his life, he conducted a large drawing and painting class for artists. He was one of the original members of the Royal Canadian Academy on its formation in 1880; and in 1904 he was appointed a member of the Council of Arts and Manufactures of Quebec. He died in Montreal in 1914. There are several portraits by him in the Parliament Buildings at Ottawa.

**Rapid City,** a town in Marquette county, Manitoba, on the Minnedosa or Little Saskatchewan river, and on the Canadian Pacific and Canadian National Railways, 10 miles north of Brandon. It was named in 1877 after the rapids which interrupt the river flowing through it. Pop. (1934), 600.

**Rasilly, Isaac de** (d. 1635), governor of Acadia (1632-35), was a member of a family of Touraine. He became a renowned seaman, and took part in several important naval engagements. In 1626 he presented to Richelieu a memoir relating to the colonies, which resulted in the formation of the Company of New France in the following year. He was one of the members of the Company of One Hundred Associates, and after 1628 was their naval commander. In 1632 he was commissioned to receive Acadia from the English in accordance with the treaty of Saint Germain, and arrived in Acadia in August, 1632. He established himself at La Hêve, and became the head of an organization to colonize Port Royal and La Hêve. He died in November, 1635.

**Rasles, Sébastien** (1657-1724), missionary, was born at Pontarlier, France, on January 4, 1657, and entered the Society of Jesus. He was sent to Canada as a missionary in 1689; and was stationed for a year or two, first at the Abnaki mission near Quebec, and then in the Illinois country. In 1693, he was recalled to Quebec, and sent south to take charge of the Abnaki mission on the Kennebec river; and here he spent the last thirty years of his life. He became the temporal, as well as the spiritual, adviser of his flock; and thus incurred the hostility of the English. A reward of £10,000 was placed on his head; and on August 23, 1724, a party of New England militia fell on his mission station, and shot him down in front of his chapel. He was the author of *A dictionary of the Abnaki language*, published a century or more after his death, with a memoir and notes by John Pickering (Cambridge, Mass., 1833). See also N. E. Dionne, *Le Père Sébastien Rasles* (Trans. Roy. Soc. Can., 1903), J. F. Sprague, *Sébastian Ralé* (Boston, 1906), T. J. Campbell, *Pioneer priests of North America*, vol. iii (New York, 1911), and A. Beauchesne, *Le martyre du Père Rasle* (Trans. Roy. Soc. Can., 1935).

**Raspberry, Purple Flowering** (*Rubus odoratus* L., *Rosaceae*), an unarmed shrubby plant, the branches, stalks, and calyx covered with clammy glandular hairs. The leaves are large, broadly ovate, 3-5 lobed, the lobes acute and minutely toothed. The flower stalks are many-flowered, the flowers large and showy, the petals rounded, purple-rose in colour. The fruit is red, hemispherical, flat, and scarcely edible. It is found growing in woods and thickets from Nova Scotia to western Ontario.

**Raspberry, Wild Red** (*Rubus idaeus* var. *aculeatissimus* Regel-Tilling, *Rosaceae*), an upright prickly-stemmed shrub. The leaves are compound, with 3-5 oblong-ovate pointed leaflets, downy and whitish beneath. The flowers are white; the sepals very bristly; the petals as long as the sepals. The fruit is light red, falling from the receptacle when ripe. It grows in thickets and on hillsides from Labrador to British Columbia.

**Rat.** The common rat (*Rattus rattus*) is an Old World animal introduced into North America by the coming of the white man. It is destructive, a carrier of disease, and a thorough nuisance. There are three forms of this animal found in Canada: the Norway or brown rat, which is the commonest and is brown in colour; the black rat, smaller and slimmer than the Norway, and black in colour; the roof rat or Alexandrine rat, which is about the size of the Norway, but is much lighter in colour. The almost bare tail will serve to distinguish these animals from the only native Canadian rat, the bushy-tailed wood-rat (*Neotoma cinerea*), which is found in British Columbia, Alberta, and south-western Saskatchewan. The bushy-tailed wood-rat lives among rocks and in crevices along cliff faces, but will establish itself sometimes in buildings, where it becomes a nuisance owing to the noise it makes and its well-known habit of carrying off small articles. Sometimes called the "pack rat", on account of these thieving propensities, it has also earned the name of "trade rat", since it often leaves some object behind in place of the article stolen. Its fur is soft and gray in colour, and the wood-rat has none of the furtive appearance of the introduced rats. The wood-rat does not hibernate, but is active all the year round. The young number three to six in a litter; and while in the north but one litter is raised each year, in milder sections several litters are the rule.

**Ratfish,** a fish of the shallow waters of the Pacific coast of America from Alaska to California. It is of no economic importance, except for the oil in its liver, but is of considerable scientific interest. It is a relative of the sharks and rays. The group to which it belongs is called the chimæras, because of their grotesque appearance.

**Rat Portage.** See **Kenora**.

**Rat river,** a tributary of the Mackenzie river, in the Mackenzie district of the North West Territories. Its mouth is 70 miles above Aklavik. See C. C. Rogers, *On the Rat river* (Can. Geog. Journal, 1931).

**Rattray, William Jordan** (1835-1883), journalist and author, was born in London, England, in 1835, the son of Alexander Rattray. His father came to Canada, and set up in business in Toronto as a baker in 1848; and he was educated at the University of Toronto (B.A., 1858). He became a journalist, and was a contributor to the Toronto *Grumbler*, and to the *Canadian Monthly* (1872-78). In his later years he was on the editorial staff of the Toronto *Mail*. He died at Toronto on September 19, 1883. His only separate publication was *The Scot in British North America* (4 vols., Toronto, 1880-84), a compilation which hardly reflects his best qualities.

**Raudot, Jacques** (1647-1728), intendant of New France (1705-11), was born in 1647, the son of Jean Raudot, seignior of Bazarne and Coudray, and Marguerite Talon. In 1674 he was councillor in the parlement of Metz, and on May 26, 1678, he became councillor at the Cour des Aides, Paris. On January 1, 1705, he was made intendant of New France, and this post he held until 1711, devoting himself to the welfare of the colony. He returned to France and was appointed councillor of marine. He died in 1728. See R. Roy, *Les intendants de la Nouvelle-France* (Trans. Roy. Soc. Can., 1903), and *Jacques et Antoine-Denis Raudot* (Bull. rech. hist., vol. ix).

**Raven** (*Corvus corax*), the largest member of the bird family *Corvidae*, to which belong the crows, magpies, and jays. It may best be described as a large crow, and this, in reality, it is. The raven formerly occurred throughout Canada, but with the encroachment of settlement it has retreated to the rather isolated parts of the north, although an occasional pair persists in wild sections

south of the Dominion. The Canadian raven is the same species as the raven of northern Europe.

**Rawdon,** a township in Montcalm county, province of Quebec, situated on the river Lac Ouareau, 8 miles from Ste. Julienne, on the Canadian National Railway. In 1799 the place was named in honour of Francis Rawdon, Marquis of Hastings (1754-1826). The chief industries are sawmills and grist mills. Pop. (1931), 1,066.

**Raymond, William Odber** (1853-1923), clergyman and historian, was born at Woodstock, New Brunswick, on February 3, 1853, the second son of Lieut.-Col. Charles W. Raymond. He was educated at the Woodstock grammar school and at the University of New Brunswick (B.A., 1876; M.A., 1891; LL.D., 1901); and he was ordained a priest of the Church of England in 1879. From 1878 to 1884 he was stationed at Stanley, New Brunswick; and from 1884 to 1920 he was rector of St. Mary's Church, Saint John, New Brunswick. In 1908 he became archdeacon of Saint John. After retirement from active parochial work, he removed to Toronto; and here he died on November 23, 1923. In 1879 he married Julia Nelson, of Saint John; and by her he had one son and one daughter. He was elected a fellow of the Royal Society of Canada in 1906; and he was an outstanding authority on the history of the Maritime provinces of Canada. In addition to numerous papers contributed to the *Transactions* of the Royal Society of Canada, the *Collections* of the New Brunswick Historical Society and other periodicals, he wrote *The history of the river St. John* (Saint John, New Brunswick, 1905), and he edited the valuable *Winslow papers* (Saint John, New Brunswick, 1901).

**Raymond,** a town in the Lethbridge district of Alberta, on the Canadian Pacific Railway, 350 miles south of Edmonton. It was named in 1902 after the elder son of Jesse W. Knight, a prominent Mormon. It is in a mixed farming district, and is particularly noted for its sugar beets and honey. The district is partially covered by irrigation. It has a weekly newspaper (*Recorder*). Pop. (1934), 1,849.

**Rayon Industry.** See **Textile Industry** and **Pulp-and-Paper Industry.**

**Rays.** See **Skates.**

**Read, David Breakenridge** (1823-1904), lawyer and historian, was born at Augusta, Upper Canada, on June 13, 1823, the third son of John Landon Read, merchant, and Janet, daughter of David Breakenridge. He was educated at Upper Canada College, Toronto; and was called to the bar of Upper Canada in 1845 (Q.C., 1858). For thirty years he was a bencher of the Law Society of Upper Canada, and he was the author of *Lectures on the Judicature Act* (Toronto, 1881). In 1858 he was mayor of Toronto. During his later years he devoted himself to historical and biographical research; and he published *The lives of the judges of Upper Canada* (Toronto, 1888), *The life and times of General John Graves Simcoe* (Toronto, 1890), *The life and times of Major-General Sir Isaac Brock* (Toronto, 1894), *The rebellion of 1837* (Toronto, 1897), and *The lieutenant-governors of Upper Canada and Ontario* (Toronto, 1900). He died in Toronto on May 11, 1904. He married Emily, daughter of Norman Ballard, of Picton, Ontario; and by her he had three daughters and one son.

**Reade, John** (1837-1919), journalist and poet, was born at Ballyshannon, county Donegal, Ireland, on November 13, 1837, the son of Joseph Reade and Frances Smyth. He was educated at Queen's College, Belfast, and came to Canada in 1856. He first studied law, and then theology; and in 1864 was ordained a clergyman of the Church of England. He had, however, before this interested himself in journalism; and in 1870 he left the church to become literary editor of the Montreal *Gazette*. This position he held for the rest of his life, conducting for many years a column entitled "Old and New", under the initials "R. V." In 1870 he published a volume of verse, *The prophecy of Merlin, and other poems* (Montreal); and he contributed to literary periodicals and to the transactions of learned societies a large number of papers on a great variety of subjects. In 1882 he was appointed one of the charter members of the Royal Society of Canada; and in 1896 he was elected a fellow of the Royal Society of Literature of Great Britain. In 1906 he was made an LL.D. of the University of Ottawa. He died, unmarried, at Montreal, on March 26, 1919.

**Ready, John** (d. 1845), lieutenant-governor of Prince Edward Island (1824-31), was a British army officer who was in 1820 appointed a member of the Executive Council of Lower Canada, and in 1824 lieutenant-governor of Prince Edward Island. His tenure of office, which lasted until 1831, was very popular and successful; and after his return to England he became a major-general and governor of the Isle of Man. It was while holding this position that he died, on July 10, 1845.

**Rebellion of 1837-8.** Toward the end of the year 1837 there broke out in both Upper and Lower Canada an armed rebellion. The causes of this rebellion were in both provinces fundamentally the same. The Constitutional Act of 1791 had given to both of the Canadas a constitution which threw power into the hands of an official oligarchy. There was in each province an elected Legislative Assembly; but the influence of the Assembly even over legislation was negative. A bill passed by the Assembly had to pass also the nominated Legislative Council; it had to receive the assent of the Crown, in the person of the governor or lieutenant-governor; and it might even be reserved for the signification of the pleasure of the Home government. Over the executive government, the Assembly had virtually no control. The Executive Council, like the Legislative Council, was appointed by the Crown; and the Assembly could not exert over it the power of the purse, as the House of Commons was able, even at that time, to exert the power of the purse over the executive government in Great Britain, for the simple reason that most of the revenues of the provinces came from the British exchequer or were derived from sources under the control of the British government. All the Assembly did was to vote money for local objects, such as the building of roads and bridges; and for it to try to "withhold supply" would merely have been to cut off its nose to spite its face. In these circumstances, the official class in both Upper and Lower Canada had almost untrammelled control of the executive government, and possessed a veto even on legislation.

The constitutional issue, however, it should be added, was obscured and confused by other considerations; and these differed in each province. In Upper Canada the constitutional issue was complicated by the fact that the official oligarchy—known as the "Family Compact"—identified itself with the claims of the Church of England, though the adherents of this church were in a decided minority in the province; and thus the political struggle took on the colour of a religious issue, into which economic grievances entered as well. In Lower Canada, the constitutional issue was overshadowed by the racial issue; for the Assembly in Lower Canada came to be predominantly French-speaking, while the executive government was in the hands of English-speaking officials, or of French-speaking officials who had thrown in their lot with the English. Thus, in Lower Canada, there came to be, as Lord Durham (q.v.) said, "two nations war-

ring within the bosom of a single state". The religious issue was less prominent in Lower Canada, because of the privileged position which the Roman Catholic Church had obtained under the Quebec Act; and economic grievances, though not absent, merely contributed to the bitterness of the racial struggle.

Between the rebellions in the two provinces there was some slight connection; for there is no doubt that the rebels in Upper Canada were, before the rebellion, in communication with those in Lower Canada, and joint action had been agreed upon. But here the connection ceased; and it is therefore desirable to treat the two rebellions separately.

*The Rebellion in Upper Canada.* Until the summer of 1837, the leader of the advanced wing of the Reform party in Upper Canada, William Lyon Mackenzie (q.v.), conducted his agitation for reform along constitutional lines; but by that time he had come to despair of achieving anything by constitutional methods, and had begun to boast of his "rebel blood". In the autumn of 1837, he busied himself with visiting various parts of rural Upper Canada, and obtaining the names of volunteers who would rise in rebellion; and he actually formed a secret committee or council of war in Toronto. At last, it was arranged, after consultation with the leaders of the *patriote* party in Lower Canada, that the rebels in Upper Canada should assemble at Montgomery's tavern, north of Toronto, on December 7, and proceed to occupy Toronto, which had been divested of troops in view of the threatening state of affairs in Lower Canada. The government, however, seems to have got wind of the fact that mischief was afoot; and the rebel council of war in Toronto sent out word that the date of assembly should be advanced to December 3. The result was that on December 3 only a fraction of the force expected gathered at Montgomery's tavern; and the advantage of surprise was lost. Mackenzie made one half-hearted attempt to advance on Toronto; but his force fled in disorder when they encountered a small picket, and September 7 found him still at Montgomery's tavern, awaiting reinforcements. Meanwhile, the loyalist militia were pouring into Toronto; and on December 7 they took the offensive. Three columns of militia advanced on Montgomery's tavern; and after a brief exchange of shots, in the course of which only one man was killed, the rebels broke and fled.

In the western part of the province, there was also a brief insurrection, under Dr. Charles Duncombe (q.v.); but it was quelled even more ignominiously than that near Toronto.

Mackenzie succeeded in escaping to the United States by way of the head of lake Ontario; and early in 1838 set up a provisional government on Navy island in the Niagara river. A body of Canadian militia, under Capt. Drew (q.v.), succeeded in "cutting out" his supply-ship, the *Caroline;* and shortly afterwards he was compelled to retire to the United States, where he was imprisoned for breach of the neutrality laws. He found, however, many sympathizers in the United States, especially among the Irish Americans; and during 1838 there were a number of disturbances along the Canadian border, organized by the so-called "Hunters' Lodges" which had been formed to help the Canadians cast off the yoke of British rule. The most serious of these was near Prescott, where a filibustering force under a Pole named Niles von Schoultz (q.v.) invaded Canada, and was defeated at what is known as the battle of the Windmill, on November 16, 1838. In the first week of December, another force of filibusters landed at Windsor, but were dispersed and driven back across the Detroit river by Colonel Prince (q.v.). By the end of 1838, the

government of the United States at last, though somewhat tardily, took action to put an end to these disturbances; and no further trouble ensued.

*The Rebellion in Lower Canada.* The outbreak of the rebellion in Lower Canada would appear to have been precipitated by a misunderstanding on the part of the authorities. The first half of November, 1837, saw in Montreal a number of disturbances in which the loyalists or "constitutionalists" clashed with a number of *patriotes*, who called themselves "Fils de la Liberté", after the French revolutionists. The Roman Catholic Church in Lower Canada, which openly disapproved of rebellion, frowned on these disturbances; and a priest advised Louis Joseph Papineau (q.v.), the leader of the *patriotes*, to leave Montreal. Papineau, with Thomas Storrow Brown (q.v.) and Dr. Edmund Bailey O'Callaghan (q.v.), left Montreal for the Richelieu valley; and the authorities jumped to the conclusion that they had left to organize a revolt. On November 16, therefore, warrants were issued for their arrest on a charge of high treason. The same day there was an encounter between a small force of loyalist cavalry and a party of armed habitants on the road between Montreal and St. Johns. These events brought the rebellion to a head. A considerable body of rebels gathered at the village of St. Charles, under Thomas Storrow Brown, and another body at St. Denis under Dr. Wolfred Nelson (q.v.). Papineau was at St. Denis, but he took no part in the rebellion, and in fact hostilities had hardly begun when he escaped over the border to the United States. The rebels under Nelson repulsed at St. Denis, on November 23, a column of troops under Colonel C. S. Gore (q.v.); but on November 25 another column, under Lieut.-Col. Wetherall, succeeded in dispersing the rebels at St. Charles. The rebels at St. Denis thereupon evacuated their position, and withdrew to the

United States. Meanwhile, even more serious trouble had been brewing to the north of Montreal. Here, at the village of St. Eustache, a strong force of rebels had gathered under Amury Girod (q.v.) and Dr. Chénier (q.v.), and were terrorizing the countryside. On December 14, Sir John Colborne (q.v.), the commander-in-chief of the forces, himself commanded a force which moved north, and carried the village by storm.

With the defeat of the rebels at St. Eustache, the rebellion was virtually at an end; and it is worthy of note that it was confined to only two localities, the Richelieu valley and the parishes north of Montreal. There was no outbreak in Montreal itself, or in Three Rivers, or in Quebec—largely, no doubt, because of the loyal attitude of the Roman Catholic Church. On February 28, 1838, a body of refugees under Robert Nelson (q.v.) and Dr. Côté (q.v.) re-crossed the border at Lacolle; but they were driven back across the border by loyalist militia, and their leaders were arrested by the American authorities.

*Bibliography.* A valuable bibliography of books and pamphlets and other material relating to the Rebellion of 1837-8 has been published by the Toronto Public Library (Toronto, 1924). For the rebellion in Upper Canada, reference should be had to J. C. Dent, *The story of the rebellion of 1837 in Upper Canada* (2 vols., Toronto, 1885), D. B. Read, *The rebellion of 1837* (Toronto, 1897), W. S. Wallace, *The Family Compact* (Toronto, 1915); and A. Dunham, *Political unrest in Upper Canada* (London, 1927). For the rebellion in Lower Canada, the chief sources are R. Christie, *History of the late province of Lower Canada* (6 vols., Quebec and Montreal, 1848-55); L. N. Carrier, *Les évènements de 1837-1838* (Quebec, 1880); C. A. M. Globensky, *La rebellion de 1837 à St. Eustache* (Quebec, 1883); L. O. David, *Les patriotes de 1837-38* (Montreal, 1884); and A. D. DeCelles, *The patriotes of '37* (Toronto, 1916).

**Recall,** a constitutional device whereby an elected representative in the legislature may, on petition of a fixed number of his constituents, be compelled to submit himself for re-election before his term of office expires. It is a device borrowed from the United States, where it is in force in some states; but the only province in Canada to adopt it has been Alberta, which passed legislation instituting the recall in 1935. It is, however, a device wholly alien to the British constitutional practice, which regards the representative of a constituency not as a delegate, but as a free agent.

**Reciprocity,** a term commonly used in Canada in reference to an agreement with the United States involving mutual reductions in customs duties. The agitation for reciprocity became of political importance in Canada in 1846 during the period of discontent that followed the repeal of the Corn Laws by Great Britain. The British government was accordingly induced to open negotiations at Washington for a reciprocal agreement including the five North American colonies. The dispute over the rights of Great Britain and of the United States in the North Atlantic fisheries complicated the negotiation for reciprocity, but increased the anxiety of both governments to reach a general settlement. At length in June, 1854, a fortuitous combination of circumstances, including the decline in the opposition of the northern protectionists and of the southern pro-slavery party, enabled Lord Elgin (q.v.), and W. L. Marcy, the American secretary of state, to negotiate the treaty.

Under the terms of the Elgin-Marcy treaty, the United States and the British North American colonies (Canada, New Brunswick, Nova Scotia, Prince Edward Island, and Newfoundland) each removed the duties upon a considerable list of natural products. The most important were grain, flour and breadstuffs, animals, meats, fruit, fish, poultry, tallow, coal, timber, and lumber. American fishermen were admitted to the colonial fisheries on the Atlantic coast, while British subjects received a similar privilege in eastern American coastal fisheries north of the thirty-sixth parallel. British and American shipping had access, upon equal terms, to the St. Lawrence, the Canadian canals, and lake Michigan. The treaty undoubtedly imparted a considerable impetus to trade between the United States and the colonies, which more than doubled between 1854 and 1865. The prosperity of the period was, however, to a large extent, the result of other factors, including the rapid development of the area around the Great lakes and of the American middle west, the construction of railways, and the American Civil War. The trade developed under the treaty has been described as a "commerce of convenience": the principal articles of importation into Canada—grain, flour, meat, livestock, coal, etc.—were largely the articles which the colonies chiefly exported to the United States.

As early as 1856, American protectionists, particularly the manufacturing and shipping interests of the state of New York, began an agitation against the treaty. Canadian tariff increases, in 1858-9, upon dutiable importations from the United States enabled opponents of reciprocity to claim that Canada had violated the spirit of the treaty. During the Civil War, the allegedly pro-southern sympathies of Great Britain and of the colonies increased northern opposition to the reciprocity agreement. Economic and political forces, therefore, combined to bring about the abrogation of the treaty by the United States in March, 1866.

Between 1866 and 1900 Canada made repeated but abortive efforts to secure another reciprocity treaty. In the period after Confederation the Macdonald government attempted to negotiate an agreement, and in 1869 Sir John Rose

(q.v.), then minister of finance, made an unsuccessful visit to Washington. Hope of securing a reciprocity agreement was temporarily destroyed by the Treaty of Washington of 1871, in which important fishery and navigation privileges were conceded to the United States, without the provision for reductions in duty, except upon fish. In 1874, George Brown (q.v.) and Sir Edward Thornton, the British minister at Washington, negotiated a draft treaty, with Hamilton Fish, the American secretary of state. The treaty, which was to operate for twenty-one years, provided for tariff reductions upon natural products, agricultural implements, and manufactures; but it was rejected by the United States Senate. During the eighties the Liberal party, through the influence of Erastus Wiman (q.v.) and Goldwin Smith (q.v.), was committed to the policy of unrestricted reciprocity with the United States. In the election of 1891, Sir John Macdonald (q.v.) made telling use of the argument that the Liberal policy would lead to the annexation of Canada. Commissioners were despatched to Washington by the Conservatives in 1892-3, and by the Liberals in 1898-9, but were alike unsuccessful in securing a treaty.

During the following decade there was little discussion of reciprocity. In 1911 negotiations between President Taft and W. S. Fielding (q.v.), the Canadian minister of finance, resulted in a reciprocal arrangement which was to be enacted by concurrent legislation in the two countries. The agreement provided for free trade in the natural products of the farm (grain, fruits, vegetables, and farm animals), low rates of duty upon natural products in secondary form (meats, canned goods, flour, etc.) and upon a variety of articles including agricultural implements and engines, building material, and partly finished lumber. Pulpwood was to be admitted free by the United States when the provinces withdrew the embargo upon the exportation of pulp-wood from government-owned lands. The necessary legislation was passed by the United States Congress; but the Laurier government, which fought a Dominion election chiefly upon the issue of reciprocity, was defeated.

No further negotiations for reciprocity occurred between the two countries for over twenty years. After passage of the Reciprocal Trade Agreements Act in the United States, negotiations were opened between the Canadian and American governments in the latter part of 1934. The accession to power of the Liberals in Canada in the autumn of 1935 was followed by the King-Hull agreement at Washington on November 15. The treaty was to be in operation until December 31, 1938. According to its provisions, the United States reduced the duties upon some sixty commodities imported from Canada, including cattle, horses, whiskey, sawed boards, planks, deals, and sawed timber, cheddar cheese, maple sugar, and seed potatoes. Free entry to the American market was guaranteed to a number of products including newsprint paper, woodpulp, pulpwoods, and shingles of wood. Canada extended to the United States the benefit of the intermediate tariff in its entirety. Specific reductions below existing most-favoured-nation rates were made in respect of eighty-eight tariff items, including products in the groups of agriculture, textiles, iron and steel, machinery, agricultural, industrial and domestic, and electrical apparatus. Each country agreed to accord to the other unconditional most-favoured-nation treatment in respect of custom duties and related matters. Concessions by Canada to the other parts of the British Empire and by the United States to Cuba, the Philippine islands, the Virgin islands, American Samoa, etc., were not included within the scope of the treaty.

See F. E. Haynes, *The Reciprocity Treaty with Canada of 1854* (Baltimore, 1892, publications of the American Economic Association, vol. vii, no. 6); Donald C. Masters, *The Reciprocity Treaty of 1854* (London, 1937); Charles C. Tansill, *The Canadian Reciprocity Treaty of 1854* (Baltimore, 1922); United States Tariff Commission, *Reciprocity and commercial treaties* (Washington, 1919); John W. Dafoe, *Clifford Sifton in relation to his times* (Toronto, 1931); Edward Porritt, *Sixty years of protection in Canada, 1846-1907* (London, 1908); *Trade and tariff relationships between Canada and the United States* (Report by joint Canada-United States Committee, maintained by Canadian Chamber of Commerce and Chamber of Commerce of the United States, 1934).

**Recollets.** The Order of Friars Minor Recollets or Recollects of St. Francis (O.F.M.), extinct since 1897, was one of the four branches constituting the Friars Minor of the Observance, who were separated from the Conventuals in 1517 by decree of Pope Leo X. The Recollet or Recollect monks, who retired in "recollection houses" in religious contemplation or thought, first made their appearance in France about the year 1570. The many difficulties they first encountered were rewarded in 1579 when the General of the Observatines granted them semi-autonomous custodies, and more particularly in the year 1612 when Pope Paul V finally conceded them their own provinces under an apostolical commissary. The Recollets soon became very conspicuous figures. The Order developed rapidly, adding recruits from all classes of society, and soon attained renown.

One of their most glorious titles is that of having been chosen as the first missionaries to be sent to Canada. Champlain (q.v.) himself, authorized by the King and with the sanction of Paul V, brought them over "à pied d'œuvre". The names of these pioneers of the Catholic faith were Fathers Denis Jamet, superior, Jean Dolbeau and Joseph Le Caron, and lay-brother

Pacifique Duplessis. In the month of June, 1615, they established themselves at Quebec, Tadoussac, Three Rivers, and Montreal, the new parish being placed under the patronage of the Immaculate Conception. In the month of August, they began their missionary work in Huronia. They were the first to establish schools in Quebec and Three Rivers. In 1625, the Recollets called to their assistance the Jesuits from Paris, offering them hospitality for a whole year and sharing with them the care of the Indian missions, an unselfish gesture of considerable bearing on the future. As early as 1619 we find them in Acadia, where they looked after the welfare of the settlers for a period of 30 years, and shared their labours with the Capuchins sent by Richelieu. Expelled from Quebec under the Kirke régime in 1629, the Recollets did not return when Quebec was restored by the treaty of St. Germain-en-Laye, three years later. During this period they had sent to Canada 18 missionaries, two of whom died in Quebec.

At the request of the people and of Intendant Talon (q.v.), they returned to Canada in 1670. From Quebec, Three Rivers, and Montreal they extended their activities to the Gaspé peninsula, Newfoundland, and Acadia, where they enjoyed many consolations, but also suffered considerable hardship. At times they served as chaplains to some of the discoverers, for instance to Cavelier de La Salle (q.v.) on the Mississippi. They established branches of the Third Order, thus grouping together their benefactors and other faithful disciples of St. Francis. They spared no pains in their endeavour to be of service to the French troops and Canadian soldiers. At the battle of Carillon they shared the honours of the day when Father Félix de Bérey, though wounded, saved one of the flags. We are indebted to Sagard (q.v.), Chrétien le Clerc (q.v.), Sixte le Tac (q.v.), Louis Hennepin (q.v.), and

Hyacinthe Lefèbvre for their historical contributions. And finally, they remained steadfast at their post in Acadia till the day of Le Grand Dérangement; and the memory of the Pieds-Nus— Recollets and Capuchins—will always be cherished among the Micmacs and white alike.

The history of the Recollets in Canada now is being written in Montreal and Paris. During the last thirty years, two able writers, the Rev. Fathers Odoric Jouve and Hugolin Lemay, O.F.M., have enriched Franciscan history with valuable contributions. Father Jouve has published Les Franciscans et le Canada (Quebec, 1915), Le Frère Didace Pelletier (Quebec, 1910), and Le Père Gabriel de La Ribourde (Quebec, 1912); and Father Hugolin Lemay has published L'Établissement des Recollects à Montréal (Montreal, 1911), L'Établissement des Recollects à Plaisance (Quebec, 1911), L'Établissement des Recollects à Percé (Quebec, 1911), Les Recollects missionaires en Acadie (Lévis, 1912), Le Père Joseph Denis (2 vols., Quebec, 1926), and a number of papers contributed to the Transactions of the Royal Society of Canada. Notable among these is a paper by Father Hugolin Lemay, Bibliographie des travaux édités ou imprimés en Europe sur les Récollets du Canada (Trans. Roy. Soc. Can., 1933).

**Red Bank,** a village in Northumberland county, New Brunswick, 12 miles from Newcastle. Pop. (1934), 250.

**Redbud,** a tree, also known as the Judas-tree, is a member of the Leguminosae family, and has many characters of the locust trees. One species (Cercis canadensis Linnaeus) occurs in the southern part of Ontario. Being a small tree with rose-pink to purple or red flowers, it is favoured for ornamental planting. The leaves are roundish heart-shaped, without teeth on the margin, and about three inches in diameter. The fruit is similar to that of black locust, but the pods are not borne on a central stalk, each having a stalk of its own. Redbud is of no importance for its wood, and is found only occasionally, being quite a rare tree now.

**Redcliff,** a town in the Medicine Hat district of Alberta, on the South Saskatchewan river, and on the Canadian Pacific Railway, 7 miles north-west of Medicine Hat. It is named after the red cliffs of the South Saskatchewan river. It has a glass factory, a foundry, brick plants, and a weekly newspaper (*Review*). Pop. (1931), 1,192.

**Red Cross Society.** The Canadian Red Cross Society was organized in 1896, as the first overseas branch of the British Red Cross. Until after the World War its activities were devoted to the care of the sick and wounded of armies at war and of victims of disasters. By the Treaty of Versailles all national Red Cross Societies were invited to assume the larger task of striving continuously to improve health, prevent disease, and mitigate suffering. Besides continuing its duty of caring for soldiers disabled by war service, the Red Cross in Canada originated and has maintained a number of activities directed towards the fulfilment of these purposes. For several years it financed courses of training for public health nurses in five universities, and subsidized many rural municipalities to ensure their employment. It devised the plan of establishing Red Cross outpost hospitals in pioneer districts, of which 42 are presently in operation. It has organized junior branches in Canadian schools, and through them has inspired two million children to live healthfully. It provides simple instruction in home nursing and nutrition, and it operates a seaport nursery in Halifax, where immigrant women and children are cared for on their arrival in Canada. The Society is organized in provincial divisions. The headquarters are in Toronto, and the National Commissioner is Dr. J. L. Biggar.

**Red Deer,** a city in Alberta, on the Red Deer river, and on the Canadian Pacific and Canadian National Railways; 95 miles north of Calgary and 98 miles south of Edmonton. The first settlement in the neighbourhood was at a ford of the Red Deer river, where the trail from Calgary to Edmonton crossed the river three miles west of the present site of Red Deer. This was known as Red Deer Crossing, a name soon abbreviated to Red Deer; and when the Calgary and Edmonton Railway reached the Red Deer river in 1891, the name was transferred to the settlement that grew up about the railway station. The city is in a mixed farming and cattle-raising district, and has grain elevators, creameries, bottling works, fruit and grocery warehouses, and a candy factory, as well as a provincial training school, a hospital, a convent, a court house, a weekly newspaper (*Advocate*), and a bi-weekly newspaper (*Optimist*). Pop. (1931), 2,344.

**Redemptorist Fathers.** The Order of the Most Holy Redeemer (commonly called The Redemptorists, or The Redemptorist Fathers, with C.SS.R. for their initials) was founded in 1732 at Scala, a small town near Naples, by St. Alphonsus de Liguori, a Neapolitan nobleman. The congregation was founded exclusively to preach popular missions. Teaching, except in its own preparatory colleges and seminaries, does not come within the scope of the congregation. Retreats to priests and religious communities in general are accepted, as also indoor or closed retreats to the clergy and laity. Of course, the apostolate of the pen is encouraged in a congregation founded by such a writer as St. Alphonsus.

The government of the congregation is monarchial. There is a superior general, called rector major, having his residence in Rome. He is elected for life by a general chapter, or meeting of superiors. Six consultors are appointed to advise the rector major in the government of the congregation. They hold office as long as the rector major holds his. A general procurator manages the temporal affairs of the congregation, and is its agent near the Holy See.

The congregation is now divided into 21 provinces and 18 vice-provinces, covering nearly all parts of the globe. Provincials and vice-provincials are appointed by the rector major for a term of three years. A father rector, assisted by two consultors, presides over each house in the province.

In North America, the congregation comprises four provinces, two in the United States, and two in Canada, the French-Canadian province of Ste. Anne de Beaupré and the English province of Toronto. (The National Shrine of Good St. Anne is in the care of the Redemptorists.) In all there are now 6,318 Redemptorists scattered in the 21 provinces and the 18 vice-provinces. Out of that number 3,253 are priests and 1,645 are lay-brothers. The rest is made up of clerical students and novices. In Canada, the congregation numbers 200 Fathers. The French-Canadian province of Ste. Anne de Beaupré has had a vice-province in Indo-China since 1925, where 15 Fathers are organizing mission work and training local recruits for the congregation.

The Redemptorist's life strikes a middle course between the purely active and the purely contemplative. "Apostles abroad and Carthusians at home" is the motto. The greatest devotion is fostered towards the Virgin Mary, the special patroness of the congregation; and particular devotion to the Blessed Sacrament, the Passion, and the Divine Infancy is a characteristic of the Redemptorists.

In 1787, the first Redemptorists crossed over the Alps and set foot in Poland. Thence, after untold troubles and persecutions, the congregation spread slowly but surely in Austria, Germany, Belgium, Holland, England, and the other countries of Europe. In 1832, the Redemptorists were seen for the first time in America. In 1879, they came from Belgium and settled down at the Shrine of Ste. Anne de Beaupré. This was the beginning of what has now developed into the prosperous provinces of Ste. Anne de Beaupré and Toronto.

Among the worthies of the congregation, besides St. Alphonsus, there are two canonized saints, St. Clement Hofbauer (d. 1820), who established the congregation on this side of the Alps, and the celebrated St. Gerard Majella (d. 1755), a lay-brother surnamed the Wonderworker. There are nine Venerables and twelve Servants of God, one of whom is a Canadian, Father Alfred Pampalon, who died at Ste. Anne de Beaupré in 1896. See Fr. Stebbing, *The Redemptorists* (London, 1924), and Fr. J. Byrne, *The Redemptorist centenaries* (Philadelphia, 1932).

**Redemptoristine Sisters.** The history of the Redemptoristine Nuns of the Order of the Most Holy Redeemer is closely connected with that of the Redemptorist Fathers (q.v.). Their common origin dates back to St. Alphonsus of Liguori, whom the church has solemnly recognized as the founder of the two branches of the Most Holy Redeemer. They are a cloistered order devoted to the apostolate of sacrifice and prayer; and were first established in Canada at Ste. Anne de Beaupré, in 1905.

**Redhead** (*Nyroca americana*), a wild duck belonging to the diving duck group (see **Duck**), which nests throughout the prairie region of Canada. Although it is classified with the more open-water species, it frequents the marshes and smaller bodies of water on migration. It occurs regularly in the east in the autumn and spring. Like most of the ducks favoured for food and sport, its numbers are decreasing. The male redhead has a reddish-brown head, and is dark on the back; the breast is black, and the remainder of the underparts is white. The female is dully coloured with brown and gray.

**Redistribution,** a familiar feature of Canadian political life, is the legislative process whereby the boundaries of electoral constituencies are re-arranged prior to an election, in such a way as to improve the chances of the party in power. The decennial census of the Dominion is generally cited as the excuse for redistribution, but that it is an excuse only is revealed by the fact that the number of voters in constituencies varies often in the ratio of one to five. Urban constituencies almost invariably have a much larger electorate than rural. The first outstanding example of the art of redistribution was the Redistribution Bill introduced into the Canadian parliament by Sir John Macdonald (q.v.) in 1882, when the boundaries of constituencies were manipulated in such a way as to "hive the Grits". The idea was derived from the United States, where it was known as the "gerrymander" a term derived from the name of Elbridge Gerry, who, when governor of Massachusetts in 1810, caused the voting districts of the state to be so altered that he was sure of re-election. Since 1882 the device has been frequently employed by Canadian politicians. When a party is in power that relies chiefly on the votes of rural constituencies, these are increased in number; but when a party is in power that relies on the votes of urban constituencies, these are increased.

**Red lake** is in the English river basin, north-west of lac Seul, in Patricia district of northern Ontario. The lake has an area of 69 square miles. Rich gold deposits were discovered on the shores of the lake in 1925 by 4 prospectors, the Howey brothers, George McNeeley, and W. F. Morgan. In 1926 Howey Gold Mines was incorporated; the company was placed on a profitable basis, and Howey became Canada's lowest-grade gold mine and its lowest-cost producer. A new departure at Red Lake was the use in mining development of aeroplanes, piloted by crack, war-time fliers. The town of Red Lake has now a population of about 2,500. See B. F. Townsley, *Mine-finders* (Toronto, 1935).

**Red Mulberry.** See **Mulberry.**

**Red Osier Dogwood.** See **Dogwood.**

**Redpath, Peter** (1821-1894), merchant and philanthropist, was born at Montreal, Lower Canada, on August 1, 1821, the son of John Redpath, a sugar manufacturer. He was educated in Montreal, studied business methods in England, and entered his father's sugar refinery. In 1864 he was appointed a member of the board of governors of McGill University; and his gifts to McGill University were on a princely scale. He endowed a chair of natural philosophy; he presented to the university a museum and a library building; and he made gifts to the library of much valuable historical material. He was also for some years president of the Montreal General Hospital. In 1879 he retired from business, and went to live in England. Here he died, at Chiselhurst Manor House, on February 1, 1894. In 1847 he married Grace, daughter of William Wood, of Bowden, Manchester, England. He left no children. See Sir J. W. Dawson, *Peter Redpath* (Montreal, 1894).

**Redpoll,** a name applied to certain small birds belonging to the family *Fringillidae*, to which belong also the sparrows, the finches, and the buntings. They are the North American representatives of the old world linnets. Redpolls are smaller than the common sparrow; they have small sharp bills, a dull crimson cap, a dark chin spot, and a streaked gray, brown, and white body plumage. Males have a rosy suffusion on the breast. These birds nest in the far north, visiting settled portions of Canada in the winter.

**Red river** rises near the sources of the Mississippi, in western Minnesota in about lat. 47° 7′ and long. 95° 25′, flows between the states of Minnesota and North Dakota, crosses the boundary into Manitoba, and enters lake Winnipeg at its southern end. The river's principal tributaries in the United States are the Sheyenne and the Red lake, and in Canada the Assiniboine, which enters the Red from the west at the city of Winnipeg. The Red is 665 miles long, of which 525 are in the United States. In the first 100 miles of its course it forms the line of connection between a multitude of small lakes. It was discovered by La Vérendrye (q.v.) or his sons in 1732-3, and subsequently became an important fur-trading area. After the establishment in 1812 of Selkirk's colony under the auspices of the Hudson's Bay Company, the valley of the Red became the scene of bitter strife between the colonists and the traders of the North West Company. The struggle was terminated by the amalgamation of the two companies in 1821. In 1870 the valley of the Red was again the scene of hostilities during the Riel rebellion which preceded the entry of Manitoba into the Dominion of Canada.

**Red River Colony.** See **Red River Settlement.**

**Red River Settlement,** a colony founded on the banks of the Red river, near the mouth of the Assiniboine river, by Lord Selkirk (q.v.) in 1811. Having obtained from the Hudson's Bay Company the grant of the district of Assiniboia, comprising 116,000 acres in the valleys of the Red and Assiniboine rivers, Selkirk collected a party of Scottish colonists, and sent them out by way of Hudson bay in the summer of 1811, under the leadership of Miles Macdonell (q.v.). This party, numbering about 90, reached the Red river in 1812; and a second, and smaller, party, sent out in 1812, reached the Red river in 1813. The colony received subsequent reinforcements in 1814, and especially in 1815, when a party of 100, under

Robert Semple (q.v.), arrived. From the first the colony encountered the hostility of the North West Company, which regarded Selkirk's colonizing project as a direct threat against its line of communications with the fur-bearing regions farther west. Numbers of the colonists were induced to desert, and received free transportation to Montreal; and every means was employed to intimidate the rest. Twice the settlement was broken up by the Nor'Westers. On June 19, 1816, the conflict culminated in the affair at Seven Oaks, in which Semple and twenty of his settlers were killed by the *bois brûlés* under Cuthbert Grant (q.v.). In 1817 the colony was re-established by Selkirk; and it became the nucleus of the first genuine settlement in western Canada. Until 1833, the settlement was administered by a governor and council appointed by Selkirk or his heirs; but from 1833 to 1870, it came under the council appointed by the Hudson's Bay Company for the northern department of Rupert's Land. Thereafter it became part of the province of Manitoba. See J. Halkett, *Statement respecting the Earl of Selkirk's settlement of Kildonan upon the Red river* (London, 1817); S. H. Wilcocke, *A narrative of occurrences in the Indian countries of North America* (London, 1817); A. Ross, *The Red river settlement* (London, 1856); J. J. Hargrave, *Red river* (Montreal, 1871); A. Begg, *The creation of Manitoba* (Toronto, 1871); R. G. MacBeth, *The Selkirk settlers in real life* (Toronto, 1897); G. Bryce, *The romantic settlement of Lord Selkirk's colonists* (Toronto, 1909); and L. A. Wood, *The Red river colony* (Toronto, 1915). See also **Kildonan.**

**Red River Rebellion.** See **North West Rebellions.**

**Redroot.** See **Amaranth.**

**Redstart** (*Setophaga ruticilla*), a member of the wood warbler family of birds, *Compsothlypidae*. It is considerably smaller than the common sparrow;

16

the male is black, marked with orange and white, and the female is greenish marked with yellow and white. The species is peculiar in possessing certain characters of the bill which approach those of the flycatchers. It is found throughout the forested part of Canada. The name redstart was applied to the species by the early settlers who were, apparently, reminded of an unrelated European bird, known as the redstart, because of certain markings on the tail. "Start" is from the Anglo-Saxon *steort*, meaning a tail.

**Red Trillium.** See **Wake Robin.**

**Redwing.** See **Blackbird.**

**Reed lake** is in northern Manitoba, near the head of the Grass river, between the 100th and 101st meridians of west longitude. The original name was Rood lake, the translation of the Cree Indian name. The lake has an area of 78 square miles.

**Reesor, David** (1823-1902), senator of Canada, was born at Markham, Upper Canada, on January 18, 1823, of German descent. He was the founder and for a number of years the editor, of the Markham *Economist*. In 1860 he was elected to represent the division of King's in the Legislative Council of Canada; and in 1867 he was summoned by royal proclamation to the Senate of Canada. He sat in the Senate until his death on April 27, 1902. He married Emily, daughter of Daniel Macdougall, and sister of the Hon. William Macdougall (q.v.); and by her he had one son and four daughters.

**Referendum,** a constitutional device whereby a question with which the legislature does not feel itself capable of dealing is referred to the electorate in a popular vote. With the analogous idea of the "initiative", it has been borrowed from the United States; and though the "initiative", by means of which legislation may be initiated by the electorate, has never formally found lodgment in Canadian constitutional practice, there have been a number of cases where the referendum has been resorted to, and many more where it has been advocated or demanded. In 1902, for instance, the Ross government in Ontario submitted the question of the prohibition of the sale of liquor to a direct vote of the people in a referendum; and it has been a common practice in municipal government in Canada to refer specific questions to the electors, especially at election time. It is clear, however, that both the referendum and the initiative are alien to the spirit of British parliamentary government. See W. B. Munro, *American influences on Canadian government* (Toronto, 1929).

**Reform Party.** See **Liberal Party.**

**Refrigeration.** When the production of certain Canadian foods exceeded the consumption at the place and time of production the problem of preservation had to be solved. During the decade from 1880 to 1890, several ice-cooled storage warehouses were erected, by A. A. Ayer at Montreal, by J. L. Grant at Ingersoll, by others at Stratford and London. The first cold storage warehouse in Canada to be equipped with mechanical refrigeration was in Montreal in 1894. Two years later the Dominion government offered a bonus of $100 to any creamery erecting a cold storage warehouse according to a specified air-circulating system. This was continued until 1931, when practically every creamery in Canada had complied with the conditions. Small mechanical refrigerating machines were soon available, and later came into general use when pasteurization was required. The next development came from a need to transport perishable foods from one part of the country to another. The dairy commissioner of Canada arranged with the railways for regular ice-car services for butter over stated routes. Eight such routes were operated in 1895, and in a few years 60 weekly cars were operating on a regular schedule.

Motor transport has of recent years caused a decline in this service. The first attempt to provide safer ocean transport for Canadian dairy products was in 1895, when ice-cooled insulated chambers were constructed in a sufficient number of steamships to provide a weekly service from Montreal to ports in the United Kingdom. In a few years all the new ships of the regular lines were fully equipped with refrigerated space. A system of inspection was inaugurated and maintained at ports of departure and landing. Reports of inspectors on condition of foods on arrival, on packing, on ventilation, on damage through handling, and on thermograph records were the basis of subsequent improvements.

The Cold Storage Act of 1907 provided for subsidies to encourage the erection of public cold storage warehouses. In 1934, out of a total of 562 warehouses in Canada, 66 were public and were receiving this subsidy.

Refrigeration has been of even greater value in the marketing and export of meat than of dairy products. To avoid the necessity of shipping live stock across the country and by water to outside markets, a complete system of preparation of meats has been developed by stockyards, slaughter houses, packing and refrigerated transport by rail and steamship. Thus livestock products have become one of the most profitable of Canada's resources.

To care for surplus stocks of fish at certain seasons large fish freezing warehouses were built at Prince Rupert, Charlottetown, and Saint John, and additions made to subsidized warehouses at other points on the Atlantic and Pacific coasts.

When experiments were tried for preserving and exporting fruits on the same principles, certain difficulties presented themselves. Here packers were dealing, not with prepared or preserved foods like meat, butter, or cheese, but with food in a living, growing state. At Grimsby a warehouse was erected for packing and shipping to distant points the more tender fruits, peaches, pears, tomatoes, and grapes. The first shipments were unsuccessful; the heat generated by the fruit itself counterbalanced the cooling power of ice, and the fruit in the middle of a package ripened too quickly and was not marketable on arrival. A precooler was devised to remedy this defect by reducing the temperature immediately after picking, and the process has now become effective for almost all fruits. Here too inspection plays an important part.

The economic value of refrigeration for Canadian products has been not only in the preservation of perishable foods and the increase of the length of time they can be used, but also in the variety of foods obtainable at all times. Safe and reliable transportation of products by rail and water has provided the markets with a uniform supply throughout the year and has tended to keep prices constant.

**Refuse, Disposal of.** Refuse may be classified as either sewage or garbage. In the pioneer days of Canada, the disposal of these presented few problems. They were either buried or burnt, or the garbage was fed to pigs. But with the growth of large urban communities, the problem of the disposal of refuse has become acute. Refuse that does not decay—such as ashes, broken glass and crockery, tin cans, paper, and other like materials—can still be buried, or "dumped" where ground has to be filled in. But garbage that does decay must be treated in reduction plants; and human waste must be carried off by sewerage systems. Sewerage systems were introduced into the larger urban centres in Canada nearly one hundred years ago; and all Canadian cities and most Canadian towns now have sewers to carry off both human waste and surplus water from the streets. But this has not proved everywhere a satisfactory solution, since it has resulted too often in the pollution of the water supply, and has been a fertile source of disease. In an increasing number of places the sewage is now treated in "disposal plants" so as to kill the germs contained in it; and it is then sold to farmers as fertilizer. Garbage collection and disposal was first entrusted in centres of population to private contractors; but the practice has now become almost universal in cities and towns to entrust its collection to paid scavengers, employed by the municipality. Allied to the task of garbage collection in most cities and towns is that of street-cleaning. This is done by paid servants of the municipality who flush the streets with water, or clean them with brooms and shovels, and cart away the refuse. The disposal of refuse has become, in the larger centres of population in Canada, one of the chief tasks of municipal government.

**Regent inlet.** See **Prince Regent inlet.**

**Regina,** the capital city of the province of Saskatchewan, is situated at an altitude of 1,885 feet, on the Canadian Pacific and Canadian Northern Railways, 357 miles west of Winnipeg, and about 100 miles north of the United States border. The word Regina is Latin for "queen", and commemorates Queen Victoria. The name was suggested in 1882 by Princess Louise, Duchess of Argyll, the Queen's daughter and wife of the governor-general. After the Canadian Pacific Railway was completed, it became expedient to remove the capital of the North West Territories from Battleford to a central point of the line. In 1882 it was announced by the lieutenant-governor that the crossing at Pile of Bones creek was to be the site of a new seat of government and headquarters of the Royal North West Mounted Police, whose chief station then was Fort Walsh. Waskana was the Sioux Indian name for "Pile of Bones", an accumulation of buffalo bones where pemmican had been made. At that time

the only promise of the present capital was a few tents pitched on the open prairie. The selection of Regina was severely criticized. On March 31, 1883, the Regina *Leader* said: "New buildings are rising. The railway traffic is increasing. Arrangements are in progress for digging a public well. Churches are about to rise. A citizen has been born in Regina and in time such an event will be no longer singular. The hotels are full. Around Regina for some 20 miles the land is taken up, and this is the reason why people have faith in the most maligned city the world ever saw." On the creation of the province of Saskatchewan in 1905, the first legislature of the province chose Regina as the capital, after Saskatoon, Prince Albert, and Moose Jaw all had advanced strong claims for that honour. The city was incorporated in 1903.

To-day Regina is a well-planned city of beautiful homes, with imposing government buildings. The Parliament Building occupies a splendid site, and the municipal buildings are ornamental. Regina is the western headquarters of the Royal Canadian Mounted Police. There are several fine parks. The public schools are modern, and the Regina College, Campion College, a provincial normal school, and a collegiate institute all combine to make the city an important educational centre. The city owns the industrial section, which was set aside for manufactories and warehouses, and where railway tracks were laid for the convenience of plants, factories, and stockyards. The largest distributing centre of farm machinery in Canada is here. There are also grain elevators, flour-mills, factories, meat-packing works, wire and steel works, a huge oil refinery, an abattoir, automobile works, paint, varnish, and glass plants. The *Leader-Post* and the *Daily Star* are the daily newspapers. Pop. (1931), 53,209. See M. Complin, *Floreat Regina* (Canadian Geographical Journal, 1934).

THE BUSINESS DISTRICT OF REGINA, SASKATCHEWAN

From the West

**Regina College,** a co-educational residential institution situated in the city of Regina, Saskatchewan, was founded in 1912 by the Methodist Church. In 1934 it became amalgamated with the provincial university and is now managed as the southern branch of the university, which is situated in Saskatoon. Since the amalgamation Regina College has given up all high school work. It is a junior college offering the first and second years of the Arts and Science course leading to the B.A. degree. There is also a Conservatory of Music and a School of Art. The total attendance for all departments is a little more than five hundred, with a total staff of thirty-one. Dr. E. W. Stapleford has been principal since 1915.

**Regiopolis College,** a Roman Catholic academic institution founded by Bishop Macdonell (q.v.) in Kingston, Upper Canada, in 1837. It was at first merely "a Roman Catholic Seminary"; but in 1866 an Act was passed by the parliament of United Canada conferring university powers on Regiopolis College. In 1869, however, the legislature of Ontario withdrew the annual grant which it had made for two years to the college; and the college then succumbed to its financial difficulties. See *The universities of Canada, their history and organization* (Toronto, 1896).

**Reid, James** (1769-1848), chief justice, was born in Scotland in 1769, and came to Canada about 1788. He studied law in the office of John Reid, clerk of the court of common pleas at Montreal, and was called to the bar of Lower Canada in 1794. In 1807 he was appointed a judge of the court of King's Bench at Montreal; and in 1825 he became chief justice of this court. In June, 1838, he became a member of the Executive Council of Lower Canada; but a few months later he resigned both from the Council and from the bench, on pension. He died at Montreal on January 19, 1848. See F. J. Audet, *James Reid* (Les Annales, 1924).

**Reid, John Dowsley** (1859-1929), minister of customs for Canada (1911-21), was born at Prescott, Ontario, on January 1, 1859, the son of John Reid. He was educated at Queen's University, Kingston (M.D., C.M., 1890), but practised medicine for only a short time, and became eventually the manager of the Imperial Starch Company, Prescott. From 1891 to 1921 he represented Grenville in the Canadian House of Commons; and he was minister of customs in the Borden cabinet from 1911 to 1917, and minister of railways and canals from 1917 to 1921. In 1921 he was appointed to the Senate of Canada. He died at Prescott on August 26, 1929. In 1899 he married Ephie, daughter of John Labatt, of Hamilton, Ontario; and by her he had one son and one daughter.

**Reid, Mary Augusta,** *née* **Hiester** (1854-1921), painter, was born at Reading, Pennsylvania, in 1854, the daughter of Dr. Hiester. In 1885 she married George A. Reid, a Canadian artist, and in 1886 she came to Canada. She had studied painting in Philadelphia and in Paris, France; and in 1888 she was elected a member of the Ontario Society of Artists. In 1896 she became an associate of the Royal Canadian Academy. Beginning as a painter of flowers and still life, she achieved success also in landscapes, gardens, interiors, and mural decoration. She died at Toronto on October 4, 1921. A memorial exhibition of her work was held in Toronto after her death.

**Reid, Sir Robert Gillespie** (1842-1908), contractor and financier, was born at Coupar Angus, Perthshire, Scotland, in 1842. He became a contractor, and in 1865 went to Australia, where he engaged in gold mining and the construction of public works. In 1871 he came to Canada, and here he made a reputation first as a bridge-builder. He built the international bridge across the Niagara river, the bridge at Sault Ste. Marie, and the

Lachine bridge, at Montreal, as well as the international bridge across the Rio Grande between Mexico and Texas and the bridges across the Colorado at Austin, Texas, and across the Delaware at the famous water gap in Pennsylvania. He also took part in the building of the Canadian Pacific Railway; and the Jackfish Bay section of this railway, north of lake Superior, was his work. In 1890 he transferred his energies to Newfoundland, and here he engaged in railway-building, in the operation of telegraphs and steamships, and the exploitation of natural resources on a scale which amounted to the acquisition by him of the "whole realizable assets" of the island. In 1901 he became president of the "Reid-Newfoundland Company"; but his health broke down under the strain of his labours, and during his later years his work was carried on by his sons. He died at Montreal on June 3, 1908. In 1865 he married Harriet Duff; and by her he had three sons and one daughter. In 1907 he was created a knight bachelor.

**Reiffenstein, John C.** (1784?-1840), soldier and merchant, was born at Frankfort-on-the-Main, Germany, about 1784. He entered the British army, and came to Halifax, Nova Scotia, about 1806 as ensign and adjutant in the 98th Regiment. He was appointed a staff adjutant in 1812, and he saw service during the War of 1812 at Miami, Fort Stephenson, and at Moraviantown. It was he who brought the report of Procter's defeat at Moraviantown to headquarters. After the war he resigned from the army, and became a prominent merchant in Quebec. He died in 1840. In 1807 he married in Halifax a Miss Carr; and by her he had several children. See B. Sulte, *Mélanges historiques*, vol. xiv (Montreal, 1928).

**Reindeer Industry.** In 1929 the Canadian government entered into an agreement with the Lomen Reindeer Corporation, which had been successful in introducing the reindeer into Alaska, to deliver a herd of 3,000 reindeer at the delta of the Mackenzie river. The trek, which began at Buckland point on Kotzebue sound in western Alaska, and ended in the Kittigazuit peninsula in the Mackenzie district of the North West Territories, about 40 miles east of the Mackenzie river, took five years; but it was at last brought to a successful conclusion, and it is hoped that the herd will form the nucleus of an abundant food supply for the Eskimo, whose food supplies are now being threatened with exhaustion. It is possible also that as the herd multiplies, and as new herds are established, the reindeer may become a source of commercial profit. See Max Miller, *The great trek* (Garden City, New York, 1935), *Introduction of reindeer into Canada* (Geographical Journal, 1933), and J. Russell Smith, *The reindeer industry in America* (Scottish Geographical Magazine, 1924).

**Reindeer lake** is on the boundary between northern Saskatchewan and northern Manitoba, between the 56th and 58th parallels of north latitude. It is connected by a serpentine strait with lake Wollaston towards the north, and on the south it empties into the Churchill river. The name is a translation of the Indian. The lake is very deep, and its waters are remarkably clear. It has an area of 1,765 square miles, of which 245 are in Manitoba and 1,520 in Saskatchewan.

**Religious History.** See **History, Religious.**

**Religious of the Sacred Heart of Jesus.** See **Society of the Sacred Heart of Jesus.**

**Remembrance Day.** See **Armistice Day.**

**Rémy, Daniel de, Sieur de Courcelle.** See **Courcelle, Daniel de Rémy, Sieur de.**

**Renaud, Emiliano** (1875-1932), pianist and composer, was born at St. Jean de Matha, Quebec, on June 26,

1875. He studied music in Montreal, Vienna, and Berlin; and in 1904 he returned to Montreal, where, with an interval spent in the United States, he lived until his death on October 3, 1932. He was the composer of a large number of musical works, chiefly concert pieces. See Sœurs de Ste. Anne, *Dictionnaire biographique des musiciens canadiens* (Lachine, Quebec, 1935).

**Renfrew,** a county in eastern Ontario, is bounded on the west by Nipissing and Hastings counties, on the south by Addington, Frontenac, and Lanark counties, and on the north-east by the Ottawa river; and a long narrow strip runs north-west along the Ottawa river. It is called after Renfrewshire in Scotland. Most of the early settlers came from the Highlands of Scotland, and engaged at first mainly in lumbering. The main body of the county is about 40 by 40 miles, and the narrow tip runs for about 45 miles along the Ottawa river to the north-west. The county town is Pembroke. Pop. (1931), 52,227.

**Renfrew,** a town in Renfrew county, Ontario, on the Bonnechère river, 8 miles from its confluence with the Ottawa river, and on the Canadian National and Canadian Pacific Railways, 65 miles west of Ottawa. The town takes its name from the county, which was named after Renfrewshire, in Scotland. Renfrew has all the modern municipal facilities. The municipality owns a large power plant. The principal occupations of the inhabitants are in creameries, flour mills, woollen mills, blanket factories, and making refrigerators. The iron, mica, and graphite mines in the vicinity are of economic importance. Renfrew has several churches, a collegiate institute, a vocational school, a kindergarten school, public and separate schools, a public library, a hospital, and good hotels. It has a weekly newspaper (*Mercury*). Pop. (1931), 5,296.

**Repentigny,** a village in L'Assomption county, Quebec, on the north shore of the St. Lawrence, 3 miles south of St. Paul l'Ermite, a station on the Canadian National Railway. It is a summer resort. Pop. (1934), 600.

**Reptiles.** See **Snakes, Turtles,** and **Lizards.**

**Reservation of Bills.** See **Disallowance.**

**Reserve,** a coal-mining town in Cape Breton county, Nova Scotia, 6 miles from Glace Bay. When the General Mining Association owned all the coal mines in Cape Breton county, the company's operations were confined at first to Pictou and Sydney Mines, and the coal-seams outside of Glace Bay were held "in reserve". The settlement at this place came therefore to be known as "Reserve Mines", and latterly "Reserve". The nearest railway station is at Dominion, on the Sydney and Louisbourg Railway. Pop. (1934), 2,200.

**Resolution.** See **Fort Resolution.**

**Resolution island** is a small island in the entrance to Hudson strait, off Baffin land, in the Franklin district of the North West Territories. The island was named by Sir Thomas Button (q.v.) after his vessel, when in 1612 he explored the south-western portion of Hudson bay. It is about 36 miles long, and lies between lat. 61° to 62° and long. 65°.

**Resplendent mountain** is in the Cariboo district of British Columbia, south-east of mount Robson, in Mount Robson Park. The name is descriptive. It is in lat. 53° 05', long. 119° 07', and has an altitude of 11,240 feet.

**Responsible government,** the term by which parliamentary government, or that form of government under which the executive is responsible to the legislature, is known in Canada. See A. B. Keith, *Responsible government in the Dominions* (rev. ed., 2 vols., Oxford, 1927), and Rosa W. Langstone, *Responsible government in Canada* (London, 1931). See also **Government** and **History, Constitutional.**

**Restigouche,** a county in northern New Brunswick, bordering on the Restigouche river and the bay of Chaleur, and bounded on the south by Madawaska, Victoria, Northumberland, and Gloucester counties. It was created a county in 1837, and was named after the Restigouche river, which is the largest of the many streams that drain its mountainous and heavily forested area. Its northern boundary is traversed by the Canadian National Railway. Chief town, Dalhousie. Pop. (1931), 29,859.

**Restigouche,** a village in Bonaventure county, Quebec, on the Restigouche river, 2 miles from Cross Point station, on the Quebec Oriental Railway. The name is of Micmac origin, but its significance is uncertain. The village is the chief settlement of the remnants of the Micmac tribe; and a mission for the Micmac has existed there since 1745. The population, partly white and partly Indian, is engaged in farming and lumbering; and the village has an important saw-mill. Pop. (1934), 300. See Fr. Pacifique, *Ristigouche* (Bulletin de la Société de Géographie de Québec, 1925-7).

**Restigouche river** rises in Madawaska county, New Brunswick, flows in a north-easterly direction across Restigouche county, and empties into Chaleur bay; during the last part of its course it forms the boundary between Quebec and New Brunswick. Cartier (q.v.) in 1534 explored Chaleur bay to its head, although he did not actually ascend the river. After 1750 settlers come in considerable numbers on the Quebec side of the river's mouth, and founded Petit Rochelle. This was destroyed in 1760 by an English fleet after they had vanquished a French fleet in the river's mouth. The Restigouche is 200 miles in length, 3 miles wide at its mouth, and drains a fertile and well-timbered area of 5,000 square miles. Its principal tributaries are the Matapedia, Patapedia, Kedgwick, and Upsalquitch. The tide flows up the Restigouche for 24 miles, of which 18 are navigable for large ships. It is one of the finest salmon rivers in the world. Fish-breeding operations are carried on on the Restigouche, opposite the mouth of the Matapedia. Good salmon-fishing may also be enjoyed on the Upsalquitch. The scenery in the course of the Restigouche is grand and beautiful, particularly in the part where it passes through the mountainous country in which rise the great streams of New Brunswick and those of the United States emptying into the Atlantic ocean. The principal towns on its banks are Dalhousie at its mouth and Campbellton at the head of navigation.

**Reston,** a village in Manitoba, on the Canadian Pacific Railway, 189 miles west of Winnipeg. It was named in 1890 after Reston, in Berwickshire, Scotland. The chief industries are grain-growing and stock-raising; and it has a weekly newspaper (*Recorder*). Pop. (1934), 650.

**Revelstoke,** a city in British Columbia, on the Columbia river, 380 miles north-east of Vancouver, is in the district of Kootenay, and is served by the Canadian Pacific Railway, of which it is a divisional point between Calgary and Vancouver. The name of the city commemorates the first Lord Revelstoke, head of the British banking firm of Baring Brothers, who took a considerable part of the first bond issue of the Canadian Pacific Railway. The name was first applied to the railway station in 1886. The city has four churches, a hospital, a library, and public and high schools. There is an artificial-ice plant, a saw-mill, and a brewery. The neighbourhood is a prominent tourist centre, with fishing and big game hunting. A fine scenic road winds up mount Revelstoke to 5,000 feet above the city. On the summit is a natural flower garden of rare beauty, and the scenery is magnificent. Pop. (1931), 2,736.

**Revelstoke National Park** is the westernmost of the national parks of Canada. It is in British Columbia, in the valley of the Columbia river; and its centre of administration is the town of Revelstoke. Mount Revelstoke, 7,000 feet high, behind the town is in the heart of the park; and on the top of this mountain is a level park-like plateau of over 2,000 acres, from which magnificent vistas may be had of the Columbia and Illecillewaet valleys. The total area of the park is about 100 square miles. It was dedicated by the Prince of Wales (later King Edward VIII) in 1919.

**Revolutionary War.** See **War of the American Revolution.**

**Rexton,** a village in Kent county, New Brunswick, on the Kent Northern Railway, and on the Richibucto river, 3 miles south of Richibucto. It was formerly known as Kingston; but the name was changed to Rexton to distinguish it from Kingston in King's county Pop. (1934), 600.

**Rho, Joseph Adolphe** (1835-1905), artist, was born at Gentilly, Lower Canada, on April 1, 1835, the son of Alexis Rho and Herménégilde St. Germain. Little is known of his early years; but in middle age he acquired a reputation as a sculptor and painter of religious subjects. He also painted portraits. He died at Bécancour, Quebec, on August 6, 1905. He was twice married; and by his first wife he had seven children. See G. Bellerive, *Artistes-peintres canadiens-français* (Quebec, 1925).

**Rhodium,** a whitish-gray hard metal belonging in the platinum group. When pure it is not acted upon by acids, but when alloyed with other metals it may be dissolved in aquaregia. It is employed in electroplating, and when alloyed with platinum it is used in windings in certain types of electric furnaces. Canadian production is obtained from the nickel-copper ores of Sudbury.

**Rhyolite,** a volcanic rock either porphyritic or felsitic in texture. The phenocrysts are usually quartz and orthoclase, and the ground mass may be either crystalline or glassy. The name comes from the Greek word indicating "to flow", and refers to the flow structure frequently seen in this rock.

**Rice.** See **Wild Rice.**

**Rice lake** is in Northumberland county, Ontario, north of Cobourg. It is about 15 miles from lake Ontario and lies nearly south-west and north-east. From the north the river Otonabee, flowing from a chain of lakes, empties into Rice lake, which is drained into the bay of Quinte by the Trent river. This route was followed by Champlain (q.v.) in 1615 in his journey with the Hurons to attack the Iroquois. The name of the lake is derived from the wild rice which grows upon its shore. It is 25 miles long, and 4 or 5 miles wide.

**Richard, Edouard** (1844-1904), historian, was born at Princeville, Lower Canada, on March 14, 1844, the son of the Hon. Louis Richard and Hermine Prince. He was educated at the College of Nicolet and at McGill University, and was called to the bar in Quebec in 1868. For seven years he practised law in Arthabaskaville, Quebec, in partnership with Sir Wilfrid Laurier (q.v.); and from 1872 to 1878 he represented Megantic in the Canadian House of Commons. From 1878 to 1883 he was sheriff of the North West Territories; and for a number of years thereafter he lived in Winnipeg. He devoted much time to the study of the history of the Acadians, and in 1895 he published two volumes of his work on *Acadia.* A French translation of this work was published by H. d'Arles in three volumes in 1916-21. In 1897 he was employed by the Canadian government to undertake historical research in Paris, France, the results of which were published in the Canadian Archives Reports for 1899,

1904, and 1905. He died at Battleford, North West Territories, on March 27, 1904. In 1896 he was elected a fellow of the Royal Society of Canada, and was made a Litt.D. of Laval University.

**Richard,** a village in Saskatchewan, on the Shellbrook branch of the Canadian National Railway, 82 miles southeast of Battleford. Pop. (1934), 250.

**Richards, Albert Norton** (1822-1897), lieutenant-governor of British Columbia (1876-81), was born at Brockville, Upper Canada, on December 8, 1822, the youngest son of Stephen Richards and Phoebe Buell. He was educated at the district grammar school, and was called to the bar of Upper Canada in 1848 (Q.C., 1863). He represented South Leeds in the Legislative Assembly of Canada from 1863 to 1864, and in the Canadian House of Commons from 1872 to 1874; and from December, 1863, to January, 1864, he was solicitor-general for Upper Canada in the Sandfield Macdonald administration. In 1869 he was appointed attorney-general of Manitoba, and accompanied the Hon. William McDougall (q.v.) in his abortive attempt to assume the government of Manitoba. He then went to British Columbia, and in 1871 was called to the bar in that province. For several years he was legal agent of the Dominion government in British Columbia; and in 1876 he was appointed lieutenant-governor of the province. His period of office terminated in 1881; and he then retired to private life. He died at Victoria, British Columbia, on March 6, 1897. He married (1) in 1849 Frances (d. 1853), daughter of Benjamin Chaffey, of Somersetshire, England; and (2) in 1854 Ellen Chaffey, daughter of John Cheslett, of Somersetshire.

**Richards, Stephen** (1820-1894), lawyer and politician, was born at Brockville, Upper Canada, in 1820, the second son of Stephen Richards and Phoebe Buell. He was educated at the Johnstown district grammar school and

at Potsdam Academy, New York; and was called to the bar of Upper Canada in 1844 (Q.C., 1858). From 1867 to 1875 he represented Niagara in the Legislative Assembly of Ontario; and from 1867 to 1871 he was first commissioner of crown lands and then provincial secretary in the Sandfield Macdonald administration in Ontario. From 1876 to 1879 he was treasurer of the Law Society of Upper Canada. He died at Toronto on October 4, 1894, and was buried in Brockville. He was married to Susan, daughter of Benjamin Chaffey, of Somersetshire, England.

**Richards, Sir William Buell** (1815-1889), chief justice of the Supreme Court of Canada (1875-9), was born at Brockville, Upper Canada, on May 2, 1815, the eldest son of Stephen Richards and Phoebe Buell. He was educated at the Johnstown district grammar school and at Potsdam Academy, New York; and was called to the bar of Upper Canada in 1837 (Q.C., 1850). From 1848 to 1853 he represented Leeds in the Legislative Assembly of Canada; and from 1851 to 1853 he was attorney-general for Upper Canada in the Hincks-Baldwin administration. In 1853 he was appointed a puisne judge of the court of Common Pleas in Upper Canada; and in 1873 he became chief justice of this court. In 1875, when the Supreme Court of Canada was formed, he became its first chief justice; and from July to October, 1876, he was deputy governor of Canada, during the absence of Lord Dufferin (q.v.) in British Columbia. He retired from the bench in 1879; and he died at Ottawa on January 26, 1889. In 1846 he married Deborah Catharine (d. 1869), daughter of John Muirhead, of Niagara. He was created a knight bachelor in 1877; and in 1885 he was awarded the Confederation medal.

**Richard's Landing,** a village in the Algoma district, Ontario, on St. Josephs island, 25 miles south-east of Sault Ste. Marie. Pop. (1934), 400.

Richards, mount, is in Alberta, in lat. 49° 01' and long. 113° 56'. It is named after Captain (later Admiral) G. H. Richards, R.N., second commissioner on the British Boundary Commission, Pacific to the Rockies, who made hydrographic surveys of the British Columbia coast in 1856-63.

Richards, mount, is in the Somenos district of Vancouver Island, British Columbia. It is in lat. 48° 51', long. 123° 40', and has an altitude of 1,100 feet. It is named after Captain (later Admiral) G. H. Richards, R.N., second commissioner in the British Boundary Commission, Pacific to the Rockies, who made hydrographic surveys of the British Columbia coast in 1856-63.

Richardson, Hugh (1826-1913), administrator of the North West Territories, was born at London, Upper Canada, in 1826, the son of Richard Richardson and Elizabeth Sara Miller. He studied law, and was admitted to the bar of Upper Canada in 1847. Later, he went to the West, and became legal adviser of the lieutenant-governor of the North West Territories from 1876 to 1887. From 1887 to 1903 he was one of the judges of the Supreme Court of the North West Territories; and from 1897 to 1898 he was administrator of the North West Territories. He died at Ottawa on July 15, 1913.

Richardson, James (1791-1875), bishop of the Methodist Episcopal Church in Canada (1858-75), was born at Kingston, Upper Canada, on January 29, 1791, the son of Captain James Richardson, of the provincial marine. He served in the provincial marine during the War of 1812, and lost an arm at Sackett's Harbour. In 1818 he joined the Methodist Episcopal Church, and became a local preacher. In 1824 he became an itinerant minister; in 1832 he was appointed editor of the *Christian Guardian;* and in 1858 he was elected bishop of the Methodist Episcopal Church of Canada. He died at Clover Hill, Toronto, on March 9, 1875. In 1813 he married Rebecca Dennis, of Kingston; and by her he had several children. See T. Webster, *Life of Rev. James Richardson* (Toronto, 1876).

Richardson, John (1755?-1831), merchant and executive councillor of Lower Canada, was born at Portsoy, Banffshire, Scotland, about 1755, the son of John Richardson and a daughter of George Phyn, of the Corse of Monelly. He was thus, through his mother, a first cousin of both James Phyn (q.v.) and John Forsyth (q.v.). He came to America in 1773, and entered the employ of Phyn and Ellice at Schenectady. During the American Revolution he saw service on a privateer. In 1787 he removed to Canada, and entered the employ of Robert Ellice and Co. This firm, however, was dissolved in 1790; and Richardson became a partner in its successor, which was known as Forsyth, Richardson and Co. This firm became one of the firms that supplied the XY Company; and on the union of the XY and North West Companies in 1804, its members became partners in the North West Company. He represented Montreal in the Legislative Assembly of Lower Canada from 1792 to 1796, and from 1804 to 1808; in 1804 he was appointed a member of the Executive Council of the province; and in 1816, a member of the Legislative Council. In 1817 he was one of the founders of the Bank of Montreal. He died at Montreal on May 18, 1831. For a fuller account of his life, see Adam Shortt, *The Hon. John Richardson* (Journal of the Canadian Bankers' Association, 1921). Some of his letters have been published by E. A. Cruikshank in the *Papers and Records* of the Ontario Historical Society, 1905.

Richardson, Sir John (1787-1865), explorer and author, was born at Nith Place, Dumfries, Scotland, on November 5, 1787. He was educated at Edinburgh University (M.D., 1816); and in 1807 he qualified as a member of the Royal

College of Surgeons. From 1807 to 1815 he served as a naval surgeon in the Napoleonic wars; but in 1815 went on half-pay. He accompanied Sir John Franklin (q.v.) on his journeys of discovery in north-western America in 1819-22 and in 1825-7; and on the latter occasion, he was in charge of the party that explored the shores of the Arctic ocean from the mouth of the Mackenzie to the mouth of the Coppermine. He contributed the natural history notes to Franklin's *Narrative* of his first expedition, and an account of his discoveries, as well as other matters, to Franklin's *Narrative* of his second expedition. In 1848, when it was decided to send a search expedition after that of Franklin, he was appointed to command it, with Dr. John Rae (q.v.) as second-in-command; but he returned to England in 1849, leaving Rae in charge. He died at Grasmere, England, on June 5, 1865. He was elected a fellow of the Royal Society in 1825, and he was knighted in 1846. Besides many scientific publications, he was the author of *An Arctic searching expedition* (2 vols., London, 1851). See Rev. J. McIlraith, *Life of Sir John Richardson* (London, 1868).

**Richardson, John** (1796-1852), soldier and author, was born at Queenston, Upper Canada, on October 4, 1796, the eldest son of Dr. Robert Richardson and Madeleine, daughter of Col. John Askin, of Detroit. He was educated at Detroit and Amherstburg. He served as a cadet during the earlier part of the War of 1812, but was taken prisoner at Moraviantown in 1813, and spent a year in captivity in the United States. He then obtained a commission in the British army, and went to England. In 1818 he was placed on half pay; and he lived in London until 1834, devoting part of his time to literary work. From 1834 to 1837 he served with the British Auxiliary Legion in Spain, attaining his majority, and winning the cross of the military order of St. Ferdinand. In 1838 he returned to Canada; and in 1840 he settled at Brockville, Upper Canada. Here he edited successively *The New Era, or Canadian Chronicle* (1840-2) and *The Canadian Loyalist* (1843-4). In 1845 he was appointed superintendent of police on the Welland canal; but this post was abolished in 1846. For several years he lived in Montreal; and about 1850 he went to New York. Here he died, in lonely poverty, on May 12, 1852. About 1830 he married in England a wife whose Christian names were Maria Caroline; she died at St. Catharines, Canada West, on August 16, 1845.

As an author, Richardson tried his hand at various types of literature. His first publication was a poem, *Tecumseh, or The warrior of the west* (London, 1828). He then wrote several works of fiction, *Écarté, or The salons of Paris* (3 vols., London, 1829), *Kensington gardens in 1830* (London, 1830), *Wacousta, or The prophecy: A tale of the Canadas* (3 vols., London, 1832), and *The Canadian brothers, or The prophecy fulfilled* (2 vols., Montreal, 1840), the latter republished under the title *Matilda Montgomerie* (New York, 1851). His most valuable works, however, were autobiographical and historical: *Movements of the British Legion* (London, 1837), *Personal memoirs* (Montreal, 1838), *The war of 1812* (Brockville, 1842; new ed., by A. C. Casselman, Toronto, 1902), *Eight years in Canada* (Montreal, 1847), and *The Guards in Canada* (Montreal, 1848). After going to New York he published a number of cheap novels, *Hardscrabble* (New York, 1850), *Wau-nan-gee, or The massacre of Chicago* (New York, 1850), *The monk knight of St. John* (New York, 1850), and *Westbrook, or The outlaw* (New York, n.d.). An anonymous article published by him in 1849, entitled *A trip to Walpole island and Port Sarnia*, has been republished, with notes, by A. H. U. Colquhoun (Toronto, 1923). See W. R. Riddell, *John Richardson* (Toronto, 1923), and A. C. Casselmann (ed.),

*Richardson's War of 1812* ('Toronto, 1902).

**Richardson, Robert Lorne** (1860-1921), journalist and author, was born at Balderson, Lanark county, Ontario, on June 2, 1860, the son of Joseph Richardson and Harriet Thompson. In 1882 he went to Winnipeg, and in 1889 he became the founder and editor of the Winnipeg *Tribune*. From 1896 to 1900 he represented Lisgar in the Canadian House of Commons. He died at Winnipeg on November 6, 1921. He was the author of two novels, *Colin of the ninth concession* (Toronto, 1903), and *The Camerons of Bruce* ('Toronto, 1906).

**Richardson, mount,** is in Alberta, north-east of Lake Louise railway station in the Rocky mountains. It is named after Sir John Richardson (1787-1866), the surgeon and naturalist.

**Richelieu,** a county in Quebec, bounded on the north by the river St. Lawrence, on the west by Verchères county, on the south by St. Hyacinthe county, and on the east by Yamaska county. It is watered by the Richelieu river, after which it is named. County town, Sorel. Pop. (1931), 21,483.

**Richelieu,** a village in Rouville county, Quebec, on the Richelieu river, and on the Central Vermont Railway, 10 miles from St. John, and half a mile from Chambly Canton. Pop. (1931), 524.

**Richelieu river** rises in the state of Vermont, but assumes the appearance of a river only after flowing out of lake Champlain, which is on the boundary between Quebec and the United States. It flows into the St. Lawrence at lake St. Peter. In 1609 Champlain (q.v.) ascended the river to attack the Iroquois, and in 1642 it was named by Governor Montmagny (q.v.) after Cardinal Richelieu (1585-1642). Despite the erection of various French forts along the river, it served as the route by which both French and English colonists repeatedly attacked each other.

In 1759-60 Amherst's army advanced up the river to Montreal, and in 1775 Ethan Allen and his American revolutionaries followed the same route. In 1814 an invading American force was repulsed at Lacolle mill on the Richelieu. The river is about 80 miles long, and the area of its basin within the province of Quebec is 1,450 square miles. It is broader and more rapid in the former than in the latter part of its course, and expands near its centre into the basin of Chambly. The Richelieu forms an important part of the navigation between the St. Lawrence and Hudson rivers, with the latter of which it is connected by the Chambly canal, lake Champlain, and the Champlain canal. The valley of the river is one of the most beautiful and most fertile in the province of Quebec. See Arthur H. Moore, *The valley of the Richelieu* (St. Johns, Quebec, 1929), and E. Goulet, *La région du Richelieu* (École des Hautes Études de Montréal: Études économiques, vol. v, Montreal, 1935).

**Richey, Matthew** (1803-1883), Methodist preacher, was born in Ramelton, in the north of Ireland, on May 25, 1803. His parents were Presbyterians, but at the age of fourteen he became converted to Methodism, and shortly afterward sailed for Canada. He was ordained a minister of the Methodist Church in 1825, and in 1836 he was appointed principal of Upper Canada Academy in Cobourg, Upper Canada. From 1841 to 1843 he was in Toronto, and thence he was moved successively to Kingston and Montreal. In 1849 he was appointed acting president of the Canada Methodist Conference, and in 1851 president. In 1856 he was chosen president of the "Methodist Conference of Eastern British America". He died in Halifax, Nova Scotia, on October 24, 1883. He published *The internal witness of the Spirit the common privilege of Christian believers* (Charlottetown, 1829); *Sermon preached for the benefit of the poor* (Halifax, 1833); *Sermon on the* *death of the Rev. William McDonald* (Halifax, 1834); *Short and scriptural method with Antipedo-baptists* (Halifax); *Memoir of the late Rev. William Black* (Halifax, 1839); *Sermons delivered on various occasions* (Toronto, 1840); *Two letters addressed to the "Church" exposing the intolerance and bigotry of that journal* (Toronto, 1843); *An address at the inauguration of the Young Men's Christian Association* (Halifax, 1854); *Britain's refuge, a discourse on the fall of Sebastopol* (Halifax, 1855); *Sermon on the death of Rev. Wm. Bennett* (Halifax, 1858); *Sermon on the death of Rev. W. Croscombe* (Halifax, 1860); and *Plea for the confederation of the colonies of British North America* (Charlottetown, 1867).

**Richey, Matthew Henry** (1828-1911), lieutenant-governor of Nova Scotia (1883-8), was born at Windsor, Nova Scotia, on June 10, 1828, the eldest son of the Rev. Matthew Richey (q.v.) and Louisa Matilda Nicholls. He was educated at the College School, Windsor, at Upper Canada College, and elsewhere, and was called to the bar in 1850 (Q.C., 1873). He was elected to the city council of Halifax in 1858, and held the office of mayor from 1864 to 1867, and from 1875 to 1878. In 1878 he was returned to the Canadian House of Commons in the Conservative interest for Halifax city and county, and was re-elected in 1882. On July 4, 1883, he was appointed lieutenant-governor of Nova Scotia, and his term of office lasted until 1888. He died in Halifax on February 21, 1911. In June, 1854, he married Sarah Lavina, daughter of the Hon. J. H. Anderson. For several years he was a governor of Dalhousie College; and he was president of the Nova Scotia was president of the Nova Scotia Historical Society (1893-5). In 1884 he received the honorary degree of D.C.L. from Mount Allison University.

**Richibucto,** a village in Kent county, New Brunswick, on the Richibucto river, and on the Kent Northern Railway, 40 miles from Chatham. It is named after the Richibucto river, near the mouth of which it is situated. The name is of Micmac origin, but its aboriginal form is uncertain. One authority gives *Lichibouktouck*, meaning "river which enters the woods". The chief industries are lumbering, farming, and fishing; and it has a harbour, with government wharf and two private wharves. Pop. (1934), 1,200.

**Richibucto river** rises in Kent county, New Brunswick, and flows north-west into the gulf of St. Lawrence, near the north-west entrance into Northumberland strait. The name is probably a Micmac word meaning "river which enters the woods". This district was extensively settled by Acadians both before and after the expulsion of 1755. The tide flows 25 miles up the mouth of the river, which is navigable for small vessels for a distance of 15 miles.

**Richmond, Charles Gordon Lennox, fourth Duke of** (1764-1819), governor-general of Canada (1818-19), was born in 1764, the only son of Lord George Henry Lennox and Louisa, daughter of the fourth Marquis of Lothian. From 1790 to 1806 he represented Sussex in the British House of Commons; and in 1806 he succeeded his uncle in the dukedom. From 1807 to 1813 he was lord-lieutenant of Ireland; and in 1818 he was appointed governor-general of Canada. He died of hydrophobia, contracted from the bite of a pet fox, near Richmond, Upper Canada, on August 28, 1819. In 1789 he married Lady Charlotte, daughter of Alexander, fourth Duke of Gordon; and by her he had several children. See E. A. Cruikshank, *Charles Lennox, the fourth Duke of Richmond* (Ont. Hist. Soc., Papers and Records, 1927).

**Richmond,** a county in Nova Scotia, situated at the south-western extremity of Cape Breton island. It was created in 1836, when it was cut off from Cape Breton county; and it was named after the Duke of Richmond (q.v.), who was

RIDEAU HALL, GOVERNMENT HOUSE, OTTAWA, ONTARIO

governor-general of British North America in 1818-19. Chief town, Arichat. Pop. (1931), 11,098.

**Richmond,** a county in southern Quebec, bounded on the north by Arthabaska county, on the west by Drummond and Shefford counties, on the south by Sherbrooke and Compton counties, and on the east by Wolfe county. It was named after the Duke of Richmond (q.v.), governor-general of British North America in 1818-19. For electoral purposes it is combined with Wolfe county. County town, Richmond. Pop. (1931), 24,956.

**Richmond,** the shire-town of Richmond county, Quebec, is on the St. Francis river, and on the Canadian National Railway, 77 miles south-east of Montreal. The settlement was named in 1818 in honour of the Duke of Richmond (q.v.). The town is the centre of a rich agricultural district, making large shipments of dairy produce to Montreal and Quebec. The principal manufacturing establishments are shoe factories, a sash-and-door factory, and granite works. Richmond is the seat of St. Francis College. Pop. (1931), 2,596.

**Richmond,** a village in Russell county, Ontario, on the Goodwood river, and on the Canadian Pacific Railway, 15 miles from Ottawa. It was founded by disbanded veterans of the 99th and 100th Regiments in 1818, and was named after the Duke of Richmond (q.v.), who visited the settlement and died near it in 1819 from hydrophobia. Pop. (1931), 405.

**Richmond Hill,** a village in York county, Ontario, on Yonge street, 10 miles north of Toronto. It was originally known as Mount Pleasant, but was renamed in 1819 in honour of the Duke of Richmond (q.v.), and was incorporated in 1872. It is in a farming and market-gardening district, and has a grain elevator, a high school, and a weekly newspaper (*Liberal*). Pop. (1931), 1,295. See M. Teefy, *Annals of an old*

*post-office on Yonge street* (Ont. Hist. Soc., Papers and Records, 1915).

**Richter, John George** (1854-1932), insurance expert, was born near Hespeler, Ontario, on September 18, 1854. In 1883 he became general manager of the London Life Insurance Company, and in 1920 its president; and he had not a little to do with the development of life insurance in Canada. He died in London, Ontario, on October 11, 1932. In 1890 he was elected a fellow of the Actuarial Society of America. See F. Landon, *John George Richter* (London, Ontario, 1935).

**Rideau Canal.** See **Canals.**

**Rideau Hall,** the name of the official residence of the governor-general of Canada in Ottawa. The house, which is in a park of 88 acres, was originally built by the Hon. Thomas McKay (q.v.) about 1840. In 1865 it was leased to the Canadian government as an official residence for the governor-general, after being renovated, and it was purchased in 1868 at a cost of $82,000. The name was given to it by its first owner, from its proximity to the Rideau canal. See F. J. Audet, *Thomas McKay, Rideau Hall and Earnscliffe* (Canadian Historical Association, Report, 1932).

**Rideau lake,** in Leeds county, Ontario, is on the height of land between the valleys of the Ottawa and St. Lawrence valleys. It empties into the Ottawa by the Rideau river, and into lake Ontario by the Cataraqui river; and it is the grand summit level of the Rideau canal. It is 24 miles long, and has an average width of 6 miles.

**Ridgetown,** a town in Kent county, Ontario, on the Michigan Central and Père Marquette Railways, 20 miles east of Chatham, and 5 miles north of lake Erie. It is so named from the ridge on which it is situated, and which divides the northern and southern watersheds of Kent county. It is in a rich farming and tobacco-growing country; and has three grain elevators, a large canning factory, a public library, a collegiate institute, an experimental farm, with an agricultural school, and a weekly newspaper (*Dominion*). Pop. (1931), 1,952.

**Ridgeway, battle of.** This was an episode in the Fenian raid of 1866. See **Fenian Raids.**

**Riding Mountain,** a village in Manitoba, on the Prince Albert branch of the Canadian National Railway, near Riding mountain, and 7 miles north of Bernie. The name, first applied to the mountain, would appear to have reference to the buffalo chase, which was often carried on near the mountain. Pop. (1934), 150.

**Riding Mountain National Park,** a reservation in Manitoba set aside by the Canadian government in 1930.

**Ridley College,** a residential school for boys at St. Catharines, Ontario, on the western bank of the old Welland canal. It was founded in 1889 by a number of laymen and clergymen connected with the Church of England in Canada, with the object of imparting to pupils a sound education on reasonable lines, with adequate religious and moral instruction, and of placing pupils in a healthy locality, away from the distractions and temptations of city life. It was first known as Bishop Ridley College, but in 1900 the name was shortened to Ridley College. The principals have been the Rev. J. O. Miller, D.C.L. (1889-1921), and H. C. Griffith, M.A., LL.D. (1921—). It is the largest purely residential school in Canada and has an enrolment of 220 boys, who are housed in the four dormitory buildings that comprise the upper and lower and intermediate schools. See O. J. Aldom, *Ridley College* (Municipal Review of Canada, 1934).

**Ridout, Thomas** (1754-1829), surveyor-general of Upper Canada (1810-29), was born at Sherborne, Dorsetshire, England, on March 17, 1754, the son of George Ridout. He emigrated to Maryland in 1774; and spent the period of the American Revolution trading with the West Indies and France. In 1787 he was captured by the Indians and was brought to Canada. He obtained employment in 1792 in the commissariat department of Upper Canada, and in 1793 in the surveyor-general's office. In 1799 he was appointed joint acting surveyor-general of the province; and in 1810 surveyor-general. From 1812 to 1816 he was a member of the Legislative Assembly for the east riding of York and Simcoe county; in 1825 he was appointed a member of the Legislative Council of Upper Canada; and he sat in the Council until his death, at York (Toronto), on February 8, 1829. He was twice married, (1) in 1776 to Isabella, sister-in-law of John Donovan, postmaster of Hancock, Virginia, by whom he had one son; and (2) in 1789 to Mary, daughter of Alexander Campbell, a United Empire Loyalist, of Fort Edward, bay of Quinte. by whom he had seven sons and five daughters. See Matilda Edgar, *Ten years of Upper Canada* (Toronto, 1890), with portrait.

**Ridout, Thomas Gibbs** (1792-1861), cashier of the Bank of Upper Canada (1822-61), was born near Sorel, Lower Canada, on October 10, 1792, the third son of Thomas Ridout (q.v.). He came with his parents to Newark (Niagara), and then to York (Toronto), when his father entered the service of the government of Upper Canada; and he was educated under the Rev. John Strachan (q.v.) at Cornwall, Upper Canada. During the war of 1812 he was deputy assistant commissary general for Upper Canada, and he remained in the commissariat until 1820. In 1822 he was appointed cashier (or general manager) of the Bank of Upper Canada, and he continued in this position until shortly before his death on July 29, 1861. He was twice married, (1) in 1825 to Anne Maria Louisa, daughter of Daniel Sullivan, by whom he had two sons and one daughter; and (2) in 1834 to Matilda

Ann, daughter of Hollingsworth Bramley, of Yorkshire, England, and by her he had six sons and five daughters.

**Riedesel, Friedrich Adolphus, Baron von** (1738-1800), soldier, was born at his ancestral castle of Lauterbach, in Hesse, Germany, on June 3, 1738. He became an officer in the army of the Duke of Brunswick; and in 1776 he was sent to America, with the rank of major-general, in command of the force of German mercenaries lent to the British government by the Duke of Brunswick. He commanded this force throughout the remainder of the American revolutionary war; and he returned to Europe, with the remnants of his force, in 1783. He continued in Europe his military career, and in 1787 was promoted to the rank of lieut.-general. In 1794 he was appointed commandant of the city of Brunswick; and here he died on January 6, 1800. His papers were published by Marc von Eelking under the title *Leben and Wirken des herzoglich braunschweig'schen General-Lieutenants Friedrich Adolph Riedesel, Freiherrn zu Eisenbach* (3 vols., Leipzig, 1856), and were partially translated into English by W. L. Stone under the title *Memoirs and letters and journals during his residence in America* (2 vols., Albany, 1868). His wife, Friederike Charlotte Luise, Freifrau von Riedesel (1764-1808), who accompanied him to America, published *Die Berufs-Reise nach America* (Berlin, 1801), and this has been twice translated, first under the title *Letters and memoirs relating to the war of American independence* (New York, 1827), and secondly, by W. L. Stone, under the title *Letters and journals relating to the war of the American Revolution* (Albany, 1867). See G. Monarque, *Un général allemand au Canada: Le Baron Friedrich Adolphus von Riedesel* (Montreal, 1927).

**Riel, Louis** (1844-1885), leader in the North West rebellions of 1870 and 1885, was born at St. Boniface, Manitoba, on October 23, 1844, the son of Louis Riel and Marguerite Boucher, a half-breed woman, and grandson of Jean Baptiste Riel, a native of Berthier, Lower Canada. He was educated at the Seminary in Montreal, and then returned to the West. In 1869 he became secretary of the *Comité national des Métis*, an organization formed to resist the establishment of Canadian authority in the North West. Later in the same year he was elected president of the provisional government set up by the rebels. He escaped from the country in August, 1870, on the arrival of the expeditionary force under Wolseley; but in 1873, and again in 1874, he was elected to represent Provencher in the Canadian House of Commons. In 1874, on taking the oath, he was expelled from the House; and in 1875 a warrant of outlawry was issued against him. He took refuge in Montana, and there he remained until, in the summer of 1884, he was invited to return to Canada to organize the half-breeds of the North West Territories so as to obtain redress of their grievances. The outcome of his visit to Canada was a second rebellion in the North West. On the defeat of the rebels at Batoche, on May 12, 1885, by General Middleton (q.v.), Riel was captured. He was tried at Regina, in July, on the charge of high treason, was found guilty, and on November 16, 1885, was hanged in the Mounted Police barracks at Regina. Riel was a man of some ability, but of an unbalanced mind; and over the question of his sanity opinions are still divided. See J. E. Collins, *The story of Louis Riel* (Toronto, n.d.); *Louis Riel, martyr du Nord-Ouest* (Montreal, 1885); *La Reine vs. Louis Riel* (Ottawa, 1886); *Le véritable Riel* (Montreal, 1887); C. K. Clarke, *A critical study of the case of Louis Riel* (Queen's quarterly, Kingston, Ontario, 1905); A. H. de Trémaudan, *Louis Riel and the Fenian raid of 1871* (Can. hist. rev., 1923); Sir J. Pope, *Correspondence of Sir John Macdonald* (Toronto, 1921); A. G. Morice, *Diction-*

17

*naire historique des Canadiens et des Métis français de l'ouest* (Quebec, 1908), and *A critical history of the Red River rebellion* (Winnipeg, 1935).

**Riel Rebellions.** See **North-West Rebellions.**

**Rigaud,** a town in Vaudreuil county, Quebec, on the Ottawa river, at the mouth of the Rigaud river, and on the Canadian Pacific Railway, 46 miles west of Montreal. It is named after the seigniory of Rigaud, granted in 1732 to Pierre and François Rigaud, sons of the Marquis de Vaudreuil (q.v.). It has important stone quarries, and is in a prosperous farming and market-gardening district. It has also a well-known classical and commercial college, a convent, and a weekly newspaper (*L'Interrogation*). It was created a village in 1881, and a town in 1911. Pop. (1931), 1,099.

**Rigolette.** See **Fort Rigolette.**

**Rimbey,** a village in the Wetaskiwin district of Alberta, on the Canadian Pacific Railway, 100 miles south-west of Edmonton. It was named after the first settlers, three brothers by the name of Rimbey. It has a hospital and a weekly newspaper (*Record*). Pop. (1934), 300.

**Rimouski,** a county in Quebec on the south shore of the St. Lawrence river between Témiscouata and Matapédia counties. It is named after the Rimouski river; and its county town is Rimouski. Pop. (1931), 33,151, mainly confined to the shores of the St. Lawrence.

**Rimouski,** a town in Rimouski county, Quebec, is situated on the south shore of the St. Lawrence river, 180 miles north-east of Quebec. The name is derived from a Micmac or Malecite Indian word, according to some authorities, meaning "home or retreat of dogs", but more probably "land of the moose", as in the days of the pioneer settlers moose abounded in the surrounding forests. The first settler

who built on its site was Germain Lepage, who settled there in 1696; and for this reason, by canonical erection, the parish was given the name of St. Germain. It is on the main line of the Canadian National Railway, formerly the Intercolonial, and has a regular ferry service with the settlements on the north shore of the St. Lawrence. Close to the town there is an aerodrome and air mail station. It is the seat of the Roman Catholic bishop of Rimouski, and has a cathedral, a bishop's palace, a seminary, a normal school of the Ursulines, and an agricultural college. The principal industry is lumbering, and it has saw mills and wood-working establishments of various kinds; but agriculture also flourishes, and it is a centre for dairying and truck-gardening. It has a weekly newspaper (*Progrès du Golfe*). Pop. (1931), 5,589. See Abbé Charles Guay, *Chronique de Rimouski* (2 vols., Quebec, 1873-4).

**Rimouski river,** a stream which rises in two branches in the interior of Rimouski county, Quebec, and empties into the St. Lawrence near the town of Rimouski. The name is derived from a Micmac word signifying "dog-house" or "haunt of dogs," or more probably "land of the moose."

**Ripley,** a village in Bruce county, Ontario, on the Canadian National Railway, 8 miles south-east of Kincardine. It was incorporated in 1925. Pop. (1931), 442.

**Ripon,** a village in Papineau county, Quebec, on the North Nation river, 15 miles from Papineauville. It was named after either the first Earl of Ripon (1782-1859), prime minister of Great Britain in 1827-8, or after Ripon, a cathedral city in Yorkshire, England. Pop. (1931), 443.

**Ristigouche.** See **Restigouche.**

**Ritcey's Cove.** See **Riverport.**

**Ritchie, John William** (1808-1890), judge, was born at Annapolis, Nova Scotia, on March 26, 1808, the son of the Hon. Thomas Ritchie. He was educated privately, and in 1831 was called to the bar of Nova Scotia. In 1839 he was appointed law clerk of the Legislative Council of Nova Scotia; and this position he held until 1860. In 1864 he was appointed a member of the Legislative Council, and from 1864 to 1867 he was solicitor-general of the province. In 1866 he was a representative of Nova Scotia at the conference in London which resulted in the framing of the British North America Act; and in 1867 he was called by royal proclamation to the Senate of Canada. In 1870 he was appointed a judge of the Supreme Court of Nova Scotia; and in 1873 he became a judge in equity. He resigned from the bench in 1882; and he died at his home at Belmont on December 18, 1890. In 1838 he married Amelia, daughter of the Hon. W. B. Almon. In 1878 he was elected first president of the Nova Scotia Historical Society. See L. G. Power, *Our first president: The Hon. J. W. Ritchie* (Coll. Nova Scotia Hist. Soc., 1918).

**Ritchie, Sir William Johnstone** (1813-1892), chief justice of Canada (1879-92), was born in Annapolis, Nova Scotia, on October 28, 1813, the son of the Hon. Thomas Ritchie and Elizabeth Wildman Johnstone. He was educated at Pictou Academy, and was called to the bar of New Brunswick in 1838 (Q.C., 1854). From 1847 to 1851 he represented the city and county of Saint John in the House of Assembly of New Brunswick. In 1855 he was made a puisne judge of the Supreme Court of New Brunswick, and in 1865 he became chief justice of the province. On October 8, 1875, he was appointed a puisne judge of the Supreme Court of Canada, and in 1879 he was made chief justice of Canada. From July 6, 1881, to January, 1882, he acted as deputy governor of Canada during the absence of Lord Lorne (q.v.) in England, and again from September 6 to December, 1882. On March 5, 1884, he was appointed

deputy to the governor-general, Lord Lansdowne (q.v.). He died at Ottawa on September 25, 1892. He married (1) in 1843, Martha Strang of St. Andrew's (d. 1847), and (2) in 1854 Grace Vernon, daughter of Thomas Nicholson of Saint John. He was created a knight bachelor in 1881. He published *The Chesapeake; before Mr. Justice Ritchie, with his decision thereon* (Saint John, New Brunswick, 1864), and *Observations of the Chief Justice of New Brunswick on a bill entitled "An Act to Establish a Supreme Court for the Dominion of Canada," presented to parliament on May 21, 1869, by the Hon. Sir John A. Macdonald, K.C.B.* (Saint John, New Brunswick, 1870).

**Ritter, Henry** (1816-1853), painter, was born in Montreal, Lower Canada, in 1816. He studied painting in Hamburg and Düsseldorf, Germany; and he was notable especially for his pictures of the sea. He died on December 21, 1853.

**River Beaudette,** a village in Soulanges county, Quebec, on the St. Lawrence river, at the mouth of the Beaudette river, and on the Canadian National Railway, 24 miles east of Cornwall. The name is derived from the fact that at the mouth of the river there was left a small bed (*beaudette*), from which the river acquired its name. Pop. (1934), 228.

**River Hébert,** a village in Cumberland county, Nova Scotia, on the Hébert river, and on the Joggins branch of the Canadian National Railway. It is named after a *coureur-de-bois* named Hébert, who had a fort here about 1749. There are coal-mines in the vicinity. Pop. (1934), 2,000.

**Riverhurst,** a village in the Swift Current district of Saskatchewan, on the Canadian National Railway, 110 miles north-west of Regina. It has five grain elevators and a weekly newspaper (*Courier*). Pop. (1934), 300.

**River John,** a village in Pictou county, Nova Scotia, on the river of the same name, and on the short line of the Canadian National Railway, 20 miles from Pictou. It is said to be named after an early settler, John Patuguin.

**River Philip,** a village in Cumberland county, Nova Scotia, on the Philip river, and on the Canadian National Railway, 28 miles from Amherst. It is said that the village is named after a popular physician named Philip who lived here. Pop. (1934), 950.

**Riverport,** a village in Lunenburg county, Nova Scotia, on the La Have river, 9 miles from Lunenburg station on the Canadian National Railway. It was one of the fishing stations established by Nicholas Denys (q.v.); and fishing is still the chief occupation. Until 1904 it was known as "Ritcey's Cove"; but in that year its name was changed by Act of parliament to Riverport. Pop. (1934), 650.

**Rivers,** a town in Manitoba, on the main line of the Canadian National Railway, 88 miles west of Portage la Prairie. It was named in 1908 after Sir Charles Rivers Wilson, chairman of the board of directors of the Grand Trunk Railway. It is a railway divisional point, is in a good farming district, and has a weekly newspaper (*Gazette*). Pop. (1934), 724.

**Riverside,** a town in Essex county, Ontario, on the south shore of the Detroit river, and on the radial line of the Hydro-Electric Commission, 3 miles east of the centre of Windsor. It was incorporated in 1921, and is almost wholly a residential town, having a waterfront of between three and four miles. It is within easy reach of both the Chrysler and the Ford motor plants; and its rapid growth is partly explained by its proximity to these plants and to Greater Windsor. Pop. (1931), 4,432. See *Report of administrative and financial survey of the corporation of the town of Riverside*, prepared for the Town Coun-

cil by the Citizens' Research Institute of Canada (Toronto, 1930).

**Riverton,** a village in Manitoba, on lake Winnipeg, at the mouth of the Icelandic river, 40 miles north of Winnipeg Beach. It was known until 1914 as Icelandic River. Pop. (1934), 210.

**Rivière Blanche.** See **St. Ulric.**

**Rivière du Loup,** a city in Témiscouata county, Quebec, is situated at the junction of the Rivière du Loup with the St. Lawrence, on the south side of the latter river, 116 miles below Quebec city. It is on the main line of the Canadian National Railway (formerly the Intercolonial), and the Témiscouata Railway gives it connection with Edmundston, New Brunswick, and the state of Maine. In 1850 it was incorporated under the name Fraserville, after Alexander Fraser (q.v.), whose family held the seigniorial rights in the district; but it was later given its present name, after the river on which it is situated and which had been so named on account of the number of timber wolves found in the vicinity. It is the centre of one of the finest agricultural and lumbering regions in the province of Quebec, and has saw mills, machine shops, a pulp mill, a furniture factory, and large railway repair shops. It contains five churches, three convents, a hospital, a court house, and several good hotels; and it is a popular summer resort. It has a weekly newspaper (*Le St. Laurent*) Pop. (1931), 8,800.

**Rivière du Loup en haut.** See **Louiseville.**

**Rivière du Sud.** See **Henryville.**

**Rivière Madeleine,** a village and harbour in Gaspé county, Quebec, on the south shore of the gulf of St. Lawrence, 111 miles east of Matane. It has a wharf, from which pulpwood and fish are exported. Pop. (1934), 300.

**Rivière Ouelle,** a village in Kamouraska county, Quebec, situated on the south shore of the St. Lawrence, on the Canadian National Railway, 80 miles north-east of Quebec city. In 1690 a settlement was founded here by René Ouellet, and named in his honour. Pop. (1931), 1,475. See E. Croff, *Nos ancêtres à l'œuvre: A la Rivière-Ouelle* (Montreal, 1931).

**Roads.** The first roads in Canada were winding Indian trails, along which the aboriginal inhabitants of the country made their way in single file through the forest or over portages. They were auxiliary to the waterways as a means of travel. The first highway in Canada was that built in the early years of the eighteenth century between Quebec and Montreal. The first highways in Upper Canada were Yonge street and Dundas street; and in 1817 overland communication by road was opened between Montreal and York (Toronto). But these roads were at first little more than cuttings in the forest, made by felling the trees, uprooting the larger stumps, and in swampy places laying logs crosswise so as to form a "corduroy road". In the winter, these roads were fairly passable for sleighs; but in the spring and summer they were so bad that as late as 1834 the road between Kingston and Toronto was so impassable that the mails had to be brought in on horseback. One of the reasons why the early roads in Canada were so bad was that they were built by means of "statute labour". The law threw on the local inhabitants the duty of keeping the roads in repair. The first attempt at improvement of the roads came when they were leased to private companies or individuals, who drained them and "surfaced" them, and levied a toll on those who used them. Toll-gates were once a prominent feature of Canadian roads. But it was not until the people of Canada, through their elected representatives, began to employ expert engineers to build roads and keep them in repair that the era of "good roads" began to dawn in Canada. The cities were the first to adopt this system of looking after their roads; then the counties followed suit; and, finally, the provinces established departments of highways, which have built province-wide arteries of traffic. This development was stimulated, in the early years of the nineteenth century, by a "Good Roads" movement or agitation, which enlisted popular support for the improvement of provincial highways. Recently, also, the Dominion government has embarked, with the help of the provinces, on the project of a national highway stretching from Halifax to Vancouver. The problem of building roads that will endure in Canada's winter climate has been progressively solved; the early dirt and corduroy roads gave place a hundred years ago to macadamized roads and plank roads, and these in turn have given way on the chief highways to surfaces of brick, asphalt, or concrete. The improvement of Canadian roads in the twentieth century has, of course, been greatly stimulated by the development of the motor-car.

The roads of Canada still await their historian; but some useful local studies have been published, generally in the *Transactions* of local historical societies, such as K. M. Lizars, *Early roads in York* (Women's Canadian Historical Society of Toronto, Transaction No. 12, 1912-3); W. H. Breithaupt, *Early roads and transportation in Upper Canada* (Waterloo Historical Society, Seventh Annual Report, 1919); W. C. Moberley, *History of the Cariboo wagon road* (Vancouver, 1908); D. Murphy, *The building of the Cariboo road* (British Columbia Historical Association, Report, 1925); Rev. I. Caron, *Le chemin de la rive nord du Saint-Laurent: Québec-Montréal* (Bull. rech. hist., 1925); and M. W. Wallace, *The old stage road along lake St. Clair* (Ont. Hist. Soc., Papers and Records, 1928). See also **Transportation.**

**Robb, James Alexander** (1859-1929), minister of finance for Canada (1925 and 1926-9), was born at Huntingdon, Quebec, on August 10, 1859, the son of Alexander Robb and Jenny Smith. He was educated at the Huntingdon Academy and became a prosperous flour-miller. From 1906 to 1908 he was mayor of Valleyfield, Quebec; and from 1908 to his death he represented Huntingdon and Châteauguay-Huntingdon in the Canadian House of Commons. In 1921 he became minister of trade and commerce in the King administration; in 1923 he was transferred to the portfolio of immigration and colonization, and in 1925 to that of finance. This portfolio he resumed on the return to power of the King government in 1926, and he held it until his death at Toronto on November 11, 1929.

**Roberton, Thomas Beattie** (1879-1936), journalist and author, was born in Glasgow, Scotland, on October 20, 1879. He emigrated to Canada in 1910; and in 1918 he joined the staff of the *Winnipeg Free Press*. He became associate editor-in-chief of this newspaper; and he died in Winnipeg on January 13, 1936. He was the author of a volume of historical essays entitled *The fighting bishop* (Ottawa, 1926), and after his death some of his fugitive journalistic writings were collected and published under the title, *T.B.R.: Newspaper pieces* (Toronto, 1936).

**Robertson, Colin** (1779?-1842), fur-trader, was born about 1779, and entered the service of the North West Company as a clerk prior to 1804. He was employed mainly in the English river department; but in September, 1809, he was dismissed from the service by John McDonald of Garth (q.v.). In 1814 he entered the employ of Lord Selkirk (q.v.) and the Hudson's Bay Company; and in 1818 he was the chief officer of the Hudson's Bay Company in the Athabaska district. In 1819 he was arrested by the Nor'Westers, but escaped, it was said, by breaking his parole. In 1820, he went to England, and was in London when the negotiations in regard to the union of the North West and Hudson's Bay Companies were in progress; and his letters, preserved in Hudson's Bay House, are one of our chief sources for the history of these negotiations. In 1821 he was made a chief factor of the Hudson's Bay Company, and was placed in charge at Norway House. In 1824 he was transferred to Fort Churchill; in 1826, to Island lake; and in 1830, to Swan river. He had leave of absence from 1832 to 1837; but from 1837 to 1839 he had charge of the New Brunswick district. He retired in 1840, with a pension. In 1841 he was elected to represent the Lake of Two Mountains in the first Legislative Assembly of United Canada; but he died at Montreal on February 3, 1842, from the effects of being thrown from his cariole the preceding day. His eldest son, Colin Robertson, Jr., died at Montreal on November 29, 1844, aged 23.

**Robertson, Gideon Decker** (1874-1933), minister of labour for Canada (1918-21 and 1930-3), was born at Welland, Ontario, on August 26, 1874. He became a railway telegrapher and station agent, and from 1907 to 1914 was chairman of the telegraphers' organization of the Canadian Pacific Railway. In 1914 he was elected a vice-president of the Order of Railway Telegraphers. He was appointed a member of the Canadian Senate and was sworn of the Privy Council in 1917, and in 1918 became minister of labour in the Borden government. He retired from office on the defeat of the Meighen government in 1921, but was re-appointed minister of labour in the Bennett government in 1930. He died on August 5, 1933.

**Robertson, James** (1839-1902), superintendent of Presbyterian home missions (1881-1902), was born in the village of Dull, Perthshire, Scotland, on April 24, 1839, the son of James Robertson and Christina McCallum. He came to Canada with his parents in 1855 and was educated at the University of Toronto, at Princeton University, and at the Union Theological Seminary, New York. In 1869 he was ordained a minister of the Canada Presbyterian Church; and from 1869 to 1874 he was stationed at Norwich, Ontario. In 1874 he accepted the charge of Knox Church, Winnipeg; and in 1881 he was appointed superintendent of missions in Western Canada. This post he continued to fill until his death, at Toronto, on January 4, 1902; and "the story of his work is the history of the Presbyterian Church in Western Canada." In 1888 he was made a D.D. of the Presbyterian College of Montreal; and in 1895 he was elected moderator of the Presbyterian Church in Canada. In 1869 he married Mary Anne Cowing, of Blandford, Oxford county, Ontario; and by her he had two daughters. See C. W. Gordon, *The life of James Robertson* (Toronto, 1908).

**Robertson, John Ross** (1841-1918), journalist, historian, and philanthropist, was born in Toronto on December 28, 1841, the son of John Robertson, of Toronto, and Margaret, daughter of Hector Sinclair, of Stornoway, Isle of Lewis, Scotland. He was educated at Upper Canada College, and early entered journalism. In 1866 he founded the *Daily Telegraph* (1866-71) in Toronto; and in 1876 he founded the *Evening Telegram*. The success of this paper laid the foundation of a large fortune, and enabled its proprietor to indulge his passion for philanthropy and for historical collections. He was the founder and benefactor of the Hospital for Sick Children, Toronto; and the John Ross Robertson collection of Canadian historical pictures in the Toronto Public Library was his creation. From 1896 to 1900 he sat in the Dominion House of Commons for East Toronto; and he rose to high rank in the Masonic order. He wrote *The history of freemasonry in Canada* (2 vols., Toronto, 1900); and he published *Robertson's Landmarks of Toronto* (6 vols., Toronto, 1894-1914), and *The diary of Mrs. John Graves Simcoe* (Toronto, 1912). In 1914 he was elected a fellow of the Royal Society of Canada; and he died in Toronto on May 30, 1918. He was twice married, (1) to Maria Louisa Gilbee (d. 1886), and (2) to Jessie Elizabeth Holland. By his first wife he had two sons.

**Robertsonville,** a village in Megantic county, Quebec, on the Quebec Central Railway, 5 miles north-east of Thetford Mines. It was founded in 1909, the year of the opening of the asbestos mines in the vicinity; and was named after the Hon. J. G. Robertson, a former president of the Quebec Central Railway. Pop. (1931), 671.

**Roberval, Jean François de la Rocque, Sieur de** (1500?-1560?), colonizer, was born either in Languedoc or in Picardy, about 1500. In 1541 he was commissioned by the king of France viceroy and lieutenant-general of New France, and appointed to command an expedition to follow up the discoveries of Jacques Cartier (q.v.). He set sail in 1542, and spent the winter of 1542-3 at Cartier's former headquarters near Quebec. In 1543, however, he returned with his colonists to France. There is reason for believing that he died about 1560. See N. E. Dionne, *Jean François de la Rocque, Seigneur de Roberval* (Trans. Roy. Soc. Can., 1899), and H. P. Biggar, *A collection of documents relating to Jacques Cartier and the Sieur de Roberval* (Ottawa, 1930).

**Roberval,** a town in the county of Lake St. John, Quebec, situated on lake St. John and on the Canadian National Railway, 190 miles north-east of Quebec city. The place was named after Jean François de la Rocque, sieur de Roberval (q.v.), first viceroy of New France. Roberval is the centre of a good dairying district. There are butter and cheese factories, and three flour mills. Excellent fishing and hunting are to be had in the neighbourhood. Pop. (1931), 2,770.

**Robie, Simon Bradstreet** (1770-1858), president of the Legislative Council of Nova Scotia (1827-38), was born at Marble Head, Massachusetts, in 1770, the son of Thomas Robie. Early in the American Revolution he was brought to Halifax, Nova Scotia, by his parents, who were loyalists; and he was educated at Halifax. About 1790 he was called to the bar of Nova Scotia; and in 1799 he was elected to represent Truro in the General Assembly of the province. In 1806 he was elected to represent Halifax county, and this seat he retained in the Assembly until 1824. In 1815 he was appointed solicitor-general of the province, and in 1817 he was elected speaker of the Assembly. Both these offices he held until 1824, when he was appointed master of the rolls in Nova Scotia. At the same time he became a member of both the Executive and Legislative Councils; and in 1827 he was appointed president of the Legislative Council. He resigned from the bench in 1834; he ceased to preside over the Legislative Council in 1838; and he resigned from the Council in 1848. The rest of his life he spent in retirement, and he died at Halifax on January 3, 1858. See I. Longworth, *Honorable Judge Robie* (Acadiensis, 1901).

**Robin** (*Turdus migratorius*), the familiar member of the thrush family, *Turdidae*, which is so widely distributed in Canada as to be known by everyone. Although the American robin is not distantly related to the Old World bird of that name, there is but slight resemblance, except in the warm colour of its breast. This feature and its habit of frequenting the proximity of man's habitations are the only points which prompted the application of the name "robin" to the New World bird by the early settlers. Young robins have streaked breasts, which is one superficial character that reflects their relationship with the thrush family.

**Robinson, Beverley** (1723-1792), loyalist, was born in Virginia in 1723, the son of the Hon. John Robinson, speaker of the House of Burgesses of Virginia. He served under Wolfe (q.v.) at the capture of Quebec in 1759; and at the outbreak of the American Revolution he raised the Loyal American Regiment. This regiment he commanded throughout the war. In 1784 he went to New Brunswick, and was appointed a member of the first Council of the province; but he did not take his seat, as he very soon went to England. He lived at Thornbury, near Bath, until his death in 1792. He married Susanna, daughter of Frederick Philipse; and by her he had several sons.

**Robinson, Sir Charles Walker** (1836-1924), soldier and author, was born at Beverley House, Toronto, on April 3, 1836, the fourth and youngest son of Sir John Beverley Robinson, Bart. (q.v.). He was educated at Upper Canada College and at Trinity University, Toronto (D.C.L., 1879); and in 1857 he obtained a commission as a second lieutenant in the Rifle Brigade. He served in the Crimean War, in the Ashanti War, and in the Zulu War; and from 1892 to 1895 he was commander of the forces in Mauritius, with the rank of major-general. He retired from the army in 1898; and he died in London, England, on May 20, 1924. In 1884 he married Margaret Frances, daughter of Lieut.-Gen. Sir Archibald Alison, Bart.; and by her he had two daughters. He was the author of *Wellington's campaigns* (3 vols., London, 1905-8), *Canada and Canadian defence* (London, 1910), and *The life of Sir John Beverley Robinson, Bart.* (London, 1904). He was created a K.C.B. in 1923.

**Robinson, Christopher** (1763?-1798), loyalist, was born in Westmoreland county, Virginia, about 1763. He was educated at the College of William and Mary; and early in the American Revolution he took refuge in New York, and obtained a commission in the

Queen's Rangers (1st American Regiment), commanded by Lieut.-Col. John Graves Simcoe (q.v.). In 1783 he went to Nova Scotia, and took up land in Wilmot; but in 1788 he removed to Lower Canada, and in 1792 he settled in Upper Canada. In 1796 he was elected to represent Lennox and Addington in the Legislative Assembly of Upper Canada; and he died at York (Toronto) on November 2, 1798. In 1784 he married Esther, daughter of the Rev. John Sayre, formerly of Fairfield, Connecticut; and by her he had three sons and two daughters.

**Robinson, Christopher** (1828-1905), lawyer, was born at Beverley House, Toronto, on January 21, 1828, the third son of Sir John Beverley Robinson, Bart. (q.v.). He was educated at Upper Canada College and at King's College, Toronto (B.A., 1846), and in 1850 was called to the bar of Upper Canada (Q.C., 1863). From 1856 to 1872 he was reporter of the court of Queen's Bench; and from 1872 to 1885 he was editor of the *Law reports*. He was counsel in many of the most famous cases in Canadian legal history, and in several international arbitrations; and he occupied an outstanding position at the Canadian bar. He repeatedly declined judicial preferment, and in 1894 he declined the honour of knighthood. He died at Toronto on October 21, 1905. In 1879 he married Elizabeth Street, daughter of the Hon. Josiah Burr Plumb (q.v.); and by her he had three sons and one daughter. In 1902 he was elected chancellor of Trinity University, Toronto; and from the University of Toronto he received in 1903 the degree of D.C.L.

**Robinson, Sir Frederick Philipse** (1763-1852), provisional lieutenant-governor of Upper Canada (July-September, 1815), was born near near New York in September, 1763, the fourth son of Colonel Beverley Robinson (q.v.). He became an ensign in his father's regiment, the Loyal Americans, in 1777,

and he served throughout the American Revolutionary War. Toward the end of the war he transferred to a British regiment; and in 1794-5 he served with distinction in the West Indies. He was a senior staff officer during the Peninsular War; and in 1814 he returned to America as commander of the forces in Upper Canada. In July, 1815, he was appointed provisional lieutenant-governor of Upper Canada; and he held this position until the arrival in Canada, in September, 1815, of Francis Gore (q.v.). From 1816 to 1821 he held appointments in the West Indies; in 1825 he was promoted to be lieutenant-general, and in 1841 general. He died at Brighton, England, on January 1, 1852. In 1815 he was created a K.C.B., and in 1838 a G.C.B. His journal of the expedition to Plattsburg in 1814 has been published in the *Journal of the Royal United Service Institution*, August, 1916. See D. B. Read, *The lieutenant-governors of Upper Canada* (Toronto, 1900).

**Robinson, Sir John Beverley, Bart.** (1791-1863), chief justice of Upper Canada, was born at Berthier, Lower Canada, on July 26, 1791, the second son of Christopher Robinson (q.v.), an officer of the Queen's Rangers, and Esther, daughter of the Rev. John Sayre. He was educated at Kingston and at Cornwall, Upper Canada, under John Strachan (q.v.), who became his friend and patron; and he entered upon the study of law. In the campaign of 1812 he served under Isaac Brock (q.v.) as a militia officer; and in 1813 he was appointed acting attorney-general of the province. On the conclusion of peace he was appointed solicitor-general, and in 1818 attorney-general. In 1821 he was elected to the Legislative Assembly of Upper Canada for the town of York, and he continued to sit in the House, and act as attorney-general, until he was, in 1830, appointed chief justice of Upper Canada, speaker of the Legislative Council, and president of the Executive Council. He resigned the presidency of the Executive Council about 1832; and he ceased to be a member of the Legislative Council at the Union of 1841; but he held the office of chief justice until, in 1862, he was appointed first president of the Court of Error and Appeal. Shortly after this, on January 30, 1863, he died at Beverley House, Toronto.

He was a man of great ability and scrupulous integrity. During the period of his political career (1821-41), he was one of the guiding spirits of what came to be known as the "Family Compact"; and no more striking refutation could be found of the traditional view of the "Family Compact" than his connection with it. As a judge he has had few equals in the history of Canadian judicature.

In 1817 he married in London, England, Emma, daughter of Charles Walker, of Harlesden, Middlesex, England; and by her he had four sons and four daughters. He was made a C.B. in 1850; and he was created a baronet of the United Kingdom in 1854. In 1853 he was elected the first chancellor of the University of Trinity College, Toronto. His only important publication, outside the sphere of law, was *Canada and the Canada bill* (London, 1840). See Maj.-Gen. C. W. Robinson, *Life of Sir John Beverley Robinson, Bart.* (Edinburgh and London, 1904).

**Robinson, John Beverley** (1821-1896), lieutenant-governor of Ontario (1880-7), was born in York (Toronto), Upper Canada, on February 21, 1821, the second son of Sir John Beverley Robinson, Bart. (q.v.). He was educated at Upper Canada College; and he was aide-de-camp to Sir Francis Bond Head (q.v.) during the rebellion of 1837. He was called to the bar of Upper Canada in 1844. In 1857 he was elected mayor of Toronto; and in 1858 he was elected to the Legislative Assembly of Canada as one of the members for Toronto. He represented Toronto in the Legislative Assembly

and in the Canadian House of Commons until 1872; from 1872 to 1874 he represented Algoma; and from 1878 to 1880 West Toronto. From March to May, 1862, he was president of the council in the Cartier-Macdonald ministry; but this was the sole occasion on which he held a cabinet position. From 1880 to 1887 he was lieutenant-governor of Ontario. He died at Toronto on June 19, 1896. In 1847 he married Mary Jane, second daughter of the Hon. Christopher Alexander Hagerman; and by her he had five children, of whom the eldest, John Beverley, succeeded to the baronetcy. See D. B. Read, *Lieutenant-governors of Upper Canada and Ontario* (Toronto, 1900).

**Robinson, Peter** (1785-1838), executive councillor of Upper Canada, was born in New Brunswick in 1785, the eldest son of Christopher Robinson (q.v.), an officer of the Queen's Rangers, and Esther, daughter of the Rev. John Sayre. His parents came to Upper Canada in 1792, settling first at Kingston, and then in 1798 at York. In the War of 1812 he commanded a rifle company at the capture of Detroit; and in 1813 he distinguished himself in the defence of Michilimackinac. In 1817 he was elected to the Legislative Assembly of Upper Canada for the east riding of York; and in 1824-5 he was instrumental in settling a large number of Irish immigrants in the neighbourhood of Peterborough, which was named after him. He was appointed commissioner of crown lands, with a seat in the Executive and Legislative Councils, in 1827; and he continued in this office until the resignation of the whole executive council, as the result of a disagreement with Sir Francis Bond Head, in 1836. He died, unmarried, in Toronto, on July 8, 1838.

**Robinson, William Benjamin** (1797-1873), executive councillor of Canada, was born at Kingston, Upper Canada, on December 22, 1797, the third son of Christopher Robinson (q.v.), an officer of the Queen's Rangers, and Esther, daughter of the Rev. John Sayre. From 1830 to 1857, with the exception of the years 1841-4, he represented the county of Simcoe in the Legislative Assembly of Upper Canada and united Canada; and in 1844-5 he was for a short time inspector-general, with a seat in the Executive Council, and in 1846-7 chief commissioner of public works. He was also one of the commissioners of the Canada Company. He died at Toronto on July 18, 1873. He married Ann Elizabeth (or Eliza Ann), daughter of William Jarvis (q.v.); but had no children.

**Robinson, Sir William Cleaver Francis** (1834-1897), governor of Prince Edward Island (1870-3), was born on January 14, 1834, the fifth son of Admiral Hercules Robinson. He entered the service of the Colonial Office in 1858 as private secretary to his elder brother, Sir Hercules Robinson, afterwards first Baron Rosmead, who was lieutenant-governor of St. Kitts. In 1866 he himself was appointed governor of the Falkland islands, and from 1870 to 1873 he was governor of Prince Edward Island. It was during his administration, and partly as a result of his judicious counsels, that the inclusion of Prince Edward Island in the Canadian confederation took place in 1873. After leaving Prince Edward Island he occupied successively important posts as governor in Western Australia, the Straits Settlements, South Australia, and Victoria; and he retired from active service in 1895. He died in South Kensington, London, England, on May 2, 1897. In 1862 he married Olivia Edith Dean, daughter of the Right Rev. Thomas Stewart Townsend, bishop of Meath, and by her he had three sons and two daughters. He was created a C.M.G. in 1873, a K.C.M.G. in 1877, and a G.C.M.G. in 1887. He was a musical composer of some note, and was the author of a number of well-known songs.

**Robitaille, Theodore** (1834-1897), lieutenant-governor of the province of Quebec (1879-84), was born at Varennes, Lower Canada, on January 29, 1834, the son of Louis Adolphe Robitaille, notary public. He was educated at the seminary of Ste. Thérèse, at Laval University, and at the University of McGill College (M.D., 1858). He practised for many years as a physician and surgeon at New Carlisle, Bonaventure county, Quebec; and in 1861 he was elected the representative of Bonaventure county in the Legislative Assembly of Canada. This constituency he represented, first in the Assembly, and after 1867 in the House of Commons, continuously until 1879. In 1873 he became receiver-general in the Macdonald government, but held office for only a few months when the government resigned. From 1874 to 1878 he was one of Sir John Macdonald's "Old Guard" in the House; and when, in 1879, Letellier de St. Just (q.v.) was dismissed from the lieutenant-governorship of Quebec, he was appointed to the vacant post. His term of office lasted until 1884; and in 1885 he was appointed to the Senate of Canada. He died at New Carlisle, Quebec, on August 18, 1897. In 1867 he married Marie Josephine Charlotte Emma, daughter of P. A. Quesnel, and granddaughter of the Hon. F. A. Quesnel (q.v.).

**Roblin, Sir Rodmond Palen** (1853-1937), prime minister of Manitoba (1900-15), was born in Sophiasburgh, Prince Edward county, Ontario, on February 15, 1853, of United Empire Loyalist descent. He was educated at Albert College, Belleville. In 1877 he migrated to Manitoba, and he became a successful farmer on a large scale at Carman, Manitoba. In 1889 he was elected to represent Dufferin in the Manitoba legislature; and from 1889 to 1899 he was leader of the Conservative opposition. In 1900 he succeeded Sir Hugh John Macdonald (q.v.) as prime minister of Manitoba; and he held power until 1915, when he was compelled to resign as the result of charges of political corruption brought against his government in connection with the building of the parliament buildings in Winnipeg. He retired from public life; and he died at Hot Springs, Arkansas, on February 16, 1937. In 1875 he married Adelaide Demill (d. 1928); and by her he had four sons. He was created a K.C.M.G. in 1912. See A. R. Ross, *Thirty-five years in the limelight: Sir Rodmond P. Roblin and his times* (Winnipeg, 1936).

**Roblin,** a village in the Dauphin district of Manitoba, on the Canadian National Railway, 215 miles north-west of Winnipeg. It was named in 1904 after Sir Rodmond Roblin (q.v.), prime minister of Manitoba from 1900 to 1915. It is in a farming district, and has five grain elevators, a high school and collegiate, and a weekly newspaper (*Review*). Pop. (1934), 680. There is also a village of this name in Richmond township, Lennox county, Ontario, 11 miles north-west of Napanee. Pop. (1934), 300.

**Robson, John** (1824-1892), prime minister of British Columbia (1889-92), was born at Perth, Upper Canada, on March 14, 1824, the son of John Robson and Euphemia Richardson. He was educated at the Perth grammar school; and in 1859 he emigrated to British Columbia. In 1861 he founded at New Westminster the *British Columbian*, the first newspaper on the mainland of British Columbia; and in its columns he waged the battle for constitutional government in the province. In 1867 he was elected to represent New Westminster in the Legislative Council of British Columbia; and he was one of the foremost advocates of Confederation. In 1869 he removed to Victoria, and became editor of the Victoria *Colonist*. From 1871 to 1875 he represented Nanaimo as a Liberal in the provincial legislature, and from 1882 to 1892 he represented again New Westminster, where he had resumed in 1879 publication of the *British Columbian*. In 1883 he was appointed provincial secretary and minister of mines, finance, and agriculture in the Smithe administration; and in 1889 he became prime minister of the province. He died in London, England, on June 29, 1892. In 1854 he married Susan, daughter of Captain Longworth, of Goderich, Upper Canada.

**Robson, mount,** is in the Cariboo district of British Columbia, south of Berg lake, and near Robson river, in Mount Robson Park. It is in lat. 53° 07', long. 119° 08', and has an altitude of 13,068 feet. The origin of the name is in doubt. See Edmond S. Meany, *The name of mount Robson a puzzle* (Washington Historical Quarterly, 1928).

**Rocanville,** a village in Saskatchewan, on the Canadian Pacific Railway, 130 miles east of Regina. The chief industries are stock-raising and grain-growing. It has four grain elevators, and a weekly newspaper (*Record and Gazette*). Pop. (1934), 400.

**Rocheblave, Philippe François de Rastel, Chevalier de** (d. 1802), soldier, was born in France, the son of the Marquis de Rocheblave, and entered the French army. He was retired on half-pay after the peace of 1748, and afterwards came to Canada. He became an officer in the colonial troops, and served throughout the Seven Years' War. At the end of the war he retired to the Illinois country; and from 1765 to 1773 he seems to have been in the Spanish service. He returned to the British Illinois in 1773, however, and in 1776 he was left in command at Kaskaskia. Here he was captured, on July 4, 1778, by George Rogers Clark, and was sent a prisoner to Virginia. In 1780 he joined the British forces in New York, and in 1781 he was back in Quebec. At the close of the American Revolution, he settled with his family at Varennes,

MOUNT ROBSON, BRITISH COLUMBIA

near Montreal. He represented the county of Surrey in the Legislative Assembly of Lower Canada from 1792 until his death, which took place on April 3, 1802. See D. Girouard, *La famille de Rocheblave* (Bull. rech. hist., 1898).

**Rocheblave, Pierre Rastel de** (1764?-1840), fur-trader, was born about 1764, the son of Philippe François Rastel de Rocheblave (q.v.). He became a wintering partner of the XY Company in 1798; and in 1802 was in opposition to John McDonald of Garth (q.v.) at Fort Augustus. On the union of the XY and North West Companies in 1804, he became a wintering partner of the North West Company, and was placed in charge of the Assiniboine district. From 1807 to 1810 he was again in the Athabaska department; from 1810 to 1812 he was in charge of the Pic, on lake Superior; and in 1814 he was appointed agent of the North West Company in regard to the south-west trade. In 1816 he became a partner in McTavish, McGillivrays, and Co.; and from 1816 to 1821 he was one of the agents of the North West Company, at the annual meetings at Fort William. In 1821 he retired from the fur-trade; but on the failure of McTavish, McGillivrays, and Co. in 1825, and the subsequent return of Simon McGillivray (q.v.), he was placed in temporary charge of the Montreal office, until the Hudson's Bay Company took charge of it. From 1824 to 1827 he represented Montreal West in the Legislative Assembly of Lower Canada; in 1832 he was appointed a member of the Legislative Council of Lower Canada, and in 1838 of the Special Council; and from 1838 to his death he was a member of the Executive Council of the province. He died in Montreal on October 5, 1840. In 1819 he married Elmire (d. 1886), daughter of Jean Bouthillier; and by her he had two daughters. See D. Girouard, *La famille de Rocheblave* (Bull. rech. hist., 1898).

**Rock Bass.** See **Sunfish.**

**Rock-cod** (*Sebastodes*), a large group of marine, spiny-finned fishes, quite unrelated to the true codfish. About a dozen species occur off the Pacific coast of Canada. Only one species of the group occurs in Atlantic waters, and it is usually called rose-fish. Many of the rock-cods are brightly coloured, deep-water ones being often a brilliant red. They are caught in considerable numbers as food fish. The flesh is rather coarse and only of moderate flavour.

**Rock Cress.** See **Cress.**

**Rocket.** See **Winter Cress** and **Sea Rocket.**

**Rock Island,** a village in Stanstead county, Quebec, on the Tomofobia river, 33 miles south of Sherbrooke. The village, established in 1892, is on a rocky island in the river; hence its name. It is the industrial centre of three villages; Rock Island and Stanstead Plain, Quebec, and Derby Line, Vermont. These three places are geographically and commercially one town of 3,000 inhabitants, on the Quebec Central Railway. There is a weekly newspaper (*Stanstead Journal*). Rock Island has several churches, an Ursuline convent, a girls' college, two commercial colleges, and a public library. It is the seat of Stanstead College. The industries include the manufacture of textiles and house furnishings. A park, on lake Memphremagog, and good fishing and hunting are attractions for tourists. Pop. (1931), 1,418.

**Rockland,** a town in Russell county, Ontario, on the Ottawa river, and on a branch line of the Canadian National Railway, 20 miles east of Ottawa. It has flour and lumber mills. Pop. (1931), 2,118.

**Rocks.** See **Geology.**

**Rockwood,** a village in Wellington county, Ontario, on the Speed river, and on the Canadian National Railway, 7 miles east of Guelph. It was formerly noted for its famous Rockwood Academy. See Rev. A. B. Sherk, *A pioneer academy* (Ont. Hist. Soc., Papers and Records, 1926).

**Rocky Mountain House.** There were five trading-posts in western Canada, that were, at one time or another, known by this name:

(1) A North West Company post on the North Saskatchewan river, about a mile above the mouth of the Clearwater river. It was built by John McDonald of Garth (q.v.) in 1802, though an earlier structure had been erected in 1799; and it was strongly fortified, being in the heart of the Blackfoot country. It was the uppermost permanent post of the North West Company on the Saskatchewan river. It was taken over by the Hudson's Bay Company in 1821, and remained in operation until 1875. It was sometimes known as Blackfoot Post.

(2) A Hudson's Bay Company House on the North Saskatchewan, near the mouth of the Clearwater river, officially known as Acton House, but generally called Rocky Mountain House.

(3) Jasper House (q.v.), which was originally known as Rocky Mountain House.

(4) A North West Company post on the north bank of the Peace river, at the mouth of Middle river, built by Simon Fraser (q.v.) in 1805, and known as Rocky Mountain House, Old Hudson's Hope, and Rocky Mountain Portage Fort. It was taken over by the Hudson's Bay Company in 1821, but was closed in 1825.

(5) A North West Company post on the Mackenzie river, in lat. 62° 15', built by John Thomson (q.v.) in 1800. It was soon abandoned, and was described in 1805 as Old Rocky Mountain Fort. Its ruins are still visible near the mouth of the Nahanni river.

**Rocky mountains,** a range (or rather a series of ranges) of mountains, paralleling the west coast of North America, and extending from New Mexico to the Arctic circle. They were formed in post-Mesozoic times by a thrust of the sea bottom of the Pacific against the solid Precambrian nucleus of the continent, crumpling up the flat-lying deposits of the Palæozoic and Mesozoic periods so as to form high ridges and jagged peaks. These mountains are known by geologists as the Corderilla; and in Canada they comprise four distinct ranges—the Rocky mountains proper, which lie immediately west of the prairies or interior continental plain, the Selkirk and Gold ranges, the Coast range, and a partially submerged range represented by Vancouver island and the Queen Charlotte islands. The Rocky mountains proper, which mark the boundary between the provinces of Alberta and British Columbia, rise to a height of between 10,000 and 12,500 feet (though in the Yukon and Alaska they rise to a height much greater than this); and the more easterly ranges slope gradually toward the Pacific ocean. The Rocky mountains are, despite their height, remarkable for the number of passes through them. Of these the most notable are the Peace River pass, by which it was first crossed by Sir Alexander Mackenzie (q.v.) in 1793, the Yellowhead pass, the Howse pass, the Kicking Horse pass (used by the Canadian Pacific Railway), the Vermilion pass, the Kananaskis pass, the Crowsnest pass, the Kootenay pass, and the Boundary pass. The exploration of the Rocky mountains has been a very gradual process, conducted by fur-traders, by government surveyors, by railway engineers, and by mountain-climbers. The literature relating to the Rocky mountains is extensive; but the most important books are A. P. Coleman, *The Canadian Rockies* (Toronto, 1911); W. D. Wilcox, *The Rockies of Canada* (3rd ed., New York, 1909); L. J. Burpee, *Among the Canadian Alps* (Toronto, 1914); Sir James Outram, *In the heart of the Canadian Rockies* (Toronto, 1923); J. M. Thorington, *The glittering mountains* *of Canada* (Philadelphia, 1925); J. N. Wallace, *The passes of the Rocky mountains along the Alberta boundary* (Calgary, 1927), and the numerous articles relating to the Rocky mountains in the *Canadian Alpine Journal* (1907—).

**Rocky Mountains National Park,** with an area of 3,961.50 square miles, is in Alberta, on the eastern slope of the Rocky mountains. It is traversed by the main line of the Canadian Pacific Railway and by a through motor highway. The scenery is characteristic of the eastern slope of the Rockies— rugged mountain ranges extending in parallel ranks north and south for nearly 150 miles, and containing many regions of surprising alpine loveliness and grandeur. Animal life is abundant; and the park is especially noted for its Rocky Mountain or Bighorn sheep, though deer, elk, and bear roam also through it. Its administrative centre is Banff, from which roads and trails lead in every direction. Among the outstanding places of beauty and interest in the park are lake Louise, Paradise valley, and Moraine lake in the valley of the Ten Peaks. In the northern part of the park lies a vast and little known region containing a bewildering array of snow-peaks, ice-fields, and glaciers, including the southern half of the great Columbia *mer de glace.*

**Roddick, Sir Thomas George** (1846-1923), surgeon, was born at Harbour Grace, Newfoundland, on July 31, 1846, the son of John Irvine Roddick and Emma Jane Martin. He was educated at Truro, Nova Scotia, and at McGill University (M.D., 1868), and practised surgery in Montreal. In 1875 he was appointed professor of clinical surgery in McGill University; and from 1901 to 1908 he was dean of the faculty of medicine in this university. From 1896 to 1898 he was president of the British Medical Association; and in 1900 he was made an honorary F.R.C.S. (Eng.). He entered the Canadian militia in 1868, saw service in the Fenian raid of 1870, and was deputy surgeon-general in the North West expeditionary force of 1885. From 1896 to 1904 he represented Montreal West, as a Conservative, in the Canadian House of Commons. He died at Montreal on February 20, 1923. He was twice married, (1) in 1880 to Marion (d. 1890), daughter of William McKinnon, and (2) in 1906 to Amy, daughter of J. J. Redpath, of Chislehurst, England. He was an LL.D. of Edinburgh University (1898) and of Queen's University, Kingston (1903), and a D.Sc. of Oxford University (1904); and in 1914 he was created a knight bachelor.

**Rodney,** a village in Elgin county, Ontario, on the Michigan Central and Père Marquette Railways, 30 miles north-east of Chatham. It is the centre of a bean-growing and tobacco-raising district; and it has also flour and planing mills, basket, woodenware, and pickle factories, a high school, and a weekly newspaper (*Mercury-Sun*). Pop. (1931), 736.

**Roe, Henry** (1829-1909), clergyman and author, was born at Henryville, Lower Canada, on February 22, 1829, and was educated at Bishop's College, Lennoxville (B.A., 1855; M.A., 1867; D.D., 1879; LL.D., 1896). In 1873 he became professor of divinity in Bishop's College, and from 1882 to 1891 he was dean of the faculty and vice-principal. He died at Richmond, Quebec, on August 3, 1909. For many years he was the Canadian correspondent of the London *Guardian;* and he was the author of a number of books and pamphlets, including *Bicentenary sermons* (Montreal, 1862), *Purgatory, trans-substantiation, and the mass examined* (Quebec and Montreal, 1863), *Advantages and means of keeping up reading among the clergy* (Montreal, 1864), and *The story of the first hundred years of the diocese of Quebec* (Quebec, 1893).

**Roebuck, John Arthur** (1801-1879), English politician, was born at Madras, in India, in 1801. In 1815 he emigrated to Canada with his step-father, John Simpson (q.v.), and he was educated in Canada. Returning to England in 1824, he was entered at the Inner Temple and was called to the bar in 1831 (Q.C., 1843). In 1832 he was returned as member for Bath in the first reformed parliament; and he became an outstanding radical. In 1835 he was appointed agent in England for the House of Assembly of Lower Canada; and in 1838 he was heard at the bar of the House of Lords in opposition to Lord John Russell's Canada bill. In his later years he represented Sheffield almost continuously. He died at Westminster on November 30, 1879. In 1878 he was made a privy councillor. He was the author of *Remarks on the proposed union of the Canadas* (Quebec, 1835), *Existing difficulties in the government of the Canadas* (London, 1836), and *The colonies of England* (London, 1849). See R. E. Leader, *Life and letters of John Arthur Roebuck* (London, 1897).

**Roes Welcome,** a strait leading northward from Hudson bay between Southampton island and the mainland. Foxe named an island in the strait after Sir Thomas Roe (1580-1644), who assisted Foxe in his expedition; and the name has since been transferred to the strait.

**Rogers, Benjamin** (1837-1923), lieutenant-governor of Prince Edward Island (1910-5), was born at Bedeque, Prince Edward Island in 1837, and became an export merchant. From 1878 to 1893 he was a member of the Legislative Assembly of the island, and was several times a member of the Executive Council. From 1910 to 1915 he was lieutenant-governor of Prince Edward Island. He died at Alberton, Prince Edward Island, on May 16, 1923.

**Rogers, David McGregor** (1772-1824), member of the Legislative Assembly of Upper Canada, was born on November 23, 1772, the second son of James Rogers (q.v.). He came with his father to Fredericksburgh on the bay of Quinte in 1784, and took up later a large military grant at West Lake. In 1796 and in 1800 he was elected a member of the Legislative Assembly for Prince Edward county, and from 1804 to 1816 he sat for the county of Northumberland, to which he had removed. He was out of the legislature from 1816 to 1820; but in 1820 was again elected for Northumberland. He died on July 13, 1824. In 1802 he married Sarah Playter (d. 1810), of York (Toronto), and in 1811 Elizabeth Playter (d. 1825); and of his first marriage he had two sons and two daughters.

**Rogers, James** (1726?-1792), loyalist, was born in New Hampshire about 1726, the third son of James Rogers and Mary McFatridge. During the Seven Years' War he was a captain in Rogers' Rangers, and was present at the captures of Louisbourg, Quebec, and Montreal. He then settled in Vermont; but he took up arms again during the American Revolution, and in 1778 was gazetted a major in the King's Rangers. During the later stages of the war he was in command at St. Johns. In 1784 he settled at Fredericksburgh on the bay of Quinte with a number of his Rangers; and here he died in 1792. In 1763 he married Margaret, daughter of the Rev. David McGregor, Londonderry, New Hampshire; and by her he had two sons and three daughters. See W. Rogers, *Rogers, ranger and loyalist* (Trans. Roy. Soc. Can., 1900).

**Rogers, Robert** (1731-1795), soldier, was born in Dumbarton, New Hampshire in 1731, the second son of James Rogers and Mary McFatridge. In 1755 he organized a company of scouts, known as Rogers' Rangers, for service against the French, and he served throughout the Seven Years' War. In 1760 he was commissioned to take possession of the western lake posts. At the outbreak of the American Revolution he organized the Queen's Rangers, and later, in 1779, the King's

Rangers. He died in London, England, on May 18, 1795. He published his *Journals* (London, 1765) and *A concise account of North America* (London, 1765; Dublin, 1770); and he was the author of *Ponteach, a tragedy* (London, 1776). His *Journals* have been re-published by F. B. Hough (Albany, 1883). His journal of 1760-1 has been edited by V. H. Paltsits in the *Bulletin* of the New York Public Library for April, 1933. See W. Rogers, *Rogers, ranger and loyalist* (Trans. Roy. Soc. Can., 1900); R. E. Day, *Robert Rogers* (Quarterly Journal of the New York State Historical Association, 1928); and J. J. Mayer, *Major Robert Rogers* (New York History, 1934).

**Rogers, Robert** (1864-1936), minister of public works for Canada (1912-17), was born at Lachute, Quebec, on March 2, 1864, the son of Lieut.-Col. George Rogers. He was educated in Montreal, and in 1881 he went to Clearwater, Manitoba, where he became a storekeeper. From 1896 to 1889 he represented Lisgar in the Canadian House of Commons; but in 1899 he was elected to represent Manitou in the Manitoba legislature, and he retained this seat until 1911. From 1900 to 1911 he was minister of public works in the Manitoba government; and in 1911 he was for a time acting prime minister of the province. Later in 1911 he resigned his provincial portfolio, to become minister of the interior in the Borden government at Ottawa, and was elected to represent Winnipeg in the Canadian House of Commons. In 1912 he became minister of public works, and he retained this portfolio until the formation of the Union government in 1917, when he retired temporarily to private life. He was re-elected to represent Lisgar in the Canadian House of Commons in 1925 and in 1930; but never again held office under the crown. He died in a sanitarium at Guelph, Ontario, on July 21, 1936. In 1888 he married Aurelia Regina Widmeyer; and by her he had one son.

**Rogers, Robert Vashon** (1843-1911), lawyer and author, was born in Kingston, Ontario, in 1843, the youngest son of the Rev. R. Vashon Rogers, head-master of the Kingston Grammar School. He was educated at Queen's University, Kingston (B.A., 1861; hon. LL.D., 1895), and was called to the bar in 1865 (Q.C., 1889). He died at Kingston on May 2, 1911. He was the author of *Wrongs and rights of a traveller* (Toronto, 1875; new ed., under title *The law of the road*, Edinburgh, 1881), and *The law and medical men* (Toronto, 1884).

**Rogers pass,** the route through the Selkirk mountains in British Columbia adopted by the Canadian Pacific Railway for their main line. It lies between the Hermit and Sir Donald ranges of the Selkirk mountains, north of Glacier station, in Glacier park. It was named after Major A. B. Rogers, the "railway pathfinder", who explored it in 1881. See A. O. Wheeler, *Rogers pass at the summit of the Selkirks* (Canadian Alpine Journal, 1929).

**Roland,** a village in Manitoba, on the Canadian National and Canadian Pacific Railways, 66 miles south-west of Winnipeg. It is in a farming and stock-raising district, and has three grain elevators, stock-yards and abattoir, a high school, and a weekly newspaper (*News*). Pop. (1934), 650.

**Rolland, Jean Roch** (1785?-1862), judge, was born about 1785, and was called to the bar of Lower Canada in 1806. In 1830 he was appointed a judge of the Court of King's Bench, and in 1847 he became chief justice of this court. He retired from the bench in 1855, and he died on August 5, 1862, at the manor-house of Sainte-Marie de Monnoir, Lower Canada. In 1821 he married Marguerite, daughter of Colonel Jean-Baptiste-Philippe-Charles d'Esti-mauville, Baron de Beaumouchel.

18

**Rolph, John** (1793-1870), physician and politician, was born at Thornbury, Gloucestershire, England, on March 4, 1793, the son of Dr. Thomas Rolph and Frances Petty. His father emigrated to Upper Canada about 1810, and he followed his family in 1812, but later returned to England to study law and medicine. He remained in England until 1821, was called to the bar at the Inner Temple, and became a member of the Royal College of Surgeons. On his return to Canada, he settled at Charlotteville, Norfolk county, Upper Canada, was called to the bar of Upper Canada, and practised concurrently law and medicine. In 1828, dissatisfied with a decision of Mr. Justice Sherwood (q.v.), he threw off his gown, and ceased to practise law; and in 1829 he was officially licensed to practise medicine. In 1831 he settled in York (Toronto), and he played henceforth an important part in the history of medicine in Upper Canada. From the first he undertook the instruction of medical students, and in 1843 he founded in Toronto a medical school, known as the Toronto School of Medicine, which later became the medical school of Victoria University, and was an important rival of the medical department of King's College.

Law and medicine, however, did not suffice to exhaust his energies. From 1824 the 1830 he represented Middlesex, and from 1836 to 1837 he represented Norfolk in the Legislative Assembly of Upper Canada; and he became one of the leaders of the Reform party in the province. In 1836 he accepted the invitation of Sir F. Bond Head (q.v.) to become, with Robert Baldwin (q.v.), a member of the Executive Council of Upper Canada; but two weeks later he resigned with all his colleagues, both Tory and Reform. In 1837 he was implicated in the Mackenzie rebellion, and was compelled to flee the province. He went to Rochester, New York, and there practised medicine until 1843, when the amnesty granted by the Canadian legislature permitted him to return to Toronto. He became one of the founders of the "Clear Grit" party; and in 1851 he was elected to represent Norfolk in the Legislative Assembly of Canada. In 1851 he became commissioner of crown lands in the Hincks-Morin administration, and in 1853 president of the council; but in 1854 he voted in the House against his colleagues, and precipitated the fall of the government. In 1857 he retired from parliament and from political life; and he died at Mitchell, Ontario, on October 19, 1870. In 1834 he married at Kingston, Upper Canada, Grace, daughter of George Henry Haines, formerly of Leicester, England; and by her he had three sons and one daughter. See W. Canniff, *The medical profession in Upper Canada* (Toronto, 1894).

**Rolph, Thomas** (*fl.* 1833-1844), physician and author, came to Canada from England in 1833. He was a member of the Royal College of Surgeons in England, and in 1835 he began practice as a physician in Ancaster, Upper Canada. In 1839 he was appointed a Canadian immigration agent in the British Isles; and he retained this position until 1843. He settled in Portsmouth, England, where he died. He was the author of *A brief account, together with observations made during a visit to the West Indies, and a tour through the United States of America, in parts of the years 1823-33; together with a statistical account of Upper Canada* (Dundas, Upper Canada, 1836; 2nd ed., London, 1842), and *Emigration and colonization* (London, 1844).

**Romaine.** See **Muskwaro.**

**Romaine river** is in Saguenay county, Quebec, and flows into the gulf of St. Lawrence on its north shore opposite the Mingan islands. The name is a corrupted form of an Indian word meaning "difficult". The river is 250 miles long and drains a basin of 1,800 square miles; it is fed by several considerable lakes including Burnt, Tshimi-komon, and Long. There are several falls in the river. It abounds in fish including gray salmon-trout, muskin-onge, pike, and carp. The river-bed, except in rapids, is formed of fine sand, and the river flows between low-lying hills. The forest in this area has been considerably damaged by fire.

**Roman Catholic Church.** *The Church under French Rule, 1534-1763.* Catholicism came to Canada through the instrumentality of the French. It is certain that a priest accompanied Jacques Cartier (q.v.) on the first of his three voyages to Canada and celebrated mass at Gaspé, on July 7, 1534. Al-though Cartier did not found a colony in the country he claimed for Francis I of France, his voyages were motivated among other things by the hope of spreading Catholic truth to the pagans of the new lands.

Sporadic efforts were made in Acadia to establish a colony in the last half of the sixteenth century, but it was not until Samuel de Champlain (q.v.) found-ed Quebec in 1608 on a site controlling the approach to the heart of North America that a regular and enduring colony was established. Believing that Catholicism was a religion for all nations, Champlain brought from France Franciscan Recollets in 1615 with the hope of teaching the faith to the Iroquois, Algonkian, and Huron tribes. Two of the priests stayed in Quebec to minister to the needs of the colonists; Father Le Caron went west from Quebec, along the shores of the St. Lawrence and north up the Ottawa into the heart of the Huron tribes. Father d'Olbeau went east among the Montagnais of the Saguenay district. For ten years they journeyed back and forth trying to implant the seed of Christ's message on hearts that were unusually stony and dull. Realizing the importance of their task and their own inability to cope with the prodigious undertaking alone, the Recollets invited the Jesuits to

come to their aid. Accordingly, Fathers Brébeuf (q.v.) and Lalemant (q.v.), with several other heroic priests, came to Canada in 1625, and began their illus-trious labours. The work of evangelizing the Indians was, however, seriously impeded by the avarice in the hearts of the company of merchants to whom the French king had ceded the colony. Furs were more precious than souls to these men, and the means they used to procure furs often undid months of moral teaching of the "black-robes". Louis XIII and Richelieu acting upon vehement protests from Champlain and the clergy suppressed the company, and replaced it by the "Company of the One Hundred Associates", which pledged hearty coöperation with the priests in evangelical work.

In 1628 Acadia fell to the English under David Kirke (q.v.), and the following year Quebec was also forced to surrender. Canada was under English control, and practically all the mission-ers had to return to France. The treaty of Saint-Germain-en-Laye, however, re-stored Canada to France in 1632.

Richelieu again sent out the Jesuits, and under the reëstablished Company of One Hundred Associates, under whom Champlain was the governor, missionary work flourished for a time. Upon the advice of Father Lajeune, it was found very beneficial to establish missions among the settled Indian tribes, but quite useless to try to work among those who constantly moved from place to place. In two localities, at least, the priests were successful in persuading meandering tribes to settle down. At Three Rivers and at another place near Quebec, settlements were established and missions formed. In the meantime, on the island of Miscou at the mouth of Chaleur bay, the Jesuits established a mission which enabled them to visit the peoples of Gaspé, Acadia, and Cape Breton. In 1664 the Recollets once more took charge of Gaspé and Acadia.

The mother church at Quebec like-wise developed. The Ursuline sisters, aided by the generosity of Madame de la Peltrie (q.v.) came from France to look after girls' education. Nursing sisters, under Marie de l'Incarnation (q.v.), were placed in charge of the Hôtel Dieu, the hospital endowed by Richelieu's niece, the Duchess d'Aiguillon.

The Company of One Hundred Associates had been granted lucrative monopolies in trade. In return for these, they were pledged to bring to Canada three hundred Catholic settlers annually, and in addition three priests to supervise their spiritual needs. So absorbed were they in fur-trading, however, that they neglected to see that the colonies grew in numerical and religious strength. France herself was distracted from attention because of European troubles. Each year the Iroquois, the particular enemy of the French, became more and more bold in harassing and threatening even Quebec. Montmagny (q.v.), the governor, in 1641 had to conduct a spirited campaign against them.

It was at this time that Montreal was founded. Because of the tepid support of the company, Quebec was not satisfactorily developed. In France under the inspiration of Father J. J. Olier, the saintly founder of the Sulpicians, and Father Jérôme de la Dauversière, the Company of Notre Dame de Montréal was formed. This company in 1640 purchased, from the Company of the One Hundred Associates, the island of Montreal, and secured the gallant Chomedey de Maisonneuve (q.v.) to direct the foundation and development of the new colony. Maisonneuve, with a courageous band of zealous Christians, including Jeanne Mance (q.v.), the future foundress of the Hôtel Dieu, landed at Montreal (Ville Marie) on May 18, 1642. For thirty years the young colony faced extinction from the savage onslaughts of the Iroquois, but the bravery of Maissoneuve, Lambert Closse, and young Dollard (q.v.), time and again saved Montreal. In 1653 Marguerite Bourgeoys (q.v.), the foundress of the Congregation of Notre Dame, came to Montreal to begin an educational development which was to bear rich harvest in Canada and the United States in the years to come. The first Sulpicians came to Canada under Father de Quesluys in 1657, being sent by their founder, Father Olier.

During these years the zealous and courageous Jesuits pursued their thankless labours among the Indians. By enduring indescribable hardships and Christ-like sacrifices, they were able to build between Georgian bay and lake Simcoe thriving missions among the Hurons. Father Bressani (q.v.) wrote in 1648: "In spite of persecution, want, famine, war, and pestilence, there is not a single family which does not count some Christians." The tone and culture of the Hurons was slowly but surely improving; the progress began to comfort the priests for their difficult duties. However, the progress was not for long. The tameless Iroquois from the south set out on the war path bent on utter extermination of their foes. One by one the Huron villages were attacked and burned and their people butchered. In the spring of 1648 St. Joseph's was wiped out. St. Louis, despite good fortifications, met the same disaster, as did St. Mary's and St. Ignace. Fathers Daniel (q.v.), Lalemant (q.v.), Brébeuf (q.v.), Garnier (q.v.), and Charbonel fell in the onslaught, victims for Christ. These Canadian martyrs were canonized by Pope Pius XI in 1925.

In Quebec the Company of One Hundred Associates maintained control of political and commercial affairs of New France till 1663, when Louis XIV and Colbert made the colony a royal province, under a Sovereign Council, consisting of the governor, the bishop, and five councillors. This body was enlarged in 1674, and again in 1703, to include an intendant, attorney-general, a clerk, and twelve councillors.

Ecclesiastical hierarchy began in Canada in 1659. François de Montmorency-Laval (q.v.) was appointed vicar apostolic of New France with the title of bishop of Petræa. He landed on June 16, 1659, but had first to contest his authority with the archbishop of Rouen, France. Whether rightly or wrongly, the latter looked upon Canada as subject to his jurisdiction in matters spiritual. He had sent a number of missioners and colonists to Canada, and had appointed Father de Queylus (q.v.) as his vicar-general. His authority up to the time of Laval's arrival was unquestioned, and he had received no notice from the Holy See of the new appointment. The conflict of jurisdiction, however, resulted in Queylus's recall to France. Matters were definitely settled when Clement X erected the see of Quebec into a regular diocese depending solely on Rome (1674). Five years after his recall, Queylus returned to Canada, and was warmly welcomed by Bishop Laval, who made him his vicar-general.

Bishop Laval's greatest battle was against the liquor traffic, which threatened the civilization and salvation of the Indians and the welfare of New France. He was forced by the commercial greed of civil authorities to threaten excommunication to traffickers in liquor. By his strong stand against Governor d'Avaugour (q.v.), Governor de Mézy (q.v.), Intendant Talon (q.v.), and Frontenac (q.v.), he braved the disfavour of the civil authorities rather than surrender his pastoral care of souls and Christian morality. Under the Viceroy Tracy (q.v.), church and state were more at peace.

Two campaigns against the Iroquois (1665-6) reduced the Indians to inaction for twenty years, and enabled the colony to develop. In 1668 Bishop Laval opened a preparatory seminary, and ten years later a theological seminary for the training of his clergy. In 1672 there were outside of Quebec at least twenty-five parishes that needed priestly administrations. The clergy were supported by a tax on the faithful of a thirteenth part of their crops (1663). Later, this was reduced to one twenty-sixth, with the king promising to make up the rest.

Missionary work had gone on apace between 1660 and 1680. On lake Superior the Jesuit Father Allouez (q.v.) founded two missions (1665). Fathers Dablon (q.v.) and Marquette (q.v.) established another at Sault Ste. Marie. The western shores of lake Huron and the southern shores of lake Ontario and the St. Lawrence saw the ministrations of the Jesuits. Father Albanel (q.v.) went as far north as the Hudson bay. In 1673 Louis Joliet (q.v.) and Father Marquette set out from Canada and discovered the great Mississippi. The Sulpicians pushed their evangelical work to the territory lying between the Illinois and the Ohio rivers; the Recollets (Franciscans) founded four missions, Three Rivers, Ile Percée, River St. John, and Fort Frontenac (Kingston).

Bishop St. Valier (q.v.) succeeded Laval, who retired in 1684. The new bishop founded the General Hospital at Quebec and freed the seminary staff from parochial duties. When the English admiral Phips (q.v.) attacked Quebec (1690) with thirty-two ships, Bishop St. Valier's pastoral letter did much for the city's defence.

The eighteenth century witnessed France's growing neglect of, and England's increasing interest in, Canada. Colonists from New France were few and far between, so that Canada was forced to rely for her preservation on her own strength. Canada's population in 1739 was but 42,000 as compared with that of the colonies of New England, which in 1706, numbered 262,000. England first directed her attention to Acadia which was very weak defensively. In 1710 Port Royal fell, and by the Treaty of Utrecht (1713), France ceded to England Acadia, Newfoundland, and the Hudson's bay territory. Although missionary work in the east did not cease, it was often impeded by the English authorities. One of the blackest pages of English history in America is that which deals with the expulsion of the Acadians from their homes. Lawrence (q.v.) scattered these defenseless and sorrowing families through the American colonies. Longfellow's poem "Evangeline" deals with this pitiable episode.

Bishop St. Valier died in 1727, and Bishop Duplessis-Mornay was appointed, but never came to Canada. His co-adjutor, Bishop Dosquet, succeeded him in 1733, and laboured particularly in the field of education. Bishop Lauberivière (q.v.), his successor, died upon his arrival at Quebec of typhoid fever (1740), and the last bishop under the French régime was Bishop Pontbriand (q.v.).

In 1759 General Wolfe (q.v.) captured Quebec, and Bishop Pontbriand took refuge with the Sulpicians at Montreal, where he died before the city was taken by the English. The Treaty of Paris, on February 10, 1763, ceded Canada to England.

*The Church under British Rule, 1763—.* The early Church in Canada had to contend against the forces of nature, the rugged winters, the immense distances from supplies both in France and in Canada, and the slow difficult transportation of men, stores, and news; she had to stave off hostile Indians, and later withstand unfavourable civil governments, anxious for gain, but indifferent to the strengthening of their colonies and their religion. But now that New France had fallen into the hands of Great Britain, a vigorously Protestant country and a traditional foe to all things French, it looked as though the 65,000 French Catholics in Canada could neither survive as Catholics nor as Frenchmen. As events turned out, however, it became evident

that Catholicism benefited by coming under British rule. Less than thirty years after France lost Canada, the Church in France was torn asunder by the Revolution, and since that time the government of that country would have been a bitter foe to the development of Catholicism in Canada. England was at first somewhat hostile to the Church, but later, placing more importance on stabilizing the country for state reasons than splitting it for a religious purpose, she made wise concessions that have benefited both the country and Catholicism.

It is not an astounding thing that, at the outset, Great Britain should have attempted to Anglicize her new subjects in both language and religion. It was inevitable. She meant to bring this about not by open violence, but by control through legislation. At the surrender of Quebec and Montreal, the British conceded the free exercise of the Catholic religion, the right of priests and missionaries to perform their duties; but they would not recognize a Catholic hierarchy. The Treaty of Paris states: "His Britannic Majesty agrees to grant the liberty of the Catholic religion to the inhabitants of Canada and will in consequence give the most precise and most effectual orders that his new Roman Catholic subjects may profess the worship of their religion according to the rites of the Romish Church, as far as the laws of Great Britain permit." In the last phase lurked the danger. It was not long before the Home government and the colonial government exchanged communications which plainly reveal the policy of Anglicizing and Protestantizing the new Catholic subjects.

In general, the Catholic clergy were loyal to their new civil government. The Church, an unnational institution, has ever tried to support lawfully constituted authority; on this occasion, the vicars general and most of the priests instilled into their flocks the obligation of political obedience to the English king. However, if the state attempted to legislate and dictate in any matter which the church regarded as under the ægis of the church and not the state, she presented firm and unshakable opposition.

The chapter of vicars general met at Quebec and petitioned the king to fill the vacant see of Quebec, and recommended for royal assent, M. de Montgolfier, the Sulpician superior at Montreal. Governor Murray (q.v.) disliked Montgolfier's strictness, and prevented the government's acquiescence. After a time Abbé Briand (q.v.) received the approval of Murray and the British government. Accordingly, he was consecrated in France and returned to Canada under the title of superintendent —but not bishop; this was a title reserved for the head of the Church of England in Canada.

The religious orders seemed doomed to extinction. They were permitted to take no novices. Their property was to pass into the hands of the state. In 1774 the Jesuits and Recollets were dispossessed. It was likewise illegal for Superintendent Briand to recruit priests from France or England. It was only when the French Revolution forced many exiles into England that the government permitted exiled French priests to enter Canada (1793).

In the meantime, Great Britain's American colonies were in revolt. England, wishing more for a loyal colony than for a victory in a religious quarrel, realized she must conciliate her Canadian subjects. Through the wisdom of Guy Carleton (q.v.) she granted them by the Quebec Act, 1774, liberties hitherto withheld. When the Americans attacked Quebec (1775) they found the French Canadians, led by Superintendent Briand and the priests, loyal to the British crown.

In 1784 Briand retired, and was succeeded by Superintendent d'Esglis (q.v.), who named as his successor Jean

François Hubert (q.v.). When the latter began his control of the Church (1789), he and two of his coadjutors, M. Bailli de Messein and M. Denaut, successfully combated a plan to establish a mixed university for Catholics and Protestants alike, which was to be subsidized out of the revenues of the Jesuit estates. It was because the state was to have complete control of education that Catholic opposition arose.

The Constitutional Act of 1791, which divided Canada into two provinces, Upper and Lower Canada, each with a separate government, restated guarantees of liberty for the Catholic religion; yet the instructions to Governors were still sent from England and these permitted much leeway for personal interpretation by the governors. What freedom the Church experienced in previous years was more due to the benevolence of the governors, especially Lord Dorchester, than to the law.

Superintendent Denaut (1793-1806) had a very difficult problem confronting him during his régime. A strong party undertook to deprive French Canadians of their institutions and religion. Chief Justice Monk (q.v.), Attorney-General Sewell (q.v.), the Anglican Bishop Mountain (q.v.), and Herman Witsius Ryland (q.v.), civil secretary to the governors of Canada for twenty years, were the leaders. They desired to subject the Church to the state in the matter of erecting parishes and appointing pastors; and they hoped to establish an exclusively Protestant school system. They obtained from the legislature in 1801 a law which established a corporation under the name of "The Royal Institution for the Encouragement of Public Instruction." Superintendent Denaut along with his clergy so strongly opposed the institution that it failed completely.

Bishop Plessis (q.v.) was destined to achieve the organization of the Canadian Church. He aimed at obtaining civil recognition of bishop and clergy without forfeiting any right or privilege of the Church in religion or education. So prudently and kindly did he conduct his business with the government that he won their respect, despite the fact that he would not yield one iota from his claim to full spiritual jurisdiction. By his whole-hearted loyalty to the Crown and vigorous pastoral letters during the American War of 1812, during which French Canadians fought bravely for Canada, he was granted a seat in the Legislative Council, and his title and dignity of bishop were recognized for the first time.

Later, he obtained governmental approval for the creation of vicariates apostolic in Upper Canada, Nova Scotia, and Prince Edward Island. In 1819 he succeeded in calming the alarm in England, and winning the government's assent to his elevation to the dignity of archbishop of the metropolitan see at Quebec with two suffragans. Upper Canada was placed under Bishop Alexander Macdonell (q.v.), and Prince Edward Island and New Brunswick under Bishop McEachern. In 1820, Bishop Provencher (q.v.) was appointed to rule over the North West, and Bishop Lartigue (q.v.) was placed over Montreal, though they were not, as yet, independent bishops. Thus it was that the great Archbishop Plessis by his prudence, loyalty, and charm won for the Church the right to organize the great archdiocese for more efficient care of souls. He died in 1825 genuinely mourned by church and state.

Bishop Panet (q.v.) succeeded Plessis. During his régime, education both primary and secondary greatly advanced. French Canadians numbered 380,000 in 1832. Kingston (1826) and Charlottetown (1829) were erected to episcopal sees. Archbishop Signay's episcopate (1832-50) was marked by several calamities, a cholera scourge (1834), civil war (1837-8), fires that ruined Quebec city (1845), and the typhus fever which Irish immigrants brought from Ireland when driven out by the famine and eviction of 1847.

The long-standing question of the property of the Sulpicians, which their enemies had coveted since the conquest, was finally settled justly by Queen Victoria by an ordinance of the Privy Council. This declared the Seminary of St. Sulpice the lawful owner of its holdings.

For some time plans had been afoot to unite Upper and Lower Canada with the hope that Protestantism and English would soon crush out Catholic and French influence in the country. The bill was introduced in the House of Commons in England (1822), but the vigilance of Bishop Plessis and the petition of 60,000 people, taken to London by Papineau (q.v.) and Neilson (q.v.), brought about the withdrawal of the bill. However, the union of Upper and Lower Canada, which was bitterly feared by French Canada, was effected in 1840. The Act, contrary to expectation, turned out very favourably to the liberty and progress of Catholicism. That broad-minded governor, Lord Elgin (q.v.), used his strong influence to make the Act deeply satisfactory to Catholicism. In addition to this, Canada owes to this just governor her religious liberty, for it was through his instrumentality that the Act of 1851 was passed which declared that "Free exercise and enjoyment of profession and religious worship, without distinction or preference, are permitted by the constitution and laws of this province of Canada to all the subjects of Her Majesty in the said province."

The impetus given Catholicism in Canada by this Act may be seen in the fact that under Archbishop Signay (q.v.) of Quebec, his successor, Archbishop Turgeon (q.v.) and Bishop Bourget (q.v.), successor of Bishop Lartigue of Montreal, five religious communities of men and sixteen of women either arose from Canadians or came to Canada from France. The number of sees increased: Toronto (1841), Halifax (1842), St. John, New Brunswick (1842), Arichat, Nova Scotia (1844), Ottawa (1847), St. John's, Newfoundland (1847). The first Council of Quebec, since it was raised to a metropolitan see, was held in 1851 with Montreal, Kingston, and Toronto as suffragans. Under the guidance of Meilleur (q.v.), the superintendent of education, primary, secondary, and higher education greatly advanced. In the thirteen years of his office, school attendance increased from 3,000 in 1842 to 127,000 in 1855. New colleges were opened at Joliette (1846), St. Laurent (1847), Rigaud (1850), St. Marie de Monnoir (1853), Lévis (1853). The Canadian clergy had long felt the need of a Catholic university, and Laval was inaugurated in 1854, and canonically established by a bull of Pius IX in 1876. Archbishop Taschereau (q.v.) was made the first Canadian cardinal in 1886. Quebec, the mother see of Canada, at present presided over by the fourth Canadian cardinal, His Eminence Rodrigue M. Villeneuve, O. M.I., has as suffragans Three Rivers (1852), Rimouski (1867), Chicoutimi (1878), Nicolet (1885), and Gaspé (1905). Montreal is an archbishopric, with St. Hyacinthe (1852), Sherbrooke (1874), Valleyfield (1892), and Joliette (1904) as suffragans.

*Western Canada.* The Church in the West had likewise her rugged, zealous pioneers who faced unbelievable hardships to fulfill the command given so long ago, "Going, therefore, teach ye all nations . . ." The Jesuit Fathers Messaiger, Aulneau, and Cocquart carried the Gospel into the West (1733-41) in the band of the great explorer La Vérendrye (q.v.). Father Aulneau and the eldest son of La Vérendrye perished along with nineteen men at the hands of the Sioux. Father Cocquart was the first priest to reach the present sites of Winnipeg and Portage la Prairie.

Lord Selkirk's colonists came to the shores of Hudson's bay in 1811, and to the Red river in 1812, under the care of Captain Miles Macdonell (q.v.), a Catholic who believed firmly in the need of religion as the basis of a state. Strained relations between men of the North West Company (French and *Métis*) and the Hudson's Bay Company (Scotch and Irish under English control) made Macdonell intent on procuring priests for the West. His earnest requests, seconded by those of Lord Selkirk, prevailed upon Bishop Plessis to send Father Provencher (q.v.) and Father Dumoulin. On the banks of the Red river, Abbé Provencher founded the first western Canadian mission in 1818. Two years later he was consecrated bishop. The rest of his life was spent zealously labouring for the development of the West; he fostered education, encouraged agriculture, and brought recruits to aid in his onerous tasks, and dispatched missioners even to the Western coast. In 1844 he was made vicar apostolic of the North West, and in 1847 bishop of St. Boniface; the same year Modeste Demers (q.v.) was named bishop of Vancouver. The great band of Oblate Fathers, to whom the West owes a lasting debt, first came to the land of perhaps their greatest labours, on the invitation of Bishop Provencher. One of them, Alexandre Taché (q.v.), was to succeed Bishop Provencher in the see of St. Boniface (1853). This heroic man nobly and energetically carried on the great work of his predecessor. Bishop Faraud was appointed vicar apostolic of Athabaska in 1862. Taché was made archbishop of St. Boniface in 1871, and his coadjutor Bishop Grandin (q.v.) was named bishop of the new see of St. Albert (1871), to which was added in 1890 the vicariate apostolic of Saskatchewan. This vicariate became the see of Prince Albert in 1908. The great Archbishop Langevin (q.v.) was consecrated for the metropolitan diocese of St. Boniface in 1895. In 1911 the vicariate apostolic of Keewatin and in 1912 the vicariate apostolic of Hudson's bay were added to the metropolitan province of St. Boniface. Regina was raised to a diocese in 1910, and in 1915 to an archdiocese with Gravelbourg (1930), Prince Albert (1933), Saskatoon (1933), and St. Peter's Abbey, Muenster, Saskatchewan, as suffragans. Edmonton was a bishopric which in 1920 was elevated to a metropolitan province with Calgary (1913), Grouard, and Mackenzie (1901) as suffragans. The last metropolitan province is Vancouver, which includes Vancouver, Victoria (1847), Nelson (1936), and the vicariate apostolic of Yukon and Prince Rupert (1916). In 1911 the Right Rev. Nicetas Budka was appointed ordinary of all Ruthenian priests in Canada, with his seat at Winnipeg.

In 1869 political disturbances arose in the Red river district which came very near having serious consequences. When the newly created Dominion of Canada sought the acquisition of the territories of the Hudson's Bay Company, which had chartered rights in the western plains, they sent surveyors into the colony of Assiniboia; these men began dividing and subdividing land which naturally the inhabitants of the West resented—for the surveyors had, as yet, no legal right to the territory. Louis Riel (q.v.) and a band of westerners forcibly stopped the work. After many parleys and conferences, both in the West and at Ottawa, after military forces had been mustered on both sides to strengthen the arguments of the contending parties, a serious civil war was narrowly averted. The arrival of Bishop Taché from Rome, where he had been visiting, helped greatly in effecting a peaceful settlement. Practically all the claims of the westerners were embodied in the Manitoba Act (1869), which became the constitution of a new Canadian province in the Confederation of Canada.

A similar grievance arose in Saskatchewan. Riel again took the lead of the *Métis* (1884-5) against the white invasion. But he had lost all prudence, being a victim of mental derangement. Bloodshed was not this time avoided. Riel was hanged, despite the fact that he was judged of unsound mind by alienists. In both of these unfortunate episodes, the Church at last succeeded in placating the bitter feelings of political, national, and religious enemies.

The Manitoba school question was a particularly bitter chapter in the history of the West. When Manitoba entered Confederation in 1869, a provision in the Act stipulated that no legislation was to be made against "any right or privilege with respect to the denominational schools which any class of persons have by law or practice in the province at the union." Under the Greenway government, and supported by the Canadian Supreme Court, separate Catholic schools were done away with, and French was abolished in the schools and courts and legislature (March, 1890). Archbishop Taché and the Catholics of the West were heartbroken. The compensation which the Privy Council thought was justly owing the Western Catholics is still to be settled, though Laurier (q.v.) did try to solve the matter by a compromise unsatisfactory to Catholics.

*Ontario.* In 1803 a very distinguished priest, Father Alexander Macdonell (q.v.), arrived in Upper Canada with a band of Scotch soldiers who had seen service in quelling revolts in Ireland. For them and their families Father Macdonell obtained grants of land in Glengarry. Bishop Denaut appointed Father Macdonell pastor of St. Raphael, and later, in 1807, vicar general. In the War of 1812 Vicar-General Macdonell mustered his men in defence of Canada, and was rewarded by a seat in the Legislative Council of Ontario. In 1826 he was consecrated bishop of Upper Canada, an independent diocese with the see at Kingston. In 1889, Kingston was made an archdiocese with Peterborough (1882), Alexandria (1890), Sault

Ste. Marie (1904) as suffragans. Toronto became a bishopric in 1841, and an archbishopric in 1870, with London (1855) and Hamilton (1856) as suffragans. Ottawa became a bishopric in 1847, and an archbishopric in 1886, with Pembroke as a suffragan (1898).

The first permanent apostolic delegate to Canada, Mgr. D. Falconio, took up his residence at Ottawa in 1903.

*The Maritimes.* Halifax in 1842 was made a bishopric, and in 1852 an archbishopric, with suffragans at Charlottetown (1829), Saint John (1842), Antigonish (1844), Chatham (1860), and Moncton (1937). In Newfoundland, St. John's was made a bishopric in 1847, and an archbishopric in 1904, with suffragans at Harbour Grace (1856) and St. George (1904).

In Canada to-day there are more than twenty-five communities of priests, about twelve of brothers, and close to eighty of sisters. The total population of Catholics in Canada greatly exceeds 3,000,000; there are over 4,000 priests, in 3,000 parishes. In perhaps no country of the world is religion as free and as respected as in Canada.

*Bibliography.* The literature relating to the Catholic Church in Canada is voluminous, including a very large number of parish histories, especially in French Canada. The best general account is to be found in the Abbé H. A. Scott, "The Roman Catholic Church east of the Great lakes," and the Rev. A. G. Morice, "The Roman Catholic Church west of the Great lakes," in A. Shortt and A. G. Doughty (eds.), *Canada and its provinces*, vol. xi (Toronto, 1913). The authority on the history of the Church during the French régime is the Abbé A. H. Gosselin, *L'église du Canada* (4 vols., Quebec, 1911-7), though reference should also be had to M. Eastman, *Church and state in early Canada* (Edinburgh, 1915). Histories of the Church in particular parts of Canada are the Rev. J. C. Macmillan, *The history of the Catholic*

*Church in Prince Edward Island* (Quebec, 1913), the Very Rev. W. R. Harris, *The Catholic Church in the Niagara peninsula* (Toronto, 1895), and the Rev. A. G. Morice, *History of the Catholic Church in western Canada* (2 vols., Toronto, 1910), the last of which has been published also in French under the title, *Histoire de l'église catholique dans l'ouest canadien* (1912).

**Romance Languages.** See **Modern Language Instruction.**

**Rondeau,** a village and harbour in Kent county, Ontario, on the north shore of lake Erie. It is a coal depot of the Père Marquette Railway, 12 miles south-east of Chatham. Pop. (1934), 200.

**Rose, George MacLean** (1829-1898), publisher, was born in Wick, Caithnessshire, Scotland, on March 14, 1829. He was educated at the Wick Academy, and was apprenticed as a printer in the office of the *John o' Groat Journal*. He came to Canada in 1851, and established a printing shop in Montreal. In 1856 he removed to Upper Canada, and for two years was a journalist. In 1858 he entered the publishing business, and in 1865 he became a partner in the firm of Hunter, Rose, and Co., Ottawa. In 1871 this firm moved from Ottawa to Toronto, and for many years was one of the most enterprising of Canadian publishing houses. It published the *Canadian Monthly* (1872-8), and its successor, *Rose-Belford's Canadian Monthly* (1878-82). In 1886-8 Rose brought out also two volumes of a *Cyclopedia of Canadian biography*. He died at Toronto on February 10, 1898. In 1856 he married Margaret, daughter of William Manson, of Oxford county, Upper Canada; and by her he had several children.

**Rose, Sir John, Bart.** (1820-1888), minister of finance for Canada (1868-9), was born at Turriff, Aberdeenshire, Scotland, on August 2, 1820, the son of William Rose and Elizabeth Fyfe. He was educated at King's College, Aberdeen; and in 1836 he came with his parents to Canada. He served as a volunteer in the loyalist forces in the rebellion of 1837. In 1842 he was called to the bar of Lower Canada (Q.C., 1848); and he built up a large practice in Montreal. In 1857 he was elected to represent Montreal in the Legislative Assembly of Canada, and became solicitor-general for Lower Canada in the Macdonald-Cartier administration. In 1858 he became minister of public works in the Cartier-Macdonald government; but in 1861 he retired from office, though he continued to sit for Montreal. He was a delegate at the London Conference of 1866-7, at which the final arrangements in regard to the Canadian Confederation were made; and in 1868 he became the second finance minister of the Dominion, representing Huntingdon in the Canadian House of Commons. In 1869 he resigned to join the banking firm of Morton, Rose, and Co., of London, England; and he left Canada, though he continued to act as an unofficial representative of Canada in London. He became a well-known figure in London society; and in 1883 the Prince of Wales appointed him receiver-general of the duchy of Lancaster. He died suddenly on August 24, 1888, while a guest of the Duke of Portland, at Langwell, Caithness. He married (1) in 1843 Charlotte (d. 1883), widow of Robert Sweeny (q.v.), and daughter of Robert Emmett Temple, of Rutland, Vermont, by whom he had five children; and (2) in 1887 Julia, daughter of Keith Stewart Mackenzie, of Seaforth, and widow of the ninth Marquis of Tweeddale. He was created a baronet of the United Kingdom in 1870, a K.C.M.G. in 1872, a G.C.M.G. in 1878, and a privy councillor in 1886. See M. H. Long, *Sir John Rose and the high commissionership* (Can. hist. rev., 1931).

**Roseau river,** a tributary of the Red river which has its source near the lake of the Woods. It was an old canoe route between the lake of the Woods and the Red river. The name is the French equivalent for "Reed river."

**Rosebrugh, Abner Mulholland** (1835-1914), physician and author, was born hear Galt, Upper Canada, on November 8, 1835. He was educated at Victoria College, Cobourg (M.D., 1859), and practised medicine in Toronto. He devoted himself chiefly to the study of ophthalmology and medical electricity; and he invented various electrical devices. He died in Toronto on November 6, 1914. He was the author of *An introduction to the study of the optical defects of the eye* (Toronto, 1866), *Chloroform, and a new way of administering it* (Toronto, 1869), *A handbook of medical electricity* (Toronto, 1885), and *Recent advances in electro-therapeutics* (Toronto, 1887).

**Rose, Early Wild** (*Rosa blanda* Ait., *Rosaceae*), a low shrub, 1-3 feet high, blossoming from June to July, along the fence rows and in moist rocky places. It is entirely unarmed, with the possible exception of a few straight slender prickles on the stem. The compound leaf has from 5 to 7 oblong-lanceolate, simply-toothed leaflets; the base of the leaf stalk bears broad leafy expansions or stipules. The large rose-pink flowers are either solitary or in few-flowered clusters; the fruit is globose and scarlet when ripe. It extends from Newfoundland to Ontario.

**Rose-fish.** See **Rock-cod.**

**Rosemary, Bog** (*Andromeda glaucophylla* Link., *Ericaceae*), an evergreen shrub with thick, evergreen, linear leaves, white beneath, with a close fine pubescence; the branchlets and bud scales are smooth. The flowers are pink or white and borne in clusters, each flower borne on a curved stalk; the calyx lobes are whitish and spreading; the corolla is globose; the stamens 10. It may be found growing in bogs from Labrador to Manitoba, blooming from May to July.

**Rosetown,** a town in Saskatchewan on the Saskatoon and Calgary branch of the Canadian National Railway, and on the Moose Jaw and Edmonton branch of the Canadian Pacific Railway, 72 miles south-west of Saskatoon. It is in a general farming district, and has a high school, a convent, a hospital, and a weekly newspaper (*Eagle*). Pop. (1931), 1,553.

**Roseway.** See **Port Roseway.**

**Rosiers, cape,** a promontory on the south shore of the St. Lawrence river, in Gaspé county, Quebec, so called after the wild rose-bushes formerly found there.

**Ross, Alexander** (1783-1856), fur-trader and author, was born in Nairn-shire, Scotland, on May 9, 1783. He emigrated to Canada in 1805, and for several years he taught school in Glengarry, Upper Canada. In 1810 he entered the service of the Pacific Fur Company, and he took part in the founding of Fort Astoria. In 1813, when Astoria was handed over to the Nor'-Westers, he became a clerk in the North West Company; and he remained on the Pacific slope until after the union of the North West and Hudson's Bay Companies in 1821. He retired from the fur-trade in 1825, and settled in the Red River district. He became sheriff of Assiniboia; and from 1835 to 1850 he was a member of the Council of Assiniboia. He died at the Red River Settlement on October 23, 1856. He was the author of *Adventures of the first settlers on the Oregon or Columbia river* (London, 1849), *The fur-hunters of the far West* (2 vols., London, 1855), and *The Red River settlement* (London, 1856). Some of his letters have been published in *Transaction No. 63* of the Manitoba Historical and Scientific Society. See G. Bryce, *Alexander Ross* (Can. mag., 1917), and *Alexander Ross, fur-trader, author, and philanthropist* (Queen's Quarterly, 1903).

**Ross, Alexander McLagan** (1829-1900), provincial treasurer of Ontario, was born in Dundee, Scotland, on April 20, 1829, the son of Colin Ross and Elizabeth McLagan. He came with his parents to Canada in 1834, and was educated at Goderich, Upper Canada. He entered the Bank of Upper Canada, and was later an officer of the Royal Canadian Bank and the Canadian Bank of Commerce. From 1875 to 1890 he represented West Huron in the Legislative Assembly of Ontario; and from 1883 to 1890 he was provincial treasurer. In 1890 he was appointed clerk of the county court, York county, Ontario; and he died at Toronto on September 29, 1900.

**Ross, Alexander Milton** (1832-1897), naturalist, was born at Belleville, Upper Canada, on December 13, 1832, the son of William Ross and Frederika Grant. He was educated at the common school in Belleville, but at the age of eleven had to leave school to earn a livelihood. He went to New York, and became a compositor on the *Evening Post*, then edited by William Cullen Bryant, the poet. At the same time he studied medicine, and in 1855 he obtained the degree of M.D., and was admitted a member of the College of Physicians and Surgeons. He became actively interested in the anti-slavery campaign, and was a personal friend of John Brown, the abolitionist. He served as a surgeon in the American Civil War; and after the war he took service as a surgeon in the Mexican army. About 1870 he returned to Canada, and devoted himself to the study of Canadian flora and fauna. He died at Detroit, Michigan, on October 27, 1897. In 1857 he married Hester Harrington; and by her he had one son. He published the following books and pamphlets: *Recollections of an abolitionist* (Montreal, 1867); *The birds of Canada* (Toronto, 1871); *Butterflies and moths of Canada* (Toronto, 1873); *The flora of Canada* (Toronto, 1875); *The forest trees of Canada* (Toronto, 1875); *Catalogue to illustrate the animal resources of the*

*Dominion* (Toronto, 1876); *Ferns and wild flowers of Canada* (Toronto, 1877); *Mammals, reptiles, and fresh water fishes of Canada* (Montreal, 1878), and *Memoirs of a reformer* (Toronto, 1893). See F. Landon, *A daring Canadian abolitionist* (Michigan History Magazine, 1921).

**Ross, Dunbar** (1800?-1865), solicitor-general for Lower Canada, (1853-7), was born at Clonakilty, Ireland, about 1800. He emigrated to Canada in youth, was called to the bar of Lower Canada (Q.C., 1853), and practised law in Quebec. From 1850 to 1851 he represented Megantic in the Legislative Assembly of Canada, and Beauce from 1854 to 1861. From 1853 to 1857 he was solicitor-general for Lower Canada. He died at Quebec on May 16, 1865. Under the *nom-de-plume* of "Zeno" he published a pamphlet entitled *The "Crise" Metcalfe, and the Lafontaine-Baldwin cabinet defended* (Montreal, 1844), and under his own name *The seat of government of Canada, its Legislative Council, and "double majority" question* (Quebec, 1858).

**Ross, Mrs. Ellen,** *née* **McGregor** (d. 1892), author, was born in Banff, Scotland, the daughter of Capt. McGregor. She married first a journalist of Inverness named Stalker; and after his death she married, secondly, a banker of Inverness named Alexander Ross. With her second husband she emigrated to Canada, and settled in Montreal. Left a widow in Montreal, she turned to writing for support. In addition to a number of stories contributed to American magazines and newspapers, she published *Violet Keith* (Montreal, 1868), *The wreck of the White Bear* (Montreal, 1871), *A legend of the Grand Gordons* (Montreal, 1873), and *The legend of the holy stones* (Montreal, 1878). She died in Montreal in 1892.

**Ross, Sir George William** (1841-1914), prime minister of Ontario (1899-1905), was born near Nairn, Middlesex county, Ontario, on September 18, 1841, the son of James Ross and Ellen McKinnon. He was educated at the Toronto Normal School and at Albert University, Belleville (LL.B., 1883). For many years he was a teacher and school inspector. From 1872 to 1883 he represented West Middlesex in the Canadian House of Commons; he then entered the Mowat administration in Ontario as minister of education, and was elected to the Legislative Assembly for West Middlesex. On the retirement of A. S. Hardy (q.v.), he became prime minister of Ontario, and held office until the government was defeated at the polls in 1905. He continued to sit in the legislature, as leader of the opposition, until 1907, when he was appointed a senator of Canada. In 1911 he was chosen as Liberal leader in the Senate; and he held this position until his death in Toronto on March 7, 1914. He was thrice married, (1) in 1862 to Christina (d. 1872), daughter of Duncan Campbell, (2) in 1875 to Catharine (d. 1902), daughter of William Boston, and (3) in 1907 to Mildred, daughter of John Robert Peel. In 1911 he was created a knight bachelor. He was an LL.D. of St. Andrew's University (1888), of Victoria University (1892), of the University of Toronto (1894), of McMaster University (1902), and of Queen's University (1903); and in 1896 he was elected a fellow of the Royal Society of Canada. With William Buckingham (q.v.) he collaborated in *The life and times of the Hon. Alexander Mackenzie* (Toronto, 1892), and he was the author of *The school system of Ontario* (New York, 1896), *The senate of Canada* (Toronto, 1914), and a large number of pamphlets and public addresses. As a public speaker he was almost unrivalled among Canadians of his day. His reminiscences were published under the title, *Getting into parliament, and after* (Toronto, 1913). See Margaret Ross, *Sir George W. Ross, a biographical study* (Toronto, 1924).

**Ross, James** (1811-1886), principal of Dalhousie College and University (1864-85), was born at West River, Pictou, Nova Scotia, on July 28, 1811, the son of the Rev. Duncan Ross. He was ordained a minister of the Presbyterian Church in 1835; in 1842 he became editor of the *Presbyterian Banner;* and later he became principal of the Presbyterian Theological Seminary at West River, and after 1858 at Truro. When this college was merged with Dalhousie College in 1863 he was appointed principal of Dalhousie, and professor of ethics and political economy. He resigned in 1885, and he died at Dartmouth, Nova Scotia, on March 15, 1886.

**Ross, James** (1835-1871), journalist, was born in the Red River Settlement, in the North West, on May 9, 1835, the son of Alexander Ross (q.v.). He was educated at St. John's College, Winnipeg, and at the University of Toronto (B.A., 1857). In 1858 he was assistant classical master to Upper Canada College; but in 1859 he returned to the North West, and from 1860 to 1864 he was editor and proprietor of the *Nor' Wester*, the only newspaper at that time in the Canadian West. After serving for a time on the editorial staff, first of the Hamilton *Spectator*, and then of the Toronto *Globe*, he returned a second time to the West, and was admitted to the bar of the North West Territories. In 1870 he was appointed chief justice under the provisional government set up by Louis Riel (q.v.). He died at Winnipeg on September 20, 1871.

**Ross, James** (1848-1913), contractor, was born at Cromarty, Scotland, in 1848, the son of Captain John Ross, a shipowner, and Mary McKeddie. He was educated at Inverness Academy, and emigrated to the United States in 1868. He held positions as a resident engineer on various railways in the United States, and later in Canada. In 1883 he took charge of the construction of the Canadian Pacific Railway west of Winnipeg; and he became one of the most successful railway contractors in Canada. He became associated with Sir William Mackenzie (q.v.), and installed electric railway systems in Montreal, Toronto, London, and Winnipeg. He was president of the Dominion Coal Company, the Dominion Iron and Steel Company, the Dominion Bridge Company, and other important corporations. He died in Montreal on March 20, 1913. In 1872 he married Annie, daughter of John Kerr, Kingston, Ontario.

**Ross, Sir James Clark** (1800-1862), naval explorer, was born in Wigtonshire, Scotland, on April 15, 1800, the son of George Ross of Balsarroch, and the nephew of Sir John Ross (q.v.). He entered the Royal Navy in 1812, and in 1819-20, in 1821-3, and in 1824-5 he accompanied Parry (q.v.) on his Arctic explorations. In 1829-33 he accompanied his uncle, Sir John Ross (q.v.) on his second expedition to the Arctic; and he discovered the magnetic pole on June 1, 1831. In 1839-43 he made a successful voyage of discovery in the Antarctic; and in 1843 he was knighted. In 1848-9 he commanded an expedition sent out in search of Sir John Franklin; and in his later years he was regarded as "the first authority on all matters relating to Arctic navigation". He died at Aylesbury, England, on April 3, 1862. In 1828 he was elected a fellow of the Royal Society; and he was the author of *A voyage of discovery in the southern and antarctic seas* (2 vols., London, 1847).

**Ross, John** (d. 1787), fur-trader, first appears in the fur-trade licences in Canada in 1779. In 1780 he was in partnership with Peter Pangman (q.v.). He became a partner in the venture organized by Gregory, McLeod, and Co. in 1783, and was placed in charge of the Athabaska district. In the spring of 1787 he was killed in a scuffle with some of the men of Peter Pond (q.v.), the North West Company partner who was opposed to him.

**Ross, Sir John** (1777-1856), explorer, was born on June 24, 1877, the fourth son of the Rev. Andrew Ross, minister of Inch, Wigtonshire, Scotland, and Elizabeth, daughter of Robert Corsane, provost of Dumfries. He entered the Royal Navy in 1790, but served in the merchant marine until 1799, when he returned to the Navy. He was on active service during the remainder of the Napoleonic Wars; and in 1812 he was promoted to the rank of commander. In 1818 he was appointed to the command of an expedition for the discovery of the north-west passage, which resulted in the re-discovery of Baffin's bay. In 1829 he made another attempt to discover the north-west passage; and on this occasion he was ice-bound for four years. On his return to England, he was created a knight bachelor; and in 1839 he was appointed British consul at Stockholm. He returned to England in 1846, and in 1847 he urged on the Admiralty the immediate dispatch of an expedition for the relief of Sir John Franklin (q.v.), but his advice was rejected. In 1850-1 he himself made an expedition for the relief of Franklin, but he did not penetrate farther than Lancaster sound. He died at London, England, on August 30, 1856. He published *A voyage of discovery* (London, 1819), *Narrative of a second voyage in search of a north-west passage* (2 vols., London, 1835), and *Rear-admiral Sir John Franklin: A narrative of the circumstances and causes which led to the failure of the searching expeditions sent by government and others* (London, 1855), as well as other works on naval subjects.

**Ross, John** (1818-1871), senator of Canada, was born in county Antrim, Ireland, on March 10, 1818. He came to Canada with his parents as a child, and was educated in the district school at Brockville, Upper Canada. He was called to the bar of Upper Canada in 1839, and practised law in Toronto. In 1848 he was appointed a legislative councillor of Canada; and during the fifteen years preceding Confederation he repeatedly held office in the government. From 1851 to 1853 he was solicitor-general for Upper Canada, and from 1853 to 1854 attorney-general; from 1854 to 1856 he was speaker of the Legislative Council; in 1858 he was for a few months receiver-general; and from 1858 to 1862 he was president of the Council and minister of agriculture. In 1867 he was called to the Senate of Canada by royal proclamation; and in 1869 he became speaker of the Senate. He died near Toronto, Ontario, on January 31, 1871. In 1851 he married Augusta Elizabeth, daughter of the Hon. Robert Baldwin (q.v.). From 1852 to 1857 he was a government director of the Grand Trunk Railway, and for a time he was president of the railway.

**Ross, John Jones** (1832-1901), prime minister of Quebec (1884-7), was born at Quebec, Lower Canada, on August 16, 1832, the son of G. McIntosh Ross and Marie Louise Gouin. He was educated at the Quebec Seminary, and in 1853 was admitted to practice as a physician. He represented Champlain in the Legislative Assembly of Canada from 1861 to 1867, and in the Canadian House of Commons from 1867 to 1874. In 1867 he was elected also to represent Champlain in the Legislative Assembly of Quebec; but later in 1867 he was appointed to the Legislative Council of the province. From 1873 to 1884 he was a member of successive governments in the province of Quebec, and from 1884 to 1887 he was prime minister. In 1887 he was appointed a senator of Canada; from 1891 to 1893 he was speaker of the Senate; and in 1896 he was a member of the Tupper administration without portfolio. He died on May 4, 1901. In 1856 he married Arline, daughter of Lieut.-Col. Lanouette, of Champlain, Lower Canada.

**Ross, Victor Harold** (1878-1934), business man and author, was born in Walkerton, Bruce county, Ontario, in 1878, the son of Donald Wilson Ross.

He was educated in the public schools of Walkerton and Windsor, and became a journalist in Toronto. For many years he was financial editor of the Toronto *Globe;* but in 1917 he joined the staff of the Standard Oil Company. In 1919 he was elected a director of Imperial Oil Limited; and he became ultimately vice-president of this company. He died in Toronto on February 23, 1934. He was the author of *Petroleum in Canada* (Toronto, 1917), and *A history of the Canadian Bank of Commerce* (2 vols., Toronto, 1920-2).

**Ross, William** (1780?-1855), fur-trader, was born in Ross-shire, Scotland, about 1780. For several years he served as an ensign in the 11th Regiment of Foot. Then he entered the service of the Hudson's Bay Company, and was successively in charge at Oxford House, at Nelson House, and at Fort Churchill. After his retirement, he lived at Ottawa, Canada West; and there he died on January 12, 1855.

**Ross, William** (1825-1912), minister of militia and defence for Canada (1873-4), was born at Boularderie island, Nova Scotia, on December 20 1825, the son of John Ross and Robina McKenzie. He was educated at the village school, and became a village postmaster. From 1859 to 1867 he sat for Victoria in the Legislative Assembly of Nova Scotia, and from 1867 to 1874 in the Canadian House of Commons. In 1873 he was appointed minister of militia and defence in the Mackenzie government; but he resigned in 1874 to accept the post of collector of customs at Halifax, Nova Scotia. He re-entered the House of Commons as member for Victoria in 1900; and in 1905 he was called to the Senate. He died at Ottawa on March 17, 1912. In 1855 he married Eliza (d. 1910), daughter of Peter Moore, North Sydney, Nova Scotia. He was a lieutenant-colonel in the Canadian militia; and he was a grand master of the Freemasons of Nova Scotia.

**Ross, William Benjamin** (1854-1929), leader of the Conservative party in the Senate of Canada (1926-9), was born in Prince Edward Island in 1854. He was educated at Dalhousie University, and was called to the bar of Nova Scotia in 1878. He was called to the Senate of Canada in 1912, and was appointed leader of the Conservative party in the Senate in 1926. He died at Guelph, Ontario, on January 10, 1929.

**Ross Cox, mount,** is on the boundary between British Columbia and Alberta, in the Kootenay district, at the headwaters of Alnus creek, Wood river, in the Rocky mountains. It is in lat. 52° 27', long. 118° 01', and has an altitude of 9,840 feet. It is named after Ross Cox (q.v.), author of *Adventures on the Columbia river* (London, 1832).

**Rosseau lake,** the most north-easterly of the Muskoka lakes (q.v.). It is connected with lake Muskoka by the Indian river and lift-locks at Port Carling, and with lake Joseph by a canal at Port Sandfield. It is named after a family of early settlers named Rousseau.

**Rossignol lake** is in Queen's county, Nova Scotia, 30 miles south south-east of Annapolis. From it flows the Mersey river, at the mouth of which is Liverpool. It was called after the early French trader named Rossignol, whose property and ships were confiscated in 1604 near Liverpool by Monts (q.v.), and his party, who founded Port Royal. Rossignol wandered off into the wilderness, and is said to have died on a small island near the north end of the lake. The lake is 11 miles in length.

**Rossland,** a city in the West Kootenay district, British Columbia, is situated near the United States boundary, 235 miles east of Vancouver. It was named after Ross Thompson, the founder of the townsite. It is served by the Canadian Pacific Railway, and is the centre of a dairying, ranching, and fruit-growing region. In the surrounding country there is an extensive gold-copper-silver mining area, from which since 1895 over $86,000,000 in gold alone has been extracted. The Consolidated Mining and Smelting Company of Canada at Tadanac employ over 2,500 workers in their smelter, and many of these live in Rossland. Lumbering is also an outstanding industry. The town has four churches, a hospital, an armoury, and a weekly newspaper. (*Miner*). Pop. (1931), 3,700.

**Rossville,** a mission station in Manitoba founded in 1840 by the Methodist church. It was situated near Norway House (q.v.), and was named after Donald Ross, chief factor of the Hudson's Bay Company at Norway House. See Rev. John Ryerson, *Hudson's Bay; or, A missionary tour of the territory of the Hon. Hudson's Bay Company* (Toronto, 1855).

**Rosthern,** a town in Saskatchewan, on the Canadian National Railway, 50 miles south-west of Prince Albert and 40 miles north-east of Saskatoon. The origin of the name is uncertain. It was evidently given by the engineers or townsite agents of the Qu'Appelle, Long Lake, and Saskatchewan Railway and Steamship Company when the railway was built. According to one story, there was a creek running through the townsite, and one of the railway construction men named Ross was drowned in it, whence the place was given the name of Ross Tarn, later corrupted to Rosthern. According to another story, a native named Ross had a farm near the station when the railway was built; and the place was named after him, though the explanation of the termination "thern" is not easily found. The chief industry is wheat-growing; and some of the finest wheat in the world is grown here. The town has five grain elevators, a flour-mill, two high schools, an opera house, and two weekly newspapers (*Saskatchewan Daily News* and *Der Bote*, the latter in German). Pop. (1931), 1,412.

**Rothesay,** a village in King's county, New Brunswick, on the Kennebecasis river, and on the Canadian National Railway, 9 miles north-east of St. John. The name is said to have been suggested by one of the titles of the Prince of Wales (afterwards King Edward VII), who embarked here for Fredericton in 1860, and who was Duke of Cornwall and Rothesay. Pop. (1934), 300.

**Rothsay,** a village in Wellington county, Ontario, on the Conestogo river, 16 miles from Elora, on the Canadian National Railway. Pop. (1934), 300.

**Rothwell, Mrs. Annie.** See **Christie, Mrs. Annie Rothwell.**

**Rottenburg, Francis, Baron de** (1757-1832), president and administrator of Upper Canada (1813), was born on November 4, 1757, at Dantzig in Poland. From 1782 to 1791 he served as an officer in the French army; and from 1791 to 1794 he commanded a battalion of infantry under Kosciusko, the Polish patriot. He then entered the British army; and in 1810 he was sent to Canada. In 1811, with the rank of major-general, he was appointed commander of the forces in Lower Canada; and he commanded the left division of the British army in Canada throughout the War of 1812. From June 19 to December 12, 1813, he was president and administrator of Upper Canada. He returned to England in 1815, and he died at Portsmouth, England, on April 24, 1832. He was knighted in 1818, and was promoted to the rank of lieutenant-general in 1819. In 1799 he published a book entitled *Regulations for the exercise of riflemen and light infantry* (War Office, London). See D. B. Read, *The lieutenant-governors of Upper Canada and Ontario* (Toronto, 1900), and *Lieut.-general Baron Francis de Rottenburg* (Society for Army Historical Research, 1931).

**Rottermund, E. S., Comte de** (1813-1858), a European geologist who was for many years employed as chemist or inspector of mines on the staff of the crown lands department of united Canada. He died near Geneva, Switzerland, in 1848. His wife was a daughter of the Hon. P. D. Debartzch (q.v.). He was the author of several reports on the geology and minerals of Canada, notably a report on the geological exploration of lakes Huron and Superior (Toronto, 1857).

**Roubaud, Pierre Antoine** (*fl.* 1742-1787), adventurer, was a native of Avignon, France, who entered the Society of Jesus, and came to Canada in 1742 as a missionary. He served for many years among the Abnaki at St. François du Lac. After the Conquest, he ingratiated himself with General Murray (q.v.); and was used by the British authorities as a secret agent. In 1764, having been repudiated by the Jesuits, he was sent by Murray to London, where he seems to have been of service to the government. His character was, however, thoroughly disreputable, and he sank lower in the social scale until, in 1787, he disappeared from view. In 1782-4 he assisted Ducalvet (q.v.) in his negotiations with the British government, and then betrayed to the authorities the information thus acquired. He was described by Sir Guy Carleton (q.v.) as "a man of genius . . . but void of truth, without one spark of honour or of honesty." See D. Brymner, *Report on Canadian archives, 1885* (Ottawa, 1886).

**Rougemont,** a village in Rouville county, Quebec, on the Central Vermont Railway, 18 miles from St. Hyacinthe. It is named after Captain de Rougemont, who was in command at Fort Ste. Thérèse in 1666. Pop. (1931), 429.

**Rouge river** has its principal source in a series of lakes between the counties of Joliette and Montcalm. Its principal branch, flowing in a southerly direction, crosses these two districts and Labelle, Terrebonne, and Argenteuil counties, and enters the Ottawa between the village of Grenville and Pointe au Chêne. The river is 150 miles in length and drains a basin of about 1,780 square miles; it is navigable for rafts for 85 miles. Its banks are high and formed of sandy soil. For half a mile inland from its banks, the soil is generally composed of a light alluvium. The district once abounded in pine; but, owing to its exploitation, birch, poplar, spruce, and fir are now more plentiful. There is also a small river of this name that flows into lake Ontario, 17 miles east of Toronto.

**Rouges.** See **Parti Rouge.**

**Rouillard, Eugène** (1851-1926), geographer, was born at Quebec, Canada East, on June 4, 1851, the son of Nicolas Rouillard and Marie Elisa Legris dit Lépine. He was educated at Laval University (LL.B., 1875; LL.D., 1916), and was admitted a notary public in 1876. Until 1893 he was prominent in the journalism and politics of Quebec; but in 1894 he was appointed an inspector of crown lands in the province of Quebec, and he retained this post until shortly before his death at Quebec on October 16, 1926. In 1907 he was instrumental in reviving the Société de Géographie de Québec, became its secretary-treasurer, and contributed many articles to its *Bulletin;* and in 1915 he was elected a fellow of the Royal Society of Canada. He was the author of *Les bibliothèques populaires* (Quebec, 1890), *Étude sur la colonisation dans les cantons de Témiscouata, Matane, Rimouski, Bonaventure, et Gaspé* (Quebec, 1899), *Noms géographiques de la province de Québec et des provinces maritimes empruntés aux langues sauvages* (Quebec, 1906), *La côte nord du Saint-Laurent et le Labrador canadien* (Quebec, 1908), and *Dictionnaire des rivières et des lacs de la province de Québec* (Quebec, 1914). See *In memoriam Eugène Rouillard* (Bulletin de la Société de la Géographie de Québec, 1926).

**Rouleau, Charles Edmond** (1841-1926), soldier and author, was born at Ste. Anne de la Pocatière, Lower Canada, on September 18, 1841, the son of Charles Rouleau and Sophie Lebrun. In 1865 he served in the Canadian militia during the Fenian raids; and from 1868 to 1870 he was a zouave in the Papal army at Rome. On his return to Canada, he became a journalist. He died at Quebec on December 24, 1926. He was the author of *Souvenirs de voyage d'un soldat de Pie IX* (Quebec, 1881), *Rome et le Canada* (Quebec, 1885), *Le guide du cultivateur* (Quebec, 1890), *L'émigration, les principales causes* (Quebec, 1896), *Légendes canadiennes* (Quebec, 1901), *La Papauté et les zouaves pontificaux* (Quebec, 1905), and *Les zouaves canadiens* (Quebec, 1924).

**Rouleau, Raymond Marie** (1866-1931), cardinal of the Roman Catholic Church, was born at Isle Verte, Quebec, in 1866. He was educated at the Seminary of Rimouski, entered the Dominican Order in 1886, and was ordained a priest in 1892. He became the first prior of the house of the Dominicans in Ottawa in 1900; and in 1923 he was elected bishop of Valleyfield, Quebec. In 1926 he became archbishop of Quebec, and in 1927 he was decorated by the pallium and was made a cardinal, the third Canadian to be thus honoured. He died at Quebec on May 31, 1931.

**Rouleau,** a village in the Moose Jaw district of Saskatchewan, on the Portal section of the Canadian Pacific Railway, 32 miles south-east of Moose Jaw. It is in a rich agricultural district, and is the headquarters of a chain of grain elevators and a chain of lumber yards. It has a hospital and a weekly newspaper (*Enterprise*). Pop. (1934), 500.

**Rous, John** (d. 1760), naval officer, was in command of a Boston privateer which raided the French posts on the coast of Newfoundland, in 1744. He took part in the capture of Louisbourg

in 1745, and was given the rank of captain of the royal navy. He was engaged in the defence of the coast of Nova Scotia in 1749; was in command of the squadron sent against Beauséjour in 1755; and took part in the expedition against Cape Breton under Lord Loudon in 1756. He commanded the *Sutherland* at the capture of Louisbourg in 1758; and in 1759 was with Admiral Saunders at the siege of Quebec. He settled at Halifax, and was sworn a member of the Council of Nova Scotia in 1754. He died in 1760.

**Rousseau, Jean Baptiste** (1758-1812), fur-trader, was born in 1758, the son of Jean Bonaventure Rousseau, who received in 1770 a licence to trade "at Toronto". The son, following the father, became a fur-trader at the mouth of the Humber river, near Toronto, and was "the last citizen of the old French Toronto, and the first of the new English York." In 1795, however, he removed to Ancaster, Upper Canada; and he died, while on a visit to Niagara, on November 16, 1812. See Percy J. Robinson, *Toronto during the French régime* (Toronto, 1933).

**Rousseau, Pierre** (1827-1912), priest and author, was born at Nantes, France, on February 11, 1827, entered the Sulpician order, and was ordained a priest in 1852. He came to Canada in 1854, and spent most of his life in Montreal, where he died on February 8, 1912. He was the author of *Vie de M. Pierre-Louis Billaudèle, grand-vicaire et dixième supérieur du séminaire de Montréal* (Montreal, 1885), and *Histoire de la vie de M. Paul de Chomedey, sieur de Maisonneuve* (Montreal, 1886).

**Routh, Sir Randolph Isham** (1787-1858), executive councillor of Lower Canada, was born at Poole, Dorsetshire, England, in 1787, the son of the Hon. Richard Routh, sometime chief justice of Newfoundland. He entered the British army, served in the Peninsular War and at Waterloo, and in 1826 was appointed commissary general in Canada. From 1838 to 1841 he was a member of the Executive Council of Lower Canada formed by Lord Durham (q.v.). He died in London, England, on November 29, 1858. In 1841 he was made, for his services in Canada, a knight bachelor, and later he received the decoration of K.C.B. His second wife, whom he married in Quebec in 1830, was Maria Louise, daughter of the Hon. Jean Thomas Taschereau (q.v.).

**Routhier, Sir Adolphe Basile** (1839-1920), judge and author, was born at St. Placide, Lower Canada, on May 8, 1839, the son of Charles Routhier, a veteran of the War of 1812, and Angélique Lafleur. He was educated at the seminary of Ste. Thérèse and at Laval University, Quebec (B.A., 1858) B.C.L., 1860; Litt.D., 1880; LL.D., 1883); and he was called to the bar of Lower Canada in 1861 (Q.C., 1873). In 1873 he was appointed a puisne judge of the Superior Court of Lower Canada, and in 1904 he became chief justice. He retired from the bench in 1906, and he died at St. Irénée-les-Bains, Quebec, on June 27, 1920. As an author, he displayed the greatest versatility. In prose, he published the following: *Causeries du dimanche* (Montreal, 1871), *En canot* (Quebec, 1881), *Les grands drames* (Montreal, 1889), *Conférences et discours* (2 vols., Montreal, 1889 and 1905), *De Québec à Victoria*, (Quebec, 1893), *La reine Victoria et son jubilé* (Quebec, 1898), *Québec et Lévis* (Montreal, 1900), *Quebec* (Montreal, 1904), an historical drama entitled *Montcalm et Lévis* (Quebec, 1918), and two novels, *Le centurion* (Quebec, 1909), translated into English by Lucille P. Borden (St. Louis, 1910), and *Paulina* (Quebec, 1918). Under the pseudonym of "Jean Piquefort", he published also *Portraits et pastels littéraires* (Quebec, 1873). In poetry he published a volume entitled *Les échos* (Quebec, 1873); but his chief production was the national song, *O, Canada*. In 1862 he married

Marie Clorinde, daughter of J. O. Mondelet, Montreal. In 1882 he was chosen a charter member of the Royal Society of Canada, and he was president of the society in 1915-6. In 1911 he was created a knight bachelor. See Abbé E. J. Auclair, *Sir Adolphe Routhier* (Revue canadienne, 1920).

**Rouville, Jean Baptiste Melchior Hertel de** (1748-1817), legislative councillor of Lower Canada, was born at Three Rivers in 1748, the son of René Ovide Hertel de Rouville (q.v.). In 1761 he went with his father to France; but he returned to Canada in 1772. In 1775 he took part in the defence of Fort St. John against the Americans, was taken prisoner, and spent a year and a half in captivity. From 1792 to 1796 he represented the county of Bedford in the Legislative Assembly of Lower Canada; and in 1812 he was appointed to the Legislative Council. He died at Chambly, Lower Canada, on November 30, 1817. By his wife, Marie-Anne Hervieux, he had eight children, of whom six died young. See P. G. R., *René-Ovide Hertel de Rouville* (Bull. rech. hist., 1915).

**Rouville, Jean Baptiste René Hertel de** (d. 1859), legislative councillor of Lower Canada, was the son of the Hon. Jean Baptiste Melchior Hertel de Rouville (q.v.). He was an officer in the Canadian Voltigeurs, and fought at Châteauguay in 1813. From 1824 to 1830 he represented Bedford in the Legislative Assembly of Lower Canada, and from 1837 to 1838 he sat in the Legislative Council. He died at Belœil, Lower Canada, on January 14, 1859. In 1816 he married Anne-Charlotte Boucher de la Broquerie; and by her he had several children. See P. G. R., *René Ovide Hertel de Rouville* (Bull. rech. hist., 1915).

**Rouville, René Ovide Hertel de** (1720-1793), judge, was born at Port Toulouse, Ile Royale (Cape Breton), on September 6, 1720, the son of Jean-

Baptiste Hertel de Rouville, commandant at Port Toulouse, and Marie-Anne Beaudoin. From 1747 to 1760 he was the sub-delegate of the intendant at the St. Maurice forges. He left for France in 1761, but returned soon afterwards to Canada, and was appointed in 1765 grand-voyer for the district of Montreal. In 1775 he was appointed a civil judge at Montreal, and in 1779 a judge of the court of common pleas. This post he held until his death at Montreal on August 12, 1793. He was twice married (1) in 1741 to Marie-Louise-Catherine André de Leigne (d. 1766), by whom he had five children, and (2) in 1767 to Charlotte-Gabrielle Jarret de Verchères (d. 1808), widow of Pierre-Joseph Raimbault de Saint-Blin. See P. G. R., *L'hon. René Ovide Hertel de Rouville* (Bull. rech. hist., 1906 and 1915).

**Rouville,** a small county in Quebec, in the valley of the Richelieu. It is bounded on the north by St. Hyacinthe county, on the east by Shefford county, on the south by Iberville county, and on the west by Chambly county. It is named after Jean Baptiste Hertel, sieur de Rouville, who was granted a seigniory here in 1694. For electoral purposes the county is combined with St. Hyacinthe county. Pop. (1931), 13,776.

**Rouyn,** a town in Témiscamingue county, Quebec, on lake Osisko, and on the Nipissing Central and Canadian National Railways, 55 miles east of Kirkland Lake, and 450 miles north of Toronto. It is named after the township in which it is situated, which derives its name from an officer of the Royal Roussillon regiment, who fought under Montcalm (q.v.) at Quebec in 1759. It is the centre of a copper-gold mining district, and has churches, schools, a hospital, two theatres, several good hotels, and a weekly newspaper (*Rouyn-Noranda Press*). The motive power for its mining industry is provided by the hydro-electric plant at the Quinze rapids, at the head of lake Timiskaming, which has a capacity of over 60,000 horse-power. Pop. (1934), 3,225.

**Rowan, Sir William** (1789-1879) administrator of Canada (1853-4), was born in county Antrim, Ireland, in 1789, the eighth son of Robert Rowan, of Mullens and Garry, county Antrim. He entered the British army in 1803, and saw service in the Peninsular War, at Waterloo, and in Canada. From 1832 to 1839 he was civil and military secretary to Sir John Colborne (q.v.); and in 1849 he was appointed commander-in-chief of the British forces in North America. From August 1853, to June, 1854, he was administrator of the government of Canada, during the absence of Lord Elgin (q.v.); and in 1855 he returned to England. He rose to the rank of field-marshal; and he died in Bath, England, on September 26, 1879. He was knighted in 1856.

**Rowand, John** (1787-1854), fur-trader, was born in Montreal, Canada, in 1787, the son of an assistant surgeon in the Montreal General Hospital. He entered the service of the North West Company as an apprentice clerk, and was stationed in 1804 and 1805 at Fort des Prairies, and in 1806 on the lower Red river. In 1807 he returned to the Saskatchewan; and in 1808 he built a fort on the site of what is now the city of Edmonton. Here he remained, with brief intervals, for most of the rest of his life. He was made a partner of the North West Company shortly before the union of 1821; and in 1821 he became a chief trader in the Hudson's Bay Company. In 1823 he was placed in charge at Fort Edmonton; and in 1826 he was promoted to the rank of chief factor. He died at Fort Pitt on the Saskatchewan on June 1, 1854. He married an Indian girl who saved his life when he was thrown from his horse on the prairies in his early days in the West; and by her he had several children. One of his sons entered the service of the North West Company; and another, who was educated at Edinburgh Uni-

ROUYN, QUEBEC

*Photograph by Royal Canadian Air Force*

versity, became a successful physician at Quebec. See R. Mitchell, *John Rowand, chief factor* (Beaver, 1935).

**Rowan Tree.** See **Mountain Ash.**

**Rowing.** This is one of the few ancient arts or pastimes that has persisted through the centuries. It was not, however, until the beginning of the nineteenth century that rowing ceased to be looked upon as a pursuit fit only for professional watermen. It was not until 1829 that the first boat-race between Oxford and Cambridge, for instance, took place; and it was not until 1839 that the first regatta took place at Henley, on the Thames, in England. In Canada, the first regatta took place on Toronto bay in 1848. In 1855 an eight-oared crew from Saint John, New Brunswick, defeated the champion crew of the United States at Boston. In 1858 a Canadian regatta was held on Halifax harbour; and in 1867 a four-oared crew from Saint John, New Brunswick, won the world's championships at the exhibition in Paris, France. It has been, however, mainly in the single sculls that Canadians have distinguished themselves. Ned Hanlan (q.v.) won the championship of the world in 1880, and defended it successfully on six subsequent occasions. Many national championships were won by Jacob Gaudaur, William O'Connor, and Eddie Durnan, the nephew of Hanlan, who held the championship of America from 1905 to 1926. Other distinguished exponents of the art of rowing in Canada have been Joseph Wright, senior, Lou Scholes, Robert Dibble, Joseph Wright, junior, and Jack Guest. Amateur rowing really began in Canada in 1880, when the Canadian Association of Amateur Oarsmen was formed. For an exhaustive account of the history of rowing in Canada, whether in single or double sculls, or in four-oared or eight-oared races, see Robert S. Hunter, *Rowing in Canada since 1848* (Hamilton, Ontario, 1933).

**Rowsell, Henry** (1806-1890), printer and publisher, was born in London, England, in February, 1806. He emigrated to Canada in 1833, and established a printing and publishing business in Toronto, Upper Canada. For many years he was printer to the University of Toronto. He retired from business in 1880; and he died in Toronto on July 29, 1890.

**Roxton Falls,** a village in Shefford county, Quebec, on the Black river, and on the Canadian Pacific Railway. It is named after Roxton, a village in Bedfordshire, England. The chief industries are mixed farming and lumbering. Pop. (1931), 760.

**Roy, Charles** (d. 1844), printer, was the son of a French soldier who settled in Canada after the British conquest. He was an apprentice in the printing shop of John Neilson (q.v.), proprietor of the *Quebec Gazette;* and in 1806 he was the printer of the famous *Le Canadien* newspaper at Quebec. He died at Quebec on December 3, 1844. See *L'imprimeur Louis Roy* (Bull. rech. hist., 1918).

**Roy, Paul Eugène** (1859-1926), Roman Catholic archbishop of Quebec (1925-6), was born at Berthier, Quebec, on November 9, 1859, and was educated at Quebec and at Paris, France. He was ordained a priest of the Roman Catholic Church in 1886, and in 1908 was appointed coadjutor archbishop in 1920, and archbishop in 1925; and he died at Quebec on February 20, 1926. He was the author of a biographical sketch of *L. A. Olivier* (Lévis, 1891); and a collection of his addresses was published under the title *Discours religieux et patriotiques* (Quebec, 1927).

**Roy, Joseph Edmond** (1858-1913), historian, was born at Lévis, Quebec, on December 7, 1858, the son of Léon Roy, N.P., and Marguerite Lavoye. He was educated at Laval University (LL.B., 1880; Lit.D., 1898), and was admitted to practice as a notary public in 1880.

From 1908 to his death he was attached to the Public Archives of Canada; and he made an important *Report on the archives of France relating to Canadian history* (Ottawa, 1911). He died at Quebec on May 8, 1913. In 1885 he married Lucienne Carrier, of Lévis, Quebec. In 1891 he was elected a fellow of the Royal Society of Canada, and in 1908 he was its president. His chief publications were *Le premier colon de Lévis* (Lévis, 1884), *Histoire de la seigneurie de Lauzon* (5 vols., Lévis, 1897-1904), *Histoire du notariat au Canada* (4 vols., Lévis, 1899-1902), and a number of papers in the transactions of the Royal Society of Canada. From 1898 to 1913 he edited *La Revue de Notariat* (Lévis).

**Roy, Louis** (*fl.* 1793-1797), printer, was the son of a French soldier who settled in Canada after the conquest. He was apprenticed as a printer in the printing office of John Neilson (q.v.), proprietor of the *Quebec Gazette;* and in 1793 he came to Newark (Niagara), Upper Canada, and for two years published the *Upper Canada Gazette or American Oracle*, an official journal. In 1795 he went to Montreal, and published there the *Gazette de Montréal.* He died in New York, but the date of his death is not known.

**Royal, Joseph** (1837-1902), journalist, historian, and lieutenant-governor of the North West Territories (1888-93), was born at Repentigny, Lower Canada, on May 7, 1837, of humble parentage. He was educated at St. Mary's Jesuit College, Montreal, and in 1857 joined the staff of *La Minerve*, Montreal. The next year he founded the short-lived *L'Ordre*, Montreal; in 1864 he was one of the originators of the *Revue Canadienne;* and in 1867 he founded *Le Nouveau Monde* (1867-81). In 1864 he was called to the bar; and in 1870 he went to the North West. Here he established in 1870 *Le Métis* (afterwards *Le Manitoba*); and the same year he was elected to the first Legislative Assembly of

Manitoba for St. François-Xavier West. He continued a member of this House until 1879, and was successively speaker of the Assembly (1871-2), provincial secretary (1872-4), provincial secretary and minister of public works (1874-6), attorney-general (1876-8), and minister of public works (1878). From 1879 to 1888 he was a member of the Canadian House of Commons for Provencher; and in 1888 he was appointed lieutenant-governor of the North West Territories. On the expiration of his term of office in 1893 he returned to Montreal, and became editor of *La Minerve*. He died in Montreal on August 23, 1902. In 1894 he was elected a member of the Royal Society of Canada. Most of his literary work appeared in fugitive form in periodicals; but he published separately *La vallée de la Mantawa* (Montreal, 1869), and *Le Canada, république ou colonie?* (Montreal, 1894), and there was published posthumously an *Histoire du Canada 1841 à 1867* (Montreal, 1909). See Abbé G. Dugas, *L'hon. M. Joseph Royal* (Revue Canadienne, 1902); and L. A. Prud'homme, *L'honorable Joseph Royal* (Trans. Roy. Soc. Can., 1904).

**Royal American Regiment,** a light infantry regiment in the British army, composed chiefly of Americans, formed in 1755. It saw service in the Seven Years' War, and was an important unit in the American Revolutionary War. Unlike most other loyalist regiments it was not disbanded after 1783, but became ultimately one of the battalions in the King's Royal Rifle Corps. See Lieut.-Col. Lewis Butler, *The annals of the King's Royal Rifle Corps* (2 vols., London, 1913-1923).

**Royal Architectural Institute of Canada,** a society founded in August, 1907, and incorporated on April 1, 1912, with a view to facilitating the interchange of knowledge of the science of architecture and of generally promoting the welfare of the architectural profession in Canada. It is allied with the Royal Institute of British Architects, and has seven associations in affiliation. The society has issued a monthly *Journal* since 1924.

**Royal Assent.** See **Disallowance.**

**Royal Astronomical Society of Canada,** a society devoted to the advancement of astronomy and the allied sciences, founded in 1890 as the Astronomical and Physical Society of Toronto. In 1900 it became the Toronto Astronomical Society, and in 1903 assumed its present name. The society issued yearly volumes of *Transactions* (which included its annual report) until 1902, when publication was continued under the title of *Papers and proceedings*. Since 1907 the latter has been replaced by the *Journal*, until 1915 a bi-monthly magazine, and now issued monthly. The *Observer's handbook*, first published in 1907 as the *Canadian astronomical handbook*, has been issued yearly ever since, with the exception of the year 1909-10.

**Royal Bank of Canada.** The name of the Royal Bank of Canada does not adequately convey the manifold activities of this Canadian institution with over 700 branches in Canada and with nearly 100 branches established in thirty-two foreign countries including Cuba, the British and French West Indies, Haiti, Dominican Republic, Argentina, Brazil, British Guiana, British Honduras, Costa Rica, Porto Rico, Panama, Colombia, Peru, Uruguay, Venezuela, as well as in London, New York, Paris, and Barcelona, nor does the average business man realize the wide and varied service this bank is able to render without going outside its own organization.

The Royal Bank of Canada has done much to foster Canadian trade at home and abroad and the value of its service to exporters and importers lies, not in its regular banking business alone, but also in its willingness at all times to supply information regarding markets and marketing conditions, tariffs and confidential credit reports, etc. The value of this type of service is to be found in the fact that information is gathered direct by managers who are not only on the spot, but know intimately local conditions.

In sixty-five years, the Royal Bank of Canada has grown from a purely local bank into an institution of international importance, and to-day holds a foremost position amongst the great banks of the world. Founded over sixty-five years ago in the city of Halifax, during the height of the American Civil War, the Royal Bank of Canada, then known as the Merchants Bank of Halifax, started in a very modest way, but through sound business principles, foresight, faith in the Dominion and in its own development, it has to-day a history of phenomenal growth to its credit. To-day, it stands at the head of Canadian chartered banks. It has the largest number of branches, both within the Dominion and abroad, and its business is yearly showing enormous increases. It is recognized as one of the world's leading financial institutions.

*History.* First established by a few prominent citizens of Halifax on May 2, 1864, this foundation of the present bank met with immediate success, and during the first five years of its operation, earnings averaged nine per cent. per annum. After Confederation a federal charter was applied for, and on June 22, 1869, royal assent was given to an Act incorporating "The Merchants Bank of Halifax", with an authorized capital of $1,000,000, of which only one-half was at first offered for subscription. On October 18, of the same year the first general meeting of shareholders was held, and the first board of directors was chosen. At that first meeting it was shown that the paid-up capital was $300,000, the reserve fund $20,000, while deposits were $284,656. The current loans amounted to $266,970, with total assets of $729,163.

The business of the bank increased to such an extent that President Kinnear found that he was unable to devote his whole time to the duties of the office, and Thomas E. Kenny, a son of one of the original founders, was elected his successor. The new president brought a policy of expansion to the bank which is to this day one of the outstanding features of the Royal Bank of Canada. Soon after taking over his duties, the new president had visions of expanding his institution and a number of branches were opened in the Maritime provinces. At the fourth annual meeting he was able to make the announcement that during the year 1872, with current loans amounting to $1,278,850, the bank had not lost one dollar by bad debts. A dividend of eight per cent. was declared, and $40,000 were added to the reserve.

In 1873 several banks in Nova Scotia failed and had to close their doors, but despite the business depression of the time, at the annual meeting of that year, the president announced the usual dividend, and another $40,000 was added to the reserve. In the two following years, 1874 and 1875, despite the trade reaction following the Civil War, this fund was augmented by $50,000 and $30,000 respectively.

During the first six years of its existence the bank had increased its paid-up capital from $300,000 to $900,000; its reserve fund now stood at $180,000, and its assets had risen to $2,594,917. Branches had also by this time been opened on Prince Edward Island.

In 1876 the Bank had outgrown its original home. One of the best sites in Halifax was chosen, and the new building was occupied in May, 1879. In 1882 trade and financial conditions had improved, and the bank commenced on its branch extension policy again, opening up several branches in New Brunswick. The trade with Halifax at this period in the bank's history was largely sea-borne, and merchants had long been carrying on an exchange of commodities with the West Indies, the Bermudas, and the Bahamas. In the hope of creating a new field for the activities of the bank, its chief accountant was sent to Bermuda with instructions to survey the ground for the opening of a branch at Hamilton. Upon his return, this official reported with certain misgivings upon the success of the venture, but that he had made arrangements for the establishment of a branch. This and another branch were ultimately closed after several years of service.

In the year 1883 the paid-up capital stock was increased to $1,000,000. The directors declined to purchase the Merchants Bank of Prince Edward Island, and, at a little later date, refused a similar proposal from the Maritime Bank of Canada, which had its headquarters at Saint John, New Brunswick.

With the passing into the hands of the receiver of two of Nova Scotia's largest industries, the Merchants Bank of Halifax suffered a severe loss. The profits for the year were wiped out, and the reserve fund was drawn upon for $80,000. The strength of the institution, however, was made manifest by the fact that within the period of three years the loss had been made good and the reserve fund had been restored to its former strength.

*National Beginnings.* In 1887 it was decided to extend operations to the city of Montreal in an effort to make the bank a national institution. A branch was opened in Montreal. Step by step, the Merchants Bank of Halifax became firmly established there, and new branches were opened in many directions. Through several years of depression and the suspicion in England of all foreign securities, which had a temporary check upon Canada, the Merchants Bank of Halifax stood firm and steadily strengthened its ground. Year by year it added to its reserve fund, and in 1895 increased its paid-up capital to $1,500,000. In this year also Newfoundland suffered its second great disaster by the failure of all its banks in the capital city, and a branch of the Merchants Bank of Halifax was opened in St. John's to assist in the restoration of banking accommodation. In 1897, renewed expansion was determined upon. Branches were opened in Nelson and Rossland, British Columbia, and at the port of Vancouver, and in the following year at Grand Forks, Nanaimo, and Victoria. In 1898, following the close of the Spanish-American War and a month after the signing of the Peace of Paris, by which Cuba was granted independence, a branch was opened in Havana.

Confidence in the bank soon gathered strength, with the result that the Havana branch was but the forerunner of over fifty branches to-day encircling the Caribbean sea and stretching far down the eastern coast of South America. Through this foreign connection, it was soon found necessary to open a branch in New York and later, in the year 1899, in Ottawa. Before the close of that year a further $500,000 capital stock was issued, and at the annual meeting in 1900 an additional $1,000,000 was authorized. At this same meeting it was felt that owing to the enormous international growth of the bank a more comprehensive title should be chosen, and a change in name to "The Royal Bank of Canada" was recommended and approved. Parliamentary sanction was applied for and granted, and the present name of the bank came into force on January 2, 1901.

The Cuban business of the bank continued to grow steadily. Both the Banco de Oriento and the Banco del Comercio were purchased, and added to the influence of the bank throughout the island.

At the annual meeting held on February 14, 1906, the shareholders approved of the proposal to move the headquarters of the bank from Halifax to Montreal. Parliamentary sanction was obtained, and the head office was established in Montreal on March 2, 1907. There was a further new stock issued, and additional funds were added to the reserve. About this time also, the bank more than doubled its branches. Fifty were opened in Ontario and the North West, five more were established in Cuba, while a number of other branches were opened in the West Indies.

During the last three decades a vigorous policy of expansion has been followed. The assets of the Union Bank of Halifax were purchased by the Royal Bank of Canada on November 1, 1910; of the Traders Bank of Canada on September 1, 1912; of the Quebec Bank on January 2, 1917, and of the Northern Crown Bank on July 2, 1918; of the Bank of Central and South America in February, 1925; and of the Union Bank of Canada on September 1, 1925. The two latter amalgamations greatly increased the bank's facilities for serving the business and industrial needs of the Dominion at home and abroad. In addition to the mergers already mentioned two important connections in its foreign field came to the bank through taking over in 1912 the Bank of British Honduras, and in 1914 the Bank of British Guiana.

During the years of war, the Royal Bank of Canada made loans to the Imperial and Dominion governments aggregating $345,000,000 for the purchase of munitions, war supplies, and grain. In 1915 distinction was reflected upon the bank when the order of knighthood was conferred upon its president, Sir Herbert S. Holt.

One of the proudest pages in the history of the bank is that written by 1,493 members of its staff between the years 1914 and 1918, when they, together with hundreds of thousands of Canada's sons, served in the Great War.

During the war period the business of the bank grew enormously. Its assets increased by more than $54,000,000 in 1916, by $82,000,000 in 1917, and by $92,000,000 in 1918. The branches of the bank established in foreign countries with which Canada has close trade relations have proved of inestimable value and of the utmost importance from a national viewpoint. They have increased the facilities afforded to Canadian exporters, importers, and manufacturers to a very great extent.

Over sixty-five years ago the Royal Bank of Canada started in one room in Halifax as a purely local organization. To-day the bank is an international force in its daily business transactions, with 700 branches in Canada and Newfoundland and nearly 100 branches in foreign lands, together with a world-wide chain of correspondents.

The paid-up capital of the Bank is $35,000,000, with a reserve fund of $21,383,000. At the end of November, 1933, its total assets were $729,000,000, with deposits of $600,000,000.

The Royal Bank of Canada is well and favourably known the world over, and to-day is one of the most progressive of the leading banking institutions in the world.

**Royal Canadian Academy of Arts,** a society formed in 1880, after the model of the Royal Academy in Great Britain, at the instance and under the patronage of the Marquis of Lorne (q.v.), then governor-general of Canada, and his wife, the Princess Louise, who was herself an amateur artist. The charter members, whose names were approved by the Marquis of Lorne, numbered thirteen painters and five architects and were entitled to bear after their names the letters R.C.A. In addition to these, there were a somewhat larger number of associate members, who were designated A.R.C.A. Future members and associate members were elected by the academicians themselves; and this has meant that the Academy has been a self-perpetuating body—a fact which has at times given rise to criticism.

One of the first objects to which the Academy devoted itself was the establishment of a National Gallery, and a beginning was made with this project as early as 1882, though it was not until 1913 that the National Gallery was placed on its present basis. The Academy has also sponsored annual art exhibitions, held at various centres in Canada, and it has fostered art education in Canada. The presidents of the Academy have been the following: Lucius O'Brien (1880-90), O. R. Jacobi (1890-93), Robert Harris (1893-1906), G. A. Reid, (1906-9), W. Brymner (1909-18), Homer Watson (1918-22), G. Horne Russell (1922-6), Henry Sproatt (1926-9), and Sir Wyly Grier (1929—). Since 1910 the secretary of the Academy has been E. Dyonnet. See Hugh G. Jones, in collaboration with E. Dyonnet, *History of the Royal Canadian Academy of Arts* (n.p., 1934).

**Royal Canadian Institute,** a professional society established in Toronto in 1849 as the Canadian Institute, and incorporated by royal charter on November 4, 1851. Its objective, in particular, was the acquisition of knowledge pertaining to the surveying, engineering, and architectural professions, and, in general, the encouragement and advancement of the physical sciences, the arts and manufactures, by research and the dissemination of scientific knowledge. The society maintains a library (housed in the University of Toronto Library) of the publications of most of the scientific societies of the world. In August, 1852, the society commenced the publication of the first series of its monthly, the *Canadian Journal*. From January, 1856, to January, 1878, the second series consisted of 15 volumes, and was entitled the *Canadian Journal of Science, Literature, and History*. From 1879 to April, 1890, it was published under the title of *Proceedings of the Canadian Institute* (third series, 7 vols.), and in October, 1890, it was continued, and is still being published, as *Transactions*. A minor series of the *Proceedings* of the Institute, containing short papers, was issued concurrently with the *Transactions* from 1897 to 1904. The Institute also published *Annual reports* from 1886 to 1904 (1901-4 entitled *Annual archaeological reports*), and three *Year books and annual reports* for the years 1912-3, 1913-4, and 1916-7. On April 2, 1914, the name of the Canadian Institute was changed to the Royal Canadian Institute.

**Royal Canadian Mounted Police,** a constabulary force maintained by the Dominion government, detachments of which are now stationed in all the provinces of Canada, as well as in the Yukon and the North West Territories, as far north as Ellesmere island. It had its origin in the formation in 1873 of the North West Mounted Police (which became in 1904 the Royal North West Mounted Police), a small body of civil constabulary organized by the Canadian government to police the prairie country in the then North West Territories. The North West Rebellion of 1869-70 and the troubles with American whiskey-pedlars in the prairie country had demonstrated the necessity of a force to police the western country; and in May, 1873, Sir John Macdonald (q.v.) introduced into parliament a bill for the formation of a mounted constabulary after the model of the Royal Irish Constabulary. The force, though it was under semi-military discipline and wore the scarlet tunic of the British army, was essentially a civil body, with a minimum of what Sir John Macdonald called "fuss and feathers." It was recruited in eastern Canada; and in 1874, after a train journey *viâ* Chicago to Fargo, North Dakota, trekked over the prairies to Fort Macleod (now Calgary), where it established its wilderness headquarters. It numbered only a little over 200 officers and men; and though its numbers were gradually increased, it per-

formed a marvellous feat in keeping for many years the King's peace among the hitherto lawless Indians and whites on the western prairies. Many are the tales of its fearlessness and devotion to duty. It failed, through lack of numbers, to cope with the North West Rebellion of 1885; but that rebellion might have been much more serious had it not been for its splendid work. During the Klondike gold rush of 1898, the Police proved again their sterling worth; during the South African War they provided many men and officers for the 1st Canadian Mounted Rifles and the Strathcona Horse; and in more recent times they have undertaken the policing of the vast territories acquired by Canada in the Arctic circle.

With the filling-up of the western prairies, however, and the creation in 1905 of the provinces of Saskatchewan and Alberta, the task originally assigned to the police largely disappeared. In 1920, therefore, they were at last merged with the Dominion Police, which had been maintained for the policing of government property at Ottawa and elsewhere; and the combined force was re-named the Royal Canadian Mounted Police, though the famous and familiar uniform of the Royal North West Mounted Police was retained. The headquarters of the force was removed from the west to Ottawa; and the force was charged primarily with the enforcement of the laws of the Dominion, especially the criminal code. Any province, however, may enter into an agreement with the Dominion for the services of the Mounted Police to enforce provincial laws upon payment for these services; and most of the provinces have made such an agreement.

The force is commanded by a commissioner, with a deputy commissioner; and the subordinate commissioned officers are known as assistant commissioners, superintendents, and inspectors. The total personnel of the

Police at present (1935) numbers over 2,500.

The romantic history of the Royal North West Mounted Police has given rise to a considerable body of literature. In addition to the annual reports of the commissioner, which are among the most interesting of all Canadian government reports, reference should be made to Sir Cecil Denny, *The riders of the plains* (Calgary, 1905), E. J. Chambers, *The North West Mounted Police* (Ottawa, 1907); A. L. Haydon, *The riders of the plains* (London, 1910); S. B. Steele, *Forty years in Canada* (Toronto, 1915); R. B. Deane, *Mounted police life in Canada* (London, 1916); R. G. MacBeth, *Policing the plains* (Toronto, 1921); F. J. E. Fitzpatrick, *Sergeant 331* (New York, 1921); T. M. Longstreth, *The silent force* (New York and London, 1927); Douglas S. Robertson, *To the Arctic with the Mounties* (Toronto, 1934), and Harwood Steele, *Policing the Arctic* (Toronto, 1935).

**Royal Canadian Volunteers,** a regiment of the British army raised in Canada on May 19, 1796. It was disbanded on September 28, 1802. A list of the officers is to be found in Neilson's *Quebec Almanac* for 1799.

**Royal Military College,** the only national educational institution in Canada, was founded by an Act of parliament passed in 1874 under the government of Alexander Mackenzie (q.v.). Its object was to provide a military education for prospective officers of the Canadian militia and the British army. The College was opened in Kingston, Ontario, in 1876, on the site of the old naval dockyard. A four-year course of instruction in mathematics, civil engineering, surveying, physics, chemistry, French, and English was inaugurated; and a high standard has been maintained by the college from that day to this. To be eligible for admission, a candidate must have passed the matriculation examination in some Canadian university; vacancies are allotted to the provinces of Canada in proportion to their population, and are filled in the order of merit obtained by the candidates in the examination for their own province. Graduates of the Royal Military College are admitted to the law schools of most Canadian provinces, on the same terms as university graduates, and to the third year of most engineering schools in Canada. A valuable feature of the College is its military discipline: students are "gentleman cadets", wear a military uniform, and are under similar regulations to those prevailing at Sandhurst, Woolwich, and West Point. The graduates of the College have had an enviable record, not only in the wars of the Empire, where many of them have won great distinction, but also in civilian life, where many of them have risen to positions of great trust and responsibility. See Major-Gen. H. A. Panet, *The Royal Military College* (Canadian Geographical Journal, 1931).

**Royal Mint.** In 1860, at the time of the Fraser river gold-rush, a government assay office was established at New Westminster, British Columbia; and in 1862 this operated as a mint. A number of gold coins of $10 and $20 in value were struck; but the operation of the assay office as a mint was shortlived, and the few gold coins it struck are worth fabulous prices. It was not until the Yukon gold-rush that the idea of establishing a mint in Canada came again to the fore; and it was not until 1908 that the Royal Mint in Ottawa was opened as a branch of the Royal Mint in London, England. See J. H. Campbell, *The Royal Mint and its branches* (Canadian Geographical Journal, 1931).

**Royal North West Mounted Police.** See **Royal Canadian Mounted Police.**

**Royal Ontario Museum.** See **Museums.**

**Royal Proclamation of 1763,** the instrument of government, issued on

THE ROYAL MILITARY COLLEGE, KINGSTON, ONTARIO

*Photograph by Royal Canadian Air Force*

October 7, 1763, that introduced civil government into Canada. It placed the affairs of "the province of Quebec", the boundaries of which it defined, under a governor and council, until "the state and circumstances" of the colony admitted of the calling of a general assembly. It also introduced into the colony "the laws of Our Realm of England." For a brief study of the Proclamation, see W. S. Wallace, *The beginnings of British rule in Canada* (Can. hist. rev., 1925).

**Royal Society of Canada,** a society formed in Montreal in 1881 through the efforts of the Marquis of Lorne (q.v.), governor-general of Canada, for the promotion of literature and science within the Dominion, its membership to consist only of those Canadians distinguished in arts, science, and letters. The *Proceedings and transactions* of the society published since 1882 (series 1, 1882-94, vols i-xii; series 2, 1895-1906, vols. i-xii; and series 3, 1907-36, vols. i-xxx) contain the contributions of the Fellows and papers from other sources presented by them, and are thus comprised of valuable historical monographs and scientific papers. The society has been instrumental in promoting many matters of public interest, such as the establishment of standard time, the prevention of the use of poisonous phosphorus in the manufacture of matches, the purchase of a large deflecting telescope for the National Observatory, the creation of scientific research stations connected by wireless, the establishment of the Public Archives of Canada, the National Museum, the Quebec Tercentenary and the Quebec Battlefields Commission, the National Sites and Monuments Board, and the National Research Council. The sections into which the society is divided now number five: (1) French literature, history, archæology, sociology, political economy, and allied subjects; (2) English literature, history, archæology, etc.; (3) mathematical, chemical and phys-

ical sciences; (4) geology, palæontology, mineralogy, geography, and allied subjects; and (5) biological sciences. The society has its headquarters at Ottawa. In 1932 it published a volume entitled *Fifty years retrospect, 1882-1932* (Toronto).

**Royal William,** the name of a paddle-wheel steamship, built at Quebec in 1831, which was the first ship to cross the Atlantic with steam as her main motive-power. She made the crossing from Quebec to London in 1833 wholly under steam. One or two other vessels had previously used steam to assist their sails in crossing the Atlantic; but none had used steam only. See W. Wood, *The record-making Royal William* (Canadian Geographical Journal, 1933).

**Rue Anemone** (*Anemonella thalictroides* (L.) Spach., *Ranunculaceae*), a low, slender-stemmed perennial rising from a cluster of thickened tuberous roots. There are 1 or 2 compound radical leaves, with rounded leaflets, and a whorl of stem leaves at the top of the stem which surround a flat-topped cluster of white or pinkish flowers, with from 5 to 10 oval petal-like sepals, and numerous stamens. It is common in the woods in spring from Quebec to Manitoba, and is very similar to the wood anemone, with which it grows, except that it bears its flowers in clusters.

**Rundle, mount,** is in Alberta, in the Rocky mountains park, between the Bow and Spray rivers. It was named after Rev. Robert Terrill Rundle, Methodist missionary to the Indians of the North West from 1840 to 1848. The name appears on the Palliser Expedition map, 1859.

**Rupert river** rises in lake Mistassini, in the province of Quebec, and flows in a westerly direction into Rupert bay in the south-east end of James bay. It was discovered by the explorer Henry Hudson (q.v.), who spent the winter of 1610-1 at its mouth. In 1668 the first trading-post of what later became the Hudson's Bay Company was established here by the explorer and fur-trader Groseilliers (q.v.). The river was named after Prince Rupert, the moving spirit in forming the company. It is 275 miles long, and drains a basin of 1,600 square miles. It is an impetuous river, and has been estimated as capable of producing over a million horse-power. Sea trout and whitefish ascend the river. Its banks are formed, in some parts, of a rich, clayey soil, and is wooded with spruce, poplar, and birch. In other parts the soil is poor and sandy and wooded with gray pine.

**Rupert's House,** the oldest trading-post of the Hudson's Bay Company on Hudson bay. It was built by Groseilliers (q.v.) in 1668 at the mouth of Rupert river, and was originally known as Fort Charles. In 1670 it was named Rupert's House, and in 1677 it was re-built and strengthened. In 1686 it was captured by the French, and renamed Fort St. Jacques. The English re-captured it in 1693, the French in 1695, and the English in 1696. By the Treaty of Ryswick, it reverted to the French, and it remained in their hands until the Treaty of Utrecht in 1713 restored it to the Hudson's Bay Company. It is still in operation.

**Rupert's Land,** the name applied to the territories granted by Charles II in 1670 to the Hudson's Bay Company, from the fact that Prince Rupert, the cousin of Charles II, was the first governor of the company. Rupert's Land comprised all those territories watered by rivers flowing into Hudson bay. The Hudson's Bay Company, in the course of time, invaded other territories, watered by rivers flowing into the Arctic ocean, the Pacific ocean, and the Mississippi valley; and in 1821 it was confirmed in its monopoly of these. In 1869 "Rupert's Land and the North West Territory" was transferred to Canada, on condition that the Hudson's Bay Company received £300,-000 by way of compensation, and re-tained certain blocks of land about its trading-posts and one-twentieth of the arable land in the ceded territories. Rupert's Land ceased then to exist as a territorial entity; but the name still persists as that of an ecclesiastical province of the Church of England in Canada. See E. H. Oliver (ed.), *The Canadian North-West* (2 vols., Ottawa, 1914).

**Rural Credit,** in its broadest sense, may be taken to include all credit provided to farmers irrespective of its form, term, or source. Short-term credit relates to funds provided for the pur-pose of meeting the operating expenses of the farm and covers a term not ordinarily exceeding nine months. Long-term or mortgage credit in Canada refers to advances for terms exceeding five years. Intermediate credit, as the name implies, includes loans for periods not covered by the above. In the sense used, rural credit dates from the early days of Canadian agriculture and consti-tutes an essential element in its growth.

Prior to the development of adequate transportation facilities in Canada, the term "rural credit" could be confined very largely to the temporary accommo-dation provided by merchants and storekeepers to the early settlers, to "emergency" advances by governments in times of distress, and to the credit terms of land settlement agencies. The early banks, although making loans to farmers, rose primarily in connection with lumber and fur rather than with agriculture, with consequent attempts to adapt a form of credit preëminently commercial to the needs of the farming community. Commercial credit, despite its obvious limitations, remained domi-nant until the era of canal and railway construction resulted in the integration of rural settlements and the presence of a reliable overseas market for surplus farm products.

The shift from fur to lumber follow-ing 1821 meant a radical change in the whole structure of credit. The impetus given to immigration and settlement and to improvements in transportation and communication resulted in heavy capital expenditures. Long-term investments became a necessity. The movement as a whole was cumulative, capital expenditures in one direction necessitating the same in others. The impact of industrialism on agriculture meant a greatly increased demand for heavier capital expenditures on farming operations, and hence for some means of providing the required funds.

It was the demand for more adequate credit facilities that led to the rise of the early building societies. Developments following 1850 intensified the need of capital supplies and the legislation of the fifties and sixties reflects the necessity for encouraging the mobilization of these for developmental purposes. When defects in the operation of the early terminating societies became apparent, they were gradually replaced by the permanent building societies, which were later to play an important part as channels for the investment of overseas funds in Canadian agriculture. The whole trend of events was such as to stress the increasing importance of capital. The rise of land values following the railways, the move to increased mechanization in agriculture, and the necessity for improvements in buildings and drainage were indicative of the change. By Confederation modern lines of development had been laid down.

In the period of gradual expansion which followed 1867, private enterprise turned more and more to agriculture as a field for investment, particularly in the case of farm mortgages for the provision of capital to farmers for permanent improvements and for the increase or acquisition of holdings. With short term funds, the disorganization of the mercantile system favoured the continuance of store debts as an important source of accommodation, although the emphasis of the banks upon liquidity following 1871 tended to restrict bank loans to farmers. Government activities were confined largely to encouraging ventures in which joint effort was essential, to fostering agricultural associations as a means of assisting farmers to coöperate in their own interest, and to providing emergency assistance in times of temporary adversity.

Physical factors such as the deepening of canals, the building of transcontinental railways, and the increasing efficiency of ocean steamship connections served to strengthen the influence of external forces upon Canadian development. The effects of these were translated largely in terms of the chief export staple, wheat. The funds necessary for these changes were obtained largely from the British Isles, with agriculture playing an increasingly important part in the balancing of the country's international indebtedness. The services of the permanent building societies as channels of investment were invaluable to an expanding agriculture, and for a quarter of a century these occupied the centre of the stage in eastern Canadian farm finance. Their importance declined only towards the close of the century with the rise of domestic capital and the competition of individual investors. The difficult times of the nineties, the keen competition among lenders in the east, and the greater possibility of diversification of assets, were factors hastening the departure of corporate lenders from the farm mortgage field in eastern Canada. Western expansion following 1900, however, furnished a new outlet for funds available for farm lending, which flowed westward to aid in another period of growth. Here again, high returns, the attraction of funds from abroad in large volume, the rise of new lending institutions, and the extension of the old were followed by strong competition, narrowing margins of profit and a falling off in the funds borrowed for agricultural purposes. The year 1912 and the early part of 1913 marked the culmination of a period remarkable for the expansion achieved, and by 1914 a "sail-trimming" year was in prospect.

Greater difficulties were encountered in meeting the requirements of agriculture for short-term and intermediate credits. With the exception of the Caisses Populaires of Quebec, which had their beginning in 1900, no institutions developed specifically for the purpose of meeting these needs, and as a result the period witnessed attempts to adapt agencies organized primarily for other purposes to the needs of agriculture. The local merchants, the banks, and the implement companies remained the chief agencies upon which the farmer had to rely. The situation, as now, tended to vary with the type of farming operations both as to the need for such credit and as to the nature of the security available.

Government activities before the World War, although remaining in the background, were an important factor in farm lending. In the case of the more permanent improvements, government measures continued to encourage action in cases where joint efforts on the part of the farmers were necessary, as exemplified in drainage, dyking, and irrigation improvements. Again, government encouragement to agricultural associations and to dairying and allied industries helped to relieve the situation in the case of short-term credits, with emergency advances also assisting in this respect. Grants, and to a smaller extent loans and guarantees of loans, were made to agricultural associations as a means of encouraging improvements, exhibitions, promising developments, and the advancement of agriculture in general. Substantial amounts were advanced for the promotion of dairying and for drainage and dyking improvements, while large expenditures were made on colonization roads and like projects. Developmental measures rather than rural credit as such describe the main theme of government action before the War, but they served as forerunners of later government activities in the narrower field of rural credit. Toward the close of the period of rapid expansion following 1900, resulting maladjustments became apparent, and the pressure for more direct government intervention in rural credit increased. The exigencies of the war period strengthened the tendency and resulted in the entry of government lending bodies into the field of farm credit. The first beginnings of restrictive legislation affecting lender-borrower relationships, the amendments to the Bank Act, the passing of seed grain Acts, and the advent of government lending, were features of the war years. Rural credit now became more explicitly a concern of governments, provincial at first, Dominion later.

Although private lenders, both individual and corporate, turned to war bonds and similar investments in the war years, with the close of hostilities large sums were again available for investment in farm loans and played an important part in the expansion years of the twenties in the prairie provinces. Insurance companies were particularly active in this field, and large amounts were invested in farm mortgages in the years following the War. Agricultural difficulties in the twenties and restrictive legislation, however, had the effect of checking the movement, and with the coming of the depression years farm lending by private agencies practically ceased. Small amounts have been advanced to safeguard loans outstanding, while the activities of the Colonization Finance Corporation have greatly assisted in this respect, but for the most part private sources of mortgage credit are practically closed. In the case of long-term farm credit, the tendency has been to overlook the importance of individual creditors as well as the holding of such agencies as the railway companies, the Hudson's Bay Company, and the loaning companies in the western provinces, where the agreement of sale as an instrument for the disposal of farm properties has long played an important part. With short-term credits, store credit and fresh advances by the banks have greatly dwindled in the hard-hit areas. On the other hand, the progress of the credit unions in the Maritime provinces gives promise of meeting a long-felt want in these regions. No provision for intermediate credit is present with the exception of the credit terms of the implement companies and the very limited operations of the Dominion Agricultural Credit Company, organized in 1931.

Until recently, government lending, save in Ontario, had been important more because of its effects and what it signified than because of the actual amounts involved. It had its beginning in the prairie provinces in 1917 when the government of the province of Manitoba took an active part in mortgage and short-term lending, the latter more particularly after the rural credit societies had broken with the banks. In the same year, the Alberta Coöperative Credit Societies Act was passed, while Saskatchewan made provision for the use of government funds for mortgage loans to farmers. In each case, the lending body is either in process of being wound up or is operating upon a very restricted basis.

In the maritime regions, land settlement rather than rural credit as such has been stressed. In British Columbia, the Agricultural Act of 1915 failed to attain any importance, giving way to the Land Settlement and Development Act of 1917, in which provision was made for advances to promote settlement. The Nova Scotia Farm Loans Act of 1919 has also remained unimportant, although various land settlement Acts providing for guarantees of loans or advances in aid of settlement as a means of relieving unemployment have attracted more attention. Land settlement activities have also been the chief interest in New Brunswick and Prince Edward Island, and no farm lending of any consequence has been done in either of these provinces.

In 1921, Ontario followed Manitoba's example by making provision for loans for mortgage and short-term purposes. Although little lending on short term has been done, large sums have been advanced upon the security of farm mortgages. At present, the plan is operating upon a very restricted basis, with substantial losses in prospect. In Quebec the legislation of 1931 passed to promote "the return to land" has been an important factor in the rural credit of the province. Close coöperation, in addition to subsidies in interest, have been given in connection with loans made in the province by the Canadian Farm Loan Board. The Dominion body was set up in 1927 as a federal lending agency and enabling legislation was passed by most of the provinces. Up to 1934 the Board pursued a very conservative lending policy. Legislation passed in that year, however, gives indication of a considerable extension of the activities of the Board in all parts of Canada.

In addition to the activities outlined, government advances to farmers for seed grain, feed, and fodder have been made over a long period, and particularly in the western provinces. Such advances have become very important in the drought area since 1929, with Dominion assistance being invoked to a very considerable extent. Loans for livestock encouragement and drainage improvements have also been made in most provinces over a long period. The activities of the Soldiers' Settlement Board have been a further important factor in rural credit, very large amounts having been advanced since its organization in 1919. Finally, government intervention in the direction of debt adjustment has assumed a new importance since 1929, although provincial boards have been operating in the prairie provinces since the early twenties. The Farmers' Creditors' Arrangement Act of 1934 marked the intervention of the federal government in matters pertaining to the adjustment of farmers' debts throughout the Dominion.

Present indications point to government intervention in rural credit for some time to come. The implications are social and political as well as economic, and relate to problems associated with the financing of a complex industry in which conditions and outlook vary widely over the different parts of the country.

*Bibliography.* See *Report of the Agricultural Credit Commission of the province of Saskatchewan* (Regina, 1913); *Report of Alberta commissioners on the American commission for the study of agricultural credit in European countries* (Edmonton, 1914); *Report of committee on rural credits, Ontario* (Toronto, 1921); *Report of committee on rural credits, Manitoba* (Winnipeg, 1922); H. M. Tory, *Report on agricultural credit* (Ottawa, 1924), also *Supplementary report* (Ottawa, 1925); *Report of the Royal Commission on Banking and Currency in Canada* (Ottawa, 1933); W. A. Mackintosh, *Economic problems of the prairie provinces* (Toronto, 1935); and W. T. Easterbrook, "Agricultural credit in Canada" (Ph.D. Thesis, Toronto, 1937).

**Rush** (*Juncaceae*), a large family of grass-like or sedge-like plants with simple, pithy or hollow stems, and clusters of small, regular, greenish flowers. As a rule these plants are found in wet soil and along the borders of streams during the summer. They are very difficult of determination, and are thus not of much interest to the amateur botanist. The flowers are lily-like in structure, having 3 sepals, 3 petals, 6 stamens, and a 3-celled pistil.

**Rush-Bagot Convention,** an agreement signed in 1817 by Richard Rush, acting secretary of state in the government of the United States, and Sir Charles Bagot (q.v.), British minister at Washington, whereby the United States and Great Britain undertook to maintain on the Great lakes and lake Champlain only four war vessels each of not more than 100 tons burden, two on the upper lakes, one on lake Erie, and one on lake Champlain. Since 1817 Great Britain, and later Canada, have permitted the United States to have on occasion larger ships on the Great lakes for use as training ships; but permission for this deviation from the terms of the convention has always been obtained in advance, and is an evidence of the confidence felt in Canada in the pacific intentions of the United States government. See C. H. Levermore, *The Anglo-American agreement of 1817* (Boston, World Peace Foundation pamphlet, vol. iv, no. 4, 1924).

**Russell, Benjamin** (1849-1935), judge and author, was born at Dartmouth, Nova Scotia, on January 10, 1849, the son of Nathaniel Russell. He was educated at Mount Allison University (B.A., 1868; M.A., 1871; D.C.L., 1893), and was called to the bar in Nova Scotia in 1872. He was elected to represent Halifax in the Canadian House of Commons in 1896, and Hants in 1900; and in 1904 he was appointed a puisne judge of the Supreme Court of Nova Scotia. This post he held for over thirty years; and he died in office at Halifax on September 21, 1935. He was the author of several legal works and of an *Autobiography* (Halifax, Nova Scotia, 1932).

**Russell, George Horne** (1861-1933), painter, was born at Banff, Scotland, in 1861. He studied art in London, and came to Canada in 1890. He specialized in portrait-painting; but he was also a painter of landscapes and marines. Elected an associate of the Royal Canadian Academy of Arts in 1909, he became a fellow in 1918; and from 1922 to 1926 he was president of the Academy. He died at St. Stephen, New Brunswick, on June 25, 1933.

**Russell, Peter** (1733-1808), president and administrator of Upper Canada (1796-9), was born at Cork, Ireland, in 1733, the son of Capt. Richard Russell, 14th Foot. He entered the army at an early age, but in 1772 sold his commission and came to America as one of the secretaries of Sir Henry Clinton. At the close of the American Revolutionary War he returned to England; and in 1791 he came out to Canada with Simcoe (q.v.) as inspector-general of Upper Canada. In 1792 he was appointed a member of the Executive and Legislative Councils of the province; and from 1796 to 1799 he was the administrator of the government, with the title of president. He died at York (Toronto) on September 30, 1808; and his property was willed to his sister, Elizabeth Russell, who left it to William Warren Baldwin (q.v.). His *Correspondence* is being collected and edited for the Ontario Historical Society (Toronto, 1932— ) by E. A. Cruikshank and A. F. Hunter. See D. B. Read, *The lieutenant-governors of Upper Canada* (Toronto, 1900).

**Russell,** a county at the eastern extremity of the province of Ontario, is bounded on the north by the Ottawa river, on the west by Carleton county, on the south by Stormont and Dundas counties, and on the east by Prescott county, with which it was long united, and still is for judicial purposes, L'Orignal in Prescott county being its county seat. It was set apart in 1798, and was named after the Hon. Peter Russell (q.v.). It is about 18 by 23 miles in area. Pop. (1931), 18,487.

**Russell,** a village in Russell county, Ontario, on the Castor river, and on the Ottawa and New York Railway, 19 miles south-east of Ottawa. It has a number of small industries, a public library, and a weekly newspaper (*Leader*). Pop. (1931), 828.

**Russian Immigration.** Russians, generally, may be classified as Great Russians, in the north, White Russians, in the west, and Little Russians, in the south. Most of the immigrants to Canada from Russia have been Germans, Jews, Lithuanians, or Poles. Practically none of the Great Russians, or Russians proper, have been among the immigrants to Canada. Those who stoutly maintain they are "Russ" are Little Russians. They are closely allied to the Ruthenians of Galicia and Bukowina (see **Galician immigration**), and hardly require separate treatment. The languages are cognate, and the social conditions much the same. See James S. Woodsworth, *Strangers within our gates* (Toronto, 1909).

**Russian Thistle,** or Tumble Weed (*Salsola Kali* L. var. *tenuifolia* G. F. W. Mey, *Chenopodiaceae*), a very bushy annual weed with alternate, filiform-awl-shaped, prickly-pointed leaves. The inconspicuous flowers are sessile, single in the axils of the leaves; the calyx is 5-parted, enclosing the fruit; the stamens are 5. The stem snaps very readily at the soil line, and the round bushy head of the plant is blown across the country giving it the local name of "tumble weed". It is very abundant and is becoming a pernicious weed in many sections of the North West.

**Rutherford, John Gunion** (1857-1923), veterinary surgeon, was born at Mountain Bank, Peeblesshire, Scotland, on December 25, 1857, the son of the Rev. Robert Rutherford. He was educated at the Glasgow High School, came to Canada in 1875, and studied at the Ontario Agricultural College and at the Ontario Veterinary College (V.S., 1879). In 1884 he settled at Portage La Prairie, Manitoba; and in 1885 he served as veterinary officer with the North West field force during the Riel rebellion. From 1892 to 1896 he represented

Lakeside in the Legislative Assembly of Manitoba; and from 1897 to 1900 he represented Macdonald in the Canadian House of Commons. In 1902 he was appointed veterinary director-general for Canada, and in 1906 live stock commissioner. In 1918 he became a member of the board of railway commissioners, and this post he held until his death at Ottawa on July 24, 1923. In 1887 he married Edith, daughter of Washington Boultbee, of Ancaster, Ontario. He was created a C.M.G. in 1910.

**Ruthven,** a village in Essex county, Ontario, on the Père Marquette Railway, 28 miles east of Sandwich. Pop. (1934), 300.

**Rutile.** See **Titanium.**

**Ruttan, Henry** (1791-1871), author, was born at Adolphustown, Upper Canada, in 1792, the son of William Ruttan, a United Empire Loyalist. From 1820 to 1824 and from 1836 to 1841 he represented Northumberland in the Legislative Assembly of Upper Canada; and in 1837 he was elected for a short time speaker of the Assembly. From 1827 to 1857 he was sheriff of the Newcastle district; and in his later years he devoted much attention to the subject of ventilation. He died at Cobourg, Ontario, on July 31, 1871. He was the author of *Lectures on the ventilation of buildings* (Cobourg, 1848), and *Ventilation and warming of buildings* (New York, 1862).

**Ryan, William Thomas Carroll** (1839-1910), poet, was born in Toronto, Canada, on February 3, 1839, the son of Thomas Ryan and Honor Carroll. He was educated at St. Michael's College, Toronto, and served as a volunteer in the Crimean War when still in his 'teens. From 1859 to 1867 he was enlisted in to 100th Regiment (Royal Canadians). He then returned to Canada and engaged in journalism, first at Ottawa, then at St. John, and then at Montreal. He died at Montreal on March 24, 1910. In 1870 he married Mary Ann McIver, of Ottawa, the author of a volume of *Poems* (Ottawa, 1870). He published *Oscar, and other poems* (Hamilton, 1857), *Songs of a wanderer* (Ottawa, 1867), *Picture poems* (Ottawa, 1884), and *Poems, songs, ballads* (Montreal, 1903).

**Ryckman, Edward Baird** (1866-1934), minister of national revenue (1930-3), was born at Huntingdon, Quebec, on April 16, 1866, the son of the Rev. Edward Bradshaw Ryckman and Emmaline Baird. He was educated at Victoria University, Cobourg (B.A., 1887; M.A., 1889; LL.B., 1890) and at Osgoode Hall, Toronto; and was called to the bar in 1890 (K.C., 1908). He practised law in Toronto, and from 1921 to his death he represented East Toronto in the Canadian House of Commons. He was minister of public works in the short-lived Meighen administration of 1926; and from 1930 to 1933 he was minister of national revenue in the Bennett government. He died at Toronto on January 11, 1934. In 1895 he married Mabel Louise, daughter of Edward Gurney; and by her he had two sons and two daughters.

**Ryerse** or **Ryerson, Samuel** (1752-1812), loyalist, was born in New Jersey in 1752, the third son of Luykas Ryerson. He was a captain in the 4th New Jersey Volunteers (Loyalists) during the American Revolutionary War; and in 1783 he took refuge in New Brunswick. In 1794 he removed to Upper Canada, where he obtained a large grant of land near Long Point on lake Erie. Port Ryerse, Norfolk county, is named after him. He became lieutenant of the county of Norfolk, judge of the London district court, and a lieut.-colonel of the militia. He died in June, 1812. In 1783 he married Sarah Underhill, widow of Capt. Davenport; and by her he had two sons and one daughter. The form of his name was changed from Ryerson to Ryerse as a result of its having been so spelt in his militia commission. See A. W. Ryerson, *The*

*Ryerson genealogy* (Chicago, 1916), and L. J. Ryerson, *The genealogy of the Ryerson family in America* (New York, 1902).

**Ryerson, Adolphus Egerton** (1803-1882), clergyman, controversialist, and educationist, was born in the township of Charlotteville, Norfolk county, Upper Canada, on March 24, 1803, the fourth son of Colonel Joseph Ryerson (q.v.), a United Empire Loyalist, and Mehetabel Stickney. He was educated at the district grammar school; and in 1825 he entered the ministry of the Methodist church. After serving in various places as a Methodist preacher, he was in 1829 chosen editor of the *Christian Guardian*, the organ of the Wesleyan Methodist Church, and, except for the years 1831-3 and 1837-8, he continued to edit this journal until 1840. He became known as a powerful controversialist, attacking especially the exclusive claims of the Church of England to the Clergy Reserves; and he acquired a great influence over the Methodist electors of the province. He leaned at first toward the Reform party; but in 1833 he came out in opposition to William Lyon Mackenzie (q.v.), of whose extreme course he disapproved, and in 1837 his influence was a powerful factor on the loyalist side. He was also influential in securing in 1844 the victory of the administration formed by Sir Charles Metcalfe (q.v.).

In 1841 he was appointed the first president of the University of Victoria College, at Cobourg; and in 1844 he accepted the position of chief superintendent of education for Upper Canada. This position he retained until 1876; and the educational system of Ontario was largely his creation. In 1848 he established the *Journal of Education;* and this periodical he edited until his retirement in 1876.

He was twice married, (1) in 1828 to Hannah, daughter of John Aikman, and (2) in 1833 to Mary, daughter of James Rogers Armstrong, of Toronto.

By his first wife he had two children, who died young; and by his second wife, one son and one daughter. He was a D.D. of the Wesleyan University, Middletown, Connecticut (1842) and an LL.D., from Victoria University, Cobourg (1861). An indefatigable controversialist, he published many pamphlets, of which the most notable were *Claims of the churchmen and dissenters of Upper Canada brought to a test* (Kingston, 1828), *The affairs of the Canadas* (London, 1837), *The clergy reserve question* ('Toronto, 1839), *Sir Charles Metcalfe defended* (Toronto, 1844), *Letters in reply to the attacks of the Hon. George Brown* (Toronto, 1859), *University reform* (Toronto, 1861), and *The new Canadian dominion* (Toronto, 1867). His chief work was his history of *The loyalists of America, and their times* (2 vols., Toronto, 1882), and he was also the author of a history of *Canadian Methodism* (Toronto, 1882). His autobiography was published posthumously by J. G. Hodgins (Toronto, 1883).

See C. B. Sissons, *Egerton Ryerson, his life and letters* (Toronto, 1937); Rev. E. Ryerson, *"The story of my life"*, ed. by J. George Hodgins (Toronto, 1883); N. Burwash, *Egerton Ryerson* (Toronto, 1903; new ed., revised by C. B. Sissons, 1926); J. G. Hodgins, *Ryerson memorial volume* (Toronto, 1889); J. H. Putman, *Egerton Ryerson and education in Upper Canada* (Toronto, 1912); L. J. Ryerson, *The genealogy of the Ryerson family in America* (New York, 1902); and A. W. Ryerson, *The Ryerson genealogy* (Chicago, 1916).

**Ryerson, George** (1792-1882), clergyman, was born near Fredericton, New Brunswick, on March 8, 1792, the eldest son of Colonel Joseph Ryerson (q.v.). He came to Upper Canada with his parents in 1799, and settled at Port Ryerse, on lake Erie. He served as a subaltern in the Norfolk militia during the War of 1812, and was severely wounded at the battle of Lundy's Lane.

He was educated at Union College, in the United States. In 1819 he was ordained a minister of the Methodist Church; later he took orders in the Church of England; and finally he became a minister of the Catholic Apostolic Church. For many years he was the head of this body in America. He died at Toronto, Ontario, on December 19, 1882. He was thrice married, (1) about 1821 to Sarah, daughter of Thomas Rolph, M.D., by whom he had one son and two daughters; (2) to Sophia Symes, by whom he had one daughter; and (3) to Isabel Dorcas, daughter of the Hon. Ansel Sterling, of Connecticut, by whom he had one son. See W. Canniff, *George Ryerson* (Belford's magazine, 1878; reprinted in *Annual Transactions* of the United Empire Loyalists' Association, vol. vi, 1914).

**Ryerson, George Ansel Sterling** (1854-1925), physician and author, was born at Toronto on January 21, 1854, the son of the Rev. George Ryerson (q.v.). He was educated at the Galt Grammar School, at Trinity University, Toronto (M.B., 1875; M.D., 1876), and at Victoria University (M.D., C.M., 1892). In 1880 he was appointed professor of ophthalmology and otology in the Trinity Medical School; and he was a member of many medical societies, including the Royal College of Physicians and Surgeons, Edinburgh. He saw service in the Fenian raid; he served as a medical officer in the North West Rebellion of 1885 and the South African war; and he rose to the rank of major-general in the Canadian militia. In 1896 he was one of the founders of the Canadian Red Cross Society; and from 1896 to 1898 he was president of the United Empire Loyalists' Association. From 1893 to 1898 he represented Toronto East in the Legislative Assembly of Ontario. He died in Toronto on May 20, 1925. In addition to a number of pamphlets on various subjects, he was the author of an autobiography entitled *Looking backward* (Toronto, 1924).

**Ryerson, John** (1800-1878), clergyman, was born in the township of Charlotteville, Norfolk county, Upper Canada, on June 12, 1800, the fourth son of Colonel Joseph Ryerson (q.v.). In 1820 he was ordained a minister of the Wesleyan Methodist Church, and he continued in the ministry for fifty-eight years. In 1854 he visited the Hudson's Bay territories on a missionary tour, and he published a description of this expedition in *Hudson's Bay; or a missionary tour in the territory of the Hon. Hudson's Bay Company* (Toronto, 1855). He died at Simcoe, Ontario, on October 5, 1878. By his wife, Mary Lewis, he had one son and three daughters.

**Ryerson, Joseph** (1761-1854), loyalist, was born in New Jersey on February 28, 1761, the second son of Luykas Ryerson. He fought throughout the American Revolutionary War on the British side, as an officer in the Prince of Wales Regiment (New Jersey); and in 1783 he settled in New Brunswick. Here he married, in 1784, Sophia Mehetabel Stickney, reputed to have been the first white woman born in Canada after the British conquest; and by her he had six sons and two daughters. In 1799 he removed to Upper Canada, and settled in Charlotteville, Norfolk county. In 1800 he was appointed high sheriff of the London district, and lieutenant of the county of Norfolk. He became a colonel in the militia; and, with his three eldest sons, fought in the War of 1812. He died on August 9, 1854.

**Ryland, Herman Witsius** (1760-1838), clerk of the executive council of Lower Canada (1793-1838), was born in Northampton, England, in 1760. In 1781 he came to America as assistant deputy-paymaster-general of the British forces, and served throughout the last stages of the American Revolutionary War. On the evacuation of New York in 1784, he returned to England with

Sir Guy Carleton (q.v.); and when Carleton, as Lord Dorchester, was appointed governor-general of British North America under the Act of 1791, Ryland came out to Canada in 1793 as his secretary. He was appointed both civil secretary and clerk of the executive council, and for many years he exercised a great influence on the government of Canada. He was the confidential adviser of Sir James Craig (q.v.), but was dismissed from office by Sir George Prevost (q.v.) as civil secretary in 1812. He continued, however, as clerk of the executive council until his death; and he was appointed in 1813 a member of the Legislative Council. He died at Beauport, near Quebec, on July 20, 1838. A selection of his papers is printed in R. Christie, *History of Lower Canada*, vol. vi (Quebec, 1854). See F. J. Audet, *Herman Witsius Ryland* (Trans. Roy. Soc. Can., 1929).

**Ryswick, Treaty of.** This was the treaty between Great Britain and France, signed on September 20, 1697, whereby King William's War was brought to an end. It provided for the restoration of all territories captured by either party during the war, and for the appointment of commissioners to determine the respective rights of the two countries in Hudson bay.

# S

**Saanich inlet,** a long narrow bay on the west side of Saanich peninsula, on the south-east coast of Vancouver island. It is 14 miles long, and varies in width from 4 miles to ¼ mile.

**Sabine, Sir Edward** (1788-1883), soldier and author, was born in Dublin, Ireland, on October 14, 1788. He entered the British army as an artillery officer in 1803, and served in Canada during the War of 1812. He was astronomer in the first Arctic expedition of Sir John Ross (q.v.) in 1818, and in the expedition of Sir William Edward Parry (q.v.) in 1819-20. He made a series of voyages with the object of investigating the variations in the magnetic needle; and his researches resulted in the establishment of magnetic observations throughout the British Empire, one of which was opened in Toronto in 1841. In 1818 he was made a fellow of the Royal Society, and from 1861 to 1871 he was its president. He died at Richmond, England, on June 26, 1883. He was created a knight of the Bath in 1869. He contributed the natural history notes to Sir W. E. Parry, *First Arctic voyage* (London, 1821); and he was the author of *An account of experiments to determine the figure of the earth* (London, 1825), and *The variability of the intensity of magnetism upon many parts of the globe* (London, 1838).

**Sable, cape,** the south-western extremity of Nova Scotia. It is named from the French word *sable* or *sablon* (sand). Lying to the south of it is an island known as Cape Sable island.

**Sable island,** an island in the Atlantic ocean, 170 miles east of Halifax, Nova Scotia. It is about 25 miles long, and a mile in breadth, and stretches from east to west in the form of a thin crescent moon. It is formed of sand, and is merely the visible portion of a vast sand bank or shoal, 75 miles in length and 10 miles in width. It owes its name to the fact that *sable* is French for "sand". It was probably discovered by some of the first navigators to North America, for it appears on Reinel's map of 1565 as Santa Cruz, and also on the Cabot mappemonde of 1544. When the Marquis de la Roche (q.v.) landed here in 1598 he found on the island wild cattle, which had obviously been left by earlier visitors, who had possibly been shipwrecked. He himself was compelled to leave on the island for five years fifty of his colonists, and only eleven of these survived. Since then the island has had a grim history. Shipwrecks have been so numerous that it has been called "the graveyard of the Atlantic". The first relief establishment on the island was initiated by the government of Nova Scotia in 1801; and in 1873 the Dominion government, which had taken over control of the island, built two powerful lighthouses, and instituted a coastguard service. There are no trees on the island; but vegetables are grown, and a race of wild ponies finds means of livelihood. It is apparent that the island is shrinking in size, since 200 years ago it was twice as long and twice as wide as it is now. See Rev. G. Patterson, *Sable island* (Trans, Roy. Soc. Can., 1894), and *Supplementary notes on Sable island* (Trans. Roy. Soc. Can., 1898), and D. W. Rosebrugh, *The graveyard of the Atlantic* (Can. Geog. Journal, 1932).

**Sable River,** a village in Shelburne county, Nova Scotia, on the river Sable, and on the Canadian National Railway, 16 miles north-east of Shelburne, and 29 miles south-west of Liverpool. It has lumber mills. Pop. (1934), 850.

**Sabrevois,** a village in Iberville county, Quebec, on the Richelieu river, and on the Quebec Southern Railway, 7 miles from St. Johns. It is named after the seigniory in which it is situated, which was granted in 1750 to the Sieur de Sabrevois. Pop. (1934), 150.

**Sackett's Harbour, Battle of.** This was an attack made by the British on the naval headquarters of the Americans at the south-east corner of lake Ontario on May 28-9, 1813. The British fleet, under Sir James Yeo (q.v.), with 1,000 troops on board, under Sir George Prevost (q.v.), made a descent on Sackett's harbour, and the British had victory within their grasp when Prevost, with his characteristic over-caution and indecision, ordered a retreat.

**Sackville,** a town in Westmorland county, New Brunswick, is situated at the edge of the famous Tantramar dykelands, created by the early French settlers near the head of Chignecto bay, 127 miles east of Saint John. It is on the main line of the Canadian National Railway, and from it a branch line runs to cape Tormentine to the ferry that connects New Brunswick and Prince Edward Island. It was named after Lord Sackville, commander of the British forces in 1758. It was incorporated as a town in 1902. The district about it has very fine farms, special attention being given to the cultivation of small fruit, especially strawberries. The town has a number of industries, chief among them being two large stove foundries. It is the seat of Mount Allison University (q.v.); and it has a ladies' college, a commercial college, and two semi-weekly newspapers (*Post* and *Tribune*). Pop. (1931), 2,234.

**Sacré-Cœur de Jésus,** the name applied among the French Canadians to the village of East Broughton (q.v.), in Beauce county, Quebec.

**Sadlier, Mrs. Mary Anne,** *née* **Madden** (1820-1903), was born at Cootehill, county Cavan, Ireland, on December 21, 1820, the eldest daughter of Francis Madden. She came to Canada in her youth, and in 1846 she married James Sadlier (d. 1869), a member of the firm of D. and J. Sadlier, publishers, New York, Boston, and Montreal. Most of her life was spent in New York, and there she became a friend of Thomas D'Arcy McGee (q.v.). In her later days, she returned to Montreal; and there she died on April 5, 1903. She was the author of numerous romances of Irish life, in America and in Ireland; and she edited, with a biographical introduction, *The poems of Thomas D'Arcy McGee* (New York, 1869).

**Sagard-Théodat, Gabriel** (d. 1650), missionary and author, was a lay brother in the Recollet order who came to Canada in 1623. He spent about one year in the Huron country; and then returned to France, where he wrote and published two books based on his experiences in Canada, *Grand voyage du pays des Hurons* (Paris, 1632), and *Histoire du Canada* (Paris, 1636), the latter of which was mainly an enlargement and revision of the former. Both works were reprinted in Paris by Tross in 1865-6. Sagard died in 1650.

**Saguenay,** a county in Quebec, on the north shore of the river and gulf of St. Lawrence, stretching from the 70th parallel of latitude to the eastern boundary of the province of Quebec. It is named after the Saguenay river. It is bounded on the west by Chicoutimi county, and on the north by Labrador; and it includes the island of Anticosti. Chief town, Tadoussac. Pop. (1931), 19,577.

**Saguenay river** flows out of lake St. John, Saguenay county, Quebec, and

5 miles below Tadoussac discharges into the St. Lawrence on its north side. The name is an Indian word which has been interpreted as "water that flows out", "inundation", or "ice having holes in it"; but all are doubtful. The river was discovered by Jacques Cartier (q.v.) in 1535; and by 1600 Tadoussac had become the centre of the fur-trade between French traders and the Montagnais Indians who acted as middlemen between them and the Algonkian tribes further north. The Saguenay remained primarily a fur-trading area, both under the French and the British, until after the Napoleonic wars, when William Price organized the lumbering industry along the river. Settlement by French Canadians in the river valley followed the work of the timber-cutters.

The river, one of the largest tributaries of the St. Lawrence, is 405 miles in length to the head of the Peribonka, 1½ miles in width at Tadoussac, receives the waters of many tributaries, and drains a basin of 3,600 square miles. It is famous for its grand and picturesque scenery. It flows out of lake St. John by a double channel, of which one arm is called Grande-Décharge, and the other Petite-Décharge. The first half of the river's course runs through a wilderness of pine and spruce; it abounds in waterfalls and is navigable only for canoes. At the foot of the turbulent cascades of the upper Saguenay is Chicoutimi, and about 10 miles below it there recedes from the river a beautiful expanse of water know as Ha! Ha! bay, so called, it is said, from the disgust of the explorers who mistook it for the main river. Between this bay and the mouth of the river is some of the most picturesque river scenery in the world. In this part of the river, which sometimes reaches a depth of more than 1,000 feet, is encompassed on each side by gigantic walls such as capes Trinity and Eternity; the first of these rises 1,500 and the second 1,700 feet above sea level. On the south shore near cape Trinity is Le Tableau or the Blackboard, an enormous face of sheer black rock. The Saguenay is navigable to Chicoutimi, and is visited in the summer by large numbers of tourists. It is one of the best salmon-fishing rivers in the world, and abounds in sea trout. The uproarous current of La Grande-Décharge has been harnessed to give 540,000 horse-power of electricity, and at Chute à Caron, where the river is forced through a stone chasm, it gives 800,000 horse-power. Around lake St. John many other power projects are to be developed to feed pulp-and-paper plants, such as at Dolbeau. The river flows through a district rich and fertile with half a million acres of cultivated farmlands. See Arthur Buies, *La Saguenay et la vallée du lac St. Jean* (Quebec, 1880); *Le Saguenay et le bassin du lac Saint-Jean* (Quebec, 1896); Blodwen Davies, *Saguenay* (Toronto, 1930); and George Tremblay, *Monographie de Tadoussac, 1535-1922* (Chicoutimi, 1922), and *Les premières pages de l'histoire du Saguenay* (Canadian Historical Association Report, 1925).

**Saindon,** a village and parish in Matapedia county, Quebec, in the Matapedia valley, near Amqui. Pop. (1931), 2,355.

**St. Agapit de Beaurivage,** a parish in Lotbinière county, Quebec, on the St. Agapit river, and on the Canadian National Railway, 27 miles south of Lévis. Pop. (1931), 760.

**St. Aimé,** a parish in Richelieu county, Quebec, on the Yamaska river, 25 miles from St. Hyacinthe. Pop. (1931), 790.

**St. Albans Raid,** an attack made from Canadian soil by a number of Confederate ex-soldiers on the town of St. Albans, Vermont, in October, 1864. See L. N. Benjamin (ed.), *The St. Alban's raid* (Boston, 1865).

**St. Albert,** a village in Alberta, on the Athabaska branch of the Canadian National Railway, 5 miles from Ed-

CAPE TRINITY, SAGUENAY RIVER, QUEBEC

monton. It was named after Father
Albert Lacombe (q.v.), and the name
dates from 1861, when Bishop Taché
chose the spot for a mission station.
Pop. (1934), 700.

**St. Alexandre,** a village in Iberville
county, Quebec, on the Canadian National Railway, 9 miles from St. Johns.
Pop. (1931), 300.

**St. Alexis,** a village in Montcalm
county, Quebec, on the Canadian National Railway, 12 miles south-west of
Joliette. It is in a general farming district, in which dairying and tobacco-
growing are also carried on. Pop. (1931),
490.

**St. Alexis de la Grande Baie,** a
village in Chicoutimi county, Quebec,
on the south shore of Ha! Ha! bay. It
was incorporated as a village in 1908.
The post-office is named Grande Baie.
Pop. (1931), 1,790.

**St. Ambroise,** a village in Chicoutimi
county, Quebec, on the north bank of
the Saguenay river. It was incorporated
as a village in 1917. Pop. (1931), 375.

**St. André.** See **St. Andrews.**

**St. André Avellin,** a village in
Papineau county, Quebec, on the Petite
Nation river, 8 miles from Papineau-
ville. Pop. (1931), 444.

**St. Andrews,** the county town of
Charlotte county, New Brunswick, on
Passamaquoddy bay, 60 miles west of
Saint John, and 3 miles east of the
United States boundary. It is a terminus
of the Canadian Pacific Railway, has a
commodious harbour, and is a fashion-
able summer resort. The origin of the
name is uncertain; but it is probable that
it dates back to the French period, and
the tradition is that a French priest
once celebrated mass here on November
30 (St. Andrew's day), and named the
point St. Andrews. Fishing is the chief
industry of the inhabitants. Pop. (1934),
1,065. See Grace Helen Mowat, *The
diverting history of a loyalist town* (St.
Andrews, New Brunswick, 1932).

**St. Andrews,** a village in Argenteuil
county, Quebec, on the North river,
three miles from its junction with the
Ottawa, and on the Canadian Pacific
Railway, 45 miles west of Montreal,
and 6 miles south of Lachute. It was
formerly known as St. Andrews East,
to distinguish it from St. Andrews in
Glengarry county, Upper Canada; and
it is to-day known also as St. André.
It was first settled toward the end of
the eighteenth century by Scottish and
American veterans of the American
Revolutionary War; and it was for a
time a place of considerable importance.
It was here that in 1803 the first paper-
mill in Canada was built. It had a
Presbyterian church as early as 1821.
To-day it is chiefly the centre of an
agricultural district. Pop. (1930), 1,520.
See B. N. Wales, *Memories of old St.
Andrews and historical sketches of the
seigniory of Argenteuil* (Lachute, Quebec,
1934).

**St. Andrews,** a village in Stormont
county, Ontario, on the river Raisin, 6
miles north of Cornwall. It is sometimes
known as St. Andrews West to distinguish it from St. Andrews in Argenteuil county, Quebec. Pop. (1934), 150.

**St. Andrews,** a village in Manitoba,
on the Red river, and on the Canadian
Pacific Railway, 16 miles north of
Winnipeg. It was originally known as
Sault à la Biche; but the Selkirk settlers
re-named it St. Andrews, and a post-
office was established here in 1870.
Pop. (1934), 900.

**St. Andrew's College** is a residential
school for boys near Aurora, Ontario,
20 miles north of Toronto. It was
founded in Toronto in 1899. Organized
at first as a joint stock company, it became in 1911 by special legislation a
public trust administered by a board of
governors. Though originally established
through Presbyterian effort, St. Andrew's has become interdenominational.
Its first home was Chestnut Park, in
Toronto, the former residence of the

Hon. D. L. Macpherson (q.v.); and its first headmaster was the Rev. George Bruce, whose health compelled his retirement in 1900. He was succeeded by the Rev. D. Bruce Macdonald, under whose administration the school achieved immediate success. In 1906 the school migrated to new and commodious buildings in north Rosedale, in Toronto; and in 1926 it was removed to its present beautiful site near Aurora. Here, in a property of 219 acres, it is fully equipped with Upper and Lower School residences, classroom building, gymnasium, swimming-pool, and chapel. It has accommodation for 160 boys. The headmasters have been the Rev. George Bruce (1899-1900), the Rev. D. Bruce Macdonald, LL.D. (1900-1935), and K. G. B. Ketchum, B.A. (1935—).

**St. Andrew's College,** in Saskatoon, Saskatchewan, was established in 1913 as the Presbyterian Theological College, Saskatoon, in affiliation with the University of Saskatoon. Classes were opened in 1914, and the present building was completed in 1923. In 1924 the name of the college was changed to St. Andrew's College; and in 1925, on the completion of church union (q.v.), it became a college in connection with the United Church of Canada. It has a residence which houses about 100 students, most of whom are undergraduates of the University of Saskatchewan. It gives instruction only in divinity; and it has over 40 students in divinity, with 16 post-graduate students. It has a teaching staff of six professors. The principals of the college have been the Very Rev. E. H. Oliver (q.v.), and the Rev. D. S. Dix (1936—).

**St. Andrews Lock.** See **Canals.**

**St. Anselme,** a village in Dorchester county, Quebec, on the Etchemin river, and on the Quebec Central and Canadian National Railways. Pop. (1931), 738.

**St. Augustin,** a village in Portneuf county, Quebec, situated on the Cana-

dian National and Canadian Pacific Railways, 14 miles west of Quebec. In 1679 the parish was placed under the patronage of St. Augustin in honour of Augustin Saffray de Mézy, a governor of New France. The industries are in agriculture: farming, market-gardening, dairying, and fruit-growing, for the Quebec city market. Pop. (1931), 1,546. For a history of the parish see Auguste Béchard, *Saint Augustin* (Quebec, 1885).

**St. Barnabé island,** in the St. Lawrence river, is in Rimouski county, Quebec, opposite the town of Rimouski. It was probably so named because it was first seen by Champlain (q.v.) on June 11, the festival of St. Barnabé. See P. Lacombe (pseud.), *La terre paternelle* (Quebec, 1877), reprinted in J. C. Taché, *Les Sablons (L'île de Sable) et l'île Saint-Barnabé* (Montreal, 1885).

**St. Benoît,** a village in the county of Two Mountains, Quebec, on the Canadian National Railway, 33 miles west of Montreal. This parish and the neighbouring parish of Ste. Scholastique were named after a brother and sister, St. Benoît and Ste. Scholastique, who founded a community of Benedictines. Pop. (1931), 306.

**St. Benoît Joseph Labre,** a village and parish in Matapedia county, Quebec, near St. Antoine de Padoue. Pop. (1931), 1,648.

**St. Boniface,** a city in Manitoba, on the east side of the Red river opposite Winnipeg, and on the Canadian National and Canadian Pacific Railways. The name of the city commemorates an English missionary called "the apostle of Germany". It originated with Abbé (later Bishop) Provencher (q.v.), who arrived at the Red river in 1818 and placed a temporary chapel "under the patronage of St. Boniface". The name was applied to the settlement in 1819. The city was incorporated in 1908. It is the seat of the Roman Catholic archdiocese of St. Boniface; its cathedral is the largest west of Toronto, and one of the most beautiful in the Dominion. There are three public schools, three collegiate institutes, a Roman Catholic college, four churches, and a convent. The industrial establishments include factories for sheet metal, breweries, flour mills, furniture works, and a shop for the manufacture of car wheels. St. Boniface has become a grest livestock centre; there are two abattoirs. Two fine bridges span the river to Winnipeg; and an electric railway connects the two cities. Winnipeg and St. Boniface harbour is controlled by one commission, consisting of five commissioners, three appointed by the city of Winnipeg and two by St. Boniface. A weekly newspaper (*Norwood Press*) is published. Pop. (1931), 16,305.

**St. Boniface College.** See **University of Manitoba.**

**St. Casimir,** a village in Portneuf county, Quebec, situated on the Ste. Anne's and White rivers, and on the Canadian National Railway, 50 miles north-east of Quebec city. The village was named to commemorate Casimir Dury, who subscribed liberally towards the erection of the church in 1836. There is a commercial academy, a convent, and a home for the aged and orphans. The industrial establishments are foundries, aërated-water works, engine shops, lumber mills, and an agricultural implement factory. Pop. (1931), 1,880.

**St. Castin, Jean Vincent d'Abbadie, Baron de** (1652-1707), soldier, was born in Béarn, France, in 1652, the son of Jean Jacques d'Abbadie de St. Castin, whose estate was made a barony in 1654. The son entered the army, and was sent to New France in 1665 as an ensign. In 1668 he returned to France, but in 1670 he was sent a second time to North America, this time as an officer in the garrison of the fort at Pentagoët (now Castine) at the mouth of the Penobscot river. Here he spent most of the rest of his life. About

1680 he married Mathilde Mataconando, the daughter of the chief of the Abnaki; and he obtained over these Indians an unrivalled influence. He died in France, whither he had returned on business, some time in 1707. His eldest son, Bernard Anselme d'Abbadie Baron de St. Castin (1689-1728), succeeded him as chief military adviser of the Abnaki. See R. Le Blant, *Un figure légendaire de l'histoire acadienne: Le baron de St. Castin* (Dax, 1934).

**St. Catharines,** a city in Lincoln county, Ontario, on the Welland canal, and the Canadian National Railway, 35 miles south-east of Hamilton. The city is named after Catharine Askin Robertson (d. 1796), the first wife of the Hon. Robert Hamilton (q.v.), a member of the first Executive Council of Upper Canada. A Church of England mission station was established about the year 1792 in Grantham township, where St. Catharines now stands. The city is connected by electric railways with Port Dalhousie, Niagara Falls, Welland, Port Colborne, Merritton, and Thorold. St. Catharines is the seat of Ridley College, and contains twenty-seven churches, ten public and four separate schools, a collegiate institute, a business college, a free library, a hospital, and a sanatorium for consumptives. The mineral springs located in the city make it an excellent health resort. The Canadian Henley regatta is held here annually. St. Catharines is the centre of the Niagara fruit belt, which extends westward from the Niagara river along the southern shore of lake Ontario. Apples, stone-fruits, grapes, and berries are grown in abundance; and this section is peopled with prosperous fruit-farmers who make St. Catharines their purchasing market. It is doubtful if any other region of the British Empire produces so great an amount and variety of stone-fruits as does this district. The equable climate, and the warm night winds from the adjacent water masses have much to do with this good fortune. There are many other industries, the principal being textile plants, metal plants, paper-mills, food-product manufactories, canneries for fruit and vegetables, and the preparation of grape juices, wines, jams, marmalade, meat products, macaroni, etc. An evening newspaper (*Standard*) is published. Pop. (1931), 24,753.

**St. Césaire,** a village in Rouville county, Quebec, on the Yamaska river, and on the Central Vermont Railway, 35 miles east of Montreal. Both an agricultural and industrial centre, it owes its prosperity to extensive farming, gardening, and tobacco-growing, as well as to maple products and canning industries, a sash-and-door factory, a sawmill, and a bindery. Pop. (1931), 1,051. See A. Gervais, *Album-souvenir du centenaire de Saint-Césaire* (St. Hyacinthe, 1923).

**St. Chad's College,** in Regina, Saskatchewan, was founded in 1907 by the Right Rev. John Grisdale, fourth bishop of Qu'Appelle, as St. Chad's Hostel, for the training of candidates for holy orders in the Church of England. The present buildings on College Avenue, Regina, were erected in 1911; and in 1914 the name of the Hostel was changed to St. Chad's College. The College is affiliated with the University of Saskatchewan, and has the power of granting degrees in divinity. The teaching staff consists of the warden, the sub-warden, and three visiting lecturers. The wardens have been the Rev. C. R. Littler (1907-9), the Rev. G. N. Dobie (1909-33), and the Rev. R. J. Morrice (1935—).

**St. Charles,** a village in St. Hyacinthe county, Quebec, on the east side of the Richelieu river, opposite St. Marc, and 9 miles from St. Hilaire, on the Canadian National Railway. The village was a centre of the Lower Canada Rebellion of 1837. Here, on October 23, 1837, the rebels gathered in force, and proclaimed a republic, to be known as the "Confederation of the Six Counties"; and here on October 25, 1837, they were scattered by a column of British troops under Col. Wetherall. After the battle, the village was burnt by the soldiers. It was re-built, however, and created a parish in 1845, and a village in 1924. Pop. (1931), 246.

**St. Charles,** a village in Bellechasse county, Quebec, on the Canadian National Railway, 9 miles east of Lévis. It is a railway junction, and was incorporated as a village in 1914. It is named after Charles Couillard, seignior of Beaumont, who gave the land for the parish church in 1748. Pop. (1934), 673.

**St. Charles des Grondines,** a village in Portneuf county, Quebec, 4 miles from Grondines station on the Canadian Pacific Railway. Pop. (1931), 429. See also **Grondines.**

**St. Chrysostôme,** a village in Châteauguay county, Quebec, on the Rivière des Anglais, 4 miles from Aubrey station on the Canadian National Railway. It was incorporated a village in 1902. Pop. (1931), 636.

**St. Clair lake** and **river,** in Kent county, Ontario, at the south-west angle of Ontario, and between this province and the state of Michigan. Both were discovered in 1670 by the Sulpician missionaries, Dollier de Casson (q.v.) and Galinée (q.v.). They were named by La Salle (q.v.), who, with Hennepin (q.v.), reached this district on St. Clare's day 1679. The lake is 571 feet above sea level and 6 feet higher than lake Erie. It is 30 miles in length, 24 at its greatest and 12 in its mean breadth, and has an area of 460 square miles. It receives the Thames, Clinton and other rivers, and is drained into lake Erie by the Detroit river.

**St. Clements,** a village in Wellesley township, Waterloo county, Ontario, 10 miles south of Kitchener, and 7 miles from St. Jacobs station, on the Canadian National Railway. Pop. (1934), 300.

**St. Clet,** a village in Soulanges county, Quebec, on the Canadian Pacific Railway, 35 miles west of Montreal. Pop. (1931), 300. See Abbé A. C. Dugas, *Notes sur la paroisse de Saint-Clet* (Le Paroissien, 1906).

**St. Columba,** a settlement in Cape Breton county, Nova Scotia, 5 miles from Iona station on the Canadian National Railway. It was named in 1903 in honour of "the apostle of Caledonia", who founded the monastery at Iona. Formerly it was known as Grand Narrows Rear.

**St. Côme,** a village and parish in Joliette county, Quebec, on L'Assomption river, 35 miles from Joliette. It was founded in 1862 by a group of Acadians from Ste. Jacques de Montcalm. Pop. (1934), of the parish, 1,000.

**St. Côme,** a village in Beauce county, Quebec, 70 miles south of Lévis, and 19 miles from the international boundary. It is partly situated in the township of Linière, and is sometimes called Linière, after Linière Taschereau, one of the seigniors of Beauce. It is mainly a lumbering centre. Pop. (1931), 667.

**St. Croix island** is a very small island in the St. Croix river, near its mouth on Passamaquoddy bay. The island is about 1/6 of a mile in length, and not more than 125 yards in breadth, and has an area of about 5 acres. It lies in lat. 45° 07′ 44″, and long. 67° 08′ 03″. The only inhabitants are the keeper of the light-house and his family. The most interesting thing about the island is its history. The date of discovery is not certain, but it was the first spot chosen in Canada for a settlement, when Monts (q.v.) and his company landed there in 1604. With the region around, it might have formed the centre of French power in Acadia, but the settlement was abandoned in 1605, owing to the severe winter and illness amongst the settlers. In 1796-9, the island played an important part in boundary controversies, and the determination of what was the St. Croix river. The Commission of 1798 finally placed the mid-line of the river as the boundary between New Brunswick and the United States, thus casting St. Croix island as a possession of the United States. The island has had several names, the one most often (and still) used being Dochet; but St. Croix was the name given to it in 1604 by Monts, as stated in Champlain's narrative, and Lescarbot (q.v.) explains that it was suggested by the resemblance of the rivers meeting above the island to a cross. From the island the name was extended to the river. See W. F. Ganong, *Dochet (St. Croix) island* (Trans. Roy. Soc. Can., 1902).

**St. Croix river** rises in Grand lake on the border between New Brunswick and Maine, and flowing in a general south south-east direction enters Passamaquoddy bay, an inlet of the bay of Fundy. Throughout its course the river forms the boundary between New Brunswick and the United States. It was discovered in 1604 by Monts (q.v.) and Champlain (q.v.), who founded an ill-fated colony at its mouth only to remove their establishment to Port Royal in the following spring. French settlement commenced in this district in 1684, settlers from New England began to arrive after 1763; and later the district was extensively settled by Loyalists. The St. Croix is about 125 miles in length, and is navigable for vessels of light draft to St. Stephen. Above this its course is broken by a succession of falls and rapids, which afford good water-power, and upon which an extensive milling business is carried on. Canoes can ascend the river to its source.

**St. Cyrille,** a village in Drummond county, Quebec, on the Canadian National Railway, 4 miles north-east of Drummondville. It was incorporated as a village in 1905, and was placed under the patronage of St. Cyrille in honour of the first settler in the district. Cyrille Brassard. Pop. (1931), 725.

**St. Davids,** a village in Lincoln county, Ontario, on the Michigan Central Railway, 5 miles west of Niagara Falls. It was named after Major David Secord, a Canadian militia officer in the War of 1812. In the early days of Upper Canada, it was a village of some importance; and one of the earliest newspapers in the province, the *St. David's Spectator*, was published here in 1816. Its importance has now declined. Pop. (1934), 300.

**St. Denis,** a village in St. Hyacinthe county, Quebec, on the river Richelieu, 6 miles from Contrecœur, which is on the Canadian National Railway. In 1694 the settlement was named after Barbe Denis, wife of Louis de Gannes, to whom the seigniory was granted. The village is in a good dairying district; and it has butter and cheese factories, and saw, flour, and planing mills. The population of the parish in 1931 was 1,065, and the village, 689. For the history of the parish, see J. B. A. Allaire, *Saint-Denis-sur-Richelieu* (St. Hyacinthe, 1905).

**St. Dunstan's University** is a Roman Catholic institution of learning, situated on the Canadian National Railway, 2 miles from Charlottetown, Prince Edward Island. It was founded as a diocesan college, under the name of St. Dunstan's College, in 1855; and in 1892 it was affiliated with Laval University, Quebec. In 1917 it was incorporated under the name of St. Dunstan's University, with power to confer degrees. It has a residence, with accommodation for 100 students; and the domestic arrangements are in charge of a community of sisters. There are three courses: the commercial course, the high school course, and the university course. The last course is for four years; and on its completion, the student may obtain the Arts degree from Laval University.

**Ste. Adelaide de Pabos.** See **Pabos.**

**Ste. Adèle,** a village in Terrebonne county, Quebec, on the Canadian Pacific Railway, 15 miles north of St. Jérôme. It is a popular country resort, being situated on Long lake and on a spur of the Laurentian mountains; and it is also the centre of a general farming and dairying district. Pop. (1931), 433. See Abbé E. Langevin-Lacroix, *Histoire de la paroisse de Sainte-Adèle* (Montreal, 1927).

**Ste. Agathe des Monts,** a town in Terrebonne county, Quebec, situated on the North river, and on the Canadian Pacific Railway, 64 miles northwest of Montreal. The first settlers were Irish, and the place was probably named after their patron church at Rome. The town, incorporated in 1915, contains Anglican and Roman Catholic churches. There are saw-mills, grist-mills, and sash-and-door factories. The words "des Monts" (of the mountains), forming part of the name of the town, refer to the Laurentian mountains, on the slopes of which the place is built. There are more than thirty lakes in the district; and with good fishing, hunting, and ski-ing as well as excellent scenery, St. Agathe has become a renowned summer and winter resort. Pop. (1931), 2,949.

**Ste. Anne de Beaupré,** a town in Montmorency county, Quebec, situated on the north shore of the St. Lawrence river, 21 miles east of Quebec, with which it is connected by an electric railway, and to which it is easily accessible by road and water. The first settlers established themselves here about 1657, and named the site in honour of a saint revered by all French Canadians. The foundation stone of the first chapel built at Ste. Anne was laid by Ailleboust (q.v.), governor of New France. The present church, in combined Gothic and Romanesque styles, is one of the largest and most beautiful churches in North America. Ste. Anne de

STE. AGATHE DES MONTS, QUEBEC

*Photograph by Canadian Pacific Railway*

Beaupré is famous throughout North America as a pilgrimage centre. Farming, dairying, and bee-culture constitute the chief occupations of the inhabitants. There is a commercial college and a convent in the town. Pop. (1931), 1,901. See Robert Rumilly, *Sainte Anne de Beaupré* (Paris, 1932).

**Ste. Anne de Bellevue,** a town in Jacques Cartier county, Quebec, situated on the Ottawa river at the confluence of lake St. Louis and lake of Two Mountains, and on the Canadian National and Canadian Pacific Railways, 21 miles west of Montreal. In 1672 Louis and Gabriel de Berthé received a grant here, and named the place Bellevue because of its appearance. The parish was named St. Louis, but the name was changed to Ste. Anne about 1715 at the request of the Rev. M. de Breslay, by way of thanksgiving for favours he received. In the early days of the fur-trade, it was the point of departure for the canoes leaving for the West. The *voyageurs* sang "at Ste. Anne's their parting hymn." It is now a residential town, and the seat of Macdonald College. There are three churches, a convent, and a large military hospital. The industries include carriage factories, lumber mills, and a publishing house. Pop. (1931), 2,417.

**Ste. Anne de Chicoutimi,** a village in Chicoutimi county, Quebec, on the north shore of the Saguenay river, opposite the city of Chicoutimi. It was incorporated as a village in 1893. Formerly the post-office was named Tremblay. Pop. (1931), 1,102.

**Ste. Anne de la Pérade,** a village in Champlain county, Quebec, on the north shore of the St. Lawrence, at the mouth of the Ste. Anne river, and on the Canadian Pacific Railway, 58 miles from Quebec, and 121 miles from Montreal. It was created a village in 1912, and was named after the seigniory of Ste. Anne de la Pérade, which took its name from the first seignior, François

Xavier Tarieu de Lanaudière, Sieur de la Pérade. Pop. (1931), 926. See *Autrefois et aujourd'hui à Sainte-Anne de la Pérade* (Three Rivers, 1895).

**Ste. Anne de la Pocatière,** a village and parish in Kamouraska county, Quebec, on the south shore of the St. Lawrence river, and on the Canadian National Railway, 47 miles south-west of Rivière-du-Loup. It derives its name from Marie Anne Juchereau, widow of the Sieur de la Combe Pocatière, to whom the seigniory of La Pocatière was granted in 1672; she combined her Christian name with that of the seigniory, and this became later the name of the parish. It is chiefly an agricultural community; but it has also a few industries, such as a furniture factory and sash-and-door factories, and it is an important educational centre. It is not only the seat of a famous classical college, founded in 1827, but it has also a well-known school of agriculture, with an experimental farm conducted by the Dominion government. Pop. (1934), of the parish, 2,800. See N. E. Dionne, *Ste. Anne de la Pocatière* (Lévis, 1900).

**Ste. Anne des Chênes,** a village in Manitoba, on the Canadian National Railway, 30 miles from Winnipeg. A post-office was opened here in 1871, under the name of Pointe du Chêne; but the name was changed to Ste. Anne des Chênes in 1873, after the scrub-oaks (*chênes*) found in the neighbourhood. Pop. (1934), 1,000.

**Ste. Anne des Monts,** a village and parish in Gaspé county, Quebec, on the Gaspé highway, 57 miles north-east of Matane, the nearest railway station. It was founded in 1815, by settlers from Ste. Anne de la Pocatière; and was for many years famous as a primitive French-Canadian village remote from railways and the incidents of modern life. Its industries are general farming, cod-fishing, and lumbering. Pop. (1930), 2,150. See Effie Bignell, *St. Anne of the mountains* (Boston, 1912).

**St. Edmond du Lac au Saumon.** See **Lac au Saumon.**

**Ste. Dorothée,** a parish in Laval county, Quebec, situated at the south-western extremity of île Jésus. It was created a parish in 1868. Pop. (1930), 1,165. See Abbé E. Langevin-Lacroix, *Sainte-Dorothée: Cinquante ans de vie paroissiale* (Montreal, 1919).

**Ste. Famille,** a village and parish in Montmorency county, Quebec, on the north shore of the island of Orleans, opposite Ste. Anne de Beaupré. It was founded in 1661, and is the oldest parish on the island. It has a church that dates from 1742, and has a number of old houses of much antiquarian interest. Pop. (1934), of the parish, 850.

**Ste. Flavie,** a village and parish in Rimouski county, Quebec, on the south bank of the St. Lawrence river, 3 miles north of Mont Joli, the nearest railway station. It is the point where the Matapedia highway joins the highway around the Gaspé peninsula. Pop. (1931), 795.

**Ste. Foy,** a village in Quebec county, Quebec, situated on the St. Lawrence river, 5 miles north-east of Quebec city, and 2 miles from Cap-Rouge station on the Canadian National Railway. The place was named after a village in France, but was changed to that of Notre Dame de Foy when the parish was established in 1698. After several years, however, the original name prevailed over that of Notre Dame de Foy because of its being older and shorter than the latter. After the battle of the Plains of Abraham, when Quebec was in the hands of the English, Lévis (q.v.) made an attempt to recover the city. On April 28, 1760, he defeated General Murray (q.v.) on the Ste. Foy road, and laid siege to Quebec; but when some English frigates arrived in the river, he was forced to retire to Montreal. Ste. Foy has an interesting church, in the Renaissance style of architecture. The village is the centre of a good dairying district, and has a large butter factory. Pop. (1931), 1,973. See H. A. Scott, *Notre-Dame de Sainte-Foy* (Quebec, 1902).

**Ste. Hélène, Jacques LeMoyne, Sieur de** (1659-1690), soldier, was born on April 16, 1659, the second son of Charles LeMoyne de Longueuil (q.v.) and Catherine Primot. He accompanied his brothers Iberville (q.v.), and Maricourt (q.v.) on the expedition against the English posts on Hudson bay in 1686; and in 1690 he was second-in-command of the raiding party which destroyed the village of Schenectady. He was mortally wounded on October 20, 1690, during the siege of Quebec; and he was buried at the Hôtel-Dieu in Quebec on December 4.

**Ste. Julienne,** a village and parish in Montcalm county, Quebec, on the St. Esprit river, and with a station on the Canadian National Railway, 37 miles north of Montreal. The population of the parish, which is chiefly agricultural, is about 1,200.

**St. Elias, mount,** in the Yukon and Alaska, is in lat. 60° 17' 50", long. 140° 56', and has an altitude of 18,008 feet. It is so named on Jeffrey's reprint of a Russian map, dated 1761; and it was seen by Bering (q.v.) on July 16, 1741, four days before St. Elias day (July 20), on which an island was named after the saint.

**St. Eloi, Battle of.** See **World War.**

**Ste. Luce.** See **Luceville.**

**Ste. Madeleine,** a village in St. Hyacinthe county, Quebec, on the Canadian National Railway, 38 miles east of Montreal. It is the centre of an agricultural district. Pop. (1931), 375.

**Ste. Marguerite river,** in Saguenay county, Quebec, flows in a southerly direction into the gulf of St. Lawrence on its north shore, a short distance above the bay of Seven Islands, between the 66th and 67th meridians of west longitude. It is navigable for schooners and barges up to the first rapid, and, in its course, receives the waters of many tributaries. Between the first rapids and the Grand portage are 25 salmon pools; the river also contains gray trout, pike, whitefish, shad, etc. It is 165 miles in length, and drains a basin of 3,200 square miles.

**Ste. Marguerite river,** the greatest tributary of the Saguenay river, is in Saguenay and Chicoutimi counties, Quebec. The river, which is formed by the union of two main branches, the northeast and north-west, enters Ste. Marguerite bay on the left bank of the Saguenay, 10 miles from its mouth. The Ste. Marguerite is very swift, and rapids occur after the fifteenth mile from its mouth. Above them are waterfalls of 75, 80, and 90 feet in height. The river abounds in salmon, and the country adjoining its mouth is suitable for agriculture. For a distance of 14 miles from its mouth, mountains border the north-west branch which contains falls of 75 and 100 feet in height.

**Ste. Marie,** a village in Beauce county, Quebec, on the Chaudière river and on the Quebec Central Railway, 40 miles south of Quebec city. In 1737 the settlement was named in honour of Marie Claire Fleury de la Gorgendière, wife of the seignior. Thousands of pilgrims are attracted annually to the chapel of Ste. Anne. The village contains a college, a hospital, and a public library. The chief industries are shoe factories, flour-mills, foundries, and creameries. There is a weekly newspaper (*Le Guide*). Pop. (1931), 1,598.

**Ste. Martine,** a village and parish in Châteauguay county, Quebec, on the Châteauguay river, and on the Canadian National Railway, 30 miles from Montreal. Pop. (1931), of the parish, 1,449.

**St. Ephrem de Tring,** a village and parish in Tring township, Beauce county, Quebec, on the Quebec Central Railway, 16 miles south of Tring Junction. The parish was created in 1864, and the village in 1897, and they were named after Éphrem Proulx, who

gave the land for the church. Pop. (1931), 470.

**Ste. Praxède de Brompton.** See **Bromptonville.**

**Ste. Rose,** a town in Laval county, Quebec, situated on the river Jésus, and on the Canadian Pacific Railway, 17 miles from Montreal. The name of the settlement was adopted for religious purposes from the parish in 1845. The centre of a good dairying district, the town has three creameries. Pop. (1931), 1,661.

**Ste. Rose du Lac,** a village in the Dauphin district of Manitoba, on the Canadian National Railway, south of lake Dauphin. Pop. (1931), 339.

**Ste. Scholastique,** the county town of the county of Two Mountains, Quebec, on the Canadian Pacific Railway, 33 miles from Montreal, and 90 miles from Hull. It was named after Ste. Scholastique, who, with her brother St. Benoît, founded an early community of Benedictines. It was incorporated as a village in 1855, and is the centre of a farming and dairying district. It contains a convent and a school of the Christian brothers. Pop. (1931), 794.

**Ste. Thècle,** a village in Champlain county, Quebec, on the Canadian National Railway, 76 miles north-east of Joliette. It was incorporated as a village in 1909, and was named Ste. Thècle, probably because Ste. Thècle was a contemporary of the patron saint of the nearby town of St. Tite. Pop. (1931), 748.

**Ste. Thérèse,** a town in Terrebonne county, Quebec, situated on the river Ste. Thérèse, and on the Canadian Pacific Railway, 20 miles from Montreal. The name of the parish is Ste. Thérèse de Blainville. In 1714 the seigniory was regranted to Suzanne and Anne Marie Thérèse, the two daughters of the first grantee, Sidrac Dugué. The daughter of Anne Marie Thérèse married one Blainville, hence the name Ste. Thérèse de Blainville. The principal manufactures are pianos, furniture, and butter. There are Protestant and Roman Catholic churches, a college, a model school, a convent, and a hospital. Pop. (1931), 3,292.

**St. Eugène,** a village in Prescott county, Ontario, on the Canadian Pacific Railway, 14 miles south-east of Prescott. Pop. (1934), 800.

**St. Eusèbe de Stanfold.** See **Princeville.**

**St. Eustache,** a parish and village in the county of Two Mountains, in the province of Quebec, situated on the river Mille-Isles near its outlet from the lake of Two Mountains. The village is 21 miles west of Montreal, on the Canadian National Railway. The parish was founded in 1768, and was named in honour of Eustache Lambert, seignior of Mille-Isles. The village was the scene of the battle fought in 1837 between the rebels under Chénier (q.v.) and the loyalist forces under Sir John Colborne (q.v.). The church, which was built in 1783, was bombarded during the battle, and the marks made by cannonballs may still be seen on the façade and on the sides. St. Eustache is in a rich agricultural district; and its proximity to the lake of Two Mountains has caused it to become a renowned summer resort. There are several canning and butter factories in the village. The population of the parish is 1,600, and of the village, 1,187.

**St. Evariste,** a village in Frontenac county, Quebec, on the Quebec Central Railway, 24 miles south of Beauceville. Pop. (1931), 654.

**St. Faustin,** a village in Terrebonne county, Quebec, on the Canadian Pacific Railway, 76 miles north-west of Montreal. It is a popular summer resort, and has a number of lakes for fishing and hunting in the neighbourhood. General farming and lumbering are also carried on. Pop. (1931), 391.

**St. Félicien,** a village in Lac St. Jean county, Quebec, situated on the Ashuapmuchuan river, and on the Canadian National Railway, 16 miles north-west of Roberval. Settlers began to establish themselves here in 1868. The parish was named in honour of Félicien Girard, who had conducted a mission here. The village was incorporated in 1905. There are cascades and rapids on the river capable of being hydro-electrically developed to the extent of 300,000 horse-power. Immense forests are in the neighbourhood, and the village has several large sawmills. General farming and dairying are thriving industries, the latter keeping in operation cheese and butter factories. Moose is hunted in the vicinity, and there is fishing to be had in the lakes and rivers. Pop. (1931), 1,599.

**St. Foy.** See **Ste. Foy.**

**St. Francis lake,** in Ontario and Quebec, is a widening of the St. Lawrence river, 35 miles south-west of Montreal. It is 28 miles long and 2 miles wide, and has an area of 85 square miles, of which 20 are in Ontario and 65 in Quebec.

**St. Francis lake** and **river.** The lake is in the county of Frontenac, Quebec, about 60 miles north-east of Sherbrooke, and discharges by a narrow channel into Aylmer lake. This is drained by the St. Francis river, which flows south-west, and then, turning sharply to the north-west at Lennoxville, flows into the St. Lawrence, on its right bank at lake St. Peter. Both the lake and river are named after François de Lauzon, who in 1635 was granted a large tract of land bounded on one side by the river. The lake is 21 miles in length, and has an area of 8,294 acres. It abounds in fish, and is surrounded on every side by lofty, wood-covered mountains, some containing iron ore. The river is 150 miles in length, and drains a basin of 3,375 square miles. It contains several falls and rapids, but is navigable at low water for about 10 miles for vessels drawing less than 4 feet.

**St. Francis river** rises in the county of Témiscouata, Quebec, and flows in a south-easterly direction until its junction with the St. John. Between lake Pohénégamook and the mouth of the river, it constitutes the boundary between Maine and Canada. It is navigable for canoes to the mouth of the lake. The shores of the river are very pronounced up to a distance of a mile, and the plateau between them has a fertile soil. The river is 60 miles in length.

**St. Francis Xavier University,** an institution of higher learning established in Antigonish, Nova Scotia, under Roman Catholic auspices, in 1855, as St. Francis Xavier College. It grew out of a college for the training of pastoral clergy established at Arichat in 1853. Its first home at Antigonish was a wooden building, built from the proceeds of half of a legacy bequeathed to the diocese of Arichat and a contribution from the French Society for Foreign Missions. A fairly comprehensive curriculum was offered, including English, French, Latin, Greek, Hebrew, philosophy, physics, and mathematics; and in 1866 full university powers were conferred on the college by an Act of the legislature of Nova Scotia. In 1880 new buildings were erected; and extensions to these were made in 1888 and 1895. A convent was built for the Sisters of St. Martha, in whose hands the domestic economy of the institution was placed. The central building was enlarged to its present size in 1898, when the south wing was built, in 1911 the Somers chapel, in 1916 the university gymnasium and the university library, in 1921 the Memorial Rink, and in 1922 the central heating plant. In 1882 an Act was passed placing the university under a board of governors; and on this board, under an Act of 1921, three alumni, annually elected, sit. In 1894 Mount St. Bernard College for women was affiliated with the university. The university has now a staff of 26 professors and a registration of over 200 students. The chancellor of the university is the Roman Catholic bishop of Antigonish; and the president is the Right Rev. H. P. MacPherson, D.D., D.C.L.

**St. François du Lac,** the county town of Yamaska county, Quebec, on the west bank of the St. Francis river, opposite Pierreville, and on the Canadian National Railway, 70 miles from Montreal. It is the centre of an agricultural community, and near it are the famous Abenakis Mineral Springs. Pop. (1931), 718.

**St. Gabriel de Brandon,** a village in Berthier county, Quebec, picturesquely situated, at an altitude of 900 feet, on lake Maskinongé, on the Canadian Pacific Railway, 24 miles north of Joliette. The place was named to commemorate the archangel Gabriel in 1836 by a visiting missionary. The village was incorporated in 1892. St. Gabriel is an attractive summer resort. Lumbering is the chief industry, supplying the material for twenty sawmills and for factories which manufacture furniture, caskets, matches, sashes and doors. Pop. (1931), 1,530. See *Histoire de Saint-Gabriel de Brandon: A travers les registres et en marge* (Montreal, 1917).

**St. George, Laurent Quetton de** (d. 1821), soldier and merchant, was one of a number of French royalist officers who emigrated to Canada in 1798, and settled at Windham, in the township of Markham, north of York (Toronto), Upper Canada. He alone among his fellow colonists prospered. He engaged in the fur-trade, and in 1802 he opened a general store on York (Toronto). Later he opened branches of his business at Orillia, Niagara, Amherstburg, and elsewhere. He returned to France in 1815, and left his property to be administered by John Spread Baldwin. He died at Orleans, France, on June 8, 1821. He was twice married, (1) to the daughter of Jean Baptiste Vallière, the blacksmith of the Windham colony, and (2) after his return to France to Adèle de Barbeyrac de St. Maurice. By his first marriage he had one son and one daughter; and by his second marriage a son, Henri de St. George, who came to Canada in 1846 or 1847, and administered his father's Canadian property until his death at Oak Ridges, near Toronto, in 1893. See N. E. Dionne, *Les ecclésiastiques et les royalistes français réfugiés au Canada* (Quebec, 1905); Lucy E. Textor, *A colony of émigrés in Canada* ('Toronto, 1905); and W. S. Wallace (ed.), *A merchant's clerk in Upper Canada* (Toronto, 1935).

**St. George,** a town in Charlotte county, New Brunswick, at the mouth of the Magaguadavic river, and on the Shore Line Railway, 45 miles from St. John. The origin of the name is conjectural, but perhaps it was given in imitation of other names of saints, particularly St. Andrews, in the neighbourhood. The parish was created in 1786. It has a harbour, from which are shipped pulp, pulpwood, and lumber. Pop. (1931), 1,087.

**St. George,** a village in Dumfries township, Brant county, Ontario, on the Canadian National Railway, 10 miles north of Brantford. Pop. (1934), 600.

**St. Georges,** a village in Beauce county, Quebec, situated on the banks of the Chaudière river, and on the Quebec Central Railway, 61 miles south of Lévis. The first settlers arrived here about 1736. It was here that the Americans under Arnold (q.v.), in 1775, came in contact for the first time with Canadian habitations. St. Georges was named in honour of Abbé Georges Payette, and the village was established in 1807. The chief occupations of the inhabitants are lumbering, farming, market-gardening, and dairying. Pop. (1931), 1,543. See P. Angers, *Les seigneurs et premiers censitaires de St. Georges-Beauce* (Beauceville, 1927).

**St. Georges,** a village in Champlain county, Quebec, half a mile from the station of Garneau Junction on the Canadian National Railway. It was incorporated as a town in 1915, under the name of "Turcotte", after some of the early settlers; but the name was changed to St. Georges in 1919. The post-office is named Blondin. Pop. (1931), 733.

**St. Georges d'Henryville.** See **Henryville,** and see also Fr. J. D. Brosseau, *St. Georges d'Henryville et la seigneurie de Noyan* (St. Hyacinthe, (1913).

**St. Gérard,** a village in Wolfe county, Quebec, on the Quebec Central Railway, 40 miles north of Sherbrooke. It is situated midway between lakes Weedon and Aylmer, and was known until 1905 as Lac-Weedon. In that year it was renamed by Bishop Larocque (q.v.) in honour of St. Gérard-Magella, whose canonization ceremonies the bishop had recently attended in Rome. Pop. (1931), 519.

**St. Germain, Hyacinthe** (1838-1909), author, was born at Repentigny, Lower Canada, on September 23, 1838, the son of Pierre Venant St. Germain; and he died at Danville, Quebec, on December 8, 1909. He was the author of *Charles Héon, fondateur de la paroisse de St. Louis de Blandford* (Quebec, 1905), and *Souvenirs et impressions de voyage au Nord-ouest Canadien* (Arthabaska, 1907).

**St. Germain, Venant** (or **Venance**) **Lemaire** (1751-1821), fur-trader, was born at the Lake of Two Mountains in 1751, the son of Bernardin Lemaire *dit* St. Germain and Marie-Joseph Lefèbvre. He became a fur-trader, and was trading to Grand Portage as early as 1777. In 1784 he was second-in-command under Edward Umfreville (q.v.) in the journey of exploration from lake Nipigon to lake Winnipeg. In 1790 he was elected a member of the Beaver Club in Montreal; but he was never apparently a partner of the North West Company, being rather a free trader trading under agreement with the Company. In 1795 he married Catherine Pichet; and by her he had several children. He died at Repentigny, Lower Canada, in 1821. He is not to be confused with the Venant St. Germain (probably his half-breed nephew), who was killed at Pembina in 1804. See F. J. Audet, *Venant St. Germain* (Bull. rech. hist., 1932), and R. Douglas, *Nipigon to Winnipeg* (Ottawa, 1929).

**St. Germain-en-Laye, Treaty of.** This was a treaty of peace signed between Great Britain and France on March 29, 1632. By it Quebec, Cape Breton island, and Port Royal in Acadia, all of which had been captured by the British, were restored to France.

**St. Guillaume,** a village in Yamaska county, Quebec, on the Canadian Pacific Railway, 10 miles from Yamaska. It was placed under the patronage of St. Guillaume (St. William) in honour of Charles William Grant (q.v.), who gave the land for the church and presbytery. It is the centre of an agricultural community. Pop. (1931), 907. See F. L. Desaulniers, *Notes historiques sur la paroisse de St. Guillaume d' Upton* (Montreal, 1905).

**St. Helens island,** in the St. Lawrence river, lies opposite the east end of the city of Montreal. It was named by Champlain (q.v.), in honour of his wife, Hélène Boulé, in 1611. In 1672 it was granted to Charles LeMoyne, sieur de Longueuil (q.v.); and it remained in the possession of the Longueuil family until 1812, when it was acquired by the crown. For over 50 years it was used as a garrison for British troops in Canada.

**St. Henri,** a village in Lévis county, Quebec, on the Etchemin river, and on the Quebec Central Railway, 7 miles south of Quebec. Pop. (1931), 453.

**St. Henri de Mascouche.** See **Mascouche.**

**St. Hilaire,** a village in Rouville county, Quebec, on the Richelieu river, opposite Belœil, and on the Canadian National Railway, 22 miles east of Montreal. It was created a village in 1912; but it was created a parish in 1799. Pop. (1931), 700.

**St. Hugues,** a village in Bagot county, Quebec, on the Yamaska river, and on a branch of the Canadian Pacific Railway, 14 miles north-east of St. Hyacinthe. It was named after an early seignior, Hugues LeMoyne de Martigny, who was the founder of the parish. It has lumber and grist mills. Pop. (1931), 482.

**St. Hyacinthe,** a county in southern Quebec, in the Richelieu valley, bounded on the north by Richelieu county, on the west by Verchères county, on the south by Rouville county, and on the east by Bagot county. It is named after Hyacinthe Simon Delorme, who purchased here in 1753 the seigniory granted to Pierre François de Rigaud, sieur de Vaudreuil, in 1748. Chief town, St. Hyacinthe. Pop. (1931), 25,854.

**St. Hyacinthe,** a city in St. Hyacinthe county, Quebec, is situated on the Yamaska river. It is on the main line of the Canadian National Railway from Montreal to Portland, and through a branch line has connection with the Canadian Pacific Railway. The first settlers arrived about 1768. It was incorporated as a town in 1849, and as a city in 1857. It is an industrial centre, with cotton and woollen mills and a famous organ factory; machinery, boots and shoes, clothing, etc. are also among its products. It is the seat of a Roman Catholic cathedral, and has a famous classical college, conducted by the Dominicans. It has two weekly newspapers (*Le Clairon* and *Le Courrier de St. Hyacinthe*). Its name is derived from the first of the Christian names of Hyacinthe Simon Delorme, who purchased the seigniory in 1753. Pop. (1931), 13,448, of which 98 per cent. is

French-speaking. See C. P. Choquette, *Histoire de la ville de Saint-Hyacinthe* (St. Hyacinthe, 1930).

**St. Ignace, Jeanne Françoise Juchereau, Mère** (1650-1723), mother superior and historian, was born at Quebec on July 7, 1650, the daughter of Jean Juchereau de La Ferté and Marie Gifford. She entered the Hôtel-Dieu of Quebec at the age of 12 years, and took the name of Sœur St. Ignace. She became mother superior of the Hôtel-Dieu; and she died on January 14, 1723. In her last years she compiled the history of the Hôtel-Dieu of Quebec; and this was later published in France under the title *Histoire de l'Hôtel-Dieu de Québec* (Montauban, 1751).

**St. Ignace island** is in lake Superior, in the Thunder Bay district of Ontario. It is named after the founder of the Jesuit order, and is found on the Bellin map of 1755.

**St. Isidore,** a village in La Prairie county, Quebec, one mile from St. Isidore Junction, and 4 miles from St. Isidore Laprairie, on the Canadian National Railway, 24 miles south of Montreal. Pop. (1931), 474. See *Centenaire de la paroisse Saint-Isidore* (n.p., 1934).

**St. Jacobs,** a village in Waterloo county, Ontario, on the Conestogo river, and on the Canadian National Railway, 8 miles north-west of Kitchener. The village is named after Jacob Snider, who purchased a saw-mill here in 1850, and built a grist mill in 1851. Pop. (1934), 500.

**St. Jacques,** a village in Montcalm county, Quebec, situated on the river Ouareau, and on the Canadian National Railway, 16 miles north of L'Assomption. The settlement was founded in 1772 by a number of Acadians who returned here from exile at Boston. The parish was named in honour of Jacques Degeay, and was known as St. Jacques de l'Achigan until 1917, when the village was incorporated as St.

Jacques. There is a beautiful church, of Romanesque style, which attracts visitors to the village. The chief occupation of the farmers of the district is tobacco-growing, and this has given birth to several factories in the village for the preparation of tobacco for pipe and cigarette smoking. Pop. (1931), 1,529.

**St. James,** a suburb of Winnipeg, Manitoba, on the Assiniboine river, and on the Canadian Pacific and Canadian National Railways, adjoining Winnipeg on the west. It is a residential district, and has a weekly newspaper (*Leader*). Pop. (1934), 13,768.

**St. Janvier de Weedon.** See **Weedon Centre.**

**St. Jean.** See **St. Johns.**

**St. Jean Baptiste, Festival of.** See **Société St. Jean Baptiste.**

**St. Jean Port Joli,** a village and parish in L'Islet county, Quebec, on the south bank of the St. Lawrence river, and on the Canadian National Railway, 60 miles from Quebec. The parish was founded in 1721, and the church dates from 1779. In the church is buried Philippe Aubert de Gaspé (q.v.), the author of *Les anciens canadiens*, whose family were for many years lords of the seigniory of St. Jean Port Joli. Pop. (1934), of the parish, 2,500.

**St. Jérôme,** a city in Terrebonne county, Quebec, on the river Du Nord, and on the Canadian Pacific and Canadian National Railways, 33 miles north-west of Montreal. It was founded in 1832, but for many years did not progress, until Father Labelle (q.v.) opened up for colonization the country north of Montreal. Then it became the distributing centre of an active colonization area and an important industrial centre. It was incorporated as a village in 1856, as a town in 1881, and as a city in 1894. The water-powers derived from the river Du Nord furnish light and power for numerous industrial plants, chief among which are pulp-and-paper mills, a spinning mill, a shoe factory, a foundry, several sash-and-door factories, a rubber factory, and sawmills. It contains a convent, a college of the Christian brothers, a court house, and a weekly newspaper (*L'Avenir du Nord*). It has also acquired some fame as the scene of an annual series of performances of the "Passion" (similar to those of Oberammergau in Bavaria), in the production of which many hundred actors take part. Pop. (1931), 8,967. See E.-J.-A. Auclair, *Saint-Jérôme de Terrebonne* (St. Jérôme, 1934), and J. J. Grignon, *Le vieux temps* (St. Jérôme, 1921).

**St. Jérôme,** a village in Lac St. Jean county, on the south shore of lake St. John, and on the Canadian National Railway, 150 miles north of Quebec. It is in an agricultural and lumbering district. Pop. (1931), 1,235.

**St. Jerome's College,** in Kitchener (formerly Berlin), Ontario, is an institution of higher learning for Roman Catholics of German extraction. It was founded in 1864 in a log-house in the village of St. Agatha, in Waterloo county, by Father Louis Funcken, C.R., a native of Holland. In 1866 the college was moved to Berlin (now Kitchener); and it has remained almost exclusively under the care of members of the Congregation of the Resurrection. The college building was burnt to the ground in 1908; but new buildings were erected almost immediately. The principals of the college have been Fathers Louis Funcken (1864-90), the Very Rev. Theobald Spetz (1890-1901), Father John Fehrenbach (1901-5), the Rev. A. L. Zinger (1905-19), the Rev. W. A. Benninger (1919-26), the Rev. L. J. Siess (1926-9), the Rev. R. S. Dehler (1926-36), and the Rev. William G. Borko (1936—). See Rev. T. Spetz, *History of St. Jerome's College* (Schoolman, Golden Jubilee Number, Berlin, Ontario, June, 1915).

**St. John,** a county in New Brunswick, on the north shore of the bay of Fundy, bounded on the west by Charlotte county, on the north by King's county, and on the east by Albert county. It was created in 1785, and was named after the river St. John, which has its mouth in this county. It is watered also by the Kennebecasis and other rivers. Parts of the county are agricultural; but the chief occupations of the inhabitants are maritime. Chief town, Saint John. Pop. (1931), 61,613.

**Saint John,** the largest city in New Brunswick, is in St. John county, on the north side of the bay of Fundy, at the head of the bay into which the St. John river flows, 190 miles north-west of Halifax, on the Canadian Pacific and Canadian National Railways. It is the Canadian terminus of the Shore Line Railway from Maine, United States. Saint John takes its name from the river discovered by Champlain (q.v.) on St. John the Baptist day, June 24, 1604; and the city fathers have expressed the desire that the city should be known as "Saint John", rather than as "St. John". No settlement was made until 1635, when Charles de La Tour (q.v.) erected a fort in the harbour, and in subsequent years traded in furs with the Indians. In 1654 La Tour lost his fort when the English captured Acadia, but three years later Acadia was ceded to France. In 1745 the English again took possession of the fort, and in 1758 a garrison was established under the command of Colonel Monckton (q.v.). No permanent settlement was made until 1783, when the Loyalists arrived and founded the present city. It was incorporated two years later. For two years it was known as Parr or Parrtown, a name given to it by request of Governor Parr (q.v.) of Nova Scotia. The part of the present city lying west of the harbour was named Carleton in 1784, in honour of Sir Guy Carleton (q.v.), commander-in-chief of the British forces in North America. The name was dropped on its union with Saint John in 1889, but still survives in common usage, where the Carleton side of the harbour is referred to. In fact, the city of Saint John comprises three distinct towns: East Saint John, north of Courtenay bay, the main town built on the peninsula projecting into the harbour on its east side, and Carleton or West Saint John. In 1912 Saint John adopted the commission form of government, and was the first city in Canada to do so. It was also the first Canadian city to be incorporated.

Saint John has high standing as a port, because of its geographical position and on account of the fact that the harbour is never frozen over. The average range of spring tides in the harbour is 27¼ feet, and of neaps 13 feet. Owing to this the currents produced are exceedingly complex; and the high tides of the bay cause the famous Reversing falls. Though fog is in some seasons frequent, it is chiefly in the less busy summer months. A new reinforced pier, 700 feet long, designed for a depth of 35 feet of water at low tide, has been constructed and has been in use since 1934. The drydock is one of the largest in the world. The port has constant steamer communication with the United States and the British Isles. Numerous passenger steamers communicate with ports in the Maritime provinces, with Montreal, and with ports on the St. Lawrence route. The passenger traffic with these ports is especially large in the summer season. Trade with the West Indies forms an important feature of the trade of the port. The harbour is nationalized, and is administered by a federal board of commissioners. There is a well-equipped airport for both land- and sea-planes.

The buildings of the city are largely modern, because of severe fires in 1877 and 1931; there are, however, some fine old buildings. The new General Hospital building cost $2,000,000. The educational institutions comprise high, public, vocational, and private schools, and business colleges. There are many churches, two public libraries, a museum, large exhibition buildings and grounds. The city is an important industrial centre, with a large sugar refinery, saw, cotton, and pulp mills, foundries, boiler and engine shops, clothing and furniture factories, and a shipbuilding plant. There is a morning (*Telegraph-Journal*) and an evening (*Times-Globe*) newspaper. Pop. (1931), 47,514. See Peter Fisher, *History of New Brunswick* (Saint John, 1921); James Hannay, *History of New Brunswick* (2 vols., Saint John, 1909); D. R. Jack, *Centennial prize essay on the history of St. John* (Saint John, 1883); F. W. Wallace, *The romance of a great port* (Saint John, 1935) and T. G. Roberts, *Saint John* (Canadian Geographical Journal, 1934).

**St. John island.** See **Prince Edward Island.**

**St. John, lake**, is in Chicoutimi county, Quebec, 192 miles north of the city of Quebec. It was named in 1647 by Father De Quen, who was the first missionary in this region. The Montagnais sometimes called it "flat lake". The lake lies in an immense valley, and into it empty many large rivers and streams, including the Mistassini, Péribonka, and Kocuatien on the north, the Ashuapmuchuan and Ouiatchouanish on the west, the Ouiatchouan on the south-west, and the Metabetchouan, Kushpahiganish, and Belle Rivière on south. By means of some of these rivers, and their lakes and tributaries, communication from lake St. John may be had through the Batiscan or St. Maurice with the St. Lawrence and through the Gatineau with the Ottawa. The lake empties by the Grande and Petite Décharge, on its east side, into the Saguenay river, which empties into the St. Lawrence. The lake contains a number of beautiful islands, and abounds in fish, including the celebrated ouananiche. On its shores are inexhaustible quarries of limestone and extensive beds of fine

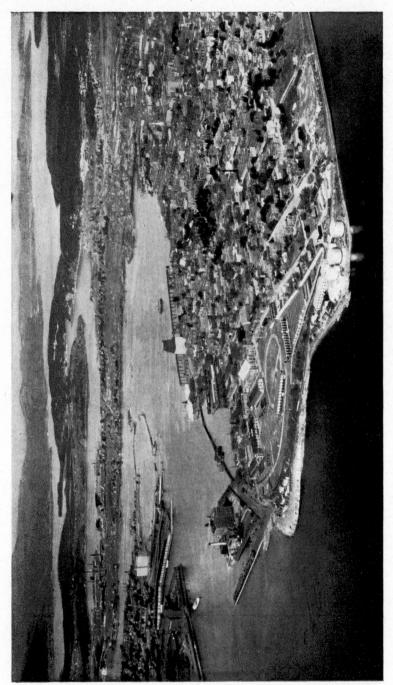

THE HARBOUR OF SAINT JOHN, NEW BRUNSWICK

*Photograph by Royal Canadian Air Force*

morl. Around the lake are a dozen flourishing parishes, connected by steamboat with each other and with the town of Roberval, which is the most important distributing centre in the valley of that name. The area of the lake is 375 square miles.

**St. John river,** the principal river of New Brunswick, rises in Quebec and Maine, between the 70th and 71st meridians of west longitude. It flows north-east to its junction with the St. Francis, in latitude 47° 10', and longitude 68° 54', and then follows an east-south-east course to the Grand falls. From the junction of the St. Francis to a point 3 miles above the falls, a distance of 75 miles, the boundary between Maine and New Brunswick is located in the middle channel or deepest water of the river. After its entry into New Brunswick, the direction of the river is nearly south to about latitude 46°, where it bends and flows east for about 100 miles to its junction with the outlet from Grand lake. Below that it flows in a broad channel due south-south-east and discharges into the bay of Fundy below the city of Saint John. It is 399 miles in length, and drains a basin of 26,000 square miles.

The principal tributaries of the St. John are the Alagash, Aroostook, and Oromocto on the right bank, and the St. Francis, Madawaska, Tobique, Nashwaak, Salmon, and Kennebecasis on the left bank. The river is navigable for vessels of 120 tons to Fredericton, 80 miles from the bay of Fundy; small steamers ascend to Woodstock, 75 miles further up, and occasionally to the Grand falls. Above the falls it is navigable for small steamers to the mouth of the Madawaska, and from this point boats and canoes can ascend almost to its sources. The valley of the St. John is noted for its fertility as well as for its picturesque beauty. Grand falls, where the river has a perpendicular descent of 70 or 80 feet, are particularly noted as a scenic spectacle. Fredericton presents a beautiful prospect of elms, domed legislative buildings, and comfortable homes with lawns and gardens. Below it one encounters a variety of scenery; the willows of Sunbury county and the elms of Queen's are replaced by evergreen in King's county. The lower part of the river between Brown's Flat and Saint John is popular with vacationists, and its banks are dotted with summer homes. Below Westfield, the entrance of the Kennebecasis is marked by bold, rocky headlands which are closely wooded. At Saint John, above the mouth of the river, are the famous reversible falls; here the river is forced through a narrow aperture between two points and gives the impression of a fall which runs in either direction according to the movement of the tide. The upper reaches of the St. John are an important lumbering area for pine and other timber; and salmon fishing is carried on towards its mouth.

The river was named upon its discovery by Monts (q.v.) and Champlain (q.v.) on the day of St. John the Baptist, June 24, 1604. The first recorded settlement was a temporary fishing village in 1612, on an island in the Long Reach above the site of Westfield. In 1635, on the site of Saint John, La Tour (q.v.) built his famous fort, which was taken by his rival, Charnisay (q.v.), in 1645, retaken by La Tour in 1650, and captured by an English expedition in 1654. Although Acadia was returned to France in 1657, it was not until considerably after 1700 that any number of Acadians came to settle in the St. John valley. Settlement from New England commenced in 1762 and, after 1783, the greater part of Loyalist settlement in New Brunswick was in the St. John valley.

See E. Ward, *An account of the river St. John* (Fredericton, 1841); J. W. Bailey, *The St. John river in Maine, Quebec, and New Brunswick* (Cambridge, Mass., 1894); W. O. Raymond, *The river St. John* (Saint John, 1910), and

M. G. Otty, *The river of the loyalists* (Canadian Geographical Journal, 1931).

**St. John river,** in Saguenay county, Quebec, flows into the gulf of St. Lawrence, on its north shore, opposite the north-western end of Anticosti, 385 miles below the city of Quebec. It is 130 miles long, drains a basin of 2,700 square miles, and is navigable for boats and canoes for 30 miles. It is a salmon river, and the adjacent country abounds in game. From its mouth for a distance of three miles, the soil is suitable for the growth of potatoes and oats. The principal timber in the district is white spruce, fir, birch, alder, and willow.

**St. John river,** in Gaspé county, Quebec, flows east and empties into Gaspé bay as Douglastown. It is also called the Douglastown river. It is a good salmon river and navigable for boats and canoes to its source. The country to the north is mountainous; but, to the south, it is wooded with white pine, spruce, larch, cedar, birch, etc. The river is about 40 miles in length, and drains a basin of 440 square miles.

**St. Johns,** a county in Quebec, bordering on the Richelieu river, and adjacent to Iberville county. Chief town, St. Johns. Pop. (1931), 17,649.

**St. Johns,** a city in St. Johns county, Quebec, is situated on the Richelieu river, about 25 miles southeast of Montreal. It is served by the Canadian National, Canadian Pacific, Central Vermont, Quebec, Montreal, and Southern, Delaware and Hudson, and Rutland Railways, and it has a direct waterway with New York city, *viâ* the Hudson river, lake Champlain, the Richelieu river, and the St. Lawrence. It is one of the most historical spots in Canada. Champlain (q.v.) passed its site in 1609, when the Richelieu was known as the "Rivière des Iroquois". In the year 1775 St. Johns was the "key to Canada". The British concentrated their forces there, and,

under Major Preston, withstood Montgomery's advance for a period of a month. It played a prominent part in the Rebellion of 1837-8. It still has military importance, for it has a fine military barracks, and a training school for Canadian cavalry. It has excellent educational institutions, chief of which is St. John's College, a classical Catholic college for boys. An industrial centre, it produces clay products, sewing machines, sugar machinery, knitted goods, furniture, etc. It has an English weekly newspaper (*News and Eastern Townships Advocate*) and a French weekly newspaper (*Canada Français*). It is supposed to have been named after Jean Fréderic Phélypeaux, Comte de Pontchartrain, French minister of marine at the time of the building of the fort on its site in 1748. Pop. (1931), 11,256, of which 85 per cent. is French-speaking.

**St. John's College.** See **University of Manitoba.**

**St. John's Wort** (*Hypericum perforatum* L., *Hypericaceae*), a much-branched perennial herb with very acrid juice, the stem somewhat 2-edged, the leaves linear-oblong with transparent dots which are easily observed when held to the light. The flowers are numerous, borne in leafy branched clusters; the petals are bright yellow dotted with black along the margins, 5 in number, lanceolate in shape; the stamens are numerous, in 3 or more clusters. This plant is a pernicious weed in open fields and along roadsides, and is very difficult to eradicate. It blooms from June to September.

**St. Joseph,** a village and parish in Beauce county, Quebec. The village is on the Chaudière river, and on the Quebec Central Railway, 38 miles south of Quebec city. The parish was named in honour of Joseph Fleury, son of the first seignior of the place. The village was incorporated in 1889. It contains a church, a convent, a college and an orphanage. The chief resources of the district are agricultural products. A weekly newspaper (*La Vallée de la Chaudière*) is published. The population of the village is 1,625, and of the parish 3,125.

**St. Joseph,** a village in Richelieu county, Quebec, is situated on the Richelieu river, at the south-west end of lake St. Peter, on the Canadian National Railway, 50 miles north-east of Montreal. The parish was named in honour of Mgr. Joseph Larocque (q.v.), bishop of St. Hyacinthe. The village was established in 1907. Boat-building and farming are the chief occupations of the inhabitants. Pop. (1931), 1,869.

**St. Joseph,** a village and parish in St. Hyacinthe county, Quebec, on the Canadian Pacific Railway, 25 miles from Farnham. Pop. (1931), 783.

**St. Joseph d'Alma,** a town in lake St. John county, Quebec, situated on Alma island, which lies between the Petite Décharge and the Grande Décharge, by which the waters of lake St. John flow into the Saguenay river. The town was incorporated in 1924. The island received its name from the battle of Alma, fought in the Crimea in 1854. Pop. (1931), 3,970.

**St. Joseph de Carleton.** See **Carleton,** and see also Abbé E. P. Chouinard, *Histoire de la paroisse de Saint-Joseph de Carleton* (Rimouski, 1906).

**St. Joseph de Grantham,** a village in Drummond county, Quebec, on the Canadian National Railway, 5 miles from Drummondville. It has been recently incorporated, and is in the heart of a rich agricultural district. Pop. (1931), 2,812.

**St. Joseph de Soulanges.** See **Cedars.**

**St. Joseph island** is in the Algoma district of Ontario, in the channel between lake Huron and lake Superior, 20 miles south-west of Sault Ste. Marie. It is 19 miles long, and 15 miles wide. When the British abandoned Michili-

mackinac in 1796, they built a fort on St. Joseph island, the remains of which are still to be seen; and there was a garrison on the island until 1828, when it was transferred to Penetanguishene.

**St. Joseph lake** is in northern Ontario, north-west of lake Nipigon, in latitude 51° 10', and longitude 90° 31' to 91° 30'. It receives the Catlake river and discharges, by the Albany river, into James bay. It is 35 miles long, has an average breadth of 10 miles, and has an area of 187 square miles.

**St. Joseph lake,** in the county of Megantic, Quebec, south of the St. Lawrence river, is connected by a narrow channel with lake William, and empties into the river Clyde.

**St. Joseph lake,** in Portneuf county, Quebec, is 24 miles north of the city of Quebec. It is very deep in the middle and abounds in fish. A magnificent tourist hotel has been erected on its shore, and there are a number of fine residences in the vicinity. It is 8 miles long, 1 to 3 miles wide, and 534 feet above sea-level.

**St. Joseph's College** is the affiliated college of the University of Alberta that attends more particularly to the religious requirements of the Catholic students who attend the University. Incorporated under an Act of the Legislature of the province of Alberta, on April 8, 1926, the College building was begun in May of the same year on a six-acre plot granted by the province for that special purpose. The corner-stone was laid on September 22, 1926, and the College opened its doors at the beginning of the autumn term, 1927. The first rector was Brother Rogation, who was replaced in the summer of 1933 by the present rector, Brother Memorian. An agreement was entered upon with the University of Alberta whereby St. Joseph's College is admitted to full participation with the Arts and Science faculties of the University. Since its inception, the College has worked in the closest harmony with the University, and there is every evidence that it will, in due course of time, make a valuable contribution to the university life of the prairie provinces. The board of governors of St. Joseph's College is composed of the archbishop of Edmonton, the bishop of Calgary, the dean of Arts, the rector of the College, the bursar, and two members from outside the University.

**St. Joseph's University,** at St Joseph, New Brunswick, on a height dominating the valley of Memramcook, was founded in 1864 by the Rev. Father Camille Lefèbvre, and is under the direction of the Congregation of the Holy Cross (C.S.C.). It was incorporated in 1868 under the name of "Collège St. Joseph", and received at that time a provincial charter authorizing it to grant university degrees. In 1898, by an amendment to the charter, the college was re-named "Université du Collège Saint-Joseph"; and in 1928, by a new amendment, the name was changed to "Université Saint-Joseph", or St. Joseph's University. The courses of study are divided into three departments, the preparatory or model school course, the academical course, and the university course. It grants the degrees of Bachelor of Commercial Science, Bachelor of Letters, Bachelor of Science, and Bachelor of Arts. It has a staff of 38 instructors of all grades, and over 250 students, nearly half of whom are in the university course.

**St. Jovite,** a village in Terrebonne county, Quebec, on the Canadian Pacific Railway, 82 miles north-west of Montreal. It is a popular country resort, with good hotels, hunting, and fishing; and is also in a general farming district. Pop. (1931), 981.

**St. Jude,** a village in St. Hyacinthe county, Quebec, on the Quebec, Montreal, and Southern Railway, 15 miles from St. Hyacinthe. Pop. (1934), 700.

**St. Julien, Battle of.** See **World War.**

**St. Justin,** a town in Maskinongé county, Quebec, on the Canadian National Railway, 30 miles west of Three Rivers. The settlement was founded in 1848, and was named after the wife of Sir Hector Langevin (q.v.). There are high water falls on the Maskinongé river in the district; and good water-power is available for St. Justin's industries, which include creameries, cheese factories, saw-mills, and sash-and-door factories. There is a weekly newspaper (*L'Echo de Saint-Justin*). Pop. (1931), 1,442.

**St. Lambert,** a city in Chambly county, Quebec, on the south shore of the St. Lawrence, opposite the island of Montreal, with which it is connected by the Victoria bridge. It is on the Canadian National and other railways entering Montreal from the south, and is an important railway centre. It is really a suburb of Montreal, and has a high school, two academies, a convent, and several parks. It was incorporated as a city in 1921. Its name is derived from that of Lambert Closse, a noted Indian fighter who came to Montreal with Maisonneuve (q.v.), and was killed in 1662. Pop. (1931), 6,075.

**St. Laurent,** a town in Jacques county, Quebec, is situated on the Canadian National Railway, 6 miles north-west of Montreal, with which it is connected also by electric railway. A mission was founded here in 1720. A village was established in 1845; and the town was incorporated in 1901. The place was named in remembrance of an old hill of Ville-Marie. Pop. (1931), 5,348.

**St. Laurent,** a parish in Montmorency county, Quebec, on the south shore of the island of Orleans, 6½ miles by road from Ste. Pétronille. It is the most important parish in the island from the industrial standpoint, and it is also one of the oldest parishes in the province, its registers going back to 1679. Pop. (1934), 683. See Abbé D. Gosselin, *Pages d'histoire ancienne et contemporaine de ma paroisse natale, St. Laurent, île d'Orléans* (Quebec, 1904).

**St. Lawrence Canals.** See **Canals.**

**St. Lawrence Deep Waterways.** See **St. Lawrence Waterways Project.**

**St. Lawrence, gulf of,** a western inlet of the north Atlantic ocean, washing the shores of Newfoundland, Quebec, New Brunswick, Nova Scotia, and Prince Edward Island. It has three openings into the Atlantic ocean—the strait of Belle Isle, between Newfoundland and Labrador; the gulf of Canso, between Cape Breton island and Nova Scotia; and a far wider passage between Cape Breton island and the island of Newfoundland, with the island of St. Paul in the middle. To the west the gulf narrows into the estuary of the St. Lawrence river, from which it derives its name. It contains many islands, the largest of which are Prince Edward island and Anticosti, but important groups of islands are the Magdalen islands and the Bird islands. It is famous for its fisheries; but it is perhaps best known as the channel of traffic, connecting as it does one of the busiest routes of maritime trade with one of the most extensive systems of inland navigation in the world. For its history, see S. E. Dawson, *The St. Lawrence basin* (London, 1905).

**St. Lawrence island.** See **Cape Breton island.**

**St. Lawrence river,** one of the most beautiful and magnificent rivers in the world, and the final link in the great water system, including the Great lakes, which extends inland in Canada for 1,900 miles (to the head of the St. Louis river, Minnesota) and drains an area of 309,500 square miles. The St. Lawrence issues from lake Ontario about 44° 10' lat. and 76° 30' long., and after pursuing a north-easterly course,

enters the gulf of St. Lawrence at a line drawn from point des Monts to cape Chat. From its head to St. Regis on the south bank, the river forms part of the boundary between Canada and the United States. The width of the river varies from less than a mile to 3 or 4 miles and, towards the gulf, to 60 miles. The distance across its mouth is about 40 miles. Its principal tributaries are the Ottawa, the St. Maurice, the Batiscan, and the Saguenay rivers.

The river was discovered in 1535 by Jacques Cartier (q.v.), who ascended it to the Indian village of Hochelaga on the present site of Montreal. On August 10, the feast of St. Lawrence, Cartier entered Pillage bay, on the north shore of the gulf, which he named St. Laurent bay, and the name was eventually applied to the gulf and river. The history of the St. Lawrence might almost be termed the history of the French-Canadian people. Fur-trading commenced at Tadoussac during the sixteenth century; colonization commenced with the founding of Quebec by Champlain (q.v.) in 1608; and New France developed in the St. Lawrence area during the seventeenth and eighteenth centuries. In this period the St. Lawrence basin served as the route by which the French extended the fur-trade further and further into the continent. After the conquest the same route was utilized by the North West Company. With the rapid development of the North American hinterland, particularly the Canadian north-west, the St. Lawrence assumed a new importance as a great avenue of trade with Europe. Since the early part of the nineteenth century, competition between the St. Lawrence and rival American routes for control of this transit trade has been an important factor in North American economic development.

Near the head of the St. Lawrence are the Thousand islands, a great tourist attraction because of their charming scenery. Between Prescott and

Montreal occur 8 series of rapids, of which the most important are the Long Sault, Coteau, Cedars, Cascades, and Lachine. These rapids, the quickest water in the world that is navigable for steamships, are also a great tourist attraction. Around the rapids have been constructed a series of canals, the Lachines, Soulanges, Cornwall, Point Farron, Rapid Plat, and Galop. Between lakes St. Francis and St. Louis occurs a total drop of 83 feet. Here the Beauharnois power project is under development. Below Montreal the river flows placidly through a level country with almost continuous settlement on both sides. Twenty miles below Quebec the Laurentians emerge on the river, and follow the north shore past the mouth of the Saguenay. On the south the Appalachians emerge at Matane and continue along the south shore, forming the table-land of Gaspé. The waters of the river are very clear, and contain a great variety of fish, including sturgeon, salmon, whitefish, and herring. The tide is first felt at Three Rivers, and below Quebec the St. Lawrence becomes a tidal river with a rise in the tide of 16 feet. It is open for navigation from the end of April to the beginning of December. Ocean-going vessels can ascend the river to Montreal. Although the Great lakes system is navigable for vessels drawing 20 feet, the present St. Lawrence canal system has a capacity of only 14 feet. The treaty for joint action of Canada and the United States to improve navigation in the upper St. Lawrence has never been approved by the United States Senate. A service of small vessels and railway at present connects the system of large lake boats with that of ocean-going vessels. Montreal is the great point of trans-shipment of Canadian exports to deep-sea vessels and of imports to the railways and smaller lake boats. The St. Lawrence is crossed by 5 bridges, including the Victoria Jubilee bridge at Montreal and a cantilever bridge with a central

span of 1,800 feet, 7 miles above Quebec.

See G. W. Browne, *The St. Lawrence river* (New York and London, 1905); S. E. Dawson, *The St. Lawrence basin and its border-lands* (London, 1905); Douglas MacKay, *Some fresh glimpses of a familiar river* (Canadian Geographical Journal, 1930); Bernard K. Sandwell, *The St. Lawrence waterway* (Canadian Geographical Journal, 1930); H. G. Moulton and others, *The St. Lawrence navigation and power project* (Washington, D.C., 1929); and R. Blanchard, *La région du fleuve Saint-Laurent entre Québec et Montreal* (Grenoble, Études canadiennes, deuxième série, 1936).

## St. Lawrence Waterway Project.

By this project it is proposed (1) to complete a channel for navigation of a minimum depth of 27 feet from Montreal to lake Superior, and (2) to provide for the production, as it is needed, of all the hydro-electric power which may be obtained from the St. Lawrence river between Montreal and lake Ontario. Improvements in navigation and plans for the production of power (see **Canals** and **Ontario Hydro-Electric System**) have hitherto been carried through piecemeal. The chief feature of the present proposal is its comprehensive character, combining as it does both power and navigation, and including the entire stretch from the lower St. Lawrence to the head of the Great lakes.

To complete the scheme it would be necessary (*a*) to dredge out some shallow stretches, notably in the lake St. Clair region, (*b*) to construct compensating works at certain points for the regulation of water levels, (*c*) to build a new lock between lakes Superior and Huron, (*d*) to construct canals and other works between Montreal and lake Ontario. For the whole distance of 1,200 miles between Montreal and Fort William there would be only about 125 miles of restricted channels, 55 of these being canals with only 18 locks. The Welland canal was completed by the Canadian government in 1930 to allow for a possible depth of 30 feet, and therefore constitutes an integral part of the entire scheme.

Interest centres chiefly on the stretch of about 181 miles between Montreal and lake Ontario, the work on which is by all odds the most expensive and difficult part of the project. For 115 miles below lake Ontario the river is traversed by the international boundary, with the province of Ontario on one side and the state of New York on the other. The remaining 66 miles from Cornwall to Montreal lie wholly within Canada and almost entirely in the province of Quebec. In the international stretch over 2 million horse-power of energy could be produced, and would be shared equally by Ontario and New York. In the Quebec stretch about 1 million horse-power could be produced from the Lachine rapids, lying immediately above Montreal, and about 2 million horse-power in the Beauharnois section, where a canal and power works are under construction. It is proposed in the international section to provide for navigation not by side canals, but by damming back the water to a sufficient height to flood the rapids out.

The project became an important subject of public discussion in both Canada and the United States soon after the World War, and engineers were appointed by the two governments to investigate. They reported favourably on June 24, 1921. An enlarged board provided much more detailed plans and estimates on November 26, 1926. This report estimated the cost of a 27-foot channel from Montreal to the head of lake Superior, with the works necessary for the production of 948,000 horse-power in the St. Lawrence, at a cost of some $560,000,000. Additional estimates were made of the amounts necessary for the production of the total available power, but the figures did not include the cost of the deepening of harbours, alterations in wharves, etc., or interest on the money during the period of construction.

The proposal aroused widespread opposition and support in both countries, and was made the subject of numerous investigations, both public and private. Opinion was sharply divided throughout both countries, not least in Ontario and New York, which were intimately concerned. The government of Quebec and important business interests in Montreal adopted a position of strong hostility. Advocates argued that the waterway would provide cheaper transportation for heavy products to and from the centre of the continent, and in particular would lower the cost of exporting grain; that the production of power was essential and should only be carried through by a comprehensive scheme including navigation; and that the cost would be moderate in view of the prospective advantages. Opponents denied that the channel would be extensively used by large vessels and argued that the reduction in transportation charges would be negligible. In particular, they attacked the estimates of costs as altogether inadequate and misleading. One American authority estimated that, if the cost were retired over a period of fifty years, the share of the United States alone might run to $1,750,000,000.

On July 18, 1932, the Canadian and American governments completed the negotiation of a treaty by which Canada was to complete the waterway through the wholly Canadian section lying within the province of Quebec; the United States was to complete the improvements above lake Erie; and both countries were to co-operate in the international section of the river below lake Ontario. The agreement was complicated by the fact that in each country improvements for navigation are within the jurisdiction of the federal government, while the control of water-power is under the provincial or state governments. The cost of improvements necessary for navigation was by the treaty to be shared equally, each country being given credit for work already completed. The cost of works necessary for power was to be undertaken by the provincial and state governments concerned. The highly contentious question of diversion of water through the Chicago drainage canal was also dealt with by a clause providing for a reduction of the diversion to a reasonable amount. The ratification of the treaty would have necessitated the completion of agreements with regard to power between the two federal governments and their respective state and provincial governments. The treaty failed, however, to gain the necessary two-thirds vote in the American Senate, being upheld, on March 14, 1934, by 46-42. It was, therefore, not submitted to the Canadian parliament. President Roosevelt declared that he had no intention of abandoning the project, and it appeared by the end of 1936 that the question was likely to be re-opened at an early date.

See C. P. Wright, *The St. Lawrence deep waterway: A Canadian appraisal* (Toronto, 1935), with bibliography; G. W. Stephens, *The St. Lawrence waterway project* (Montreal, 1930); H. G. Moulton and others, *The St. Lawrence navigation and power project* (Washington, 1929); L. R. Thomson, *The St. Lawrence problem* (Engineering Journal, April, 1929); and R. S. MacElwee and A. H. Ritter, *Economic aspects of the Great lakes-St. Lawrence ship channel* (New York, 1921). A voluminous literature has been published by the Great Lakes-St. Lawrence Tidewater Association, Washington, D.C.; and excellent annual surveys are to be found in the *Canadian Annual Review.*

**St. Leger, Barry** (1737-1789), soldier and author, was born in 1737, a nephew of Viscount Doneraile. He entered the British army in 1756 as an ensign in the 28th Regiment, and he served in America throughout the Seven Years' War. In the American Revolutionary war, he commanded the expedition against Fort Stanwix in 1777. He became commander-in-chief of the British forces in Canada, with the rank of brigadier-general, in 1784; but his name disappears from the army lists in 1785. He died in 1789. He was the author of a valuable *Journal of occurrences in America* (London, 1780).

**St. Léonard d'Aston,** a village in Nicolet county, Quebec, on the Nicolet river, and on the Canadian National Railway, 98 miles from Montreal. It was incorporated as a village in 1912, and is in a prosperous farming and dairying district. Pop. (1931), 610.

**St. Leonards,** a village in Madawaska county, New Brunswick, on the St. John river, and on the Canadian Pacific and Canadian National Railways, 11 miles north-west of Grand Falls. Pop. (1934), 865.

**St. Liboire,** a village in Bagot county, Quebec, on the Canadian National Railway, 15 miles east of St. Hyacinthe. It was named after the Abbé Liboire Girouard, the curé of St. Simon, who helped in founding the parish. Pop. (1931), 528.

**St. Liguori,** a village and parish in Montcalm county, Quebec, 2 miles from Montcalm, a station on the Canadian National Railway. Pop. (1931) of the parish, 1,000. See Abbé A. C. Dugas, *Histoire de la paroisse de Saint-Liguori* (Montreal, 1902).

**St. Lin.** See **Laurentides.**

**St. Louis,** a village in Kent county, New Brunswick, on the St. Louis river, 10 miles north of Richibucto. Pop. (1934), 300.

**St. Louis lake,** an expansion of the St. Lawrence river, south of Montreal island, and 9 miles above the city of Montreal. The river Ottawa enters the lake by two channels on its west side. It was named in 1611 by Champlain (q.v.), who was the first European to pass over the north shore of the lake. The district was opened for settlement in 1666, when La Salle (q.v.) founded the village of Lachine at the north-east extremity of the lake. This part of the island is, with the exception of Montreal itself, the most ancient and perhaps the most historical part of the whole island. Here in 1689 occurred the famous Lachine massacre at the hands of the Iroquois. In 1812-13 the district was the seat of operations of an important detachment of British troops. Lachine, moreover, was the principal warehouse of the fur-traders of the North West Company which rivalled the Hudson's Bay Company until their amalgamation in 1821. The lake is 20 miles long, 7 miles wide at its greatest breadth, and has an area of 57 square miles. See Désiré Girouard, *Lake St. Louis, old and new* (Montreal, 1893), and *The old settlements of lake St. Louis* (Montreal, 1892).

**St. Louis river** runs through Beauharnois county, Quebec, and empties into the St. Lawrence river on its south bank at lake St. Louis, at the head of the Beauharnois canal. It is 20 miles in length and drains a basin of 90 square miles.

**St. Luc, Lacorne.** See **Lacorne, St. Luc de.**

**St. Lusson, Simon François Daumont, Sieur de** (d. 1673), French official, arrived in Canada in 1663, as a deputy of the intendant of New France. In 1770 Talon (q.v.) sent him to the west to search for copper-mines and to establish friendly relations with the Indians. On June 14, 1671, he concluded a treaty with the western Indians at Sault Ste. Marie, and took possession of the western country in the name of the French king. He appears to have died in 1673.

**St. Magloire de Bellechasse,** a parish and village in Bellechasse county, Quebec. The village is 8 miles from the station of St. Camille, on the Quebec Central Railway. See the Abbé Wilfrid Roy, *Saint-Magloire de Bellechasse* (Quebec, 1925).

**St. Malachie,** a parish in Dorchester county, Quebec, on the Canadian National Railway, 15 miles from St. Anselme. It was originally known as East Frampton; but the name was changed in 1845 to St. Malachie, in honour of the saintly eleventh-century Archbishop Malachy of Armagh. Until 1860 the settlement was mainly English-speaking; but it is now predominantly French-speaking. Pop. (1931), 1,354. See Abbé J. A. Kirouac, *Histoire de la paroisse de Saint-Malachie* (Quebec, 1909).

**St. Marc-des-Carrières,** a village and parish in Portneuf county, Quebec, two miles from Lachevrotière station on the Canadian Pacific Railway, and 44 miles west of Quebec. The parish was established in 1902, and named after St. Mark's church in Rome. The operation of quarries in the locality furnished the suffix to the name. The village was incorporated in 1918. The chief occupations of the inhabitants are lumbering and quarrying for limestone. Pop. (1931), 1,997.

**St. Margaret bay,** an indentation in the south-east coast of Nova Scotia, about 25 miles west of Halifax harbour. It was named by Champlain (q.v.) "Le Port Saincte Marguerite", and its shores were first settled by settlers from Lunenburg in 1783.

**St. Margarets Bay,** a village in Halifax county, Nova Scotia, on the Halifax and South-Western Railway, 22 miles from Halifax. Pop. (1934), 600.

**St. Martin lake,** between lakes Manitoba and Winnipeg and between the 51st and 52nd parallels of north latitude, in Manitoba. It was called St. Martin's lake on the map of Assiniboia of 1811. It has an area of 125 square miles.

**St. Martins,** a village and harbour in St. John county, New Brunswick, on the bay of Fundy, 30 miles east of Saint John. The nearest railway is at Hampton Junction, 28 miles to the north. Being situated on Quaco bay, it is sometimes known as Quaco. Pop. (1931), 1,195.

**St. Mary river,** in southern Alberta, flows in a north-easterly direction to its junction with the Oldman river south of Lethbridge, and lies between the 112th and 113th meridians of west longitude. The Blackfoot Indian name for the river means "banks damming the river."

**St. Mary river,** a tributary of the Kootenay river, into which it discharges at Steele, in the Kootenay district of British Columbia. The river is 58 miles in length, and is named after the mission station of "Holy Head of Mary."

**St. Mary river,** in Guysborough county, Nova Scotia, flows in a south-easterly direction into the Atlantic ocean.

**St. Mary river** joins lakes Superior and Huron, and forms part of the international boundary line between Ontario and the state of Michigan. The head of the river, at the south-eastern extremity of lake Superior is on a line drawn between Gros cap and point Iroquois. After following a south-easterly direction, the river enters lake Huron by two channels. Around the Sault Ste. Marie or rapids near the head of the river, canals have been constructed on both the Canadian and American shores to overcome the 18-foot difference in level between lakes Superior and Huron. These two canals, consisting of four locks on the American, and one on the Canadian side, are the greatest ship-highway in the world. Below the "sault", the scenery is very picturesque; the river spreads out in some places into lakes, and at others rushes through narrow rapids or winds around beautiful islands. It was discovered in 1623 by the French explorer, Étienne Brûlé (q.v.), and was named after the mission of "Sainte Marie du Saut", which was founded in 1641 by the Jesuit missionaries, Raymbaut and Jogues (q.v.). The river subsequently became part of the fur-trading route to the north-west of the French *voyageurs*, and later of the North West Company. It was the North West Company that built the first small lock on the Canadian side in 1797-8. See also **Canals.**

**St. Mary's College,** in Halifax, Nova Scotia, was founded in 1839 as St. Mary's Seminary. In 1841 it was constituted St. Mary's College by Act of the provincial legislature, and was empowered to grant degrees. For many years it enjoyed a precarious existence; but in 1903 it was reorganized by Archbishop O'Brien (q.v.), and a new site was acquired. In 1913 it was placed in charge of the Christian Brothers of Ireland; and in 1918 an Act of the provincial legislature re-affirmed its status as a university. Since 1913 its presidents have been the Rev. Brother P. J. Culhane (1913-19), the Rev. Brother W. B. Cornelia (1919-22), the Rev. Brother P. J. Culhane (1922-5), the Rev. Brother C. C. Sterling (1925-31), and the Rev. Brother W. B. Cornelia (1931—).

**St. Mary's College,** Winnipeg. See **St. Paul's College.**

**St. Mary's,** a town in Perth county, Ontario, on the river Thames, and on the Canadian Pacific and Canadian National Railways, 20 miles north of London. It was named in honour of Mary, daughter of the Rev. John Strachan (q.v.), and wife of T. Mercier Jones, commissioner of the Canada Company. Settlement began in 1841; and the place was incorporated as a village in 1854, and as a town in 1863. It is sometimes called the "Stone Town", from the fact that it is largely built of stone drawn from nearby quarries, which provided an almost inexhaustible supply of stone for masonry and cement. It has a collegiate institute, a public library, and a weekly newspaper (*Journal-Argus*). Pop. (1931), 3,802.

**St. Mary's strait.** See **St. Mary river.**

**St. Maurice,** a county in Quebec, fronting on the north bank of the St. Lawrence, between Champlain and Maskinongé counties. It is named after the St. Maurice river, which empties into the St. Lawrence here. Chief town, Three Rivers. Pop. (1931), 69,095.

**St. Maurice,** a village and parish in Champlain county, on the St. Maurice river, and on the Canadian Pacific Railway, 10 miles north of Three Rivers. The registers of the parish date from 1743. Pop. (1931), 1,714. See *Historique de la paroisse de Saint-Maurice* (Bull. rech. hist., 1929).

**St. Maurice Forges,** an early iron industry in Canada, on the right bank of the St. Maurice river, 9 miles north-west of Three Rivers. The forges began operation, under government auspices, in 1737; and they continued in operation until 1883. See. B. Sulte, *Les forges Saint-Maurice* (Mélanges historiques, vol. vi, Montreal, 1920); D. Dubé, *Les vieilles forges il y a 60 ans* (Three Rivers, 1933), and R. C. Rowe, *The St. Maurice forges* (Can. Geog. Journal, 1934).

**St. Maurice river** is, with the exception of the Ottawa, the largest tributary of the St. Lawrence. It is 325 miles in length and drains an area of 16,200 square miles. It rises in the mountains separating the watershed of the St. Lawrence from that of Hudson bay, and, after flowing in a south-easterly direction, discharges into the St. Lawrence by three mouths at the city of Three Rivers. Its principal tributaries are the Mattawin, Mékinac, Bastonnais, Croche, Vermilion, Trench, Manouan, Shawinigan, Rat, Flamand, and Ribbon. The St. Maurice is navigable for 70 miles above Grandes Piles. It has several falls, of which the most important are the Shawinigan, Grand' Mère, and La Tuque; the first two are a great tourist attraction. The river expands into numerous lakes and contains a number of beautiful islands, although none of great extent. Both the St. Maurice and its tributaries abound in fish. The river crosses a mountainous region, and its banks, which are generally high, are covered with groups of majestic trees. The St. Maurice was discovered by Jacques Cartier (q.v.) in 1535, and was later named (probably) after Maurice Poulin, Sieur de la Fontaine, who was granted the seigniory in 1668. During the sixteenth century, the headwaters of the St. Maurice were a part of the route over which was conducted the early fur-trade between the French and the Indians to the north of the Saguenay. By the year 1603, after expulsion of the agricultural Indians from the St. Lawrence basin, the Hurons and Algonkin were able to bring their furs down the St. Maurice to Three Rivers. With the subsequent penetration of the St. Lawrence basin by the fur-trader, the Maurice route, like the Saguenay route before it, declined in importance. See G. Sénécal, *La Tuque et le haut Saint-Maurice* (École des Hautes Études commerciales de Montréal, Études économique, vol. iii, 1933).

**St. Michael's College,** one of the federated colleges of the University of Toronto. It was founded in 1852 by Bishop de Charbonnel (q.v.), the second Roman Catholic bishop of Toronto, who brought into his diocese some Basilian fathers, to whom he entrusted the task of preparing young men for the priesthood. Instruction was carried on at first in a wing of St. Michael's Palace, the home of the bishop; but in 1855 the cornerstone of the present building was laid, on land adjacent to that set apart for the University of Toronto. This building has been repeatedly extended, and new buildings have been acquired or built, until the college is now spread over a very considerable area. In 1881 St. Michael's was affiliated with the University of Toronto, being the first of the denominational colleges of Ontario to seek affiliation; and in 1887 it was federated with the University. For many years, however, it remained on a basis of federation which was in some respects incomplete; and it was only in 1910 that it became an Arts college in the University, on the same footing as Victoria and Trinity Colleges. The long connection of St. Michael's with the University of Toronto, culminating in the arrangement by which it has become a component part of the University, has been a great source of strength to University, since it meant that the University was able to count from an early period on the good-will of the large and influential element in Ontario which has belonged to the Roman Catholic communion, and this at a time when several Protestant denominations in the province were denouncing it as "a godless institution." The College has continued under the superintendence of the Basilian fathers; and the superiors of the College have been the Rev. Father Soulerin (1852-65), the Rev. Father Charles Vincent (1865-86), the Rev. Father Daniel Cushing (1886-9), the Rev. Father J. R. Teefy (1889-1904), the Rev. Father Daniel Cushing (1904-6), the Rev. Father N. Roche (1906-10), the Rev. Father F. G. Powell (1910-13), the Rev. Father R. McBrady (1913-16), the Rev. Father H. Carr (1916-25), and the Rev. Father J. J. McCorkell (1925—).

**St. Michel,** a village and parish in Bellechasse county, Quebec, on the Boyer river, and a port on the St. Lawrence river, 4 miles from St. Michel station, on the Canadian National Railway. Pop. (1934), of the parish, 1,700. See R. P. Marie-Antoine, O.F.M., *St. Michel de la Durantaye: Notes et souvenirs* (Quebec, 1929).

**St. Moïse,** a village in Matane county, Quebec, on the height of land between the St. Lawrence river and Chaleur bay, and on the Canadian National Railway, 70 miles north of Matapedia. It is in a lumbering district,

but farming is also carried on. Pop. (1931), 911.

**St. Nicolas,** a village and parish in Lévis county, Quebec, on the south shore of the St. Lawrence river, and on the Canadian National Railway, 15 miles west of Lévis. It is one of the oldest parishes in North America, dating back to 1694; and a Jesuit mission to the Abnaki was established here in 1683. The parish is connected with the north shore of the St. Lawrence by the Quebec bridge. Pop. (1931), 851. See H. Magnan, *La paroisse de Saint-Nicolas* (Quebec, 1920).

**St. Norbert,** a village in Manitoba, on the La Salle and Red rivers, and on the Emerson division of the Canadian National Railway, 10 miles south of Winnipeg. Pop. (1934), 450.

**St. Ours, Charles Louis Roch de** (1753-1834), legislative councillor of Lower Canada, was born in New France on August 24, 1753. During the American Revolution he served as an officer in the Canadian militia, and for a time was aide-de-camp to Sir Guy Carleton (q.v.). In 1785 he travelled through Europe, and was received at the English, French, and Prussian courts. From 1808 to 1834 he was a member of the Legislative Council of Lower Canada. He died on November 11, 1834; and in 1792 he married Marie-Josephte Murray.

**St. Ours, François Roch de** (1800-1839), legislative councillor of Lower Canada, was born at the manor-house of St. Ours, Lower Canada, on October 23, 1800, the son of Charles Louis Roch de St. Ours (q.v.) and Marie-Josephte Murray. From 1824 to 1832 he represented the county of Richelieu in the Legislative Assembly of Lower Canada, and in 1832 he was appointed to the Legislative Council. In 1837 he was made sheriff of Montreal. He died at Montreal on September 11, 1839. See E. Z. Massicotte, *Le shérif François-Roch de Saint-Ours* (Bull. rech. hist., 1919).

**St. Ours, François-Xavier de** (1717-1759), soldier, was born in Canada on December 12, 1717, the son of Pierre de St. Ours and Hélène-Françoise Céloron. He entered the military service and rose rapidly in rank. He was one of the commanders of the militia in the attack on Fort George in 1757, and at the head of a few Canadians, drove back the forces of the English. After the battle of Ticonderoga in 1758, he was one of three officers specially mentioned by Montcalm for bravery. He commanded the right wing of the French army at the battle of the Plains of Abraham in 1759, and he was killed at the head of his troops. He married, in 1747, Thérèse Hertel de Cournoyer, and had by her nine children.

**St. Ours, Paul Roch de** (1747-1814), legislative councillor, was born in Canada on September 5, 1747, the son of Roch de St. Ours and Charlotte Deschamps. He became a member of the legislative council of Quebec in 1775, and in 1787 he introduced a bill limiting the application of French civil law. In 1792 he became a member of the first executive council of Lower Canada, and was a member until his death on August 11, 1814. He married Marie-Joseph Godfroy de Tonnancour.

**St. Ours,** an incorporated town in Richelieu county, Quebec, on the east bank of the Richelieu river, opposite St. Roch, and 6 miles south of Contrecœur. It is named after the seigniory in which it is situated, and which was granted in 1672 to Pierre de St. Ours, a captain in the Carignan regiment. It has some flour-mills, a box factory, and a shoe factory, as well as a college and a convent. Pop. (1931), 615. See Abbé A. Couillard-Després, *Histoire de la famille et de la seigneurie de Saint-Ours* (2 vols., Montreal, 1915-7).

**St. Pacôme,** a village in Kamouraska county, Quebec, on the Canadian National Railway, 40 miles south-west of Rivière-du-Loup. The name was given in allusion to the poverty of the inhabitants, St. Pacôme having been an anchorite. The village derives its subsistence from agriculture and saw-mills. Pop. (1931), 1,235.

**St. Patrick,** a summer resort in Témiscouata county, Quebec, on the St. Lawrence river, 5 miles west of Rivière-du-Loup.

**St. Patrick's College,** an academic institution founded in Ottawa in 1929, under Roman Catholic auspices. It was designed as a college for English-speaking Roman Catholic boys and young men in the Ottawa district, since the University of Ottawa, though it offers a bilingual course, is predominantly a French-Canadian institution. The English-speaking Oblates of Canada were invited to take charge of the college; and its founder was the Rev. Dennis Finnegan, O.M.I. The high school department was opened in temporary quarters in September, 1929; the new buildings of the college on Echo Drive, Ottawa, were completed in 1930; and in 1931 the Arts course was inaugurated. In 1934 seven students graduated with B.A. or B.Sc. The rectors of the college have been the Rev. E. Killian (1929-30), the Rev. T. Kennedy (1930-31), the Rev. J. Moriarty (1931-3), the Rev. P. J. Phelan (1933-5), and the Rev. A. L. Cormican (1935—).

**St. Paul des Métis,** a village in the Athabaska district of Alberta, on the north Saskatchewan, and on the Canadian National Railway, 125 miles northeast of Edmonton. It was founded by Father Lacombe (q.v.) about 1894 as a half-breed (*métis*) settlement. It has six grain elevators, a flour mill, saw-mills, a fruit-canning factory, a creamery, and a power-plant, as well as a high school, a convent, a hospital, and a weekly newspaper (*Journal*). Pop. (1931), 938.

**St. Paulin,** a village in Maskinongé county, Quebec, on the Canadian National Railway, 34 miles north-east of Joliette. Pop. (1931), 700.

**St. Paul's Bay.** See **Baie St. Paul.**

**St. Paul's College,** in Winnipeg, is one of the colleges of the University of Manitoba. It was founded in 1926 for English-speaking Catholic students, with the Oblate Fathers in charge, after the bilingual course at St. Boniface University was discontinued. Housed at first in temporary quarters, it acquired in 1931 the building of old Manitoba College. From 1931 to 1933 the College was under the direction of the archbishop and the diocesan clergy; but in 1933 it was placed in charge of the Jesuit Fathers of the Upper Province of Canada (the name by which the English-speaking Jesuits in Canada are known). In 1936 St. Mary's College in Winnipeg, conducted by the sisters of the Holy Names of Jesus and Mary, became the women's department of St. Paul's College. Connected with the College is also St. Paul's High School. The principals of the College have been the Rev. A. Simon, O.M.I. (1925-31), the Rev. C. B. Collins, D.D. (1931-3), and the Rev. J. S. Holland, S.J. (1933—).

**St. Peter lake,** an expansion of the St. Lawrence river, in Quebec, between Sorel and Three Rivers. It was discovered by Jacques Cartier (q.v.) in 1535 on his second voyage. It receives many rivers, the largest of which is the St. Francis from the south-east. In the south part of the lake are many islands. It has been made navigable for large ocean vessels. It is 35 miles long, 10 miles at its greatest breadth, and has an area of 130 square miles.

**St. Peters,** a seaport village in Richmond county, Nova Scotia, on St. Peter's bay, an inlet of the Atlantic ocean, 32 miles from Port Hawkesbury. The place was called "San Pedro" by the Portuguese; and Denys (q.v.), who settled here in 1755, named it "St. Pierre". It is on the Canadian National Railway, and a short canal here connects St. Peter's bay with the Bras d'Or lakes. The total population of the district is about 1,200.

**St. Peters,** a village in Kings county, in Prince Edward Island, on St. Peters bay, and on the Canadian National Railway, 32 miles east of Charlottetown. Pop. (1934), 500.

**St. Peters Canal.** See **Canals.**

**St. Pie,** a village in Bagot county, Quebec, on the Canadian Pacific Railway, 8 miles south of St. Hyacinthe. It was created a village in 1904. Pop. (1931), 858.

**St. Pierre,** a village in Montmagny county, Quebec, on the Canadian National Railway, 5 miles south-east of Montmagny. The village was named in honour of Pierre Blanchet, the founder of the church in this parish, in 1848. St. Pierre is in a good dairying district; the village has three butter factories. Pop. (1931), 1,350.

**St. Pierre de Durham.** See **L'-Avenir.**

**St. Pierre island** lies south-west of the Miquelon islands, in the gulf of St. Lawrence, 17 miles south of the coast of Newfoundland. Except for the years 1713-63 and 1793-1814, when it was occupied by the British, it has been French territory since 1635. With the Miquelons, it is now all that remains of the French empire in North America. Though its area is only 10 square miles, it has been an important centre of trade. For centuries, the French fishermen on the banks of Newfoundland have used it as a *pied à terre;* and, during the period of "prohibition" in the United States, it enjoyed a boom as a centre for "rum-running". It is fortified, and has several lighthouses. The chief town is St. Pierre. Pop. (1935), about 4,000. See Mrs. C. A. Randall, *Picturesque St. Pierre* (Can. mag., 1897); D. Gauvin (comp.), *Almanach du cen-*

*tenaire, 1816-1916, Saint-Pierre et Mique-lon* (Paris, n.d.); A. Martineau, *Esquisse d'une histoire de Saint-Pierre et Mique-lon* (Revue de l'Histoire des Colonies Françaises, 1928), and F. Louis-Legasse, *Evolution économique des îles Saint-Pierre et Miquelon* (Paris, 1935).

**St. Polycarpe,** a village in Soulanges county, Quebec, on the Delisle river, and on the Ottawa division of the Canadian National Railway, 4 miles from Coteau Junction. Pop. (1931), 495.

**St. Raphael,** a village in Bellechasse county, Quebec, on the banks of the Rivière-du-Sud, 7 miles south of St. Vallier. The village is named after the Rev. François Raphaël Paquet, curé of St. Gervais from 1806 to 1838. It is in the centre of a farming, dairying, and lumber district; and it has a power-development plant. Pop. (1931), 619.

**St. Raphael,** a village in Glengarry county, Ontario, 20 miles north of Cornwall, and 4 miles from Green Valley station on the Canadian Pacific Railway. It is sometimes known as St. Raphael West, to distinguish it from St. Raphael in Bellechasse county, Quebec. Pop. (1934), 100.

**St. Raymond,** a village in Portneuf county, Quebec, situated on the St. Anne river, and on the Canadian National Railway, 36 miles north-west of Quebec. The parish was founded in 1842, and was named in honour of Raymond Nonnat. The village was organized as a municipality in 1898. It is beautifully situated on both banks of the river, requiring three large bridges for road and railway traffic. It has several saw-mills, a paper-mill, brick-yards, a brush factory, and two butter factories. Pop. (1931), 1,772.

**St. Rédempteur,** a village in Lévis county, Quebec, on the Chaudière river, and near Chaudière station on the Canadian National Railway, 12 miles west of Lévis. Most of the inhabitants are railway employees. Pop. (1931), 657.

**St. Regis,** a village in Huntingdon county, Quebec, at the junction of the St. Regis and St. Lawrence rivers, and adjacent to the international boundary, where the 49th parallel of latitude meets the St. Lawrence. It was formerly an important Iroquois village, and its population is still largely of Indian origin.

**St. Rémi,** a village in Napierville county, Quebec, on the Canadian National Railway, 30 miles south of Montreal. The parish was founded in 1833, and was named to commemorate Daniel de Rémi, who was governor of New France in 1665. Farming, dairying, and market-gardening are carried on with considerable success. The village has a large canning factory, saw-mills, and lumber-dressing establishments. Pop. (1931), 1,135.

**St. Romuald,** a village and parish in Lévis county, Quebec, on the south shore of the St. Lawrence, near the Quebec bridge, and on the Canadian National Railway, 4 miles from Lévis. It was formerly an important marine centre. It is now headquarters for a number of industrial concerns, notably a lumber plant, a monumental-stone works, and a textile factory. It is also the site of a Trappist monastery. Pop. (1934), of the parish, 4,000. See Abbé J. Demers, *La paroisse de Saint-Romuald d'Etchemin* (Quebec, 1906).

**St. Siméon,** a village in Charlevoix county, Quebec, on the north shore of the St. Lawrence, 20 miles north-east of Murray Bay, the terminus of the Canadian National Railway. It was incorporated as a village in 1911. It is a port of call for the Saguenay steamers and for the ferry from Rivière-du-Loup. Pop. (1931), 875.

**St. Stephen,** a town in Charlotte county, New Brunswick, is situated at the head of tide water on the St. Croix river, and on the Canadian Pacific and Shore Line Railway, 85 miles west of Saint John, and lies opposite the

United States town of Calais, with which it is connected by an international bridge. It was formerly a lumbering and shipbuilding centre, but these industries have disappeared; and it is now the home of confectionery, soap, and shoe factories, etc. At Milltown, which, although a separate municipality, is for practical purposes a part of St. Stephen, there is a large cotton mill. The site of St. Stephen was laid out for the Loyalists before New Brunswick became an independent province. The names of saints were given to the different parishes. In the case of St. Stephen it appears that the name was suggested by the name of a member of the surveying party (Stephen), and the word "saint" was added. An earlier name of the place was Schoodic Falls. It has a hospital and a weekly newspaper (*St. Croix Courier*). Pop. (1931), 3,437.

**St. Stephen's College,** a divinity school of the United Church of Canada in Edmonton, affiliated with the University of Alberta. It was formed in 1925 by the union of Alberta College, founded by the Methodist Church in 1903, and Robertson College, founded by the Presbyterian Church in 1910. The College has a staff of 5 professors, and a registration of about 20 students. The principals have been the Rev. John M. Millar (1925-30), and the Rev. A. S. Tuttle (1930—).

**St. Telesphore,** a village and parish in Soulanges county, Quebec, on the Baudet river, and on the Canadian Pacific Railway, 44 miles west of Montreal. Pop. (1934), of the parish, 1,000.

**St. Thomas,** a city in Elgin county, Ontario, situated on Kettle creek, 15 miles south of London, and 120 miles west of Toronto, on the Canadian National, Canadian Pacific, Père Marquette, Michigan Central, and Wabash Railways. The city was named after Colonel Thomas Talbot (q.v.), who was private secretary to Governor Simcoe, and who

received a grant of 5,000 acres in the county and settled there in 1803, subsequently bringing in other settlers. In 1817 the place was no more than a hamlet, chiefly under the hill at the extreme west end of the present city. The hamlet in the valley was at one period named Stirling, but as the village grew and spread up the hill and along the crest of the heights above the creek, it acquired its present name. The city has several churches, a collegiate institute, an industrial training school, a ladies' college, a business college, seven public schools and one separate school. St. Thomas is known as the railway city; many passenger and freight trains leave daily. There are three large railway shops, foundries, planing-mills, sawmills, a packing house, a lithographing plant, brush and broom factories, a shoe factory, and a butter and cheese factory. The city is surrounded by a rich agricultural and fruit district. The *Times-Journal* is published daily. Pop. (1931), 15,430.

**St. Thomas de Montmagny.** See **Montmagny.**

**St. Timothée,** a village in Beauharnois county, Quebec, on the south shore of the St. Lawrence, a short distance from the Beauharnois canal, and 6 miles from Valleyfield. It was incorporated as a village in 1929. Farming and market-gardening are carried on in the neighbourhood. Pop. (1931), 511.

**St. Tite,** a village in Champlain county, Quebec, situated on the Kapibouska river, 33 miles north of Three Rivers, on the Canadian National Railway. The parish was founded in 1859, and named in honour of the Roman saint. The village contains a convent, a college, and a hospital. Lumbering is the chief occupation of the inhabitants. Pop. (1931), 1,969.

**St. Tite des Caps,** a village and parish in Charlevoix county, Quebec, near the mouth of the Ste. Anne river, 35 miles below Quebec, and 7 miles from St. Joachim, the nearest railway station. It is described as "des Caps" because it is situated at the foot of the headlands (*caps*) behind cape Tourmente. Pop. (1934), of the parish, 1,435.

**St. Ulric,** a village in Matane county, Quebec, on the south shore of the St. Lawrence river, and on the Canada and Gulf Terminal Railway, 10 miles west of Matane. The railway station is named Rivière-Blanche, from the Blanche river, which empties into the St. Lawrence here in a series of little white falls. General farming, fishing, and lumbering are the chief occupations. Pop. (1931), 973.

**St. Valier, Jean Baptiste de la Croix Chevrières de** (1653-1727), Roman Catholic bishop of Quebec (1687-1727), was born at Grenoble, France, on November 14, 1653. He took holy orders, and became one of the chaplains to Louis XIV. In 1685 he came to Canada as vicar-general of the diocese of Quebec; and in 1687 he succeeded Laval (q.v.) as bishop of Quebec. He administered the affairs of the diocese for forty years, and he died at Quebec on December 26, 1727. He was the author of *Estat présent de l'église et de la colonie française dans la Nouvelle-France* (Paris, 1688; reprinted, 1856). See Abbé A. Gosselin, *Mgr. de St. Valier et son temps* (Evreux, 1899).

**St. Victor de Tring,** a village and parish in Tring township, Beauce county, Quebec, on the Quebec Central Railway, 8 miles south of Tring Junction. It was named in honour of Victor Hudon, a wholesale merchant of Montreal, when the parish was created in 1864. The village was created a municipality in 1922. It is in an agricultural district. Pop. (1931), 478.

**St. Vincent de Paul,** a village and parish in Laval county, Quebec, on the south shore of île Jésus, and on the Canadian Pacific Railway, 9 miles from Montreal. The parish was founded in 1743, and has been a prosperous farming and market-gardening district, adjacent to Montreal. It has been for many years a popular summer resort, but the erection of an immense dam above it on the Des Prairies or Back river, providing a source of cheap electric power, promises to transform it into an industrial area. It has a penitentiary, a college of the Marist brothers, and a convent of the sisters of Providence. Pop. (1934), of the parish, 2,000. See Abbé E.-J. Auclair, *Une page d'histoire locale* (Revue Canadienne, 1911).

**St. Vital,** a suburb of Winnipeg, Manitoba, on the Winnipeg Electric Railway, 5 miles north of Winnipeg. It has a weekly newspaper (*St. Vital Lance*). Pop. (1934), 10,402.

**St. Vital de Lambton.** See **Lambton.**

**St. Walburg,** a village in Saskatchewan, on the Canadian National Railway, 81 miles north-west of Battleford. It has three grain elevators and a weekly newspaper (*Enterprise*). Pop. (1934), 388.

**St. Wenceslas,** a village in Nicolet county, Quebec, on the Canadian National Railway, 23 miles west of Victoriaville. It was incorporated as a village in 1922, and is in a farming and dairying district. Pop. (1931), 300.

**St. Williams,** a village in Norfolk county, Ontario, on the Canadian National Railway, 4 miles from Port Rowan, Pop. (1934), 300.

**St. Zotique,** a village in Soulanges county, Quebec, on the north shore of the St. Lawrence, and on the Canadian National Railway, 2 miles from Coteau Junction. Pop. (1931), 216.

**Salaberry, Charles Michel d'Irumberry de** (1778-1829), soldier, was born at Beauport, Lower Canada, on November 19, 1778, the son of Ignace Michel Louis Antoine d'Irumberry de Salaberry (q.v.). In 1794 he obtained a commission in the 60th Regiment, and he served in the British army throughout the Napoleonic Wars. In 1810 he came to

Canada as aide-de-camp to General De Rottenburg; and in 1812 he was commissioned to raise among the French Canadians the Canadian Voltigeurs. In 1813 he defeated a superior American force at Châteauguay; and in 1817 he was created, in recognition of his services, a C.B. In 1818 he was appointed a member of the Legislative Council of Lower Canada, of which his father was already a member. He died at Chambly, Lower Canada, on February 27, 1829. In 1812 he married Marie-Anne-Julie, daughter of Jean-Baptiste-Melchior Hertel de Rouville, seignior of Chambly; and by her he had four sons and three daughters. See P. G. Roy, *La famille d'Irumberry de Salaberry* (Lévis, 1905), and F. Taylor, *L'hon. Chs. Michel de Salaberry* (Revue canadienne, 1868).

**Salaberry, Charles René Léonidas d'Irumberry de** (1820-1882), soldier and civil servant, was born at Chambly, Lower Canada, on August 27, 1820, the son of Lieut.-Col. Charles Michel d'-Irumberry de Salaberry (q.v.). From 1855 to 1860 he was employed by the Hudson's Bay Company as an engineer in the North West; and in 1869 he was one of the commissioners appointed by the Dominion government to investigate the grievances of the *Métis* of the Red River district. With his fellow-commissioners he was arrested and imprisoned by Louis Riel (q.v.). He was the organizer and first lieut.-colonel of the 9th Voltigeurs of Quebec; and in 1869 he was appointed a superintendent of woods and forests for the province of Quebec. He died at L'Assomption, Quebec, on March 25, 1882. He married (1) in 1849 Marie-Victorine Cordélia Franchère (d. 1855), (2) in 1869 Louise-Joséphine Allard (d. 1877), and (3) in 1880 Marie-Louise Baby. By his first marriage he had three children, and by his second four. See P. G. Roy, *La famille d'Irumberry de Salaberry* (Lévis, 1905).

**Salaberry, Ignace Michel Louis Antoine d'Irumberry de** (1752-1828), legislative councillor of Lower Canada, was born at Beauport, near Quebec, on July 4, 1752, the youngest son of Michel d'Irumberry de Salaberry and Madeleine-Louise, daughter of Ignace Juchereau Duchesnay de Saint-Denys, seignior of Beauport. He was educated at the Quebec Seminary and in France. In 1775 he took part in the defence of Quebec against the Americans, and in 1777 he was with Burgoyne at Saratoga. He was a member of the Legislative Assembly of Lower Canada from 1792 to 1796. In 1808 he was appointed an honorary member of the Executive Council of Lower Canada; and in 1817 a member of the Legislative Council. He died at Quebec on March 22, 1828. In 1778 he married Françoise-Catherine, daughter of Joseph Hertel de St. François, seignior of Pierreville; and by her he had eight children. He was popularly known as "Couronel Salumari." See P. G. Roy, *La famille d'Irumberry de Salaberry* (Lévis, 1905).

**Salamanders** are tailed amphibians. They are commonly mistaken for lizards (q.v.), but the latter, being reptiles, are covered with scales, while salamanders, being amphibians, are naked-skinned. Salamanders deposit their eggs in the water as frogs do, and these develop into tadpoles, which later are metamorphosed into salamanders of the adult form. Jefferson's salamander (*Ambystoma jeffersoniam*), which is black marked with traces of pale blue and the spotted salamander (*A. maculatum*), black with yellow spots, are widely distributed. The tiger salamander (*A. tigrinum*) found in the prairie provinces; the long-toed salamander (*A. macrodactylum*) is found from the Rocky mountains to the Pacific. The mud puppy (*Necturus maculosus*), a permanently aquatic species, which retains its external gills throughout life, is one of the largest tailed amphibians, sometimes reaching a length of fifteen inches or more. The newts, small, bright-coloured forms which spend some time in the water at spawning time, but at other seasons are terrestrial, are widely distributed. The Pacific newt (*Triturus torosus*) of British Columbia differs from that found in the rest of the country (*Triturus viridescens*). The newts are greenish when in the water, but reddish on land. Another widely distributed species is the little red-backed salamander (*Plethodon cinereus*). This is a small cylindrical-bodied animal, two to four inches long, with a reddish or ashy-coloured streak down its back. It lives in moist woods, never going to water even at spawning time. Several other less common species are found in different parts of Canada.

**Salem,** a village in Nichol township, Wellington county, Ontario, 2 miles north-west of Elora, the nearest railway station. Pop. (1934), 400. There are also small villages of this name in Yarmouth county, Nova Scotia, 2 miles from Yarmouth, and in Albert county, New Brunswick, 2 miles from Hillsborough.

**Salisbury,** a village in Westmorland county, New Brunswick, on the Canadian National Railway, 12 miles from Moncton. Pop. (1934), 300. There is also a small village of this name in Bruce county, Ontario.

**Salisbury island** is in the Hudson strait in the Franklin district of the North West Territories. It lies to the east of Bell island, off the eastern coast of Southampton island, and is in lat. 63° 27′, long. 76° 40′. It is about 29 miles long and 22 miles at its widest. It was named by Hudson (q.v.), according to Foxe's narrative, after Sir Robert Cecil, fourteenth Earl of Salisbury (1563-1612), who was principal secretary of state in England from 1596 to 1612.

**Salish,** a linguistic group inhabiting the south-easterly part of Vancouver island, the neighbouring islands, southern British Columbia, and the adjacent states. On Vancouver island they adjoin the Nootka-Kwakiutl, and on the mainland the Kutenai and Déné. The Salishan are usually regarded as of two great divisions, coast and inland. These are subdivided into smaller groups, of whom the Comox, Cowichan, Songhees, Squamish, Lillooet, Thompson River, Shuswap, Okanagan, Flathead, and Nisqually are the principal. The coast Salish lived in houses not unlike those of Nootka (q.v.), with roofs almost flat, and sometimes six hundred or even a thousand feet in length. Such communal dwellings were occupied by related family groups, each having its own section. The inland Salish had dwellings for summer and winter use. The former was a light frame lodge formed by a gable resting on the ground. The winter house was the Keekwillie hole; that is, a hole twenty-five or thirty feet in diameter dug to a depth of four or five feet, with a conical roof of beams, and cedar boards covered with earth. On the coast they were fish-eaters; but in the interior they lived largely by hunting, though fish formed a considerable portion of their diet. The custom of flattening the head by pressure during cradle-life was general amongst them, though not universal. They, however, did not use the labret or lip-piece so common amongst the Haida, Tlingit, and Tsimshian. The purpose of both customs was to indicate high birth. Amongst their customs was the potlach, which also prevailed amongst the Nootka, Haida, and other tribes. It was a great ceremonial feast at which goods, usually blankets, were given away, under certain conditions, to mark some event in the donor's life and to increase his social position. Some Salish tribes buried their dead, others placed the coffins in trees. The coast Salish were expert basket-makers and skilled in weaving. They had a breed of fleece-bearing dogs which were regularly shorn. From their wool and that of the mountain goat they manufactured blankets and cloth. The Salish believed in guardian spirits or totems. To obtain his totem, the Salish endured prolonged fasts, forced vomitings, and exhausting exercises enervating the body and rendering real and vivid the dream or vision of the looked-for spirit. Some, at least, of the Salish tribes had a vague notion of a future existence in a spirit land, which, however, was not the happy hunting-ground of the North American Indian, but something quite undesirable. They seem to have worshipped the sun, and to have had an idea that the dead would return from the land of the shades. In 1907 their number was estimated at 12,000; in 1909 it was found to be 10,264. See C. Hill-Tout, *The far west: The home of the Salish and Déné* (London, 1907), and James Teit, *Traditions of the Thompson River Indians* (Boston, 1898).

**Salmo,** a mining town in the Kootenay district of British Columbia, on the Salmo river, and on the Great Northern Railway, 25 miles south of Nelson. Pop. (1930), 300.

**Salmon,** the name originally applied to the salmon inhabiting the north Atlantic off the coasts of northern Europe and North America, now usually called Atlantic salmon (q.v.). Various other species more or less closely related to the true salmon are also commonly referred to as salmon, notably the five species of so-called Pacific salmon (q.v.). The Arctic char in Hudson bay and off the northern coast of Canada is also commonly called salmon.

**Salmon Arm,** a city in the Yale district of British Columbia, is situated on the southern arm of Shuswap lake, 75 miles east of Kamloops, and 75 miles west of Revelstoke. It is on the main line of the Canadian Pacific Railway, and is the centre of a fruit-growing and dairying district having a population of about 4,000. The name was derived from the immense salmon runs for spawning up the Salmon river, adjoining the city. The arm of the lake was named Salmon Arm, and this name was applied to the city when it was incorporated. It has a high school, a farmers' exchange, a creamery, electric light, waterworks, and a weekly newspaper (*Observer*). It is also a summer resort. Pop. (1931), 830.

**Salmon river,** in the Cariboo district, British Columbia, rises a little east of Stuart lake, and flows in a general south south-east direction, and enters the Fraser river about 19 miles north of Prince George. It is 122 miles in length, is navigable for canoes, and abounds in salmon.

**Salmon river,** in the Yale district of British Columbia, flows north-east into Salmon arm, Shuswap lake. It is 70 miles long.

**Salmon river,** in New Brunswick, rises in two branches, in the neighbourhood of the Miramichi and Richibucto rivers and flows south-west into Grand lake, in Queens county. It is 70 miles in length, of which 20 are navigable for small vessels.

**Salmon river,** in Lake St. John county, Quebec, rises in a series of small lakes east of Lake St. John, and discharges into the river Ashuapmuchuan, north of St. Félicien. It is 50 miles in length, and drains an area of 390 square miles. Between the 9th and 40th miles from its mouth the river are almost continuous rapids. For 24 miles above the river's mouth the adjacent land is for the most part level; above that, although more rocky, it is of good quality. Timber in this area has been extensively devastated by fire.

**Salmon river,** in the Sayward district, Vancouver island, British Columbia, flows north-west into Salmon bay on the south side of Johnstone strait. It is 46 miles in length.

**Salmon river** rises in Frontenac county, Ontario, and flows through Lennox and Addington counties into the bay of Quinte in Hastings county

SCENES IN A SALMON CANNERY ON THE SKEENA RIVER, BRITISH COLUMBIA

**Saltcoats,** a town in Saskatchewan, on the Canadian Pacific Railway, 114 miles north-east of Regina. It is named after the village of Saltcoats, in Scotland. It is in a mixed farming district, and has six grain elevators. A weekly newspaper (*Observer*) is published. Pop. (1934), 460.

**Salt Industry.** The commercial production of salt in Canada dates from the discovery of bedded deposits of salt in south-western Ontario in 1866. Since then salt has been produced in several other provinces of Canada. A large deposit of rock salt was discovered at Malagash, Nova Scotia, in 1917, and another at Gautreau, Westmorland county, New Brunswick, in 1921. Brine wells were discovered at Waterways, Alberta, in 1920. Salt is now produced, not only in south-western Ontario and in the Maritimes, but also at Neepawa, Manitoba, at Simpson, Saskatchewan, and at La Saline, Alberta. See L. Heber Cole, *The salt industry of Canada* (Ottawa, 1931), and *The salt industry in Canada* (Can. Geog. Journal, 1934).

**Salvation Army.** The Rev. William Booth, the founder of this organization, was a minister of the Methodist Church in England; finding that the churchless masses seemed to be beyond the reach of the ordinary services, he gave up this connection, and in July, 1865, organized the Christian Mission in the east end of London. In August, 1878, it received the name of the "Salvation Army"—an appropriate name, considering its religious character and its military organization. William Booth was soon hailed as "General", and many of his evangelists as "Captains". The growth of the Army throughout the world has been phenomenal, as have been also its social and religious achievements. In the earlier days, because of the stern discipline, General Booth was called a merciless autocrat, and the methods and severe restrictions of the Army were widely criticized. But the storm passed, and to-day in most quarters the Army is recognized as worthy of genuine respect.

The first appearance of the Army in Canada seems to have been in London, Ontario, in 1882; and in this year also it was officially recognized and officered. In 1884 Canada was constituted a separate command. Two years later, General Booth visited Canada, where he found a nation in the making. He came again in 1894, 1903, and 1907, being welcomed with much enthusiasm. With his wide outlook he sought to promote immigration from the Mother Country, and also strove for social amelioration of the needy. In one year, the Army sent out to Canada 4,000 immigrants. In later days, on the General's eightieth birthday, Earl Grey (q.v.), then governor-general, sent him the message: "There are many in Canada better and happier for your life's work." Though London, England, continues as the international headquarters of the Army, Toronto is the headquarters for the wide district including Canada, Newfoundland, the Bermudas, and Alaska, in which there are now (1936) 689 centres, an actual membership approximating 40,000, and a very large following. The present territorial commander is Commissioner John McMillan. The great variety of work carried on by the Army in Canada is shown in the following facts: it has 18 shelter and food depots, 18 hostels, 2 general hospitals, 8 maternity hospitals, 3 rescue homes, 5 old people's homes, 4 children's homes, and carries on prison work in the penitentiaries and provincial gaols, and police court work in all the main centres of Canada. The enormous expense of these widespread activities is borne by the voluntary contributions of the members and the gifts of the public. Underneath and behind all this social service are the spiritual aims of the Army; evangelism remains, as always, its true objective. The official organ of the Army is the *War Cry.*

The Salvation Army is not a sect; it does not claim to be a church, but seeks the good-will of all churches. General Booth's "stand was definitely upon the central work of conversion; after conversion there was nothing but a life of unselfish devotion." This conviction—the necessity of the renewal of the human heart—the Army shares with its distinguished founder in its world-wide service.

See Harold Begbie, *Life of General William Booth* (New York, 1920); and also *The Salvation Army Year Book* (London, England).

**Sambro,** a fishing port in Halifax county, Nova Scotia, on the west side of Sambro harbour, near cape Sambro, at the western entrance to Halifax harbour. The name appears to be a corruption of the name of Sesambre island, near St. Malo, France. Pop. (1934), 400.

**Sanctuary Wood, Battle of.** See **World War.**

**Sanderling** (*Crocethia alba*), one of the smaller members of the bird family *Scolopacidae*, which is one of the groups of shore birds to which belong the woodcock, snipe, and sandpiper. The species is primarily a frequenter of sandy beaches on migration. In the spring the sanderling is rather dark above, but variegated with paler markings. The neck and breast are washed with reddish ochre, and the remainder of the underparts is white. In the autumn they are much more extensively white below, and paler above. Sanderlings nest in the Arctic.

**Sanderson, Joseph Edward** (1830-1913), ecclesiastical historian, was born at York (Toronto), Upper Canada, on January 13, 1830, the son of John Sanderson and Margaret Crawford. He was educated at the University of Toronto (B.A., 1855; M.A., 1858), and in 1856 he was ordained a minister of the Methodist Church. He served in many charges in eastern Canada; and

he was the founder and first principal of the Ontario Ladies' College, Whitby, Ontario. He died at Sault Ste. Marie, Ontario, on August 3, 1913. Among other works he published *The first century of Methodism in Canada* (2 vols., Toronto, 1908-10).

**Sandham, Alfred** (1838-1910), historian and numismatist, was born in Montreal, Lower Canada, on November 19, 1838, the son of John Sandham and Elizabeth Tait. He was educated at the common schools, but left school at an early age, and was mainly self-educated. In 1864 he was appointed general secretary of the Young Men's Christian Association in Montreal; and this post he held for eleven years. In 1869 he was one of the founders of the Antiquarian and Numismatic Society of Montreal; and from 1872 to 1874 he was the editor of the *Canadian Antiquarian and Numismatic Journal*. In 1878 he removed to Toronto, and from 1878 to 1882 he was secretary of the Toronto Young Men's Christian Association. He then went into religious journalism, and started *The Christian Witness*, a journal that proved very successful from a financial point of view. He died in Toronto on December 25, 1910. His chief publications were *Coins, tokens, and medals of Canada* (Montreal, 1869), with *Supplement* (Montreal, 1872), *McGill College and its medals* (Montreal, 1872), *Montreal past and present* (Montreal, 1872), and *History of Montreal Young Men's Christian Association* (Montreal, 1873). In 1857 he married Christina Houston, and he had by her several children. See R. W. McLachlan, *Biographical notes on Alfred Sandham* (Canadian Antiquarian and Numismatic Journal, 1911).

**Sandham, Henry** (1842-1910), painter and illustrator, was born in Montreal, Lower Canada, on May 24, 1842, the son of John Sandham and Elizabeth Tait, and younger brother of Alfred Sandham (q.v.). He assisted his father, who was a house decorator, and taught himself the rudiments of painting. After some assistance from Jacobi (q.v.) and other Canadian artists, he went to Europe to study painting; and in 1880 he settled in Boston, Massachusetts. He executed illustrations for the American magazines, and at the same time he had great success as a painter of battle and historical scenes. "He was an excellent draughtsman" (E. Morris), and was a charter member of the Royal Canadian Academy of Arts in 1880. He died in London, England, on June 21, 1910; and a memorial exhibition of his chief paintings was held in the Imperial Institute, London, in June, 1911. In 1865 he married Agnes, daughter of John Fraser, a Canadian journalist; and by her he had six children, two of whom reached maturity.

**Sand-launce,** or sand-lance, are small, slender, silvery marine fishes. They live along shore, where they bury themselves in the sand in shallow water. On account of their great abundance, they are of considerable importance, especially as food for salmon. One species occurs on the Atlantic and another on the Pacific coast of Canada.

**Sandpiper,** a word used in a general sense for the smaller members of one of the shore bird families, namely *Scolopacidae*, which also includes the woodcock, snipe, curlew, godwits, etc. Although members of this group could quite fittingly be designated as "sandpiper", their common names do not carry this appellation. On the other hand, several of these birds are regularly given this name with a specific prefix. Some of the commoner and more widely distributed species so designated are the spotted sandpiper (*Actitis macularia*), the semipalmated sandpiper (*Ereumetes pusillus*), the red-backed sandpiper (*Pelidna alpina*), and the least sandpiper (*Pisobia minutilla*).

**Sandstone,** a sedimentary rock consisting of grains of minerals or rocks cemented together. It is consolidated sand, and may be cemented by calcium carbonate, silica, or some iron compound. The original sands may possibly represent material transported by streams or ground upon beaches, or it may have been the result of wind transportation. Usually the stone is of uniform grain as the result of the sorting action of water. When the mineral grains in the sandstone are largely feldspar, the rock is called arkose. A sandstone which is easily quarried and dressed is called freestone. Sandstone is one of the most important rocks used in building, and it is also employed in making grindstones.

**Sandwich,** formerly the county town of Essex county, Ontario, on the Detroit river, opposite Detroit, and on the Canadian Pacific and Canadian National Railways. It was originally settled during the French régime, and was known as L'Assomption; under the English régime it was known first as South Side, and then, when Detroit was evacuated by the British in 1796, and the British subjects moved across the river, it was named Sandwich, after the town of Sandwich in England. It was one of the most important places in the western part of Upper Canada; and it was here that in 1830 the first newspaper in the western part of the province (the *Sandwich Emigrant*) was published. In more recent years, with the growth of Windsor, it has become mainly a residential town, though it has a number of industries. It is the site of Assumption College, and has high and separate schools and a weekly newspaper (*Home News*). In 1935 it was merged with the city of Windsor, to which it was adjacent, and it has now therefore no corporate existence. Pop. (1931), 10,715. See F. Neal, *The township of Sandwich* (Windsor, Ontario, 1909).

**Sandy lake,** in the Patricia district of Ontario, lies south-east of Island lake, about the 93rd meridian of west longitude. It is drained by the Severn river north-eastward into Hudson bay. It has an area of 270 square miles.

**Sangster, Charles** (1822-1893), poet, was born at Kingston, Upper Canada, on July 16, 1822, the son of a shipwright at the Navy Yard. He had only a common school education, and from 1838 to 1849 was employed in the ordnance office, Kingston. He then engaged in journalism, and from 1850 to 1861 was sub-editor of the Kingston *Whig*. In 1867 he obtained a post in the Canadian civil service at Ottawa, and this he held until his death at Kingston, on December 19, 1893. He published *The St. Lawrence and the Saguenay, and other poems* (Montreal, 1856); and *Hesperus, and other poems and lyrics* (Montreal, 1860). His manuscripts are now in the Library of McGill University. See Rev. E. H. Dewart, *Charles Sangster* (Can. mag., 1896).

**Sangster, John Herbert** (1831-1904), educationist and physician, was born in London, England, on March 26, 1831, the son of John Alexander Sangster and Jane Hayes. He came to Canada in his youth, and was educated at Upper Canada College and at Victoria University, Cobourg (M.A., 1861; M.D., 1864). He became, first, a schoolteacher; and from 1865 to 1871 he was headmaster of the Normal School in Toronto. In 1874 he was an unsuccessful candidate, against Goldwin Smith (q.v.), for election to the Council of Public Instruction in Ontario. Soon afterward, he abandoned teaching for the practice of medicine; and became a country physician at Port Perry, Ontario. He died on January 27, 1904. He was twice married, (1) in 1851 to Mary Price, of Toronto, and (2) in 1871 to Caroline Elizabeth McCausland, of Toronto.

**San Juan island** is in Juan de Fuca strait, between Haro and Rosario straits, in the state of Washington, east of the south-eastern end of Vancouver island. It was named in 1791 by the Spanish commander Eliza, and at this time appears on his chart. It is 15 miles long, and has a maximum width of 7 miles. Years ago the Hudson Bay Company established a sheep farm on it, and it is about the only island in its group of any value for colonization, and that is small. Its ownership, with other islands in the vicinity, was unsettled for years, a dispute arising between the United States and Great Britain over the treaty of 1846. In 1859, they compromised on a plan of joint occupation. Finally in 1871, by the Washington Treaty, the German Emperor was made arbitrator, and he decided in 1872 in favour of the United States. The island was really of value to either country only as a right of way to its own possessions. See Viscount Milton, *History of the San Juan water boundary question* (London, 1869), and E. H. Wilson, *San Juan island* (Beaver, 1927).

**Sapsucker,** a name properly used, with descriptive prefixes, for at least two species of woodpeckers found in Canada, although it is occasionally misapplied to other smaller members of this family (*Picidae*). The yellow-bellied sapsucker (*Sphyrapicus varius*) occurs in forested parts of Canada from the mountains of the west to southern Quebec and Cape Breton island. Other forms occur in the West. Sapsuckers feed almost exclusively at shallow drillings, which they make in closely arranged rows through the outer bark of trees. They consume both the sap which flows from these wounds and the insects attracted to the sap.

**Sarbach, mount,** is in Alberta, west of the Mistaya river in the Rocky mountains. It is called after Peter Sarbach, a Swiss guide.

**Sarcee.** See **Sarsi.**

**Sardine.** The true sardine of Europe is *Sardinia pilchardus*, which is usually known as pilchard in England. It belongs to the same family as the marine herring. A closely related species occurs off the west coast of North America, from California to British Columbia. In Canadian waters it is taken in large numbers off the west coast of Vancouver island, where it is used in making oil and fish meal. It is canned to only a very limited extent. The annual production in normal times is valued at about two million dollars. The young of the common marine herring are sometimes packed under the name of sardines.

**Sardis,** a farming settlement in the New Westminster district, British Columbia, on the New Westminster-Chilliwack branch of the British Columbia Electric Railway, 3 miles south of Chilliwack. Pop. (1930), 500.

**Sarnia,** a city in Lambton county, Ontario, at the mouth of the St. Clair river on lake Huron, 60 miles west of London, and served by the Canadian National and Père Marquette Railways. Sarnia is the Roman name of the isle of Guernsey, where Sir John Colborne (q.v.) was governor before he went to Canada. The town was surveyed, laid out, and first settled in 1833, and called "The Rapids", after the rapids at the foot of the lake. In 1836, after the town had become larger, the name was changed to Port Sarnia; it was changed to the present form in 1886. This is an important trans-shipping point for lumber, grain, coal, etc. The traffic from here is very heavy on the Great lakes during the season of navigation. The limits of Sarnia harbour include all the waters of the St. Clair river between the Canadian shore and the international boundary in the middle of the stream and extending from the head of the river at the outlet of lake Huron to the foot of the river at the entrance of St. Clair flats, a distance of 30 miles. The first two miles below the outlet of lake Huron constitute a wide, deep, and sheltered harbour of refuge. The waters include the inlet known as Sarnia bay. Here vessels make their winter haven; and here also immense rafts of logs are handled. The water in the river runs very swiftly, but in the bay it is slack,

and vessels are not exposed to any ice movement. The city has twelve churches; public, high, and technical schools; a public library; and a daily newspaper (*Canadian Observer*). There are steam ferries to the United States; and a tunnel under the St. Clair river connects Sarnia with Port Huron, Michigan. The principal industrial establishments are lumber mills, a large oil refinery, flour mills, foundries, machine shops, grain elevators, and steel works. Pop. (1931), 18,191.

**Sarrazin, Michel** (1659-1734), physician, was born in Burgundy, France, in 1659, and studied medicine. He emigrated to Canada in 1685, and in 1686 was appointed surgeon-major to the troops in the colony. In 1697 he was appointed physician to the king; and he played an important part in the early development of medicine in Canada, as well as in the early study of natural history. In 1707 he was appointed a member of the Superior Council; and he died at Quebec in 1734. In 1712 he married Marie-Anne Hazeur; and by her he had seven children. See A. Vallée, *Michel Sarrazin* (Quebec, 1927).

**Sarsaparilla** (*Aralia nudicaulis L., Araliaceae*), an herb with a very short stem which scarcely rises above the ground, and which bears a single long-petioled compound leaf and a naked flower stalk. The leaflets are oblong to ovate, pointed and toothed. The flowers are borne in compound clusters and the fruit is black. It may be found in moist woodlands from Newfoundland westward. The root is aromatic, and used as a substitute for the official sarsaparilla.

**Sarsi,** a small tribe of the great Athapaskan or Déné race. The name is said to be derived from a Blackfoot word meaning "not good." Their hunting grounds were on the eastern side of the Rocky mountains, between the headwaters of the Athabaska and the North Saskatchewan, and thus in proximity to the Blackfoot. Sir Alexander Mackenzie (q.v.) about 1800 estimated them at thirty-five tents or 120 men, though David Thompson (q.v.), a few years later, placed them at ninety tents or 650 persons in all, and gave them credit for raising, not stealing, horses. At present they are on a reserve near Calgary and are supposed to be about 200, all told. In 1888, the Rev. E. F. Wilson described them as inferior to the Blackfoot, and not so fine and tall a race. They lived in tipis in the summer, and in low log-huts, plastered with mud, in the winter. Polygamy was common amongst them, as amongst most of the plains Indians. They knew how to cauterize with burning touchwood, and understood the use of vapour baths. Their diseases were treated by their medicine men who, to the accompaniment of beating drum or shaking rattle, pretended to catch the bad spirit that caused them.

**Saskatchewan.** The province of Saskatchewan, which in Cree means "Rapid river", extends from the international boundary in the south to lat. 60° in the north, a distance of 761 miles, and from long. 110°, styled the fourth meridian, eastward 393 miles in the south and 277 miles in the north to the second meridian, and comprises 251,700 square miles. Of the 152 million acres of land included therein, about 80 million are potential agricultural land, of which about 55 million are occupied. The greater part of the province lies on the second of the three prairie "steppes" or levels, and has a general elevation of between 1,000 and 2,000 feet. The south-western corner is on the third level, the Cypress hills reaching a maximum elevation of 4,500 feet. The two great river systems, the Beaver-Churchill in the far north and the Saskatchewan in the centre, traverse the province from west to east, seeking an outlet into Hudson bay. Each drains an area of more than 100,000 square miles. The Assiniboine, with its tributaries the Qu'Appelle and the Souris, drains the south-eastern corner, and joins the Red river at Winnipeg. These rivers are of relatively small use for purposes of transportation, because of their swift currents, shifting sand bars, variable volume, rapids, and the blocking of their outlets by ice for a considerable part of the year.

The southern third of the province, including the Regina plains of over 3,000 square miles, is in the main treeless prairie. Its brown soils, rich in nitrates and potash, yield wheat of the finest quality. The quantity is limited only by the annual rainfall, which may vary from 7 to over 20 inches in the west and from 10 to 26 in the east. Fortunately, the larger portion falls during the growing season. For reliable crop production a rainfall of 12 inches per year, or $7\frac{1}{2}$ inches for the warm season, is necessary. In some areas of the south-west of the province, in about 40 per cent. of the years, the rainfall is less than this minimum, while in the south-east the percentage is around 20.

The central third, the "Park Belt" of dark soils, has a greater precipitation and more trees. It is well watered, and is suitable for livestock, as well as for the growing of grain. The risk of early frost is greater in this area. Garnet and Reward wheat can be matured on the northern boundary of the park belt, over 350 miles north of the southern boundary.

The northern third is dotted with lakes. The two largest, Athabaska in the west and Reindeer in the east, cover over 1,500 square miles each. Fish and furs are found in abundance in this region.

Extensive deposits of lignite coal (at one time estimated to contain about fifty billion of tons), brick, and china clays occur in the south of the province. Gold and copper are mined in the north, near the Manitoba boundary, and are found in promising quantities near the Alberta boundary.

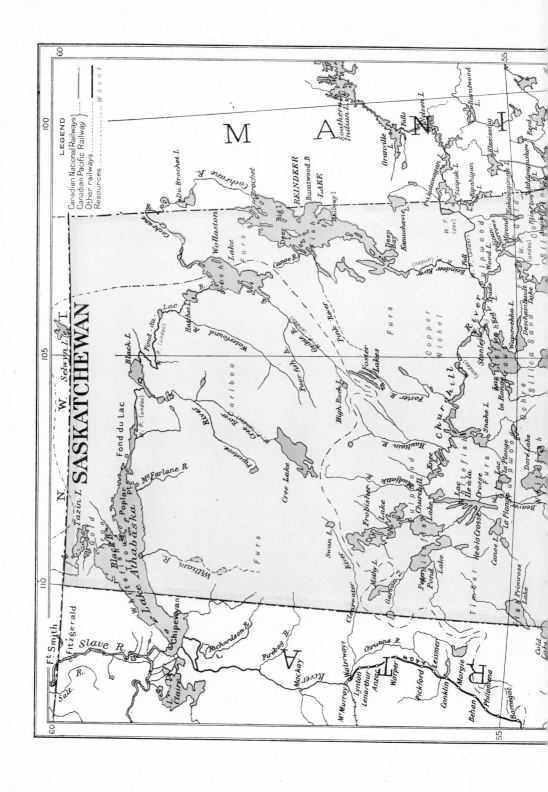

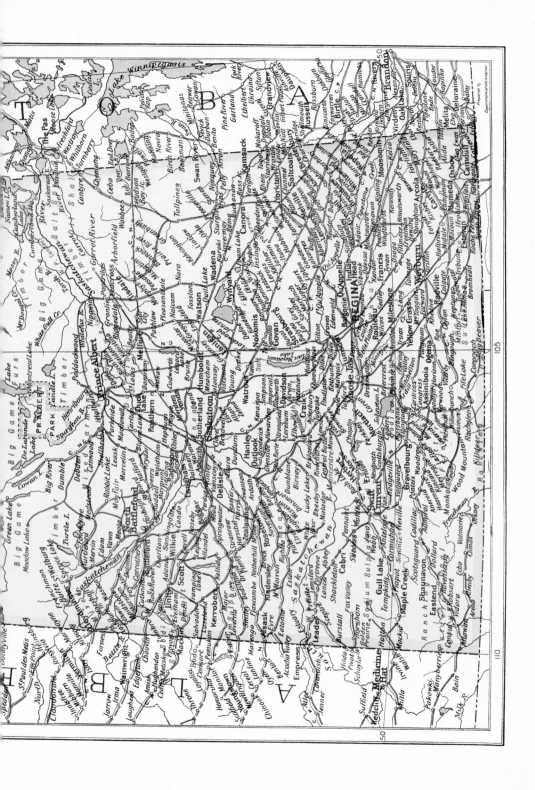

Prepared by
Department of the Interior

*History.* The territories now comprised within the province of Saskatchewan were originally an important area in the early fur-trade in the West. The first white man to reach this area was probably Henry Kelsey (q.v.), a servant of the Hudson's Bay Company, who penetrated into the interior in 1691. The French fur-traders reached this area about the middle of the eighteenth century; and Fort Paskoyac on the Saskatchewan was built, probably by one of La Vérendrye's sons, about 1750, and Fort à la Corne, farther west, a year or two later. The first agricultural operations in the Canadian west were conducted by the Chevalier de la Corne (q.v.) in the Carrot valley, in Saskatchewan, in 1754. Cumberland House, the first trading-post built by the Hudson's Bay Company in the interior, was established on the Saskatchewan in 1774; and in the heyday of the fur-trade Saskatchewan was dotted with trading-posts of the Hudson's Bay and North West Companies. About these posts there grew up small settlements, composed mostly of half-breeds; but settlement in Saskatchewan did not really begin until about 1870, after the Hudson's Bay Company's territories had been acquired by the Dominion of Canada. The influx of settlers, the building of the Canadian Pacific Railway, and other causes produced in 1885 what is sometimes known as the Saskatchewan rebellion, which was brought to an end at the battle of Batoche; but this rebellion delayed for some time any considerable settlement on the western prairies, and it was only with the adoption of a vigorous immigration policy by the Laurier government, under the inspiration of Sir Clifford Sifton (q.v.), that the vacant prairies of Saskatchewan began to be filled. By 1905 the population of Saskatchewan was such that it was, with Alberta, created a separate province.

*Industries.* Saskatchewan is primarily an agricultural province. In 1930 agriculture yielded 57.85 per cent. of the value of the net production of the industries of the province, while manufactures accounted for only 13.72 per cent. For purposes of comparison it may be noted that the percentages for Prince Edward Island were 76.80 and 6.16, and for Ontario, 20.17 and 51.31.

The *Canada Year Book* for 1934-5 reports that the gross agricultural wealth of Saskatchewan in 1933 was estimated at $1,163,850,000; that of Ontario, at $1,389,313,000. The gross value of the production of all industries in Ontario averages more than six times that of Saskatchewan.

For the years 1927-32 practically one-third of the total acreage of field crops for Canada was in Saskatchewan, but not more than one-fourth of their value. Low prices and poor yields, due to drought, caused the value of field crops in Saskatchewan to decline from $348,000,000 in 1928 to $70,347,000 in 1931. For spring wheat, the most important of the field crops in Saskatchewan, the area, yields, and values were:

| | *Area* | *Bush. per Acre* | *Total yield* | *Average price* | *Total Value* |
|---|---|---|---|---|---|
| 1925-29 | | | | | |
| Average... | 13,465,533 | 17.7 | 237,879,000 | $1.00 | $237,828,400 |
| 1930........ | 14,324,000 | 14.4 | 206,700,000 | .47 | 97,149,000 |
| 1931........ | 14,961,000 | 8.9 | 132,466,000 | .38 | 50,337,000 |
| 1932........ | 15,543,000 | 13.0 | 202,000,000 | .30 | 60,600,000 |
| 1933........ | 14,743,000 | 8.7 | 128,004,000 | .47 | 60,162,000 |
| 1934........ | 13,262,000 | 8.6 | 114,200,000 | .61 | 69,662,000 |
| 1935........ | 13,206,000 | 10.2 | 135,000,000 | .60 | 81,000,000 |

*Population.* The population of the area now known as Saskatchewan increased from 91,279 persons in 1901, to 257,763 in 1906 (the year following the establishment of a provincial government) and 930,977 in 1936. An increase of 401,153 occurred between 1901 and 1911. In 1931 over two-thirds (68.44 per cent.) were classified as rural. The four largest cities were Regina (53,209), Saskatoon (43,291), Moose Jaw (21,299), and Prince Albert (9,905). The Canadian-born formed 66 per cent. of the total, the British 10 per cent., and the foreign-born 24 per cent. According to racial origin 46.4 per cent. of the population were of British origin, and 50.2 per cent. of other European races. The numbers were: Teutonic, 170,988 (German, 129,232); Scandinavian, 72,774 (Norwegian, 29,755); Slavic, 132,179 (Ukrainian 63,400); Latin, 65,728 (French, 50,700); Asiatic, 4,419; and Indians, 15,268 (11,718 in 1911). The largest religious groups were the United Church of Canada, 243,399; Roman Catholic, 233,979; Anglican, 126,837; Lutheran, 113,676; Presbyterian, 67,954; Mennonite, 31,388; Greek Orthodox, 31,126; Jewish, 5,047; and Doukhobor, 7,956 (of whom less than 1,000 were living in "communities").

*Government.* When it was proposed to extend provincial rights and powers to the North West Territories, there was division of opinion with regard to the best method of doing this. One proposal favoured the extension of the boundaries of the province of Manitoba westward and the erection of one new province. Public opinion in the Territories favoured the erection of two provinces by dividing the Territories either by a line running east and west or a line running north and south. The latter suggestion was adopted in 1905, since it gave greater variety to each province. Had the horizontal division prevailed the southern province would have developed more quickly than the northern, but would have been subject to greater vicissitudes of fortune.

Each province was given a single-chamber legislature. The provinces were divided into constituencies, each represented in the legislature by one member, except in the larger cities. Saskatchewan was empowered to select its capital. Regina, the old capital of the North West Territories and the headquarters of the Mounted Police, was chosen. An Executive Council, consisting of a prime minister and eight ministers of the Crown, is responsible for the administration of the province through twelve departments of government. These ministers have oversight also of certain commissions, boards, and bureaux, with varying measures of independence, such as the Telephone, Civil Service, Power and Liquor Commissions, the Farm Loans and Local Government Boards.

The agencies for local government, each with power to borrow money and levy taxes, exceeded 7,000 in 1936. Of these 4,905 are school districts, 499 being classed as urban. The municipalities include 8 cities, 81 towns, 382 villages, 302 rural municipalities, and 171 local improvement districts. There were 1,155 telephone companies, 22 union hospital districts, 25 drainage districts, and one Hail Insurance Association operating in 135 rural municipalities in 1935. The urban municipalities are limited in area, and graded according to population (50 within a square mile being the minimum for a village, 500 for a town, and 5,000 for a city), and are endowed with different powers and rights. The rural municipality, corresponding in some measure to the county in eastern Canada, is the collecting agency for all rural activities—for schools, hospitals, telephones, hail insurance, etc. It has been stated that "less than one-third of the taxes collected are actually municipal taxes."

The judicial system of the province comprises a Court of Appeal with a chief justice and four justices, a King's Bench with a chief justice and six justices, and judicial districts, 21 in number and served by 18 judges. The justices and district court judges are appointed by the Dominion government, while the police magistrates of the cities and the magistrates who hold court elsewhere in the province are appointed by the provincial government.

The Royal Canadian Mounted Police, appointed and supported by the Dominion by an agreement between the provincial and Dominion governments, are responsible for the maintenance of law and order in all areas of the province beyond the jurisdiction of the special police of the cities. In 1936 the province gave the Dominion $225,000 for this service.

The School Act passed by the Saskatchewan legislature in 1905 continued provision for separate schools in accordance with the Dominion statute establishing the province. In 1935 there were 24 Roman Catholic separate and 6 Protestant separate school districts out of a total 5,123. The Secondary Education Act, passed in 1906, authorized high school districts, with trustees and levy distinct from those of the School Act. There were 18 high school districts in 1936, and in three of them there are vocational schools. It was found necessary to extend the right to give instruction in high school subjects to schools operating under the School Act. Some opened a high school room giving instruction beyond grade eight, others under the name of continuation school included grade eight with the higher grades. In 1936 there were 3,396, mostly one-roomed rural schools, giving instruction to 11,396 pupils, of whom about 85 per cent. were in grades nine and ten. There were also 2,495 schools districts operating high school and continuation rooms under the School Act, giving instruction to 13,972 pupils and receiving $290,204 in high school grants; while 18 secondary school districts enrolled in the collegiates, high schools, and vocational schools 10,390 pupils and re-

ceived $250,150 in high school grants. Three normal schools and a faculty of education in the University of Saskatchewan provide the training required by teachers. The first normal school was opened in Regina in 1892 by Premier Haultain of the North West Territories.

In 1907 the legislature, in an Act based upon the recommendations of the Toronto University Commission, authorized the establishment of a university to be supported by the province, and given the exclusive right to confer all degrees except in theology. In 1935 the University of Saskatchewan had ten faculties, including agriculture, with a total enrollment, including summer school, night classes, etc., of 3,148.

The provincial department of health is responsible for two mental hospitals, one in Battleford and one in Weyburn, and three sanatoria, in Fort Qu'Appelle, Prince Albert, and Saskatoon, where residents of the province suffering from tuberculosis are treated free of charge. This beneficent provision has effected a marked reduction in the mortality rate for tuberculosis. Over three score of the 302 rural municipalities have engaged medical men on full-time basis to be responsible for the medical care of the people of the municipality. In a number of other municipalities, the services of doctors are engaged on a part-time basis.

*Finances.* When the province was erected, provision was made for a subsidy from the Dominion based upon population, and also for the revenue of the school lands set apart for the support of schools in every township surveyed. These lands were held in trust by the Dominion until 1930, when they were transferred in trust to the province. The province began without any public debt, but with liability for setting up the machinery of government in a sparsely settled territory, with many and great problems and small resources. The expenditures of the province chargeable to revenue have in 25 years increased sixfold, while the population has not quite doubled. In 1911 the annual expenditures were $2,699,603; in 1936 they were $16,124,689. They increased from $5.48 *per capita* for a population of 492,432 in 1911 to $17.32 *per capita* for a population of 930,977 in 1936. The capital debt of the province in 1936 consisted of a funded debt (stocks or debentures) amounting to $124,446,375 and an unfunded debt of $68,189,135 in the form of treasury bills of a maturity of one year or less, issued mainly to the Dominion for relief expenditures. A sinking fund of $9,585,192 reduced the net public debt to $183,050,317 at April 30, 1936. In February, 1937, the Finance minister of the Dominion reported that Saskatchewan had borrowed $51,898,717 from the Dominion for relief, and that $17,-960,000 of this would be written off, thus further reducing the net debt of the province. This was an acknowledgment that the disasters caused by the seven years of drouth had become a national obligation. Of the funded debt 44 per cent. was revenue-bearing, consisting of moneys advanced to the Farm Loan Board, the Coöperative Wheat Producers, the Telephones, the Power Commission, the Elevators, and the Co-operative Creameries. Public improvements (bridges and highways) were responsible for 23.7 per cent., and public buildings for 18 per cent. of the funded debt.

*Municipal Finance.* While the receipts and expenditures of the cities for municipal purposes during the years 1929 to 1934 increased slightly, those of the rural municipalities decreased greatly. The tax collections of the rural municipalities for all purposes reached $18,274,880 in 1929, and dropped to $10,055,370 in 1935, a decline of 44 per cent. This decline was disastrous for rural schools and telephones. In 1935 the rural municipalities owed the school districts $6,508,905 and the telephone companies $3,338,244. Nearly every

telephone company was forced to default some principle and interest due on debentures. Fortunately, 80 per cent. of the telephone debenture indebtedness ($17,537,665) had been paid before the depression. The revenues of the rural school districts (including grants as well as taxes) had declined from $8,455,017 in 1929 to $3,487,250 in 1935. The brunt of this decrease fell upon teachers' salaries. During this period salaries were reduced by 57 per cent., and the total of unpaid salaries to rural teachers rose to $662,263 in 1935. Default on principle and interest on school debentures rose from a negligible amount in 1926 to $1,265,037 in 1935. The total of the debenture indebtedness for municipal purpose of the rural municipalities, less sinking funds, was only $124,753 in 1935, yet two-thirds of it was in default.

The urban picture shows a debenture indebtedness of over $30,000,000. There was practically no default in the cities. The sinking funds in the cities, except in the smallest city, are sufficient to meet all debts as they fall due. The towns were less fortunate, showing 12 per cent. overdue. The villages, like the rural municipalities, showed about one-half of the debenture indebtedness overdue. Yet the total amount overdue is less than half a million dollars out of a total of thirty millions for all urban municipalities. The schools in the towns and villages, because of shrinkage in tax collections, suffered, but not so badly as those in the rural districts. Payments for teachers' salaries from 1929 to 1935 were reduced 57 per cent. in rural districts, 48.3 per cent. in towns, and 34.5 per cent. in cities.

This distressful picture is the result of a combination of small yields of crops due to drought, of low prices due to the depression, and of the ravages of wheat rust, especially in 1935. While the gross agricultural wealth of Saskatchewan at one time rivalled that of Ontario, the income from agriculture in

Saskatchewan declined from 1925 to one-fifth in 1931 and to one-third in 1935. This appalling decline was responsible for the great demand for relief. From September 1, 1929, to January 31, 1936, $86,689,356 was spent on relief, of which $20,577,335 was for rural direct relief, $6,865,448 for urban direct relief, $18,826,219 for fodder and feed for stock, and $15,908,-373 for seed grain. The cost was more for stock and seed grain than for food, clothing, and fuel for direct relief. Of the aggregate gross expenditure for relief for the foregoing period, 68.1 per cent. or $59,270,740 was chargeable to the provincial government. Of this amount the Dominion has since assumed responsibility for $17,960,000.

*Bibliography.* See N. F. Black, *History of Saskatchewan and the old North West* (Regina, Saskatchewan, 1913); A. L. Burt, *The romance of the prairie provinces* (Toronto, 1930); E. H. Oliver, *The beginning of white settlement in northern Saskatchewan* (Trans. Roy. Soc. Can., 1925), *The settlement of Saskatchewan to 1914* (Trans. Roy. Soc. Can., 1926), *Economic conditions in Saskatchewan, 1870-1881* (Trans. Roy, Soc. Can., 1933), and *The beginnings of agriculture in Saskatchewan;* W. A. Mackintosh and W. L. G. Joerg (eds.), *Canadian frontiers of settlement* (9 vols., 1933-7); and the *Report* of the Saskatchewan Taxation Commission, 1936.

**Saskatchewan mountain** is in Alberta at the headwaters of the North Saskatchewan river in the Rocky mountains. It is in lat. 52° 06', long. 117° 06', and has an altitude of 10,964 feet. It is named after the Saskatchewan river.

**Saskatchewan river,** the longest river in the prairie provinces, flows across Alberta, Saskatchewan, and Manitoba. Its northern branch rises in the Rocky mountains in Alberta in the angle between the British Columbian boundary and the 52nd parallel of north latitude. It follows a north-east direction to Pointe aux Pins, winding among the mountain spurs near its source, then runs north north-east to its junction with Bighorn river, where it turns and flows eastward to Rocky Mountain House. From this point to Edmonton the general direction of the river is north-east; it continues in the same direction to the 54th parallel of latitude, which it skirts before turning south-east toward Battleford. Below Edmonton the North Saskatchewan is a quiet winding river with heavily wooded banks, always steep but never sheer, and varying in height from 200 to 300 feet. In the 200 miles above Battleford are about 20 stretches of fairly fast and somewhat broken water. Near the 107th meridian of west longitude, the North Saskatchewan turns abruptly north-east and runs in this direction until its junction with the South Saskatchewan at the Forks, near the 105th meridian of west longitude. For 200 miles between Battleford and Prince Albert the river abounds in shallows and bars. Above the Forks is Cole fall and a series of rapids, where the river narrows between ever-heightening banks. The South Saskatchewan also rises in the Rocky mountains in the south-west angle of the province of Alberta and flows in an easterly direction, past its junction with the Bow river, to Medicine Hat, where it turns abruptly and flows in a north-westerly direction to a point near the Alberta-Saskatchewan boundary; here it turns eastward. Near this boundary it is joined by the Red Deer river. Near the 107th meridian the river turns and proceeds in a north-westerly direction until, as a broad, sedate stream, it joins the North Saskatchewan. The united Saskatchewan then flows north-east to Cumberland lake, whence it flows south-east through Cedar lake into lake Winnipeg. Above Cumberland lake the main channel has been blocked by driftwood and silt, and the river deflected through innumerable marshes, swamps, and sloughs. The marshes and sloughs between Cumberland lake and lake Winnipeg are probably the finest region in North America for the shooting of geese and ducks. To the head of the Bow river the Saskatchewan is 1,205 miles in length, and drains an area of 158,800 square miles.

As far north as Prince Albert, the valley of the Saskatchewan is fitted to sustain a dense agricultural population, and the great Canadian wheat-growing industry has to a great extent developed in this area. The North Saskatchewan is navigable for barges from Rocky Mountain House to Edmonton, and between Edmonton and Carlton, a distance of about 500 miles, for small steamers, during a period of about two months. Between Carlton and lake Winnipeg the North Saskatchewan and the Saskatchewan are well suited for navigation, except for the rapids below Cole falls, the section above Cumberland lake, and about 20 miles between Cedar lake and lake Winnipeg.

The name of the river is derived from the Cree *Kisiskatchewan*, meaning "swift current." The Saskatchewan was discovered by La Vérendrye (q.v.) and his sons before 1741, and in 1748 was explored to the Forks by Noyelles (q.v.), with two of La Vérendrye's sons. The French established a number of trading posts on the river before 1763 in their effort to cut off the fur-trade of the Hudson's Bay Company. The Saskatchewan was later used by the North West Company, and after 1821 by the Hudson's Bay Company, as part of the route over which was conducted the fur-trade with the Mackenzie area. Until shortly before 1869 the Saskatchewan area was an important source of pemmican, one of the staple supports of the fur-trade. See Lewis R. Freeman, *The nearing north* (New York, 1928).

**Saskatchewan, University of.** See **University of Saskatchewan.**

**Saskatoon,** a city in Saskatchewan, is situated on the South Saskatchewan river, and is the geographical and commercial centre of northern Saskat-

chewan, as well as the educational capital of the province, being the seat of the University of Saskatchewan, (affiliated with which are Emmanuel College, St. Chad's College, and St. Andrew's College), of the provincial Normal School, Agricultural College and Experimental Farm, of the Dominion Forestry Station, and of the Provincial School for the Deaf and Dumb. It is the only large city between Winnipeg and Edmonton, being almost midway between the two. The portion of the city on the east side of the river was originally known as East Saskatoon, and the portion on the west side West Saskatoon; but as population increased, confusion resulted, and the name of East Saskatoon was changed to "Nutana", a word of Indian origin which is claimed by some to mean "first-born", as it was the first settlement. The name "Saskatoon" is derived from the Cree word *Mis-sask-quah-too-mina*, or *Mis-sask-a-too-mina*, sometimes contracted to "Sask-a-too-mina", a name given to a berry used in the making of buffalo pemmican, found in profusion in the vicinity. The site was selected, and named in 1882 by John N. Lake, acting for the Temperance Colonization Society of Toronto, which had purchased 100,000 acres of land for $200,000.

The townsite was surveyed in 1883, but the first railway did not arrive until 1890. In 1901 Saskatoon was incorporated as a village; in 1903 as a town; and in 1906, as a city. Five bridges cross the river within the city limits, two for vehicular and pedestrian traffic, and three serving the Canadian Pacific and Canadian National Railways. The modern city is a result of the union of the villages of West Saskatoon, Nutana, and Riversdale. Since 1906 the city's expansion has been very rapid, due largely to the fact that it is the distributing centre of a vast farming region of great fertility. It has an elevator with a capacity of 5,500,000 bushels, stock yards, an abattoir, cold

SASKATCHEWAN'S PROVINCIAL LEGISLATIVE BUILDINGS, SITUATED ON
THE SHORES OF WASCANA LAKE AT REGINA

A SUMMER EVENING ON WASCANA LAKE, REGINA, SASKATCHEWAN

storage plants, and a number of industrial concerns. There is also a civic aviation field, and aerodromes. Saskatoon has three collegiate institutes, a technical school, a normal school, two hospitals, a daily newspaper (*Star-Phoenix*), published both in the morning and the evening, a weekly newspaper for Ukrainians (*New Pathway*), and a number of weekly and monthly periodicals, such as the *Western Producer* (weekly) and the *Western Teacher* and the *Western Retailer* (monthly). Pop. (1931), 43,291.

**Saskeram lake,** in Manitoba, near the Saskatchewan boundary, lies between the 53rd and 54th parallels of north latitude. The name is a corruption of the Indian word for "service berry."

**Sassafras** (*Sassafras variifolium* (Salisb.) Ktze., *Lauraceae*), a small tree or shrub with yellowish to greenish-yellow twigs, and spicy aromatic bark. The ovate leaves are either entire or 3-lobed, the lobes being small and irregular in shape. The flowers are greenish-yellow, borne in naked clusters in the axils of the leaves and appearing with the leaves; there are 9 stamens in 3 rows. The fruit is a drupe on a reddish club-shaped stalk. This tree is typical of rich woods in southern and western Ontario, and is an overlap from a more southerly vegetation.

**Saugeen river,** a stream which rises in the highlands of western Ontario, and after flowing in a north-westerly direction for over 100 miles, empties into lake Huron at Southampton. It has many tributaries, and it is interrupted by numerous rapids. Saugeen is a Huron word signifying "river mouth."

**Sauger.** See **Pike-perch.**

**Sault-au-Récollet,** a former town in Laval county, Quebec, on the north shore of the island of Montreal, facing on the Back or Des Prairies river, 2½ miles from Bordeaux station on the Canadian Pacific Railway. It was originally an Indian mission founded by the

Sulpicians in 1696. Settlement began in 1730; the parish was established in 1834; and a village was incorporated in 1910. In 1914 the village was incorporated as a town; and in 1916 the town was annexed to Montreal. The name is derived from the fact that at the nearby falls on the Des Prairies river a Recollet father, Nicolas Viel, was drowned in 1625. See Rev. R. Desrochers, *Le Sault-au-Récollet* (Montreal, 1936).

**Saulteaux,** a division of the Chippewa (q.v.), so named from the fact that their meeting-place was the falls (Sault) of Sault Ste. Marie. For a description of them, see Peter Grant, "The Sauteaux Indians", in L. R. Mason, *Les bourgeois de la Compagnie du Nord-ouest, deuxième série* (Quebec, 1890). See also **Chippewa.**

**Sault Ste. Marie,** a city in the district of West Algoma, Ontario, is situated on the St. Mary's river, which connects lake Huron with lake Superior. It is on the Canadian Pacific and Algoma Central and Hudson Bay Railways; and has steamboat connection with all the Great lake ports. Before the white man came, it was a meeting-place of the Indian tribes, and was known as Pawiting, or Bawating, meaning "turbulent or bounding waters". Étienne Brûlé (q.v.) visited the spot in 1622, and Jean Nicolet (q.v.) in 1634. The first name assigned to the place by the French was Sault Gaston, in honour of a brother of Louis XIII. The name was changed to Sault Ste. Marie on the establishment of a permanent mission there in 1669. A French fort was built in 1751, and maintained until the British conquest of Canada, when it was taken over by a British garrison in 1762. In 1783 the North West Company established a post at Sault Ste. Marie. Owing to the difficulty of the portage at this point, the company began the construction of a lock for the transportation of canoes and boats from lake Huron to lake Superior. The lock was completed in 1799, but was destroyed during the War of 1812, and likewise the trading-post. After the War the post was rebuilt, and in 1821, when the Hudson's Bay Company absorbed the North West Company, it was handed over to them. In 1858 Algoma was organized as a judicial district, with headquarters at Sault Ste. Marie, which was incorporated as a town in 1887; and in this year the Canadian Pacific Railway entered the town, and the international bridge over the rapids was completed. In 1888 work was commenced on the construction of the ship canal, which was first opened for traffic in 1895. The town was incorporated as a city in 1912. It is a great industrial centre, having steel works, pulp-and-paper mills, car shops, etc. The country about it abounds in minerals, and the forests contain much valuable timber. It is named after the cataract in the river, the Sault Ste. Marie or falls of St. Mary. It has a collegiate institute, a technical school, two public libraries, ten public and five separate schools, and an evening newspaper (*Star*). Pop. (1931), 23,082. See E. H. Capp, *The story of Baw-a-ting, being the annals of Sault Ste. Marie* (Sault Ste. Marie, 1907), and R. Whitaker, *Sault Ste. Marie, Michigan and Ontario: A comparative study in urban geography* (Bulletin of the Geographical Society of Philadelphia, July, 1934).

**Sault Ste. Marie Canal.** See **Canals.**

**Saumarez, Sir Thomas** (1760-1845), president and administrator of the province of New Brunswick (1813-14), was born in the island of Guernsey in 1760. He became a subaltern in the British army in 1776, distinguished himself as a junior officer in the War of the American Revolution, and rose to the rank of general in 1838. In 1812 he was appointed commandant of the British troops in Halifax; and from August 17, 1813, to August 13, 1814, he was president and administrator of the government of New Brunswick.

He died in the island of Guernsey in 1845.

**Saunders, Sir Charles** (1713?-1775), sailor, was born in Somersetshire, England, about 1713, and entered the Royal Navy in 1727. In 1759 he was promoted to be vice-admiral of the blue, and appointed commander-in-chief of the fleet which carried the army of James Wolfe, (q.v.) to Quebec. To his efficiency and cordial co-operation, the fall of Quebec in 1759 was in no small measure due. He was created a knight of the Bath in 1761; and in 1770 he was promoted to the rank of admiral. From 1754 to his death he represented Heydon in Yorkshire in the House of Commons. He died in London on December 7, 1775; and he was buried in Westminster Abbey. See Edward Salmon, *Life of Admiral Sir Charles Saunders* (London, 1914).

**Saunders, Edward Manning** (1829-1916), clergyman and historian, was born in the Annapolis valley, Nova Scotia, on December 20, 1829, the son of David Saunders and Elizabeth Rhoades. He was educated at Acadia University (B.A., 1858; M.A., 1863; D.D., 1882) and at Newton Institute, Massachusetts. He was ordained a minister of the Baptist Church in 1858; and for many years he was the pastor of the First Baptist Church in Halifax. In his later years he was the pastor of the First Baptist Church in Ottawa. He died at Toronto on March 15, 1916. He was the author of several historical works, *The history of the Baptists of the Maritime provinces* (Halifax, 1902), *Three premiers of Nova Scotia* (Toronto, 1909), and *The life and letters of the Right Hon. Sir Charles Tupper* (2 vols., London, 1916).

**Saunders, John** (1754-1834), chief justice of New Brunswick (1822-34), was born in Virginia on June 1, 1754. He fought throughout the American Revolution on the loyalist side, as an officer in the Queen's Rangers, and in

1783 he went to England. Here he studied law at the Middle Temple, and in 1787 was called to the bar. In 1790 he was appointed an assistant judge of the Supreme Court of New Brunswick, and he took up his residence in Fredericton, New Brunswick, in 1791. In 1822 he was made chief justice of the Supreme Court; and he died at Fredericton on May 24, 1834. In 1790 he married Ariana Margaretta Jekkyl; and by her he had one son, the Hon. John Simcoe Saunders (q.v.), and two daughters. See J. W. Lawrence, *The judges of New Brunswick and their times* (St. John, New Brunswick, 1907).

**Saunders, John Simcoe** (1795-1878), president of the Legislative Council of New Brunswick (1866-78), was born at Fredericton in 1795, the only son of the Hon. John Saunders (q.v.). He was educated at Worcester College, Oxford (B.A., 1815), and was called to the bar of Nova Scotia in 1819, and to that of Lower Canada in 1820. In 1834 he was appointed advocate-general of New Brunswick, in 1840 surveyor-general, and in 1845 provincial secretary. He was made a member of the Legislative Council in 1833, and in 1866 he became its president. This position he occupied until his death at Fredericton on July 25, 1878. He married Elizabeth Sophia, daughter of the Rev. George Stone, rector of Stow Maries, Essex, England. He was the author of *The law of pleading and evidence in civil actions* (London, 1828). See J. W. Lawrence, *The judges of New Brunswick* (St. John, New Brunswick, 1907).

**Saunders, William** (1836-1914), agricultural scientist, was born in Devonshire, England, on June 16, 1836, and came to Canada with his parents in 1848. He became a manufacturing chemist at London, Upper Canada, and in 1868 he acquired a farm for the purpose of scientific experimentation. In 1886 he was appointed director of the newly-formed Experimental Farms

Branch of the Dominion Department of Agriculture; and he continued in charge of this branch until his retirement on pension in 1911. During this time he originated many promising varieties of fruit and grain; and, in particular, he inaugurated the researches which resulted in the discovery by his son, Sir Charles Edward Saunders, of the famous Marquis wheat, which is now the basis of the best wheat of the Canadian North West. He died at London, Ontario, on September 13, 1914. He married Sara Agnes, daughter of the Rev. J. H. Robinson; and by her he had several sons, one of whom, Sir Charles has been carrying on his work as cerealist at the Central Experimental Farm, Ottawa. In 1882 he was selected a charter member of the Royal Society of Canada, and in 1906 he was elected president of the Society. He was an LL.D. of Queen's University (1896) and of the University of Toronto (1904). He was the author of *Insects injurious to plants* (Philadelphia, 1883), and of a great number of scientific papers and reports.

**Sauteux.** See **Saulteaux.**

**Savary, Alfred William** (1831-1920), jurist and historian, was born in Plympton, Digby county, Nova Scotia, in 1831. He was educated at King's College, Windsor (B.A., 1854; M.A., 1857), and was called to the bar of Nova Scotia in 1861. He represented Digby in the Canadian House of Commons from 1867 to 1872; and from 1876 to 1907 he was the county court judge for Annapolis, Digby, and Yarmouth. He died at Annapolis Royal, Nova Scotia, in 1920. He was the joint author, with W. A. Calnek, of a *History of the county of Annapolis* (1897), and he published a *Supplement* to this (1913); he was the author also of *The Savery families of America* (Boston, 1887); and he edited *David Fanning's narrative* (1908). See T. C. Mellor, *Life of Judge Savary* (Annapolis Royal, Nova Scotia, 1922).

**Savigny, Mrs. Annie Gregg** (d. 1901), novelist, was the wife of Hugh P. Savigny, provincial land surveyor, of Toronto, Ontario, and died, a widow, at Toronto on July 10, 1901. She was the author of *A heart-song of to-day: A novel* (Toronto, 1886), *A romance of Toronto* (Toronto, 1888), *Lion, the mastiff* (Toronto, 1895), and *Three wedding rings* (Toronto, n.d.).

**Saw-bill.** See **Merganser.**

**Sawfish** are shark-like rays (q.v.), with greatly elongated snouts armed on the sides with many sharp spikes. The use of the "saw" is not known. Some believe it to be used to hack pieces of flesh from large fish and whales; others state that it is used to stir up the animals from the sea-floor. Sawfish occur chiefly in tropical and subtropical waters; they seldom stray into Canadian waters, but have been recorded on the Atlantic coast of Canada.

**Sawyer, Artemas Wyman** (1827-1907), president of Acadia University (1869-96), was born in Rutland county, Vermont, on March 4, 1827, and was educated at Dartmouth College (A.B., 1847). From 1855 to 1860 he was professor of classics at Acadia University, Nova Scotia; from 1869 to 1896 he was president; and in his later years he remained as professor of psychology and Christian evidences. He died at Wolfville, Nova Scotia, on August 5, 1907.

**Sawyer, William** (1820-1889), portrait-painter, was born at Montreal, Lower Canada, in 1820, of English parents. He entered a law office in Montreal, but finding law distasteful, began to study art. In 1851 he went to study in New York, and later in London, Paris, and Antwerp. On his return to Canada, he settled in Kingston, Ontario, and became a successful portrait-painter. Several of his pictures are to be found in public buildings at Kingston and Ottawa—notable among them being his portrait of Sir John Macdonald (q.v.) in the Kingston City Hall. He

died at Kingston, Ontario, on December 9, 1889.

**Sawyer beetles** often cause serious damage to skidways of logs left in the woods through the summer and to fire killed timber. The gray and the black sawyer are the two most common species. The presence of these insects is easily recognized by the cone-shaped heaps of borings on skidways and around the base of burned trees. In June, July, and August the beetles lay their eggs in niches which they cut in the bark. The larvæ usually complete their development in two years; they feed for several days on the surface of the wood just under the bark, after which they bore deeply into the logs. These beetles are normally abundant in nearly all regions of eastern Canada. Placing logs liable to attack in water deep enough to float them, covering the skidways with balsam brush or dusting them with lime sulphur are the usual methods of control.

**Sawyerville,** a village in Compton county, Quebec, on the Eaton river, and on the Maine Central Railway, 25 miles east of Sherbrooke. It was incorporated as a village in 1892; and it is named after an early settler, Josiah Sawyer. Pop. (1934), 700.

**Sayabec** (say'-bĕc), a village in Matapedia county, Quebec, on the Sayabec river, at the head of lake Matapedia, and on the Canadian National Railway, 48 miles from Rimouski. The name is a Micmac word signifying "obstructed river", in allusion doubtless to the beaver dams and log jams which made navigation of the Sayabec river impossible. It was created a municipality in 1895, and it is in a prosperous agricultural district. Lumbering is also a thriving industry; and the surrounding district abounds in game and fish. Pop. (1931), 3,060.

**Sayer, John** (1750?-1818), fur-trader, was born about 1750, and first appears in the fur-trade in 1780, when he was granted a licence to send one canoe to Michilimackinac. He engaged in the fur-trade in the Fond-du-Lac district; and as early as 1793 he was described by J. P. Perrault (q.v.) as "an agent of the [North West] Company" in this region. In 1799 he was "proprietor" in charge of the Fond du Lac department; but he retired from the fur-trade about 1806, and went to live at St. Annes, on the island of Montreal. In 1810 he was elected a member of the Beaver Club of Montreal, though he does not appear to have attended any of its meetings. Ross Cox (q.v.) met him at St. Annes in September, 1817; and he died here on October 2, 1818, aged 68 years. He was apparently married to a French-Canadian half-breed; for he had a half-breed son, named Guillaume Sayer, who was the leader of a half-breed rising on the Red river in 1844. John Charles Sayer, who was a clerk and interpreter in the service of the North West Company in 1815, and was concerned in the Selkirk troubles of that year, would appear to have been another son.

**Scadding, Henry** (1813-1901), clergyman and author, was born at Dunkeswell, Devonshire, England, on July 29, 1813, the son of John Scadding, at one time factor to Colonel John Graves Simcoe (q.v.). He came to join his parents in Canada in 1821, and was educated at Upper Canada College and St. John's College, Cambridge (B.A., 1837; M.A., 1840; D.D., 1852). In 1838 he was admitted to holy orders in the Church of England; and after teaching for several years in Upper Canada College, he became in 1847 rector of the church of the Holy Trinity in Toronto. He retired from active parochial work in 1875, and devoted himself to literary and scholastic pursuits. He published a large number of pamphlets on historical, literary, and religious subjects; but his chief work was *Toronto of old* (Toronto, 1873), an admirable essay in local history. Later he collaborated with J. C. Dent (q.v.) in a volume entitled

*Toronto, past and present* (Toronto, 1884), and with G. Mercer Adam (q.v.) in *Toronto, old and new* (Toronto, 1891). He died in Toronto on May 6, 1901. In 1841 he married Harriett Eugenia (d. 1843), daughter of John Spread Baldwin, Toronto. From 1870 to 1876 he was president of the Canadian Institute; and in 1885 he was awarded by the Canadian government the Confederation medal.

**Scallops.** These are marine shellfish or molluscs which are being exploited in Canadian fisheries, marketing at over $100,000 annually. There are six species found on the Atlantic coast, all of which are marine.

**Scandinavian immigration.** The Scandinavians (Icelandic, Norwegian, Swedish, and Danish) are among the best immigrants to Canada. They have settled in the four western provinces, of which Alberta has by far the greatest share. Here they are practically all farmers, and as prosperous and successful as the country possesses. In 1931 there were over 228,000 Scandinavians in Canada. They come from peoples who are accustomed to a vigorous climate; acquainted with agriculture, forestry, and fishing; and noted for their honesty, hospitality, patriotism, and love of freedom. As they come from countries with highly-developed educational systems, the standard of literacy among the Scandinavians is high. They are very ambitious. Since they are anxious to become Canadian citizens, they become quickly assimilated. Inter-marriage with Anglo-Saxons is common; and the Scandinavians rapidly acquire English, and become interested in the activities and in the life of the state. In addition, they are a sociable people and, whenever settled in large numbers, have their own social and political organization. Scandinavian newspapers are published in western Canada. The Scandinavians are a religious people, and practically all are Protestants; the Lutherans are much the strongest in

24

number, but the Mission Friends and the Baptist and United Churches also have their adherents.

In every western province the Icelanders, in particular, have exerted an influence out of all proportion to their numbers. They are a sober, industrious, and thrifty people. They have their representatives in the legislatures and in practically every public office. They are largely represented in the teaching profession, and have provided several professors in Canadian universities. They have some of the cleverest doctors and lawyers, and some of the shrewdest business men in the West. During the Great War, the Icelanders were well represented in the Canadian army. Most of the Swedes, Norwegians, and Danes in Canada have taken up homesteads and are prospering as farmers, although small colonies are found in most of the cities and in many towns and villages. The great proportion of these people in Alberta come from the northern American states, and have adapted themselves to Canadian institutions and Canadian ways. They have not confined themselves merely to the production of wheat, but are turning their attention also to dairying and to mixed farming. See J. T. M. Anderson, *The education of the New-Canadian* (New York, 1918); W. G. Smith, *A study in Canadian immigration* (Toronto, 1920); and James S. Woodsworth, *Strangers within our gates* (Toronto, 1909).

**Scarborough,** a village in York county, Ontario, on lake Ontario, and on the Canadian National Railway, 4 miles east of Toronto. It was named by Mrs. Simcoe, the wife of Colonel Simcoe (q.v.), in 1793, because of the resemblance of the shore line to the Scarborough cliffs in England. Settlement began soon after 1793, and the village is one of the oldest centres of population in western Ontario. It has a high school and a weekly newspaper (*York County Post*). Pop. (1934), 200. See D. Boyle, *The township of Scarborough, 1796-1896* (Toronto, 1896).

**Scatcherd, Henry** (1823-1876), politician, was born in Wyton, near London, Upper Canada, on November 10, 1823, the eldest son of John Scatcherd and Anne Farley. He was educated at the London grammar school; and he was called to the bar of Upper Canada in 1848. From 1861 to 1867 he represented West Middlesex in the Legislative Assembly of Canada, as a Reformer, and after 1867 he represented the riding of North Middlesex in the Canadian House of Commons until his death at Ottawa on April 15, 1876. In 1851 he married Isabella, daughter of Thomas Sprague; and by her he had two sons. See W. Horton, *Memoir of the late Thomas Scatcherd* (London, Ontario, 1878).

**Schanck, John** (1740-1823), admiral, was born in Scotland in 1740, and entered the British naval service in 1758. In 1777 he was placed in charge of the naval establishment on lake Champlain and the Great lakes with the rank of lieutenant; and he defeated the American flotilla on lake Champlain on October 11-13, 1777. He was promoted to the rank of captain in 1783, to that of rear-admiral in 1805, vice-admiral in 1810, and admiral in 1821. He retired on half-pay, however, in 1802; and he died in the summer of 1823. He married a sister of Sir William Grant (q.v.), attorney-general of Quebec in 1776-7.

**Scheelite.** See **Tungsten Minerals.**

**Schist,** thinly laminated metamorphic rocks which split quite readily along certain parallel planes. This cleavage is the result of pressure and movement in older rock which causes certain easily cleavable minerals to arrange themselves in parallel position. Some of the more important varieties are mica schist, chlorite schist, and hornblende schist.

**Scholefield, Ethelbert Olaf Stuart** (1875-1919), librarian and historian, was born at St. Wilfrid's, Ryde, Isle of Wight, in 1875, the son of the Rev. Stuart Clement Scholefield. He came to British Columbia in 1887, on the appointment of his father as rector of St. Paul's Church, Esquimalt; and he was educated at Victoria, British Columbia. In 1901 he was appointed librarian and archivist to the Legislative Assembly of British Columbia; and he held this post until his death at Victoria, British Columbia, on December 24, 1919. With F. W. Howay, he was joint author of *British Columbia* (4 vols., Vancouver, 1914), and he published a series of valuable *Memoirs* of the provincial archives of British Columbia.

**Schomberg,** a village in King township, York county, Ontario, on the Holland river, and on the Metropolitan Electric Railway, 35 miles north-west of Toronto. It was originally known as Brownsville; but was re-named after the Duke of Schomberg, who was killed at the battle of the Boyne in 1690. Pop. (1934), 300.

**School of Practical Science.** See **Science, Applied,** and **University of Toronto.**

**Schools.** See **Education.**

**Schreiber, Mrs. Charlotte Mount Brock,** *née* **Morrell** (1834-1922), artist, was born at Woodham Mortimer, Essex, England, in 1834, the daughter of the Rev. Robert Price Morrell. She studied art in London, and exhibited at the Royal Academy. She became the second wife of Leymouth George Schreiber of Toronto in 1875, and with him came to live in Canada, first at Deer Park, near Toronto, and later at Springfield-on-the-the-Credit. She became a charter member of the Royal Canadian Academy of Art in 1880, and was a constant exhibitor at Canadian exhibitions, especially of figure studies. In 1898 she returned to England, and she lived at Paignton, South Devon, until her death in 1922.

**Schreiber, Sir Collingwood** (1831-1918), civil engineer, was born in Essex, England, on December 14, 1831, the son of the Rev. Thomas Schreiber and Sarah, daughter of Admiral Bingham, R.N. He came to Canada in 1852, and engaged in railway engineering. In 1873 he became chief engineer of the government railways, and in 1880 he succeeded Sir Sandford Fleming (q.v.) as chief engineer of the Canadian Pacific Railway. These positions he held until 1892, when he was appointed chief engineer of the Department of Railways and Canals. In 1905 he became general consulting engineer to the Dominion government; and he died at Ottawa on March 22, 1918. He was twice married, (1) to Caroline (d. 1892), daughter of Lieut.-Col. A. H. MacLean, 41st Regiment; and (2) in 1898 to Julia Maude, youngest daughter of Hon. Mr. Justice Gwynne, of the Supreme Court of Canada. He was created a C.M.G. in 1893, and a K.C.M.G. in 1916.

**Schreiber,** a village in the district of Thunder Bay, Ontario, is situated on the north shore of lake Superior, 128 miles east of Port Arthur and on the main line of the Canadian Pacific Railway. The municipality was incorporated on August 10, 1901. There are no industries, it being merely a railway terminal point. The surrounding district is very hilly and rocky, and there is but little farming. It was named after Sir Collingwood Schreiber (q.v.), who in 1880 succeeded Sir Sandford Fleming (q.v.) as chief engineer of the Canadian Pacific Railway. Pop. (1934), 1,000.

**Schultz, Sir John Christian** (1840-1896), lieutenant-governor of Manitoba (1888-95), was born at Amherstburg, Upper Canada, on January 1, 1840, the son of William Schultz and Eliza Riley. He was educated at Oberlin College, Ohio, at Queen's University, Kingston, and at Victoria University, Cobourg (M.D., 1860). He practised medicine at Fort Garry (Winnipeg). During the North West rebellion of 1869-70 he was one of the leaders of the loyalist party, was seized and imprisoned by Louis

25

Riel (q.v.), and was sentenced to death, but escaped. From 1871 to 1882 he represented Lisgar in the Canadian House of Commons, as a Liberal-Conservative. In 1882 he was called to the Senate of Canada; and in 1888 he became lieutenant-governor of Manitoba. His term of office came to an end in 1895; and he died on May 13, 1896. In 1894 he was elected a fellow of the Royal Society of Canada; and in 1895 he was created a K.C.M.G. He married, in 1868, at Winnipeg, Agnes Campbell Farquharson, of Georgetown, British Guiana. See J. C. Hopkins, *J. C. Schultz* (Week, October, 1894); bibliography in *Proc. Roy. Soc. Can.*, 1894.

**Schultz lake,** at the northern end of the Dubawnt river, between the 64th and 65th parallels of north latitude, North West Territories. It was named by J. B. Tyrrell after Sir John C. Schultz (q.v.), lieutenant-governor of Manitoba (1888-95). It has an area of 110 square miles.

**Schumacher,** a town in the Cochrane district of Ontario, on the Timmins branch of the Temiskaming and Northern Ontario Railway, 2 miles east of Timmins. It serves the Hollinger and McIntyre mining areas. Pop. (1934), 2,000.

**Science, Applied.** The teaching of engineering or applied science began much later in Canada than that of arts, medicine, law, or theology. The first course in engineering given in a Canadian university would appear to be that offered in McGill College, under the influence of Sir William Dawson (q.v.), in 1855. In 1856 general courses in applied science were established in McGill, in connection with the faculty of Arts; and though these were temporarily discontinued in 1870, owing to lack of funds, they were revived in 1878, and the faculty of applied science in McGill University was established. This faculty has achieved since that time a world-wide reputation, and it

has given to Canada many of her most distinguished engineers. It was not until after Confederation that the first steps were taken in Ontario to establish "a College of Technology." In 1871 the Sandfield-Macdonald government, a few months before its defeat, made a grant for this purpose; but for several years instruction was confined to evening classes for working-men, and it was not until 1878 that the School of Practical Science in Toronto opened its doors to students. This school was at first separate and distinct from the University of Toronto, though some of the professors of the University gave instruction in it; but in 1887 it was affiliated to the University, and in 1900 it became the faculty of applied science in the University. "S.P.S." (as the school was familiarly known, and is still known) has, like the faculty of applied science in McGill, trained many of Canada's most famous engineers. Military engineering, including many phases of applied science, has, of course, been taught in the Royal Military College at Kingston, Ontario, since its inception in 1875. The School of Mining in Queen's University was established in 1893. To-day applied science is taught in most, though not all, Canadian universities.

The introduction of applied science as a subject of instruction in secondary schools in Canada dates only from the beginning of the twentieth century. See **Education, Technical.**

**Scobie, Hugh** (1811-1853), journalist, was born at Fort George, Invernessshire, Scotland, on April 29, 1811. He was educated at the Tain Academy; and in 1832 he emigrated to Canada. In 1838 he founded the *British Colonist* newspaper at Toronto; and in 1850 he began the publication of the *Canadian Almanac*. He died at Toronto on December 4, 1853.

**Scollard, David Joseph** (1862-1934), Roman Catholic bishop, was born at Ennismore, Ontario, on November 4,

1862. He was educated at St. Michael's College, Toronto, and at Laval University; and was ordained a priest of the Roman Catholic Church in 1890. He was consecrated bishop of Sault Ste. Marie in 1905, and he administered this diocese until his death at North Bay, Ontario, on September 7, 1934.

**Scotch Village,** a settlement in Hants county, Nova Scotia, on the Kennetcook river, 12 miles from Windsor. Pop. (1934), 670.

**Scoter,** a name restricted in Canada to members of the group of sea ducks which are predominately black in colour and are further characterized by their swollen and frequently vividly coloured bills. The word scoter, with specific prefixes, is used to designate three forms occurring in Canada. These are the white-winged scoter (*Melanitta deglandi*), the surf scoter (*Melanitta perspicillata*), and the American scoter (*Oidemia americana*). All three species breed well to the north in Canada. The white-winged scoter is more frequently seen on inland lakes than the other two.

**Scotia Junction,** a village in the Parry Sound district, Ontario, at the junction of the Canadian National Railway lines between Toronto and North Bay and between Renfrew and Parry Sound. The nearest community centre of importance is Burks Falls, 11 miles to the north. Pop. (1934), 100.

**Scotland,** a village in Brant county, Ontario, on Malcolm creek, and on the Toronto, Hamilton, and Buffalo Railway, 6 miles from Burford. Pop. (1934), 500.

**Scotstown,** a town in Compton county, Quebec, on the Canadian Pacific Railway, 44 miles east of Sherbrooke, and 25 miles west of Megantic. It was incorporated as a town in 1892, and was named after John Scott, manager of the Glasgow Canadian Land and Fur Company, which founded the settlement. Pop. (1931), 1,189.

**Scott, Ephraim** (1845-1931), clergyman and editor, was born in Hants county, Nova Scotia, on January 29, 1845, and was educated at Dalhousie University (B.A., 1870; M.A., 1875) and at the Presbyterian College, Halifax (D.D., 1905), as well as at the Free Church College, Edinburgh. He was ordained a minister of the Presbyterian Church in 1875; and until 1891 he was engaged in pastoral work in Nova Scotia. He then became editor of *The Presbyterian Record*, published by the Presbyterian Church in Canada; and he conducted this periodical for 30 years. In 1921 he was elected moderator of the Presbyterian Church in Canada. He died at Montreal on August 7, 1931.

**Scott, Henri Arthur** (1858-1931), priest and historian, was born at St. Nicholas, Quebec, on September 3, 1858, the son of Maurice Scott and Lucie Guay. He was educated at Laval University (B.A., 1878; D.D., 1888; Litt.D., 1902), and he was ordained a priest of the Roman Catholic Church in 1882. He was parish priest at Ste. Foye, near Quebec, from 1893 to his death in 1931. He was the author of *Notre Dame de Sainte Foy* (Quebec, 1902), *Grands anniversaires: Souvenirs, historiques et pensées utiles* (Quebec, 1919), *Bishop Laval* (Toronto, 1926), and *Nos anciens historiographes et autres études d'histoire canadienne* (Lévis, 1930).

**Scott, Sir Richard William** (1825-1913), secretary of state for Canada (1874-8 and 1896-1908), was born at Prescott, Upper Canada, on February 24, 1825, the son of W. J. Scott, M.D., and Sarah Ann McDonell. He was privately educated, was called to the bar of Upper Canada in 1848 (Q.C., 1867), and practised law in Bytown (Ottawa). He represented Ottawa in the Legislative Assembly of Canada from 1857 to 1863, and in the Legislative Assembly of Ontario from 1867 to 1873. In 1871 he was elected speaker of the latter house; but on the fall of the Sandfield Macdonald government, he resigned this position and accepted the office of commissioner of crown lands in the Blake and Mowat administrations (1871-3). In 1874 he was called to the Senate of Canada, and was appointed secretary of state in the Mackenzie administration. He retired from office with his colleagues in 1878, but in 1896 he resumed the secretaryship of state in the Laurier government, and retained it until his resignation in 1908. From 1902 to 1908 he was also government leader in the Senate. He was the father of the Separate School Act of 1863, and of the Canada Temperance Act, sometimes called the "Scott Act", of 1878. He died at Ottawa on April 23, 1913. In 1853 he married Mary (d. 1905), daughter of John Heron, of Dublin, Ireland. He was made an LL.D., of Ottawa University in 1889; and in 1909 he was created a knight bachelor.

**Scott, Thomas** (1746-1824), chief justice of Upper Canada (1806-16), was born in Scotland in 1746, the son of the Rev. Thomas Scott, a clergyman of the Church of Scotland. He was educated for the ministry of the Church of Scotland, and became a "probationer"; but on the advice of Sir John Riddell, Bart., of Roxburghshire, in whose family he had been employed as tutor, he went to London to study law at Lincoln's Inn. He was called to the English bar in 1793; and in 1800 he received the appointment of attorney-general of Upper Canada. He arrived in York (Toronto) in 1801, and performed the duties of attorney-general until 1806. He was then appointed chief justice of the province, with a seat in the Executive and Legislative Councils; and he retained this position until 1816. He died at York (Toronto), on July 29, 1824. He does not appear to have been married. See W. R. Riddell, *Thomas Scott* (Ont. Hist. Soc. Papers and Records, 1923); and D. B. Read, *Lives of the judges of Upper Canada* (Toronto, 1888).

**Scott, Thomas** (d. 1870), loyalist, was an Orangeman from Ontario who went west before 1869, and was engaged for a time as a labourer under the Canadian government road superintendent. He was taken prisoner by the provisional government of Louis Riel (q.v.) on February 17, 1870, and after being tried by a sort of court martial, was shot at Fort Garry on March 4, 1870, at the early age of 24. His execution roused profound feeling in Ontario, and was one of the chief causes of the Wolseley expedition to the Red river. See A. H. de Trémaudan (ed.), *The execution of Thomas Scott* (Can. hist. rev., 1925).

**Scott, William** (1812?-1891), clergyman and author, was born about 1812, and in 1839 was ordained a minister of the Wesleyan Methodist Conference in Upper Canada. He died at Ottawa on October 5, 1891. He was the author of *The teetotaller's handbook* (Toronto, 1860) and *Letters on superior education in its relation to the progress and permanence of Wesleyan Methodism* (Toronto, 1860).

**Scott Act.** See **Prohibition.**

**Scott, cape,** the extreme north-west point of Vancouver island, British Columbia. It was named in 1786 by Captains Lowrie and Guise after David Scott, a merchant of Bombay, who had assisted in fitting out their expedition.

**Scottish Immigration.** There were Scots who found their way to Canada during the French régime, as a result probably of the "auld alliance" between Scotland and France. Abraham Martin (q.v.), after whom the Plains of Abraham were named, was a native of Edinburgh; the Chevalier de Ramezay (q.v.) was a scion of the Scottish house of Ramsay; and the Chevalier de Johnstone (q.v.), who was an aide-de-camp of Montcalm (q.v.), was a Scottish Jacobite. Strangely enough, one of the finest regiments in Wolfe's army, Fraser's Highlanders, was also composed largely of Scottish Jacobites; and of this regiment several officers and about 300 men settled in Canada after the conquest. This was the spearhead of Scottish immigration into Canada; and because of the clannishness of the Scots it was followed by repeated subsequent waves of Scottish immigration. The *Hector* brought in 1773 the first Scottish immigrants into Nova Scotia; the North West Company, which acquired a vast commercial empire in the fur-bearing regions of the North West, was predominantly an association of Scots; the first real settlement in the North West, that established by Lord Selkirk (q.v.) in 1811 on the Red river, was almost wholly composed of Scottish Highlanders; and in the great emigration of the years from 1830 to 1850, Scottish immigrants were no small proportion of the total. This influx of Scotsmen into Canada was the result of political and economic conditions in Scotland. The suppression of the rebellion of 1845 in Scotland and the subsequent turning of Highland estates into sheep-runs turned the thoughts of the Scottish people to the New World. Some of these went to the American colonies that later became the United States; but the Scottish colonists in New York and the Carolinas proved, in the War of the American Revolution, to be among the most devoted adherents of the British crown, and after the war a considerable part of the Loyalist immigration into Canada was of Scottish origin. Those Scots who settled after 1783 in Glengarry, in what was later the province of Upper Canada, were afterwards joined by clansmen who came direct from Scotland; and, though the total immigration of Scots into Canada never perhaps exceeded in numbers the immigration of Englishmen or Irishmen, their influence has nevertheless been profound. John Morley, when he visited Canada in 1906, was so impressed by the dominance of Scottish influence in Canada that he described Canada as "a backyard of Scotland." See W. J. Rattray, *The Scot in British North America* (4 vols., Toronto, 1880-84); G. Bryce and W. W. Campbell, *The Scot in Canada* (2 vols., 1911); and J. M. Gibbon, *Scots in Canada* (London, 1911).

**Scott, mount,** is on the boundary between Alberta and British Columbia. It is in lat. 52° 27', long. 118° 03', and has an altitude of 10,826 feet. The name was suggested by G. E. Howard in 1914, after Captain Scott, commander of the British Antarctic expedition, who died in 1913.

**Scouring Rush.** See **Horsetail.**

**Scriven, Joseph Medlicott** (1819-1886), hymn-writer, was born at Seapatrick (Bambridge), county Down, Ireland, on September 10, 1819, the son of Capt. James Scriven and Jane Medlicott. He was educated at Trinity College, Dublin (B.A., 1842) and at the Addiscombe Military College. In 1844 he emigrated to Canada. Here he taught school at Woodstock and Brantford, Upper Canada, and served as tutor in the family of Commander Pengelley, a retired naval officer, near Bewdley, on Rice lake. He was a member of the Plymouth Brethren communion, and wrote hymns, one of which, entitled *What a friend we have in Jesus*, has become world-famous. He died near Bewdley, Ontario, on August 10, 1886, and was buried in the Pengelley burial-ground. A collection of his verses was published under the title *Hymns and other verses* (Peterborough, Ontario, 1869).

**Scriver, Julius** (1826-1907), legislator, was born in Hemmingford, Lower Canada, on February 5, 1826, of United Loyalist stock. He was educated at the University of Vermont; and he became a prosperous merchant in his native town. He represented the county of Huntingdon in the Canadian House of Commons from 1869 to 1900, and he was on his retirement from politics "the father of the House." He died at Quebec on September 5, 1907.

**Scugog lake** and **river.** The lake, a very pretty sheet of water, between Ontario, Durham, and Victoria counties, in Ontario, is drained by the river which flows in a north-easterly direction into Sturgeon lake. The name is an Indian word meaning "submerged land." The lake in its present form owes its existence to a family named Purdy, who moved to Lindsay in 1837 and built a dam across the Scugog river; this raised the height of water in the lake by 4 feet. The lake is indented with numerous bays; and in the centre of the lake is a considerable island, on which is located the village of Scugog. The lake is 25 miles long and 5 miles broad. See Rev. F. G. Weir, *Scugog and its environs* (Port Perry, Ontario, 1927).

**Sculpin.** The sculpins are a large family of fishes characteristic of the northern seas; a few species are found also in the fresh waters of northern North America, Asia, and Europe. They range is size from a weight of fifteen pounds in the case of the great sculpin (*Scorpaenichthys marmoratus*) of the Pacific, to tiny forms about an inch in length. Nearly twenty species are found off the Pacific coast of Canada, but only half a dozen off the Atlantic coast. Freshwater species are in general small and few in number. Most of the species live on the bottom in shallow water, but a few frequent considerable depths. They are characterized by their very large wing-like pectoral fins. They are of no value as food.

**Sculpture.** See **Art.**

**Sea-bass,** a large family of spiny-finned fishes most prevalent in warm seas. A few kinds of some value as food occur in Canadian waters. The white perch (*Morone americana*) is a small species found along the coast of the Maritime provinces of Canada, often landlocked in fresh water. The striped bass (*Roccus lineatus*) is a large and important food fish of the Atlantic coast, but is not common in Canadian waters;

introduced artificially into Pacific coast waters, it is, however, now common in California. The white bass (*Lepibema chrysops*) is quite similar to the striped bass. It occurs in the Great lakes, where it is a commercial species of minor importance.

**Sea Cucumbers** are sausage-shaped echinoderms which, unlike starfish and sea urchins, to which they are related, have a very flexible body and swim about in a horizontal position with an undulating motion. There are nineteen species recorded from the Pacific coast of Canada and fifteen from the Atlantic.

**Seaforth,** a town in Huron county, Ontario, on the Canadian National Railway, 21 miles south-east of Goderich. The town-site was laid out about 1850, and the town was named after Seaforth in Scotland. It was incorporated as a village in 1868, and as a town in 1874. Its chief industries are a creamery, a tannery, a furniture factory, an agricultural implement works, a shoe factory, and saw, flax, and flour mills. It has a collegiate institute, a public library, and two weekly newspapers (*Huron Expositor* and *News*). Pop. (1931), 1,686.

**Seagram, Joseph Emm** (1841-1919), distiller, horseman, and politician, was born in Galt, Ontario, in 1841, the son of Octavius Augustus Seagram and Amelia Styles. He was educated at the grammar school of Dr. Tassie (q.v.) in Galt; and in 1870 entered the employ of a firm of millers and distillers in Waterloo, Ontario, of which he became sole proprietor in 1883. He was a devotee of the turf; in 1906 he became president of the Ontario Jockey Club; and he had a stable which on numerous occasions won the King's Plate in Ontario. From 1896 to 1908 he represented Waterloo in the Canadian House of Commons. He died at Waterloo on August 18, 1919. In 1869 he married Stephanie Erb (d. 1909); and by her he had several children.

**Seal.** The members of two families of the *Pinnipedia*, a group of flesh-eating mammals highly modified for aquatic life, are commonly referred to as "seals". These families are the *Otariidae* and the *Phocidae*. The seals of the family *Phocidae*, the hair seals or earless seals, have no external ears, and have the hind feet united to the tail. The harbour seals (genus *Phoca*) are the common small seals of the Atlantic and Pacific coasts, and they also occur in the Arctic ocean. The harp or Greenland seal (genus *Phoca*) found along the Atlantic coast and north into the Arctic is much hunted for its oil, and forms the greater part of the catch of the Atlantic seal-hunters. The ringed seal (genus *Phoca*) is a small seal found in the Arctic and the north Atlantic. This is an important food animal of the Eskimo. The bearded seal (genus *Erignathus*), found in the Arctic seas, is also an important source of food for the Eskimo. The gray seal (genus *Halichoerus*) ranges along the Atlantic coast and north into the Arctic. The hooded seal (genus *Cystophora*) occurs along the Atlantic coast, and is also hunted by the seal hunters for its oil.

The family *Otariidae* have external ears and the hind feet are free from the tail, so that these seals are able to move about readily on land. Included in this group are the sea-lions and the fur seals. The steller sea-lion (genus *Eumetopias*) is the common large seal of the Pacific coast. This animal has been slaughtered in some areas on the complaint of commercial fishermen that it destroys great numbers of salmon and other fish. There is doubt as to the truth of these charges, and in any event wholesale slaughter of any animal usually brings other evils in its train. In no case should mass killings be permitted until careful studies have proved that an animal is inimical to mankind, and that no great harm is likely to follow its destruction.

The Alaska fur seals (genus *Callorhinus*) gather in great herds on the Pribilof islands during the breeding season, and then swing far south in a great circular migration which brings some of these animals into the coastal waters of British Columbia. The seal skin of the fur-trade is obtained by plucking out the long coarse outer hairs and leaving the fine soft under-fur, which is then dyed a rich brown. This fur is not so popular as it once was, and so the fur seal, once threatened with extermination, may now escape that fate owing to the lessened demand for its pelt.

Seals feed mainly on squids, crustaceans, and fish. Their adaptation to aquatic life may be seen from their ability to dive to a depth of two hundred feet, remain submerged for as long as twenty minutes, and swim for some distance at a speed of twenty miles an hour.

**Sea-lion.** See **Seal.**

**Seal lakes** are two large lakes in the New Quebec territory, Quebec. The Upper Seal lake, which has an area of 260 square miles, discharges through the Little Whale river into Hudson bay; and the Lower Seal lake, which has an area of 130 square miles, discharges into Hudson through the Nastapoka river. The lakes are named after the seals caught in them.

**Sea Otter.** The sea otter (*Enhydra lutris*) formerly frequented the bays and islands along the Pacific coast of Canada, but now, owing to incessant pursuit, it seldom comes to land, living far offshore on the vast floating beds of kelp. Fish, crustaceans, sea urchins, and other marine creatures living among these beds provide the food of this rare creature. This animal, once so abundant along the Pacific coast of North America, is now almost extinct. When the explorer Bering (q.v.) found these otters in abundance off the coast of Alaska in 1741, the slaughter began. The great beauty of the fur and consequent value attracted hunters in much the same fashion as the beaver of the mainland did; and the sea otter has suffered the same fate. Lack of agreement between the nations affected allowed the slaughter to continue, till in 1896 the hunting of sea otters began to be unprofitable. This was almost the end. In 1911 an international treaty was arranged, restricting the killing of otter and providing heavy penalties, but the harm has been done. The remedy came too late, and it is unlikely that the sea otter will ever become numerous again. The price of sea-otter skins, perhaps the finest of all furs, has risen steadily throughout the years till now a good pelt commands between $2,000 and $3,000. It was the sea otter's death warrant to be so valuable.

**Seargeant, Lewis James** (1825?-1905), general manager of the Grand Trunk Railway (1890-96), was born in England about 1825. He became connected with the South Wales Railway; and in 1874 he came to Canada as traffic manager of the Grand Trunk Railway. In 1890 he was appointed general manager of this railway; but in 1896 he retired, and was appointed a director. He died at London, England, on November 28, 1905.

**Sea Rocket** (*Cakile edentula* (Bigel.) Hook, *Cruciferae*), a fleshy annual plant common along the Atlantic coast and along the shores of the Great lakes. The leaves are bluntly ovate, fleshy waxy, and toothed. The flowers are purplish, the typical cruciform of this family. The pods are fleshy and 2-jointed.

**Seath, John** (1844-1919), educationist, was born at Auchtermuchty, Fifeshire, Scotland, on January 6, 1844, the son of John Seath and Isabel Herkless. He was educated at Glasgow University and at Queen's University, Belfast, Ireland (B.A., 1861). In 1862 he came to Canada, and became a school-teacher. He taught successively at Brampton, Oshawa, Dundas, and St. Catharines,

Ontario. In 1884 he was appointed an inspector of high schools in Ontario; and in 1906 he was appointed superintendent of education for Ontario. This post he occupied until his death, at Toronto, on March 17, 1919. In 1873 he married Caroline Louisa McKenzie, of Dundas, Ontario; and by her he had one son. He was an LL.D. of Queen's University, Kingston (1902) and of the University of Toronto (1905); and he was the author of a number of text-books and other educational publications. See J. Squair, *John Seath and the school system of Ontario* (Toronto, 1920).

**Seaton, Sir John Colborne, first Baron.** See **Colborne, Sir John, first Baron Seaton.**

**Sea Urchins,** a group of Echinoderms represented on the west coast of Canada by six species and on the Atlantic coast by three species. Two of the species are common to both coasts and the Arctic seas.

**Sebago salmon,** land-locked Atlantic salmon found in some lakes in New Brunswick and Maine. See **Ouananiche.**

**Sechelt,** a village and summer resort in the New Westminster district of British Columbia, on the north shore of Georgia strait, 30 miles north-west of Vancouver. There is an Indian village in the vicinity; and the village is named after the Salish sub-tribe to which the Indians belong. Pop. (1930), 450.

**Second Chambers.** Under the old colonial constitution, all the provinces of British North America had originally second chambers of the legislature, known as Legislative Councils. The members of these Legislative Councils were appointed by the Crown, generally on the recommendation of the local executive government. When Upper and Lower Canada were united in 1841, this feature of the constitution was continued; but in 1856 an Act was passed amending the constitution of the Legislative Assembly of Canada so that, while the existing members continued to sit during their lifetime, the elective principle was to be gradually introduced. This experiment, however, did not prove wholly successful; and when the Dominion of Canada came into existence in 1867, the elective principle was discarded. The Senate of Canada, composed of members appointed by the Crown, became an important feature of the government of Canada; and though there have been repeated proposals for its amendment or abolition, it has continued to the present unaltered. In the provinces, however, the fate of second chambers has been different. Ontario began its existence in 1867 with only a single chamber; and since then all the other provinces of Canada have followed its example, except Quebec. British Columbia abolished its upper house when it entered Confederation in 1871; Manitoba, in 1876; New Brunswick, in 1892; Prince Edward Island, in 1893; and Nova Scotia, in 1928. When Alberta and Saskatchewan were created provinces in 1905, they, like Ontario, became unicameral. See F. X. A. Trudel, *Nos chambres hautes* (Montreal, 1880), and Sir J. A. R. Marriott, *Second chambers* (Oxford, 1927). See also **Government, Legislative Council**, and **Senate.**

**Secord, Mrs. Laura,** *née* **Ingersoll** (1775-1868), heroine, was born in Massachusetts in 1775, the daughter of Thomas Ingersoll and Sarah, daughter of Gen. John Whiting. After the American Revolution she came with her parents to Upper Canada, and here she married Sergeant James Secord, of the First Lincoln Militia. In the summer of 1813, while American troops were billeted in her house at Queenston, she came into possession of knowledge of American plans for a surprise attack on Beaver Dams; and she made her way through the American lines, and warned Lieut. James Fitzgibbon (q.v.), in command at Beaver Dams, of the projected attack. She lived for many years after-

wards; and died at Chippawa, Ontario, on October 17, 1868. See S. A. Curzon, *The story of Laura Secord* (pamphlet, Toronto, 1891); Mrs. E. J. Thompson, *Laura Secord* (Niagara hist. soc., no. 25, 1913); and W. S. Wallace, *The story of Laura Secord* (Toronto, 1932).

**Secretan, James Henry Edward** (1854-1926), civil engineer and author, was born in 1854, and for many years was on the surveying staff of the Canadian Pacific Railway. In his later years he was a civil servant at Ottawa; and he died at Ottawa, suddenly, on December 22, 1926. He was the author of *To the Klondyke and back* (London, 1898), *Out west* (Ottawa, 1910), and *Canada's great highway: From the first stake to the last spike* (Toronto, 1924).

**Sedgwick, Robert** (1613?-1656), soldier, was born in Bedfordshire, England, about 1613, and emigrated to New England in 1636. He took a foremost part in organizing the militia of Massachusetts, and in 1652 was elected major-general of the colony. In 1653 he went to England, and was commissioned by Oliver Cromwell to command an expedition against the Dutch of Manhattan island; but before he was able to launch his attack, peace was signed with the Netherlands, and he therefore turned his expedition against the French in Acadia. In 1654 he captured the French forts at Port Royal and at the mouth of the St. John river. He was then sent by Cromwell on an expedition against the Spanish West Indies; and he died in Jamaica on May 24, 1656.

**Sedgewick,** a village in Alberta, on the Canadian Pacific Railway, 100 miles south-east of Edmonton. It was named in 1906 after the Hon. Robert Sedgewick, a judge of the Supreme Court of Canada. It has a newspaper (*Community Press*). Pop. (1931), 338.

**Seechelt.** See **Sechelt.**

**Seigniorial Tenure.** The form of land tenure introduced into Canada during the French régime was that which existed at that time in France, and was an outgrowth of the feudalism of the Middle Ages. It was a system whereby the weak man placed himself under the protection of the strong man, and rendered certain services in return for the protection he received. In France this system had given rise to grave abuses, since the seignior had already, when Canada began to be settled, laid greater stress on his privileges than on his obligations; and the seigniorial system in France was destined to become one of the chief causes of the French revolution. But in Canada the seigniorial system, because of the primitive conditions in the New World, had a new lease of life; and it proved a not ineffective system of land tenure and settlement.

The beginnings of the system date back in Canada to the commission granted to La Roche (q.v.) in 1598, which authorized him to make grants of land *en seigneurie*. At first, few grants were made. Until the organization of the Company of New France in 1627, only three seigniories were granted. Under the Company of New France (1627-63), about sixty grants were made. Then, under the system of royal government, a large number of seigniories were granted; and New France became organized, from the standpoint of land tenure, wholly on a seigniorial basis.

Various tenures characterized the system. There were grants of land *en franc aleu noble* and *en franc aleu roturier*, the former carrying with it a patent of nobility, and the latter resembling the English freehold. There was the tenure *en franche aumône*, corresponding to the English tenure of frankalmoign, under which religious foundations held their land. The most common tenures, however, were *en fief* or *en seigneurie, en arrière-fief*, and *en censive* or *en roture*. The tenure *en fief* or *en seigneurie* was that by which the seignior held directly of the crown. Under it, he was obliged

to perform military service and to pay a relief or *quint* to the crown when the seigniory changed hands, except by direct succession—the *quint* being one-fifth of the mutation price of the seigniory, though part of this was always remitted. After 1711, the seignior was also compelled to sub-infeudate his seigniory—an obligation peculiar to Canada, which did much to people the seigniories of New France. Grants *en arrière-fief* were few in Canada; and most of the lands granted by the seigniors were *en censive* or *en roturier*. This was the tenure by which the *censitaire* or *habitant* held his land. The obligations incumbent on the *censitaire* were the payment of *cens et rentes*, a rent payable either in money or in kind, or in both (according to the terms of the grant), the *corvée* or obligation to work for the seignior on certain specified days (usually, in New France, three days in the year), and the payment of *lods et ventes*, or a twelfth of the mutation price, when the holding changed hands, except by direct descent. The seignior had also what were known as *droits de banalité*—that is, the right of compelling the censitaire to make use of the seigniorial grist-mill or the seigniorial bake-oven. In actual practice, in Canada, this resulted in the seignior being compelled to provide his *habitants* with a seigniorial mill at a loss to himself; and only one case is recorded of the *habitants* being compelled to use the seigniorial bake-oven.

The truth is that in Canada the seigniorial system took on something of the primitive vigour which it enjoyed in the Middle Ages, when it grew up. The seigniorial mill was a godsend to the *habitants*, who would without it have had no means of grinding their grain; and it often served as a centre of defence against the Iroquois. The seigniorial system, indeed, gave New France a defensive strength out of all proportion to its population; and it gave rise to few of the abuses which made it unpopular in Old France. After the British conquest, however, when the English law of free and common socage came into effect in those districts which had not been granted under seigniorial tenure, the system became gradually an anachronism. The *quint* and the *lods et ventes* became an unreasonable burden, as did the *corvée;* and the defensive strength of the seigniorial system lost its value. After many years of agitation, the system was abolished by the Canadian legislature in 1854, under an arrangement whereby the seigniors were to be compensated for the loss of their seigniorial rights. In many cases, full advantage was not taken of the provisions of this Act, with the result that the shell of the seigniorial system still exists in the province of Quebec, and there are seigniories where the *habitants* still pay *rentes constitués* to the seignior.

The best account of the seigniorial system in Canada is still W. B. Munro's *The seigniorial system in Canada* (New York), with his *Documents relating to the seigniorial system in Canada* (Toronto, The Champlain Society, 1908). Reference may be made also to W. B. Munro, *The seigneurs of old Canada* (Toronto, 1915), T. Guérin, *Feudal Canada* (Montreal, 1926), Dorothy A. Heneker, *The seigniorial régime in Canada* (Quebec, 1927), and G. E. Marquis, *Le régime seigneuriale* (Quebec, 1931). Excellent accounts of the history of individual seigniories are to be found in J. E. Roy, *Histoire de la seigneurie de Lauzon* (6 vols., Montreal, 1897-1907), and G. M. Wrong, *A Canadian manor and its seigneurs* (Toronto, 1908; new ed., 1926).

**Seismology,** the branch of science which treats of earthquakes, has made considerable progress in Canada. So far as the historical period is concerned, Canada has been singularly free from earthquakes; but it has not been entirely free. What appears to have been a serious earthquake occurred in the St. Lawrence valley in 1663. A slighter quake was felt in this region in 1870. In 1899 a great earthquake shook Alaska, and was no doubt felt in the adjacent Canadian territory. Another quake, the most serious in Canada for more than two centuries, affected the whole of the St. Lawrence valley on February 28, 1928, but caused little damage. On November 18, 1929, a quake occurred about 300 miles south of Newfoundland, and the tidal wave that resulted caused some damage in Newfoundland. With an object of studying earthquakes, the Dominion government has established in Canada five seismological stations, at Halifax, Ottawa, Toronto, Saskatoon, and Victoria. See *Canada Year Book*, 1931.

**Sekani,** a group of the Athapaskan or Déné family, divided into nine tribes, having their habitat on the upper Peace and Fraser rivers, roaming both slopes of the Rockies and adjacent forests and plains, from 54° to 60°. Their name means "people among the rocks." They are nomadic hunters. Fishing they regard as unmanly; and fish they will not voluntarily eat. For their trade, Simon Fraser (q.v.) in 1805 built Fort McLeod at the headwaters of the Peace; but their trading rendezvous now is Fort Norman on the Mackenzie. Though they were regarded as merciless and blood-thirsty, they are, says Father Morice, absolutely honest, and a trader may leave his store unlocked without fear of theft. Anything taken from his stock by them being replaced by its exact equivalent. They do not use tents, but even in winter sleep in brush huts open to the weather. They pay small attention to their dead, merely pulling down the brush hut over the remains, or placing the body in a rude coffin on a scaffolding, or leaving it on the ground covered with his inverted birch-bark canoe. Petitot (q.v.) estimated their number at between 300 and 400 persons. See A. G. Morice, *The Great Déné race* (Vienna, 1926).

**Selby, Prideaux** (d. 1813), receiver-general of Upper Canada, came to Canada as a subaltern in the 5th Regiment, and became assistant secretary of the department of Indian affairs. In 1804 he was appointed a judge of the district court of the Western district in Upper Canada; and in 1808 he became receiver-general of the province and a member of the Executive Council. He died about the end of April, 1813.

**Selenium** is an element that is closely related to sulphur in its properties, and exists in at least three modifications: vitreous selenium, when it is melted and cooled quickly; crystalline selenium, when precipitated from certain solutions; and so-called metallic selenium, when it is fused and cooled slowly. In nature selenium is found mixed with sulphur, for it has been found that selenium and sulphur mix in all proportions. The substance as found in nature is called selen-sulphur. Most of the selenium however, is combined with metals to form extremely rare minerals. The commercial source of the element is entirely as a by-product, and originally it was obtained from sulphuric acid plants. The chief source at present is a residual slime from electrolytic copper refining. It was produced in Canada for the first time in 1931 at the Ontario Refining Company's electrolytic refinery at Coppercliff, Ontario. Selenium is chiefly used in the glass and rubber industries. The metallic modification of selenium is rapidly coming into use because of its remarkable property of changing its electrical conductivity with changes in the intensity of light to which it may be subjected, so that it is employed in the construction of instruments for the telegraphic transmission of sketches and in the photo-electric cell or electric eye. It has also been used to some extent in gas buoys and for exploding torpedoes.

**Selkirk, Thomas Douglas, fifth Earl of** (1771-1820), philanthropist, was born at St. Mary's Isle, Kirkcudbrightshire, Scotland, on June 20, 1771, the seventh and youngest son of Dunbar Douglas, fourth Earl of Selkirk. He was educated at Edinburgh University; and here he was a member of a club for the discussion of social and political questions, of which Sir Walter Scott was also a member. In 1799, on the death of his father, all his brothers having died previously, he succeeded to the Scottish earldom of Selkirk; and he immediately began to formulate plans for relieving the distress consequent upon the economic revolution then in progress in the Highlands of Scotland. He proposed emigration of the evicted "crofters" to British North America; and in 1803 he planted his first colony of Highlanders in Prince Edward Island. At the same time he was connected with the establishment of a similar colony at Baldoon, near lake St. Clair, in Upper Canada. His chief project, however, was the establishment of a settlement in the Red river valley, in what is now Manitoba. With a view to the founding of this colony, he acquired financial control of the Hudson's Bay Company, and obtained from the company in 1811 the cession of forty-five millions of acres in the Red river valley. In 1811 he sent out a party of settlers, under Miles Macdonell (q.v.), by way of Hudson bay, and in 1812 a second party; and these established themselves near the site of the present city of Winnipeg—the first body of colonists in the North West.

In these proceedings Selkirk was actuated by the purest and most altruistic motives; but he failed to take into account the certain hostility of the North West Company to his plans for the colonization of the Red river valley. The Nor'Westers, who were the inheritors of the French fur-trade in the west, disputed the right of the Hudson's Bay Company to dispose of the territory in the Red river country; and they resolved to break up the Selkirk settlement. Twice they drove the settlers from their homes; and on June 19, 1816, a miniature battle took place at Seven Oaks, near Fort Douglas, between the Nor'Westers and the Selkirk settlers, under Robert Semple (q.v.), whom the Hudson's Bay Company had sent out as governor. In this skirmish Semple and twenty of his men were killed. Meanwhile, Selkirk was on his way to the Red river from Canada, with a force of disbanded soldiers; and when news reached him of the Seven Oaks affair, he seized the North West Company's headquarters at Fort William, on lake Superior, arrested a number of the officers of the North West Company, and sent them back to Canada for trial. The following spring he pushed on to the Red river, reinstated his colonists, and restored order. The battle was then transferred to the courts. The North West Company brought action against Selkirk for having conspired with others to ruin the company's trade in the West; and the trials, which took place in 1818, resulted in the defeat of Selkirk, who was ordered to pay heavy damages. Selkirk returned to England broken in health; and he died at Pau, in the south of France, on April 8, 1820. He was survived by his wife, Jean, daughter of James Wedderburn-Colvile, whom he married in 1807, and by whom he had one son and two daughters.

A clear and forceful writer, Selkirk published, in addition to several pamphlets on political subjects, the following works dealing with his emigration projects: *Observations on the present state of the highlands of Scotland* (London, 1805), *A sketch of the British fur-trade in North America, with observations relative to the North West Company of Montreal* (London, 1816; New York, 1818), and *A letter to the Earl of Liverpool . . . on the subject of the Red River settlement in North America* (privately printed, London, 1819). Two anonymous pamphlets on *The civilisation of the Indians of British North America*

(London, 1807) have also been attributed to him.

See G. Bryce, *Life of Lord Selkirk* (Toronto, n.d.) and *Mackenzie, Selkirk, Simpson* (Toronto, 1905); C. Martin, *Lord Selkirk's work in Canada* (Oxford, 1916); Helen I. Cowan, *Selkirk's work in Canada* (Can. hist. rev., 1928); *Narrative of occurrences in the Indian Country of North America* (London, 1817); *A statement respecting the Earl of Selkirk's settlement upon the Red river* (London, 1817); *The communications of "Mercator"* (Montreal, 1817); *Trials of the Earl of Selkirk versus the North West Company in 1818* (Montreal, 1819); *Report of the proceedings connected with the disputes between the Earl of Selkirk and the North West Company* (London, 1918); A. Macdonell, *A narrative of the transactions in the Red river country* (London, 1819); and W. S. Wallace, *The literature relating to the Selkirk controversy* (Can. hist. rev., 1932).

**Selkirk,** a town in Manitoba, on the west bank of the Red river, at the head of deep-water navigation, and on the Selkirk branch of the Canadian Pacific Railway, 24 miles north-east of Winnipeg. It is named after the fifth Earl of Selkirk (q.v.). It is the chief port of lake Winnipeg; and the greater part of the products of northern Manitoba are trans-shipped here, especially fish and lumber. It has saw and planing mills, rolling mills, a steel plant, a box factory, a flaxboard insulation plant, and boat-building establishments; and it has a high school, a general hospital, a hospital for the insane, a public library, and a weekly newspaper (*Record*). Pop. (1931), 4,486.

**Selkirk,** a village in Haldimand county, Ontario, 10 miles south-west of Cayuaga, and 7 miles from Nelles Corners, the nearest railway station. Pop. (1934), 500.

**Selkirk mountains,** a division of the Columbia system, in the Kootenay district of British Columbia, between the Kootenay and Columbia rivers on the east, and the Columbia river and Upper and Lower Arrow lakes on the west. See A. O. Wheeler, *The Selkirk range* (2 vols., Ottawa, 1905-6), and A. O. Wheeler and Elizabeth Parker, *The Selkirk mountains: A guide for mountain pilgrims and climbers* (Winnipeg, 1912).

**Selkirk Settlement.** See **Red River Settlement.**

**Sellar, Robert** (1841-1919), journalist and author, was born in Glasgow, Scotland, on August 1, 1841, and came to Canada as a child. He became a a journalist on the staff of the Toronto *Globe;* and in 1863 he founded the *Canadian Gleaner* at Huntingdon, Quebec. He retained the direction of this paper until his death at Huntingdon, on November 30, 1919. He was the author of *The history of the county of Huntingdon* (Huntingdon, 1888), *Disabilities of Protestants in the province of Quebec* (Huntingdon, 1890), *Hemlock, a tale of the war of 1812* (Huntingdon, 1890), *Gleaner tales* (Huntingdon, 1895), *The tragedy of Quebec* (Huntingdon, 1907), *Morven* (Huntingdon, 1911), *The U.S. campaign of 1813* (Huntingdon, 1913), *True makers of Canada* (Huntingdon, 1915), and *George Brown and Confederation* (Toronto, 1917). See G. Lanctot, *Un régionaliste anglais, Robert Sellar* (Bull. rech. hist., 1935).

**Selwyn, Alfred Richard Cecil** (1824-1902), director of the Geological Survey of Canada (1869-95), was born at Kilmington, Somerset, England, on July 28, 1824, the son of the Rev. Townshend Selwyn, canon of Gloucester cathedral, and Charlotte Sophia, daughter of Lord George Murray, bishop of St. David's. He was privately educated, and became an assistant geologist on the staff of the Geological Survey of Great Britain. From 1852 to 1869 he was director of the Geological Survey of Victoria, Australia; and from 1869 to his retirement on pension in 1895 he was director of the Geological Survey of Canada. He died at Vancouver, British Columbia, on October 18, 1902. In 1852 he married Matilda Charlotte (d. 1882), daughter of the Rev. Edward Selwyn, rector of Hemingford Abbots, Huntingdonshire. He was a fellow of the Royal Society, of the Geographical Society, and of the Royal Society of Canada. Of the last society he was president in 1896. In 1881 he was made an LL.D. of McGill University; and in 1886 he was created a C.M.G. A bibliography of his scientific papers and reports is to be found in *Trans. Roy. Soc. Can.*, 1894.

**Selwyn, mount,** is in the Kootenay district of British Columbia, south-east of Glacier in the Dawson range of the Selkirk mountains. It is in lat. 51° 09', long. 117° 24', and has an altitude of 11,013 feet. It was named after A. R. C. Selwyn (q.v.), director of the Geological Survey of Canada. There is also a mount Selwyn in the Cariboo district of British Columbia, south-west of the confluence of the Peace river and Selwyn creek. It has an altitude of 6,200 feet.

**Semitic Languages.** See **Oriental Languages.**

**Semlin, Charles Augustus** (1836-1927), prime minister of British Columbia (1898-1900), was born in Upper Canada in 1836, of United Empire Loyalist descent. He became a school teacher; but in 1862 he went to British Columbia, at the time of the Cariboo "gold fever", and settled at Cache Creek, British Columbia. From 1871 to 1876, and from 1882 to 1903, he represented Yale in the Legislative Assembly of British Columbia; and in 1898 he became prime minister of the province, with the portfolios of public works and agriculture. He was dismissed from office in 1900, and he retired from political life in 1903. He died, unmarried, at Ashcroft, British Columbia, on November 3, 1927.

**Semple, Robert** (1766-1816), governor of the Hudson's Bay Company's territories (1815-16), was born in Boston, Massachusetts, in 1766. His parents espoused the loyalist cause during the American Revolution; and at the close of the Revolution he went into business in London, England. In the course of business he travelled extensively in South Africa, Spain, Italy, Asia Minor, the West Indies, Brazil, Venezuela and Germany; and he wrote *Walks and sketches at the Cape of Good Hope* (London, 1803), *Observations on a journey through Spain and Italy* (London, 1807), *A second journey in Spain* (London, 1810), *Sketch of the present state of Caracas* (London, 1812), and *Observations made on a tour from Hamburg through Berlin to Gothenburg* (London, 1814). He also wrote a novel, *Charles Ellis, or the friends* (London, 1814). In 1815 he obtained through the influence of Lord Selkirk (q.v.), an appointment as governor or chief agent of the Hudson's Bay Company in North America, in succession to Miles Macdonell (q.v.); and he arrived at the Red River settlement in September of that year. In March, 1816, he seized and destroyed the fort of the North West Company at Red River; and on June 19 he came into armed collision with a party of Nor'Westers at Seven Oaks. In the fight which ensued he and twenty of his men were killed.

**Senate,** the name applied in 1867 to the second chamber or upper house of the legislature of the Dominion of Canada. The members of the Senate were to be appointed by the Crown, on the recommendation of the government of the day; and the qualifications of a senator were that he should be 30 years of age, should be a natural-born or naturalized subject of the crown, should be seised of a freehold of the value of $4,000, should have real and personal property to the value of $4,000, and should be resident in the province for which he is appointed. The number of senators was fixed at first at 72, of whom 24 were appointed for Ontario, 24 for Quebec, and 24 for the Maritime provinces (12 for Nova Scotia and 12 for New Brunswick). In 1915 the British North America Act was amended by the British parliament, so as to increase the number of senators to 96. Of these Ontario, Quebec, and the Maritime provinces each had 24; but there were to be 10 senators from Nova Scotia, 10 from New Brunswick, and 4 from Prince Edward Island, and there were to be 24 from the western provinces, 6 from British Columbia, Alberta, Saskatchewan, and Manitoba. There have been repeated agitations for the abolition or reform of the Senate, but hitherto without success. It was the opinion of no less acute an observer than Sir Clifford Sifton (q.v.) that the Senate has never balked the will of the House of Commons except when it had the people of Canada behind it. This may be an overstatement; but it is at least true that when the Senate has blocked legislation it has had the support of a large element in the country behind it. The Senate is not permitted to initiate legislation involving the expenditure of public funds. See Sir George Ross, *The Senate of Canada, its constitution, powers, and duties, historically considered* (Toronto, 1914), and R. A. MacKay, *The unreformed Senate of Canada* (Oxford, 1926). See also **Government** and **Second Chambers.**

**Seneca.** See **Iroquois.**

**Sénécal, Louis Adélard** (1829-1887), senator of Canada, was born at Varennes, Verchères county, Quebec, on July 10, 1829. He had a limited education, but became an important figure in the economic life of the province of Quebec. He built steamships, railways, saw-mills and grist-mills; and he was interested in cotton-mills, pulp-factories, electric-light plants, and timber limits. He took also an active part in politics, first as a Liberal, and then as a Conservative; and he was a member of the

Canadian House of Commons for Yamaska from 1867 to 1871, and for Drummond and Arthabaska from 1867 to 1872—the only member to represent two constituencies at the same time in the history of the Dominion. On January 25, 1887, he was appointed to the Senate of Canada; but he died, shortly afterwards, on October 11, 1887.

**Senneville,** a village in Jacques Cartier county, Quebec, on the shore of the lake of Two Mountains, at the north-western extremity of the island of Montreal. It is named after a French officer, Capt. Le Ber de Senneville, who lived in Montreal about 1682. It was created a village in 1895, and is a popular summer resort. Pop. (1931), 473.

**Separate Schools.** This is a term generally understood to mean Protestant schools in Quebec and Roman Catholic schools in Ontario, Saskatchewan, and Alberta. To be accurate, however, certain modifications must be made this statement. In the strict sense, there are no separate schools in Quebec, but only dissentient schools or schools of the denominational minority. Again, there are a few Protestant separate schools in Ontario where the majority of the ratepayers are Roman Catholics. Properly, then, a separate school is established by the denominational minority only where that minority prefers to support such a school rather than patronize the public school. Outside of the province of Quebec, the first school established under provincial authority in any district is the public school. The denominational minority may then apply for a separate school in the same area, assuming the payment of taxes for the support of that separate school only. With a few exceptions in Alberta, separate schools are supposed to be limited to the elementary grades; in Ontario some are allowed to conduct classes which correspond to the first year in high school, while Protestant dissentient schools in Quebec include high school grades.

The first use of the term separate schools in Ontario was in 1843 when the amendments to the Act of 1841 authorized the erection of separate schools, either Protestant of Roman Catholic, wherever the minority denomination had 15 school children. In 1885 the Taché Act defined the administration of trustees and granted the right to collect taxes from their patrons on the same principles as applied to public schools. The Separate School Act of 1863 provided for the creation of schools in rural districts, gave them a share in both municipal and provincial grants, regulated inspection, and fixed certain standards in qualification of teachers. At the present time provincial educational authorities exercise administrative and academic control over separate, as over public, schools in matters of inspection, curricula, teachers, etc.

Manitoba has achieved the present school system only after bitter controversy over both sectarian and racial questions. The first provincial legislation provided for the establishment of separate schools for Roman Catholics. In the twenty years that followed, Protestant sections increased greatly in proportion, and the work done in the separate school decreased in quality, with the consequences that the Public School Act of 1890 required all to be free and non-sectarian, and gave no share of the legislative grant to denominational schools. This led to prolonged litigation, a Privy Council judgment, and a remedial bill introducing the Laurier-Greenway compromise of 1897, which allowed some religious teaching and in some cases the appointment of Roman Catholic teachers. By the Coldwell amendments of 1912, a questionable definition of terms admitted several Roman Catholic teachers to one school and denominational instruction in schools sharing the legislative grant. These amendments were repealed four years later.

Legislation in the North West Territories was increasingly favourable to separate schools, and culminated in the ordinance of 1884, which gave full privileges to separate schools of either denomination in the conduct of classes, choice of subjects and textbooks, and licensing of teachers. From that date, however, several ordinances were passed each curtailing more radically the rights previously granted. The Saskatchewan Act, stating the constitution for the newly created province in 1905, supported this limitation of privilege, but the years that followed were filled with bitter controversy, on optional taxation, on distribution of taxes of corporations, on language issues, and on political disputes. Alberta, the other province to emerge from the territories in 1905, followed an entirely different course. No political or sectarian divisions diverted the attention from the fundamental aim of improving educational conditions; there was no rigid line of demarcation between the two classes of school supporters; minorities usually agreed to a peaceful compromise.

The dissentient schools in Quebec are Protestant or Roman Catholic, according to the faith of the local minority. All schools are admittedly conservative in spirit and curricula, but the province shares with British Columbia the distinction of having the most progressive and economical unit of administration, i.e., the municipality. On the whole, there is a spirit of freedom and tolerance manifested to a marked degree in the relations between dissentient and Roman Catholic schools.

Bilingualism has been a special problem in the Canadian school system, as privileges granted to minorities have been claimed for language minorities as well as for denominational minorities. In Ontario the dispute has been, for the most part over the circular of instructions commonly referred to as Regulation 17, which proceeded on the principle that, in separate schools in French-speaking communities, English should be made the language of instruction as early as possible. The Merchant Report in 1927 advised a policy of intelligent tolerance, a plan of gradual introduction of English instead of coercion, and more adequate professional training of teachers. Advantages granted at one time to language minorities in Manitoba and Saskatchewan have been, to a large extent, withdrawn, because the problem is in reality a multilingual one; a large population speaking German, for instance, could claim the same rights as the French population. In Alberta the authorities have treated the French minority generously, and harmony on language as on regilion characterizes the administration of the school system in Alberta.

See J. C. Hodgins, *Legislation and history of separate schools in Upper Canada, 1841-1876* (Toronto, 1897); C. B. Sissons, *Bi-lingual schools in Canada* (Toronto, 1917); W. H. G. Armstrong, *Separate schools* (n.p., 1918), and G. M. Weir, *The separate school question in Canada* (Toronto, 1934).

**Sept Isles,** a fortified trading-post on Sept Isles bay, in the lower St. Lawrence. It was built about 1650, and was one of the earliest of the King's posts, as well as the most easterly. After the British conquest, it was leased to the North West Company; and in 1821 it was taken over by the Hudson's Bay Company. It was closed in 1859, but was re-opened in 1870, and has been in operation up to the present.

**Seranus** (pseud.). See **Harrison, Mrs. Susie Frances.**

**Sericite,** a scaly mineral, usually light-coloured, which is an important constituent of many schists. The composition of the mineral is doubtful, but in most cases it is probably a very fine-grained variety of muscovite.

**Serpentine,** a soft mineral with a sub-resinous to greasy or earthy lustre. In colour it is usually some shade of

green, but varies from nearly white to
nearly black. It is usually in massive
form, and in sufficient quantity to be
considered as a rock. It also occurs in
fibrous form giving what is known as
chrysotile asbestos (see **Asbestos**). The
massive material is used to some extent
as a building and ornamental stone,
but in Canada it is more important as
the material which contains the fibrous
variety in veins. Serpentine results from
the alteration of olivine, and more particularly from the olivine rock known as
peridotite. Large deposits of serpentine
occur at Thetford Mines and Black
lake, Quebec.

**Servantes de Jésus-Marie.** The
Congregation of Servantes de Jésus-
Marie was founded at Notre-Dame-des-
Neiges de Masson, in the diocese of
Ottawa, on May 24, 1895, by the Abbé
Alexis Louis Mangin, and by Mlle.
Eleanor Potvin (in religion, Sister Marie-
Zita-de-Jésus), with the especial object
of offering prayers for priests, before
the Most Holy Sacrament, which is
perpetually exposed in the chapel of
each monastery. The Congregation comprises three classes of nuns: the Sisters
of the Choir, the Auxiliary Sisters, and
the travelling Sisters. The costume consists of a white woollen cloth gown; of
a white woollen scapular, similar to
the gown; of a girdle of blue wool; of a
veil of dark wool; and of a rosary of
beads carved from natural wood and a
silver bosom-cross. Since 1902, the
mother-house of the Congregation has
been at Hull, Quebec. The Congregation
has also three other houses, one at
Rimouski (1918), one at Cap-de-la-
Madeleine (1927), and the other at
Shawinigan Falls (1930).

**Serviceberry,** a tree, frequently
called shad bush. It is the name of a
species of the genus *Amelanchier Medicus*.
Most of the species are shrubs, but some
of them reach tree size. June-berry (*A.
canadensis* (Linnaeus) *Medicus*) ranges
from Nova Scotia to lake Superior, but
is nowhere abundant; western service-

berry (*A. florida* Lindley) is found from
Alaska southward through British
Columbia, and may also get on to the
prairies in Alberta and Saskatchewan.
The leaves resemble those of choke-
cherry, being oval in shape, and finely
and sharply serrate, but the fruit is
sweet and edible and contains several
seeds rather than a single seed, as in
the case of the cherry. The trees flower
early in the spring, before the leaves are
fully out, and are quite showy. The
wood is occasionally used for handles,
fishing-rods, bows, and small turnery,
but is not sold in the lumber market.

**Service-Tree. See Mountain Ash.**

**Servite Fathers.** The Servites of
Mary (O.S.M.) have three religious
communities at present in Canada, each
of which is attached to a parish. The
house in Ottawa, the residence of the
vicar-provincial, with a novitiate and
an apostolic school, is the most important. In Montreal is the Church of
Our Lady of Mount Carmel, to which
is attached an orphanage conducted by
the Sisters of the Servants of Mary.
Another house in Montreal, that of Our
Lady of Defence, is especially noted as
being the most beautiful church in
Montreal, owing to its interior decora-
tions executed by the famous Italian
artist Guido Nincheri. The Servants of
Mary came to Canada for the express
purpose of overseeing the Italian colonization. Had immigration not been so
restricted a much more elaborate programme would have been undertaken
in accordance with the wishes of the
ecclesiastical authorities, and more members of the order would have been sent
to carry out this work across the
Dominion. There is also a religious
house in Vancouver, but this is under
the supervision of the American province.

The Servites were founded in 1233 by
the supernatural apparition of the
Blessed Virgin to the Seven Holy
Founders. These seven Holy Founders
were canonized simultaneously by Pope

Leo XIII in 1888, a unique fact in the history of the Church. To-day the order has houses in the following countries: Italy, France, England, Belgium, Austria, Hungary, United States of America, Argentina, and Canada, and has missions in Brazil and South Africa (Swaziland).

**Setting lake** is in northern Manitoba, in the basin of the Gross river, about the 55th parallel of north latitude. It is named from the practice of setting fish-nets in the lake; the Indian name for the lake means "fishing with a net." It has an area of 65 square miles.

**Seul, lac,** is an extension of the English river, in the Kenora district of northern Ontario. It has an area of 416 square miles.

**Seven Islands.** See **Sept Isles.**

**Seven Oaks,** the name of a locality near the Red River Settlement, about three miles north of the present city of Winnipeg, where an encounter took place on June 19, 1816, between a party of half-breeds in the service of the North West Company and a party of Hudson's Bay Company settlers, under Governor Semple (q.v.). Semple and about twenty of his party were massacred. See A. H. Trémaudan, *Une page d'histoire de la nation métisse* (Canada Français, 1928).

**Seven Persons,** a village in Alberta, on the Canadian Pacific Railway, 16 miles from Medicine Hat, and on the Seven Persons river. The name is a translation of the Indian name for the river. Pop. (1934), 300.

**Seven Sisters mountain** is in Range 5 of the Coast district of British Columbia, east of the Skeena river, and southeast of Cedarvale railway station. It has an altitude of 9,140 feet.

**Seventh Day Adventists.** Of the various Adventist denominations on the American continent, the Seventh Day Adventists are by far the strongest and most numerous. Their founder was William Miller of Low Hampton, N.Y.,

who lectured much on the prophecies of Daniel and John the Evangelist. The premillennial coming and reign of Jesus Christ was fundamental in his teaching. He proclaimed the belief that the end of the world would be in 1843, and that Christ would come to reign. This prophecy proved unfounded, but large numbers still continued to hold to his main belief; the accepted faith is that He will come in person, but at a date unknown, and that there will be the triumph of the righteous and the destruction of the unrighteous. The Adventists accept the seventh day of the week as the Sabbath, and baptize by immersion.

Their first church in Canada was formed about 1880 at South Stukeley, Quebec; at present, scattered over the Dominion, they have 150 churches and 8,203 communicants. The 1931 census reports the Seventh Day Adventists population in Canada as 16,026, mostly in Alberta, Saskatchewan, and Ontario.

Part of the North American division is the Canadian Union Conference, which includes six smaller Conferences. Winnipeg is the headquarters, and the officers are a president, who holds office for eight years, and an executive committee. The denomination has two junior colleges, one at Lacombe, Alberta, and one at Oshawa, Ontario; its licentiates and ministers complete their required course of study at one of the several Adventist colleges in the United States. It has also a hospital at Sidney, British Columbia, called the Rest Haven Sanitarium. Consult James White, *The life and labours of William Miller* (Battle Creek, Michigan, 1875), and the *Seventh Day Adventist Year Book* (Washington, D.C.).

**Seven Years' War,** the name applied to the final or culminating phase of the century-long struggle between Great Britain and France for supremacy in North America. It is so named because war was formally declared in 1756, and peace was signed only in 1763; but

26

actually hostilities broke out in North America in 1754, and military operations were in full swing in 1755.

*Bibliography.* The chief accounts of the Seven Years' War in North America are to be found in Capt. J. Knox, *An historical journal of the campaigns in North America* (2 vols., London, 1769; new ed., by A. G. Doughty, 3 vols., Toronto, The Champlain Society, 1914); T. Mante, *History of the late war in North America* (London, 1772); G. E. Hart, *The fall of New France* (Montreal, 1888); F. Parkman, *Montcalm and Wolfe* (2 vols., Boston, 1884), and *A half century of conflict* (2 vols., Boston, 1892); A. G. Bradley, *The fight with France for North America* (Westminster, 1900); William Wood, *The fight for Canada* (London, 1904); and George M. Wrong, *The fall of Canada* (Oxford, 1914), *The conquest of New France* (New Haven, 1918), and *The rise and fall of New France* (2 vols., London, 1928). See also **History, Military.**

**Severn Bridge,** a village in the Muskoka district, Ontario, on the Severn river, and on the Canadian National Railway, 14 miles north of Orillia. Pop. (1934), 300.

**Severn river,** in the northern part of Patricia district, Ontario, flows northeast through Severn lake and empties into Hudson bay near the 56th parallel of north latitude. It was discovered in 1631, and was named New Severn, after the Severn in England, by Captain Thomas James (q.v.) of Bristol. The Hudson's Bay Company in 1688 established at the mouth of the river a trading-post which was in the following year captured by the French under Iberville (q.v.). By the Treaty of Utrecht, the English acquired permanent control of the area. The river is a large one, but difficult for navigation. Canoes sometimes take this route in passing from lake Winnipeg to Hudson bay. The river is 420 miles long, and drains an area of 38,600 square miles.

**Severn river,** between Simcoe county and Muskoka district, Ontario, flows north-west out of lake Simcoe, into Georgian bay. It was probably visited by Étienne Brûlé (q.v.), a protégé of Champlain (q.v.), between 1611 and 1615, and was discovered by Champlain himself in 1615. It has several rapids and falls, and runs through very beautiful scenery. It is about 20 miles in length.

**Sewage Disposal.** See **Refuse, Disposal of.**

**Sewell, Jonathan** (1766-1839), chief justice of Lower Canada (1808-38), was born at Cambridge, Massachusetts, on June 6, 1766. He was educated at the grammar school in Bristol, England; and in 1785 he emigrated to New Brunswick, where he studied law in the office of Ward Chipman (q.v.). In 1789 he settled in Quebec, and was called to the bar of the province of Quebec. In 1793 he was appointed solicitor-general of Lower Canada, and in 1795 attorney-general; and he represented the borough of William Henry in the Legislative Assembly of the province from 1796 to 1808. In 1808 he was appointed chief justice of Lower Canada and president of the Executive Council; and in 1809 he became also speaker of the Legislative Council. He resigned the presidency of the Executive Council in 1829, and the office of chief justice in 1838; but he continued as speaker of the Legislative Council until his death at Quebec, on November 12, 1839. He was an LL.D. of Harvard University; and he published the following: *A plan for the federal union of the British provinces in North America* (London, 1814); *On the advantages of opening the river St. Lawrence to the commerce of the world* (London, 1814); *An essay on the juridical history of France so far as relates to the law of Lower Canada* (Quebec, 1824); and, in collaboration with others, *Plan for a general legislative union of the British provinces in North America* (London, 1824). He was one of the earliest advocates of the federation of the British North American provinces. See F. J. Audet, *Les juges en chef de la province de Québec* (Revue du Droit, 1925), and P. G. Roy, *Les juges de la province de Québec* (Quebec, 1933).

**Sewell, William George** (1829-1862), journalist and author, was born in Quebec in 1829, the grandson of the Hon. Jonathan Sewell (q.v.). He studied law, but in 1853 he became a journalist in New York. He died in Quebec in 1862. A few years before his death, he went to the West Indies in search of health; and while there he wrote *Ordeal of free labour in the British West Indies* (New York, 1861; 2nd ed., London, 1862).

**Sewellel.** See **Mountain Beaver.**

**Seymour, Frederick** (1820-1869), governor of British Columbia, was born on September 6, 1820, the fourth son of Henry Augustus Seymour, of Pembroke College, Cambridge. He entered the service of the Colonial Office; and was successively assistant colonial secretary of Tasmania, special magistrate of Antigua, president of Nevis, superintendent of Honduras and lieutenant-governor of the Bay islands, and lieutenant-governor of Honduras. In 1864 he was appointed governor of the mainland of British Columbia; and he held this post until his death on June 10, 1869, on board H.M.S. *Sparrow Hawk*, off the coast of British Columbia. His régime was marked by his opposition to the union of British Columbia with Canada. In 1865 he married Florence Maria, daughter of the Hon. and Rev. Sir Francis Stapleton, Bart. See F. W. Howay, *The attitude of Governor Seymour toward Confederation* (Trans. Roy. Soc. Can., 1920).

**Shad,** a valuable food fish related to the marine herring. It is a native of the eastern coasts of America, but has been introduced into the Pacific ocean off California, and from there it has spread northward to Alaska. It is not abundant in Pacific waters of Canada. In the Atlantic, it has been so exploited that its numbers are much reduced. It is confined to the immediate coastal waters, and in Canada the gulf of St. Lawrence marks its northern limit.

**Shad Bush.** See **Serviceberry.**

**Shaganappi,** or "North West iron", signified thongs of rawhide used formerly in the Canadian west for rope or cord. It was an important factor in the development of the North West, and was one of the most important gifts of the Indian to the white man. Out of it was made the harness of the Red river carts and of the dog-sleds of the country farther north. The name is derived from an Algonkian word meaning "a thong of rawhide." A corresponding term is babiche (q.v.). It has been said that "shaganappi and Scotchmen made the North West."

**Shag Harbour,** a village in Shelburne county, Nova Scotia, on the Atlantic ocean, and on the Canadian National Railway, 6 miles from Barrington Passage. It is named after the shag, or crested cormorant, which formerly frequented the harbour. Pop. (1934), 500.

**Shakespeare,** a village in Perth county, Ontario, on the Canadian National Railway, 7 miles east of Stratford. Pop. (1934), 500.

**Shale,** a sedimentary argillaceous rock formed by a partial consolidation of clay. By an increase in the amount of quartz, it grades through argillaceous sandstone toward sandstone; while by an increase in lime we have calcareous shales and argillaceous limestones. In colour, shales range from gray, through greenish, bluish, or yellowish colours almost to black. The best grades of shale are used in the manufacture of brick, and certain varieties when mixed with limestone are burned to make Portland cement.

**Shallow Lake,** a village in Grey county, Ontario, on the Canadian National Railway, 10 miles from Owen Sound. Pop. (1934), 650.

27

**Shank, David** (d. 1831), soldier, was a loyalist who received in 1777 a commission in the Queen's Rangers. He served throughout the American Revolutionary War, and in 1783 returned to England on half-pay. When the Queen's Rangers were revived in 1791, on the appointment of Colonel Simcoe (q.v.) as lieutenant-governor of Upper Canada, he was employed in raising the regiment, and brought it out to Canada in 1792. He was gazetted major in 1794 and lieut.-colonel in 1798; and remained in command of the regiment until his return to England in 1799. In 1803 he was appointed lieut.-colonel of the Canadian Fencibles. He rose to the rank of lieut.-general; and he died at Glasgow, Scotland, on October 16, 1831.

**Shank, John.** See **Schanck, John.**

**Shanly, Charles Dawson** (1811-1875), poet and art critic, was born in Dublin, Ireland, on March 9, 1811, the son of James Shanly. He came to Canada with his parents in 1836, and settled in Middlesex county, Upper Canada. He was a writer of occasional verse, and he edited a short-lived periodical entitled *Punch in Canada*. In his later years he was an art critic in New York. He died at Arlington, Florida, whither he had gone in search of health, on April 15, 1875.

**Shanly, Francis** (1820-1882), civil engineer, was born at Stradbally, Queen's county, Ireland, on October 29, 1820, the fifth son of James Shanly. He came to Canada with his parents in 1836, and settled in Middlesex county, Upper Canada. He became a civil engineer, and played an important part in the "railway era" in the Canadas. With his brother, Walter Shanly (q.v.), he built the Hoosac tunnel in Massachusetts. In 1880 he was appointed chief engineer of the Intercolonial Railway. He died suddenly, in a sleeping car of the Grand Trunk Railway, between Kingston and Brockville, on September 13, 1882.

**Shanly, Walter** (1819-1899), civil engineer, was born at "The Abbey", Stradbally, Queen's county, Ireland, on October 11, 1819, the fourth son of James Shanly. He came to Canada in 1836 with his parents, settled in Middlesex county, Upper Canada, and became a civil engineer. From 1858 to 1862 he was general manager of the Grand Trunk Railway; and in 1869-75 he was engaged, with his brother, Francis Shanly (q.v.), in the construction of the Hoosac tunnel in Massachusetts. From 1863 to 1867 he represented South Grenville as a Conservative in the Legislative Assembly of Canada; and he sat in the Canadian House of Commons for this constituency, from 1867 to 1872, and from 1885 to 1891. He died in Montreal on December 17, 1899. He was unmarried.

**Shannonville,** a village in Hastings county, Ontario, on the Salmon river, near its mouth on the bay of Quinte, and on the Canadian National Railway, 9 miles east of Belleville. Pop. (1934), 400.

**Shanty Bay,** a summer resort in Simcoe county, Ontario, on the north shore of Kempenfeldt bay, an inlet of lake Simcoe, and on the Canadian National Railway, 6 miles from Barrie. Pop. (1934), 100.

**Sharbot Lake,** a village in Frontenac county, Ontario, on the north shore of Sharbot lake, and on the Canadian Pacific Railway, 45 miles north of Kingston, and 25 miles west of Perth. Pop. (1934), 500.

**Sharks** are marine fishes, mostly of large size. They are the modern survivors of a very ancient group which were among the first true fish to inhabit the ancient seas. They differ from the typically modern fish, such as salmon, cod, bass, etc., in having a skeleton of cartilage or gristle instead of bone, in lacking true scales, the body being covered with hard, strong spines, in having the gill slits opening directly to the outside instead of under a gill cover, and in the shape of the tail, the upper lobe in sharks being much longer than the lower lobe, and having the backbone running through it. Several species occur in Canadian waters. These include the great blue shark (*Prionace glauca*) which sometimes reaches a length of twenty feet. It is a typical pelagic shark common in the tropics, occasionally straying into Canadian waters. Other species are the basking shark (*Cetorhinus maximus*), one of the largest of living sharks, said to reach a length of 36 feet, which is to be found in the Arctic and south along both coasts to Virginia and California; the Greenland or sleeper shark (*Somniosus microcephalus*), also an inhabitant of Arctic regions, occasionally ranging southward to New England and Puget Sound; the thresher (*Alopias vulpinus*), which occasionally visits the Atlantic and Pacific coasts of Canada; the porbeagle or mackerel shark (*Lamna nasus*), which is an enemy of mackerel, salmon, and other similar fish, in both Atlantic and Pacific waters; and the mud shark (*Notorhynchus maculatus*), which occurs in some numbers in British Columbia waters, where it is sometimes taken for reduction to fertilizer and oil. Other species occasionally stray into Canadian waters. The dogfishes are small littoral sharks.

**Sharon,** a village in York county, Ontario, 4 miles north of Newmarket, the nearest railway station. It was formerly the centre of a religious sect known as "the Children of Peace", founded by David Willson (q.v.); and there is still standing in the village "the Temple of Peace" built by David Willson about 1830, now preserved as a museum. Pop. (1934), 200. See J. Squair, *The temple of peace* (Women's Can. Hist. Soc. of Toronto, Transaction no. 20, 1919-20), and J. L. Hughes, *Sketches of the Sharon temple and its founder* (Toronto, 1918).

**Sharp, George** (d. 1800), merchant, was a prominent trader of Detroit and the North West in the period subsequent to the American Revolution. In 1798 he became one of the original partners of the XY Company. He died at Montreal on January 17, 1800.

**Shatford, Allan Pearson** (1873-1935), clergyman and author, was born at St. Margaret's Bay, Nova Scotia, on May 9, 1873. He was educated at King's College, Windsor (B.A., 1895; M.A., 1898; D.C.L., 1911), and was ordained a priest of the Church of England in 1896. After serving as rector of Bridgewater and North Sydney in Nova Scotia, he became assistant rector in 1906, and rector in 1912, of the Church of St. James the Apostle in Montreal. He served as chaplain to the 24th Battalion during the Great War, and was awarded the O.B.E. He died at his summer home in Nova Scotia on August 16, 1935. He was the author of a *Memoir of Herbert Symonds* (Montreal, 1921), *Six marks of a Christian* (Philadelphia, 1925), and a number of Christmas brochures, one of which he published each year.

**Shaughnessy, Thomas George Shaughnessy, first Baron** (1853-1923), president of the Canadian Pacific Railway Company (1898-1918), was born at Milwaukee, Wisconsin, on October 6, 1853, the son of Thomas Shaughnessy, of Limerick, Ireland. He entered the employ of the Milwaukee and St. Paul Railway in 1869, and in 1882 he joined the staff of the Canadian Pacific Railway. He became president of this railway in 1898, and continued as such until 1918. He died at Montreal on December 9, 1923. In 1880 he married Elizabeth Bridget Nagle, of Milwaukee; and by her he had two sons and three daughters. In 1901 he was created a knight bachelor, and in 1907 a K.C.V.O.; and in 1916 he was created Baron Shaughnessy, in the peerage of the United Kingdom. He was a D.C.L. of Trinity College, Dublin, and an LL.D. of Dartmouth College and of McGill University.

**Shaughnessy, mount,** is in the Kootenay district of British Columbia, north of Glacier. It is one of the Hermit range, in the Selkirk mountains, is in lat. 51° 23', long. 117° 32', and has an altitude of 9,380 feet. It was named after Thomas George Shaughnessy (q. v.), first Baron Shaughnessy of Montreal and Ashford, county Limerick, Ireland, formerly a chairman of the Canadian Pacific Railway Company.

**Shaunavon,** a town in the Maple Creek district of Saskatchewan, on the Canadian Pacific Railway, 200 miles south-west of Moose Jaw. It was named after Lord Shaughnessy (q.v.), who objected to the use of his name for any railway station, but who consented in this case to the use of the first syllable of his name, combined with some letters from the name of Sir William Van Horne (q.v.). It is the centre of a farming district; and it has eight grain elevators, five oil warehouses, a power station, and a weekly newspaper (*Standard*). Pop. (1931), 1,761.

**Shaw, Æneas** (d. 1815), soldier, was the second son of Angus Shaw of Tordarroch, Scotland, and Anne Dallas. He served in the Queen's Rangers under Simcoe (q.v.) in the American Revolutionary War; and in 1792 he came from New Brunswick to Upper Canada with his company of the reorganized Queen's Rangers. In 1794 he was appointed a member of the Legislative Council of Upper Canada, and later a member of the Executive Council. In 1803 he was placed on half-pay in the army, and he ceased to be a regular member of the Executive Council, though he remained an honorary councillor until 1807. In 1811 he was gazetted a major-general; and during the War of 1812 he was adjutant-general of the militia. He died near York (Toronto) on February 15, 1815. He was twice married, (1) to Ann Gosline (d. 1806), of Newton, New York, and (2) to Margaret Hickman, daughter of Capt. Poole Hickman England, 47th Regiment. By his first marriage he had seven sons and six daughters.

**Shaw, Angus** (d. 1832), fur-trader, was a native of Scotland who entered the service of the North West Company as a clerk prior to 1787. In 1789 he was at Fort L'Orignal, near the source of the Fraser river; and in 1790 he was "at Moose Hill Lake, up the Beaver river from Isle à la Crosse". In 1791 he was back at Fort L'Orignal; and in 1792 he was at Fort George. He became a partner in the North West Company between 1795 and 1799; in 1797 he was elected a member of the Beaver Club of Montreal; and in 1799 he was proprietor in charge of the Upper English river district. In 1802 he was appointed agent in charge of the King's Posts, with headquarters at Quebec; and in 1808 he became a member of McTavish, McGillivrays, and Co. He was one of the agents of the North West Company at Fort William in 1810 and 1811; but thereafter he took little part in the fur-trade, until the struggle with Lord Selkirk (q.v.) reached its height, when he was one of the partners of the North West Company arrested by the Hudson's Bay men in 1819. He continued to be a partner in McTavish, McGillivrays, and Co. after the union of 1821, when they were made Montreal agents of the Hudson's Bay Company; and his estate, which was involved in the failure of that firm in 1825, was not settled until 1847. He became a victim of pulmonary tuberculosis; and he died at New Brunswick, New Jersey, on July 25, 1832, two days after his arrival at that place. He married a sister of the Hon. William McGillivray; and she died in London, England, on March 27, 1820. But before his marriage he had a daughter, named Anna, who was born of "an Indian woman", and who was baptized in Montreal in 1797, aged 9 years.

**Shawbridge,** a village in Terrebonne county, Quebec, on the North river, and on the Canadian Pacific Railway, 42 miles north-west of Montreal. It is named after William Shaw, the first postmaster, who opened up the settlement by building a bridge across the North river. Pop. (1931), 457.

**Shawinigan Falls,** a city in St. Maurice county, Quebec, on the St. Maurice river, 20 miles from its outlet in the St. Lawrence, and on the Canadian National and Canadian Pacific Railways, 21 miles north of Three Rivers. The falls, picturesquely situated near the city, are 150 feet in height, and can develop 200,000 horse-power. They are a source of attaction to tourists. The chief industries are the manufacture of aluminum, pulp and paper, electrodes, abrasive material, cotton goods, knitted goods, stainless steel, cellophane, sashes and doors. There are five churches, five schools, a modern technical institute, and a municipal library. The city was founded in 1899, and was incorporated in 1909. Three newspapers are published (*L'Echo du Saint-Maurice, Standard* and *Review-La Revue*). Pop. (1931), 15,345.

**Shawnigan,** a settlement on Vancouver island, British Columbia, on Shawnigan lake, and on the Canadian Pacific Railway, 28 miles north of Victoria. Pop. (1934), 600.

**Shawville,** a village in Pontiac county, Quebec, on the Canadian Pacific Railway, 50 miles north-west of Hull. It takes its name from the township of Shawville, in which it and the village of Portage du Fort are situated. The chief industries are general farming, dairying, and lumbering. There is a high school and a weekly newspaper (*Equity*). Pop. (1931), 801.

**Sheaffe, Sir Roger Hale, Bart.** (1763-1851), president and administrator of Upper Canada (1813), was born in Boston, Massachusetts, on July 15, 1763, the third son of William Sheaffe and Susannah Child. He obtained a commission in the British army in 1778, and served throughout the

Revolutionary and Napoleonic wars. From 1787 to 1797, from 1802 to 1811, and again from 1812 to 1813 he was stationed in Canada. On the death of Brock (q.v.) at Queenston Heights, the command of the British forces devolved upon him; and he was commander-in-chief of the forces and president and administrator of Upper Canada until his recall to England in June, 1813. He rose to be a lieutenant-general in 1821 and a general in 1828. His death took place at Edinburgh, Scotland, on July 17, 1851. In 1810 he married Margaret, daughter of John Coffin, of Quebec. In 1813 he was created a baronet, in recognition of his services at Queenston Heights. See D. B. Read, *The lieutenant-governors of Upper Canada* (Toronto, 1900).

**Shediac,** a town in Westmoreland county, New Brunswick, on Shediac bay, in Northumberland strait, and on the Canadian National Railway, 18 miles from Moncton. The terminus of the railway is at Pointe du Chêne, 1½ miles distant from Shediac, where there is a government wharf; and Shediac bay is a sea-plane harbour, with moorings for 20 large sea-planes. The name of the town is derived from the Micmac *Es-ed-ei'-ik*, which means according to S. T. Rand (q.v.), "running far back". It is a port of entry. Pop. (1931), 1,883. See J. C. Webster, *A history of Shediac, New Brunswick* (Shediac, 1928).

**Sheep.** Mountain sheep (genus *Ovis*) are found along the Rocky mountain range and north into the Yukon and Alaska. They are sturdy animals, weighing between 100 and 300 pounds. Both sexes have horns, the ewes' medium-sized, curving horns and the rams' massive, thick, curling horns at once identifying them as sheep. The mountain sheep of North America fall naturally into two groups, northern and southern. The Rocky mountain bighorn, a member of the southern group, is found in the mountains of British Columbia and Alberta, north to the canyon of the Peace river. This sheep is gray-brown in colour, and full grown rams have magnificent curling horns. The northern sheep differ widely in colour, are smaller than the bighorn, and have less massive horns. Dall's sheep is white; Stone's sheep is very dark, almost black; and Fannin's sheep is intermediate. The ranges of these sheep overlap, and the colours tend to intergrade, making identification difficult. The habits of the various mountain sheep are similar. They are never found away from mountainous country, where their skill in climbing enables them to escape their enemies. They move to lower altitudes during the winter, and gradually work higher again with the return of warm weather. They are active during the day, and may be seen feeding and moving about at all hours. The lambs are born in early spring, usually one to two at a birth. Bears, wolves, and cougars prey on mountain sheep, and eagles snatch lambs, but man is the sheep's most persistent and dangerous enemy. The magnificent horns of this animal are trophies much sought after by sportsmen, and in many areas these sheep have been wiped out by continued hunting. See Casper Whitney, *Musk-ox, bison, sheep, and goat* (1904).

**Sheepberry.** See **Nannyberry.**

**Sheep Laurel,** or Lambkill (*Kalmia angustifolia* L., *Ericaceae*), a low shrub with narrowly oblong leaves, pale beneath and bright green above. The flowers appear in June or July in dense, lateral, deep pink clusters, the single flowers are about ½ inch across, the corolla wheel-bell-shaped and 5-lobed; there are 10 stamens, caught in the depressions of the corolla. This plant grows in bogs and damp barren grounds in the eastern part of the country. It is very poisonous, particularly to sheep, and for this reason it is often called "lambkill".

**Sheepshanks, John** (1834-1912), clergyman, was born in England in 1834, and was educated at Christ's College, Cambridge. He took holy orders in the Church of England; and from 1859 to 1867 he was the first rector of Holy Trinity church, New Westminster, British Columbia. He then returned to England, and in 1893 he became bishop of Norwich. He died on June 3, 1913. The journal which he kept in British Columbia has been reproduced in part in the Rev. D. Wallace Duthie (ed.), *A bishop in the rough* (London, 1909).

**Sheep Sorrel** (*Rumex Acetosella* L., *Polygonaceae*), a very persistent stem arising from spreading, fleshy, yellow rootstocks. The leaves are smooth and rather fleshy, and are arrow-shaped, with two distinct ear-like extensions at the base. The small flowers are unisexual, borne in much-branched, very slender spikes, the staminate being the more showy. This is a very common weed everywhere.

**Sheet Harbour,** a town in Halifax county, Nova Scotia, on the east side of a deep inlet on the Atlantic coast, 75 miles east of Halifax by road. It has a large pulp-mill. The nearest railway is at Musquodoboit. Pop. (1934), 1,500.

**Shefford,** a county in south-western Quebec, north of Brome county, east of Rouville county, south of Bagot county, and west of Richmond and Sherbrooke counties. It was named after Shefford, in Bedfordshire, England. The Yamaska river drains it, and it is traversed by the Canadian Pacific and Central Vermont Railways. Chief town Waterloo. Pop. (1931), 28,262. See C. Thomas, *The history of Shefford* (Montreal, 1877), and J. P. Noyes, *Sketches of some early Shefford pioneers* (Montreal, 1905).

**Shehyn, Joseph** (1829-1918), acting prime minister of Quebec (1898), was born at Quebec, Lower Canada, on November 10, 1829, of Irish and French-Canadian parentage. He was educated at the Quebec Seminary; and he became a wholesale dry goods merchant in Quebec. From 1875 to 1900 he was the representative of Quebec East as a Liberal in the Legislative Assembly of Quebec. From 1887 to 1891 he was provincial treasurer in the Mercier administration; from 1897 to 1900 he was minister without portfolio in the Marchand government; and in 1898 he was for some months acting prime minister. In 1900 he was summoned to the Senate of Canada, and he remained a member of the Senate until his death at Quebec on July 14, 1918. He was twice married, (1) in 1858 to Marie Zoé Virginie, daughter of Ambroise Verret, of Quebec, by whom he had several children, and (2) in 1902 to Mme. Madeleine Josephine Leduc (*née* Beliveau), of Quebec. He was the author of *Railways vs. watercourses* (Quebec, 1884), a pamphlet in which he advocated the use of the railway to Quebec in shipping to Europe. For several years he was president of the Quebec Board of Trade.

**Shelburne,** a county in south-western Nova Scotia, between Yarmouth county and Queen's county. It was created in 1799, and was named after the town of Shelburne, which was named in 1783 after the Earl of Shelburne, one of the secretaries of state in the British government. It is watered by the Clyde, Roseway, and other rivers; and its deeply-indented coast line has a number of harbours. It is traversed by the Canadian National Railway. Chief town, Shelburne. Pop. (1931), 12,485.

**Shelburne,** the shire-town of Shelburne county, Nova Scotia, is situated on Roseway river and an arm of capacious Shelburne harbour, and on the Canadian National Railway, 160 miles south-west of Halifax. At the close of the Revolutionary War a large number of United Empire Loyalists settled here. In 1783 it was known as Port Roseway, but in that year Governor Parr (q.v.) named the town and district Shelburne, in honour of Lord Shelburne, a member of the British cabinet of that day. For a time Shelburne was the largest town in British North America, but the settlers drifted away when they discovered that the soil was not suitable for the kind of crops they wished to grow. A population of 10,000 in 1785 decreased to 374 in 1816. The entrance to a good land-locked harbour is marked by a lighthouse on McNutt's island. The wharfage and warehousing accommodation are modern and commodious. The industries include fish-curing and packing, shipbuilding, gas engine works, barrel-making, box-making, lumbering, and milling. The town has seven churches, a county academy, a court house, a customs house, and a weekly newspaper (*Coast Guard*). Pop. (1931) 1,474. For fuller particulars see J. P. Edwards, *The Shelburne that was and is not*, and *Vicissitudes of a loyalist city* (Dalhousie Review, 1922), and W. O. Raymond, *The founding of Shelburne, Nova Scotia* (Coll. New Brunswick Hist. Soc., 1909).

**Shelburne,** a village in Dufferin county, Ontario, on the Canadian Pacific Railway, 16 miles north-west of Orangeville, and 57 miles south-east of Owen Sound. Its chief industries are flour and saw mills, tanneries, sandstone quarries, and a creamery. It has two grain elevators, a high school, a public library, and a weekly newspaper (*Free Press and Economist*). Pop. (1931), 1,077.

**Shellbrook,** a village in Saskatchewan, is situated about 30 miles west of Prince Albert, at the junction of the Canadian National Railway, the Prince Albert-North Battleford, and the Shellbrook-Big River lines. The first settlers came into the Shellbrook district about 1890, and took up homesteads west of the present town. The first railway reached it in 1909, and the village was incorporated in 1910. It is the centre of a wheat-growing and mixed-farming district, and has five elevators, a creamery, and a flour mill. The neighbourhood supplies large quantities of lumber. The town takes its name from the Shell river, a tributary of the North Saskatchewan, which flows in a north-easterly direction about two miles north of the town. Pop. (1931), about 550.

**Sheldrake, Sparham** (1851-1903), schoolmaster and author, was born in England in 1851, the only son of Edward Sheldrake, of Inworth Priory, Suffolk. He was educated by private tutors, and went to Cambridge University, but did not graduate. When a young man, he emigrated to Canada, and he later founded at Lakefield, Ontario, the Grove School (now the Lakefield Boys' School). He died in 1903. He was the author of *Curious facts: Prose and verse* (Toronto, 1895), and he contributed to the *Canadian Magazine*.

**Sheldrake river,** a tributary of the St. Lawrence river, in Saguenay county, Quebec, which falls into the St. Lawrence 16 miles east of the Moisie river. It has a length of 120 miles.

**Sheol, mount,** is in Alberta, south of lake Louise, in lat. 51° 23', long. 116° 13', with an altitude of 9,108 feet. It was named by S. E. S. Allen, in 1894, from the gloomy appearance of the valley at the base.

**Shepherd's Purse** (*Capsella Bursapastoris* (L.) Medic., *Cruciferae*), a very common weed, the root leaves clustered and pinnately lobed, the stem-leaves clasping, and arrow-shaped; the flowers small, white, in terminal spiked clusters; the pods triangular, flattened at right angles to the narrow partition. It is found everywhere, especially in cultivated soil and around dooryards.

**Shepody bay,** an arm of Chignecto bay, in New Brunswick. The name is popularly said to be a corruption of the French *Chapeau Dieu;* but it almost certainly derived from the Micmac *Es-ed'-a-bit.* The name first appears in its present form on a map of 1749.

**Sheppard, Edmund Ernest** (1855-1924), journalist and author, was born at South Dorchester, Elgin county, Canada West, on September 29, 1855, the son of Edmund Sheppard and Nancy Bentley. He was educated at Bethany

College, West Virginia; and his early years were spent in Texas and Mexico. He returned to Canada in 1878, and became a journalist. From 1883 to 1887 he was editor-in-chief of the Toronto *News;* and in 1887 he founded *Saturday Night*, a weekly journal which achieved a great success. His contributions to this journal, under the pseudonym of "Don", brought him a national reputation. He retired from journalism in 1906, owing to ill-health; and he died in California on November 6, 1924. In 1879 he married Melissa, daughter of Edwin Culver, of Mapleton, Ontario. He published three novels, *Dolly* (Toronto, 1886), *Widower Jones* (Toronto, 1888), and *A bad man's sweetheart* (Toronto, 1889).

**Sheppard, George** (1819-1912), journalist and author, was born at Newark-on-Trent, England, On January 5, 1819, and became a journalist. In 1850 he came to America; and from 1854 to 1857 he held a post in the actuarial department of the Canadian Life Assurance Company in Hamilton, Canada West. In 1857 he became editor of the Toronto *British Colonist;* and subsequently he was editor of the Toronto *Globe*, the Hamilton *Times*, the Quebec *Chronicle*, the Quebec *Mercury*, and chief political writer on the New York *Times*. He retired from active journalism in 1892; and he died at Jamaica Plain, Boston, Massachusetts, in 1912. He was the author of *The theory and practice of life assurance* (Hamilton, 1855), and he edited a *Cyclopedia of biography* (New York, 1865).

**Sheppard, William** (d. 1867), executive councillor of Lower Canada, lived at Fairymead, Eastern Townships, Canada, and was a member of the Executive Council of Lower Canada from 1837 to 1841. He died on July 2, 1867. To the *Transactions* of the Literary and Historical Society of Quebec he contributed *Observations on the plants of Canada described by Charlevoix in his History* (1829), and *Notes on the plants* *of Lower Canada* (1831), and to the *Annals* of the Botanical Society of Canada a paper on *The geographical distribution of the Coniferæ in Canada* (1861). To the *Transactions* of the Literary and Historical Society of Quebec, his wife contributed a paper *On the recent shells which characterise Quebec and its environs* (1829), and *Notes on some of the song birds of Canada* (1837).

**Sheraton, James Paterson** (1841-1906), first principal of Wycliffe College, Toronto, was born in St. John, New Brunswick, on November 29, 1841. He was educated at the University of New Brunswick (B.A., 1861), and he was ordained a priest of the Church of England in 1865. In 1877 he was appointed first principal of Wycliffe College, Toronto; and he continued as principal until his death at Toronto on January 24, 1906. He was the author of *Christian Science* (Toronto, 1891), *The inspiration and authority of the Holy Scriptures* (Toronto, 1893), *The higher criticism* (Toronto, 1904), and *Our Lord's teaching concerning himself* (Toronto, 1904). See *In memoriam J. P. Sheraton* (Toronto, 1906).

**Sherbrooke, Sir John Coape** (1764-1830), governor-in-chief of Canada (1816-18), was born in England in 1764, the third son of William Coape, J.P., of Farnah in Duffield, Derbyshire, who took the name of Sherbrooke on his marriage in 1756 to Sarah, one of the co-heiresses of Henry Sherbrooke, of Oxton, Nottinghamshire. He entered the British army as an ensign in the 4th Foot in 1780; and he attained the rank of full general in 1825. In 1784-5 he was stationed in Cape Breton, Nova Scotia; and during the wars with France he saw service in the Netherlands, in India, in Sicily, in Egypt, and in the Peninsula. In 1809 he was second-in-command to Wellesley, and greatly distinguished himself at the battle of Talavera. In 1810 his health gave way, and he returned to England; and in 1811 he was appointed lieutenant-governor of Nova

Scotia. During the War of 1812 the defence of Nova Scotia was conducted by him with great success; and in 1814 he led a military expedition up the Penobscot, which resulted in the capture of the port of Maine, and which to some extent offset the British failure at Plattsburg. In 1816 he became governor of Canada; but in 1818 he suffered a paralytic stroke, and was forced to send in his resignation. The rest of his life he spent in retirement at Calverton, Nottinghamshire; and he died there on February 14, 1830. In 1811 he married Katherine, daughter of the Rev. Reginald Pyndar, rector of Madresfield, Worcestershire; and she died in 1856 without issue. He was created a K.B. in 1809, and a G.C.B. in 1815. The Duke of Wellington described him as "as very good officer, but the most passionate man, I think, I ever knew." See A. P. Martin, "Memoir of Sir J. C. Sherbrooke", appended to *Life and Letters of Viscount Sherbrooke* (2 vols., London, 1893).

**Sherbrooke,** a county in Quebec, bounded on the south by Stanstead county, on the west by Shefford county, on the north by Richmond county, and on the east by Compton county. It is traversed by the Canadian Pacific, Canadian National, and Quebec Central Railways; and is watered by the St. Francis and Magog rivers. Chief town, Sherbrooke. Pop. (1931), 37,386.

**Sherbrooke,** a city in Sherbrooke county, province of Quebec, is situated at the confluence of the Magog and St. Francis rivers, 100 miles east of Montreal. It is served by the Canadian National and the Canadian Pacific Railways, and is the headquarters of the Quebec Central Railway and the Canadian terminus of the Boston and Maine Railway. It owns its own electric power plant and has developed about 20,000 horse-power, two-thirds of which is being used; should occasion arise, it could develop another 10,000 horsepower. As a result of this convenient power, and an abundance of reliable workmen, Sherbrooke has become an important manufacturing centre, and the commercial metropolis of the Eastern Townships. In and about it United States manufacturers have established branch plants, and there are many of Canadian origin, producing clothing, woollen cloth, cotton goods, silk gloves and hosiery, boots and shoes, and machinery of various kinds. In the neighbourhood asbestos, copper, and limestone are found, while the nearby forests supply birch, maple, elm, and cedar. The land about it is fertile, and it is the centre of a rich mixed farming and dairying district. It has excellent educational institutions (a university, a college, and a technical school being chief among them), five hospitals, two public libraries, an afternoon newspaper (*La Tribune*), an evening newspaper (*Record*), and two weekly newspapers (*Telegram* and *Le Message de St. Michel*). The city was named in honour of Sir John Coape Sherbrooke (q.v.). Pop. (1931), 28,933. Of these fully eighty per cent. are of French origin, but practically all the inhabitants speak both French and English.

**Sherbrooke,** a village and port in Guysborough county, Nova Scotia, at the head of navigation on the St. Mary river, and 40 miles from Antigonish, the nearest railway station. It is a shipping point for lumber and pulpwood. Pop. (1934), 1,000.

**Sherman, Francis Joseph** (1871-1926), poet and banker, was born on February 3, 1871, in Fredericton, New Brunswick, the eldest son of Louis Walsh Sherman and Alice Maxwell. He was educated at the University of New Brunswick; but did not proceed to a degree. He became a banker, and rose to be assistant general manager of the Merchants' Bank of Canada and, after the amalgamation in 1907, of the Royal Bank. He retired on pension in 1919; and he died at Atlantic City, New Jersey, on June 15, 1926. He published

one volume of verse, *Matins* (Boston, 1896), and two booklets of verse, *In memorabilia mortis* (Boston, 1896), and *A prelude* (Boston, 1897); and he collaborated with Frank Day in *The deserted city* (Boston, 1899), and with John Bodkin in *Two songs at parting* (Boston, 1899). See Charles G. D. Roberts, *Francis Sherman* (Trans. Roy. Soc. Canada, 1934).

**Sherwood, Adiel** (1779-1874), sheriff of Leeds and Grenville (1829-64), was born near Montreal, May 16, 1779, the son of Thomas Sherwood, a loyalist. In 1784 his parents settled in Elizabethtown, Leeds county, Upper Canada; and from 1829 to 1864 he was sheriff of the united counties of Leeds and Grenville. He died at Brockville, Ontario, on March 25, 1874. In 1801 he married Mary, daughter of Stephen Baldwin, of Litchfield, Connecticut; and by her he had one son and seven daughters.

**Sherwood, George** (1811-1883), receiver-general of Canada (1858-62), was born in Augusta, Leeds county, Upper Canada, on May 29, 1811, the second son of the Hon. Levius Peters Sherwood (q.v.). He was educated at the Johnstown Grammar School, and was called to the bar of Upper Canada in 1833 (Q.C., 1856). He practised law at Prescott and Brockville; and he represented Brockville in the Legislative Assembly of Canada from 1841 to 1851, and from 1858 to 1863. From 1858 to 1862 he was receiver-general, and later, for a few months, commissioner of crown lands, in the Cartier-Macdonald government. In 1865 he was appointed judge of the county of Hastings; he retired from the bench in 1881; and he died at Toronto, Ontario, on February 7, 1883. In 1883 he married Marianne, daughter of Dr. Thomas G. Keegan, of Halifax, Nova Scotia; but he had no children.

**Sherwood, Henry** (1807-1855), solicitor-general for Upper Canada (1844-6) and attorney-general (1847-8), was born in Augusta, Leeds county, Upper Canada, in 1807, the eldest son of the Hon. Levius Peters Sherwood (q.v.). He was called to the bar of Upper Canada (Q.C., 1842), and practised law, first in Prescott, and then in Toronto. From 1837 to 1840 he was reporter to the Law Society of Upper Canada; and in 1841 he was elected to represent Toronto in the Legislative Assembly of united Canada. He held this seat continuously until 1854, and during this period came to be regarded as one of the leaders of the Conservative party in the House. In 1842, and again from 1844 to 1846, he was solicitor-general for Upper Canada; and on the retirement of the Hon. W. H. Draper (q.v.) in 1847, he became attorney-general for Upper Canada, and virtual leader of the government. Defeated in 1848, he went into opposition, and he took henceforth a somewhat subordinate part in politics. He died in Kissingen, Germany, in 1855.

**Sherwood, Levius Peters** (1777-1850), judge, was born in St. Johns, Quebec, in 1777, the second son of Capt. Justus Sherwood, a loyalist from Connecticut. He was called to the bar of Upper Canada in 1803, and practised law in Brockville. From 1812 to 1816, and from 1820 to 1824, he represented Leeds in the Legislative Assembly of Upper Canada; and in 1821 he was elected speaker of the House. In 1825 he was appointed a judge of the court of King's Bench in Upper Canada. He retired from the bench on pension in 1841; and in 1842 he was appointed a member of the Legislative Council of united Canada. He died in Toronto on May 19, 1850. He married Charlotte, daughter of Col. Ephraim Jones (q.v.) and by her he had four sons and three daughters. See D. B. Read, *Lives of the judges of Upper Canada* (Toronto, 1888).

**Sherwood, William Albert** (1859-1919), painter and poet, was born at Omemee, Canada West, on August 1, 1859, and died at Toronto, Ontario, on December 5, 1919. He was a member of the Ontario Society of Artists, and an associate of the Royal Canadian Academy of Arts. He acquired a considerable reputation, both as a portrait-painter, and as a painter of *genre* pictures, such as "The gold prospector", "The Canadian rancher", and "The Canadian backwoodsman." A frequent contributor to Canadian periodical literature, he was also the author of *Lays, lyrics, and legends* (Toronto, 1914).

**Shickshock mountains,** a range of mountains in the Gaspé peninsula, in Quebec, running parallel to the St. Lawrence river. The name Shickshock is from a Micmac word signifying "rocky mountains." Champlain (q.v.) named them the Notre Dame mountains. They rise to a height of from 3,000 to 4,000 feet.

**Shiner,** the common name of a number of species of small silvery fish of the minnow family (q.v.). The common creek shiner (*Notropis cornutus*) is the largest of the shiners, sometimes reaching a length of six inches. The lake shiner (*Notropis atherinoides*), a slender, silvery minnow found only in the larger lakes and rivers, is commonly sold in the preserved condition as bait. It is found from lake Champlain to Alaska. The golden shiner (*Notemigonus crysoleucas*) is sometimes used in ponds as a forage fish for bass.

**Shin-leaf,** or Wintergreen (*Pyrola elliptica* Nutt., *Ericaceae*), a low, smooth, perennial herb with subterranean shoots, which bear clusters of thin, dull, elliptical leaves on a margined stalk. The flowers are white or greenish-white, borne on a long slender stalk or spike; the calyx lobes are 5, acute; petals 5, concave; stamens 10. It grows in dry woods and thickets from eastern Quebec to British Columbia, blooming from June to July. The name "shin-leaf" comes from an old custom of applying the leaves to bruises and sores like a "shin-plaster".

**Ship-Building.** This was once a great Canadian industry. Before Confederation, British North America was one of the four greatest ship-building centres in the world. The beginnings of the industry went back to the early days of the French régime. It was Talon (q.v.) who founded the industry in New France, and especially at the port of Quebec. La Salle (q.v.) built the first sailing-ship, the *Griffon*, on the Great lakes; and this vessel was the forerunner of a large number of ships which were built on the Great lakes, and sailed on them, before the building of the canals on the St. Lawrence brought into the Great lakes ships built elsewhere. It was only, however, after the British conquest that ship-building in British North America became an important business. Quebec became a port in which a large proportion of the population were engaged in shipbuilding; and it was significant of the importance of this industry in Quebec that it was here that in 1831 there was launched the *Royal William*, the first steamship that crossed the Atlantic wholly under its own steam. In the Maritime provinces, with their many natural harbours, ship-building had begun at an early date. In both Nova Scotia and New Brunswick ship-yards were built; and privateers from these provinces played a part in the War of 1812. It was Samuel Cunard (q.v.) of Halifax who inaugurated the first regular transatlantic steamship service across the Atlantic. By 1867 the ship-building business in British North America had reached its peak. Quebec was turning out *per annum* over 50 vessels between 1,000 and 2,000 tons; and Nova Scotia and New Brunswick were building about 300 vessels, though these were of a tonnage averaging less than 300 tons. If the tonnage built on the Great lakes, in Prince Edward Island, and in Newfoundland, were included, the total shipping tonnage produced in British North America before 1867, must have been nearly a quarter of a million tons a year.

Then came the change from wood to steel in the construction of ships. Had Canada developed her iron-and-steel industry earlier, she might have held her position in ship-building; but when steel ships came into being, Canada had neither the steel nor, later, the capital to compete with the ship-building industry in Great Britain and other countries. The result has been the almost complete disappearance of one of Canada's former industries.

See R. Roy, *Navires canadiens* (Bull. rech., hist., 1921); William Wood, *All afloat* (Toronto, 1914); C. R. Fay, *Mearns and the Miramichi* (Can. hist. rev., 1923); F. W. Wallace, *Wooden ships and iron men* (London, 1934), *In the wake of the wind ships* (Toronto, 1927), *Record of Canadian shipping* (Toronto, 1929), and *The ships of old Quebec* (Maclean's Magazine, 1932).

**Ship Harbour,** a village and port in Halifax county, Nova Scotia, on an indentation of the Atlantic coast, about 50 miles east of Halifax. It has a government wharf. The nearest railway is at Musquodoboit. Pop. (1934), 800.

**Ship head.** See **Gaspé, cape.**

**Shippigan,** a village and harbour in Gloucester county, New Brunswick, opposite the south-western end of Shippigan island, and on the Canadian National Railway. The name is from a Micmac word signifying "duck road", or a passage from which ducks fly from one place to another. Pop. (1934), 100.

**Shippigan island** is off Gloucester county, New Brunswick, just south of Miscou island, and 12 miles from Shippigan village.

**Ship Worms.** This name is applied to several organisms which bore into the wooden piles of wharfs and the hulls of ships, causing great annual loss. The wood is in time so weakened by the borings that it must be frequently replaced. The best known of these are bivalve molluscs known as *Teredo* and *Xylotrya*. The boring is accomplished by the organism rotating and cutting its way with the two valves of the shell much like a drill. As the *Teredo* penetrates farther, the diameter of the tunnel increases. The tunneling is rapid, reaching a foot in length in a month or two. Other marine animals also go by the name of ship worm, the best known of which are certain species of marine arthropods belonging to the order *Isopoda*.

**Shirley, William** (1694-1771), governor of Massachusetts (1741-56), was born at Preston, Sussex, England, on December 2, 1694. He was educated at Pembroke College, Cambridge (B.A., 1715), was called to the bar in 1720, and for eleven years practised law in London. In 1731 he emigrated, with his family, to Massachusetts; and in 1741, through the influence of the Duke of Newcastle, he was appointed governor of Massachusetts. He it was who conceived the project of attacking Louisbourg in 1745; and in 1755 he was given command of the expedition against Niagara. After the death of Braddock (q.v.), he was appointed commander-in-chief of the British forces in North America; but the failure of his expedition against Niagara brought about his recall in 1756. In 1761 he was appointed governor of the Bahamas; but in 1767 he relinquished this post, and returned to Massachusetts. He died at Shirley Place, Roxbury, Massachusetts, on March 24, 1771. His *Correspondence* has been edited by C. H. Lincoln (2 vols., New York, 1912). See G. A. Wood, *William Shirley, governor of Massachusetts* (New York, 1920).

**Shoal Lake,** a village in Manitoba, on the Canadian Pacific Railway, 171 miles north-west of Winnipeg. It is in a mixed farming and cattle-raising district; and it has six grain elevators, a creamery, and a cheese factory. There is a weekly newspaper (*Star*). Pop. (1934), 697.

**Short, Richard** (*fl.* 1761), artist, was an officer in Wolfe's army who fought at the battle of the Plains of Abraham and Ste. Foy. While he was in garrison at Quebec in 1759-60 he executed a series of twelve engravings of Quebec which were published in London in 1761, and are now much sought after by collectors.

**Shortt, Adam** (1859-1931), economist and historian, was born at Kilworth, near London, Ontario, on November 24, 1859, the son of George Shortt and Mary Shields. He was educated at Queen's University, Kingston (B.A., 1883; M.A., 1884; LL.D., 1911), and he studied at Glasgow and Edinburgh Universities. In 1885 he was appointed assistant professor of philosophy in Queen's University; and in 1892 he became professor of political science. In 1908 he resigned to become a civil service commissioner at Ottawa, and he continued in this position until 1918. He was then appointed chairman of the Board of Historical Publications of the Public Archives of Canada. He died at Ottawa on January 14, 1931. He was created a C.M.G. in 1911; and in 1906 he was elected a fellow of the Royal Society of Canada. He was an outstanding authority on the economic history of Canada, and was the author of *Imperial preferential trade from a Canadian point of view* (Toronto, 1904), *Lord Sydenham* (Toronto, Makers of Canada, 1908; 2nd ed., 1926), and many valuable papers on the history of Canadian banking contributed to the *Journal* of the Canadian Bankers' Association. He edited *Documents relating to Canadian currency, exchange, and finance during the French period* (2 vols., Ottawa, 1926); and he was co-editor with A. G. Doughty of *Canada and its provinces* (23 vols., Toronto, 1914), and of *Documents relating to the constitutional history of Canada, 1759-1791* (Ottawa, 1907; new and revised ed., 2 vols., 1918).

**Shoveller** (*Spatula clypeata*), a duck largely characterized by its bill, which is greatly broadened near the tip and equipped along its margins with remarkably long fringes, through which its food is strained from the water. The male has a dark greenish head and neck, and the body is rather gaudily patterned with browns, white, rufous, and blue. The female is dully coloured. Shovellers nest in the western part of Canada, but occur rarely in the east on migration. This species is sometimes known as the "Spoonbill".

**Showy Lady's Slipper.** See **Lady's Slipper.**

**Showy Orchis.** See **Orchis.**

**Shrews** are small mouse-like animals, with long pointed snouts and minute eyes and ears. Their soft dark-coloured fur differs from that of most mammals in that it may be stroked as easily backwards as forward. They feed mainly on insects, which they secure by searching among the leaves and debris of the forest floor. These little animals are widely distributed in Canada, penetrating as far north as the Arctic circle. There are short-tailed shrews (genus *Blarina*), long-tailed shrews (genus *Sorex*), least shrews (genus *Microsorex*), which are the smallest Canadian mammals, and the little short-tailed shrews (genus *Cryptotis*). See *North American Fauna*, no. 51 (U. S. Dept. of Agriculture, 1928).

**Shrike,** the general name for two species of birds found in Canada, which are commonly known as "butcher-birds". Their affinities are with the order of birds known as the *Passeriformes*, which includes all the great variety of insect-eating and seed-eating song birds. They are notable, however, in being adapted for a raptorial life. They feed on small mammals and birds and some of the larger insects. Shrikes are somewhat smaller than a robin, gray in general colour, and patterned with black and white. The loggerhead shrike (*Lanius ludovicianus*) inhabits the cultivated sections of southern Canada, and the northern shrike (*Lanius borealis*) nest in the North West, but occurs in settled sections in winter. See Alden H. Miller, *The North American shrikes* (Berkeley, California: University of California Publications, 1931).

**Shrimps.** There are several species of these marine arthropods taken in trawl nets in Canadian waters. The fishery is not very important, the catch realizing only about $25,000 annually. The largest of these shrimps belong to the genus *Pandalus*, which is represented on the west coast by nine recorded species and on the Atlantic coast by three species. Two of these are common to both coasts.

**Shubenacadie,** a village in Hants county, Nova Scotia, on the Shubenacadie river, and on the Canadian National Railway, 40 miles north-east of Halifax. The name is derived from the Indian word meaning "the place where the gound nut or *seguban* [Micmac potato] grows." Pop., about 1,000.

**Shuswap,** the most important of the widely spread Salish family in British Columbia. Their present home is in the neighbourhood of the Thompson river, and Shuswap and Adams lakes, adjoining on the south and west the Okanagan and Lillooet Salish tribes, and on the north the Chilcotin, a branch of the great Déné race. In former days a state of almost continual warfare prevailed between the Shuswap and Chilcotin, the effects of which still remain in their mutual distrust. In 1811, David Stuart (q.v.), who was the earliest fur-trader amongst them, spoke of the "She Whaps" as a powerful nation and well disposed, inhabiting a land rich in beavers. They were hunters and fishermen, subsisting principally on venison, salmon, roots, and berries, living in the summer usually in tents of bark or mats, and in the winter like the Salish (q.v.), in "keekwillie" houses.

Their social organization was very loose; they had no chiefs, save in so far as wealth gave influence and leadership. They had no clans or totems. Though they had the custom of the potlatch, it did not attain the important place amongst them that it held with the coastal tribes. They had no secret societies or ceremonials with dramatized myths so prevalent on the coast. Their religion was similar to that of the other Salish. Their numbers are diminishing, but it is believed that at present there are about 2,000 persons in the Shuswap tribe. See James Teit, *Traditions of the Thompson River Indians* (Boston, 1898).

**Shuswap lake** lies at the head of the South Thompson river, in the Kamloops district, British Columbia. It has an area of 123 square miles.

**Sibbald, Mrs. Susan,** *née* **Mein** (1783-1866), diarist, was born at Fowey, in Cornwall, on November 29, 1783. Her husband, Colonel Sibbald, whom she married in 1807, died in 1835; and after his death, she brought her family to Canada, and settled near Jackson's Point, on lake Simcoe. She died in Toronto on July 9, 1866. Her *Memoirs* have been published by her great-grandson, F. Paget Hett (London, 1926), with a selection of letters covering the later years of her life in Canada.

**Sicamous,** a village in the Kamloops district of British Columbia, on the Shuswap lake, and on the main line of the Canadian Pacific Railway. It is the northern terminus of the Okanagan branch of the Canadian Pacific Railway, and has a school and some government offices. Pop. (1931), 250.

**Sicotte, Louis Victor** (1812-1889), politician and judge, was born at Boucherville, Lower Canada, on November 6, 1812, the son of Toussaint Sicotte and Margaret St. Germain. He was educated at the College of St. Hyacinthe, and was called to the bar of Lower Canada in 1837 (Q.C., 1854). He was a member of the Legislative Assembly of Canada from 1851 to 1863; and from 1854 to 1857 he was speaker of the Assembly. He held office in the Taché-Macdonald administration as commissioner of crown lands from November 25, 1857, to July 29, 1858, and in the Macdonald-Cartier administration as chief commissioner of public works from August 6, 1858, to December 24, 1858. In 1862 he became, with John Sandfield Macdonald (q.v.), joint leader of the government, with the portfolio of attorney-general for Lower Canada; but, on the reorganization of the cabinet in 1863, he retired to accept the position of puisne judge of the Superior Court of Lower Canada. He retired from the bench in 1887, and he died at St. Hyacinthe, Quebec, on September 5, 1889. In 1837 he married Margaret Amelia, daughter of Benjamin Starnes, of Montreal; and by her he had eleven children.

**Siderite.** See **Iron** and **Meteorites.**

**Side-saddle Flower.** See **Pitcher Plant.**

**Sidney,** a town in Vancouver island, British Columbia, on the Saanich peninsula, and on the Canadian National Railway, 18 miles north of Victoria. It is the centre of a populous district in the Saanich peninsula and the Gulf islands; and it is connected by automobile ferries with the state of Washington and with Vancouver and New Westminster. It has numerous industries, such as brick yards, cement works, lumber mills, salmon and fruit canneries, and creameries; and there are poultry and fox farms and apiaries in the neighbourhood, while sheep and goats are raised in the Gulf islands. The Saanich peninsula is a favourite resort for tourists. There is a weekly newspaper (*Saanich Peninsula and Gulf Islands Review*). Pop. (1934), 1,000, and, with surrounding districts, 6,000.

**Sifton, Arthur Lewis** (1858-1921), judge and politician, was born at St. John's, Middlesex county, Upper Canada, on October 26, 1858, the son of John Wright Sifton (q.v.). He was educated at Wesley College, Winnipeg, and at Victoria University, Cobourg (B.A., 1880; M.A., 1888), and was called to the bar of the North West Territories in 1883 (Q.C., 1892). From 1899 to 1903 he sat in the legislature of the North West Territories for Banff, and from 1901 to 1903 he was treasurer and commissioner of public works in the Haultain administration. In 1903 he was appointed chief justice of the Supreme Court of the North West Territories, and in 1905 of the Supreme Court of Alberta. In 1910 he retired from the bench, and became Liberal prime minister of Alberta, having been elected to the Legislative Assembly of Alberta for Vermilion. In 1917 he broke with the Liberal party, and entered the Dominion government as minister of customs under Sir R. Borden. He was a member of the war committee of the cabinet, and in 1918 he was one of the Canadian delegates to the peace conference at Versailles. In 1920 he became secretary of state, and was made a member of the imperial privy council; but he died at Ottawa on January 22, 1921. In 1882 he married Mary, daughter of William Deering, of Cobourg, Ontario; and by her he had one son and one daughter. He was an LL.D. of the University of Alberta (1908).

**Sifton, Sir Clifford** (1861-1929), minister of the interior for Canada (1896-1905), was born in Middlesex county, Ontario, on March 10, 1861, the son of John W. Sifton (q.v.), later speaker of the Legislative Assembly of Manitoba. He was educated at Victoria University, Cobourg (B.A., 1880), and was called to the Manitoba bar in 1882 (Q.C., 1895). He began the practice of law in Brandon, Manitoba; and from 1888 to 1896 he represented North Brandon in the Legislative Assembly of Manitoba. From 1891 to 1896 he was attorney-general and minister of education in the Greenway administration;

and it fell to him to deal with the Dominion government in regard to the thorny question of separate schools in Manitoba. He represented Brandon in the Canadian House of Commons from 1896 to 1911; and from 1896 to 1905 he was minister of the interior in the Laurier administration. During these years he prosecuted a vigorous immigration policy, which resulted in filling the vacant spaces in the Canadian West. He resigned from office in 1905 because of disagreement with Sir Wilfrid Laurier over the educational clauses of the Acts which created the new provinces of Saskatchewan and Alberta. In 1909 he was appointed chairman of the Canadian Conservation Commission; and he retained this position until 1918. But in 1911 he opposed the proposals of Sir Wilfrid Laurier for reciprocity with the United States, and withdrew from parliament and from the Liberal party. For the rest of his life he pursued an independent, but influential course in politics, mostly behind the scenes. He gave a general support to the war government of Sir Robert Borden (q.v.), but he never again held public office or sat in parliament. He died at New York on April 17, 1929. In 1884 he married Elizabeth Arma (d. 1925), daughter of H. T. Burrows, Ottawa; and by her he had four sons. In 1915 he was created a K.C.M.G. See J. W. Dafoe, *Clifford Sifton in relation to his times* (Toronto, 1931).

**Sifton, John Wright** (1833-1912), contractor and politician, was born in Middlesex county, Upper Canada, in 1833, the son of Bamlet Sifton, who came to Canada from Ireland in 1832. For many years a farmer and oil operator, he went to the North West in 1875 and became a contractor for the construction of telegraph and railway lines. In 1878 he was elected to represent St. Clements in the Legislative Assembly of Manitoba, and he was chosen speaker of the Assembly. Defeated in the next general elections, he was re-elected for

Brandon in 1881; but was defeated again in 1883, and in 1888. He then retired from politics, and occupied various positions in the civil service of Manitoba. He died at Winnipeg on September 19, 1912. In 1853 he married Kate (d. 1909), daughter of James Watkins, Parsonstown, King's county, Ireland; and by her he had two sons, the Rt. Hon. Arthur Lewis Sifton (q.v.), the Hon. Sir Clifford Sifton (q.v.), and one daughter.

**Signay, Joseph** (1778-1850), first Roman Catholic archbishop of Quebec (1844-9), was born at Quebec on November 28, 1778. He was educated at the Quebec Seminary, and was ordained a priest in 1802. In 1826 he became co-adjutor to the bishop of Quebec, with the title of bishop of Fusala; and in 1833 he succeeded as bishop of Quebec. In 1844 he became the first archbishop of Quebec; in 1849 he handed over the administration of the diocese to his coadjutor; and he died at Quebec on October 3, 1850. During the rebellions of 1837-8, he was noteworthy for the loyal attitude which he adopted; and his *mandements*, together with a biography of him, have been printed in H. Têtu and C. O. Gagnon, *Mandements, lettres pastorales, et circulaires des évêques de Québec* (6 vols., Quebec, 1887-90).

**Siksika,** or Blackfoot, an important Algonkian confederacy of the western plains, consisting of three tribes, the Blackfoot proper, the Kainah or Bloods, and the Piegan. Of these tribes the Piegan were, and are still, numerically almost as strong as the other two combined. The origin of the name, of which "Blackfoot" is merely an English translation, is disputed; but it is believed to have reference to the blackening of the moccasins of these Indians by the ashes of prairie fires. Within recent historic times, the Blackfoot occupied most of the vast territory lying between longitude 105° and the foothills of the Rockies, and between the headwaters of the Missouri river and the valley of the

North Saskatchewan. Allied with them were the Sarsi, an Athapaskan tribe, and occasionally the Gros Ventre, though the latter retreated south before the end of the eighteenth century, and played no further part in Canadian history. With the tribes surrounding them they were at constant war, and they have been aptly described as "the Ishmaels of the prairies".

The Blackfoot have been, as far back as history and tradition go, roving buffalo-hunters, dwelling in tipis and without permanent habitation, ignorant of the art of pottery and without canoes, and without even the art of agriculture, except for the growing of a species of native tobacco. Their traditions go back to a time when they had no horses, and hunted their game on foot; but in the seventeenth century they acquired the horse from tribes farther south, who were in touch with the Spaniards in California, and later they became noted for their great horse-herds. It is probable that their supremacy on the prairies was largely due to their acquisition of the horse and later of fire-arms. Their hostility to the idea of the traders of the North West Company crossing the Rocky mountains seems to have been dictated largely by the fear that these would supply fire-arms to their enemies, the Kutenai and Salish tribes of the Pacific slope.

In their culture, the Blackfoot tribes hardly differed from the Assiniboin, though there is evidence of an earlier culture, resembling that of the tribes of the eastern forests. Both the Blackfoot and the Assiniboin wore the typical costume and ornaments of the prairie tribes, and both employed dogs and travois in transporting their household possessions. In both the social units were the bands, of which, in the three main divisions, there appear to have been at least forty-five in all. It has been said that these bands were originally gentes; but, if so, their gentile character had in historical times disappeared. Cutting across the division into bands, there was also a military and fraternal organization, similar to that existing in other plains tribes, and consisting of at least twelve orders or societies, most of which are now extinct. These societies had a great number of dances, including the annual ceremony of the sun-dance, and performed police and other duties when the bands came together in summer and pitched their skin tents in the characteristic circle. Both the Blackfoot and the Assiniboin worshipped the sun and the thunder, which they regarded as manifestations of the Great Spirit.

Estimates of the numbers of the Blackfoot at various periods are often unreliable. The best estimate appears to be that of Sir Alexander Mackenzie (q.v.) in 1801. He calculated that there were then between 2,250 and 2,500 warriors in the three tribes of the confederacy—which would give a total population of about 9,000. Earlier than this, however, the numbers of the Blackfoot must have been considerably greater; for they suffered severely in the smallpox epidemic of 1781. About the middle of the nineteenth century they were again ravaged by smallpox, as well as by measles; and in 1858 H. Y. Hind (q.v.) estimated that they numbered only 950 tents. If there were eight persons to a tent, we arrive at a total figure of 7,600. The disappearance of the buffalo later caused a further decline in the numbers of the Blackfoot; and they number now less than 5,000. About 2,200 live on the Piegan reservation in north-west Montana; and a slightly larger number on three reservations or agencies in Alberta, one for the Blackfoot, one for the Blood, and one for the Piegan.

See Mgr. E. J. Légal, *Les Indiens dans les plaines* (Lyons, 1891), and *Au Nord-Ouest canadien: Les Pieds-Noirs* (Bulletin de la Société de Géographie, Paris, série vii, tome xx); G. B. Grinnell, *Blackfoot lodge tales* (New York, 1907); L. A. Prud'homme, *Les Pieds Noirs* (Revue Canadienne, 1908); W. McClintock, *The old north trail; or Life, legends, and religion of the Blackfoot* (London, 1910); E. S. Curtis, *The North American Indian* (Norwood, Mass., 1911); C. Wissler, *The material culture of the Blackfoot Indians* (American Museum of Natural History, Anthropological Papers, vol. v), and *The social life of the Blackfoot Indians* (American Museum of Natural History, Anthropological Papers, vol. vii); and F. Linderman, *Blackfoot Indians* (St. Paul, Minn., 1936).

END OF VOLUME V